Becoming a Marriage and Family Therapist

Becoming a Marriage and Family Therapist

From Classroom to Consulting Room

D. Eugene Mead

WILEY-BLACKWELL
A John Wiley & Sons, Ltd., Publication

This edition first published 2013

Wiley-Blackwell is an imprint of John Wiley & Sons, formed by the merger of Wiley's global Scientific, Technical and Medical business with Blackwell Publishing.

Registered Office
John Wiley & Sons Ltd, The Atrium, Southern Gate, Chichester, West Sussex, PO19 8SQ, UK

Editorial Offices
350 Main Street, Malden, MA 02148-5020, USA
9600 Garsington Road, Oxford, OX4 2DQ, UK
The Atrium, Southern Gate, Chichester, West Sussex, PO19 8SQ, UK

For details of our global editorial offices, for customer services, and for information about how to apply for permission to reuse the copyright material in this book please see our website at www.wiley.com/wiley-blackwell.

Library of Congress Cataloging-in-Publication Data

Mead, D. Eugene (Donald Eugene), 1934–
Becoming a marriage and family therapist : from classroom to consulting room / D. Eugene Mead.
pages ; cm
Includes bibliographical references and index.
ISBN 978-0-470-02736-3 (cloth) – ISBN 978-0-470-02737-0 (pbk.) 1. Family psychotherapy–Practice.
2. Psychotherapy–Vocational guidance. I. Title.
RC488.5.M4879 2013
616.89′1560023–dc23

2012034627

A catalogue record for this book is available from the British Library.

Cover image: © ImageZoo/Alamy
Cover design by Nicki Averill Design

Set in 10/12 pt Minion by Aptara Inc., New Delhi, India

1 2013

This book is dedicated to the hundreds of student interns who started to become marriage and family therapists in their first practicum classes at Brigham Young University. It is also dedicated to the doctoral students who enrolled in the supervision course to learn how to supervise others becoming family therapists. Thousands of family members have benefitted from their efforts.

Contents

List of Figures, Tables, and Boxes ix

About the Author xi

Foreword xiii

Acknowledgments xvii

Part I

1 Becoming a Competent Marriage and Family Therapist 3

2 Basic Therapist Skills 17

3 The Initial Phone Call and Assessing Clients' Complaints and Goals 63

4 Establishing a Treatment Plan and Delivering the Planned Treatment 85

5 Evaluating Adherence to the Treatment Plan and Evaluating Treatment Outcomes 109

6 Terminating Therapy 135

Part II Protocols for Selected Models of Marriage and Family Therapy: Delivering Evidence-Based Treatments

Introduction to Part II 147

7 Protocol for Conducting Gottman Method Couple Therapy 149

8 Protocol for Conducting Emotionally-Focused Therapy with Couples 195

Notes 217

Appendix A Person of the Therapist Checklist 219

Appendix B Therapist Self-Soothing Procedures 221

Appendix C Standard Assessment Battery for Marital Relational Problems 223

Appendix D Written Case Progress Notes 235

Appendix E Observations of the Couples' Communication and Problem-solving Behaviors Therapist's Rating Form Based on Gottman (1999) 237

Appendix F Clinical Experience Log 239

Appendix G Preparing a Written Treatment Plan 241

Appendix H Written Treatment Summary 247

Appendix I Therapy Tailoring Skills Rating Form 249

Appendix J Homework Success: Therapist Guidelines 251

Appendix K Preparation for Supervision Checklist: Couples 253

References 257

Index 285

List of Figures, Tables, and Boxes

Figures

2.1 Questions for a semi-structured screening interview for family violence 55

4.1 An example of a marital Standard Assessment Battery scores record 87

4.2 An example of a scored marital Standard Assessment Battery record 95

5.1 Some combinations of husband's and wives' outcome rating scale and revised dyadic adjustment scale scores in terms of levels and trends indicating successful, improving, deteriorating, and extremely distressed client outcomes 122

5.2 Family therapy decision tree 127

5.3 Domains of social support used to cope with significant life stressors 130

Tables

2.1 Categories of suicide risk 34

2.2 Recommended best treatments for depression and anxiety 36

2.3 Risk factors for partner, child, and elder mistreatment 46

G.1 Example of an assessment table in a treatment plan 243

Boxes

1.1 Supervision and Split Alliances 9

2.1 The Supervisor's Role in Suicide Risk Assessment and Intervention 37

4.1 The Supervisor's Role in Establishing the Treatment Plan 91

4.2 An Example of a Treatment Plan 93

5.1 Improving Therapists' Cognitive Processes 115

7.1 Presenting the Gottman Method Couple Therapy Treatment Plan 159

About the Author

D. Eugene Mead, EdD, is emeritus professor of Marriage and Family Therapy at Brigham Young University. He is a Fellow of the American Association for Marriage and Family Therapy and a member of the American Psychological Association. Joining the Brigham Young University Child Development and Family Relationships Department in 1967 he taught marriage and family therapy for forty years. During that time he developed (a) the behavioral marital and family therapy classes, (b) the practicum classes which provide the students with opportunities to begin practice with couples and families, (c) the sex therapy class, and (d) the supervision class designed to teach doctoral students to supervise master's level marriage and family therapy students. He also taught supervision at annual meetings and Summer Institutes of the American Association for Marriage and Family Therapy.

Foreword

D. Eugene Mead's book, *Becoming a Marriage and Family Therapist*, represents a significant step in the training literature in marriage and family therapy (MFT). It marks a coming of age in that it takes more seriously than any other training volume the importance of MFTs becoming "research informed" (Karam and Sprenkle, 2010). The vast majority of MFTs will not do formal original research as part of their careers, but this volume presents a strong case for the expectation that all MFTs will use research knowledge and research instruments to inform their clinical decision making. The reader will note that the vast majority of physicians do not do original research either. But, how many of us would want to patronize a physician who did not use research knowledge and instruments (e.g., blood pressure tests) to inform clinical decision making?

As a clinical member of the American Association for Marriage and Family Therapy (AAMFT) for forty years, all as an MFT educator, I have seen a lot of models and methods of training come and go. For too much of the history of the discipline, training has relied on a series of "here is my method" volumes based largely on the experience and theoretical preferences of the authors with scant regard for supporting evidence. Typical of Mead's candor is his warning: "You should be equally cautious about adapting a new technique presented at a workshop or national meeting. Prudent therapists do not chase off after the latest theoretical model no matter how charismatic the presenter. Hyperbole should not be allowed to substitute for scientific evidence" (p. 104).

While acknowledging there are sometimes contradictory findings from research, and typically presenting both sides, Mead's guidelines for training are grounded in evidence wherever possible. I was also very impressed with his broad command of the psychotherapy research literature. Although this is a volume on MFT training, Mead draws on evidence-based insights from counseling and clinical psychology – especially where this literature addresses themes not yet reported in the MFT research literature.

As strong as his evidence-based orientation is, Mead's volume makes clear that a scientific approach is not the sterile application of principles by therapists in white lab jackets; and therefore he gives considerable attention throughout to such issues as adapting validated approaches to clients' needs and characteristics and to "self of the therapist" issues that are usually not well-addressed in empirically-oriented approaches. However, in keeping with the author's desire to operationalize what some might consider the "soft side" of therapy, Mead includes appendices of instruments he has developed like "A Person of the Therapist Checklist" and "Therapist Self-Soothing Procedures." Mead's volume is more oriented toward instrumentation than any training text I have ever reviewed.

Another thing that I appreciated about this volume is its recognition of the moderate common factors stance (Sprenkle, Davis, and Lebow, 2009) – that although empirically validated treatments have done an excellent job demonstrating that they are superior to no treatment and to many alternative treatments (like "treatments as usual"), there is currently little evidence that one empirically validated MFT treatment is superior to another. So, the research informed therapist will want to (if at all possible) use an empirically validated approach for the problem being presented since these approaches are typically more effective than common "seat of the pants" alternative treatments. At the same time, the research-informed therapist is free to chose from a range of empirically-validated models (when there are multiple models for particular issues) depending on the match of that model to the therapist's world view, the needs of the client, and the therapist's and supervisor's training and skills. So, for example, while both Emotion Focused Therapy (EFT) and Integrative Behavioral Couples Therapy (IBCT) have both produced an impressive body of evidence that they are superior to common alternatives for treating marital distress (that these treatments have demonstrated what Sprenkle et al., 2009, have called "absolute efficacy"), there is currently no research that compares the efficacy of EFT with ICBT (that addresses what Sprenkle et al., 2009, have called "relative efficacy" between MFT models).

So, as Mead notes, one factor (other things being equal) that the therapist might use in making a choice between these two treatment models might be whether the presenting problem is an "attachment injury," for which EFT would be especially well-suited; or more a communication and problem-solving issue, for which IBCT might be the more potent match. "Other things being equal" is an important qualifier since in some instances therapist or supervisor training would be an over-riding concern in choosing a model from among evidence-based approaches.

Another way in which the current volume acknowledges the moderate common factors approach is that it makes clear that the largest portion of the variance in successful outcomes in empirically validated approaches is because they activate or potentiate common change mechanisms that operate in all successful treatments. That is, the largest portion of the variance in successful treatment is not what is unique about the treatment but common change mechanisms found in all *successful* treatments. This approach does not gainsay the value of models as important roadmaps for therapeutic success since having a model/roadmap is crucial. It also does not deny that there are some unique aspects of models that are likely especially helpful to certain clients and therapists. It is rather that commonalities (such as building strong therapeutic alliances, helping people to look at their problems differently, engaging in interventions that appear credible to clients) seem to trump unique dimensions when it comes to explaining outcome variance. Also, often what model developers present as unique dimensions are just a variation of a common theme. For example, getting clients to look at their problems differently may be called promoting "insight," "reframing," or "building a new narrative." The names are different but the basic mechanisms of change are often quite similar.

For this reason, Mead devotes the first three chapters of his book to developing basic skills and addressing issues that are largely independent of specific models. Not surprisingly, he has a very comprehensive section on the therapeutic alliance and one of the best sections on split alliances (when, for example, the therapist has a strong relationship with one family member but not with another) I have seen in any text. He also addresses topics like how to be an empathic listener, learning to deal with the therapists own issues like therapist stress, transference and countertransference, personal therapy, and how best to use supervision. In fact, one of the real strengths of this volume is that in almost every chapter he has information on how the therapist can use supervision to address the issue at hand, as well as guidelines for supervisors.

Although a text for beginning therapists, this volume contains one of the most comprehensive discussions I have seen anywhere on dealing with the suicidal client and how to address issues of violence and potential violence, as well as duty to warn and reporting issues. Rather than relegating these issues to peripheral stature at the end of the volume, they are given a prominent place at the beginning – in part because research shows, for example, how widespread family violence is and how infrequently therapists ask about it directly.

During this first part of the volume the author focuses on working through the various stages of therapy in chronological order, beginning with the initial phone call and assessing the clients' complaints and goals (Chapter 3), progressing to establishing and delivering the treatment plan (Chapter 4), evaluating adherence to the treatment plan and assessing treatment outcomes (Chapter 5), and termination (Chapter 6). Throughout, virtually all suggestions are research informed. Each section is also unusually thorough as Mead specifies, for example, every issue the aspiring therapist might encounter in an initial phone call.

What is unique about this section is that it includes the first call for "continuous" assessment and evaluation using reliable and valid instruments that I have seen in any training text. There is a growing body of evidence that just as "continuous" assessment has revolutionized medicine (e.g., physicians taking blood pressure readings at every consultation and recommending blood tests daily, or more often, if conditions warrant e.g., high blood sugar), so also continuous assessment has the capacity to revolutionize psychotherapy. Scholars like Anker, Duncan, and Sparks (2009) and Lambert, Hansen, and Finch (2001) have demonstrated that therapists who get session-by-session feedback using valid instruments get better results than those who do not, independent of theoretical orientation or presenting problem. Mead specifies that therapists use brief instruments regularly (like the Revised Dyadic Adjustment Scale for Couples (RDAS; Busby, Crane, Larsen, & Christensen, 1995)) and some at each session (like the Outcome Rating Scale (ORS; Miller, Duncan, Sorrell, and Brown, 2005)). Quite refreshing is that rather than just expecting the reader to track down these instruments, where possible many are included in his detailed sets of appendices.

Part II part of the book also contains another "first" for an MFT text. Mead offers two protocols for conducting empirically validated couple therapies – "Gottman Method Couples Therapy" and "Emotion Focused Therapy" with couples. These chapters offer session by session guidelines for implementing these therapies while also incorporating the guidelines for assessment, use of instruments, development of treatment plans, and so forth that Mead has laid out previously in the volume. These protocols are not a substitute for the model developer's treatment manuals, but rather are guidelines regarding how to use them.

The third section of the volume is a detailed series of appendices that include either the assessment instruments themselves, or information regarding where they can be easily found. These appendices are not only exceptionally useful, but will also save the reader/clinician considerable time, since many are in the public domain and can be photocopied.

Taken as a whole, this book is not for the faint of heart. It is challenging – not in the sense of difficult to comprehend since it is clear and well-written – but because it is a call for clinicians to be rigorous. It is a challenge to marriage and family therapists to apply an evidence-based approach to their work not unlike what MFTs expect of the physicians to whom they take themselves and their families for treatment. It is a plea to assess thoroughly and to demonstrate progress and success with the best science available. It is a call for the field to mature beyond the "truth by assertion" offered by charismatic prophets. It is asking the field to come of age. Gene Mead would not question that there is "art" as well as "science" in therapy, but only that the former needs to be in service of the latter. I commend this book as an important contribution to the training literature. That *Becoming a Marriage and Family Therapist* was written and published, is a positive sign for the future of MFT.

Douglas H. Sprenkle
Professor Emeritus, Purdue University
Former Editor, *Journal of Marital and Family Therapy*

Acknowledgments

This text grew out of the Brigham Young University Marriage and Therapy programs' supervision courses that I taught for over forty years. I thank the University administration, faculty, and students for their many contributions. The administration provided the "Marriage and Family Therapy" program with outstanding facilities including consulting rooms with one-way-screens and audio and television recording equipment all of which greatly facilitated supervision of the student interns' therapy work. The receptionists at the clinic front desk contributed by administering assessment instruments to the arriving clients. Faculty members gave support and helpful criticism and I especially want to thank Doctors Hugh Allred, Leslie Feinauer, James Harper, Joel Moss, and Robert Stahmann for their feedback over the years.

I am especially grateful to the several hundred student interns who allowed me to supervise them in their beginning work with their marriage and family clients. Together we evolved the therapist training program described in this text.

I give special thanks to the families that gave permission to observe their sessions both to me and to the doctoral student supervisors. Without the cooperation of the couples and families who came to the clinic the student interns would not have had the opportunity to learn to become marriage and family therapists.

The author and publisher gratefully acknowledge the permission granted to reproduce the copyright material in this book. I am grateful to the authors of the 563 works that contributed to this text. I thank John Wiley and Sons for permission to quote from Wingate, Joiner, Walker, and Rudd (2004) Empirically informed approaches to topics in suicide risk assessment, *Behavioral Sciences & the Law, 22(5),* 651–665. Special thanks for permission to use material for several tables in this book. Specifically:

1 Table 2.1 "Categories of suicide risk" is based on material from Joiner, Walker, Rudd, and Jobes (1999) and Wingate, Joiner, Walker, Rudd, and Jobes (2004).
2 Table 2.3 "Risk factors for partner, child, and elder mistreatment" is based on material from Choi and Mayer (2000), Kyriacou et al. (1999), Lachs, Williams, O'Brien, Hurst, and Horwitz, R. (1997), Pillemer and Finkelhor (1988), and Tolan, Gorman-Smith, and Henry (2006).
3 Figure 2.1 "Questions for a semi-structured screening interview for family violence" is based on material from Bomba (2006), Jacobson and Christensen (1996), Lachs, Williams, O'Brien, Hurst, and Horwitz, (1997), McCloskey and Grigsby (2005), Slep and Heyman (2006), Tolan, Gorman-Smith, and Henry (2006), Welfel, Danzinger, and Santoro (2000).

Every effort has been made to trace the copyright holders and to obtain their permission for the use of copyright material. The publisher apologizes for any errors or omissions in the above lists and would be grateful if notified of any corrections that should be incorporated in future reprints or editions of this book.

Special thanks to my editor Karen Shield at John Wiley Ltd. UK who patiently put up with my taking a year-and-a-half long hiatus to serve as a mental health advisor to the Church of Jesus Christ of Latter-day Saints missionaries in Japan and South Korea. Thanks also to Stan Wakefield who acted as an agent to help me connect to Wiley UK.

Finally, I want to acknowledge the support and encouragement from my wife Sherrill and our children Stanley, Marcia, and Christine.

Part I

Chapter 1

Becoming a Competent Marriage and Family Therapist

Introduction

This book is designed to help you make the transition from the classroom to the consulting room. In the classroom you have developed verbal and theoretical knowledge of how to do therapy. In the consulting room you will begin to change your verbal-theoretical knowledge into experiential knowledge. In the classroom you learned to respond to verbal descriptions of client behaviors. In the consulting room you will learn to respond to actual client behaviors in real time. You will begin to feel the responsibility of attempting to help clients deal with the complexities of their lives. Meeting clients for the first time is both exciting and frightening. In this effort you will not be alone. You will have the support and guidance of your supervisor who is an experienced therapist. Therefore, this text is also for supervisors. It will help supervisors provide the support and guidance new therapists need as they work to become competent therapists.

As a new therapist your goal is to become a competent entry-level therapist. Wampold (2001) stated that competent therapists have successful client outcomes. Therefore, your goal should be to help clients achieve their therapy goals. Your supervisor's goals are to help you become a competent therapist while safeguarding the welfare of your clients. How can you help clients to have successful outcomes? Successful therapy appears to be a function of four factors that appear to be common to all models of therapy (Lambert & Barley, 2002).

The Role of Common Factors in Therapy Outcomes

Research over the past twenty years has found that about 80 percent of clients who undergo psychotherapy are better off than those who do not (Lambert & Barley, 2002). Research has also found that about 40–50 percent of couples and families who complete marital or family therapy have successful outcomes (Shadish & Baldwin, 2002). Why marital and family therapy should be found to be less successful than individual therapy is not known. One could speculate that the difficulty of building and maintaining multiple alliances in families may be a contributory factor (Blow, Sprenkle, & Davis, 2007).

When individual therapy models are compared with each other none of the models have been found to be more efficacious than any other (Lambert & Barley, 2002). The same is true for

Becoming a Marriage and Family Therapist: From Classroom to Consulting Room, First Edition. D. Eugene Mead.

marriage and family therapy models. When they are compared head-to-head, no marriage or family therapy model is superior (Shadish & Baldwin, 2002, 2005).

There are a few noteworthy exceptions in which specific treatments have been found to be effective for specific classes of problems (Lambert & Barley, 2002). For example, exposure treatments for anxiety, avoidance, and rituals have been found to be superior to other forms of treatment (Lambert, 1992). Similarly, exposure techniques appear to play a significant role in the treatment of panic disorder with agoraphobia (Craske, 1999; Michelson & Marchione, 1991). Also there is considerable support for cognitive behavioral therapy (CBT) as an effective treatment for depression (Clark, Beck, & Alford, 1999). However, even in these specific treatments the common factors appear to play an important part.

Common factors contributions to successful client outcomes

According to the common factors literature there are four factors that make up the variance in therapy outcomes (Hubble, Duncan, & Miller, 1999; Sprenkle, Blow, & Dickey, 1999). The four factors are (1) the *alliance*, (2) what the *clients bring* to therapy, (3) the *placebo effect*, and (4) the *treatment techniques*. The *alliance* is the relationship between the clients and the therapist and makes up 30 percent of the therapy outcome variance. What the *clients bring* to therapy makes up approximately 40 percent of the variance (Lambert & Barley, 2002) and includes their presenting problems, their readiness to change, their social skills, and their support systems (Asay & Lambert, 1999). The third factor is the client's expectations for a successful outcome, what some call the *placebo effect* of coming to therapy and makes up 15 percent of the outcome variance (Lambert & Barley, 2002). The fourth factor *treatment techniques* employed by the therapist are embodied in the therapy model used by the therapist. Therapist techniques are used to maintain the therapeutic conversation between the therapist and the clients (Frank & Frank, 1991, 2004). Treatment techniques are believed to make up the final 15 percent of the outcome variance. These four factors appear to be common to all models of therapy and seem to account for successful client outcomes in both individual psychotherapy (Lambert & Barley, 2002) and in marriage and family therapy (Sprenkle et al., 1999).

Two of these factors, what the clients bring to therapy and the placebo effect, appear to be primarily client factors and not directly open to manipulation by you the therapist. The remaining two factors, the alliance and therapy techniques are factors that you can influence.

Here I will deal with each of the common factors independently although in practice they are difficult to differentiate. For example, the placebo effect may contribute initially to the client's trust in you thus facilitating the development of the alliance. Building and maintaining the alliance is related to how you employ the treatment techniques (Blow et al., 2007). It is difficult to differentiate the role of the treatment techniques from procedures that build the alliance. The alliance is said to consist of three elements, the clients' trust in the therapist, the clients' agreement with the therapist on the goals of therapy, and the clients' agreement about the techniques needed to achieve their goals (Bordin, 1979). So, at the same time that you are working collaboratively with the clients to clarify and establish their goals they will begin to trust you. As you communicate respect and empathy and exercise care concerning their safety in the sessions, the clients come to trust that you are on their side, both as individuals and as a couple or family. In this way two of the elements of the alliance are being forged, first, agreement on goals and second, trust in you as their therapist. Next you will propose a treatment plan tailored to fit the clients' needs and goals. If the clients agree that the treatment is appropriate to help them achieve their goals then the third element of the alliance is being constructed which is agreement on the treatment methods or therapy model. Finally, the treatment model serves as a structure for a continuing conversation about the clients' problems, needs, and goals while they formulate their solutions and change their behaviors and relationships (Frank & Frank, 1991, 2004). Thus, while treatment techniques have been found to contribute only 15 percent to the outcome variance, that 15 percent is not trivial.

Although the factors labeled "what the clients bring to therapy" and "client expectations" do not appear to be open to direct manipulation by you as a therapist there are potentially several ways you can influence the clients' perceptions of the alliance. These will be discussed at length in this chapter. Perhaps what is more important is that the delivery of the therapy techniques and the skill with which they are delivered is directly under your control. It has been shown that therapist's vary in their therapy delivering skill (Luborsky et al., 1986) suggesting that therapists can learn how to deliver therapy more effectively. By improving your skills in delivering therapy, you will increase the probability that your clients will have successful outcomes (Blow et al., 2007).

The Therapeutic Alliance

As stated above, the therapy alliance has been found to account for approximately 30 percent of the total outcome variance (Asay & Lambert, 1999). The alliance consists of three factors: (a) the clients' trust in, or bonding with, the therapist; (b) agreement between clients and therapist on the therapy goals; and (c) the clients' agreement with the tasks in the treatment plan (Bordin, 1979; Heatherington & Freidlander, 1990; Johnson & Talitman, 1997; Pinsof & Catherall, 1986). As a therapist you make a positive contribution to the therapy alliance by: (a) communicating respect, caring, and empathy (see Chapter 2); (b) helping clients clarify and establish their goals (see Chapter 3); (c) establishing treatment plans tailored to those goals (Chapter 3); and (d) dealing effectively with breaches in the alliance.

In individual psychotherapy you only need to be concerned with the alliance the client makes with you as the therapist. In family therapy you must be concerned about the alliance each family member makes with you (Friedlander, Escudero, & Heatherington, 2006; Pinsof, 1995). Family members may vary in their goals for therapy. Therefore, each family member will form her or his own alliance with the therapist. When family members' differ in their alliance with the therapist, the alliance is said to be split (Beck, Friedlander, & Escudero, 2006; Thomas, Werner-Wilson, & Murphy; 2005). Pinsof and Catherall (1986) were the first to define a split alliance. Split alliances occur when one member of the family rates the alliance with the therapist high and another member of the family rates the alliance low. Split alliances may lead to clients deciding to withdraw from therapy before they have reached their goals.

The probable causes of split alliances

In family therapy there may be as many goals for coming to and for staying in therapy as there are family members in the room (Friedlander, Escudero, & Heatherington, 2006). Family members have already formed alliances between each other before they come to therapy. Alliances between family members are what Friedlander and colleagues (2006) call family allegiances and what Garfield (2004) calls family loyalty. Family members may vary in their sense of family unity from total enmeshment to wondering whether or not they intend to remain in the family. It should come as no surprise then that the alliances they form with the therapist vary (Friedlander Friedlander, Escudero, & Heatherington, 2006; Symonds & Horvath, 2004).

The causes of split alliances are not yet well understood. The family power structure may be one factor in split alliances. Differential power may be a function of differences in physical size and development or in role differences between partners and between parents and children. The power hierarchy in the family may make some members vulnerable to other members in terms of psychological and physical aggression and even abuse (see Chapter 2). Therefore, some family members will be motivated to avoid family therapy and others may be motivated to come in self-defense. You will need to be sensitive to the power issues and be prepared to provide for the safety of each family member. Power differences may also occur between family members based on gender, race, education, and control of family finances.

There appears to be support for the idea that gender influences alliances however, the results are not consistent. Quinn, Dotson, and Jordon (1997) found that wives' scores on an alliance scale predicted outcome while the husbands' scores did not. On the other hand, Symonds and Horvath (2004) found that the relationship with the outcome was greater when the male's alliance was stronger. They also found that the relationship between alliance and outcome was greater when both partners agreed on the strength of the alliance and when the strength of the alliance increased over the course of treatment. Knobloch-Fedders, Pinsof, and Mann (2004) found that individual psychological symptoms in the couple did not predict alliance formation. Similarly Mamodhoussen, Wright, Tremblay, and Poitras-Wright (2005) found that psychiatric symptoms did not predict the alliance but marital adjustment did. In both studies husband's greater marital distress was a predictor of poor alliance. In the Knobloch-Fedders study women's marital distress at intake and reports of family-of-origin issues predicted the tendency for a split alliance. However, in the Mamodhoussen study the husband's marital adjustment and wife's psychiatric symptoms were associated with split alliances.

Family secrets are another source of alliance difficulties in family therapy (Friedlander et al., 2006). Some family members fear that the secrets will come out while others worry that they will not. In these circumstances the issue of safety in the therapy sessions is a serious issue for family members and therefore for the therapist. As a therapist you must address concerns about safety in the therapy system from the beginning of therapy starting with the initial phone call (See Chapter 3).

It is likely that the therapist will be working with split alliances when spouses or family members have mixed motives, are concerned about differential power, and are concerned about family secrets. Heatherington and Friedlander (1990) and others (Mamodhoussen et al., 2005; Symonds & Horvath, 2004) have empirically verified the existence of split alliances between family members and the therapist. Symonds and Horvath found strong correlations between alliance and outcome when the partners agreed on the strength of the alliance and when the strength of the alliance increased from Session 1 to Session 3. Similarly, Safran, Muran, Samstag, and Stevens (2002) found evidence in individual psychotherapy that alliance predicts positive outcomes if found to be about average, as measured by alliance assessment instruments, or if the scores increase over the course of treatment.

Johnson, Wright, and Ketring (2002) found that in family therapy the alliance scores for family members predicted changes in psychiatric symptom distress for mothers, fathers, and adolescents. Agreement with the therapist on the therapy tasks domain of the alliance was the greatest predictor of the outcome for both mothers and adolescents while agreement on the therapy goals domain was greatest for fathers. Beck et al. (2006) also looked at alliances in families in a qualitative study with four cases. Interestingly, they found direct measures of split alliances with the therapist in only two of the four cases. In the study Beck et al. (2006) found that most of the problems centered on the lack of agreement between family members on goals for being in therapy, rather than disagreeing with the therapist on therapy goals. In two of the cases, which included husbands and fathers, most of the conflict appeared to be between spouses.

It seems clear that as a therapist you will need to guard against forming reciprocal emotional triangles with either partner (Bowen, 1978; Rait, 1998; Thomas et al., 2005). Triangles that form between you and any family member or groups of family members – such as aligning with the parents against an adolescent – seems to have the potential to form rifts in the alliances. In addition, negativity or defensiveness on your part in response to client negativity may be harmful to the client-therapist alliance.

Detecting rifts in the alliance

Client confrontation of the therapist and client withdrawal from the therapist or the treatment program often signal a rupture in the alliance (Safran & Muran,1996; Safran et al., 2002). Confrontation is observed when the client openly expresses hostility or anger toward you or the therapy process. The far more frequent signal of a rupture is client withdrawal. The client may withdraw from you, the therapy process, or from her or his own emotional processes. Examples of withdrawal include passivity or refusal to talk and coming late or missing sessions. There can be, of course, a mix of ways of expressing alliance rupture in which the client manifests angry or hostile withdrawal.

It would appear that a split alliance in couple or family therapy should be treated as a therapeutic rupture (Friedlander, Escudero, & Heatherington, 2006; Pinsof, 1995). In family therapy one family member may confront you or attack the therapy process while another family member may experience you or the process as positive and helpful. In a split alliance one family member may withdraw from the therapy process, from you, or from interaction with the other family members.

When there is a split alliance two factors are said to determine the strength of the split (Pinsof, 1994). The first is the intensity of the negative alliance of one family member balanced against the degree of positivity in another family member. The second factor is the power of the subsystem, such as the parental subsystem, to influence whether or not family members keep coming to therapy. For example, your strong positive alliance with an adolescent son may not be sufficient to balance a negative alliance with the parents. Pinsof (1994) suggests that you need to give careful attention to the alliance with the most powerful subsystem in an attempt to help the clients continue the therapy. However, this does not justify failure to attend to the alliance with the less powerful subsystems. Thomas et al. (2005) makes it clear that husbands and wives wield alliance power in different ways. Therefore, family therapists must be especially mindful of the alliance with each spouse and between the spouses.

Learning to detect split alliances

Alliance ruptures and split alliances occur frequently in therapy. It is therefore important that you become proficient at detecting and in repairing them (Safran et al., 2002). One way to learn to detect and repair split alliances is to assess the alliance at the end of each session. This is especially important in the first three sessions (Symonds & Horvath, 2004) although it remains important throughout the treatment as the alliance is constantly subject to change (Safran et al., 2002). Some therapists assess the alliance at the end of each session by asking something like, "Did I say or do anything in this session that offended you or bothered you in any way?" It takes a great deal of courage on your part to ask such questions and then to accept the feedback without defensiveness. Some therapists find it easier to use one of the many reliable and valid client self-report instruments such as the Session Rating Scale (SRS: Duncan et al., 2003), the System for Observing Family Therapy Alliances self-report form (SOFTA-s: Freidlander et al., 2006), and the Revised Helping Alliance Questionnaire-II (Haq-II: Luborsky et al., 1996). The SRS is recommended as it is short, just 4 items, takes only a minute or two to administer, and it is easily scored in session.[1]

The SRS (Duncan et al., 2003) is a forced choice instrument with the choices separated by a 10 cm line. For example, the first item, entitled "Relationship," states at the left end "I did not feel heard, understood, or respected." The opposite end the line (at the 10 cm point) states, "I felt heard, understood, and respected." Clients are asked to place a mark on the line close to the description that "best fits your experience." As clients tend to rate their alliance with the therapist high, any mark at 9 cm or less should elicit a therapist enquiry. For example, if a client marked the "relationship" item above at 9 cm or less you might ask, "What happened or didn't happen in this session that made you feel you were not heard, understood, or respected?" After listening carefully to the client's reply you should immediately begin attempting to repair the breach by first accepting responsibility for the oversight, second by validating the client's feelings and thoughts, and third by offering to make changes in subsequent sessions. For example, you might say something like, "I'm sorry I appeared to not be listening at times. You have every right to be offended by my behavior. I will make a greater effort to let you know that I really am listening in the next session. If I look like I'm not paying attention in the future will you tell me right when it happens? I really do want to make our time together as helpful as possible." The issue should be entered in your case notes to serve as a reminder to change your behavior in the next session. Continuous use of the SRS will make early detection of alliance ruptures easier and facilitate your immediate attempts to repair the alliance.

Another way for you to learn to detect alliance breaches is to use the SOFTA-o which was developed for observers to evaluate therapy alliances (Friedlander, Escudero, Horvath et al., 2006). Friedlander, Escudero, Horvath et al. recommend that you and your supervisor observe your digitally or videotaped recorded sessions and rate each family member's alliance. The SOFTA-o has a helpful training manual and an online support system to help you learn how to observe alliance breaches.[2] You will increase your ability to recognize breaches in the alliance by reviewing the recordings of your sessions and discussing the clients' alliance with your supervisor. You can greatly improve your skills as a therapist by frequently and consistently reviewing your videotapes just as athletes and performing artists benefit from reviewing videotapes of their performances.

Interventions to repair ruptured alliances

Safran and Muran (1996; Safran et al., 2002) found that therapists who are successful in repairing alliance ruptures recognized the clients' withdrawal or negative responses earlier than therapists who were not successful. As soon as you detect a breach focus the clients' attention on the behavior that indicated the rupture in the alliance. Recognize the clients' expressions of negative feelings, validate those feelings, and then help them express and clarify their feelings. According to Safran et al. (2002) repair attempts generally consist of the therapist: (a) commenting in a nondefensive, noncritical way on the here-and-now communication; (b) accepting responsibility for the therapist's cognitive, behavioral, and emotional responses to the communication; (c) expressing supporting and soothing behaviors toward the participants; and (d) making expressions of validation and appreciation. For example, if one family member expresses negative feelings toward you and the treatment program you should immediately stop and ask what happened in a noncritical, nonblaming way. You might say something like, "I'm sorry. Did I say or do something that offended you?" After the client explains you might say, "I can see how what I said may have sounded harsh. Let me say that again in a better way."

Pinsof (1994) derived several techniques from psychoanalytic theory for repairing ruptures to the alliance. Pinsof recommends focusing on the marital couples' individual and collective experiences of the therapist and the therapy experience. This recommendation fits with Safran and Muran's (2004) finding that immediate focus on the experience in the session led to alliance repair. Pinsof also recommended changing the therapy context by seeing the spouses individually.

Pinsof and Catherall (1986) recommend focusing on the client or subsystem alliance with the most power in the relationship. This may include giving the most powerful member of the dyad more individual time. Beck et al. (2006) in a qualitative study of four cases found some evidence in two of the cases that split alliances were more a function of the family members' differences in their family allegiance than in feelings about the therapist. These researchers divided the clients into family subunits for treatment as did Pinsof (1994). Beck et al. (2006) suggests that breaking the session down into subunits allows the therapist to provide a safe therapy context for everyone. However, one could equally well argue that the clients should be seen together to discuss their issues. Seeing the couple or family conjointly seems justified since the differences in the family members allegiance to each other may be the critical element in their split alliance. It seems plausible that family members will benefit from a conjoint conversation about their differing responses to (a) each other, (b) the therapist, (c) the therapy goals, and (d) the treatment interventions – even if this conversation is emotionally highly charged. In this conversation you may act as a coach, being careful not to reciprocate negativity and not to align with one family member or family subgroup against another.

Should you decide to divide the treatment into two or more separate units of the family be sure to review your policies for seeing individual family members in separate sessions before you divide them (see the extended discussion about seeing family members individually in Chapter 3). Important issues of confidentiality and triangulation should be carefully considered and discussed with the clients prior to entering into individual sessions.

Summary: Establishing and maintaining the therapeutic alliance

In summary, each family member's perception of the alliance with the therapist appears to be an important element of successful outcomes. You can facilitate the alliance by communicating respect, care, and empathy while collaborating with the clients to establish the therapy goals and the treatment methods. You will need to attend to the safety needs of each member of the family by avoiding taking sides with one family member or family subunit over another. As Alexander and colleagues (2000) put it, each family member should leave the session feeling that you are on their side (Alexander, Pugh, Parsons, & Sexton, 2000). You can also facilitate the alliance by not reciprocating client negativity. Negativity toward the therapist or the treatment may be the result of a breach in the alliance and should be addressed as soon as it is detected. Another mark of a rift in the alliance is client's avoidance or escape behavior, such as defensiveness, withdrawing from the therapy process during the session, and/or coming late to or missing sessions. You should confront – in a nondefensive, nonpunishing way – the behavior that is indicative of an alliance rupture as soon as it occurs in the session. Successful therapists make early detection and repair of alliance ruptures one of their hallmarks. Early detection of breaches in the alliance can be facilitated by administering an alliance rating instrument, such as the SRS (Duncan et al., 2003) at the end of each session.

Box 1.1 Supervision and Split Alliances

Supervisors should assist beginning therapists to recognize breaches in the therapy alliance and should support therapists' efforts to repair alliance ruptures. It takes a great deal of courage on the part of therapist-interns to ask clients about any negative feelings they may be having toward the therapy and toward them as therapists. Therefore, if you detect a potential breach in the alliance you should encourage the therapist-intern to identify and repair it. When the therapist does this the supervisor should make a point to congratulate the therapist on this accomplishment. The administration of an alliance instrument, such as the SRS (Duncan et al., 2003) at the end of each session should be encouraged as that will make it easier for therapist-interns to enquire about possible breaches in the alliance.

To help therapist-interns increase their skill at detecting alliance splits you may wish to review a recorded therapy session together using SOFTA-o (Friedlander, Escudero, Horvath et al., 2006). In this supervision session compare your observations with those of your therapist-intern. The goal should be to strengthen the intern's skill in detecting alliance splits. By helping interns learn to detect and repair split alliances supervisors will be protecting the welfare of the clients while increasing the competence of the therapist-intern.

Marriage and Family Theories and Evidence-Based Marital and Family Therapy

Family therapists and counselors use therapy models as a vehicle to help clients to establish an alliance and to change from dysfunctional to more functional behavior. The question then becomes – which model should therapist-interns be taught? Individual psychotherapy has over 250 models (Lambert & Barley, 2002) and marriage and family therapy has generated nearly as many (Becvar, 2003). What criteria may be applied to facilitate the decision about which model to use?

The traditional theories of marriage and family therapy were developed by outstanding clinicians responding to specific classes of clients often with specific classes of needs (Becvar, 2003; Sprenkle & Blow, 2004). For example, Minuchin's structural model resulted from his treatment of blue-collar families with physically ill children (Minuchin, Montalvo, Guerney, Rosman, Schumer, 1967). Haley's (1987) strategic therapy was designed for use with resistant clients. Bowen's (1978) intergenerational model derived from his work with individuals struggling to overcome attachment issues with their families of origin. Feminist theory grew out of protest against gender oriented power differentials and domestic violence cases where the female victims were blamed (Avis, 1988). Collectively these models came to be known as systems models because they are based on the concept that families form an interpersonal relationship system. A system is a closed or semi-closed set of interacting relationships and the behavior of individual family member is said to be determined by circular causality and feedback within the system (Becvar, 2003). Systems theory has served the field well until recently.

Currently, however, health maintenance organizations, government agencies, and professional accrediting bodies are demanding that mental health services provide evidence of treatment efficacy, effectiveness, and efficiency (Crane, 1995; Hayes, Barlow, & Nelson-Gray, 1999). As a result there has been a turn toward evidence-based practice both in marriage and family therapy and in the mental health field in general (Margison et al., 2000; Patterson, Miller, Carnes, & Wilson, 2004; Weisz, Jensen-Doss, & Hawley, 2006).

Evidence-based models as an alternative to theory-based models

In contrast to the theory-based systems models of marital and family therapy discussed above there are a number of evidence-based models available. Evidence-based practice in mental health is reported to have started in the United Kingdom in the 1990s and has spread to other countries (Norcross, Beutler, & Levant, 2006a). The intent of evidence-based practice is to use the most reliable and valid information to establish what works best for specific types of clients, with specific types of problems, and in specific conditions or settings. Norcross et al. point out that the American Psychological Association differentiates between practice guidelines and treatment guidelines (American Psychological Association, 2006). Practice guidelines are said to refer to how professionals conduct themselves. Treatment guidelines provide specific recommendations about which treatments work or are considered "best practice." In this text we are primarily focused on best practice treatment guidelines.

What evidence-based therapies are available to marriage and family therapists?

A number of evidence-based models for marriage and family counseling are available. For recent reviews of empirically-supported family therapy treatments see Carr (2000), Christophersen and Mortweet (2001), Fonagy, Target, Cottrell, Phillips, and Kurtz (2002), Miller, Johnson, Sandberg, Stringer-Seibold, and Gfeller-Strouts (2000), Sandberg et al. (1997), and Sprenkle (2002). Treatment guidelines or protocols for two of these evidence-based models are presented in Part II of this volume. Chapter 7 describes the Gottman Method Couples Therapy, which is based on his research into the causes of divorce (Gottman, 1999). Chapter 8 presents Johnson's emotionally-focused therapy, which was designed for couples with commitment and attachment problems (Johnson, 1996).

Selecting an Evidence-Based Model for Marriage and Family Therapy Interns

The decision about which theories, methods, and techniques to teach beginning therapists has not been resolved in mental health fields and this is especially true for marriage and family therapy (Liddle, 1991a; Liddle, Becker, & Diamond, 1997; Pinsof & Wynne, 1995a, 1995b). As stated earlier there seems to be general consensus that all therapists need to be taught the basic listening and observing skills that are required to establish and maintain a working relationship with each member of the family in treatment. Beyond that, the current debate appears to be focused on whether one of the many general theoretical models – such as Haley's (1987) problem-solving strategic model or Bowen's (1978) intergenerational model – should be taught as opposed to the one of the evidence-based models – such as Gottman's in *The Marriage Clinic* (1999). In theory MFT educators and supervisors need not be limited to either theory-based or empirically-based training approaches. Both could be taught. However, in terms of the practical demands upon the time of therapist-interns, their instructors, and their supervisors, selection of one of these approaches will severely limit the amount of time that may be devoted to any other model or method (Calhoun et al., 1998). This is especially true for trainees enrolled on a two-year clinical marriage and family therapy master's program.

The debate about theory-based models versus evidence-based models is already well discussed in clinical psychology (Beutler, 1998; Calhoun et al., 1998; Garfield, 1998; Nathan, 1998; Norcross et al., 2006a, 2006b; Persons & Silberschatz, 1998) but marriage and family therapists, while recognizing the issues (Pinsof & Wynne, 1995a, 1995b, 2000), appear to continue to focus primarily on epistemological arguments. It would appear that epistemological arguments cannot be resolved as long as they remain arguments based on words alone. Other disciplines have found that the best way to resolve these types of disputes is to submit the questions to empirical test (Liddle, 1991b; Norcross et al., 2006a). However, as Liddle (1991b) and others (Pinsof & Wynne, 1995a; Shields, 1986) point out, empirical research has not been an important part of the culture of marriage and family therapy. How much longer marriage and family therapy can maintain a credible position in the mental health field sustained primarily by epistemological arguments is an open question (Shields, Wynne, McDaniel, & Gawinski, 1994).

A step in the direction of establishing empirically supported treatments for marriage and family therapy was taken in October 1995. At that time a special edition of the *Journal of Marital and Family Therapy* entitled "The effectiveness of marital and family therapy" was published under the direction of then editor Douglas H. Sprenkle and special editors William M. Pinsof and Lyman C. Wynne. Pinsof and Wynne (1995a) established guidelines that could be used to select marriage and family therapies that have been found to be efficacious and effective.[3]

As discussed above, evidence-based therapies offer us the most promise for providing our clients with the best treatments available at any one time. These therapies have limitations of which we need to make ourselves aware. However, even with their limitations it appears better to go with the strength provided by the empirical evidence rather than depend on theory and clinical lore. The lists of best treatment will change as new research is carried out and results published. As better methods are tested and become available they should be adopted into practice. It is incumbent upon all therapists and their supervisors to continue to seek out the most efficacious and effective therapies through continuing education. It takes great intellectual courage to change from a known treatment that we are comfortable with to a new treatment (Polya, 1971). However, delivering the "best" treatment to our clients demands that we change when there is sufficient empirical evidence to warrant such a change.

Some criteria for selecting an evidence-based therapy model

If the effect on client outcomes that results from the therapy model is only 15 percent and if no model is more efficacious than any other, then the choice of a treatment model to teach beginning therapists appears to be somewhat arbitrary. However, the decision is important. To help with the decision some rules for selection of a therapy model may be set out.

First criterion: Select a treatment model with demonstrated efficacy

When you select a model find one that has been found to be efficacious for treating the clients' assessed problems. As described above a wide range of models for treatment of marital and family distress have been subjected to random clinical trials (RCT) and established as efficacious. Therefore, it should be possible to select an evidenced-based therapy that will satisfy the clients' values, needs, and goals.

Second criterion: select a model with a helpful treatment manual

Most evidence-based treatments have a treatment manual that was used to train and supervise the therapists involved in the clinical trial. Treatment manuals are useful, especially for training, as they spell out the interventions to be followed in delivering the treatment (Addis & Cardemil, 2006; Calhoun et al., 1998). This is helpful as you and your supervisor seek for ways to improve your treatment delivery (Chapter 4) and your adherence to the treatment interventions spelled out in the manual (Chapter 5). However, as pointed out earlier, therapist competence is not a function of adherence to the manual alone. One of the most important things you must learn is how to tailor the treatment to the clients' needs.

Third criterion: Select a model that can be tailored to the needs of the clients

A client-focused approach to therapy requires tailoring the therapy to the clients' needs and goals (Chapter 4). You will need to help the clients see how the model fits their needs, values, and beliefs in order to build and maintain a positive therapeutic alliance (Horvath & Bedi, 2002). Tailoring the therapy to the clients' needs starts with "Therapy Task 1: Assessment" (Chapter 3). In the assessment phase you will determine the clients' needs and goals. This is followed by "Therapy Task 2: Establishing a Treatment Plan". The treatment plan should be an evidence-based treatment, which best fits the clients' problems. If your assessment is accurate then the clients are likely to agree that the treatment plan "fits them," that is, is tailored to their needs. However, the tailoring does not stop there. As you deliver the treatment you will need to continually assess the "fit" by measuring both the alliance and the therapy outcomes (Duncan & Miller, 2006; Lambert, Harmon, Slade, Whipple, & Hawkins, 2005). If you encounter splits in the alliance then you will need to make adjustments to the way you are delivering the treatment (Safran & Muran, 1996; Safran et al., 2002). Learning to tailor the treatment to the clients' needs is an important therapist skill, which when mastered will generally lead to successful client outcomes.

Fourth criterion: Select a best-treatment model where the outcomes are measurable

The fourth rule for selection of a treatment model is that treatment outcomes should be measurable (Miller, Duncan, & Hubble, 2004). The assessment instruments need not be specific to the model but should be relevant to the class of problems that the model treats. For example, the Outcome Rating Scale (ORS: Miller & Duncan, 2004) and the Revised Dyadic Adjustment Scale (RDAS: Busby, Crane, D. R., Larson, J. H., & Christensen, 1995) work well to assess psychological symptoms and marital distress respectively. These outcome instruments are applicable for any of the evidence-based marital therapies such as Johnson's emotionally-focused therapy (Johnson, 2004), Gottman's couple therapy method (Gottman, 1999), or *Integrative Couple Therapy* by Jacobson and Christensen (1996). By assessing the therapy outcomes continuously you will be in a position to recognize trends and to make corrections to the treatment if needed. If the clients are not making progress in therapy, as determined by the outcome measures, then you should consider altering the treatment and should consult with your supervisor (see Chapter 5).

In summary

Selecting the first therapy model for use by marriage and family therapy trainees is an important decision. Select an evidence-based treatment with has a treatment manual. The choice may be made by the faculty as a whole, by a training center, or by the instructor teaching the first clinical-experience class. Once the treatment model has been selected it is recommended that beginning therapists be given sufficient time to practice with the model so that they may gain skill and confidence in its use. This may require up to one year and the opportunity to treat three or four cases employing the model (Calhoun et al., 1998).

Practicing Within Your Competence

Therapists are admonished not to practice beyond their competence and ethical and legal sanctions are often imposed on unwary therapists who stray beyond their limits (AAMFT, 1998; Knapp & VandeCreek, 1997). Most beginning therapists feel that they are practicing beyond their competence in their first clinical cases. However, therapist-interns who have studied the treatment carefully and are committed to it, who follow the treatment manual in a flexible manner, who regularly assess their clients' progress and the alliance, and who receive supervision regularly are acting within their sphere of competence. Clients who come for therapy at training clinics are made aware of the fact that they are being treated by therapist-interns under the guidance of licensed supervisors. None the less, if the clients believe that treatment can be helpful, and if they are presented with a plausible treatment for their problem that will allow them to undergo a healing experience, then they have a reasonable chance at a successful outcome (Wampold, 2001).

The Remainder of the Book

Part I of this text is designed to help you learn the five therapy tasks needed to deliver most models of therapy. Part II will help you learn to deliver selected marriage and family therapies.

You will need to learn to build and maintain an alliance with clients, which will help your clients undergo the changes in their behavior needed for successful outcomes (Frank & Frank, 2004; Horvath & Bedi, 2002; Norcross, 2002). You have begun to learn to build and maintain a therapy alliance in this chapter. In Chapter 2 you will learn to apply some basic therapist communication skills and you will learn to use the basic therapy skills to help clients explore their issues, consider alternative behaviors, and begin to make changes in their lives. In addition, in Chapter 2 you will also learn crisis management for both suicidal ideation and for family violence.

In Chapters 3 to 6 you will learn to apply the five key tasks of therapy. The five therapy tasks are; (1) Assessing the problem; (2) Establishing the treatment plan; (3) Delivering the planned treatment; (4) Evaluating treatment delivery and treatment outcomes; and (5) Terminating treatment.

- Chapter 3 will provide you with the skills you need for Therapy Task 1, which includes making the initial phone contact, introducing your clients to therapy and making your initial assessment of their problem.
- In Chapter 4 you will learn the elements of Therapy Tasks 2 and 3. Task 2 is establishing the treatment plan and includes how to develop a treatment plan and how to share the treatment plan with the clients. Therapy Task 3 focuses on how to begin delivering the planned treatment. Therapy Task 3 is continued in Chapter 5.
- Chapter 5 introduces you to the skills needed for continuing Therapy Task 3 and for Therapy Task 4 – how to evaluate your treatment delivery and how to evaluate your clients' progress toward successful outcomes. Successful outcomes lead to treatment termination.
- Chapter 6 will discuss the termination processes.

That will conclude Part I of this text. Part II provides an introduction to two empirically supported marriage treatment programs. The treatment protocols introduced in Part II are the Gottman Method Couples Therapy (Gottman, 1999) and the Emotionally-Focused Therapy (Johnson, 2004). I have selected these treatment protocols to show how the protocols can be used to treat marital problems as encountered by family therapists and counselors. Once you have assessed your clients' problems you may match one of these treatment programs to your assessment. You will then present it to your clients as a treatment plan. However, these selected therapy models are not the only empirically-supported family therapy programs and you may choose others to fit the needs of your clients as determined by you and your supervisor.

What Should You Take Away from Chapter 1?

1. There appear to be four factors which all successful therapies have in common (Hubble et al., 1999; Sprenkle et al., 1999). These four factors are (1) the *alliance*, (2) what the *clients' bring* to therapy, (3) the *placebo effect*, and (4) the *treatment techniques*. The alliance explains 30 percent of the outcome variance, what the clients bring to therapy explains 40 percent of the

outcome variance, while the placebo effect and the therapy techniques each explain 15 percent of the outcome variance.

2 The most important factor in successful therapy outcomes may be the therapy alliance. The therapy alliance is composed of (a) the clients' trust in the therapist to help them achieve their goals and meet their needs, (b) the clients' agreement that the therapist understands their goals, and (c) the clients' belief that the treatment provided by the therapist will help them achieve their goals.

3 The alliance is built and maintained by your skill in communicating respect and empathy while delivering a treatment tailored to the clients' needs, values, and beliefs. The treatment needs to be of sufficient length for the therapist and client to have a conversation about the clients' goals and needs, which lead to clients changing dysfunctional behaviors and relationships to more functional behaviors and relationships. In the course of the conversation the clients find ways to accomplish their goals and satisfy their needs.

4 Since all models are about equally effective the choice of a model should fit the clients' needs and goals. The model selected should be an evidence-based treatment that you are competent to deliver under supervision.

5 Advantages of an evidence-based treatment. Evidence-based treatments have a manual that provides you with structure and guidance. This in turn gives you and your supervisor with the opportunity to discuss and develop your treatment delivery and your alliance building enabling you to develop the competence and confidence you need to be an effective therapist.

Chapter 2

Basic Therapist Skills

Introduction

Your behavior as a therapist is a critical element in your clients' successful outcomes. In a recent review Wampold (2006) estimated that the therapist's contribution to therapy outcome is about 8 percent in controlled clinical trials and 5 percent in private practice. Treatment versus no treatment has been found to account for 13 percent of the outcome variance. Differences between treatments accounted for 0 percent to 1 percent effect and the difference between empirically-supported treatments and placebo treatments was 0 percent to 4 percent. Finally, the alliance (see Chapter 1) was found to account for 5 percent – "Clearly, the person of the therapist is a critical factor in the success of therapy" (Wampold, 2001, p. 202).

Your ability to relate to clients has been shaped by your personal life history. This has prompted some to say that therapists and counselors are born, not made. However, this would be incorrect. Some people have learned good relationship skills over their lifetime and it is always possible to learn these skills with effort and guidance (Hill, 2004). Furthermore, those with good relationship skills can improve their skills even further.

The basic therapy skills are (a) empathic listening, (b) building and maintaining a therapeutic alliance, (c) recognizing and working through your own issues, (d) conceptualizing the clients' interpersonal and intrapsychic processes, and (e) learning to reflect on and analyze one's own performance (Wampold, 2001). In Chapter 1 you were introduced to the skill of building and maintaining a therapeutic alliance. In this chapter you will be introduced to the therapist skill of applying empathic listening to family members in therapy sessions. You will also learn to recognize and work with some of your personal issues. In addition, before you begin seeing clients will need to learn crisis management for clients with suicidal ideation and for families experiencing family violence. You will learn to assess and classify suicidal ideation and the three domains of family violence: (a) partner-to-partner maltreatment, (b) adult-to-child maltreatment, and (c) elder maltreatment.

The Therapist's Contribution to the Therapy Relationship

The therapy relationship is an intense, emotional encounter between the therapist and clients (Norcross et al., 2006). As pointed out by Lambert and Barley "it is difficult to conceptually

Becoming a Marriage and Family Therapist: From Classroom to Consulting Room, First Edition. D. Eugene Mead.

differentiate between therapist variables (interpersonal style, attributes), facilitative conditions (empathy, warmth, positive regard), and the client–therapist relationship (therapeutic alliance, working endeavor)" (Lambert & Barley, 2002, p. 21). The therapist's ability to communicate empathy, warmth, and genuineness may be separated conceptually, however, it is not really possible to separate the three in practice (Bohart, Elliott, Greenberg, & Watson, 2002). Therefore, empathy will be used as our term for the facilitative conditions.

Empathic listening and responding

You can learn to be a more effective therapist by improving your skill as an empathic listener and communicator. Effective interns have been found to have higher levels of empathic understanding than less effective interns (Lafferty, Beutler, & Crago, 1991). When clients rate therapists they consistently give high marks to therapists who communicate understanding. We can have confidence in these findings because they have been found in a variety of settings and with a variety treatment models (Bohart et al., 2002; Lambert & Barley, 2002). To be more effective as a therapist you need to demonstrate understanding at the level of the client's experience, not just the client's words (Bohart et al., 2002). As a family therapist it is important that you demonstrate empathic understanding of each family member's feelings, perceptions, values, assumptions, and their views of other people and situations (Bohart et al., 2002). Bohart and associates point out that part of being empathic includes understanding that some family members may find expressions of empathy too intrusive, while highly resistant family members may find empathy too directive; still others may find an empathic focus on feelings unnatural. Attempt to understand each family member's responses to your efforts at being empathic as you attempt to respond to their other behaviors, feelings, and thoughts.

Your skills can be improved by:

- Listening to and observing your clients carefully as they share their story
- Responding using simple direct statements that show an understanding of each member's experiences in their family (Bohart et al., 2002). For example, "Mary, you feel John doesn't listen to you and John you feel overwhelmed by Mary's attempts to get you to talk."
- Attempting to validate each family member's perspective. You might say something like, "You're upset with all this fighting, and you have a right to be upset."
- Using language that is concrete, which brings strong images or feelings to mind, but leaves it open for the family members to correct if needed (Bohart et al., 2002). For example, "You appear to feel out of control, as if your plane is spiraling down and you can't seem to stop it."

Empathic statements are often an attempt to bring together the overall sense of what is happening to the family members and what they are experiencing, "Overall, you seem to feel unable to bring all this trouble to an end." Your goal is to help the family members put into words what they are experiencing. In learning to respond empathically it is important that you attempt to use more positive responses than negative responses to their behaviors (Najavits & Strupp, 1994). Using positive statements will help you to avoid sounding critical or defensive.

As you increase your ability to be empathic you will be increasing your ability to respond to the overall context, not just the immediate words. Context is said to include: (a) client variables such as impairment; (b) their presenting problems; (c) the family member's life situation, support systems, and stressors; and (d) the stage in treatment, including the improvement, they have achieved to this point (Waltz, Addis, Koerner, & Jacobson, 1993). Use of empathic statements that bring together the contextual variables in the treatment will increase your ability to communicate your understanding of the clients and their situation.

Person of the therapist variables

One of the variables that influences the clients' behavior in the session is your behavior (Mead, 1990; Norcross, 2002; Wampold, 2006). At the same time your behavior is, and should be, responsive to the clients. Therefore, the therapist–client relationship is an ongoing reciprocal cycle. Your behavior includes your affective, cognitive, and behavioral responses to the clients and to the setting – all of which are a function of your personal and professional history (Mead, 1990).

Person of the therapist in treatment delivery

As a therapist you bring two histories to the therapy session, your personal history, which is a function of all your life experiences, and your professional history, which is a subset of your personal history. As you learn to be a professional therapist you will learn techniques and interventions designed to help your clients achieve their therapy goals. However, since your professional history is a subset of your personal history your personal history will be part of your behavior as a therapist. We turn here to your personal history and how that impacts treatment delivery. Your personal feelings, thoughts, and behavior are all part of your treatment delivery.

In the treatment delivery you need to have strong responses to your clients and the events in the session. If you fail to recognize your personal responses and subsequently act on them the resulting behavior may not be beneficial to your clients. For example, when clients express strong emotions in the session you need to recognize the impact their emotions are having on you. Start by recognizing that the clients' emotional responses to you and to the current therapy experience are responses from their life histories triggered by the current therapy relationship and your behavior in the session. This is sometimes referred to as the clients' transference behavior (Crits-Christoph & Gibbons, 2002). Your emotional, cognitive, and behavioral responses to your clients are sometimes called countertransference (Gelso & Hayes, 2002). Countertransference is defined as all of your emotional reactions to your clients and may be triggered by your clients' transference behaviors. Your supervisor will play an important role in helping you to recognize and manage transference and countertransference.

When you encounter intense emotional responses in your session ask yourself, "Are my clients' emotional behaviors calling out responses I have developed in the past in my family of origin or in my current intimate relationships?" Also ask yourself, "Are my clients' emotions eliciting my 'fight or flight' responses?" In situations like this recognize that the clients' emotions are not your emotions, then help your clients express, clarify, and understand their emotions. When clients express negative responses to the treatment, or to you, recognize your automatic responses to their criticisms and try not to reciprocate with negative responses. Instead, consider these events as possible breaches in the alliance and use your skills to deal with the breach.

You may wish to use the Person of the Therapist Checklist (Appendix A) to help you review your personal responses either in the session or after the session. You should ask yourself:

- "Is my affect appropriate for the events occurring in this session or am I experiencing affective arousal, which is interfering with my performance as a therapist?"
- "Am I experiencing feeling stuck, frustrated, ambivalent, anxious, angry, fearful, or/and experiencing panic, rage, disgust, passion, sexual arousal, guilt/shame, depression, grief, optimism, or mirth?"
- "Are my thoughts centered on the clients and their behavior or am I 'out of the room' some of the time?"
- "Is my behavior congruent with the treatment being delivered?"

Your goal should be to recognize your internal responses and then act on them in a way that enhances your clients' therapy. If you are experiencing sweaty palms or feet, dry mouth, tears, tight stomach muscles, tense large muscles – such as tension in the neck, jaw, forehead, and back – during the session then do not ignore your body's warnings. Learn to apply therapist self-soothing procedures as needed (Appendix B).

You can perform therapist self-soothing by slowly taking three deep breaths then asking yourself what the therapy task is for this session and give yourself an answer. The key therapy tasks, found in Chapters 3 to 5 are: (1) assessing the clients' problems and goals, (2) developing a treatment plan, (3) delivering the planned treatment, (4) evaluating your treatment delivery and evaluating the impact of the treatment on the clients' behavior, and (5) terminating therapy. When you have refocused on the therapy task briefly review the things, relevant to the therapy task, you have done effectively so far in the session. There are sure to be many things you have done well so don't give up, keep digging them out. They do not need to be big things. The cognitive behavior required for you to complete this step is part of the self-soothing process so it is not intended as a self-blame, shame, or guilt game. Just recall all the things you have done well so far. Finally, ask yourself what you need to do next to be helpful to these clients. Give yourself several alternatives such as:

- Using "I" statements to reflect your feelings to the clients.
- Reflecting and restating the clients' behavior clearly and specifically in a nonblaming way and then asking the clients for their interpretation.
- Asking family members to describe to each other the recent events in the session.
- If necessary, excuse yourself, step out, walk around, get a drink, before returning to the session.
- If necessary seek out a supervisor or peer for consultation.

Once you have determined what you can do to continue being therapeutic to your clients implement an intervention consistent with the therapy task. If your task is delivering treatment, then select an intervention based on the "best treatment" model you are delivering. After you have implemented your intervention tell yourself to stop, listen, and observe the clients' responses. After the session consult with your supervisor about your emotional response to the clients.

Dealing with stress as a therapist

As pointed out earlier therapy is an intense, emotional encounter between the therapist and the clients (Norcross et al., 2006). You need to be prepared to meet the stresses of carrying out therapy and be especially prepared to handle stress when providing crisis management. You will need to learn to work within your emotional limits. Most therapists are not prepared to listen empathically to the primitive, violent, and sadistic material often encountered in family violence cases (Turkus, 1995). Therefore, you will need to learn to protect yourself from vicarious traumatization (Turkus, 1995). Be aware of your personal symptoms of stress and burn out. You need to be involved but not over-involved or enmeshed (Hipple & Hipple, 1983). Learn to differentiate between reasonable altruism and rescuing (Turkus, 1995). Learn to make use of your supervisor, colleagues, and personal therapist. Keep your personal social support system, such as significant others and friends, informed of the stressful nature of your work but do not violate any client confidences.

Job burnout as a form of therapist stress

In addition to investigating your reaction to the clients in a specific case you can also consider your overall reaction to the stress of your therapy work. Ask yourself, "Am I experiencing job burnout?"

Burnout may be defined as feelings of emotional exhaustion, depersonalization, and diminished personal accomplishment (Burisch, 2002; Zellars & Perrewé, 2001). Rosenberg and Pace (2006) using the Maslach Burn out Inventory (Maslach & Jackson, 1981) assessed burnout in a sample of 116 experienced clinical members of the American Association for Marriage and Family Therapy. Rosenberg and Pace found that female therapists compared to males rated themselves significantly lower on the Depersonalization subscale ($M = 2.62, 3.21$ respectively) but no significant gender differences were found on the Emotional Exhaustion and Personal Accomplishment subscales. The authors report that these findings are consistent with findings from other mental health fields.

Marriage and family therapists (MFTs) differed in levels of feelings of Personal Accomplishment and feelings of Emotional Exhaustion according to their primary work settings. MFTs in private practice rated themselves significantly higher on Personal Accomplishment than did therapists in medical settings and MFTs in academic settings. MFTs in private practice rated themselves significantly lower on the Emotional Exhaustion subscale than did MFTs in community agencies, pastoral care, and MFTs in healthcare settings.

Older therapists had lower scores on the depersonalization and emotional exhaustion subscales than did younger workers (Maslach & Jackson, 1981). Stoltenberg suggests that it is not uncommon for therapist-interns in the intermediate stages of their training to have doubts about the effectiveness of therapy and of their ability to be an effective therapist (Stoltenberg, 2005; Stoltenberg & Delworth, 1987). Those therapists who persist in training and in their careers gain in feelings of competence and overcome feelings of ineffectiveness as they have successful outcomes.

Self-help for therapist stress

If you find that you are reacting to the clients, the therapy process, or supervision in ways that are less than optimal then you may wish to initiate some self-help measures. You could use the "Therapist Self-Soothing Procedures" as mentioned above. In addition, you could make use of Weiss's (2004) self-help text. Weiss provides helpful tips for personal and professional self-care that will be of use throughout your career as a therapist or counselor. Laireiter and Willutzki (2003) present another interesting approach to therapist self-help. They discuss the use of self-practice and self-reflection to increase an intern's competence in delivering cognitive behavioral therapy. Self-practice is defined as applying the techniques and interventions that you are learning to use with clients to your own behavior. Self-reflection is concerned with increasing your interpersonal sensitivity, empathy, and competency. Self-practice and self-reflection are combined as you apply the therapy techniques you are learning to your own behavior and as you reflect on the impact of the therapy technique on you as a person. Laireiter and Willutzki hypothesized that therapists would make gains in their professional skills more than in their personal skills by using these techniques. They found some support for this hypothesis.

Social-support as help for therapist stress

Therapist-interns may receive social support from (a) colleagues, (b) supervisors and other faculty, (c) ecclesiastical leaders and family physicians, and (d) professional mental health workers (Barker & Pistrang, 2002; Bowing et al., 2004; Cowen, 1982; Milne, Cowie, Gormly, White, & Harley, 1992). Although many people receive social support from their spouse, family, and friends this source is limited for therapists because of the confidential nature of therapy. When using family members and others as a source of social support you should be careful to adhere to the rules of confidentiality and your clients' rights of privacy (AAMFT, 2007; American Psychological Association, 2002). You must not release information about clients to third parties without written consent. Therefore, when discussing cases with anyone other than your supervisor you must scrupulously avoid any details that would form a breach of the clients' confidentiality or an invasion of their privacy. Consequently, discussing specific cases with your family, spouse, or intimate other should be avoided. Treat the clients' information in the same manner you would have your personal information treated.

Help from supervisors

After a stressful therapy session discuss your responses to the clients and the session with your supervisor. Your affective, behavioral, and cognitive responses are not atypical or abnormal. Most therapists, including your supervisor, have experienced similar responses in therapy sessions. Before discussing the case it may help to review your session using the Person of the Therapist Checklist (Appendix A).

It takes a great deal of courage to tell your supervisor about the affective and cognitive responses you are experiencing toward your clients. Therapists have been known not to disclose what they perceive to be clinical mistakes, negative and positive reactions to clients, client attraction to the therapist, and therapist countertransference (Ladany, Hill, Corbett, & Nutt, 1996). Failure of therapists to disclose to their supervisors issues related to clients sometimes stems from problems in the therapist–supervisor relationship (Ellis, 2002; Gray, Ladany, Walker, & Ancis, 2001; Magnuson, Wilcoxon, & Norem, 2000; Moskowitz & Rupert, 1983; Nelson & Friedlander, 2001; Wetchler, Piercy, & Sprenkle, 1989). Therapists often cited as reasons for nondisclosure their perception of the issue as unimportant, fear of evaluation, the personal nature of the event, and negative feelings toward their supervisors. Although you may feel that there are good reasons for not sharing your feelings with your supervisor the research cited above suggests that the benefits of disclosure generally outweigh the downside.

Bernard (1988) provides some useful guidelines on how to best use your supervision time. Bernard suggests that before you go to a session with your supervisor that you review the tape or digital recording of the session and ask yourself, "Did I know what to do in the session?" "Did I know what I wanted to do?" "Was I comfortable at that point?" "Was my performance that of a professional counselor?". It is important that you learn to analyze your performance as a therapist and to take responsibility for your behavior. Then when you go to a supervision session you will be prepared to get the most from the available time – have your case progress notes prepared, have your digital recording, video, or audio tape cued to the places where you want to get help. It's also okay to have the recording cued to places you want to show that you did well as well as places where you feel you want to improve. When you leave the supervision session make sure you have a sense of direction concerning what to do in the next therapy session.

Supervision, like therapy, may be an intense emotional exchange between you and your supervisor. You may take feedback about your therapy interventions very personally. As a result you may feel anxious or even threatened by the prospect of supervision. As Bernard (1988) points out some interns resist supervision by several defensive "games" (Bauman, 1972). These resistance strategies are labeled: submission, turning the tables, I'm no good, helplessness, and projection (Bernard, 1988):

- *Submission.* The intern yields immediately to the superior knowledge of the supervisor and accepts all feedback without discussion or question.
- *Turning the tables.* The intern elicits the teacher role from the supervisor by asking numerous questions about what the supervisor would have done in the interns' previous therapy session.
- *I'm no good.* The intern works to convince the supervisor that she or he is an incompetent therapist by magnifying all the mistakes in the session thus placing the supervisor in the role of reassuring the intern that there is hope. The "I'm no good" defense may appear to be an effort to draw the supervisor into a counseling or therapist mode.

- *Helplessness.* Similar to the "I'm no good" approach the "helpless" intern focuses on her or his lack of experience and attempts to have the supervisor take full responsibility for the case.
- *Projection.* In this form of resistance to supervision the intern suggests that it is the supervision process itself which is the problem. The intern protests that she or he is inhibited when the supervisor observes the session live or when she or he must prepare a tape for the supervisor's observation. The therapist implies that the "imposition" of supervision keeps the supervisor from seeing the intern's real therapy skills.

In general when trainees talk over their therapy issues with supervisors the results are helpful (Anderson, Schlossberg, Rigazio-DiGilio, 2000; Hutt et al., 1983; Moskowitz & Rupert, 1983; Wetchler, Piercy, & Sprenkle,1989; Worthen & McNeill, 1996). However, anxiety in supervision is unavoidable. Any time we are observed by others our behavior is altered (Guerin, 1994). Performance anxiety is one source of anxiety in supervision (Liddle, 1986). Problems in the therapist–supervisor relationship are another source of anxiety in supervision (Anderson et al., 2000; Gray et al., 2001; Hutt et al., 1983; Magnuson et al., 2000; Nelson & Friedlander, 2001; Worthen & McNeill, 1996). Some interns react to supervision as if their personal agency is under attack. They find it hard to accept suggestions and resist their supervisor's directives. If you find yourself experiencing supervision anxiety or resistance ask yourself, "Why am I in supervision?" Your answer should be, "To learn to be a more competent therapist." If that is your answer, then you will want to determine what it is that is interfering with you attempts to achieve that goal.

Consider your difficulties with supervision as a problem to be solved. The steps required are (1) to clearly define the problem, (2) to develop a list of possible solutions, (3) to select the most probable solution and put it into practice for a reasonable period of time, (4) to evaluate the result, and (5) if the solution works go on and if not return to step one.

1 Define the problem: During this step stay focused on specifying the problem. As you attempt to determine the problem you are having with supervision consider the following possibilities – have you had trouble accepting correction and feedback in the past? Are you teachable? Have you had difficulties with teachers and supervisors in the past? Are you anxious, fearful, or depressed? Are you having a relationship problem with this supervisor? Are there racial, ethnic, gender, or sexual issues in your relationship with this supervisor? Do others have trouble with this supervisor? Once you have clarified your problem write it down and then go to the next step.
2 Develop a list of solutions. Keep the written statement of the problem, developed in step 1, in front of you. During this step stay focused on problem solutions and do not return to specifying the problem. To help you generate a complete list of possible solutions use brainstorming techniques such as rapidly tossing out ideas without censuring. Keep a record by recording your ideas for solutions on your MP3 player, smart phone, or other electronic device. Ask friends and colleagues to join you in developing possible solutions. When you feel you have generated a list of all possible solutions write them down. Combine any ideas that look as if they might work together. Toss out all completely ridiculous ideas. Give yourself some time to think about the possible solutions. The old adage to "sleep on it" is a good idea. However, do not take too long as an unresolved problem may generate anxiety thus exacerbating the problem. You must also consider the needs of your clients. Too much time in fixing the problem may prevent you from making timely interventions to help the clients. One solution to avoid undue anxiety or procrastination is to set a deadline. Remember that work increases as deadlines approach. Keep the deadline short. When you reach your deadline select the most plausible solution and make a plan to put it into action. The solution you are looking for should be a "win-win" solution for both you and for your supervisor. However a "win-win" solution is not always possible when the problem relates to differences between

you and your supervisor on difficult issues such as those related to a racial, ethnic, gender, or sexual nature.

3 Put your solution into action. If your solution consists of actions you can take on your own, such as overcoming obstacles to scheduling supervision appointments, then proceed to take those actions. If, for example, the action requires a personal change of attitude toward supervision and instruction on your part and you can make those changes on your own, then do so. If you need assistance in making changes in your attitude talk it over with your supervisor, another faculty member, or your personal therapist. If the problem is in your relationship with your supervisor then consider the pros and cons of approaching your supervisor directly. Is this a supervisor that can accept feedback without becoming defensive or reactant? Would approaching this supervisor be the equivalent of career suicide? For example, if the issue is of a racial, ethnic, gender, or sexual nature can a change of supervisor be arranged without difficulty? If not would it be a good idea to discuss the issue with another trusted faculty member or the department chair?
4 Observe the outcome of your solution. After you have selected a solution put the plan into action and observe the results. Set a date that will allow enough time for the solution to become effective. Evaluate the outcome and decide if you need to continue working on this solution or if the solution is not proving effective then return to the problem definition stage and try to determine if you are working on the right problem. If the problem remains the same then consult your list of potential solutions and select another. Put the next potential solution into practice and evaluate the results.
5 If the solution works continue. If not return to step 1 and follow this steps until the problem is solved.

Use of personal therapy for therapist stress

In addition to discussing your reactions to your clients and your sessions with your supervisor you may find it useful to discuss your responses to your clients with your personal therapist. It is unethical for supervisors to enter into a therapy relationship with trainees. Therefore, when your stress is acute you may seek help from a personal therapist. Personal therapy for practicing therapists has been found to be helpful (Deacon, Kirkpatrick, Wetchler, & Niedner, 1999; Farber, 1983; Norcross, 2005). Your conversations with your personal therapist need not be limited to therapy issues. Deacon et al. (1999) found that, in a sample of American Association for Marriage and Family Therapy clinical members, the majority reported that since entering the profession they have had problems relating to their families and marriages that they took to their personal therapist. Clarifying issues in your personal life with your therapist may keep your problems from becoming issues in therapy when clients bring up similar problems.

Many therapists are making use of their own personal therapy whether in response to not achieving progress with a client, to burnout, or simply as a desire to enhance their personal awareness and life satisfaction (Norcross 2005; Weiss, 2004). Norcross's review of twenty years of research found that nearly three-quarters of mental health workers in the US and Europe have made use of personal psychotherapy, often more than once. Sundland (pers. comm. December 13, 1994) reports that out of a cross-national sample of 200 mental health workers 148 reported having had personal therapy. Norcross also reported that the amount of research on the effects of the therapists' personal therapy related to outcomes for their clients is somewhat limited. However, self-reported and observer-rated positive effects of the therapists' personal therapy as having an effect on therapy processes such as warmth, empathy, genuineness, increased focus on the therapeutic alliance, and awareness of countertransference are available. Norcross states that over 90 percent of therapists who have made use of personal therapy reported that it was helpful in improving their self-esteem, work functioning, social life, and emotional expression.

According to Norcross many therapists report that the most helpful parts of their educational experiences were their personal therapy and their supervised practicum and intern experiences (Norcross, 2005). Personal therapy and supervision were both ranked above course work, reading professional journals, and classroom professors.

Learning to observe your client's clinically relevant behavior

One of the basic therapy skills is observing the clients' clinical relevant behavior in the context of the session. Behavioral therapists defined behavior as anything you can do with any part of your body (Skinner, 1953). Verbal behavior and nonverbal behavior is all behavior. Cognitive behavior or "thoughts" may be defined as internal verbal behavior. As thoughts are not readily observed they are often given special status by nonbehavioral therapists. However, when you think about it thoughts are simply behavior that cannot be easily observed. Affective or emotional behaviors are changes in the smooth muscles and glands. We describe these changes verbally by analogy. For example, we talk about a "sharp" pain, a "pounding" headache, or a response to the loss of a dear friend as "heartache." Like thoughts, some affect takes place internally and may not be readily detected by an outside observer. Some of our emotional responses are responses to external contextual variables such as the behavior of other persons or conditions in the nonsocial environment. For example, what one person says or does may elicit emotional behavior on the part of another. Viewing a mountain or an ocean at sunset may also evoke an emotional response. Affect can also be a response to the person's own cognitive behavior. For example, "I was thinking of home and I began to get all choked up and started to cry." Because the physiological changes in affective responses are not initially differentiated in the body we are taught to place specific labels on the "emotional" behavior as it relates to specific contextual variables. For example, consider crying "for happy," crying "for shame," and crying "from pain" each of which can be best understood by the context. Each of these forms of crying occur in response to different contextual events. Your goal, as a therapist-intern, is to learn to carefully observe your client's behavior and the contextual events that are antecedent and consequent to it. Of special importance are the contextual variables provided by family members for each other.

Observing "here and now" behavior

Learning to observe client behavior in the clinical context is important because the only behavior you can help the clients change is behavior that occurs in the session. You have no technology for changing behavior that occurred in the past, even if only a few seconds previously. Therefore, learning to observe the clients' clinically relevant behavior requires taking a "here and now" approach to your observations. The most important data for you to observe is the behavior your clients are exhibiting in response to you and to each other in the session.

Observing clinically relevant behavior

Your family clients' current behavior is a function of their history of interaction with each other and of their interaction in the present context. The behavior is "clinically relevant" if it is too little or too much for the current contextual situation or if it is punishing to the individual or to others. Behavior that is considered too little or too much for the current contextual situation or is punishing to the individual or to others is sometimes referred to as "dysfunctional behavior." Behavior is also "clinically relevant" if it contributes to or takes away from the survival of the individual, of the family, or of other relevant social groups. Behavior which contributes to the welfare of the individual and the group is said to be "functional."

In any social context two or more persons are interacting in relation to each other. In a social context they cannot "not" interact. The awareness of the presence of another individual changes our behavior in some way. The other individual does not need to be physically present for this interaction to take place. For example, a family member may be in one setting, say 100 miles from home, and be thinking of his or her family members back home. The thoughts (cognitive responses) may trigger emotional behavior, and may also trigger a behavioral response, such as making a phone call home.

The interaction of family member's behavior forms a reciprocal system. For example, the wife's behavior serves as an eliciting stimulus for the husband who then responds based on how he has responded in the past and on the basis of how that previous response was reinforced or punished. The husband's response then serves as a stimulus for the wife. She then, in turn, responds. The reciprocal system established by their interaction forms a pattern or cycle which continues until perturbed by changes in the environmental context.

What you observe in the consulting room is the pattern or system of interpersonal responses that have evolved over the history of the family members' relationships. Your first job is to learn to recognize the behavior each family member uses in her or his part of the pattern. Your second job is to learn to describe – in a warm, respectful, and empathic manner – their behavior and the part it plays in their system. When you have learned to describe how each member of the family influences and is influenced by the other family members' behavior, then you will be able to predict each member's behavior, at least in a general way (Skinner, 1953). When you can predict each family member's behavior you will be in a position to recommend changes to alter the pattern. In as much as those changes modify the dysfunctional behaviors in an appropriate way and increase the functional behaviors as desired by the family members then their therapy will likely be considered successful.

In the assessment sessions it is enough that you learn to observe, describe, and predict the relational patterns. In treatment delivery sessions you will intervene using the interventions set out in the treatment manual of the therapy model you are attempting to master. However, because clients may present in crisis at any time over the course of therapy you need to be prepared to manage crisis situations.

Crisis Management of Suicidal Ideation and Family Violence

When clients present in crisis, such as suicidal ideation or family violence, the situation calls for immediate attention. The first issue in crisis management is the safety of all family members. Therefore, before you complete your crisis assessment interview be sure you help your client(s) develop a safety plan. The second issue in crisis assessment, indeed in all assessments, is the need to gather sufficient information to make clinical judgments about the course of action to be taken. Assessment requires information about many areas of the client's life. A thorough crisis assessment makes use of semi-structured interviews, checklists, and reliable and valid assessment instruments. Seek information from the client(s) and, with the client's permission, seek information from other family members. Provide hope for the client and for the other family members. As quickly as possible establish a treatment plan. Initiate the plan and follow through.

Always seek supervision help as early as possible in managing a crisis. Should you be seeing clients when a crisis arises and no supervisor is observing determine if the situation is safe enough for you to excuse yourself briefly to contact your supervisor or a trusted colleague. At the very least be sure the session is being recorded. If you need to step out to contact your supervisor or arrange for videotaping you can explain to the clients that you want to make sure that they are getting the full benefit of your services and the services of your supervisor.

Crisis situations are usually filled with stress and anxiety for the clients and for the therapist. Therefore, it is important for you to have a strategy in place that allows you to deal with the clients' and your own anxiety. The guidelines provided will help you deal with your clients' anxiety. In addition you should know the community resources you can draw upon as needed (Hipple & Hipple, 1983). Your supervisor is a good source for resources in the community.

You manage your own stress better if you have a plan and if you stay grounded in your therapeutic stance (Turkus, 1995). Work within your emotional limits. As stated earlier most therapist-interns are not prepared to listen empathically to primitive, violent, and sadistic material (Turkus, 1995). Therefore, you will need to draw upon the support of your supervisor and your colleagues as you work with clients with suicidal ideation or with clients experiencing family violence. To help you deal with the stress of crisis management use your supervisor, colleagues, personal therapist, and social support systems as described earlier.

Guidelines for suicide risk assessment and intervention

It is believed that throughout the world between half a million and one million people die through suicide each year (Comtois & Linehan, 2006; Wingate, Joiner, Walker, Rudd, & Jobes, 2004). For every completed suicide it is estimated that there are fifteen to twenty attempted suicides (Spirito & Overholser, 2003). Suicidal ideation among adolescent youth is reported to be almost 100 percent (Miller & Taylor, 2005). A national survey of college students found 9.5 percent reported they had seriously considered attempting suicide and 1.5 percent reported making an attempt in the previous year (Kisch, Leino & Silverman, 2005).

Depression is perhaps the most frequent problem treated in mental health agencies. Therefore, because of the close link between depression and suicide, client suicide is not a rare event in clinical practice (Simon, 2004). Clinical psychologists in practice see about five suicidal clients per month and one in six will have a client suicide over their career (Chemtob, Bauer, Hamada, Pelowski, & Muraoka, 1989). One in six interns and one in three psychiatric residents experience the suicide of a client in their training (Bongar, 2002).

Kozlowska, Nunn, and Cousens (1997) report that almost 90 percent of trainees and supervisors reported adverse events in training situations involving crises. It has been reported that many interns and residents receive little help with crisis situations (Foulkes, 2003; Kozlowska et al., 1997). Few interns are fortunate enough to be receiving direct (live) supervision at the time a client broaches the subject of suicide as happened in the incident reported by Charles, Ticheli-Kallikas, Tyner, and Barber-Stephens (2005). It is much more common for the intern to be interviewing the client on their own. In fact, many trainees report a lack of support from their supervisors when dealing with patient violence, patient suicide, and harassment by patients (Foulkes, 2003; Kozlowska et al., 1997). These trainees felt their supervisors were disinterested and lacked empathy and understanding leaving them feeling unsupported. However, in another study 93 percent of the trainees reported receiving support and help with crisis coverage and intervention (Ladany, Lehrman-Waterman, Molinaro, & Wolgast, 1999).

It appears that therapists receive very little training in suicide risk assessment and treatment in their educational programs (Miller, Jacobs, & Gutheil, 1998; Richards & Range, 2001) and this appears to be equally true for marriage and family therapists (Berman, 2006). A review of supervision texts revealed that Lee and Everett (2004) and Mead (1990) make no mention of supervision of suicide risk while other supervision texts provide only a paragraph or two on the subject (Borders & Brown, 2005; Falender & Shafranske, 2004; Watkins, 1997).

The following guidelines are designed to help you prepare to assess suicide risk and to begin treatment of suicidal clients (Gladding, Remley, & Huber, 2001; Ladany et al., 1999; Simon, 2004). Should you have a suicidal client you should consult frequently with your supervisor because your supervisor is legally responsible for your conduct and for the welfare of your clients. In preparing to treat clients with suicidal ideation you will need to consider the legal issues that may arise. Therefore, before discussing assessment of suicidal ideation some potential legal ramifications will be discussed.

Some legal issues related to treating suicidal clients

According to Simon (2004) suicide is the most frequent cause for malpractice litigation. Treatment of depression and the frequently accompanying suicidal ideation and intent is not always successful; as a result the surviving family members of the suicidal client may initiate a lawsuit. Therefore, both you and your supervisor must consider the possibility of legal action following the suicidal death of a client. For extended discussions of malpractice litigation see Chiles and Strosahl (2005) and Simon (2004).

The best protection against a lawsuit related to a client suicide is through thorough and careful assessment of suicide risk followed by client-oriented evidence-based treatment (Chiles & Strosahl, 2005). The assessment and treatment interventions should be carefully and contemporaneously documented in your case notes (Meichenbaum, 2005; Simon, 2004; Wingate et al., 2004).

Generally in malpractice suits the court first attempts to determine if a therapist–client relationship was established. A therapist–client relationship is established when the client enters therapy. However, you may unwittingly establish a therapist–client relationship by engaging in an online phone consultation. Therefore, you should not attempt to assess or manage individuals at risk for suicide on the phone or by other electronic communications.

If the court determines that a therapist–client relationship was established then the court looks for the "four Ds." The four Ds are:" Duty of care, Deviation from a standard of care, Damage to the client, and Direct damage resulting from deviation from the standard of care" (Simon, 2004, p. 4).

1. Duty of Care. This is a legal term. As a therapist you assume a duty of care when you establish a client–therapist relationship.
2. Standard of Care. This is also a legal concept. In the United States each state varies in its definition of a standard of care. Standard of care is determined by expert witnesses. Generally a standard of care suggests that the therapist is responsible for delivering treatment and care which would be delivered by the "average" therapist. Current practice guidelines are the standard against which the courts generally determine a standard of care. Because empirical knowledge changes rapidly less than 90 percent of practice guidelines are valid after 3.6 years and half are outdated at 5.8 years (Simon, 2004). Therefore, you and your supervisor are obligated to engage in continuous upgrading of your knowledge and skills related to assessing suicide risk and treatment.
3. Direct Causation. If, as a therapist, you deviate from the standard of care it must be shown that the deviation caused harm to the client. Deviation from the standard of care may be as simple as not answering the client's phone calls. However, it would need to be shown that the deviation from the standard of care was directly related to the client's suicidal behavior.
4. Damage. This is determined in the courts by the testimony of expert witnesses. In a malpractice suit you are only liable if the client actually suffered damage as the result of your negligence in delivering standard care.

Simon (2004) and Chiles and Strosahl (2005) conclude that the best defense against a malpractice suit is the delivery of evidence-based clinical treatment in which you are fully committed to the overall care and treatment of the client. Such treatment includes adequate suicide risk assessment, good client care, and your use of good clinical judgment augmented by consultation with your supervisor. Therapists-in-training should never attempt to go solo with clients at risk for suicide. Consultation with supervisors is needed for assuring good clinical judgment. It is important to continuously and thoroughly document your therapy assessments and interventions at the time you perform the action because some courts have ruled that what was not recorded was not done. It is important that you also document your supervision consultations. Cases are settled or lost on the basis of inadequate or absent documentation.

Suicide prevention contracts

One approach taken by some therapists in an attempt to mitigate against lawsuits is the use of no-suicide contracts, also known as no-harm contracts, or suicide-prevention contracts (Drye, Goulding, & Goulding, 1973; Simon, 2004). Miller et al. (1998) found that the majority of the mental health workers they surveyed had never received training in the use of no-suicide contracts. "Obtaining a suicide prevention contract establishes that the patient is at risk for suicide. It does not establish that suicide risk has been assessed" (Simon, 2004, p. 74). Do not attempt to use "no-suicide contracts" to allay your anxiety about the client's suicidal ideation and intent (Meichenbaum, 2005; Simon, 2004). If your anxiety about treating suicidal clients is great consider this as a person of the therapist issue and seek help from your supervisor or your personal therapist.

There is no evidence that no-suicide contracts are effective in preventing suicide (Egan, 1997; Lee & Bartlett, 2005; Miller et al., 1998; Simon & Gutheil, 2002; Stanford, Goetz & Bloom, 1994; Weiss, 2001). Scholars generally agree that no-suicide contracts do not have any standing in law (Simon, 2004). Therefore, such contracts do not serve to mitigate against lawsuits. They are nothing more than a therapeutic tool. Stanford et al. (1994) and others (Weiss, 2001) suggest that the no-suicide contract may be useful in building the alliance, establishing therapy limits, and reducing client and therapist anxiety. To the extent that such contracts are effective at all may be a function of the client–therapist alliance (Simon, 2004; Stanford et al., 1994; Weiss, 2001). Therefore, your first defense against client suicide may be a strong alliance with your client. Even when the alliance is strong you should not be lulled into a false feeling of security based upon a contract with the client about suicidal behaviors (Simon, 2004; Stanford et al., 1994).

One danger from the use of a no-suicide contract may be that it causes you to limit your exploration of the client's suicidal and self-destructive fantasies (Mothersole, 1996). Failure to explore the client's thoughts, feelings, and behaviors will undoubtedly work against establishing an alliance and against effective assessment and treatment. Another risk in the use of the no-suicide contract may be the creation of an adversarial tone between client and therapist. An adversarial tone is another condition that may prevent an effective alliance from forming (Simon, 2004). Therefore, if the no-suicide contract prevents you from carrying out an effective risk assessment it will not be an effective defense against a lawsuit (Simon, 2004; Weiss, 2001).

Suicide risk assessment

Assessment and prediction of the risk of suicide has a long history in the mental health fields. However, assessment of suicide risk remains difficult (Meichenbaum, 2005). Assessment of suicide risk is not prediction of suicide. Prediction of specific future events, such as a client's committing suicide, is not possible because there are too many unknown variables. Therefore, your goal should be to attempt to determine your client's risk of suicide and to use that information to guide clinical decisions.

Joiner, Walker, Rudd, and Jobes (1999) found two critical factors in suicide risk assessment; first the client's history of previous suicide attempts and second, the specific nature of the client's self-reported current suicidal symptoms. Joiner's model will be discussed at length.

Performing a suicide risk assessment

You should perform a suicide risk assessment whenever clients express suicidal ideation or intent either directly or indirectly and whether in words or in actions. This may occur in the initial interview or in any subsequent interview. Immediately after a session in which a client reports suicidal ideation notify your supervisor. Never attempt to work with a suicidal client without the safety net of supervision (Linehan, 1999; Simon, 2004).

The primary method of assessing suicidal ideation and intent is by conducting a face-to-face clinical interview with the individual and his or her family members. Do not conduct a risk assessment on the phone or by other online media (Simon, 2004). Suicide risk assessment may best be conducted by use of a semi-structured interview followed by a suicide risk checklist to determine that all the relevant issues have been discussed. The suicide risk assessment concludes with a rational, clear, and specific procedure for establishing the risk classification. The risk classification should point directly to a program of treatment.

Using a semi-structured interview to assess suicide risk

If you have any reason to suspect suicidal ideation or intent then take the time to do a semi-structured interview. Some of the information may be available from other sources – such as the intake interview, the initial interview, or other interviews taken prior to your making a suicide risk assessment interview. There is no need to initiate questions that will lead to answers you already have. However, do not avoid asking specific questions pertaining to suicidal ideation and intent because the lack of information from the questions you do not ask will limit your ability to make a fully informed risk assessment.

In order to carry out a semi-structured interview for suicide risk assessment it is important to ask all of the questions to allow you to prepare an adequate suicide risk assessment following the interview. The questions need not be asked in order. The semi-structured interview below is based upon the work of several scholars (Jacobs et al., 1999; Joiner, Walker et al., 1999; Linehan, 1999; Simon, 2004; Wingate et al., 2004). To ensure that you ask all the questions use this checklist as you conduct the interview.

Ask your client:

- Do you have suicidal thoughts, feelings, or actions?
  - Tell me your thoughts?
  - Are you currently having suicidal thoughts?
  - Can you control your suicidal thoughts or are they involuntary?
  - When did you first have these thoughts?
  - How frequently do you have thoughts of suicide?
- Have you ever attempted suicide in the past? Tell me about each attempt? (Explore all past attempts in detail.)
- What is your suicide plan? (Ask specific questions and get the details.)
  - Do you have a specific method, time, and place?
  - Are the means available? (For example, does the client have a gun? bullets? A stockpile of pills? etc)
  - Have you written a note? Made financial plans? Given away prized possessions?

- What is your planned sequence of events?
- Have you practiced? For example, driven to a cliff or bridge? Put a gun to your head?
- How likely are you to carry out your plan? Do you think you have the courage to carry it out? Do you think you know how to carry out the plan?
- Do you wish to die? Do you want to punish someone? Do you want to escape? Are you attempting to punish yourself?
- What is causing you to want to die? What is keeping you from wanting to continue living?
- What are your beliefs about death?
  - Do you expect to have a rebirth or reunion?
  - Do you hope to connect with a significant other?
- Have you lost, or do you anticipate losing, a reason for living?
- Have you lost, or do you anticipate losing, an important family or personal relationship?
- What is your goal? (e.g., to really die, to hurt yourself and have someone find you before you die, or some other outcome?)
- What is the likelihood of rescue? For example, what are the chances that family members will come home and find you and take you to the ER?
- Are you experiencing or likely to experience painful emotional states such as loneliness, self-contempt, murderous rage, shame, guilt, or panic?
- Are you experiencing painful physical illness? (Try to determine if they are experiencing intoxication, pain, delirium, or organic impairment?)
- Are there recent or anticipated stresses in your life?
  - Are you facing loss, disappointment, humiliation, or failure?
  - Have there been or are there disruptions in your support systems, including therapy?
- Ask about violent rages, assaultive behavior, arrests, destruction of property, spending sprees, speeding tickets, sexual indiscretions, or other indications of poor impulse control.
- Is there a chaotic family history (parents divorced, frequent moves, frequent changes in care givers, and so on)?
- Is there a history of physical abuse, sexual abuse, or mistreatment?

Possible protective factors include:

- Suicide writing, if it is not in the mode of communication of resolved plans and preparations.
- Social support. Never married, divorced, widowed or living alone are at increased risk.
- Self-control skills.
- Problem-solving abilities.

As soon as possible after the suicide interview record your client's responses in your case notes. Use your video or audio record to ensure you have the details correct. If the notes are not recorded in a timely manner the courts may assume that the interview did not take place.

Adding self-report instruments to suicide risk assessment

There are no assessment instruments that predict suicide (Jacobs, Brewer, & Klein-Benheim, 1999; Linehan, 1999; Simon, 2004; Wingate et al., 2004). However, there are some client self-report instruments which you may use to augment the semi-structured suicide risk interview. One useful self-report instrument is the Depressive Symptom Index: Suicidality Subscale (Joiner, Pfaff, & Acres, 2002). Joiner, Pfaff, and Acres report that the instrument is a reliable and valid assessment of suicide ideation. The scores can range from 0 to 12 and a cutoff score of 3 was associated with a high risk profile for depression. This four item scale may serve as a brief screening device to screen clients to determine who should receive an in-depth interview. Joiner, Rudd, and

Rajab (1999) report that clients' self-reports of suicide ideation are lower than therapists' ratings as determined by follow-up measures at 6, 12, and 18 months. This may be because therapists take a better-safe-than-sorry attitude, as well they should (Joiner, Rudd, & Rajab, 1999). Wingate et al. (2004) conclude that therapists should take clients' self-reports seriously and make them a part of the therapist's suicide risk assessment.

Specifying the suicide risk factors

To meet the accepted standard of care for suicidal clients you will need to adequately assess their risk of suicide (Simon, 2004). The risk factors do not predict suicide but assist you in estimating the degree of risk (Linehan, 1999; Simon, 2004). The specific risk factors are part of a suicide assessment because of their correlation with completed suicide. Correlated factors cannot be used as predictors but should be considered with other information in making a determination of the risk for this specific client. According to Simon (2004) "Perfect assessment of suicide risk is not possible; exhaustive assessments are not necessary" (p. 27).

Suicide risk goes up as the number of risk factors increase (Simon, 2004). Linehan (1999) provides a detailed "Suicide Risk Checklist" that will help you determine that you have systematically covered all the important risk and protective factors. Following the interview you may wish to use Linehan's (1999) "Suicide Risk Checklist" to help you determine if you have covered all the relevant points. After you have completed the checklist note the number and nature of the risk factors attributed to this client at this time. Summing the number of "y" answers that you circled indicates the number of risk factors associated with this client. You must also carefully consider the nature of the factors circled and not just the number of factors. Do not assume that simply summing up the risk factors is an adequate risk assessment. The next step in suicide risk assessment is to classify the extent of the risk for this specific client at this specific time.

Classifying the risk of suicide

To classify your client's risk of suicide you will need to learn to use the best empirically supported methods and your best clinical judgment (Joiner, Walker et al., 1999; Wingate et al., 2004). Joiner and colleagues provide evidence-based guidelines to assist you to classify your client's risk of suicide as (a) nonexistent; (b) mild; (c) moderate; (d) severe; or (e) extreme. To classify your client's risk of suicide first determine if your client (1) is currently expressing suicidal ideation, (2) has made a single attempt at suicide, or (3) has made multiple attempts. Research has shown that multiple attempters are at considerably more risk than single attempters or ideators (Jacobs, 1999; Joiner, Walker et al., 1999). Second, to determine your client's suicide risk establish how your client's behavior fits into the two suicide risk factors established by Joiner, Walker et al. (1999).

Joiner, Walker et al. (1999) found two factors "resolved plans and preparations" and "suicidal desire and ideation" that summarized the risk for suicide. These factors were determined after making a factor analysis of 330 suicidal young adults' responses to the "Modified Scale for Suicidal Ideation" (Joiner, Pfaff, & Acres, 2002). The "resolved plans" factor was found to be more related to suicide attempts than to suicidal ideation. Joiner et al. (2003) found that "resolved plans" predict death by suicide but "desire and ideation" do not. Similar factors were found by Beck, Brown, and Steer (1997) using different suicide self-report scales. These two factors, "resolved plans and preparations" and "suicidal desire and ideation" are highly correlated (approximate $r = .50$). However, both are useful in helping you classify the client's suicide risk.

Review the information from your interview and your responses to the "Suicide Risk Checklist" (Linehan, 1999) to determine how well the client's responses fit or do not fit into the "resolved plans and preparations" factor or the "suicidal desire and ideation" factor (Joiner et al., 2003). The symptoms for these factors are described below.

Resolved plans and preparations

Your answers to the following questions will help you determine if your client fits the "resolved plans and preparations" category (Joiner, Walker et al., 1999). Does the client:

- Have the courage to make an attempt?
- Have the competence to make an attempt?
- Have the means and opportunity for an attempt?
- Have a specific plan for an attempt?
- Has the client made preparations for an attempt?
- How long has the client been considering suicide?
- How intense is the client's wish to die?

According to Joiner, Walker et al. (1999) anyone who has these symptoms should be classified as at least a moderate risk of suicide.

Suicidal desire and ideation

The second empirical factor in suicide risk assessment is "suicidal desire and ideation." It is composed of the following symptoms (Joiner, Walker et al., 1999; Wingate et al., 2004). Ask yourself:

- Does the client have reasons for living (see "The Reasons for Living Inventory," Linehan, Goodstein, Nielsen, & Chiles, 1983). Lack of or minimal reasons for living indicate a higher risk.
- Doe the client wish to die?
- If the client wishes to die how frequent are the client's wishes for death?
- How strong is the client's wish not to live?
- Has the client performed passive attempts to commit suicide (e.g. taking unnecessary risks with the thought of possible death)?
- How much does the client desire to make an attempt to commit suicide?
- How strongly does the client expect she or he will make an attempt?
- What are their deterrents or lack of deterrents to making an attempt?
- How often does the client talk of death and/or suicide?

Clients with the "suicidal desires and ideation" symptoms and not the "resolved plans and preparation" symptoms should not be classified as a risk for suicide unless they are (1) a multiple attempter or (2) they have notable responses in other assessment domains such as (a) significant negative life stressors, (b) any DSM Axis I (American Psychiatric Association, 2000) clinical disorders especially anxiety and mood disorders, (c) hopelessness, (d) social isolation, (e) DSM Axis II classifications especially antisocial personality disorders, for example – impulsive behavior, aggressive behavior, and irresponsible behavior.

Clients with "suicidal desires and ideation" symptoms who are multiple attempters should be classified as at moderate risk for suicide even in the absence of resolved plans and preparation symptoms.

Both sets of symptoms "resolved plans and preparations" and "suicidal desire and ideation" are of concern. However, "resolved plans" is of greater concern (Joiner, Walker et al., 1999) because among outpatients experiencing suicidal ideation at assessment the resolved plans factor was found to be more related to multiple suicide attempts, subsequent completed suicide, and a lifetime history of attempts (Joiner et al., 2003).

To fully establish your client's suicide risk classification you will need to take into account your assessment of any noteworthy findings in the "resolved plans and preparations factor" and any noteworthy findings in the "suicidal desire and ideation factor." In addition you will need to consider the following risk factors (Joiner, Walker et al., 1999; Wingate et al., 2004).

There are also additional assessment domains (AAD) to be considered:

- significant negative life stressors.
- DSM Axis I (American Psychiatric Association, 2000) clinical disorders especially anxiety and mood disorders.
- expressions of hopelessness.
- social isolation such as a sense of lack of belonging or a sense of burden to others.
- DSM Axis II classifications especially antisocial personality disorders, for example – impulsive behavior, aggressive behavior, and irresponsible behavior.

Using all the information above you may use Table 2.1 to help you classify your client's suicide risk as: (a) nonexistent, (b) mild, (c) moderate, (d) severe, and (e) extreme (Joiner, Walker et al., 1999). Once you have classified the client's suicide risk review your decisions with your supervisor.

Table 2.1 Categories of suicide risk

Categories of suicide risk				
Nonexistent	*Mild*	*Moderate*	*Severe*	*Extreme*
No history of suicide attempt No identifiable suicide symptoms No or very few other AAD[a] risk factors	(1) A multiple attempter and no other risk factors (2) Nonmultiple attempter plus: Suicidal ideation of limited intensity or duration No or mild symptoms of "resolved plans and preparation" factor No or few AAD[a] risk factors	(1) A multiple attempter and any other notable finding (2) Nonmultiple attempter plus: Moderate to severe symptoms of "resolved plans and preparation" factor (3) Nonmultiple attempter plus: No or mild symptoms of "resolved plans and preparation" factor Moderate to severe symptoms of "resolved plans and preparation" factor At least two other notable AAD[a] risk factors	(1) A multiple attempter and two or more other notable findings (2) Nonmultiple attempter plus: Moderate to severe symptoms of "resolved plans and preparation" factor At least one other AAD[a] risk factor	(1) A multiple attempter plus severe symptoms of the "resolved plans and preparation" factor (2) Nonmultiple attempter: Moderate to severe symptoms of "resolved plans and preparation" factor Severe symptoms of "resolved plans and preparation" factor Two or more AAD[a] risk factors

Source: based on Joiner, Walker et al (1999) and Wingate et al. (2004)
Note: [a]Additional Assessment Domains

When you and your supervisor agree on the risk you will be ready to establish a treatment plan and begin treatment.

Intervening with clients experiencing suicidal ideation and intention

After assessing and categorizing the clients risk for suicide you will need to arrive at a treatment plan.

Treatment for clients assessed as nonexistent or mild risk of suicide

For clients in the nonexistent and mild risk categories you might say to them something like,

> In the event that you begin to develop suicidal feelings, here's what I want you to do: First, use the strategies for self-control that we have discussed, including seeking social support. Then, if suicidal feelings remain, seek me out or whoever is covering for me, or call [suicide help number]. If, for whatever reason, you are unable to access help, or, if you feel that things just won't wait, call 911 [999 in the United Kingdom] or call or go to the ER (Wingate et al., 2004, pp. 655–656).

In addition, it would be a good idea to provide your clients with a written copy of this information as it is doubtful that they will remember it if they are anxious, depressed, or under stress. In their study Morgan, Jones, and Owen (1993) found that providing clients with information similar to this reduced single attempters' subsequent attempts by 8.56 percent.

You should document in your progress notes that you have made this statement to your client and that you have given the client a copy. As suicidal behavior can change rapidly for any number of reasons you need to continue to monitor the client's suicide risk level as you treat the problems underlying their suicidal ideation (Joiner, Walker et al., 1999).

Treatment for clients assessed as at moderate risk for suicide

For client's classified as at moderate risk for suicide you should start by making a statement similar to the one above giving them instructions about what they should do if they feel suicidal. Next recommend that they intensify treatment by increasing the frequency or duration of visits. For example, the client could be advised to meet twice a week or for 90-minute sessions. Present a treatment plan designed to reduce or replace symptom behaviors. Select an empirically supported treatment to best fit your client's needs. The most frequently recommended treatments for clients with suicidal risk are treatments for depression or anxiety. The treatment programs listed in Table 2.2 have demonstrated efficacy, have treatment manuals, and most have self-help manuals for clients.

As you deliver the planned depression or anxiety treatment work to identify and help the clients reduce stressors in their lives. Also work to help the clients increase their involvement in social support systems such as family, friends, and community organizations. Finally, find ways to reduce behaviors that interfere with therapy on the part of both yourself and your clients including: (a) behaviors leading to avoiding or escaping from sessions; and (b) behaviors that overstep the therapist's or client's limits, for example, unreasonable phone calls from clients or therapist's not returning client's calls (Linehan, 1999).

Treatment for clients assessed as severe or extreme risks for suicide

The activities prescribed for the moderate category also apply for clients in the severe and extreme risk categories. In addition Joiner, Walker et al. (1999) recommend that you should immediately consider psychiatric hospitalization. Linehan (1999), on the other hand, recommends careful consideration of hospitalization.

Table 2.2 Recommended best treatments for depression and anxiety

	Best treatments
For depression	
For individual clients	Beck, Rush, Shaw, and Emery (1979)
For couples	Beach, Sandeen, and O'Leary, (1990)
For adolescents	Clarke, DeBar, Ludman, Asamow, and Jaycox (2002) Lewinsohn, Clarke, Rohde, Hops, and Seeley, (1996)
Self-help manual for individual clients	Burns (1980)
For anxiety	
For individual clients	Craske (1999).
For couples	Craske and Zoellner (1995).
Self-help manual for individual clients	Craske, Barlow, and O'Leary (1992) and the accompanying therapist guide. Zinbarg, Craske, and Barlow (1993)

Considering hospitalization: Linehan (1999) states that there is no empirical evidence to support inpatient hospitalization as an effective deterrent to suicide. In addition, she suggests that no current research supports hospitalization as the treatment of choice, even for chronically suicidal patients. For many therapists the treatment and management of suicide risk is the most difficult part of their work as a therapist (Simon, 2004) and the decision to recommend or not recommend hospitalization may be the most difficult part of treating clients at risk of suicide (Linehan, 1999). Therefore, follow the oft repeated recommendation to consult early and often with your supervisor (Linehan, 1999; Simon, 2004).

You should consider hospitalization for a client at severe or extreme suicide risk if the client is not responding to treatment, is experiencing severe depression or anxiety, is in a crisis with which they cannot cope without serious risk of harm to themselves, and/or if they are presenting with psychotic symptoms (Linehan, 1999).

In summary, the suicide risk treatment goals should be to reduce the frequency and intensity of the client's "resolved plans and preparation" and "suicidal desire and ideation" (Joiner, Walker et al., 1999). This can perhaps best be accomplished by delivering treatments for depression and anxiety that have been found to be effective. As you work to deliver the best depression and anxiety treatments you should also be working to help your clients improve their chances for a reasonable quality of life by developing problem-solving and other life skills needed to reach their goals (Chiles & Strosahl, 2005; Joiner, Walker et al., 1999; Linehan, 1999). To accomplish these goals you will also need to work to reduce client behaviors that interfere with therapy (Linehan, 1999).

Post-crisis risk assessment

Clinical lore suggests that there is an increased risk of suicide when people begin to come out of depression or out of suicide risk. This increased risk of suicide has been hypothesized to be due to increased energy making it possible for the client to carry out a suicidal act. Wingate et al. (2004) suggest that the problem may be the persistence of subclinical depressive symptoms. Joiner, Pettit, and Rudd (2004) found that clients that have incomplete remissions of any depressive symptoms may have been more ill to begin with and this may account for their higher suicide risk following treatment. Therefore, you should be aware of any and all symptoms of depression that continue after apparently sufficient treatment. In cases in which symptoms continue it may be well to augment the treatment by increasing the frequency of visits and to consider antidepressant medications. Recurrent depression and severity of depression carry serious risk for suicidal behavior (Wingate et al., 2004).

Box 2.1 The Supervisor's Role in Suicide Risk Assessment and Intervention

Supervisors are responsible for the behavior of those they supervise (Simon, 2004). Slovenko (1980) states that "One may be held legally responsible not only for one's own faulty conduct but also for that of others" (p. 453). Therefore, supervisors may be held accountable for the errors their trainees make in diagnosis (Spitzer, Skodol, Williams, Gibbon, & Kass, 1982) and in treatment delivery (Ruscio & Holohan, 2006; Schulte & Eifert, 2002; Wilson, 1996). Spitzer and colleagues (1982) found that trainees made errors during assessment interviews. These errors were often errors of omission, that is, in assessment sessions interns failed to gather all the relevant information required to make a correct diagnosis. Subsequently when the trainees presented the case to their supervisors the supervisor also made an incorrect diagnosis. The trainee's and their supervisor's diagnoses were compared to the diagnosis of expert observers. The expert observers observed the session then entered the consulting room after the trainees had left the room to report to their supervisors. The observer then completed the interview and made a diagnosis. The trainees' and their supervisors' diagnoses were then compared with the diagnosis of the expert observer. For 30 percent of the cases there was a major disagreement and for 24 percent of the cases there was a minor disagreement. Therefore supervisors should not rely on trainee's self-reports of assessment interviews. Due to the increased emotional stress in assessing suicide risk trainees may be even more prone to error. One solution to this problem may be the use of direct supervision through a one-way screen. Charles et al. (2005) found that direct supervision of therapist-interns from behind a one way screen proved successful. Direct supervision allowed the supervisor to assist the trainees who were treating a client at suicidal risk. It may not always be possible for supervisors to carry out direct supervision. Therefore, supervisors should insist on a digital or video record of assessment sessions not viewed directly and should not rely upon the therapist-intern's self-reported diagnosis. If the intern has completed a thorough semi-structured suicide risk interview and has it on tape, then it should be possible for the supervisor to review the tape with the intern and assist in establishing the suicide risk for the client.

The therapist-intern should establish the suicide risk using the factors described in Table 2.1 after conducting a suicide risk assessment interview. The supervisor and the intern then review the therapist's suicide risk assessment. They should then review together the intern's planned treatment. Once supervisor and therapist-intern are in agreement on the suicide risk and the treatment, then the intern will be ready to begin delivering the treatment.

Continued close monitoring by the supervisor is necessary as therapists are also prone to make mistakes over the course of treatment. One mistake trainees make is changing from the planned treatment to another treatment plan either in session or from session to session (Schulte & Eifert, 2002). The mistake most often made by interns during sessions is to make frequent changes from the methods prescribed by the treatment manual to process-focused treatment (Schulte & Eifert, 2002; Wilson, 1996). Process-focused treatment is treatment that makes the relationship between the therapist and the client the center of attention rather than the interventions prescribed by the planned treatment. For many therapists and supervisors the idea of not shifting to a process-client-focused approach may seem counterintuitive. However, Schulte and Eifert's research found that the planned treatment should continue to be delivered in a way that is client and relationship focused rather than shifting to an exclusive focus on the client–therapist process. Research has shown that maintaining a focus on the planned treatment as spelled out by the treatment manual is positively related to successful outcomes (Dane & Schneider, 1998; Rounsaville, O'Malley, Foley & Weissman, 1988; Ruscio & Holohan, 2006; Schulte & Eifert, 2002; Schulte, Kunzel, Pepping & Schulte-Bahrenberg, 1992; Wilson, 1996).

As stated earlier, supervisors should be aware that interns may be more likely to make treatment errors due to the emotional stress associated with treating suicidal clients (Berman, 2006). Suicidal clients raise significant doubts in the therapist as to the therapist's competence (Simon, 2004). Anything which increases the intern's lack of confidence and reduces feelings of efficacy may increase the intern's chances of making an error in treatment delivery. Therefore the supervisor will need to increase their support for the trainee while closely monitoring the intern's treatment delivery for clients at risk of suicide (Linehan, 1999). While this may seem self-evident it appears from the research that it does not always happen. As noted earlier support is often missing in supervision (Ellis, 2002; Gray et al., 2001; Hutt et al., 1983) and supervisors' help with difficult and suicidal clients is sometimes short (Charles et al., 2005; Foulkes, 2003; Kozlowska et al., 1997).

It seems clear that supervisors need to be proactive when their supervisees are seeing clients at risk for suicide. They need to make good use of direct or videotaped supervision. Supervisors need to attend to the intern's personal affective and cognitive behavior in relationship to the suicidal responses of the clients (Berman, 2006; Linehan, 1999; Simon, 2004). Therapist's responses to suicidal clients is often fear, anger, helplessness, and hopelessness (Berman, 2006). In addition, they may become too attentive to their legal liabilities (Meichenbaum, 2005; Simon, 2004). If interns become too focused on their personal affective and cognitive behavior or their legal risks then their clinical judgment may be impaired.

Perhaps the best help that supervisors can give their trainees is to prepare them in advance to manage suicidal clients. Then when a crisis arises supervisors should be prepared to evaluate the intern's handling of the situation. Meichenbaum (2005, pp. 69–71) provides a number of questions for supervisors to use in reviewing the intern's efforts:

- What are you doing to establish a therapeutic alliance with the suicidal patient?
- What assessment strategies are you using to determine ongoing risk of suicide?
- What background factors have been assessed?
- How have you assessed for comorbidity and determined level of suicidal risk?
- What have you done explicitly to reduce the presence of risk factors?
- Have you involved family members and significant others?
- How have you gone about determining the role of medication?
- What specific psychotherapeutic interventions did you provide?

If the intern has (a) conducted a careful and thorough suicide risk assessment, (b) carefully categorized the risk, and (c) established a treatment plan that is tailored to the client's risks and needs then they should be able to answer most of Meichenbaum's questions to their own and to their supervisors' satisfaction. If the supervisor finds that the intern's answers are not sufficient then the supervisor should explore with the trainee the trainee's preparation for treating suicide risk. In addition the supervisor should discuss with the intern their affective, cognitive, and behavioral responses to the suicidal client. The supervisor should be able to help the intern through the process by maintaining a respectful and supportive attitude toward the intern's work.

Guidelines for Family Violence Risk Assessment: Partner-to-partner, Adult-to-Child, and Elder Maltreatment

The purpose of this guideline is to provide you with a model for assessing risk of family violence. The assessment of the risk of family violence is not the prediction of family violence any more than assessment of the risk of suicide is prediction of suicide. The goal is to help you determine if family violence has occurred or is occurring. If family violence has occurred or is occurring you have two responsibilities. First, you must report family violence, or in the case of child maltreatment even the suspicion of child abuse, to the proper authorities. Second, you have the responsibility to work to ensure the safety of all family members.

Family violence occurs in three domains: (1) partner maltreatment, often labeled domestic violence or intimate partner violence; (2) child maltreatment, often labeled child abuse; and (3) elder maltreatment or elder abuse. Until quite recently partner, child, and elder maltreatment were each treated as separate domains. Currently, partner-to-partner aggression and adult-to-child aggression are being considered as co-occurring events by many researchers and therapists (Appel & Holden, 1998; Slep & O'Leary, 2001). The most frequent form of elder abuse is partner-to-partner maltreatment and second is adult-child to elder-parent maltreatment (Pillemer & Finkelhor, 1988; Tolan, Gorman-Smith, & Henry, 2006). Therefore, it appears that whenever you encounter one type of violence in a family you should screen for the other types.

In considering family violence you must first determine who your clients are. One approach has been to determine who the abuser is and who the victim is. However, taking this approach immediately places you in a position of judging and blaming. Family therapists take the position that the family or marriage is their client. In family violence one or more family members may be psychologically or physically maltreated, injured, and in extreme cases the injuries may result in death. In the treatment of family violence your first goal should be to prevent further maltreatment and injury. Your second goal should be to see that all family members receive appropriate therapy.

Here I attempt to reduce the use of terms that tend to criminalize family violence. As a family therapist you should attempt to respond with empathic understanding to each family member. Therefore, the terms abuser, perpetrator, and victim will be used only sparingly and only when no other term will suffice. This may appear euphemistic but words matter and they influence our behavior. When referring to legal definitions the terms victim and abuser will be retained for ease of communication with police and the courts.

Family violence prevalence

Family violence appears to be ubiquitous and worldwide (Tolan et al., 2006). An estimated 20 to 30 percent of women and 7.5 percent of men in the United States have been physically mistreated over their lifetime (Family Violence Prevention Fund, 2008). European (Knickerbocker, Heyman, Slep, Jouriles, & McDonald, 2007) and Japanese (Arai, 2004) estimates are similar. Prevalence rates for child maltreatment or harm in the United States in 1993 were found to be 2.3 percent of the child population (1,553,800). It is estimated that 0.57 percent (381,700) of the children were physically mistreated by their caregivers (Knickerbocker et al., 2007). Prevalence of elder mistreatment in the general population of the United States was found to be 3.2 percent (1,093,560) as extrapolated from the Boston sample by Pillemer and Finkelhor (1988). Similar results for elder mistreatment have been found in Canada (Podnieks, 1992), Australia (Kurrle, Sadler, & Cameron, 1992), Japan (Arai, 2004), and Great Britain (Ogg & Bennett, 1992). Comijs, Pot, Smit, Bouter, and Jonker (1998) found a slightly higher prevalence of 5.6 percent in the Netherlands. This may be the result of methodological differences as Comijs et al. sampled somewhat more widely than other studies and included relatives, people with whom the elderly lived, and other familiar and trusted people.

The differences in prevalence reports of the various forms of family violence may be due to a lack of clear and specific definitions (Appel & Holden, 1998; Comijs et al., 1998; Knickerbocker et al., 2007). Discrepancies in ways of conceptualizing, defining, and establishing operational definitions of physical maltreatment have led to differences in reported rates. Discrepancies may also be the result of differences in the source of the information. For example, family members may disagree in their perceptions of maltreatment in their homes and agreement appears to be even lower between family members' self-reports and official reports from medical facilities and the police. Finally, the time period referenced in the report makes a difference. Some researchers have used adults' retrospective reports of their childhood (life time reports) and others have asked adults to recall incidents in just the past year. Knickerbocker and associates suggest that prevalence studies should: (1) use a representative sample of the community; (2) use clear and specific operational descriptions of partner and child maltreatment; (3) present detailed information about who performed the maltreatment and to whom; and (4) state clearly when the maltreatment occurred. In practice not all these recommendations have been met.

The prevalence rates for co-occurrence across the three domains suggest that one form of violence in the family significantly increases the risk for another form (Appel & Holden, 1998: Arai, 2004; Slep & O'Leary, 2001). These researchers report that partner-to-partner aggression is associated with an increased probability that a child in the family will be mistreated. When there is one act of partner aggression by the husband in a year there is a 5 percent chance of child mistreatment. When there is an average of one act of husband-to-partner aggression per week the chance of child mistreatment escalates to almost 100 percent. For wives when there is one act of wife-to-partner aggression in the past year there is a 5 percent chance of child maltreatment and when there is an average of one act of wife-to-partner aggression per week the ratio goes to 30 percent. Appel and Holden (1998) estimated that 6 percent of all households in the United States are characterized by both partner-to-partner and adult-to-child mistreatment which makes the co-occurrence rate for families with any form of physical mistreatment about 40 percent.

Family violence definitions

Partner-to-partner, adult-to-child, and elder maltreatment have historically been seen as separate domains as a result each has developed an independent set of definitions. In part this is because each of the domains has had a different set of stakeholders vying for public attention and support. Even within domains there has been considerable disagreement about the definitions. One of the difficulties stems from decisions about where to focus attention and energy. For example, one decision is whether to focus on only the most severe cases of maltreatment or to focus on the full range including mild forms of family conflict. Mild forms of family conflict are often seen as normative – such as sibling rivalry and corporal punishment of children – such forms of maltreatment are often accepted as typical. This leads some scholars to question whether mild forms of family aggression should be included in a definition of family violence (Tolan et al., 2006). However, if we are to fully understand how aggression in the family may lead to family violence it seems best to look at the full range of aggressive behaviors. Each of the three domains of family violence will be described separately for heuristic purposes however you should keep in mind the high rates of co-occurrence.

Adult-to-child maltreatment

Legal definitions of child abuse

Child maltreatment is most often termed child abuse in legal definitions. Legal definitions of child abuse have been established in all 50 states of the United States, in Canada, and in many countries in Europe. Legal definitions of child abuse often lack specific operational terms which therapists and others can use to clearly differentiate between problematic parenting, corporal punishment, and mistreatment (Slep & Heyman, 2006). The child abuse laws typically focus on the impact, potential impact, or risk to the child of a physical act by a parent or other adult (Heyman & Slep, 2006). In the legal definitions of child physical abuse the physical acts cover a wide range of interpersonal behaviors. Physical abuse of children includes acts such as spanking with the hand, slapping, poking, grabbing, pushing and shoving, hair pulling, restraining, shaking, throwing, biting, kicking, hitting with fist, stick, strap or other objects, scalding, burning, cutting off air supply, holding under water, and so on (Straus, Hamby, Finkelhor, Moore, & Runyan, 1998). Acts which involve injury to the face or head, or any injury to children younger than 2 years of age are considered abusive. Child sexual mistreatment requires only a qualifying act because most societies' feel that nonconsensual sexual acts with children younger than the age of consent should not be tolerated regardless of immediate impact (Slep & Heyman, 2006).

Mandatory reporting of child maltreatment

In all 50 states of the United States and in many European countries child abuse and even suspicion of child abuse requires mandatory reporting to Child Protective Services (CPS: Knickerbocker et al., 2007). Child abuse is generally reported to child protective service agencies unless there is immediate danger to the child in which case the danger should be reported to agents of the law.

Reporting and confidentiality

In states or countries where abuse reporting is mandatory it is important that your clients be informed of the necessity for you to breach confidentiality should suspicions of abuse arise (Friedrich, Olafson, & Connelly, 2004). Due to the close relationship of abuse in all three domains of family violence you should caution clients about the necessity to breach confidentiality regardless of the type of family therapy being sought – whether couple, child, or adolescent therapy. It is best if clients are cautioned before therapy begins and in many agencies it is part of the intake or initial interview procedures. Should mistreatment come up during the course of therapy you can remind the clients of your need to report and stress that this can be turned to helpful purposes. For example, if it is determined that maltreatment may be occurring then the focus of therapy can be shifted to the safety needs of all the family members as a first critical step in treatment. Once family members are safe then consideration of treatment for each family member can be undertaken.

Reporting abuse creates legal liabilities for the reporter, for the parents, and for other caregivers. Reporting of child abuse and the subsequent investigation is typically seen by parents as an intrusion into their private family lives and is not seen as helpful (Knickerbocker et al., 2007). Many parents fear the loss of their children or other parental rights. It may help for you to explain to your clients that CPS agencies generally have as their goal the elimination of all forms of abuse in the family. It is probably a good idea to consult with your supervisor about her or his experience with probable outcomes from CPS in your community and then share that information with your clients. However, be careful not to imply or promise any special treatment from CPS on the basis of the family being in therapy.

It often helps if the family members themselves initiate the report to CPS. Having the parent(s) report may protect them against charges of failure to protect the child (Family Violence Protection Fund, 2008). After discussing the nature of the report and what they might say you might suggest something like, "If you would like to call CPS you can use my phone. CPS often responds more positively if the parents initiate the report. Would you like me to dial it for you?"

You must make a report even if the family demurs. You might say something like, "I will need to report possible abuse to the proper authorities because if I do not report then I may not be able to become a licensed therapist. I can't promise anything but it sometimes helps if CPS knows that you are continuing in treatment. Therefore, I hope that we can continue to work together to make things better for every member of this family." After explaining your position take time to validate each family member's concerns. However, do not be talked out of reporting.

In addition to reporting child maltreatment or suspicion of maltreatment to the proper authorities be sure to record your action in your case notes in a timely fashion. As mentioned earlier if information concerning your actions to provide standard care for your clients does not appear in your notes then the courts may treat it as if it did not happen. In the case of family maltreatment the standard of care includes reporting to proper authorities.

Partner-to-partner maltreatment

Legal definitions of partner-to-partner abuse have been established in all 50 states of the United States, in Canada, and in many countries of Europe. These definitions vary but generally include three basic guidelines: (a) two acts of physical aggression against the partner; (b) at least two acts of physical aggression resulting in physical injury requiring medical attention; and (c) use of threats and intimidation resulting in the recipient feeling almost always fearful of the offender (O'Leary, Slep, & O'Leary, 2000). Single acts are generally not considered because young couples frequently engage in physical aggression (O'Leary, 1999).

Reporting of partner-to-partner maltreatment

Reporting of partner maltreatment appears to differ from reporting of child and elder maltreatment in two ways. First, the mandate to report partner maltreatment is often limited to medical professionals (Rodriquez, Sheldon, & Rao, 2002; Sachs, Koziol-McLain, Glass, Webster, & Campbell, 2002; Smith & Winokur, 2004). Australia appears to be an exception requiring reporting by mental health professionals as well as medical personnel (Shepherd, 2007). Second, the laws which mandate reporting of partner-to-partner aggression often require that the report be made to the police rather than to Adult Protective Services (APS) or Child Protective Services (CPS) as is the case for elder and child abuse respectively.

Mandated reporting of intimate partner violence has generated considerable controversy among female recipients of maltreatment (Rodriguez, 2001; Rodriguez et al., 2002; Sachs et al., 2002; Smith, 2001; Smith & Winokur, 2004). The majority of the women in these studies appear to be in favor of mandatory reporting. The favorable responses ranged from 92 percent to 55.7 percent in studies spanning the United States (Gielen et al., 2006; Rodriguez et al., 2001; Rodriguez et al., 2002; Sachs et al., 2002). However, in several of these studies abused women were less likely than non-abused women to favor mandatory reporting (Rodriguez et al., 2001; Rodreguez et al., 2002; Sachs et al., 2002). Many of the respondents qualified their responses suggesting that they would like to be allowed to decide if the maltreatment should be reported (Rodriguez et al., 2001; Rodreguez et al., 2002; Sachs et al., 2002). A number of respondents expressed fear that mandatory reporting would lead to further mistreatment (Coulter & Chez, 1997; Gielen et al., 2000; Sachs et al., 2002).

Elder maltreatment

Legal definitions of elder abuse

The age at which one is defined as an elder in the United States varies from state to state but is generally established as 60 or 65 years of age. Legal definitions of elder abuse are more recent than definitions of partner and child abuse and have only been enacted in 45 states of the United States and in six Canadian provinces (Welfel, Danzinger, & Santoro, 2000). Europe has lagged behind in developing legal definitions of elder abuse (Penhale, 2007). As with other forms of abuse legal definitions of elder abuse contain a wide range of acts that include intentional or negligent action by care givers or any others that cause harm to a vulnerable adult (Administration on Aging, 2007). Definitions of elder abuse typically include the following six categories: physical mistreatment, emotional or psychological mistreatment, sexual mistreatment, caregiver neglect, abandonment, and financial or material exploitation. Physical abuse is defined as intentionally inflicting pain by hitting, biting, burning, striking with a hard object, and so on. Emotional or psychological abuse includes verbal behavior that conveys disrespect, contempt, belittling, threat, and intimidation. Sexual abuse includes any nonconsensual sexual behavior of any kind. Caregiver neglect is the failure to provide food, shelter, protection, or healthcare to a vulnerable elder. Abandonment is the desertion of an elder by anyone who has assumed responsibility for the care or custody of an elderly person. Finally, financial or material exploitation is the illegal appropriation, misuse, or concealing of funds, assets, or material goods of a vulnerable elder.

The most frequent form of elder mistreatment appears to be partner-to-partner maltreatment (Comijs et al., 1998; Pillemer & Finkelhor, 1988). The second most frequent type of elder mistreatment takes place between grown-up children and their parents when elders are living with their adult-children.

Statutes for reporting elder abuse

Laws for reporting elder abuse are generally similar to the procedures for reporting child abuse (Welfel et al., 2000). However, elder abuse is reported to Adult Protective Services (APS). Welfel and associates report that mandated reporting of elder abuse is limited to 45 states of the United States and three provinces in Canada. However, it does not appear that the nations of Europe have moved to require mandated reporting of elder abuse at present (Penhale, 2007). Elder abuse laws differ from child abuse laws in that most allow older adults to refuse protective services if they chose to do so. This is designed to protect the autonomy rights of adults as much as possible. In their review Welfel and colleagues include a very detailed table of the elder abuse reporting laws state by state. This is helpful as you are responsible for knowing the mandatory reporting laws for all three forms of abuse in the community where you practice.

Convergence of family violence domains

Recently the three domains of family mistreatment have come to be seen as converging under the umbrella of family violence. As stated earlier research has shown that when there is partner-to-partner violence about 40 percent of the time there is also adult-to-child maltreatment (Knickerbocker et al., 2007; Slep & O'Leary, 2005). Adult-child to elder-parent maltreatment and co-occurring adult-child maltreatment of the adult-child's dependent children was not found in a search of the current literature. Even so it may be useful to conclude that family violence is a single phenomenon with variations based upon the participants.

Family violence appears to be an outcome of conflict resulting from the interaction between family members. Conflict in families appears to be inevitable because family members' lives are interdependent and because they share the same scarce resources (Felson, 2002). Family conflict may be verbal or physical. Both verbal and physical conflict may range from mild to severe. Even mild family conflicts may escalate to the level of family violence.

Verbal conflict includes complaints, criticism, defensiveness, contempt, threats, and active withholding of verbal and emotional responses. Active withholding of verbal and emotional behavior, what Gottman (1999) calls "stonewalling," may be considered a form of either neglect or mistreatment. A family member may use verbal or symbolic threats to evoke fear in an effort to exercise control over others (Felson, 2002). Male assaults on women are more likely to be preceded by threats. As a result, women in intimate relationships are more likely to express fear than are men (Felson, 2002; McCloskey & Grigsby, 2005). Creating conditions in which partners or children live in constant fear is considered abuse (Heyman & Slep, 2006).

Physical conflict includes (a) using physical acts which have a significant impact on the recipient or (b) which have a high potential for significant impact such as throwing a hammer at a family member but not hitting them (Slep & Heyman, 2006). Physical acts may also include withholding of resources necessary for other family members to thrive or survive, for example, withholding food, clothing, shelter, education, and access to healthcare. A frequently cited form of elder mistreatment is financial and material exploitation. All physical acts described above are considered acts of aggression (Friedrich et al., 2004) and aggressive acts can escalate into acts of violence.

As a result of family members' sexual needs and because they live in close proximity, some family conflicts are sexual in nature. For example, males' demands for sex often exceed women's due to gender differences in sexual responsiveness (Felson, 2002). Males' use of physical aggression to coerce sexual behavior from their partners or others is considered to be sexual abuse. As stated earlier child sexual mistreatment requires only a qualifying act to be considered sexual abuse (Slep & Heyman, 2006). Similarly, as stated earlier, sexual mistreatment of the elderly is defined as any nonconsensual sexual contact with an elderly person.

Additional factors which set family violence off from other forms of violence

The fact that family violence occurs between individuals with an ongoing relationship makes it different from violence between strangers (Tolan et al., 2006). Family violence may continue over extended periods of time whereas stranger-to-stranger violence is generally a one-off event.

Males who are abusive have been classified into two groups, first, a passive aggressive and dependent group also known as nonpathological family-only abusers. The second group is the generally violent antisocial abuser (Holtzworth-Munroe, Stuart, & Hutchinson, 1997; Lohr, Hamberger, Witte, & Parker, 2006). The first group has been shown to accelerate their aggressive behavior until they reach approximately age 24 or 25 and then aggression decelerates slowly until about age 70 (O'Leary, 1999). However, males who have been characterized as generally violent and antisocial tend to continue partner mistreatment or may even increase the frequency of their attacks over time (Holtzworth-Munroe, Meehan, Stuart, Herron, Rehman, 2003; Lohr et al., 2006). Surprisingly, classifying males in this way does not help predict future assaults (Hilton & Harris, 2005). In addition, it may perpetuate a misunderstanding about the role of gender in intimate partner violence (Dutton, 2007; Felson, 2002).

Partner-to-partner violence may be initiated by females or males (Tolan et al., 2006). However, because males are generally larger and stronger more females get hurt (Felson, 2002). Archer (2000) reports in a meta-analytic review of eighty-two independent studies that women were found to be slightly more likely than men to initiate intimate partner violence. In that same review it was found that women are slightly more likely than men to be injured. Straus and Gelles (1990) report similar results following their United States national survey. Dutton (2007) reports that in the Canadian General Social Survey the rates of severe abuse were about even with 8 percent of the women and 7 percent of the men reporting victimization in the past five years. It appears that the most common form of partner-to-partner violence is mutual aggression (Stets & Straus, 1992). Research seems to suggest that intimate partner violence is an equal gender phenomenon (Dutton, 2007; Felson, 2002).

Family members differ in terms of gender, age, and culturally defined roles. These differences may translate into conflicts over power and control. The fact that family conflicts sometimes escalate to physical violence is not surprising as violence is one way of exerting control, addressing grievances, and establishing one's position in the family (Felson, 2002). Power and control issues occur between partners, between adults and children, and between adult-children and their elderly parents. Conflict also occurs between siblings and it has been suggested that sibling conflict may be the most prevalent form of family violence (Straus & Gelles, 1990). However, our discussion focuses on mistreatment initiated by adults, therefore discussion of sibling conflict is not included in this text.

While control is one element in family maltreatment family members also use violence for retribution, as Felton identified "Grievances play a greater role in violence between people who know each other, for both men and women" (2002, p. 213). There are gender differences in partner grievances and gender differences alter the power structure. For example, as stated earlier, male demands for sex exceeds the supply due to gender differences in sexual responsiveness. This often results in men complaining about women withholding sex and women complaining about male pressure: "Men use women for sex and women use sex to influence men" (Felson, 2009, p. 210). Male's use of physical aggression to coerce sexual behavior from their partners may result in sexual abuse.

People sometimes use violence to project an image they wish to portray to others (Felson, 2002). Men may wish to portray an image of power in the family to avoid appearing weak or ineffective. However, men may refrain from violent behavior against women in public to avoid portraying an image of being cowardly or ineffective.

Partner violence in love triangles may be related to control issues, to grievances about justice, and to identity issues (Felson, 2002). According to Felson women are as likely to kill their partners in love triangles as are men. Men are more likely to kill their rivals than to kill their partners. Women are more likely to kill men in self-defense but this is not limited to partners.

Partner-to-partner aggression is found in high rates in both community and clinical samples. The rates appear to be highest in young, newly married couples but the rates begin to lessen after the mid-twenties (O'Leary, 1999). Although both males and females may initiate aggression adolescent males tend to be more violent than women and this continues into their early twenties. Male anger and hostility are frequently associated with violence against female partners (Felson, 2002; O'Leary, 1999). Jealousy is a factor related to partner violence for many dating and courtship couples and often appears related to attempts to end the relationship on the part of the female partner (O'Leary, 1999). Communication problems are frequently at the center of partner relationship discord (Christensen & Jacobson, 1998; Gottman, 1999). Psychological aggression frequently precedes physical aggression in marital relations (O'Leary, 1999).

Marital discord is known to decrease over couples' life spans. O'Leary (1999) notes that related factors such as male misuse of alcohol, male hostility and aggression, jealousy, and communication problems are all associated with high rates of physical aggression in the early years of marriage and tend to decline after the mid-twenties.

To summarize, family violence is aggressive behavior by one family member toward another. Family violence may be:

- Initiated by either partner.
- Mild to severe.
- Verbal or physical.
- Verbal aggression includes threats which evoke fear.

Table 2.3 Risk factors for partner, child, and elder mistreatment

Mistreatment Risk Factors		
Partner-to-partner	*Adult-to-child*	*Elder*
Individual characteristics • History of aggression and violence. • Low impulse control. • Low self-esteem. • Psychopathology. • Alcohol and drug dependence. • Gender is not a risk factor as males and females are about equal as abusers and abused. • Family of origin poor parenting. *Relationship risk factors* • Higher levels of conflict and relationship discord. • Modest negative correlations with communication quality, felt support, and relationship satisfaction. • Low relationship skills. • Felt stress in marital relationship. • Assortitative mating in which, if individuals with greater aggressive tendencies partner then there is a greater probability of partner-to-partner violence whereas if one partner does not have an assertive history there may be less of a tendency for violence. *Contextual/environmental risk factors* • Partner-to-partner violence exists across all socioeconomic levels but poverty increases the risk. • Stress, hopelessness, and financial constraints also increase risk.	*Adult individual characteristics* • History of antisocial behavior. • Poor impulse control. • Low self-esteem. • Mental health problem. • Low empathy toward the child. • Unrealistic expectations for the child's developmentally appropriate behavior. • Child physical mistreatment is not related to parents' marital status or education. *Child individual characteristics* • Younger male children and children with medical complications and disabilities are more at risk for child mistreatment. *Relationship risk factors* • There is greater risk of child mistreatment in dysfunctional families. • There is greater risk of child mistreatment in families with poor parenting skills. • Partner-to-partner violence has a negative impact on children and increases the probability of adult-to-child aggression. *Contextual/environmental risk factors* • Socioeconomic status has been found to be related to adult-to-child levels of severe violence but not to mild levels. • Parental stress and especially stress over child rearing is related to mistreatment. • Parents' perception of low social support is related to child mistreatment.	*Caregiver individual characteristics* • History of aggression and violence • Is suffering with her or his own mental illness. • Has a current substance abuse problem • Gender, is not a risk factor as males and females are about equally abused and abusers. *Elder individual characteristics* • Poor health. • Widowed are at risk for neglect and for material and financial mistreatment. • Religion, economic, and educational background are not risk factors. *Caregiver relationship factors* • Financial dependence of the caregiver on the elder has been found to be a risk factor for elder mistreatment. *Elder relationship factors* • Living with others has more in common with partner-to-partner mistreatment risk factors than living alone. • The dependence of the elder on the caregiver is not a risk factor. *Contextual/environmental risk factors* • Social isolation of the elder and the caregiver. • Spouse's perception of stress as caregiver.

Source: Based on Choi and Mayer (2000); Kyriacou et al. (1999); Lachs, Williams, O'Brien, Hurst, and Horwitz, R. (1997); Pillemer and Finkelhor (1988), and Tolan et al. (2006)

- Physical aggression includes (a) using physical acts which have a significant impact or (b) have a high potential for significant impact, on another family member.
- Neglect including the withholding of communication, affection, and other resources necessary for survival.
- Unwanted, unacceptable, and/or coerced sexual behavior.
- Financial and material exploitation, especially of the elderly.

Some factors are known to increase the risk for violence in families. Specific risk factors for family violence will be discussed next.

Risk factors for family violence

The risk factors for each of the three domains, partner-to-partner, adult-to-child, and the elder mistreatment are summarized in Table 2.3. The risk factors for mistreatment in each domain are separated into three subsets of factors (1) individual factors, (2) relationship factors, and (3) contextual/environmental factors (Tolan et al., 2006). As can be seen in Table 2.3 each of the domains have some risk factors in common with the other domains. For example, those who are likely to initiate mistreatment in any of the three domains often have a history of aggressive behavior, mental health problems, and are currently experiencing stress.

Partner-to-partner risk factors for family violence

The literature for partner maltreatment has largely focused on the male partner due to concerns about physical injury to the female and concerns about blaming the female partner (McCloskey & Grigsby, 2005; Slep & O'Leary, 2001; Tolan et al., 2006). In light of the recent findings that both genders initiate aggression and that both receive injuries it is important to treat the risk factors for family violence as gender neutral (Dutton, 2007; Felson, 2002). This will be difficult as there has been a general bias toward treating males as the aggressor and females as the victims.

Researchers have found that one of the individual risk factors for partner-to-partner maltreatment is a history of aggression and violence by the person committing the aggressive behavior (Slep & O'Leary, 2005; Tolan et al., 2006). As pointed out by Tolan and associates low impulse control and low self-esteem have also been found to be related to partner aggression. The aggressor has also been found to frequently have other mental health problems. The aggressor often has a family-of-origin history of unskilled parenting and poor family functioning. In addition, relationship factors have been shown to add to the explanation for partner mistreatment even when individual characteristics are controlled. For example, marital relationship discord is related to partner maltreatment (Holtzworth-Munroe, Clements, & Farris, 2005). There are modest inverse relations found between communication skills, partner felt support, relationship satisfaction, and partner aggression. Negativity in partner-to-partner relations has been found to play a part in marital conflict, which may be related to partner mistreatment (Fincham, Garnier, Gano-Phillips, & Osborne, 1995; Gottman, 1999).

Violent men have been reported to feel more stress during marital interaction than nonviolent men (Margolin, John, & Gleberman, 1988). However, martial stress may be mediated by marital satisfaction (Brock & Lawrence, 2008). Brock and Lawrence found, in a longitudinal study of newly married partners, that escalation in husbands' role strain is associated with reduction in husbands' marital satisfaction regardless of the adequacy of wives social support. However, when wives are receiving adequate support from their husband escalation in both the husbands' and the wives' role strain is associated with increased marital satisfaction for wives. Further research is needed to determine if husbands' support is a protective factor for partner maltreatment when both spouses are experiencing increases in role strain.

Contextual and environmental factors that contribute to partner-to-partner violence include living in poverty and financial struggles (Tolan et al., 2006). Poverty contributes to feelings of stress, hopelessness, and dependency on the part of women, all of which are factors that may prevent the female from leaving abusive relationships (Babcock, Jacobson, Gottman, & Cordova, 1994; Bornstein, 2006). There does not appear to be any literature on what prevents men from leaving abusive relationships.

Adult-to-child risk factors for family violence

Parents are required to provide guidance and control for infants and toddlers because infants and toddlers have limited ability to maintain self-control for extended periods of time (Straus & Douglas, 2008). Parents' failure to provide control and guidance, if it places a child at risk of harm, may be considered neglect, and neglect is the most frequent form of child abuse (Tolan et al., 2006). The issue is not whether infants and children need guidance but what form the guidance and control should take. It is believed by some in the West that corporal punishment is a necessary and acceptable form of child discipline. However, other methods of child guidance are available, which are just as effective (Alexander, Pugh, Parsons, & Sexton, 2000; McMahon & Forehand, 2003; Straus & Douglas, 2008). The presumed differences between corporal punishment and mistreatment will be discussed later.

Adolescent youth also require control and guidance but it is assumed that they are able to take some responsibility for their own behavior. Adolescents can assume some control over their own behavior so it becomes necessary for parents to modify the amount of control and guidance provided as their children develop and mature (Alexander et al., 2000). None the less 40 percent of parents report physically punishing their 14-year- olds in the previous year (Straus, 1994) and in the United States 13 of 1,000 children below the age of 18 years have experienced some form of mistreatment or neglect and 21 percent have suffered physical abuse (Gershoff, 2002).

Corporal punishment

Corporal punishment is defined as "the use of physical force with the intention of causing the child to experience pain, but not injury, for purposes of correction or control of the child's behavior" (Straus, 1994, p. 4). Child abuse was defined earlier as specific acts such as "hit with a hard object" and acts that have a significant impact or high potential for having a significant impact, such as shooting a gun in the direction of the child but not hitting her or him (Slep & Heyman, 2006). Severe adult-to-child aggression was described as "spanked on the bottom with bare hand, hit on bottom with something like a belt, hairbrush, a stick or some other hard object; slapped on a hand, arm, or leg; slapped on head, face, or ears; pinched; or shook" (Slep & Heyman, 2006, p. 438). In practice the difference between corporal punishment and mistreatment is often whether or not the act was brought to the attention of the CPS (Straus & Douglas, 2008). The decision made by an agent of CPS often appears to depend on whether or not the punishment made a significant impact on the child. Significant impact has been defined as (a) more than inconsequential injury, (b) more than reasonable potential for a more than inconsequential injury, or (c) a more than inconsequential fear reaction (Slep & Heyman, 2006). However, it would seem that any form of physical punishment whether defined as mistreatment or corporal punishment has the potential of causing long-term negative consequences (Straus, 1994; Straus & Douglas, 2008).

Corporal punishment of children is allowed in all 50 states of the United States whereas 19 European countries have laws or policies that prohibit parents from using corporal punishment (Straus & Douglas, 2008). Straus and Stewart (1999) report that 94 percent of parents in the

United States have spanked their children by the time the child is 3 to 4 years of age. In a meta-analysis of 88 studies extending over the last 62 years Gershoff (2002) found a strong association between parental corporal punishment and parental physical mistreatment of the same children. In Gershoff's review parents' use of corporal punishment was frequently reported by the parents as an effort to get the child to comply with their control and guidance attempts. There is evidence in the research that corporal punishment is effective in getting the child to stop what the parents perceive to be misbehavior but that the child soon returns to what they were doing prior to the punishment (Sidman, 1989). What the parents observe is that corporal punishment stops the misbehavior immediately. However, they rarely make the connection between corporal punishment and the long-term effects because they may not show up until years later. Gershoff (2002) in her meta-analytic review of 88 studies found 93 percent of the studies agreed that corporal punishment resulted in harmful effects. Specifically Gershoff found:

- In twelve of the eighty-eight studies that reported on children's mental health problems there was an association between corporal punishment and children's anxiety and depression.
- Eight studies found a relation with later adult mental health problems.
- Thirteen of the studies reported on delinquent behavior and twelve of those studies found there was a higher probability of delinquent and anti-social behavior for children who had received corporal punishment compared to those who had not.
- There was an overall decrease in the children's moral internalization, that is, there was a reduction in "their long term compliance, their feelings of guilt following misbehavior, and their tendencies to make reparations upon harming others" (Gershoff, 2002, p. 550).

Straus and Douglas (2008) assert that a number of studies – including longitudinal studies which control for Time 1 misbehavior and family and parenting characteristics – have found that children who are not spanked are better behaved and have the lowest rates of psychological problems. Thus the short-term advantage of the use of corporal punishment, that is terminating the immediate misbehavior, is strongly offset by the long-term disadvantages, which work against the parents' goal to help children learn to exercise self control.

As an evidence-based therapist you should educate your parent-clients concerning the research related to corporal punishment. As there are highly effective programs available to help parents achieve compliance from their children without the use of punishment (see for example, McMahon & Forehand, 2003) there is no need for parents to put their children at risk of the potential harmful side effects of corporal punishment. You should work to help parents give up two of the great myths of our time which are "Spanking works when other methods do not" and "Spanking may sometimes be necessary" (Straus & Douglas, 2008). The overwhelming evidence described above has shown that these are myths. Other methods work just as well as spanking and therefore, spanking is not necessary to get child compliance.

Some specific parent-to-child mistreatment risk factors

The risk factors for adult-to-child maltreatment are presented in Table 2.3. Talon et al. (2006) summarized the child mistreatment risk factors as:

- Individual child characteristics associated with risk for mistreatment suggest that male children under 3 or 4 years of age, and those with medical problems or disabilities are most at risk.
- The adult caregiver's marital status or education has not been found to be related to child physical mistreatment but a relationship does exist for child sexual mistreatment.
- Direct descendants of the adult abuser are less likely to be sexually mistreated than are other children in the family.

- Caregivers' personal low self-esteem, poor impulse control, personal mental health problems, and a history of hostile and aggressive behavior are all factors associated with child mistreatment.
- Caregivers' lack of empathy for the child and/or unrealistic expectations for the child's behavior at the child's developmental level are associated with child mistreatment.
- Relationship factors associated with risk for child mistreatment include dysfunctional families, which often have poor parenting practices and poor adult-to-child relationship skills.

As discussed earlier partner-to-partner conflict is also a risk factor for child maltreatment. Simply witnessing partner violence has a negative impact on children's development (Laszloffy, 2007). Male to female partner mistreatment is known to increase the risk for mother-child mistreatment (Knickerbocker et al., 2007). Slep and O'Leary (2001) state that this may be the result of living with a violent partner, which makes it difficult for the mother to deal with the child's behavior. This has been referred to as the "spillover effect" where the mistreatment received by the mother "spills over" to mistreatment of the child. Several studies lend support to this hypothesis (Levendosky & Graham-Bermann, 2001; Levendosky, Leahy, Bogat, Davidson, & von Eye, 2006; Margolin & Gordis, 2003).

Contextual and environmental factors related to adult-to-child maltreatment appear to be differentiated by the level of violence. Socioeconomic status has been found to be related to adult-to-child levels of severe violence but not to mild levels (Tolan et al., 2006). Parental stress and especially stress over child rearing appears to be related to child mistreatment (Margolin, John, & Gleberman, 1988). The parents' perception of low social support also appears to be related to child mistreatment.

Risk factors for elder mistreatment

The family conflict research associated with elder mistreatment is much less extensive than for the other domains of family violence (Tolan et al., 2006). Research into elder mistreatment began as recently as the 1970s in Great Britain (Penhale, 2007) and has spread to Europe (Comijs et al., 1998), Australia (Kurrle et al., 1992), Canada (Podnieks, 1992), and the United States (Pillemer & Finkelhor, 1988). The most frequent form of elder mistreatment appears to occur between spouses (Pillemer & Finkelhor, 1988; Podnieks, 1992). The next most frequent form of elder mistreatment is performed by other family members with whom the elder is living (Comijs et al., 1998). According to Pillemer and Finkelhor the rate of mistreatment in the United States was 4.1 percent for elders living with only their spouse. For those living with their adult-children the rate was 4.4 percent. However, the highest amount of elder mistreatment is between spouses because far more elders live with their spouses than with their adult-children. The problem may be deciding if partner-to-partner elder mistreatment should be classified as elder mistreatment, spouse mistreatment, or both. Perhaps the difference should be decided based upon the condition of the one who has been mistreated. If the mistreated spouse is more infirm, is suffering with dementia, or with other chronic disabilities than the spouse performing the mistreatment, then it probably should be classified as elder mistreatment rather than spouse mistreatment.

Some specific risk factors for elder mistreatment

Table 2.3 presented the risk factors for elder mistreatment. Among the individual risk characteristics for the elder maltreatment is advanced age (Choi & Mayer, 2000). Risk for elder mistreatment increases markedly for those over 60 years of age and even more markedly for each decade beyond

60 (Tolan et al., 2006). Being female increases the risk as does illness and disability. Poor health, and especially dementia puts an elder at risk. Being widowed increases the risk for neglect and/or for material and financial mistreatment by caregivers. Advanced age and dementia also increases the elder's risk for self-neglect such as failure to eat, failure to maintain personal hygiene, and failure to remain on medical regimes (Bomba, 2006). As with partner-to-partner mistreatment gender is not a risk factor because male and female elders mistreatment of each other is about equal (Tolan et al., 2006). Religion, economic factors, and educational background have not been found to be risk factors for elder maltreatment.

Caregivers' individual risk factors for elder abuse include a personal history of aggression and violence, a current substance abuse problem, or the caregiver is suffering from mental illness.

Relationship problems between elders and their children occur when the elder is living with an adult offspring and is often related to the elder's disabilities, especially dementia (Podnieks, 1992). Another caregiver relationship factor for elder mistreatment is the financial dependence of the caregiver on the elder. However, dependence of the elder on the caregiver is not a risk factor.

Contextual and environmental factors related to elder mistreatment include the social isolation of the elder and the caregiver. Most elder mistreatment is hidden perhaps for the same reasons that male aggression toward females is hidden, that is, the perpetrator does not want to appear cowardly or ineffective. Social isolation may contribute to the caregiver's ability to hide any elder mistreatment which is occurring.

Co-occurrence of risk factors for the three domains of family conflict

Tolan et al. (2006) note that risk factors for the three domains of family conflict show considerable overlap (Table 2.3). It appears important to recognize some of the multiple factors and the interrelationships that contribute to the risk of family violence. As you consider the risk factors for family conflict be aware that your clients will vary given the domain of interest. For example, the clients in partner-to-partner maltreatment consist of two adults. This differs markedly from the clients in an adult-to-child case. In adult-to-child cases three people are your clients, the person performing the mistreatment, the other parent, and the child. It is important in family therapy that your focus is not just on the individuals involved but also upon the relationships between the family members.

The co-occurrence of both partner-to-partner and adult-to-child physical maltreatment in the same family is defined as: (a) one partner is physically aggressive to the other partner and maltreats a child; (b) one partner is physically aggressive to the other partner who is maltreating a child; or (c) one or both partners are aggressive toward the other and both are maltreating a child (Knickerbocker et al., 2007). A related issue is partner-to-partner violence witnessed by the children but in which the children are not physically mistreated (Jouriles, McDonald, Norwood, & Ezell, 2001; Tolan et al., 2006). Children who witness violence between their adult caregivers have been found to be at risk for mistreatment themselves and later they may mistreatment their intimate partners (Margolin & Gordis, 2003). Children's exposure to domestic violence is an important health and social problem. In some states of the United States and in some European countries it is considered child maltreatment. However, children's exposure to partner-to-partner violence will not be discussed further here.

The variables that appear to influence the co-occurrence of partner-to-partner mistreatment and adult-to-child mistreatment are not well understood (Knickerbocker et al., 2007). Knickerbocker found support for a wide range of variables that appear to contribute to co-occurrence. Many variables for co-occurrence are similar to the risk factors for partner-to-partner mistreatment and adult-to-child mistreatment (Table 2.3). For example, intrapersonal variables such as personality characteristics, genetic predispositions, psychological symptomatic behaviors, and historical risk factors all appear to contribute to the risk of co-occurrence of partner-to-partner and adult-to-child maltreatment. Intrapersonal variables have typically been evoked when the co-occurring mistreatment is carried out by the same individual performing both partner maltreatment and adult-to-child maltreatment whether a man or a woman.

Interpersonal variables also contribute to co-occurrence. For example, Bornstein (2006) reported that both economic and emotional dependency play a role in both child mistreatment and elder mistreatment. Economic dependence plays a role in wife mistreatment. Thus emotional and economic dependency appears to play a role in co-occurrence of all three domains of family mistreatment.

In addition, environmental or contextual variables such as stressful life events and lack of social support have been found to be related to the co-occurrence of both partner and child mistreatment (Margolin, Gordis, Medina, & Oliver, 2003). Margolin et al. found that husband-to-wife physical aggression was associated with mothers' and fathers' child mistreatment when the contextual variable of parenting stress was high but not when parenting stress was low. In this study partner mistreatment was found to have negative effects on maternal parenting behavior.

Slep and O'Leary (2001) suggest that the contextual variables related to partner and parenting roles may be common variables in the co-occurrence of partner and parental maltreatment. The abuser's attributions of the child as responsible for her or his misbehavior and the abuser's attributions of negative intent by their partner appear to be related to co-occurrence. It has also been found that while marital partner's arguments over child rearing are fewer than arguments over other marital issues arguments over child-rearing practices are more likely to escalate into violence (Straus, Gelles, & Steinmetz, 1980).

Screening and assessing for family violence

Research has shown that many therapists and medical personnel are not well prepared to screen and assess for partner-to-partner violence (Agar & Read, 2002; Edin & Hogberg, 2002; Goff, Shelton, Byrd, & Parcel, 2003; Harris, Kutob, Surprenant, Maiuro, & Delate, 2002; McCloskey & Grigsby, 2005). It also appears that therapists and medical personnel are not well prepared to assess for elder mistreatment (Lachs & Pillemer, 1995; Reis & Nahmiash, 1998: Welfel et al., 2000). However, professionals do appear to be prepared to screen and assess child mistreatment (O'Leary et al., 2000; Slep & Heyman, 2006). Given that licensed professionals have trouble screening for and assessing intimate partner violence it should be no surprise that therapy interns have also been found to lack these skills (Greene & Bogo, 2002; Haddock, 2002; Todahl, Linville, Chou, & Maher-Cosenza, 2008). Therefore, supervisors should be prepared to help interns acquire the necessary training to screen for and assess all three forms of domestic violence.

Routine screening for domestic violence is necessary because intimate partner violence rates have been found to be as high as 67 percent in outpatient marital therapy clients (O'Leary, Vivian, & Malone, 1992). Adult-to-child violence also occurs at high rates with 12.4 children per 1,000 mistreated (approximately 906,000) in the United States in 2003 (Tolan et al., 2006). Elder maltreatment also occurs at high rates. Approximately 450,000 persons aged 60 and over in the United States were abused or neglected in 1996 (National Center on Elder Abuse, 2011). Therefore, failure to screen for mistreatment in the family means that many family members will be left without physical and psychological health care services (Goff et al., 2003).

It is best to screen for mistreatment in the initial interview. The usual procedure in the initial interview is to first interview all the family members involved with the presenting problem followed by separate interviews with individual family members (Chapter 3). Should the issue of mistreatment come up in the conjoint interview you should note it and defer any detailed discussion until you have administered the individual interviews. Individual interviews should be held with each family member to ensure client safety. You need to interview the family members individually because the risk of additional violence is likely to increase if the family members explore these difficult and emotional issues together (Bograd & Mederos, 1999; Holtzworth-Munroe, Meehan, Rehman, & Marshall, 2002; McClosky & Grigsby, 2005). Another advantage of individual interviews near the start of family therapy is that it increases the probability of disclosure of any mistreatment occurring in the family. Wives, for example, rarely report intimate partner violence when the male is present in the interview because they fear retaliation.

As a family therapist you should screen each case for the possibility of co-occurring partner, child, and elder mistreatment. Your clinical interviews will be more reliable and valid if they follow a semi-structured format. However, you should not rely upon interviews alone as empirical evidence suggests that written assessment instruments provide the most reliable and valid information upon which to base clinical decisions (Garb, 2005; O'Leary, Vivian, & Malone, 1992).

Use of a semi-structured interview to screen for family violence

If in your initial interview or at any time during your treatment program you have reason to suspect mistreatment in the family move to an individual interview with each family member. This is part of crisis management just the same as moving to a suicide risk assessment interview whenever you suspect suicidal ideation. As a family therapist you should work to prevent harm to all family members whether from suicide or from mistreatment. A full-scale assessment for family violence will include a detailed semi-structured interview and a battery of self-report instruments. The goal is to provide you and your clients with the information needed to maintain your clients' safety and to determine if treatment is necessary.

When conducting a semi-structured interview to determine which, if any, of the domains of family violence exist in this specific family, start by ruling out domains where possible. For example, when a family presents for couple or child therapy elder mistreatment can be quickly dispensed with if there are no elders living in or interacting with the family presenting for treatment. Simply ask something like, "Are there any family members 60 years old or older living with or associated with your family?" If the family does not include an elder member you can then dispense with screening for elder mistreatment.

If a couple is presenting for couple therapy then attempt to determine if there are children in the family. Simply ask something like, "Do you have any children living in the home with you at any time?" If they do not have children living in the home with them you can then focus on the couple and any potential for partner-to-partner maltreatment. If they do have children living in the home then keep this in mind as you take a history of the couple's presenting problem. While taking the couple history blend in questions that will help you evaluate for co-occurrence of couple and child mistreatment. If, for example, you are conducting an initial interview with a distressed couple and you are asking about the nature of their arguments, then you can add something like, "When you are having an argument with your partner are the children watching or listening? What about any older members of the family, are they watching?" Another example of blending when taking a couple history is, "So you and your partner sometimes hit each other? Does anyone hit any of the children?" Conversely if you are taking a history of parent concerns about a child's behavior you might add something like, "Parent concerns about child misbehavior sometimes spill over into people's marital relationships. Have you ever argued with each other about your roles as parents and about child discipline?" To repeat, it is necessary to screen for co-occurrence because one form of family violence is so frequently associated with the other types of aggression and mistreatment. So whenever you find an indication of one type be sure to ask about the other two.

While taking your semi-structured interview enquire about the events that preceded the abusive behaviors, the nature of the behavior, any injuries sustained, and what followed the event. When enquiring about the events preceding the event be careful not to make judgments about who is to blame and who is the victim. Avoid labeling one person as the abuser and another as the victim. Labeling one as an abuser makes that person a victim also.

Bragg (2003) cautions against asking "victim blaming" questions such as "What did you say or do to make your partner angry?" "What could you do to make your partner stop hurting you?" "Why don't you just leave?" or "Why do you put up with the violence?" Make sure you try to understand the event from the point of view of each of the participants. Assure each family member that you wish to ensure their safety and the safety of the other family members. Point out to the family members that you can best help them be safe if you fully understand the whole picture. Remember that each family member should leave the session feeling you are on their side (Alexander et al., 2000a).

Figure 2.1 presents some specific questions you might ask in a semi-structured interview to determine the nature and extent of maltreatment occurring in the family. These questions concerning family conflict are a representative sample based on the work of a number of scholars in the field (Jacobson & Christensen, 1996; Lachs & Pillemer, 1995; McCloskey & Grigsby, 2005; Slep & Heyman, 2006; Welfel et al., 2000). When assessing for mistreatment it is important for you to ask clear and specific questions because many mistreated individuals will not report mistreatment unless asked specifically (Bogard & Mederos, 1999; Edin & Hogberg, 2002; Goff et al., 2003; Harris et al., 2002; Slep & O'Leary, 2001). As a therapist you will want to develop the ability to be curious and persistent in following up the questions in the semi-structured interview. Use follow-up questions to get details of disturbing and uncomfortable behavior. Follow-up by first establishing a nonjudgmental, respectful, and compassionate stance without letting your own emotions get in the way (Bograd & Mederos, 1999). Second, follow-up using basic therapist skills in order to allow clients to tell their story (Hill, 2004). You need not ask these questions in order but it is important to cover the full range of questions. You will need as much information as possible to make informed clinical decisions about the nature of the problem and a possible course of action. If there are no children or elders associated with the family then of course it is not necessary to ask the questions about children or elders.

In taking information concerning family violence in a semi-structured interview be aware that some people use humor to mask some of their intentions. For example, someone might say in a jesting way, "George, if you don't be quiet I'm going to beat your head on the sidewalk." While the sender may protest that this is simply in jest and that she or he did not really mean it, the critical issue is the impact on the receiver. Take the time to find out what the impact of a statement like that is on the recipient by asking follow-up questions. Hurtful and threatening statements are just as hurtful and threatening when said in "jest" as when said directly.

It is permissible to use a checklist, such as Figure 2.1, to assist you to cover all of the material in the semi-structured family violence interview. Our work is no less complicated than flying a jumbo jet and you wouldn't want the pilot to decide not to use the aircraft checklist for takeoffs and landings. Your clients will find your use of a checklist acceptable, perhaps even comforting, unless you let it get between you and them. You can set the stage for its use by a statement like, "I've prepared a checklist to help me be sure I've covered everything in the interview. Your story is important to me and I don't want to leave out any critical areas." Even after using the checklist it is a good idea to close the interview by asking, "Did I miss anything important, or is there anything you want me to know before we finish today?" Once again, the purpose of the interview is to develop the information you will need to help you, in collaboration with the clients, to make important clinical decisions about each family member's safety and about possible treatment programs.

Figure 2.1 Questions for a semi-structured screening interview for family violence

When screening for:		
Partner-to-partner mistreatment	***Child mistreatment***	***Elder mistreatment***
When your partner gets angry how does she/he act? How do you act when you get angry?	When your partner gets upset with a child how does your partner act? When you get upset with a child how do you act? How do the children act?	When your partner gets upset with an elder member of the family how does she/he act? When you get upset with an elder member of the family how do you act? How does the elder act?
"Sometimes when people get mad in an argument they yell, start pushing and shoving and things like that. Does this ever happen in your house?"		
"Does it ever get worse than pushing and shoving?"		
Hand a copy of the following to your clients. During your family arguments, do you or your partner ever do any of following to each other? To a child or children? To elders in the home? Please read the whole list and circle all that apply. Slap, Grab, Punch, Kick, Bite, Push, Push to Ground, Pin to ground/wall, Pull hair, Hold, Twist arm, Hit with an object, Break objects, Tear clothes, Throw things that might hurt, Punch fist through wall, Break down a door, Beat up, Use a knife, Burn or scald, Use a gun, Strike with a belt, board, etc, Strangle/choke, Threaten to hit, Threaten to kill, Threaten harm to self/suicide, Threaten others or pets		
Do you or your partner ever get frightened or afraid in an argument with each other?	Are the children afraid in an argument with the parents?	Is an elder family member ever frightened or afraid in family arguments?
Have you or your partner ever threatened that she or he would harm children or pets?	Have you or your partner ever threatened a child or children with physical harm?	Have you or your partner ever threatened to harm an elder member of the family?
Have you or your partner ever deprived the other of basic needs such as food, shelter, protection, health care, or education?	Have you or any member of your family neglected to supply a child's basic needs for food, shelter, protection, health care, or education?	Have you or any member of your family neglected to supply an elder family member's basic needs for food, shelter, protection, or health care?
Do you or your partner force the other to engage in sexual activities?	Do you or your partner engage in sexual acts with a child or children?	Do any family members engage in non-consensual sexual behavior with elders?
		Have you or any member of the family illegally misused, appropriated, or concealed funds, assets, or material goods belonging to an elder?
		Is an elder family member neglecting to eat, follow medical regimes, maintain good hygiene, or take care of personal needs?
When any of these things happened where you or any member of your family using alcohol, prescription drugs, or street drugs?		

Source: Based on Bomba (2006), Jacobson and Christensen (1996), Lachs et al. (1997), McCloskey and Grigsby (2005), Slep and Heyman (2006), Tolan et al. (2006), Welfel et al. (2000).

Using self-report instruments to assess for the occurrence of family violence

Assessing family violence with empirically supported self-report instruments can increase the reliability and validity of your estimates of maltreatment in the three domains.

Assessing partner-to-partner mistreatment

Marital distress is an important element of partner-to-partner aggression. The Standard Assessment Battery for Marital Distress (SAB: Appendix C) may be used to assess the couple's relationship distress. The SAB instruments assess for each partner's psychological state, their perception of their relationship, their divorce potential, and their perception of the use of violence in the relationship. The SAB also screens for depression. Finally, the SAB screens for misuse of alcohol, which is often a factor in partner-to-partner and in elder maltreatment.

The information gathered about partner-to-partner mistreatment by means of the screening interview and the self-report assessment instruments will prepare you to determine if mistreatment has occurred or is occurring. Your goal in taking a full-scale assessment for the risk of mistreatment should be to determine: (a) the types of mistreatment including co-occurrence; (b) the current dimensions of the mistreatment; (c) any contributing factors or clinical issues; (d) the relationship quality and distress; and (e) dangerousness and potential lethality (Murphy & Eckhardt, 2005). Heyman and Slep (2006) provide guidelines that can be used to specify whether partner-to-partner mistreatment is occurring or has occurred. Heyman and Slep's criteria will allow you to reach a clear and definitive decision about the occurrence of partner mistreatment.

Assessing for parent-child mistreatment

To assess parent-to-child aggressive behavior Slep and O'Leary (2005) used Straus et al.'s (1998) "Parent-child Conflict Tactics Scale" (CTSPC) to classify adult-to-child aggression into mild and severe types.

- Slep and O'Leary defined corporal punishment as mild aggression using Straus' definition of corporal punishment "spanked on the bottom with bare hand, hit on bottom with something like a belt, hairbrush, a stick or some other hard object; slapped on a on hand, arm, or leg; slapped on head, face, or ears; pinched; or shook" (Straus, 1994, p. 438).
- Slep and O'Leary defined severe parent-to-child aggression using selected items from the CTSPC regarded as acts "with high potential to cause injury (i.e., hit on some part of the body other than the bottom with something like a belt, hairbrush, a stick or some other hard object; burned or scaled on purpose; beat up; hit with fist or kicked hard; grabbed around neck and choked; threatened with a knife or gun; thrown or knocked down)" (Slep & O'Leary, 2005, p. 438).

Assessing for elder mistreatment

The majority of occurrences of elder mistreatment appear to be related to elder partner-to-partner maltreatment (Pittaway, Westhues, & Peressini, 1995). Elder partner-to-partner mistreatment may be assessed by use of the SAB (Appendix C) described above for adult-to-adult mistreatment with emphasis on Straus et al.'s (1996) Conflict Tactics Scale-2.

The second most frequent form of elder mistreatment occurs between adult-children and their elderly parents when the elder is living with their children (Comijs et al., 1998; Pillemer & Finkelhor, 1988). No specific assessment instruments appear at present for this population. However, Straus et al.'s (1996) Conflict Tactics Scale-2 (CTS-2) might be adapted if you instructed the adult-child to substitute parent for partner in the stem of each question. Similarly the elder parent could substitute son or daughter for partner in the stem questions. The norms for the CTS-2 will not apply, of course, but your inspection of the results should prove informative.

Caregivers in living facilities for the elderly have also been found to mistreat their charges (Reis & Nahmiash, 1995). The Care Giver Abuse Screen (CASE) has been found to be a reliable and valid initial screen for caregiver mistreatment (Reis & Nahmiash, 1995, 1998). In a follow-up study Cohen, Halevi-Levin, Gagin II, and Friedman (2006) extended Reis and Nahmiash's indicators of abuse (IOA) and found the extended indicators of abuse (E-IOA) to be a reliable and valid assessment of elder abuse and risk for mistreatment. Another instrument to assess elder mistreatment was developed by Bomba (2006). Bomba's one page instrument may prove useful as a quick screen. Bomba (2006) provides guidelines that may be used to substantiate whether or not elder mistreatment and/or self-neglect has occurred.

Intervening with clients experiencing family violence

The purpose of screening and assessing for family violence is to determine if mistreatment has or is occurring. Once you have determined that mistreatment has occurred or is occurring your responsibility is to move to safeguard all family members and this is best facilitated by reporting your findings to appropriate authorities. When you have determined that family members are at risk you must report to designated authorities such as the Child Protective Service for children at risk or Adult Protective Services in the case of elders. Spouse-to-spouse abuse is most commonly reported to legal authorities. Child and elder maltreatment should also be reported to law officers if there is immediate danger to the child or the elder.

Prediction of future dangerousness and potential lethality requires additional actuarial procedures, which may best done by a forensic therapist (Hilton, Harris, & Rice, 2009; Quinssey, Harris, Rice, & Cormier, 2006). Therefore, consult with your supervisor about referring the case to a specialist to determine future dangerousness and potential lethality.

When you have completed your assessment of family mistreatment you should proceed to establish an appropriate treatment plan (Chapter 3). Protocols for empirically supported treatments for couples are found in Chapters 7 (Gottman, 1999), Chapter 8 (Johnson, 2004). Empirically supported protocols for parent-to-adolescent child issues may be found in Alexander et al., (2000a). McMahon and Foreman (2003) present an empirically-supported treatment for noncompliant children. At present there do not appear to be empirically supported treatments specifically designed for treating elder abuse. As mentioned earlier elder partner-to-partner abuse might best be treated with one of the couple therapies.

Enter your assessment of maltreatment in your case notes within twenty-four hours of your interview. Delayed or missing case progress notes may be treated as if the event did not happen.

Case Progress Notes

As important as case progress notes are for crisis interventions the overall importance of case notes should not be minimized. The primary purpose of case progress notes is to protect the clients' welfare by making a written record that will provide the information used to: (a) establish the clients presenting complaints and goals; (b) make a rational argument for an evidence based treatment plan for these specific clients with their specific problems; (c) provide a baseline from which to evaluate treatment progress and outcome, and (d) chronicle the treatment outcomes. Case notes should be based on facts and should not resort to special pleading or rhetoric (Bromley,

1977). They should be in good English prose avoiding use of jargon and technical language. Use plain English in your notes because in addition to serving the welfare of your clients your notes may be used to defend your performance to the average layman in a jury (Hersen & Turner, 1985).

Case progress notes are a permanent record of your professional conduct and as such they have a privileged ethical and legal status (Wilcoxon, Remley, Gladding, & Huber, 2007; Knapp & VandeCreek, 1997). Consequently, your supervisor, quality control officers, lawyers, and ethics committees may review your case notes for evidence of your competence as a therapist. They may look for evidence that you have used best treatments, adhered to the planned treatment, looked to clients' welfare, and otherwise behaved legally and ethically. Information which does not appear in your case notes will be presumed, in a court of law, not to have happened. Therefore, anything you can do to improve the quality of your case notes will be of benefit to both you and your clients. Increasing the reliability and validity of the information in your case progress notes will greatly improve their quality.

Structuring case progress notes

The specific format for case notes will vary from clinic to clinic. A general format will be described here to serve as an example (Appendix D). Case notes typically have five basic sections: (1) Session information; (2) Session summary; (3) Observations; (4) Conceptualizations; and (5) Assignments and future plans.

Session information

Case progress notes begin with the client(s) names, a client identification number, the date the clients were seen, the date the notes were completed, session number, and for marital or family therapy a list of all the clients present in the session. You may be asked to identify the type of therapy service being performed, such as assessment or treatment. If treatment is being delivered you should indicate the therapy model being used for example "functional family therapy" or "cognitive behavioral therapy for depression." The session information forms a basic set of data which may be used to chronicle the case and may also be used for heuristic and/or research purposes.

Session summary

The session summary provides a brief description of the treatment attempted and what was accomplished. As it is an abstract of what occurred in the session it is often written last. It appears first so that you and others may quickly review the previous session.

The session summary typically has three parts. You should start with a description of the therapy task planned for the session followed by a report of what was accomplished and conclude with the clients' progress. As an example of reporting the planned intervention you might say something like, "The therapy task for this session was to take an Oral History of Mr. and Mrs. Jones' marital relationship." After stating what was planned report what was accomplished. For example, "The Oral History was completed in 45 minutes." The session summary should conclude with a brief statement of the impact of the therapy task on the clients. For example, "The clients appeared to enjoy discussing their relationship history and commented that they planned to continue the discussion at home."

Observations

In this section start with your observations of the events that occurred during the session. In the progress notes it is important to separate the observed information from your conceptualizations. Use of your clinical conceptualizations will be discussed later.

Observations include information gathered from the client's self-reports in the interview and from valid and reliable assessment instruments. Observations also include a record of your ratings for client characteristics such as use of the Oral History Rating Scale (Brewer & Mead, 2008) to rate the couple's divorce potential.

Your most reliable and valid observations will be provided by the assessment instruments administered in the session. Therefore begin the observations section with a review of the assessment scores. If this was an assessment session then present a table of the instruments administered and the scores of each family member (see Table 4.1, p. 87). If this was a treatment session then start with the outcome scores that provide information about changes which have occurred since the previous session. Include other assessment scores if administered. For example, "The Beck Depression Inventory (Beck, Steer, & Brown, 1996) was administered and Ross' score was 8 and Betsy's score was 20, indicating minimal and moderate to severe depression respectively." Indicate if the assessment scores suggest improvement, staying the same, or deterioration since the previous session (see "Evaluating the clients' treatment outcomes" in Chapter 5). This is important as it will form the basis for your decisions on interventions to be performed and decisions about whether to continue the treatment or terminate.

Under Observations include a brief summary of your clients' discussion of the events since the last session. Report their perceptions of progress or lack thereof.

Include your clients' assessment scores for the therapy alliance. Your notes might say, "At the end of the session I assessed the alliance by administering the Session Rating Scale (Duncan et al., 2003). Betsy's total score was 32.1 with the items "Goals and topics" and "Overall" falling below 9. Ross' total score was 36.2 with "Relationship" and "Approach or method" falling below 9. I explored their thoughts and feelings about these alliance breaches and attempted to repair the process. I will make greater efforts in the future to meet each of their needs.

Conceptualizations

Conceptualizations are conjectures, inferences, and hypotheses which the you make from your observations (Mead, 1990). Separating observations from conceptualizations makes it possible to return to the case notes for additional hypotheses, should that prove necessary. By recording observations first it is possible to indicate the information upon which your inferences, conjectures and hypotheses are based.

Decisions about treatment interventions are a function of your observations of their current behavior, your conceptualization of their behavior, and of the therapy model you are employing. Based on this information you will provide a treatment intervention designed to move the clients' current dysfunctional behavior toward more functional behavior. For example, "Based on Betsy's depression score I recommended that we use Beech, Sandeen, and O'Leary's (1990) *Depression in Marriage* treatment and the clients agreed."

Interventions

Next provide a description of the intervention applied in this session and its impact on the clients' clinically relevant behaviors (CRBs: Kohlenberg & Tsai, 1991; Smith, Mead, & Kinsella, 1998). The intervention should be relevant to the clients' current behavior and consistent with the treatment plan. For example, "Ross and Betsy spent most of the therapy session discussing their major theme of 'Ross as the scientist' and 'Betsy as the artist.' Specifically Ross wanted to talk about Betsy's 'always being late for activities, such as Church, getting ready for work, and going to parties and other entertainments.' Betsy talked about "Ross's constant attention to details. She said 'he should just slow down and get a life'."

For behavior as described above Gottman's (1999) model would suggest helping them to have a conversation that included each other's wants and needs. Therefore your notes might indicate this by a statement such as, "I structured the session to help the client use Gottman's Dreams-Within-Conflict intervention. I provided a rationale for this intervention suggesting that it is designed to eliminate a major stressor in their lives which will combat Betsy's depression and increase her positive responses toward Ross. This makes for a win-win change for both of them. It was only necessary to restructure their discussion once with a reframe to keep them from lapsing into criticism and blaming. Furthermore, they were able to repair their failed bid for each others' support and caring on their own. While they were discussing their theme and their relationship, I began fading the amount of my reinforcement for their appropriate behaviors."

Missing information

As you write case notes from time to time you will become aware that information you need in order to understand your clients' behavior, to complete a diagnosis, or to write a treatment plan is missing. Because memories are fragile, make a record of missing information in your case notes. State clearly where information is missing and/or where additional information will help to: (a) determine the problems, complaints, or goals; (b) establish the treatment plan; or (c) determine treatment progress and outcome. For example: "It might be beneficial to measure their anxiety concerning the changes they are making to determine if interventions to reduce their stress might be appropriate."

In the Future Plans section of your case notes indicate your plan for obtaining the missing information.

Assignments and future plans

In this section provide a clear and specific description of the homework assignment. For example, "The couple was assigned to continue to practice discussing their theme at home and to record any failed bids for repair and/or soothing." If no homework was assigned, you should discuss the reason for not assigning homework in your notes.

As suggested above in this section indicate how you will attain any missing information. You might state, "In the next session I will administer the *Beck Anxiety Inventory* (Beck & Steer, 1993) to assess their level of anxiety."

Finally, provide a rationale for continuing the current treatment or task, or for moving onto a new task. For example, "Based on their current outcome assessment scores, their performance in the session, and their reports of their progress at home it appears that several more sessions will be needed to reduce Betsy's depression and lessen their marital distress."

After you have written up your case progress notes submit them in accord with the procedures established in your clinic. Most clinics require case progress notes to be submitted within 24 hours of the session. Share your case progress notes with your supervisor in your next supervision session. After you supervisor has reviewed both your session and your case progress notes ask for feedback on the session and on your progress notes. Ask your supervisor if you attended to all the elements of the session. Ask if you left out any important information in the case notes. If your supervisor recommends changes to the notes add an addendum to make the changes. An addendum is necessary as it is not good form to change notes that have been submitted. In fact in many clinics it is not possible to make changes to the original notes because submitted notes are sealed.

In addition to your case progress notes there are two additional written reports you will need to prepare for your clients' files, the treatment plan, and the termination summary. The treatment plan will be discussed in Chapter 4 and the termination summary will be reviewed in Chapter 6.

Your case progress notes, your written treatment plan, and your termination summary are professional reports which become a permanent part of the clients' file. Their primary purpose is to serve the needs of the clients. Therefore they should be written in your best style. They should be clear, specific, concrete, and complete. Remember too that your written reports may be used to support your defense should you be accused of unethical or illegal conduct.

What Should You Take Away From Chapter 2?

1 The person of the therapist makes an important contribution to the outcome of therapy. It has been found that between 5 to 8 percent of the variance in therapy outcome is due to the person of the therapist (Wampold, 2006). In addition the alliance between the client and the therapist contributes another 5 percent to the outcome variance. Treatment versus no treatment accounts for 13 percent of the outcome variance but the difference between treatment and placebo treatments only accounts for 0 percent to 1 percent, and the difference between empirically supported treatment models is only 0 percent to 4 percent. The alliance, although largely a client variable, is strongly influence by the person of the therapist. Therefore, the person of the therapist and the alliance contributes importantly to therapy outcomes.

2 Your therapy relationship is a series of intense emotional communications between you and your clients. Your ability to communicate empathy, warmth, and genuineness to your clients is a function of your personal and professional histories. It may not be possible to change your interpersonal style but you can always improve your use of the facilitative conditions, empathy, warmth, and positive regard. The key to good couple and family therapy is learning to respond to each family member with the basic therapist skills so that each family member leaves the session feeling heard and understood.

3 Therapy is an intense emotional experience. You will need to learn to deal with your personal stress by first recognizing it and second by learning to cope with it. Some ways to cope include use of: (a) personal self-help methods; (b) your supervisor; (c) your personal therapist; and (d) friends and family.

4 Another important skill is learning to observe your client's clinically relevant behavior. The here and now behavior exchanged between your clients and you in the session constitutes clinically relevant behavior. Learning to observe these patterns and help the clients change their dysfunctional patterns to more functional patterns is the essence of family therapy.

5 Before you see your first clients it is important that you develop the skills needed to deal with clients who present in crisis. Suicidal ideation and family violence are the two most common forms of crises seen by family therapists. You should be prepared to assess the risk of suicide before you see your first clients because approximately 1 in 6 interns encounter suicidal clients (Bongar, 2002) and because for every suicide there are estimated to be 15 to 20 nonfatal suicide attempts (Spirito & Overholser, 2003). In addition because family violence appears to be an almost universal problem you will also need to be prepared to screen for family violence.

6 Assessing and treating clients who have suicidal ideation requires some understanding of the related legal issues. According to Simon (2004) suicide is one of the most frequent reasons for malpractice suits. Therefore, you should be aware of the legal issues and how to protect yourself from lawsuits.

7 The best defense against legal action in the case of suicide by a client is a well-documented paper trail which demonstrates that you have carefully and thoroughly assessed the risk for suicide and taken appropriate therapeutic action. Suicide risk assessment is best done by taking a structured interview augmented by the use of empirically supported assessment instruments. Following the assessment it is important that you use empirically established methods to estimate the risk of suicide (Joiner et al., 2003). Joiner and colleagues have found that client responses that fit into the "resolved plans and preparations" factor and the "suicidal desire and ideation" factor are important in determining suicidal risk. Of these two factors the most critical is the clients resolved plans and preparations along with consideration of the client's reports of previous suicide attempts. Clients with two or more previous attempts and resolved plans and preparations are at greatest risk.

8 When you encounter a client with suicidal ideation you should involve your supervisor at the earliest possible moment. You should never attempt to go solo with clients expressing suicidal ideation.

9 Screening and assessing the risk of family violence requires skill in assessing the risk of partner-to-partner, adult-to-child, and elder maltreatment. Partner-to-partner and adult-to-child maltreatment have been found to co-occur at high rates. Therefore, when you find that one is taking place you should screen for the other as there is a reasonable probability that both are occurring.

10 The most frequent form of elder maltreatment is partner-to-partner maltreatment. The next most frequent form of elder maltreatment occurs when the elder is living with an adult-child. Elders living in the care of others are also at risk and you should be prepared to screen for elder abuse in those settings as well.

11 The most effective way to screen for family violence is by means of semi-structured interview augmented by standardized assessment instruments.

12 Case progress notes are important professional documents. They serve to demonstrate that you have behaved ethically and legally while attending to your clients' welfare by delivering the planned treatment and by assessing their progress toward successful termination.

Chapter 3

The Initial Phone Call and Assessing Clients' Complaints and Goals

Introduction

Therapy tasks are strategic operations that guide the therapist's in-session performance. Mead (1990) identified five therapy tasks which appear to be present in all therapy models. The five tasks are: Therapy task 1: Assessing the clients' complaints and goals; Therapy task 2: Establishing a treatment plan and obtaining the clients' consent to therapy; Therapy task 3: Delivering the planned treatment; Therapy task 4: Evaluating treatment delivery and evaluating the treatment outcomes; and therapy Task 5: Terminating therapy. Although these tasks appear to be found in all therapy models the amount of emphasis placed on any given task varies between models (Frank & Frank, 2004; Mead, 1990). Recently a committee of the American Association for Marriage and Family Therapy (AAMFT, 2004) organized the tasks of therapy into six primary domains: (a) Admission to treatment; (b) Clinical assessment and diagnosis; (c) Treatment planning and case management; (d) Therapeutic interventions; (e) Legal issues, ethics, and standards; and (f) Research and program evaluation. All of the AAMFT tasks appear relevant for evaluating the competence of licensed and practicing therapists. However, many of AAMFT tasks do not apply to beginning therapists. Therefore, for teaching and learning purposes it appears that Mead's five therapy tasks will suffice. Therapy task 1 will be discussed in this chapter. The remaining tasks will be discussed in subsequent chapters.

Before you can begin "Therapy task 1: Assessing the clients' complaints and goals" you will need to arrange an assessment interview with your client(s). Often a family's first contact with a family therapist is a phone call. How you handle the first phone call may determine whether family members will or will not attend therapy. The first phone call also serves to determine which family members come to the assessment session. Therefore, the first phone call is the start of the client–therapist alliance with the family. The goal of the first phone call is to get all of the family members who are involved in the problem to come to the assessment session.

The Initial Phone Call: A Semi-Structured Interview

The initial phone call will be your first contact with a family member who is initiating therapy or it may be the bridge from the intake interview to the first session. The initial phone call serves

Becoming a Marriage and Family Therapist: From Classroom to Consulting Room, First Edition. D. Eugene Mead.

three important purposes. First, and most important, it is the beginning of the client–therapist alliance (Boylin & Briggie, 1986; Norcross, 2002b; Wetchler & Gutenkunst, 2005). Second, the initial call should increase the client's reasons for wanting to come to the assessment session (Haley, 1987; Wetchler & Gutenkunst, 2005). The third goal is to negotiate which family members should attend the initial session (Boylin & Briggie, 1986; Haley, 1987; Odell & Campbell, 1998; Wetchler & Gutenkunst, 2005; Whitaker in Neill & Kniskern (1982).

If the clients do not come to the first interview you will not be able to help them. Therefore, it is important that in the initial phone call you begin establishing an alliance with the clients. This is accomplished by seeking to establish agreement on the initiating family members' therapy goals, agreement on the methods to achieve those goals, and trust in the therapist (Friedlander et al., 2006; Miller & Prinz, 2003; Noonan, 1973; Pinsof, 1995). To achieve these goals you will need to perform a semi-structured phone interview with the following seven steps: (a) making the initial contact; (b) beginning to clarifying the clients' problems and goals; (c) establishing your expectations for the assessment and feedback sessions including who should attend; (d) dealing with the clients' safety needs and providing support; (e) clarifying clinic procedures including fees; (f) providing directions to the clinic; and (g) explaining how they will meet with you when they arrive. The initial phone call is a semi-structured interview designed to ensure that the clients will attend the assessment session. Semi-structured interviews increase the probability that all of the relevant information will be conveyed to the clients while allowing you the flexibility needed to establish a trusting relationship.

It is important that you provide opportunities for the family member who is initiating therapy to actively participate in the initial phone call. Failure to elicit participation has been found to be related to early termination and may, therefore, be related to clients attending or not attending the assessment session (Attride-Sterling, Davis, Farrell, Groark & Day, 2004; Harwood & Eyberg, 2004; Johnston, 1996; Miller & Prinz, 2003; Morrissey-Kane & Prinz, 1999; Nock & Kazdin, 2001; O'Dell, 1982; Prinz & Miller, 1994).

Initiating the initial phone contact

You should make the initial phone call as soon as possible after receiving the case. It has been shown that phone contact by the therapist within four days of the client's initial call to the clinic increases the probability of the client attending the first session. By returning the client's call promptly you signal to them that they are respected and that their concerns are important (Patterson, Williams, Grauf-Grounds & Chamow, 1998). For many clients the initial call is perceived as initiating therapy (Goldstein, 2001). Therefore, your words and voice should reflect a positive and hopeful attitude that therapy can be of help, after all, 80 percent of clients who completed individual therapy reported that it was a successful experience (Asay & Lambert, 1999; Wampold, 2001). Marriage and family therapy has been found to perform at least as well, and sometimes better than individual therapy (Shadish & Baldwin, 2002). Consequently you should express your optimism about therapy and your willingness to be of help.

The initial phone call will set the tone for the remainder of your interaction with your clients. The impression you want the client to take away from this initial phone call is that you intend to make therapy safe for all family members and that you will focus on their individual needs as well as on the family relationships.

Begin the phone call by being sure you have the right person. Then give your full name and introduce yourself as a therapist-intern (AAMFT, 2001). Identify the clinic where services will be provided. Once you are sure you have the right party and you have identified yourself begin by asking if this is a good time for them to talk. Be sensitive to the fact that there may be others present where they are and they may not want to have a conversation about their problems in front of a third party. If this is not a good time to talk then ask when would be a good time to call back. Your sensitivity to their safety needs may help to establish your credibility as a person they can trust.

Clarifying the clients' problems and goals

If they are able to talk then begin by asking permission to record the session for training purposes. You could say something like, "I like to record this call so I can learn from it. Would it be alright if I record it?" If you are able to record the call you will be able to use the recording to improve your therapy skills.

Next ask how you can be of help at this time. Use your best attending and listen skills. Listen for general themes and hidden agendas and validate their concerns with respect and empathy (Patterson et al., 1998; Wetchler & Gutenkunst, 2005). Schulte and Eifert (2002) found that therapists who attended to the clients' treatment expectations had better outcomes. Research has shown that dropout rates were lower when therapists allowed the parents of adolescent boys with extreme antisocial behavior to share their expectations about the treatment process as compared to parents who were not given the opportunity to share their concerns (Miller & Prinz, 2003; Morrissey-Kane & Prinz, 1999; Prinz & Miller, 1994). Similarly, Harwood and Eyberg (2004) found that therapists who facilitated parent discussion, used fewer questions, and fewer supportive statements in the first session had fewer parents who dropped out. Others have also found a relationship between attention to parent's concerns and early dropout rates (Attride-Sterling et al., 2004; Johnston, 1996; Nock & Kazdin, 2001). Patterson and Forgatch (1985) report that increased facilitation of parent discussion was associated with lower resistance in sessions. Therefore, allowing the person who is initiating therapy to share their complaints and expectations will increase the probability of their attending the first session.

Establishing expectations for the assessment session

After clarifying the clients' expectations and goals you may begin by explaining the purpose of the assessment session. Your intention should be to build trust by educating the clients about your expectations for therapy. One of the first decisions to be made by the family member who is initiating therapy is whether or not to come to the first interview. The issue about whether to come or not is appropriate, as you should not assume that the client is fully committed at this point (Patterson et al., 1998). Therefore, you need to ask, "What might get in the way of your family coming to the first session?" Listen carefully to their concerns and try to resolve them.

One thing that may help the client become more committed is for you to explain the agenda for the assessment session. The explanation might go something like this, "The assessment session is designed to help me to get to know everyone in the family. It helps me to get as many points of view as possible. Each member of the family may have one piece of the puzzle, one part of the solution. Then, after we clarify what the problem is, we can decide if therapy is the best solution or if there is some other solution. After the assessment session we will have a feedback session. We can decide together in the feedback session if therapy is needed and if it is we can decide who should come to therapy. We can make all those decisions at the end of the feedback session. So you can see that therapy doesn't really begin until after the feedback session." Note that the reassurance that therapy does not begin until after the feedback session may be a safety factor for some clients, especially men (Jacobson & Christensen, 1996).

Setting safety needs

As you are clarifying your expectations for the assessment session with the clients you will be providing support. You will also be educating them about what will be done to provide for the safety of all the family members in the interview (Friedlander et al., 2006; Odell & Campbell, 1998; Rait, 1998). For example, it may be that family members will fear being blamed for the problem (Odell & Campbell, 1998). Therefore you should address this safety need. Make it clear that no family member is to blame for the problem. You might explain that family problems are similar to family members passing around a cold or flu bug. "No one is to blame for the cold or flu but all the family members get involved in one way or another. The same is true for family problems, no one is to blame, but all get involved." Therefore, as a family therapist you routinely invite all members of the family to come for the assessment and feedback sessions (Jacobson & Christensen, 1996).

There are some other safety needs you may need to address. Several scholars (Odell & Campbell, 2001; Patterson et al., 1998) suggest that you will need to be especially sensitive to such issues as: (a) the desire of a family member to have the therapist to themselves; (b) fears about invaded privacy and concerns about sharing private, personal, or shameful information with the therapist and/or with other family members present; (c) stigma such as shame at having a problem and fear of what others may think; (d) concerns about what other family members might do or say – for example, blowups; (e) fear of change or anxiety about trying something new; and (f) efforts to protect other family members, especially the family member identified as the one with the problem. Listen carefully for suggestions of any of these fears and if they are present take time to address them. Many of these safety needs can be addressed if you are clear and specific about confidentiality rules and family therapy procedures (Odell & Campbell, 1998).

To begin meeting the safety needs of the family members you should explain that everything that is shared in therapy is held confidential by you as required by ethical codes for mental health workers (AAMFT, 2001; American Psychological Association, 2002; National Association of Social Workers, 1996). In addition, explain that you will encourage family members not to share things that are discussed in the sessions with persons that were not in the session. State that you will do everything possible to give each family member an opportunity to share her or his point of view. The focus will be on understanding the issues and the processes, not apportioning blame. While many of the issues may be emotional, the goal will be to learn how to regulate the emotion and how to use it to communicate and solve problems better.

Another safety need concerns family secrets. Many times behaviors that are considered by a family member to be a secret – such as an affair; abuse of drugs, alcohol, or medication; frequent use of pornography; eating disorders; excessive gambling; and so on – are a concern. The initiating family member may have the concern for her or his own behavior or may be protecting another family member. If the client reveals a secret to you it may help for you to explain that family secrets are often already known or suspected by other family members. The road to healing starts when things that are secret are made open for discussion. Explain that you will help all family members to provide support for each other and to assist in finding solutions. Even if the problem is an individual one the support of family members is very important in resolving it.

Deciding who should come to the assessment session

After explaining the purpose of the assessment session ask the initiating client who she or he believes should come to the session. The decision about who should come for marital or family therapy is one of the most critical decisions that therapists and clients make together (Boylin & Briggie, 1986; Haley, 1987; Odell & Campbell, 1998; Wetchler & Gutenkunst, 2005; Whitaker in Neill & Kniskern, 1982). Family therapists typically invite all the members of the family to come for the assessment session. If the problem is with young children or adolescents then invite all the adults responsible for the child's care and the child or adolescent. If it is a marital or couple relationship problem then invite both partners to participate. While making decisions about who should come to marital therapy point out that infants and children should not be brought to marital therapy sessions. Infants and children often react to their parents' emotions and the child's reaction then distracts the parents, which disrupts the session.

The outcome of the discussion about who should come to the assessment session should be a "win-win" decision. It is not a debate between the therapist and the client. It should be a respectful sharing of ideas and values. The client should win by having the final say about who attends. As a therapist you should feel good about having shared the values and benefits of conjoint therapy. Remember to always keep the client's welfare in mind. It is, after all, the client's therapy.

The importance of getting all the family members to come to therapy has been discussed by Whitaker (Neill & Kniskern, 1982) and others (Boylin & Briggie, 1986; Hiebert & Gillespie, 1984; Odell & Campbell, 1998; Patterson et al., 1998; Wetchler & Gutenkunst, 2005). Whitaker takes perhaps the strongest stand, suggesting that the therapist must "win the battle for structure" (Neill & Kniskern, 1982). By this Whitaker means that it is important for the therapist to be in charge of the therapy process and that the therapist should maintain the right to establish who should attend the sessions. Others agree (Hiebert & Gillespie, 1984; Odell & Campbell, 1998) and there is some empirical evidence to suggest that if the therapist does not structure the therapy sessions the family members may drop out (Shields, Sprenkle, & Constantine, 1991). However, it should be noted that in the first session Whitaker quickly shifts to what he terms "the battle for initiative" (Neill & Kniskern, 1982). That is, according to Whitaker, the therapist should make it perfectly clear that the initiative for making decisions about what to do about their lives is the responsibility of the family members. Thus, while Whitaker suggests that the therapist should work collaboratively with the clients to establish that he or she is responsible for structuring the therapy sessions he is emphatic that the family members are responsible for their lives and any changes they make as a result of the treatment. In other words, the family therapist keeps the process client and family focused.

Keep in mind that your goals in the initial phone call are, first to begin to establish the alliance, second to increase their desire to come to the initial session, and only third to determine who should come. Therefore, it makes no sense for you to get into a power struggle with the initiating client over who should come. You can maintain control over the structure of the sessions by listening carefully to the client's needs and expectations and by respectfully sharing your expectations. After that you should work to find a collaborative solution that meets the client's needs. When you negotiate with the initiating family member to determine which family members should come to the initial sessions you are as much in control of the structure of the sessions as a therapist who lays down hard and fast rules. The advantage of respectfully negotiating who should come will be that you are building a stronger client–therapist alliance.

Often, if you simply make a request in a friendly and matter of fact way for all family members to attend the assessment session, then the family members will comply. Sometimes family members do not come simply because they were never invited (Odell & Campbell, 1998). Your attitude should be that all the family members should attend just as the natural order of things. None the less some clients will raise objections.

Resistance to conjoint marital or family therapy

If, in the initial phone call, you encounter resistance to conjoint marital or family therapy then you may use probes and open questions to attempt to determine what is getting in the way (Hill, 2004). If you are talking to a partner who says the other partner is unwilling then ask to talk to the unwilling partner on the phone. Always get the initiating partner's permission before contacting the second partner. Another alternative has been suggested by Wilcoxon and Fenell (1983). They recommend getting permission to send a letter to the unwilling partner. Using text messages or email may be contraindicated as electronic communications run the risk being too easily disseminated to unknown parties thereby violating confidentiality.

If the person you are talking to says that the problem is "their problem" then inquire about the problem. There are many reasons for clients to feel that they should come to therapy alone. It is also the case that some family members assume that the only the person they consider to have the problem should come to therapy. Many in the general population – and in the mental health community as well – assume that problems, and especially mental health problems, reside within the individual (Odell & Campbell, 1998; Patterson et al., 1998). Therefore, some clients believe that they should come alone for therapy or that the individual identified as the patient (IP) should be the one to attend. Similarly, if family members consider a child to be the problem then they may believe that the treatment will be for the child alone. Family therapists gently resist these opening gambits for individual therapy. There are several reasons why conjoint family therapy should trump individual therapy.

Supporting reasons for conjoint therapy

There are several strong reasons for supporting conjoint therapy over individual therapy. The first reason family therapists gently resist individual therapy is one we have already discussed. That is, family therapists assume that the problems individual family members have are shared by all family members (Brody & Farber, 1989; Karney, Story, & Bradbury, 2005; Revenson, Kayser & Bodenmann, 2005b). For example Revenson, Kayser, and Bodenmann (2005b) point out that major life stressors affect others "in the individual's social network: family, friends, coworkers, neighbors, and even whole communities" (p. 3).

The second reason family therapists resist individual therapy is that we know that when family members supply support for each other the distress they are experiencing tends to be reduced (Cohen & Syme, 1985; Coyne & DeLongis, 1986; Milne, 1999; Uchino, Cacioppo, & Kiecolt-Glaser, 1996). For example the following problems have all been found to be helped when family members supply support to each other:

- anorexia nervosa (Lock & Le Grange, 2001);
- autism (Hastings, 2003);
- breast cancer (Segrin et al., 2005);
- child behavior problems (Dadds & McHugh, 1992);
- bereavement and loss (Stroebe, Stroebe, Abakoumkin & Schut, 1996);
- depression (Chou & Chi, 2001; Zuroff & Blatt, 2002);
- heart disease (Coyne et al., 2001);
- hypertension (Earp, Ory, & Strogatz, 1982);
- marital distress (Cutrona, 1996; Revenson et al., 2005b);
- Post Traumatic Stress Disorder (Tarrier & Humphreys, 2003);
- work place issues (Bowing et al., 2004; Zellars & Perrewé, 2001)

Third, as noted earlier, there is evidence that when family members structure the therapy sessions the clients are less likely to complete therapy (Shields et al., 1991). Consequently, as an evidence-based family therapy practitioner you can and should structure the session by recommending that all family members attend the assessment and feedback sessions.

Trying to manipulate or coerce the presenting client to get other family members to come may be counterproductive by creating resistance (Ellis, 2002; Goldstein, 2001), reactance (i.e. fear of loss of freedom or agency) (Goldstein, 2001), or what Butler describes as unproductive struggle (Butler & Bird, 2000; Butler & Wampler, 1999). However, it seems ethically responsible on the part of the marriage and family therapist to present the case for conjoint therapy since conjoint family therapy is at least as effective as individual therapy and often has additional benefits.

Family therapy has been found to have a number of additional benefits over individual therapy. Conjoint therapy often reduces the amount of time in therapy (Simmons & Doherty, 1995) and therefore reduces treatment costs (Alexander, Pugh, Parsons, & Sexton, 2000b; Crane, Hillin, & Jakubowski, 2005). It has also been suggested that conjoint therapy reduces the need for family clients to return for additional therapy over the years (Odell & Campbell, 1998). The alternative to coercion or manipulation appears to be education by providing the reluctant client with the information needed to make an informed decision.

Supplemental motivation for attending conjoint therapy

If there is still hesitancy after you have explained the confidentiality rules and the expectations for the assessment session, then the you may choose to provide further help to motivate the family members to come together for therapy. No empirical studies directly related to motivating or inducing couples and families to attend therapy together were found (Burke, Vassilev, Kantchelov, & Zweben, 2002). However, one approach may be to make use of the interventions suggested in the motivational literature (Burke et al., 2002; Miller & Rollnick, 2002; Prochaska, 1994; Prochaska et al., 1994).

One way you may facilitate the initiating client's participation in the decision about who should come is to use circular and reflexive questions. Adding circular and reflexive questions has been shown to improve the alliance in family therapy in two analogue studies (Dozier, Hicks, Cornille & Peterson, 1998; Ryan & Carr, 2001). According to Dozier et al. "Circular questions reflect an exploratory intent in which the therapist is attempting to bring forth 'patterns that connect' persons, objects, actions, perceptions, ideas, feelings, events, beliefs, contexts" (p. 192). Some examples of circular questions are "Who [in the family] worries most?" or "What does your father usually do when you and your mother talk?" (Dozier et al., 1998, p. 192). Circular questions may serve to help clarify the clients' goals and help establish the alliance.

Reflexive questions are designed to start clients thinking about new possibilities, to reframe their difficulties in new ways, and to get family members to begin evolving their own solutions (Dozier et al., 1998; Ryan & Carr, 2001). For example, the therapist might say "Let's imagine there was something he was resentful about, but didn't want to tell you for fear of hurting your feelings, how could you convince him you were strong enough to take it?" (Dozier et al., 1998, p. 193). or "If there was some unfinished business between the two of you, who would be the most ready to apologize?" (Ryan & Carr, 2001, p. 69). You may bring out the client's ideas about who should attend the assessment and feedback sessions by using a reflexive question such as, "Who do you think should come for the assessment session and how would you approach them?" In addition, the client's ideas about possible solutions may then begin to be matched with possible treatment methods. Recall that agreement on goals and methods are elements of the alliance.

The motivational interviewing research may be employed to help clients decide who should come to conjoint therapy. Prochaska proposed that clients go through several motivational stages related to behavior change (Prochaska, DiClemente, & Norcross, 1992). The first is the pre-contemplative stage in which the client is unaware of the need for change or has no intention of changing in the near future. The second is the contemplative stage in which people are aware of the need to change and are giving change serious consideration. After the contemplation stage Prochaska et al. (1992) suggest that clients move to the preparation stage, which includes both intention to change and some preliminary behavioral changes. The fourth stage is the action stage in which clients change their environment to create experiences that will modify their behavior. Finally, in the fifth stage they work to maintain the changes they achieved in the action stage.

These stages are not linear but rather circular with periods of backsliding and making several attempts to change before they are successful (Prochaska et al., 1992).

In a series of twelve carefully replicated studies Prochaska (1994) and colleagues (Prochaska et al., 1994) demonstrated that movement from the pre-contemplative to the action stage occurred when clients increased their perception of the number of reasons to change and increased their perception of the negative effects of not changing. Therefore, when the client or family members are reluctant to come to conjoint family therapy the therapist may improve the probability of their doing so by helping the clients to provide their own strong set of reasons for attending conjoint therapy and a strong set of reasons why not attending conjoint therapy might be bad for them.

Some pros and cons for attending conjoint family therapy

Some pros for all the family members coming to conjoint family therapy have been suggested earlier. For example, it is known that the support family members provide each other reduces stress, shortens the time in therapy, and helps family members recover from a number of physical and mental problems. Another reason for coming to family therapy is to help set the record straight. It is known from the attributional bias research that people commonly attribute unfavorable motives to the behavior of others and more favorable causes to their behavior (Alexander et al., 1989; Bradbury & Fincham, 1990; Doherty, 1981; Schwartz, Friedlander & Tedeschi, 1986). Therefore, if only one person comes to the assessment sessions you may get a distorted view based on that person's view of the relationship problem (Epstein & Baucom, 2003). Consequently it is in each family member's self-interest to attend the assessment session. You may suggest that family members may want to be sure that you are getting it right by attending and sharing their side of the story.

You can appeal to their pecuniary needs. You could point out that we usually charge the same fee for two, three, or more family members as we charge for one. Therefore the family that comes altogether is getting good value for money (Burger, 1986).

Yet another approach is to appeal to reluctant family members to come to the assessment and feedback sessions to help the family member who is perceived to have the problem (Odell & Campbell, 1998). It may be worth pointing out to the client who is initiating therapy that your care and concern as a therapist can never replace the care and concern of family members (Odell & Campbell, 1998). According to several research studies the therapist's support cannot replace the support of one's partner if the client is married or in a committed relationship (Bodenmann, 2005). Pistrang and Barker (2005) state "There is some evidence to suggest that support from other relationships may not compensate for the lack of a confiding relationship with the partner" (p. 98).

Some additional reasons for all the family members taking part in therapy follow. Treating individual family members may require returning for more therapy later as treating the individual does not change the family system and it is the family system that maintains the dysfunctional behaviors (Simmons & Doherty, 1995). Change is not complete until there are changes in the context that controls behavior and the family unit is the most important context for many people (Jacobson & Margolin, 1979; Mead, 1990; Skinner, 1974).

Some disadvantages of not taking part in conjoint therapy appear specific to marital or couple therapy. For example, there is some reason to believe that if one spouse comes alone to therapy about marital problems then there is an increased risk of divorce. It has been found that if an individual comes to therapy for a marital problem then their relationship with their spouse changes, and not always for the better from the point of view of their partner (Phillips, 1983). Phillips reviewed the literature on individual treatment with marital clients and found that there is a high probability that the marital relationship will be disturbed as the result of individual therapy. Katz, Beach, and Anderson (1996) found that if individuals in distressed marriages undergo individual therapy, which successfully increased their global self-esteem they were then undervalued by their partner. If there are no accompanying changes in the marital relationship then one or both partners may become increasingly dissatisfied. Therefore, it is in the couple's best interest for both to attend marital therapy.

Exceptions to recommending conjoint therapy

There are exceptions to what should be the general rule that all family members be invited to attend the assessment sessions (Odell & Campbell, 1998). For example, the client making the initial call may have strong reasons for including or excluding other family members. You should consider their reasons carefully. For example, if one partner has already made a firm decision to divorce then conjoint therapy may be contraindicated. In cases of domestic violence, sexual abuse, and incest the offending family member may be excluded. However, where domestic violence between couples is concerned there is currently some disagreement between scholars about who should attend. Some scholars recommend separate treatment for the victim and the offender (Holtzworth-Munroe et al., 2002) and others suggest that conjoint therapy may be helpful (Stith, Rosen, & McCollum, 2002). You should consider these possible exceptions when you are attempting to establish who should attend therapy.

After the therapist and initiating client have collaboratively reviewed coming conjointly or alone to the assessment and feedback sessions the therapist respectfully accepts the client's decision. As stated above the outcome should be a win-win situation with the client winning by making the decision and the therapist winning by having respectfully shared the values and benefits of conjoint therapy.

Clarifying clinic procedures

Once the decision about who is to come for the assessment sessions has been made you need to turn to clarifying clinic procedures. Clarifying the procedures may add to the client's feelings of safety and trust. If you have not already discussed confidentiality issues then point out that everything that occurs in therapy will be confidential. The only exception to strict confidentiality will be the need to report abuse. This will be explained in detail in the first session unless it becomes a question at this time. If the client expresses concern you will need to take time to explain the reporting policies mentioned in Chapter 2 and which are given in more detail later in this chapter.

Next you should clarify the time expectations for the first session. For example, if the couple has agreed to come or if the parents are coming with the child or adolescent, then you should tell them that the initial session will be for two hours. The initial session takes two hours because time is needed for everyone to share their points of view. However, if it is more convenient the initial session can be split into two 1-hour sessions. If only an individual is coming then the first appointment can be for an hour. Where applicable tell them that they are charged by the session, not by the hour, so the fee will remain the same. They will get two hours for the price of one (Burger, 1986). Explain that in the first session each family member will have the opportunity to share his or her reasons for coming and they will discuss their marital or family relationships. They will also take part in an observation exercise so that you can learn how they communicate and problem solve. At the end of the first session you will share some questionnaires with them, which they will take home to complete. Explain that the questionnaires will speed up the process of deciding if therapy is needed and if so what approach might work best. A second 1-hour assessment session will be scheduled for each marital partner to individually share their point of view about the marriage. Once they have completed and returned the questionnaires you will make an appointment for a feedback session with them. The feedback session will be for 1 hour. Tell them that in the feedback session you will feedback what you have learned from the assessment sessions. Then, if therapy seems warranted, they can decide if they want to begin therapy and who should come.

Next you will need to add a discussion of the clinic fees. If your fees are on a sliding scale explain the scale. As applicable you should tell the client if you do or do not bill insurance companies, Medicare, and other third party payers. Let them know if you do or do not accept credit cards. Ask if they have any questions or concerns about the fees and attempt to resolve them.

Providing directions to the clinic

Providing directions to the clinic, if needed, is another way to increase the client's feelings of trust and safety. Begin by asking if the client knows where the clinic is located, if they do not then give clear and specific instructions as to how to find the clinic. You might start by asking how they will be coming, for example, "Will you be coming by car or by public transportation?" If they are using public transportation provide instructions about which stop is nearest to the clinic. If they are driving then provide instructions about where to park.

Next explain how to check in with the receptionist or how to find you in the building. Be sure to tell them to come a little early as the receptionist will have some paperwork for them to complete. In addition, the receptionist may ask them to complete some pre-session assessment instruments. Explain that these instruments help you keep track of their individual mental health and relationship status. This is similar to a medical doctor taking their temperature and blood pressure when they make an office visit. Finally, ask about any concerns and resolve them if possible.

Closing the initial phone interview

Remind the client about the length of the first appointment, especially if it is to be for two hours. Next set the appointment date and time by suggesting two or three dates and times that you have available and ask them to choose one. Ask if they have any final questions or concerns and attempt to resolve them. Then restate your name, the date and time of the appointment, and let them know you are looking forward to meeting them. Let them know that you will call to reconfirm 24 hours before the appointment but if they need to change an appointment they can call the receptionist at [give the clinic phone number] and leave a message for you [state your full name again]. Congratulate them on taking this important step for their marriage or family and tell them that you are looking forward to meeting with them.

Immediately after you complete the call reserve a consulting room and request videotaping if that service is available in your agency. Within twenty-four hours of the phone session write a case progress note (Appendix D) to record the information about the client's presenting problem, decisions about who should attend, and so on.

Reconfirming sessions

To increase the probability that the clients will keep the appointment make a phone call the day before the appointment to reconfirm (Ross, Friman & Christophersen, 1993; Turner &

Vernon, 1976). If the clients are unable to keep the appointment this gives you the opportunity to reschedule. It is always a good idea to make a call the day before the next session to reconfirm.

Summary

Many clients consider the first phone call as part of therapy. Therefore, you should be well prepared in advance to use the steps of the Initial Phone Call Semi-structured Interview described above. As you prepare for the initial phone call re-read the steps above. Review a videotape model of the process if one is available. Practice delivering the initial phone call with your colleagues and/or supervisor. If possible record your initial phone call with the client's permission. Review your recorded session to ensure that all the essential elements were delivered to the clients. Seek feedback on your delivery from your colleagues and supervisor. An important part of becoming a competent therapist includes making successful initial phone calls.

Remember that the goals of the first interview are to start building an alliance and to increase the probability that the all of the family members will come. In addition, in the initial call you should provide for client safety needs by: (a) clarifying the clients' problems and goals; (b) reviewing the rules for confidentiality; (c) establishing expectations for the assessment and feedback sessions; (d) dealing with concerns and providing support; (e) clarifying clinic procedures including fees; (f) providing directions to the clinic, and (g) explaining how they will meet with you when they arrive. We turn next to the assessment session.

Therapy Task 1: Assessment

Introduction

When the clients come to the assessment session your first goal is to build and strengthen the alliance with each attending family member. After that your task is to help them clarify and specify the problem and their desired outcomes (Tryon & Winograd, 2002). Your goal should be to acquire a thorough understanding of these specific clients and their problem. Once the problem is clarified you need to arrive at a treatment plan that matches your clients' needs and expectations (Arnkoff, Glass & Shapiro, 2006).

The assessment session is scheduled for two hours to allow you time to complete all the tasks required to get your clients off to a good start. In this session you will need to share detailed information about the clinic, about confidentiality, and about fees. Even if you discussed most of this in the initial phone contact it is still necessary to repeat it here as not all family members were listening to the phone conversation. In addition, you need to be sure they are clear on all the details before they sign the request for services form. After taking care of the paperwork you will use the first session to (a) take the clients' presenting problems and begin establishing their goals for therapy; (b) take a relationship history; (c) observe your clients communication and problem-solving skills; and (d) administer the assessment battery.

After completing the assessment session you should be able to answer two basic questions. "What are the clients' problems?" And "What are their goals for therapy?" In addition, at the end of the assessment session you should have developed a level of trust with all of family members by listening respectfully to each of them and by validating their points-of-view. Working to build the alliance in this session is important because many clients see the assessment session as the beginning of therapy (Cordova et al., 2001; Davidson & Horvath, 1997; Worthington et al., 1995).

To answer the question "What are the clients' problems" you will need to get a clear and specific description of the clients' complaints. Complaints are descriptions of dysfunctional behaviors.

Dysfunctional behaviors are behaviors that are seen by the one or more family member as too much, too little, or missing behavior. In addition, dysfunctional behavior is often seen as punishing to one or more family members. The contextual variables maintaining the dysfunctional and functional behaviors of family members are the relational behavior patterns of the family members. These relational behaviors are often described as the interpersonal themes, patterns, or cycles performed by the family members around what the family members consider the problem. More specifically the contextual variables are the behaviors of family members that are antecedent to and consequent of the dysfunctional behavior. When you can assist the clients to spell out these patterns then you and the clients will be in a position to predict the dysfunctional behavior. If the antecedent and consequent behaviors are open to change then the dysfunctional behavior may be changed.

However, after determining the dysfunctional behavior your job is not yet done. The second question you are attempting to answer in the assessment session is "What are their goals for therapy?" The clients generally have expectations for the outcome of the treatment. These expectations or goals may be seen as the functional behaviors family members would prefer to be performing in place of the dysfunctional behaviors. The contextual variables that structure and maintain the clients' desired outcome behaviors are generally not the same as the variables that structure and maintain the dysfunctional behaviors. Therefore, simply helping the clients to change, reduce, or remove the dysfunctional behaviors may not help them reach their goals for therapy. You will need to help the clients specify the desired behaviors and then help them create the new interpersonal patterns which will build and maintain the desired behavior.

The first hour of the assessment session is designed to allow the family members to share their issues and their perceptions of their relationship history. The second hour is designed to help you observe family members' communication and problem-solving style through direct observation. At the end of the second hour you will need to explain the assessment battery to the clients and ask them to complete it at home after the interview. Once the assessment instruments have been completed and returned you should have enough information to determine if therapy is appropriate. If therapy is appropriate then you should determine which type of therapy will prove most helpful. In addition, you should be able to determine if you are competent to deliver the planned treatment under supervision. If the treatment is outside your current training competence then referral is appropriate. For example, should the problem be primarily the couple's sexual behavior and you have not yet had training in sex therapy, then the case should be referred.

The first assessment hour

Sharing the structure of therapy sessions

Once the clients have been escorted to the therapy room and have been made comfortable the therapist begins by greeting each and every family member and taking a minute to get acquainted. Next determine if they completed the pre-session assessment instruments, such as the Outcome Rating Scale[1] (ORS: Miller & Duncan, 2004) and if they have come for couple therapy the Revised Dyadic Adjustment Scale (RDAS: Busby et al., 1995; Appendix C). If the receptionist is not able to administer these two assessments, then administer them at this time. Explain to the clients that these instruments will be used to help you keep track of their progress in therapy. It is important that the ORS and RDAS be administered in the first session as the scores for these two instruments will serve as your baseline to evaluate therapy outcomes.

Obtaining authorization for clinical services

Once the clients have competed the pre-session assessments begin sharing specific information about clinic procedures. This should be done even if they have filled out the paperwork in the lobby. Start by providing each family member with written documents that provide information about your clinic or agency, the fee schedules, and an authorization for clinical services form. In addition to having copies to share with the clients you should have a copy that they will sign and which will be kept in the case file. Tell the clients that they will be able to keep their copies so they can write on them if they wish to.

Inform the clients that you are a marriage and family therapy intern

Start by informing the clients that you are a marriage and family therapy intern and give them the name of your supervisor and her or his qualifications, for example, "My supervisor is Dr. (name) and she is a licensed marriage and family therapist." Tell them that they are free to contact your supervisor at any time should they have questions or concerns about the treatment. Give them your supervisor's office address and phone number.

Review your clinic's authorization for services form with the clients. It is necessary to do this orally, even if they have already read it, as some clients may have difficulty reading and/or understanding the information. As you read it check with each family member to ensure that they understand it. Respond to any concerns they may have. Ask them to sign it and secure it in their case file.

Observation and videotaping

Inform the clients about your clinic's policy on observation and videotaping of the sessions. In some training clinics it is required that all sessions be recorded. Explain that the recorded materials are used to help you improve your skills as a therapist. The videos will only be viewed by you, your supervisor, and the therapist-interns in your training class. All are required to adhere to the profession's code of ethics and strict confidentiality will be maintained (AAMFT, 2001; American Psychological Association, 2002; National Association of Social Workers, 1996).

Tell your clients that your supervisor is a licensed therapist, therefore they will be getting the benefit of two therapists, you and your supervisor. In addition, when a one-way screen is available your supervisor may observe the sessions directly. Inform them that to further facilitate training other therapist-interns may sometimes observe behind the screen. If they refuse permission to have their sessions recorded or observed then accept and respect their right to that position and follow the procedures in your clinic. In some training clinics it will be necessary to provide them with a referral for services of a fully licensed therapist who is not in training and therefore does not require supervision. Secure in writing the clients' permission to record and/or observe the sessions.

Confidentiality issues

Point out to the clients that all participants in therapy share a responsibility to maintain the confidentiality of the material shared in the sessions. This means that each family member has a responsibility to maintain each others' privacy outside the session concerning things shared in the session. Ask the clients to decide what confidentiality means to them and how it is to be maintained. After the clients have shared their ideas on confidentiality acknowledge their responses.

Tell them that you have some rules about confidentiality that you would like to share with them. For example, you may have a rule about chance meetings in the community and a rule about private conversations between individual family members and yourself. This is a suggested rule for chance meetings. Your rule about chance meetings might be that you will take your cue about how to respond from them. That is, should you chance to meet on the street or in a store, if they greet you, you will respond. If they choose not to acknowledge you then you will act as if they are strangers. That way they will be spared from possibly embarrassing or uncomfortable explanations to others about how they know you.

Another rule about confidentiality concerns private disclosures to you by a family member. You need to decide what your rule will be and communicate it to your clients. Repeat that all those involved in the therapy have an obligation to maintain the confidentiality of what is shared in the sessions. Then set your boundaries concerning privately shared confidences. Privately shared confidences are instances where one family member wishes to communicate something to the therapist without the other family members being aware of the communication. Private communications may be a phone call, a letter, email, text message, or a conversation with the therapist after the others have left the therapy room. In general, there are three positions that the therapist can take on privately shared confidences.

Privately shared confidences may be seen as on a continuum from keeping all confidences shared with the therapist to not accepting any privately shared out of session confidences (Margolin, 1982; Wilcoxon et al., 2007). That is, the therapist can state that anything one of the family members shares in private such as in a phone call, email, or a private conversation will be treated as confidential and not shared with other family members. At the other end of the continuum is the position that the therapist will not accept any out of session one-on-one information. Between these two poles on the continuum is the position that the therapist will decide, based on her or his clinical judgment, whether it is important to share privately divulged information with other family members. The total secrecy position allows family members to share information with the therapist that might otherwise not come out. The nonsecrecy position prevents the therapist from being in collusion with one family member to the possible detriment of other family members. The intermediate position places a heavy burden on the therapist to decide when, where, how, or if a piece of information should be disclosed (see Gladding et al., 2001 for an extended discussion of these positions).

Whatever position you take on privately shared confidences it should be clearly stated in the first session and repeated whenever an issue comes up. Your failure to explain your rules may leave one family member expecting that everything will be held in confidence while another family member may expect that everything will be shared. This places you as a therapist in a no-win position. For example, if you share something that a family member shared with you in private and that person believes that "everything will be kept in confidence" then you may be perceived to have broken trust with that family member. If, on the other hand, you do not share things you have received in private from a family member, then a family member who expects that "everything will be shared" may feel betrayed when it comes out – and it generally does. Therefore, it is imperative that you establish a firm rule that is made clear to all family members in the very beginning. The rule, once established, should be maintained consistently.

Legal limits to confidentiality

As a further note on confidentiality you can explain that without written permission from all the participants you will not release information or even acknowledge their participation in therapy to any person not in their therapy sessions (AAMFT, 2001). However, you must explain to the clients that there are situations where you are obligated by law to break confidentiality. In Great Britain, Europe, Australia, Canada, and in all 50 states of the United States it is required that therapists report child abuse or neglect. Even the suspicion of child abuse must be reported to the appropriate department for child protection and welfare. If there is immediate danger to a child the therapist must report to the appropriate local legal authorities such as the police, sheriff, or constable. Tell the clients that should it be necessary to make such a report you will discuss it with them. It is also necessary to report elder abuse to Adult Protective Services. Explain your state's requirements for reporting adult-to-adult abuse. Finally, let them know that because you care about human life you will report whenever there is perceived danger of harm to people, such as potential suicide or threats of harm to others (Simone & Fulero, 2005). Check to see that they understand each point as you go and respond to their concerns. Record that you have shared this information with the clients in your case progress notes.

Obtaining signatures on the authorization for services form

Once you have reviewed the authorization for services form with the clients and answered their questions ask all participants to sign a copy and secure it in the case file. Again they are instructed that they may keep their copies. Note that in most states children under 18 cannot sign for consent. In all cases parents must sign for underage children. Also note that in the case of divorced parents where they have joint custody both parents must sign giving permission for treatment of the child. In the case of family therapy the children may sign the authorization form signifying their assent, but not consent, to therapy. Allowing the children to sign is often helpful in establishing an alliance with the children.

Structuring the expectations for therapy

Next, identify the therapy session start and stop times saying something like, "We operate on a 50 minute session starting on the hour and ending ten minutes before the hour. This provides time for the next person who uses the room to get set up. Two hour sessions stop at ten to the hour of the second hour." Tell them about the possible duration of treatment. The number of sessions available to clients may be a function of the policies of the clinic in which you practice. If you are limited to a certain number of sessions you should explain the limits to your clients. If not, you can use the research to establish expectations for the number of sessions. Empirically-based treatments often specify the desired number of sessions in the treatment manual. You can also say something like, "Based on research about 75 to 80 percent of the clients who come for therapy achieve beneficial results in 15–21 sessions, however 20–25 percent require 45 or more sessions" (Lambert & Ogles, 2004, pp. 154).

Read and discuss with the clients the clinic or agency statement on terminating therapy or requesting another therapist. This statement should explain that they are free to drop out of therapy at any time without penalty of any sort (AAMFT, 2001). It should also mention that they are free to request another therapist. Share again with them your expectations for who should attend, "It is important for all the family members to attend therapy sessions." If the case is a marital case reiterate that in the case of marital therapy when one spouse comes alone about marital issues there are often changes in their behavior that impact the marital relationship. In the case of both marriage therapy and family therapy if all family members attend then progress may be faster, the possibility of needing additional sessions may be reduced (Simmons & Doherty, 1995), and therefore the costs may be reduced (Alexander et al., 2000; Crane et al., 2005). Finally, point out that it is not a good idea to bring infants or children to marital therapy as they often react to their parents' emotions which can detract from the session.

Review the fee schedule and secure their signatures

It is important to discuss fees in the first session. Present your agency's fee policy to your clients. Explain the policy on accepting or not accepting third party payment such as health insurance and Medicare. Also state the policy on accepting or not accepting credit cards. If you have a sliding fee schedule then put your clients at ease concerning the fees by describing the sliding fee schedule. Herron and Sitkowski (1986) reviewed the literature to determine what the effect of charging or not charging a fee has on therapy. They found no evidence that clients who pay a fee do better in therapy. They also found that fees appear to present a barrier to clients seeking therapy and remaining in it. Therefore, it appears important for your alliance with your clients that you open a discussion on fees and work to resolve the issues in a way that is satisfactory to the clients and to the agency in which you are practicing.

Fees and fee setting may require reviewing your own attitudes toward charging a fee for your services. Herron and Sitkowski (1986) note that many therapists express concerns about being in a service profession and charging fees. Greenson and Jaffe (2004), for example, express discomfort about discussing fees and Greenson personally expresses discomfort about addressing fees over the phone. If you find it is difficult for you to discuss fees with your clients then you may want to discuss this issue with your supervisor and/or take it up with your personal therapist (Deacon et al., 1999; Norcross, 2005).

When you have reached an agreement on the fee with your clients write down your agreement on the fee schedule and ask them to sign a copy for the file. Clip that copy securely in the case file. Tell them they can keep their copies of the fee agreement for their files at home.

Setting the agenda

When you have competed the preliminary paperwork begin to outline the agenda for the rest of assessment session. Point out that "We have much to accomplish together in this session." Explain that you first want to hear from each of them about why they came to therapy at this time. Tell them that after they have each had a chance to explain why they came to therapy you will ask them about their family relationships. In the second hour, after a short break, you will have them discuss their issues while you observe their interaction – either from behind the one-way screen or from a corner of the room, depending upon the facilities at your clinic. At the end of the session you will provide them with some questionnaires that they can complete at home. Ask if they have any questions and attempt to resolve their concerns. After setting the agenda move to a discussion of the clients' presenting problems.

Taking the clients' presenting problems and goals for therapy

After taking care of the paperwork and setting the agenda you are ready to attempt to determine each family member's perception of the problem and their expectations for therapy outcomes. This is usually accomplished by a series of open ended questions. For example, with a couple, you might say, "I would like to hear briefly from each of you. Who would like to start? What brings you to therapy at this time?" With a family it is often best to start with the youngest and work up. This makes it easier for the children to respond without simply reiterating what their parents have said. For example you might say to the youngest child, "What did your parents tell you about why you are here today?" Each family member should be given an opportunity to respond to each question. In addition to collecting each family member's perceptions of the issues the therapist is attempting to establish that in the therapy sessions each participant will be treated fairly and with respect. Each family member should leave the session feeling that you are on their side and that you have their best interests in mind (Alexander & Sexton, 2002). If you accomplish this then the probability of the family members returning for additional sessions will be increased.

Taking a structured marital or family history interview

After taking the clients' statements of the presenting problems the therapist interviews couples or family members to determine their views of their relationship. Many therapy manuals provide models of initial interviews designed to bring out couple or family processes. For example, the semi-structured Oral History Interview is used by Gottman (1999) as an initial interview for marital couples. Johnson (2004) and Christensen, Jacobson, and Babcock (1995) also provide initial interviews for couples. Alexander and Sexton (2002) provides guidelines for initial interviews with adolescents and their parents and McMahon and Forehand (2003) presents an initial interview for parents and their noncompliant child. The purpose of each of these semi-structured interviews is to provide family members the opportunity to interact around a systematic series of questions and procedures. By systematically interviewing each family member the therapist will develop more reliable and valid information to assist in making informed decisions.

Session break

After completing the marriage or family history interview take a 5- to 10-minute break. Explain how to find the drinking fountain and the restrooms from the therapy room. Set a time to start the second half of the session and allow them to take a break.

Assessment session: Second hour

Structuring sessions to observe clinically relevant relationship patterns

The therapist can structure sessions in such a way that family patterns emerge, can be observed, and in time predicted (Cleghorn & Levin, 1973; MacLean, 2005; Watzlawick, 1972). Each family member's behavior is controlled by the behavior of the other family members and in turn each family member's behavior influences the behavior of others. The patterns of influence exchanged by family members are not random. They form cyclic patterns that maintain themselves over long periods of time. Some of the behavior shaped by these variables is functional for the survival of individual family members. The infant's cry usually results in the attention of others who supply food, dry clothing, warmth, and so on. Some of the family behavior is functional or dysfunction for the survival of the family as a social system. The family member's behavior that is emitted in the session may be termed clinically relevant behavior (Kohlenberg & Tsai, 1991; Smith et al., 1998). It is these here and now clinically relevant behaviors that you observe and respond to in an effort to help clients change dysfunctional behaviors into more functional behaviors (Kohlenberg & Tsai, 1991).

Functional behavior is behavior that helps each family member to adapt to the environment and to survive. Individual survival is greatly enhanced through cooperation and collaboration with other family members (Ansbacher & Ansbacher, 1956; Milne, 1992; Revenson, Kayser, & Bodenmann, 2005a). Indeed, infants and young children, and thus the species, cannot survive without a relatively functional family system. There are numerous family forms, which have evolved in various cultures, all of which serve to provide for the survival of infants and children as they develop into adults. Enduring committed interpersonal relationships such as those found in well-functioning families and marriages are known to contribute to the family members' physical (Campbell, 2006; Kiecolt-Glaser & Newton, 2001) and mental health (Horwitz, White & Howell-White, 1996; Mueser, 2006; Stack & Eshleman, 1998).

Dysfunctional behavior is behavior that reduces the chances of survival for family members. As described earlier dysfunctional behavior may be defined as behavior which is too much, too little, or missing in response to the current environment. Dysfunctional behavior is often perceived as harmful or painful to the individual, to other family members, or to both. Family members may seek outside help when they perceive that the dysfunctional behavior is too harmful or too painful to be handled by their usual coping methods.

Functional and dysfunctional family behavior can best be observed when family members interact in a semi-structured environment. You can provide the clients with an opportunity to interact in the session so that you may observe their behavior. By observing their patterns in vivo you will be better able to determine the patterns that may be used to change dysfunctional behaviors to more functional behaviors.

Using semi-structured observation sessions to observe family members' communication and problem-solving style

In the second assessment hour your goal is to structure the session to be able to observe the clients communication and problem-solving processes. To accomplish this you may introduce couples to the "Comprehensive Areas of Change Item Ranking Form" (CAC; Appendix C) or for parents and adolescent children either the "Parent-adolescent Areas of Change Questionnaire" (Jacob & Seilhamer, 1985) or Watzlawick's (1972) "Structured Family Interview." With parents and younger children McMahon and Forehand (2003) present procedures for observation of parent–child interaction with children aged 3 to 8 in either the home or in the clinic. The procedures used to observe a couples' communication and problem-solving style will serve as an example of observational procedures.

A semi-structured observation session to observe couple interaction

Begin by providing each partner with a copy of the "Comprehensive Areas of Change Item Ranking Form" (CAC; Appendix C) and keep one for yourself. Ask each partner individually to put an "X" in the left hand column next to any item she or he thinks they need to discuss. You may read the items if you suspect that one or both may have difficulty reading. When they have both completed this task tell them to look over the items they have marked and rank order them in the right-hand column. Instruct them to look over each of the items they put an "X" beside on the left side of the form. Then ask them to find the item they marked which would be the easiest to talk about and to problem-solve about. Mark the easiest item with a "1" in the right hand column next to that item. Next ask them to find the next easiest item they marked in the left column and put a "2" by it in the right column. Ask them to continue in this way until they have ranked all of the items they marked. Monitor their progress and assist as needed.

When they have completed their ranking of the CAC items ask them each to share the easy item, the item that they marked with a "1" with their partner. That is, first one partner shares her or his easy item and then the other partner shares hers or his. After they have each shared their "easy" item ask them to talk to each other and to decide which of the two "easy" items they will talk about in session today. Explain that in a few minutes you will step out of the room and they will have six minutes to try to resolve the "easy" issue. While they are deciding on which easy item to use observe their processes. When they have decided, ask them to write down the "easy" item they plan to use and you do the same. Next ask them each to look at their list and pick an item which they think will be hard or difficult for them to talk about and to problem-solve about. When they have each selected a "difficult" item ask them to turn to each other and share their "difficult" item. Next they are to decide on one of two the "difficult" items to talk about today. Again observe their processes as they decide on their "difficult" item. As before, write down their choice and encourage them to do the same.

Explain to them that you will step out of the room and go behind the one-way screen, view their interaction, or alternatively, move as far away as possible into a corner of the room. When it is time to start you will signal them to start with the "easy" item by a tap on the window. They are then to begin talking about the "easy" item and try to resolve any issues they have about it. After six minutes you will tap on the window again and they can relax for a minute. After that you will tap on the window a third time and they are to talk about and attempt to resolve any issues they have about the "difficult" item. Again after six minutes you will tap on the window and they can stop. Tell them you will then return to the room. It is a good idea to have them tell you back these instructions before you leave the room to ensure that they understand the instructions.

When you are behind the screen set your kitchen timer for six minutes. Use of a timer frees you to concentrate on observing and recording their communication and problem-solving patterns rather than keeping track of the time. When you are ready to record their responses to the "easy" issue start your timer and tap on the window. Record your observations systematically based on the therapy model you are using (see for example, the "Therapist's Observation Form for Couples' Communication", Appendix E). When your timer signals that six minutes have elapsed, tap on the window. Get ready to record the "difficult" issue, start your timer and tap on the window and follow the same procedures as described above.

When you return ask them something like, "If I had been a fly on the wall at home would this have gone the same way it went here?" Ask each partner to describe how things might have been different at home. Ask them how talks like this usually end. When they have finished sharing how their discussions end at home thank them for their efforts. Validate any discomfort they may have experienced and explain that in the therapy sessions you will try to help them find ways to make such conversations much more pleasant and productive.

Administering standardized assessment instruments

After the observation session is completed you should administer the appropriate standardized assessment instruments (Appendix C). The advantage of standardized assessment instruments is that they are reliable, valid, and many have established norms. They will help you evaluate any hypotheses you have made or help to establish new hypotheses concerning your clients' behavior. The standardized assessment instruments will help you establish a treatment plan. They also provide a basis for continuously observing progress and outcomes. For example, the Outcome Rating Scale (Miller & Duncan, 2004) and the Revised Dyadic Adjustment Scale (Busby et al., 1995) may serve to help establish the difficulty of the case and may also serve as continuous measurements to evaluate the clients' progress.

Use of standardized assessment instruments

There continues to be disagreement among marriage and family therapists about the nature and function of assessment (Crews & Hill, 2005; MacLean, 2005; Sperry, 2004). According to a study by Boughner, Hayes, Bubenzer, and West (1994) only about one-third of the members of the American Association for Marital and Family Therapy (AAMFT) who responded to their survey used any kind of assessment instruments. Lavee and Avisar (2006) surveyed Israeli marriage and family therapists. Of those responding only 27.6 percent used standard assessment instruments and 56.4 percent did not use any assessment instruments. The results of these two studies suggest that at present only about 30 percent of marriage and family therapists use standardized assessment instruments.

Some marriage and family therapists believe that the primary function of assessment instruments is to arrive at a *Diagnostic and Statistical Manual of Mental Disorders* (DSM-IV-TR; American Psychiatric Association, 2000) type diagnosis (Crews & Hill, 2005). Some of the questions that arise over using the DSM are concerns about labeling clients and therefore distancing the therapist from the clients (MacLean, 2005; Odell & Campbell, 1998). Whether a DSM diagnosis distances the therapist from the client may be primarily in the attitudes of the therapist. If you approached the diagnosis as the first step in matching a treatment to the client's problems and needs, then the diagnosis can be helpful. As Wilson (1996) points out DSM diagnoses do not imply that all clients that share a diagnosis have the same etiology or that the same treatment will be equally effective for clients in that diagnosis. The DSM diagnosis is simply another tool to help you help your clients.

One problem with the DSM is that it does not deal well with the relational issues seen as critically important by many marriage and family therapists (Kaslow, 1996). However, Gollan, Gortner, and Jacobson (1996) have demonstrated that an empirically-supported, relationship-focused diagnoses for partner related depression is possible. There is no reason that other relationship-focused diagnoses could not be developed.

Some family therapists are concerned that an ethical dilemma may arise when the family therapist is required to provide a DSM diagnosis. In general DSM diagnoses focus on individual issues. Many marriage and family therapists feel that the problem is in the family members' relationships and not in individuals. This problem becomes even more acute when the diagnosis will be used to justify reimbursement by a third-party payer (Crews & Hill, 2005; Odell & Campbell, 1998). Third-party payers often limit reimbursement to specific classes of DSM diagnoses most of which do not include relational issues. Therefore, the family therapist may resort to providing a DSM diagnosis for individual family members although the problem is perceived to be a relational issue (Odell & Campbell, 1998). If the diagnosis for the individual family member is not appropriate, then ethical and legal problems may occur (Crews & Hill, 2005; MacLean, 2005; Wilcoxon et al., 2007). Therapists who supply a diagnostic label simply to collect a fee may be breaking the law or violating ethical principles. However, there are times when an individual DSM diagnosis is completely justified as in the case of a spouse with depression. In addition, there are numerous empirically supported marriage and family treatments that are appropriate for DSM type diagnoses see for example, Miller et al. (2000) and others (Baucom, Shoham, Mueser, Daiuto & Stickle, 1998; Dobson & Craig, 1998; Sandberg et al., 1997). While it would be good to have an empirically verified relationship classification system, at present we will just need to work with the diagnostic system that we have, the DSM-IV-TR (Wilson, 1996).

For Crews and Hill (2005) the ethical issues center around honest assessment and diagnosis when developing treatment plans and reporting to third-party payers. At present it appears best to acknowledge any issues related to diagnostic categories in your treatment plans and case notes and to report honestly and completely your assessment or diagnosis for both the individual family members and their relational issues (Barnett, 2004).

While some marriage and family therapists avoid doing assessments for the reasons cited above, others see assessments as important in establishing effective treatment plans (Christensen, Jacobson & Babcock, 1995; Gottman, 1999; Johnson, 2004; MacLean, 2005; Mead, 1990). The goal of assessment is to collect the information needed to make informed decisions about the clients' presenting problem and their goals for therapy.

The decision as to which assessment instruments to administer is based on (a) the clients' needs and goals as expressed in their statements of the presenting problems, (b) the clients' responses to the semi-structured interview, (c) your ratings of their processes in the observation session, and (d) the model of therapy you are using. The most common marital problems are: (a) marital adjustment or marital satisfaction; (b) marital stability or divorce potential; (c) depression; (d) domestic violence; (e) abuse of alcohol; and (f) individual psychological symptoms. For marital couples the Standard Assessment Battery (SAB: Appendix C) is useful to screen for the issues most commonly associated with marital problems. The instruments selected for the SAB were chosen because they are reliable, valid, and relatively brief. The SAB is also available in a Spanish language version (Mead, Thurber, & Crane, 2003). The Outcome Rating Scale (ORS: Miller & Duncan, 2004) and the Revised Dyadic Adjustment Scales (RDAS: Busby et al., 1995) may be administered at the beginning of each session to serve as a continuous assessment of client progress.

The SAB may be administered in the clinic or may be sent home with the clients. If the SAB is to be sent home it is suggested that you provide each spouse with a return envelope containing copies of each instrument. Ask each spouse to complete their SAB independently and return them to you. Explain that these instruments will help you get a fuller picture of their marriage. This is a "standard" package that has been found to be useful for a broad range of clients. However, they may find that some of the instruments do not seem to pertain to them specifically. Explain that it is as important to find out what does not fit as well as what does fit. Therefore, ask them to complete all of the instruments in the packet. Briefly explain each of the instruments in turn (SAB: Appendix C). For example, you might say, "The Revised Dyadic Adjustment Scale, is a measure of marital satisfaction. The Outcome Ratings Scale is a measure of current mental status. The Marital Status Inventory is a measure of marital stability. The Brief Screen for Depression is just what it says, a brief screen for depression. The Conflict Tactics Scale 2 is a measure of how issues are resolved in the marriage. Finally, the AUDIT is measure of alcohol use." Remind them that they are each to complete their packet on their own at home and it will take them about an hour. After they have completed the packet they are to seal it and return it as soon as possible. Explain that as soon as you have the assessment instruments back you will score them and make a personalized treatment. When you have prepared the treatment plan you will call them to make a feedback appointment. Ask if they have any questions and try to resolve their concerns.

A standard assessment battery for family therapy cases would include assessment of the parents' perceptions of the child's adaptive and maladaptive behaviors. It should also include a measure of the child's psychological distress. The two most frequently used assessment instruments for assessing children are the Child Behavior Checklist/6-18 (Achenbach, 1994) to assess the child's behavior and the Youth Outcome Questionnaire (Wells, Burlingame, Lambert, Hoag, & Hope, 1996) to assess psychological distress. Parent's psychological distress is measured by the ORS.

After administering the assessment instruments close the session by asking your clients to summarize the session and then administer the Session Rating Scale (SRS: Duncan et al., 2003; see Chapter 1 note 1). Score their responses to the Session Rating Scale and ask about any of the scales marked at 9 cm or lower or a total score below 36. It takes courage to ask about the clients' concerns about the session and about you. It is important to ask about their concerns because it allows you to resolve rifts in the alliance more quickly. Resolve any concerns and thank them for their efforts. Walk them out to the lobby and remind them once again that you will set up the time for the feedback session as soon as they return the assessment packages.

Write up your case progress notes within 24 hours (Appendix D). Do not wait to write your progress notes until after they return the assessments as that would delay your prompt entry of your notes. Record your observations from the observation session in your case progress notes. Share your case notes with your supervisor. When your supervisor returns your case notes make any corrections and submit the corrections as an addendum or as required by your agency. Keep a private log (Appendix F) of your therapy and supervision hours as you will need this information when applying for additional training, jobs, licensure, and clinical membership in professional organizations.

What Should you Take Away from Chapter 3?

1 The initial phone call initiates therapy in the minds of most clients. The initial phone call is a semi-structured interview designed to help you cover many of the issues that come up in the first contact with the clients. Purpose of initial phone call: (1) begin building the client–therapist alliance; (2) increase motivation to come to therapy; (3) clarify who should come to the assessment sessions.

2 Topics which may be covered in the initial phone call include: (a) making the initial contact; (b) beginning to clarifying the clients' problems and goals; (c) establishing your expectations

for the assessment and feedback sessions including who should attend; (d) dealing with the clients' safety needs and providing support; (e) clarifying clinic procedures including fees; (f) providing directions to the clinic; and (g) explaining how they will meet with you when they arrive.

3 The purpose of the assessment interview is to help you understand the clients' goals and needs so that collaboratively you and the clients can make informed decisions. Therefore, you should use methods that provide the most reliable and valid information. Reliability and validity increases with structure. Reliability and validity increases as you move from unstructured interviews and observations to structured interviews and observations and to empirically tested assessment instruments.

4 You will be using the information gathered in the assessment session to make decisions about whether the clients should come for treatment and who should come.

5 Finally, you will use the information gathered in the assessment session(s) to develop a treatment plan (see Chapter 4).

Chapter 4

Establishing a Treatment Plan and Delivering the Planned Treatment

Introduction

In this chapter you will learn the skills needed to complete Therapy Task 2: Establishing a Treatment Plan and Therapy Task 3: Delivering the Planned Treatment. The treatment plan functions to join your perception of the client's problem with the clients' perception of the problem. After you have reached agreement on the problem you can present an empirically-based treatment plan which fits with the clients' expectations for how to treat the problem. The treatment plan should meet the clients' expectations if the alliance is to be maintained and strengthened. Presenting an empirically-based treatment that has been shown to be efficacious with similar clients with similar problems will help to meet the clients' expectations. When the clients agree with the treatment plan you can begin to deliver it.

Most empirically-based treatments have a treatment manual designed to describe the treatment and its delivery. The use of treatment manuals to deliver treatment has been controversial. However, there appears to be agreement that manual guided treatment can bring about successful outcomes. The key to the successful use of a manual is continuous attention to the client–therapist alliance. One way to attend to the alliance is to tailor the interventions from the manual to the needs of your clients. Delivering the planned treatment tailored to the needs of your clients allows you to carry on a therapeutic conversation long enough for the clients to change their dysfunctional behavior to more functional behavior (Frank & Frank, 1991, 2004).

This chapter is designed to help you learn two important therapist skills. First, how to establish an empirically-based treatment plan and share it with your clients. Second, how to deliver the planned treatment by tailoring the interventions to meet the clients' needs.

Therapy Task 2: Establishing a Treatment Plan

After the assessment sessions you will have in front of you information from multiple persons and from multiple sources. Some of the information agrees, some of it contradicts, and some of it does not seem to fit in anywhere. Family members contradict themselves and each other. They also agree on some points and not on others. Some of the problems they present appear trivial

Becoming a Marriage and Family Therapist: From Classroom to Consulting Room, First Edition. D. Eugene Mead.

and others may appear life threatening. Your first job is to reassemble this information into a clear and specific description of the problem. Once the problem is clear you can propose a treatment plan to resolve it.

Organize the assessment information

You begin to develop a treatment plan by organizing all of the available information. To illustrate the process let us assume that you are preparing a treatment plan for a couple. The process is similar for a family or for an individual client. When a couple has completed and returned their Marital Standard Assessment Batteries (SAB: Appendix C) score each of the instruments. Next organize your information into tabular form as shown in Figure 4.1. You can add scores to the table from other assessment instruments as needed. For example, you could add rows to enter scores for the *Beck Depression Inventory* (Beck, Steer & Brown, 1996), and the *Beck Anxiety Inventory* (Beck & Steer, 1993) which are frequently used to help establish the clients' needs and goals. By tabling the data you will make it easier to consider all of the assessment information as you prepare the treatment plan. Tabling the data may also make missing information more apparent.

Studying the information in the table will help you take a multiple causation approach to the client information. It may help you to determine if the information forms a coherent pattern that is consistent across instruments and across respondents. It also helps you look for disconfirmations, inconsistencies, and biases (Nezu & Nezu, 1989). Everything you can do to help reduce any biases in your judgment will be of benefit to your clients. There is considerable evidence that clinical judgment can be flawed (Garb, 2005; Nezu & Nezu, 1989; Wilson, 1996). Therefore, you should work to develop procedures which work against errors in judgment.

Establish the clients' problems and goals

With your assessment data tabled you are ready to establish the clients' problems and goals. You have information from each family member and from your observations (multiple persons), which has been collected by both interviews and assessment instruments (multiple methods). Using information from multiple persons and multiple methods will help you to overcome pre-judgment biases you may have formed (Nezu & Nezu, 1989; Wilson, 1996).

To specify the problems and goals start by reviewing your case notes from the assessment sessions. Look for missing information as you review the data. Also look for patterns and recurrent cycles. Look at your notes to attempt to determine each family member's complaints and goals. How did each family member respond to the structured interview? Compare your notes, ratings, and observations with the scores from the clients' SAB. What part did each contribute to the patterns and cycles observed in the observation session?

Ask yourself (Polya, 1971):

- Is there a pattern in this data?
- Have I seen this before?
- Have I seen parts of this before?
- What is missing?
- What hypotheses does this information suggest?
- What other hypotheses does this information offer?

By carefully considering the part each family members' behavior plays in maintaining the families clinically relevant functional and dysfunctional behavior patterns you will be able to form a relational diagnosis (Kaslow, 1996). Ask yourself, "Who does what to whom and when?" Some

Figure 4.1 An example of a marital Standard Assessment Battery scores record

Instruments used in this example:
1 Therapist's Ratings on the Oral History Rating Scale (Brewer, 2004; Brewer & Mead, 2008; Buehlman & Gottman, 1996; Gottman, 1994)
2 Outcome Rating Scale (ORS) and Session Rating Scale (SRS: Miller & Duncan, 2004).
3 Revised Dyadic Adjustment Scale (RDAS: Busby, Crane, Larson, & Christensen, 1995).
4 Marital Status Inventory-Revised (Jamieson, 2007).
5 Brief Screen for Depression (Hakstian & McLean, 1989).
6 Revised Conflict Tactics Scales 2 (Straus, Hamby, Boney-McCoy, & Sugarman, 1996).
7 Alcohol Use Disorders Identification Test (Babor, de la Fuente, Saunders, & Grant, 1992).

Assessment Instrument: Oral History Rating Scale
Therapist's ratings

Factor	*Score*
Wife We-Ness	—
Husband We-Ness	—
Couple Glorifying the Struggle	—
Husband's Fondness	—
Husband's Negativity	—
Husband's Expansiveness	—
Couple Chaos	—
Wife Disappointment/Disillusionment	—
Husband Disappointment/Disillusionment	—
TOTAL DIVORCE POTENTIAL	—

Assessment Instrument: ORS	*Partner 1*	*Partner 2*
Overall	—	—
Individually	—	—
Interpersonally	—	—
Socially	—	—
TOTAL	—	—
RDAS Total	—	—
Marital Status Inventory	—	—
Brief Screen for Depression	—	—
Assessment Instrument: Revised Conflict Tactics Scales (CTS-2)		
Negotiation	—	—
Psychological Aggression	—	—
Physical Assault	—	—
Sexual Coercion	—	—
Injury	—	—
Assessment Instrument: The Alcohol Use Disorders Identification Test (AUDIT)		
Recent Alcohol Consumption	—	—
Dependence Symptoms	—	—
Alcohol Related Problems	—	—
TOTAL	—	—
Assessment Instrument: SRS		
Relationships	—	—
Goals and Topics	—	—
Approach or Method	—	—
Overall	—	—
TOTAL	—	—

common couple and family patterns are differences in: (a) desired closeness or distance; (b) control and responsibility; (c) how to communicate loving and caring behavior; (d) timing of spontaneity and play versus goal setting and planning; and (e) conventional and socially conforming behavior versus unconventional and nonconforming behavior (Alexander, Pugh, Parsons, & Sexton, 2000a; Gottman, 1999; Jacobson & Christensen, 1998). Try to determine if your clients fit into one of these patterns or some other pattern. If you understand the pattern then you will be able to predict their behavior. If you can predict their behavior then you can find a treatment plan that will allow you help them change.

Consider the possibility of a DSM-IV-TR (American Psychiatric Association, 2000) diagnosis for each family member. Some scholars have suggested that we consider the possibility of more than one DSM diagnosis for each family member (Baucom et al., 1998; Ruscio & Holohan, 2006; Schulte et al., 1992). Others have suggested that the dysfunctional behavior is under the control of the family themes and therefore DSM diagnoses are not helpful in family therapy, for example, in one handbook of family therapy there is not a single reference to the DSM (Sexton, Weeks, & Robins, 2003).

Next consider the possibility of the clients' having multiple problems. Some problems are potentially life threatening such as suicidal ideation or domestic violence. Treatment of life threatening problems takes precedence over other problems. Problems of alcohol or drug abuse will probably need to be taken care of before marital or child-rearing problems can be successfully treated (McCrady & Epstein, 1995; Roberts & McCrady, 2002). Court referred cases and adolescents referred by their parents may be too resistant or too reactant to begin treatment for their presenting problems. In such cases the first treatment plan may need to be to resolve any motivational issues (Burke, Vassilev, Kantchelov & Zweben, 2002; Prochaska & Norcross, 2001). It appears best to prioritize multiple problems and treat them serially (Eifert, Evans, & McKendrick, 1990). However, some comorbid problems, such as marital problems accompanied by depression, may be treated simultaneously if an empirically-supported treatment such as Beach, Sandeen, and O'Leary's (1990) *Depression in Marriage* is available.

Agreement between the you and your clients about the severity of the problems is also an important part of establishing the problem. Disagreements between clients and therapists about the severity of the problem has been shown to reduce the probability of reaching a mutually agreed upon termination (Croning, Malofeeva & Bucchianeri, 2007).

Do not limit your review of the clients' information to dysfunctional behavior. As you consider your assessment information ask yourself, "What are the personal strengths of the individual family members and what are the strengthens of their relationships? What are the potential controlling variables for their strengths?" Be aware of the fact that the controlling variables for their functional behavior will not be the same as the controlling variables for their dysfunctional behavior. Therefore to help them make lasting changes you will need to help them develop new patterns of more functional behaviors which they support and maintain by their day-to-day interactions.

When you have identified their problems and goals write them out. Begin identifying which problems need to be focused on at this time. Try to list the problems and goals you have identified and rank them in order of importance. How close does your list of ranked problems match with those presented by the clients? How important are these goals to the clients? Ask yourself, "Will the clients agree that these are the problems they face and the goals they want to achieve in therapy?" If you can answer "yes" then you are prepared to go begin identifying where to begin. If your proposed problems differ markedly from those of the clients you may need to rethink your analysis. Recall that the match between clients expectations for therapy and your statement of the problem is a critical part of the client–therapist alliance (Horvath & Bedi, 2002).

Using all the available information you should be able to predict, in a general way, each family member's responses related to their complaints and goals. Then, if you can predict the behavior patterns, you should be able to recognize the variables that may be changed to reduce or eliminate the complaints. You should also be able to identify the variables that can be changed to help your clients achieve their goals. Note as stated earlier that the variables that control behavior to be reduced or eliminated may not be the same as the variables controling the desired behavior. Your treatment plan will need to take into consideration both sets of variables.

Selecting the treatment plan

First consider your treatment strategy. The treatment strategy is the broad focus on the clients' most salient issues. For example, your strategy might be marital therapy for a maritally distressed couple or your strategy might be parent education for a family with a noncompliant child. The treatment strategy links the type of treatment, such as marital therapy, to a specific class of problems being experienced by your clients.

On the basis of your treatment strategy select an evidence-based treatment that has been shown to be effective with this specific class of complaints and goals. Look for a plan that has been used with clients who are reasonably similar to your clients and which has been applied in similar settings (American Psychological Association, 2006; Bonomo, Ostron & Sexton, 2001; Carr, 2000; Crane & Hafen, 2002; Denton, Walsh & Daniel, 2002; Margison et al., 2000; Norcross, Beutler & Levant, 2006b; Patterson et al., 2004).

Several factors enter into the selection of a specific evidence-based treatment. Some of these factors may pose a dilemma for you. For example, it is generally agreed that no one model of therapy is more effective than any other (Lambert & Barley, 2002; Shadish, Ragsdale, Glaser, & Montgomery, 1995; Wampold, 2001). If that is the case, then how do you make a choice? If you make the choice on the basis of science then the treatment selected should be the most efficacious and effective treatment that fits with the needs of these specific clients. For example, if you have documented that the clients are suffering from an attachment injury then the treatment of choice would be "*Emotionally Focused Therapy*" (Johnson, 2004). On the other hand if the clients problem is an inability to resolve marital conflicts then one could choose between "Integrative Behavioral Couple Therapy" (Jacobson & Christensen, 1998) or Gottman's *The Marriage Clinic* (1999). The decision often comes down to the your best clinical judgment.

However, decisions about which treatment to select based on your clinical judgment are subject to many of the decision biases described by Nezu and Nezu (1989) and Wilson (1996). For example, rigid adherence to one's theoretical position often influences therapists to look for data that is consistent with their preferred model. This is one form of bias known as the availability heuristic. The availability heuristic suggests that if one's preferred model is Emotionally Focused Therapy (EFT) then the probability of finding examples of "attachment injuries" (Johnson, 2004) in the assessment information is greater than finding examples of "harsh startups" (Gottman, 1999). Of course just the opposite would be true if you prefer Gottman's marital therapy. The problem does not go away if the supervisor selects the model. Supervisors are just as subject to decision-making biases as are therapists (Wilson, 1996). Therefore, as stated before, it appears that the selection of one marital therapy over another may be somewhat arbitrary.

Although the selection of a marital therapy model may be arbitrary it is still necessary to select a model. The benefits of using an evidence-based treatment were discussed at length earlier. For example, if a family presents with an adolescent female diagnosed as suffering from anorexia nervosa then the therapist would search the literature for evidence-based treatments of anorexia nervosa. She or he might find a range of treatments such as nutritional counseling, cognitive-behavioral therapy, behavioral therapy, individual supportive and analytic therapy, and family therapy. Of these treatments family-based treatment for adolescents with anorexia nervosa appears to have the most empirical support and all else being equal should be selected (Lock, le Grange, Agras, & Dare, 2001).

Evaluating outcome progress

Once you have established the goals and arrived at a treatment plan consider how you will evaluate treatment progress. The outcome progress measures should be relevant to the class of problems to be changed. The assessment instruments used for measuring outcomes should allow for continuous measurement so that you can receive feedback on your clients' progress session by session. As a rule outcome measures can be a general measure, such as the Outcome Rating Scale (Miller & Duncan, 2004), but they should be relevant to the problem being treated. For example if you are treating marital distress you might select the Revised Dyadic Adjustment Scale (Busby et al., 1995).

When you have selected a treatment strategy and then narrowed down the relevant treatment models to the "best practice" model write your treatment plan (Appendix G) and share it with your supervisor. Write your treatment plan in words that will be understood by your clients and be prepared to share it with them in the feedback session. As stated in Chapter 2 your written treatment plan is a professional report that becomes a permanent part of the clients' file. A complete treatment plan should answer the following questions (Nezu & Nezu, 1989):

1 Who are the clients? Describe each of the family members attending therapy.
2 What is the problem? Describe their presenting complaints and the relational patterns which maintain the complaints.
3 What are the clients' goals and how might they achieve them?
4 How will the outcomes be evaluated?
5 What will be the criteria for termination?

When you have your treatment plan written you are ready to meet with the clients in a feedback session. However, before you meet with the clients you will need to determine if the treatment is within your scope of competence (AAMFT, 2001).

Therapist competence

As a therapist-intern your scope of competence is determined by your preparation to deliver a specified treatment under supervision. Your preparation begins by studying the theoretical and practical material in the treatment manual. Then you should meet with a supervisor who has a background in the treatment model you are proposing (Milne, Baker, et al., 1999; Milne & James, 2002; Milne, James, Keegan, & Dudley, 2002). Seek ways to have the procedures modeled such as by digital recording, videotape, or role plays. Rehearse the procedures and get feedback on your performance. When you are sufficiently prepared you and your supervisor will determine that you are ready to begin delivering the treatment. If you do not have the necessary background, or if adequate supervision is not available, then you should refer the clients to a therapist who is competent (Code of Ethics, AAMFT, 2001). If it is necessary to refer the clients to another therapist then be prepared to make the referral in the feedback session.

Referrals

Competent therapists know how to make referrals. To make a referral meet with the clients and provide them with a description of their problem and their goals. Then tell them what the best treatment for that problem would be. State clearly that you are not competent to provide that treatment and therefore you are recommending that they see someone who is able to help. Be careful not to imply that you are rejecting them or making a negative judgment about their problem. Simply make it clear that you are seeking to find the best possible treatment for them at this time. If possible, supply two or three names for referral along with addresses and phone numbers. It is always helpful to your clients to have your recommended referral printed out so you can hand it to them before they leave. Ask if they have any questions and allay any concerns. Thank them for giving you the opportunity to assist them and invite them to return if they have other problems that you can help them with. A successful referral is considered a successful outcome. Your goal as a therapist is to have successful outcomes, including successful referrals.

If the treatment plan is within your scope of competence then share it with your supervisor. After consulting with your supervisor make an appoint for a feedback session with your clients.

Box 4.1 The Supervisor's Role in Establishing the Treatment Plan

Supervisors should play an active role in helping therapist-interns establish a thorough assessment of the client's issues and problems and in establishing an evidence-based treatment plan. Errors in diagnosis (Spitzer et al., 1982) and errors in treatment assignments (Schulte & Eifert, 2002; Wilson, 1996) may be avoided if the supervisor utilizes direct (live) supervision or digital or video-recorded supervision sessions to observe the therapist's performance in the assessment sessions.

The Feedback Session

Sharing the treatment plan

Call your clients and set an appointment for the feedback session. Remind them to come 15 minutes early to complete the outcome assessments such as the Outcome Rating Scale (ORS) and the Revised Dyadic Adjustment Scale (RDAS). Remind them that these assessments will help you document their treatment progress.

When the clients arrive for the feedback session see that they are seated comfortably. If the ORS and RDAS were not administered by the receptionist prior to the session then administer and score them now. After administering the progress assessments begin the session by asking if anything has changed since the last time they met with you. Use your best listening and attending skills. Review the most recent outcome assessments and attempt to determine if the assessment scores are congruent with their report about changes since the last session. Be especially aware of indications that they are currently in crisis. If your clients are in crisis then change your agenda to deal with the situation by switching to the appropriate crisis protocol.

If the clients are not in crisis then share the agenda for the feedback session. For example, tell them something like, "I am going to share back what you have shared with me. Please make corrections or add anything as I go along." Be proactive at eliciting their questions and comments throughout the interview. Remember that clients who are encouraged to participate are more likely to remain in therapy (Attride-Sterling et al., 2004; Johnston, 1996; Miller & Prinz, 2003; Morrissey-Kane & Prinz, 1999; Nock & Kazdin, 2008; Patterson & Forgatch, 1985; Prinz & Miller, 1994).

As you share your perception of the clients complaints and goals you should attempt to determine how well your perception fits with theirs. Your goal is to bring your understanding of their complaints and goals into agreement with each family members' perceptions (Lowe, 2005).

Failure to reach agreement on the therapy goals and methods may lead to early termination by the clients (Attride-Sterling et al., 2004. Lowe, 2005; Nock & Kazdin, 2008; O'Dell, 1982).

Presenting the treatment plan

Once you have shared your understanding of their problems and goals and have reached agreement then present your written treatment plan. Describe your proposed treatment plan in clear and specific terms. Include the potential benefits and the potential side effects. For example, "The treatment I recommend is based on the research of Dr. John Gottman. It has been found to be effective with couples who are having difficulties similar to yours and was developed to reduce the probability of divorce. From what you have told me you both would like to build and strengthen this marriage. Is that correct?" After getting an affirmative response get a scaled response by saying something like, "Let's check that out. On a scale from one to ten where ten means that you would do almost anything to keep the marriage going and one means you have little commitment to the marriage., where are you on that scale Jack?" "Where are you on that scale Jill?" Write down their responses and enter them later in your case progress notes.

If they disagree on the treatment plan suggest that the first thing to work out is their decision to be in therapy. Their discrepancy becomes the topic of the conversation. Help them discuss their individual goals and what that means for their relationship. Marital therapy is contraindicated if one has decided on divorce. As mentioned earlier some scholars also recommend individual therapy if there is partner-to-partner maltreatment or if one partner is having a long-term affair. If you suspect abuse or an affair suggest that you have individual assessment sessions where you can discuss their concerns privately.

Next ask them how many sessions they think it might take to reach their goals. This is important as many clients expect change to occur in five to ten sessions (Pekarik, 1985). Client expectations for treatment duration have been found to predict actual treatment duration better than any other variable (Wierzbicki & Pekarik, 1993). Therefore any discrepancy between client expectations for duration of the treatment and your expectations needs to be resolved to reduce the chances of early termination by the clients. Share with them what the treatment manual suggests as the recommended number of sessions required to complete the treatment. If the manual does not recommend a number of sessions you can share the research findings of Lambert, Hansen, and Finch (2001). Lambert et al., found that successful therapy usually takes fifteen to twenty-one sessions and for some couples it takes up to fifty.

Point out the potential side effects and benefits of the proposed treatment. For example, you might say something like,

> Therapy is sometimes difficult and sometimes brings up strong emotions. However, the point of therapy is to help you learn to deal with difficult problems and the associated emotions. The goal will be to help you learn to deal with problems effectively. I will do everything I can to make the experience safe but there are some risks. For example, you may learn new things about yourself and about your partner or other members of the family. Even so most people who complete therapy report that they benefitted from the experience.

Be sure to check with the clients frequently to determine that they understand what you are telling them. Try to resolve any concerns they may have as you go through your description of the proposed treatment.

Share possible alternative treatments. Say something like, "There are several other approaches to problems like yours. One such approach is emotionally-focused therapy and another is integrative behavioral couple therapy. I am prepared to help you using Gottman's Method Couple

Therapy (1999) but I could refer you to another therapist for one of those other treatments if you would prefer.

Tell them that "It's not necessary to make a decision right now. Many couples like to take a day or two to talk it over and decide. I'm going to send you home to decide but before I do let me explain your rights. You have the right to know what is expected in your treatment so if at anytime things are not clear just ask me and I will attempt to clarify what we are attempting to do and why. You have the right to change therapists, change treatments, or end treatment at any time. A decision not to continue this treatment will not be held against you should you wish to return for this or another treatment at any time in the future. Okay, that ends my recommendations. Any concerns or questions?"

Many clients will make a decision to begin therapy at this point. If they decide to accept the treatment plan then begin ending the session.

Ending the feedback session

End the session by asking them to complete the SRS. Score the SRS. If any items are marked below 9 cm or if the total is 36 or below consider this a breach in the alliance and use your best skills to elicit their concerns and to attempt to repair the breach. If there is no breach then ask them to summarize the session. Set a date and time for the next session which will be the first treatment session. Remind them of the duration of the treatment sessions. Then thank them for coming and praise them for working on their marriage at this time. Walk them back to the reception area carrying on a social conversation.

Write up your case progress notes within 24 hours (Appendix D). Begin graphs of the ORS and SRS scores to make evaluation of changes and trends easier.

If they decide to think about coming back for treatment then ask them to call you back in a day or two. Suggest that they call on next (state a day of the week and date). Tell them that your number is on your business card and hand them one or write your name and phone number down for them. Tell them it is important for them to let you know one way or the other. Specifying a day and date helps them reach a decision and not let it slide. Use the same procedures as above to end the session including writing your case progress notes within 24 hours. Do not wait to write your case notes until after you get their call. You will need to enter another progress note after you receive their answer.

If after two or three days they have not called you then you call them. When the clients give you their decision about entering therapy if their answer is "No" thank them for calling and remind them that they may return to the clinic anytime they feel the need for help. You then close the case by writing a Treatment Summary (Appendix H) and submitting it to your supervisor. If their answer is "Yes" then you should set an appointment for the first treatment session. See Box 4.2 for an example of a treatment plan.

Box 4.2 An Example of a Treatment Plan

The following is a case example to illustrate the use of assessment materials to establish a treatment plan. The assessment instrument details are found in Appendix C unless otherwise noted. All information in this example is fictional.

The therapist asked herself the following questions and answered them to formulate the treatment plan.

Who are the clients?

Demographics for each person in treatment. Mr. Robert and Mrs. Martina Jones are Black, members of the Methodist Church, both age 26, married 2 years and no children, he has a BA and is an information technology specialist at a bank. She has 2 years of college education and works in a health food store.

What is the problem?

Presenting problem as seen by each person in treatment. Mr. and Mrs. Jones both came to therapy complaining of "poor communication" and "increasing frequency of arguments, at least once a week and sometimes more often." Both denied any domestic violence. Neither reported any symptoms of anxiety, depression or suicidal ideation.

Clients' goals or expected outcomes. Their goals for therapy are to reduce the arguments and to be able to communicate and problem solve better.

What is the data?

Discussion of the assessment instruments and the therapist's observations. I administered the Oral History Interview (Buehlman, Gottman, & Katz, 1992, in Gottman, 1999, pp. 398 ff.). I rated the Oral History Interview using the Oral History Rating Scale (Brewer, 2004; Brewer & Mead, 2008).

Therapist's ratings of the couple's divorce potential. I rated the couple at 41 on the Oral History Rating Scale (Brewer, 2004; Brewer & Mead, 2008) which places their divorce potential in the moderate to low range (Figure 4.2). However, their self-reported divorce potential on the Marital Status Interview (Weiss & Cerreto, 1980) was 3 for Martina and 0 Robert. Martina's Marital Status Inventory-Revised score falls in the moderate category and Robert's score suggests low divorce potential (Crane, Newfield, & Armstrong, 1984; Crane, Soderquist, & Gardner, 1995). Therefore, I conclude that they are not at high risk for divorce at this time.

Evaluation of the clients' Standard Assessment Battery Scores

The "Jones" couple's baseline Outcome Rating Scale Total Scores were 18.2 and 28 for Martina and Robert respectively (Figure 4.2). Martina's ORS score is in the clinical range and Robert' score is nonclinical.

The Jones' baseline Revised Dyadic Adjustment Scores Total Scores were 38 and 44 for Martina and Robert. Martina's score is in the marital distressed range and Robert's score appears to be distressed however, it is in the indeterminate zone which is 43 to 53. Therefore Robert's score although it falls below the cutoff score of 48 cannot be classified with statistical certainty.

The couple's divorce potential was assessed using the Marital Status Inventory-Revised. Martina's score was 3 and the Robert's was 0 suggesting that potential for divorce at this time is low.

The Brief Screen for Depression scores of 20 and 7 for Martina and Robert respectively. Martina's score is just below the cutoff of 21 suggesting that depression may be issue for her. I will administer the Beck Depression Inventory (BDI: Beck et al., 1996) next session.

Scores for the Conflict Tactics Scales 2 are reported respectively as Martina's and Robert's subscale scores: Negotiation, 33 and 25; Psychological Aggression, 17 and 12; Physical

Figure 4.2 An example of a scored marital Standard Assessment Battery record

Instruments used in this example

1. Therapist's Ratings on the Oral History Rating Scale (Brewer, 2004; Brewer & Mead, 2008; Buehlman & Gottman, 1996; Gottman, 1994)
2. Outcome Rating Scale and Session Rating Scale (Miller & Duncan, 2004).
3. Revised Dyadic Adjustment Scale, (Busby, Crane, Larson, & Christensen, 1995).
4. Marital Status Inventory-Revised (Jamieson, 2007).
5. Brief Screen for Depression (Hakstian & McLean, 1989).
6. Revised Conflict Tactics Scales 2 (Straus, Hamby, Boney-McCoy, & Sugarman, 1996).
7. Alcohol Use Disorders Identification Test (Babor, de la Fuente, Saunders, & Grant, 1992).

Assessment Instrument: Oral History Rating Scale		
Therapist's ratings		
Factor	*Score*	
Wife We-Ness	5	
Husband We-Ness	3	
Couple Glorifying the Struggle	5	
Husband's Fondness	2	
Husband's Negativity	4	
Husband's Expansiveness	5	
Couple Chaos	5	
Wife Disappointment/Disillusionment	6	
Husband Disappointment/Disillusionment	6	
TOTAL DIVORCE POTENTIAL	41	
Assessment Instrument: ORS	*Wife*	*Husband*
Overall	5	6
Individually	4	7
Interpersonally	4.5	6.5
Socially	4.7	8.5
TOTAL	18.2	28
RDAS Total	38	44
Marital Status Inventory	3	0
Brief Screen for Depression	20	7
Assessment Instrument: Revised Conflict Tactics Scales (CTS-2)		
Negotiation	33	25
Psychological Aggression	17	12
Physical Assault	1	2
Sexual Coercion	0	0
Injury	0	0
Assessment Instrument: The Alcohol Use Disorders Identification Test (AUDIT)		
Recent Alcohol Consumption	0	1
Dependence Symptoms	0	0
Alcohol Related Problems	0	0
TOTAL	0	0
Assessment Instrument: SRS		
Relationships	9.3	8.5
Goals and Topics	5.8	9.3
Approach or Method	9.5	8.9
Overall	7.5	9.5
TOTAL	32.1	36.2

Assault, 1 and 2; Sexual Coercion 0 and 0; and Injury, 0 and 0 (see Figure 4.2). This information suggests that their use of negotiation skills is below the mean for wives and husbands in the normative sample. The Psychological Aggression score of 17 for Martina is slightly elevated. Taken together the low negotiation and the slightly elevated Psychological Aggression score for the wife may indicate that the couple are having communication difficulties. Physical Assault was self-reported as 1 and 2 for Martina and Robert respectively. I will interview them separately to explore further for domestic violence. Sexual Coercion and Injury were self-reported as zero for both wife and Robert.

The Alcohol Use Disorders Identification Test (Babor et al., 1992) suggests that alcohol abuse is not a factor for these individuals at this time.

Therapist's report of the observation session

After the break I structured the session to observe the clients' interaction as they discussed and attempted to solve two problems that they selected from the Comprehensive Areas of Change Item Ranking Form-Revised (Appendix C). In the observation session they specified that their arguments were about having a child and finances. Martina was observed to use "harsh startups" and this was followed by use of criticism, defensiveness, occasionally contempt on her part and some stonewalling by Robert (Gottman, 1999; also see Chapter 7 this text). More specifically I observed that when the Martina brought up the issue of having a child she was negative and critical and he responded with defensiveness. When she accused him of not wanting children he began stonewalling and complained of not being financially stable enough to have a child. He criticized her spending and she got defensive. At that point she made a rather contemptuous remark about his being afraid to ask for a raise and he retreated further into stonewalling.

Session Rating Scale

The SRS was administered at the end of the assessment session and Martina's SRS score was 32.1 and the Robert's score was 36.2. In a discussion, which followed, Robert expressed some concern that the therapist might be more on his wife's side because the therapist is a female. Martina appeared concerned that I was not listening to her concerns. I attempted to respond to their concerns. I will take more time to listen to Martina's issues in the next session and I will work to let Robert know that I am on his side just as much as I am on Martina's side.

Are there any initiation or resistance problems?

Both Robert and Martina appeared to be motivated to work in therapy. In the Oral History Interview they both expressed considerable "we-ness" Robert especially. Robert's fondness rating in the Oral History was also a positive sign. No resistance problems were encountered in the assessment session.

What is the your assessment/diagnosis of the problem?

Relational diagnosis

The primary problem appears to be marital distress centered around their difficulties communicating about Martina's dream of starting a family and his concerns about financial security. The result appears to be disappointment and disillusionment as assessed by the Oral History Rating Scale scores (Brewer, 2004; Brewer & Mead, 2008).

DSM-IV-TR Diagnosis

Deferred.

Functional analysis of the specific complaints

Both Robert and Martina are contributing to the communication difficulties by use of criticism, defensiveness, contempt, and stonewalling. She initiates these responses through the way she starts conversations about having a child. He exacerbates the problem by the way he responds to her negativity and by the way he begins conversations about their finances.

What are the treatment outcome goals?

The goals of therapy are to increase their marital satisfaction and reduce Martina's depression symptoms.

How will progress be determined for both short and long term goals?

Progress will be determined by their increased expressions of marital satisfaction in sessions and as assessed by the RDAS (Busby et al., 1995). In addition, Mrs. Jones Total ORS Score of 18.2 will be increased to the nonclinical range of 25 or above. Progress will also be observed by reductions in the use of criticism, defensiveness, contempt, and stonewalling. Long-term progress will be determined by their ability to have conversations without the use of criticism, defensiveness, contempt, and stonewalling and by the increased use of positive and supportive terms.

How will treatment outcomes be determined for both short and long term goals?

Short-term outcomes will be determined by upward trends in Martina's ORS scores. Long-term success will be a clinically significant change in her ORS score from the clinical range to the nonclinical range. For both Martina and Robert the short-term goals will be to see an upward trend in their RDAS scores. Long-term success for both will be determined by clinically significant changes in their RDAS scores from the maritally distressed to the nondistressed range.

Are there any potential blocks to attainment of the family members' goals?

There are no apparent blocks to the attainment of their goals.

What is the treatment plan?

Gottman's Marital Therapy for Couples *The Marriage Clinic* (1999) will be recommended. If Martina's depression score on the BDI is elevated I may recommend Beach, Sandeen, and O'Leary's (1990) treatment for marital distress and depression.

Specifying the treatment design

On the basis of the assessment information and on the basis of my current training in the use of the Gottman model of marital therapy I hypothesize that the basis of the arguments are the wife's concerns about starting a family and the Robert's concerns about financial stability. However, it is not these issues that are the dependent variables. The dependent or outcome variables of primary interest are the frequency, duration, and emotional intensity of their arguments. The independent or controlling variables are built into their interpersonal relationship processes, specifically the use of "harsh startups" and the resulting escalation into negativity such as criticism, defensiveness, stonewalling, and especially "contempt" in their conversations and problem-solving attempts. I further hypothesize that their goals can be achieved if the use of harsh startups and contemptuous statements are eliminated, and the use of criticism, defensiveness, and stonewalling reduced. Better stated, the goals of improved communication and problem-solving may be seen as the outcome variables. I hypothesize that to resolve their problems and achieve their goals they will need to: (a) increase the frequency of use of positive, caring expressions and acts to at least five positive exchanges to each negative exchange, and (b) develop their skills and increase their use of attending, listening, and validating each other's dreams, specifically her dream of starting a family and his dream of achieving financial stability. The contextual or independent variables that appear to control positive exchanges may be their increased frequency of recognizing and responding to each others' use of positive exchanges as outlined in interventions such as the "magic five hours" (Gottman, 1999). The contextual controlling variables for their increasing the frequency of attending, listening, and validating each others' dreams will be interventions to increase his awareness of and responsiveness to her concerns and suggestions by joining in making plans for a child or children in the future. Similarly interventions designed to increase her responsiveness to his financial concerns by entering into conversations about how they can jointly work toward increased financial security may work to validate his dreams. I predict that when these changes are implemented the couple will report fewer and less emotionally intense arguments and this will result in a clinically significant change in her psychological symptoms. It will also result in their Revised Dyadic Adjustment Scale (Busby et al., 1995) scores making a clinically significant change into the maritally nondistressed range.

Estimated number of sessions

The usual course of therapy is 14 weekly sessions (Gottman, 1999). Earlier termination is possible if their RDAS and ORS scores cross the respective cutoff lines from clinical to nonclinical.

What are the criteria for termination?

It will be time to terminate when (a) the couples' psychological outcome scores are in the nonclinical range (b) their marital adjustment scores are in the nondistressed range, and (c) the couple can have conversations about their issues in which they repair failed bids for attention and affection, and can effectively repair marital arguments on their own (Gottman, 1999).

Assignments and future plans

No homework was assigned.
Plans to collect missing information.
Administer BDI to them in the next session.

Therapy Task 3: Delivering the Planned Treatment

Therapy Task 3 is delivering the planned treatment. One of the major advantages of evidence-based procedures is that they are generally accompanied by a treatment manual. Treatment manuals are useful in learning to deliver the model and in learning to maintain treatment fidelity. Treatment fidelity with be discussed at length in Chapter 5. Treatment manuals were first developed in the course of establishing a treatment's efficacy in randomized controlled trials (RCTs). Treatment manuals spell out which procedures to follow and which procedures to avoid. Manuals were used to guide therapists as they prepared to take part in the research study. Treatment manuals were also used to determine that the therapists adhered to the treatment as prescribed. Later, treatment manuals were found to be useful to train practitioners in the use of the empirically-supported treatment. Therapists who wished to learn to practice a specific evidence-based treatment can do so by following the manual and receiving supervision.

Use of treatment manuals in training

Treatment manuals have been found to be especially useful for training beginning therapists (Calhoun et al., 1998; Moras, 1993; Norcross et al., 2006). The use of a treatment manual provides the therapist and supervisor with a criterion against which to judge the therapist's progress in carrying out the planned treatment. Therefore, your skill and confidence in treatment delivery will be enhanced by the use of a treatment manual.

Moras (1993) suggested that treatment manuals for training should contain: (a) a clear description of the problem to be treated; (b) the assessment procedures used to determine if the client has the problem; (c) a description of the interventions, which includes a rationale for the treatment and operational definitions; and (d) teaching aids such as video tapes of experts modeling the interventions. The operational definition of the intervention may include suggestions and guidelines that will help you to know what to say and do while delivering the treatment. Treatment manuals should also specify what not to say and do. Part 2 of this book provides protocols to accompany the training manuals for two couple therapy models. You can evaluate your adherence to the treatment plan by comparing your performance to the procedures recommended in the manual.

Treatment manuals

There is evidence that manual-based therapy is generally successful (Norcross et al., 2006). However, this assumption has been questioned by some (Duncan & Miller, 2006). Among those using manual-based treatments the therapists with the most sensitivity to their clients' feelings and needs have been found to be the most successful (Addis & Cardemil, 2006; Binder et al., 1993; Duncan, Nicol, & Ager, 2004; Luborsky, McLellan, Diguer, Woody, & Seligman, 1997). In almost any form of client-focused therapy the client–therapist relationship appears to be more important than the content of the treatment being delivered (Addis & Cardemil, 2006; Schulte & Eifert, 2002).

The practical usefulness of manual-based treatments

Ruscio and Holohan (2006) state that one benefit of using treatment manuals is that the treatments have been found to be efficacious for relieving the target symptoms. For example, Schulte et al. (1992) compared three groups of phobic clients, a control group, a manualized treatment group, and a group which received individually tailored treatments. The manualized treatment was found to be the most successful. Similarly Dennehy et al. (2005) found that therapists who stayed with the treatment protocol for a year were more successful with bipolar clients. Wilson (1996) suggests that other benefits of following a manualized treatment include: (a) an increased focus on the clients' active participation, (b) clear specification of the rationale and goals of the treatment, (c) greater specificity of the treatment interventions, and (d) a focus on providing systematic feedback. Therefore, maintaining the planned treatment increases the probability of successful outcomes (Eifert et al., 1997).

Beginning therapists are well advised to select one model for each class of problems they are learning to treat. For example, if you are learning to treat marital problems select one of the empirically-supported marital therapies and arrange for supervision by a supervisor who is competent in that method. Then practice, under supervision, delivering the interventions prescribed by the treatment manual until you are proficient with the model (Calhoun et al., 1998). Professional therapists are not born. They learn to be expert therapists by mastering the theory, techniques, and interventions one model at a time (Calhoun et al., 1998; Cukrowicz et al., 2005; Huppert & Abramowitz, 2003). To achieve competence with a model you will need to practice with a number of clients. To become an expert with a model Berger (2004) states that it takes almost eight years of "deliberate practice." By deliberate practice Berger means continuous practice which is "accompanied by systematic and immediate feedback" (Berger, 2004, p. 312).

Efficacious treatments

Many evidence-based models have been subjected to empirical study and found to be efficacious. Efficacious treatments are those that have been found to work under controlled conditions. For a treatment to be called efficacious it needs to have been studied in a randomized controlled trial (RCT) with clearly defined protocols, multiple outcome criteria, and independent treatment evaluations (Chambless & Hollon, 1998; Pinsof & Wynne, 1995a, b). For the treatment to be efficacious the therapists used in the clinical trials were trained using treatment manuals setting out the main procedures. In addition, the therapists were supervised in the treatment delivery to ensure compliance to the treatment manual. Many have cautioned that treatments, which have been found to be efficacious in this way may not be effective, where effective is defined as having been shown to work in everyday clinical practice (Beutler, 1998; Garfield, 1998; Kihlstrom, 2006; Messer, 2006; Nathan, 1998; Persons & Silberschatz, 1998; Pinsof and Wynne 1995a, b; Reed, 2006).

Efficacious treatments may not be effective in the field

It has been argued that efficacious treatments may not be effective in the field for several reasons. One of the most frequently cited reasons is that the clients used in the efficacy trials were carefully selected for a single diagnosis, such as social phobia or depression (Stirman & DeRubeis, 2006; Westen, 2006). It is argued that in the field clients often present with several diagnostic patterns, therefore with several illnesses, a condition known as comorbidity. Another frequent criticism of efficacy trials is that they were conducted in carefully controlled settings such as research hospitals or university clinics. Yet another criticism of efficacy studies concerns the length of time allowed for treatment. In efficacy studies the time for therapy to be completed is generally fixed whereas in the field the number of treatment sessions often varies. Finally, many critics express concern about the use of treatment manuals in efficacy studies (Duncan & Miller, 2006). Each of these arguments will be discussed below.

Single diagnosis versus multiple diagnosis or comorbidity

It is true that the clinical trials were conducted with relatively homogenous groups of clients. The tendency in research is to start with the simplest cases and then add complexity as we learn from the basic studies (Skinner, 1953). Starting with less complicated cases is not limited to research. It is also true that text book examples are of relatively "pure" cases. Text books tend to start with descriptions of clients with single symptom sets such as depression, anxiety, marital distress, acting out adolescents, noncompliant children, and so on. Few textbooks are known to present comorbid cases for beginning therapists to study. An exception is Beach, Sandeen and O'Leary's (1990) *Depression in Marriage*, which is designed to treat marital distress and depression.

Certainly future controlled clinical research with cases with mixed diagnoses will add to our knowledge of what to do in therapy. However until that time comes we should proceed with the best single diagnoses treatments available. At present, in dealing with clients with multiple problems it has been recommended that you determine, in collaboration with your clients, which of the clients' problems are the most salient (Schulte et al., 1992; Schulte & Eifert, 2002; Wilson, 1996). Once the most salient problem has been determined you should begin treatment by focusing on that problem. The clients' additional problems can then be treated serially (Eifert, Evans, & McKendrick, 1990). Taking care of one problem at a time is sound policy.

Controlled settings versus clinically representative settings

The issue about efficacy trials being limited to research hospitals and university clinics has been true in the past. However, in a meta-analysis of 90 therapy studies conducted in clinically representative conditions both manualized and nonmanualized therapy proved equally effective for treatment of individual clients (Shadish, Matt, Navarro, & Phillips, 2000). Therefore, it appears that efficacy studies of individual psychotherapy treatments can be transported successfully to typical clinical settings. The jury is still out on the effectiveness of marriage and family therapy as there have not been enough effectiveness studies in clinical settings at this time to allow for a meta-analysis of treatments in the field versus treatments in research facilities (Shadish & Baldwin, 2003).

Length of treatment in controlled versus clinical cases

As stated earlier one argument against the use of empirically-based treatments is that in efficacy studies the time for therapy to be completed is generally fixed whereas in the field the number of treatment sessions often varies. This statement is true but it does not address the real issue about the length of treatment. The most important question about length of treatment is how long does it take to reach a successful outcome? Before we attempt to answer that question we must decide what is a successful outcome. Some have argued that successful outcomes should be defined as statistically significant changes in the clients' behavior and others have argued for clinically significant changes. Others have argued that it is the clients' definition of success that determines the number of sessions (Pekarik, 1985). Statistically significant results indicate changes in outcome scores that are greater than chance. Clinically significant outcomes are changes in the clients outcome scores that have moved from the clinical range to the nonclinical range. Lambert and Ogles (2004) found that for individual therapy it typically requires 7 sessions for 50 percent of the clients to have statistically significant changes in outcome scores. Seventy-five percent of individual clients improved to the level of statistical significance following fourteen sessions. However, it generally requires twenty-one sessions for 50 percent of the clients to achieve clinically significant changes and forty-five sessions for 75 percent of the clients to reach clinical significance.

Pekarik (1985) reports that 70 percent of clients expect to attend ten sessions or less and 75 percent expect improvement in five sessions. Pekarik stated that in routine practice the number of sessions completed was three to five and many clinics report that clients only attend one or two sessions.

This appears to conform with client expectations. Client termination after three to five sessions may be a function of the fact that rapid change often occurs early in treatment and is followed by smaller incremental changes in subsequent sessions (Anderson & Lambert, 2001; Howard, Kopta, Krause, Merton, & Orlinsky, 1986; Kadera, Lambert, & Andrews, 1996). It may be that when clients perceive change in the early sessions they believe they should terminate. Therapists, on the other hand, are inclined to believe that more sessions lead to greater chances of improvement and lasting change. However Hatchett and Park (2003) argue that there is no scientific evidence for longer durations of treatment being more effective.

The length of time in therapy required to reach a successful conclusion appears to be a function of the definition of success. Many clients expect to get change in symptoms and emotional distress in five to ten sessions. When they perceive early change they assume that it is time to terminate. Pekarik (1992) reports that 37 percent of clients that terminated early stated that they did so because their problem was improved or resolved. Therapists expect treatment to last much longer than clients. Therapists in one study tended to expect therapy to last sixteen or more sessions. This discrepancy between clients' and therapists' expectations for duration of therapy suggests that therapists need to be more attentive to the client–therapist alliance and the clients' reports of treatment outcomes (Wierzbicki & Pekarik, 1993).

Criticisms of use of manuals to deliver treatment

Some feel that the use of treatment manuals limits the therapist's freedom to select the most effective parts of a treatment, to blend in other treatments from other theoretical models, and to create additional procedures on their own (Beutler, 1998; Duncan & Miller, 2006; Garfield, 1998; Nathan, 1998; Persons & Silberschatz, 1998).

Two issues present themselves in this argument. First, is staying with a single treatment model presented by a treatment manual more or less effective then blending in various treatments? Two studies have found evidence that standardized treatments are as effective as individualized treatments (Shadish, Matt, Navarro, & Phillips, 2000; Wilson, 1996). In addition, there is evidence that blending in other treatments that are assumed to be more effective does not lead to greater treatment success (Eifert et al., 1990; Wilson, 1996). Schulte and Eifert (2002) present evidence that therapists who ammend the treatment methods outlined in the treatment manual and focus on process-oriented treatment have less successful client outcomes. The evidence seems to support keeping with a single model of treatment rather than attempting to develop individualized treatments.

The second issue presented in the argument against using manuals is that using a manual prevents the therapist from creating an individualized treatment. The question arises, if you do add in interventions, either from other treatments or of your own creativity, then how do you decide what to include and what to discard? Blending interventions from other treatment programs cannot be done on an empirical basis at present. Unless empirical studies are conducted to evaluate the various components we are adding then we do not know which are the effective components (Borkovec & Castonguay, 2006; Jacobson, 1984). Unfortunately, component analysis is rarely done. Therefore, when you blend interventions from another model the outcome must remain in doubt because you are now using a treatment that has not been tested for efficacy. Taken all together the research suggests that you will be more successful if you stay with the procedures set out in the treatment manual.

Another argument against the use of manuals is that it leads to rigidity and reduced empathic responding on the part of therapists. There is some evidence that the use of manuals does lead to rigidity and does reduce therapists' empathic responses (Henry, Schacht, Strupp, Butler, & Binder,

1993). Rigidity resulting from the use of treatment manuals may come about because the therapist does not attend to the alliance or it may be the result of becoming too rule focused (see Chapter 5). There is evidence that therapists can learn to adhere to treatment manuals and to attend to the alliance if given appropriate training and supervision (Luborsky, 1990). One anecdote to rigidity is continuous assessment of the alliance. Continuous assessment of the alliance by use of a rating scale, such as the SRS (Duncan et al., 2003), can alert you to alliance difficulties before they have time to interfere with the treatment. Continuous assessment of the alliance builds in flexibility by signaling the need to change your behavior as you deliver the interventions prescribed in the manual.

Rigidity in applying manualized treatment may be a function of conforming to the rules of the manual and not attending to the relationship contingencies (Wulfert, Greenway, Farkas, Hayes, & Dougher, 1994). Research has shown that when people follow a set of rules they tend not to change their behavior when the contingencies in the context change (Catania, Shimoff, & Matthews, 1989). The clients' behaviors are the important contingencies or contextual variables which should be controlling your behavior rather than the rules of the treatment manual. The skill you should be working to acquire is how to apply the manualized treatment in a way that is responsive to the needs of your clients (see Chapter 5). With the help of your supervisor the verbal knowledge of what to do, as presented by the manual, will become part of your experiential knowledge of when and how to apply an intervention to best meet the needs of your clients.

Another reason some therapists feel constrained by empirically-supported therapies appears to be that they find the pressure to attempt to help their clients to be extremely compelling. Not being able to help is aversive. Escape from, or avoidance of, aversive situations is highly reinforcing (Skinner 1953, 1969). Therefore, when the clients do not appear to be making progress in the planned treatment it may be tempting to try combining other treatments and/or to try untested treatments, which are the result of your own creativity. Two problems appear here. First, what evidence will you accept that the clients are not making progress? Second, what evidence do you have that the integrated treatment will prove more successful? You should make your determination of client progress on the basis of their scores on reliable and valid outcome assessment instruments (see Chapter 5). In addition, you should be receiving and attending to the clients' reports of their perception of the alliance as measured by reliable and valid instruments.

When clients are not making progress you may be tempted to integrate into the planned treatment interventions that are not part of the treatment. Combining treatments or creating new treatments may result in greater client improvement but they may just as easily result in no improvement or even worse, result in client deterioration. As soon as you leave the empirically-supported treatment your ability to predict the outcome is reduced (Schulte et al.,1992; Schulte & Eifert, 2002; Wilson, 1996). When you leave the empirically-supported treatment you have become engaged in an experimental treatment. It would appear ethically and legally prudent to separate therapy practice from therapy research (AMFT, 2001; Gladding et al., 2001).

Separating clinical practice from therapy research

If you deem it necessary to incorporate other methods into the best practice model agreed to by you and your clients then you are responsible for justifying the changes. Such an approach may be considered experimental and you should seek the specific informed consent of the clients. Once you have received their consent for the experimental treatment then document their consent in your progress notes.

When we are *practicing therapy* we should use the evidence-based treatments, which have been found to be the most efficacious and effective, for a given class of clients with a given set of problems. When we are *conducting research* we should ask our clients for their informed consent prior to initiating new procedures. The new techniques may be found to be more efficacious and effective then our current "best" treatments but until they are empirically tested they should be considered experimental. When new treatments have been found to be more efficacious and effective than the treatments we are currently employing then intellectual honesty would require that we adopt the new "best treatment" (Polya, 1954). However, until there is good evidence to change we should be intellectually courageous enough to stay with the current "best treatments" (Polya, 1954).

You should be equally cautious about adapting a new technique presented at a workshop or national meeting. Prudent therapists do not chase off after the latest theoretical model no matter how charismatic the presenter. Hyperbole should not be allowed to substitute for scientific evidence.

We can concluded that the arguments about the lack of effectiveness for evidence-based treatments are largely specious. You can learn to duplicate the conditions of the efficacy trial studies by staying with the treatment protocol and ensuring that the appropriate therapeutic interventions are delivered in sufficient numbers to provide an adequate "dose" of treatment (see Chapter 5). At the same time you can learn to build and maintain the alliance by ensuring that the treatment plan is carefully fitted to the clients' goals and that the treatment interventions set out in the model are tailored to the clients' needs. Therefore, to be of maximum benefit to your clients you should go with the profession's strength and deliver evidence-based treatments along with careful attention to maintaining your alliance with your clients. This approach appears to have the greatest probability of success (Addis & Cardemil, 2006; Schulte & Eifert, 2002; Wilson, 1996).

Tailoring the treatment to your clients' needs

Tailoring the treatment to the clients needs requires attention to four elements of the therapy relationship: (a) the therapeutic alliance, (b) cohesion, (c) empathy, and (d) goal consensus and collaboration. These four elements have been found to be effective in bringing about successful outcomes (Norcross, 2002a). If you are skillful in including these four elements in therapy sessions while delivering the planned treatment you will increase the probability of having successful outcomes. To help you tailor your delivery of the manualized treatment to your clients' needs the Therapy Tailoring Skills rating form (TTS: Mead, 2007: Appendix I) was designed as a heuristic device. You can evaluate your therapy tailoring using the six TTS items: (1) Therapy Alliance; (2) Empathy; (3) Goal consensus; (4) Collaborative involvement; (5) Couple cohesion; and (6) Structuring the session.

TTS item 1: Alliance

The alliance item is based on the work of Horvath and Bedi (2002) and asks if you measured the alliance. The alliance can be assessed using one of the following instruments: (a) the Session Rating Scale (Miller & Duncan, 2004), (b) the System for Observing Family Therapy Alliances (SOFTA: Friedlander et al., 2006), or (c) the Revised Helping Alliance Questionnaire (Haq-II: Luborsky et al., 1996). Measuring the alliance is a basic step in tailoring the treatment interventions to the needs of the clients as it serves to identify early when the treatment is not working.

TTS item 2: Empathy

TTS item 2 asks if the you were able to "understand each client's thoughts, feelings, and struggles" (Bohart et al., 2002, p. 90). Respect for the clients – as expressed by the therapist's attentive listening and by expressions of care and concern for the clients' welfare – has long been associated with positive outcomes. Use of open questions, tentative restatements, and reflections will help you better understand your clients' thoughts, feelings, and efforts to cope (Hill, 2004). Assessing your use of empathy during the session should serve to remind you to continuously apply your basic therapist skills.

TTS item 3: Goal consensus

This item asks you to rate if you checked with the clients to determine if they agreed with each intervention (Tryon & Winograd, 2002). As you present each intervention from the treatment manual take the time to be sure that each family member understands the procedures and how it fits into their overall goals. They are more likely to agree with a procedure if they can see how it fits into the bigger picture. If they do not understand an intervention try to tailor it by restating it in their own words or try reframing it to fit their situation. In attempting to fit your intervention to the clients' needs do not abandon the intervention by bringing in procedures from some other model of therapy. If they are having difficulty with an intervention consider returning to a previous intervention that prepared them for this step in the program. It is assumed that if you systematically determine whether the clients agree or disagree with the interventions then, if the clients disagree, you will be in a position to tailor it to meet their needs.

TTS item 4: Collaborative involvement

Collaborative involvement assesses your skill at eliciting the clients cooperation and collaboration. Collaboration and cooperation serves to help you resolve their resistance and reactance to the interventions (Haley, 1987; Forgatch, Patterson, & DeGarmo, 2005; Tryon & Winograd, 2002). Collaborative involvement consists of helping the clients to take an active role in their treatment. One indication of cooperation is their willingness to practice the intervention in the session. Another indication of cooperation and collaboration is their willingness to complete assigned homework. Item four of the TTS serves as a reminder of your need to elicit the clients' cooperation and collaboration.

TTS item 5: Family cohesion

This item is based upon Burlingame, Fuhriman, and Johnson's (2002) review of cohesion in group psychotherapy. The item asks you to evaluate your performance in recognizing and reinforcing the family members' expressions of acceptance and support for each other. It also asks if you observed and reframed any expressions of negativity, as negativity undermines family members acceptance and mutual support (Gottman, 1999). You will have the opportunity to observe your clients' expressions of being a couple or a family unit, what Gottman (1999) terms "we-ness" if during the session you encourage your clients to practice the interventions. Expressions of care and concern for each other are important markers of family cohesion and you should take note of that behavior when it occurs and provide social reinforcement. On the other hand, couple or family members' expressions of negativity tear down cohesion and are corrosive in relationships (Alexander et al., 2000a; Gottman, 1999). You will want to gently but firmly end negativity, perhaps by reframing it as intense caring. For example, if one partner is criticizing the other then try reframing it as caring. You might suggest that "You are trying to help but it appears that you just can't seem to find any other way to express it." Reframes must be sincere, stated tentatively, and their impact carefully assessed. As Alexander et al. (2000a) suggests, reframe relentlessly until you find one that works. Working to establish the family members' cohesion is an important step in tailoring the treatment to their needs.

TTS item 6: Structure of the session

This item is also built on group cohesion research (Burlingame et al., 2002) and on the research from family therapy, which found that the therapist's failure to structure the session leads to early client dropout (Shields et al., 1991). The item asks you if you (a) specified and clarified expectations for the treatment interventions, (b) defined or redefined the rules for therapy, and (c) specified the roles needed for effective relationships.

When you present an intervention, a rule, or attempt to specify a role state it clearly and in the clients own words but avoid talking down to them. Assume that they are intelligent but unlearned in the skills required to perform the intervention. If, in the course of treatment, the clients appear to fail to comprehend the rules or their roles then do not fall into blaming the clients. Accept the responsibility for the misunderstanding and make an effort to help the clients, and yourself, past the impasse. For example, if the clients break the rule about calling you at home you could determine if they are in crisis. If they are not in crisis then you could say something like, "I'm sorry, I may have forgotten to tell you that my time at home is reserved for me and my family. If this is an emergency go to the emergency room. If it is not an emergency please call me at my office tomorrow." Burlingame suggests that your efforts to set expectations, define rules, and instruct them in appropriate roles and skills will lead to more successful outcomes.

Summary of the TTS rating form

The TTS rating form, while untested for reliability and validity, has strong face validity. It is hypothesized that if you can honestly and fairly rate your treatment tailoring at three or above after each session then you will increase the probability of successful outcomes.

Some general procedures to carry out planned treatment

Here are some general procedures that may be used in carrying out planned treatments. Detailed protocols for carrying out selected empirically supported treatment models are presented in Part II.

Using the clients' ideas

In carrying out the planned treatment show respect to the clients by first determining their understanding of the intervention you planned for this session. For example, ask them what they think they should do about the problem. If they have a plan, ask if they have tried that before and what success they have had. Clients often have ideas about how to proceed but are hesitant to use them without some outside support. If their idea seems to be in the right direction, and especially if it appears congruent with the planned treatment, then encourage them to try it. Help them to make the steps they have proposed clear and specific. Model the behavior for them using their steps and language. Then ask them to practice the procedures they have developed in the session. Have a kitchen timer and set it for 6 to 10 minutes to establish a practice interval. Coach the clients' practice by giving social reinforcement for correct actions. Social reinforcements include statements such as "umhum," "that's good," "keep going," and so on. Do this very quietly in a stage whisper while they are proceeding so as not to cause them to stop. When the timer goes off after the selected time ask them to critique their efforts. Ask them to note all the things they did right. Ask how they might do it better next time. If they went off track accept the responsibility for not making it clear. Point out one, and only one, thing they could do to make it better (Kluger

& DeNisi, 1998). Then immediately return the floor to them to practice. Again set your timer for another 6 to 10 minutes and ask them to try again. Encourage them to make it better this time. Ensure that all family members get the opportunity to practice in each session if at all possible. Continue practicing in therapy sessions until they have mastered the interventions. This may take several sessions. Caution: Do not send them home to practice until they have mastered the intervention in-session. You should only suggest that they practice at home if both you and they think they have at least an 80–90 percent chance of success (Jacobson & Christensen, 1996). In the next session get them to report on their progress and observe the outcome measures for changes in the desired direction.

Using the treatment manual interventions

If when you ask the clients what they think they should they do and they do not have a clue then make a suggestion for an intervention from the treatment manual protocols. Use material from the clients conversations and behaviors to tailor your intervention to fit their needs. Follow your suggestion by asking how they see this intervention fitting with their overall goals. Probe for specific understandings and misunderstandings. Provide social reinforcement for correct understandings and redirect misunderstandings.

Next, explain the behavior to be performed in clear specific terms and give a rationale for the intervention. For example, "I am going to teach you how to have discussions about issues that come up in your marriage, such as (cite an example from your observation of their relationship issues). The method we are going to learn is known as 'soft startups.' Research has shown that couples who consistently use harsh startups end up divorced (Gottman, 1999). Therefore, we are going to help you learn to use soft startups."

Having presented a rationale for the intervention the therapist then proceeds to give step by step instructions. If the clients have read about the intervention as part of your previous homework assignments, then ask them to provide examples of correct and incorrect applications. Otherwise explain the behavior and give examples of correct and incorrect performances (Englemann & Carnine, 1991). For example, describe both soft and harsh start ups. The explanation may be delivered by various media such as: textbook, digital video or audio recording, or verbal instruction by the therapist. Use multiple methods whenever possible. For example, if you are treating marital distress using the Gottman (1999) method recommend that the clients pick up a copy of Gottman and Silver's *The Seven Principles that Make Marriage Work* (1999) from the library or a bookstore. Make the reading assignments short and in the next session start by testing their understanding. Always follow up on homework assignments (Appendix J). Homework assignments have been shown to speed up client improvement but if you do not follow up the clients will soon disregard them. When the clients report on their homework be sure to provide social reinforcement for correct understandings. When there are misunderstandings take the responsibility by saying something like "I probably didn't make this clear. Let me try again" and re-explain the procedure. Give correct and incorrect examples and get them to differentiate between the two (Engelmann & Carnine, 1991).

Model the behavior to be performed after you have explained the intervention. When you model the behavior use the material they have generated about their complaints and/or goals. To avoid resistance try not to use the term "role play." Ask them for a recent example of the issue in question. Then simply present the situation and model the behavior you wish them to perform. Model doing the procedure both correctly and incorrectly. Test for their understanding by having them point out what you did right and what you did wrong to help them distinguish between correct and incorrect performance (Engelmann & Carnine, 1991).

In summary

How you begin treatment predicts the outcomes. You will make a good beginning by organizing all the information from your assessment session. Based on this information establish a treatment plan designed to meet the needs of these specific clients with their specific problems. Match their problems to an evidence-based treatment that has been developed for similar clients with similar problems. Share your plan in consultation with your clients. When you have their agreement on the nature and severity of the problem and on the recommended treatment model then you will have established a treatment contract. The next step is to begin to implement the planned treatment. It has been found that use of treatment manuals provide solid guidance for treatment delivery. Follow the structure provided by the treatment manual to increase the probability of successful outcomes. Further guidance in how to adhere to the treatment manual will be given in the Chapter 5.

What Should You Take Away from Chapter 4?

1. An evidence-based treatment plan is developed from all the information gathered in the assessment session. You should seek the most reliable and valid information to use in developing the treatment plan. The most reliable and valid information is gathered by use of structured interviews, structured observations, and reliable and valid assessment instruments. The assessment information should be organized systematically in a table to help you make informed clinical judgments. Based on all the best information available you should select the evidence-based treatment most is closely matched to the clients values, problems, and goals. The treatment plan should be tailored to the clients' needs and values in order to have the greatest probability of helping them successfully achieve their goals.
2. The treatment plan should be written in words that will be easily understood by the clients. The written treatment plan should be reviewed by your supervisor and then entered in the case file.
3. You should present your perception of the clients' problems and goals to the clients in a feedback session and seek their agreement. When the clients agree that you understand their problem then present your evidence-based treatment plan and seek their agreement.
4. Presentation of the treatment plan includes explaining the treatment procedures, the expected number of sessions required to complete the treatment, the risks and benefits of the treatment, and the clients' rights to refuse the treatment or to terminate without prejudice by the therapist or the clinic.
5. If the clients agree to the treatment plan then the therapist and clients have a therapy contract. You are ethically and legally obligated to complete the therapy contract by delivering the planned treatment.
6. The therapist delivers the evidence-based treatment using the treatment manual as a guideline. The treatment manual interventions must be tailored to the clients. This requires attention to the therapy process and the clients' resistance, reactance, or lack of motivation. However, research has shown that therapists who deviate from delivering the planned treatment and pay extended attention to the process have less successful outcomes. Therefore, if it is necessary to attend to process variables, for example, to heal a breach in the alliance, the therapist should do so and then quickly return to the planned treatment.

Chapter 5

Evaluating Adherence to the Treatment Plan and Evaluating Treatment Outcomes

Introduction

When you present a treatment plan to the clients and they accept you have established a therapeutic contract. The contract stipulates that you will deliver the planned treatment and that the treatment will help the clients meet their needs and reach their goals. As a result you have both an ethical and a legal obligation to deliver the treatment as promised (Wilcoxon et al., 2007; Knapp & VandeCreek, 1997). Not only do you have an obligation to deliver the planned treatment but you also have an obligation to show that it is related to the outcome. In this chapter you will continue with Therapy Task 3: evaluating your adherence to the planned treatment and also Therapy Task 4, which is to evaluate your clients' progress toward successful outcomes.

Therapy Task 3: Evaluating Adherence to the Planned Treatment

Adherence to the treatment plan is also known as maintaining program integrity or program fidelity (Waltz et al., 1993). All three terms refer to the degree to which the procedures specified by the treatment manual are carried out as prescribed. Adhering to the treatment manual is important for several reasons. The first reason for adhering to the planned treatment is for the good of the clients. Research has found that adhering to the empirically-supported treatment has a greater likelihood of leading to successful outcomes

The second reason for assessing treatment fidelity is to provide you with confidence that the treatment you delivered resulted in the obtained outcome. Assessment of treatment adherence is important whether the treatment is successful or not successful. If your treatment is not successful and you have not assessed treatment fidelity then it will be hard to know if treatment failure is due to incomplete or inadequate delivery of an effective treatment or due to the wrong treatment (Bellg et al., 2004). Without evidence of treatment fidelity it will not be possible to determine if positive results are due to (a) an effective treatment, (b) unknown active elements added to the intervention, or (c) weak or inactive elements which were left out (Borrelli et al., 2005; Dane & Schneider, 1998; Gresham, Gansel, & Noell, 1993; Henggeler et al., 1997; Miller, Moyers et al., 2005; Waltz et al., 1993; Wilkinson, 2006).

Becoming a Marriage and Family Therapist: From Classroom to Consulting Room, First Edition. D. Eugene Mead.

Another reason for adhering to the treatment plan is to fulfill your therapeutic contract. Should there be a disagreement about the therapy outcomes one question that will be asked is was the treatment delivered? If you have not assessed treatment fidelity over the course of treatment it may be difficult to find sufficient information to support your claim that the treatment was delivered fully and competently. Therefore you are well advised to assess and document your treatment adherence over the course of treatment.

Determining adherence to the treatment protocol

Treatment fidelity requires that you deliver the treatment fully and fairly. There are several steps needed to ensure full and fair treatment delivery. First, you will need to determine that you have delivered all the treatment interventions as set out in the treatment manual. Second, you will need to determine that you have tailored the treatment to your clients' needs sufficiently to maintain the client–therapist alliance. Third, in each session you will need to ensure that your clients understand and are able to perform the treatment interventions. Fourth, you will need to determine that the clients are able to perform the interventions successfully in their home and other settings outside the session. Finally, you will need to establish that you have completed the full course of the treatment as specified in the treatment manual to ensure that the clients receive the maximum effect or "dose" (Bellg et al., 2004; Borrelli et al., 2005; Dane & Schneider, 1998; Howard, Moras, Brill, Martinovich, & Lutz, 1996).

Using the manual to evaluate treatment adherence

Other issues related to treatment manuals were discussed in Chapter 4. In this chapter the concern is with the use of the treatment manual to ensure that you have delivered the specified treatment. The treatment described in the manual has been found to be efficacious for a specific class of symptomatic behaviors. Consequently (as dicussed in Chapter 4) any substantial deviation from the treatment manual will result in a new, untested treatment with unknown efficaciousness (Ruscio & Holohan, 2006). Therefore, to maintain treatment fidelity you should stay with the manualized treatment.

Failure to maintain fidelity to the treatment program throughout the course of therapy has been shown to lead to poor outcomes (Henggeler et al., 1997; Schulte & Eifert, 2002; Wilson, 1996). Experienced therapists have been found to fail to maintain treatment adherence later in therapy (Dennehy et al., 2005; Margison et al., 2000). This may explain why less experienced therapists often have as much or more success than more experienced therapists. For example, Stolk and Perlsez (1990) reported that second year students in a marriage and family therapy masters' degree program had less successful outcomes than first year students. Therefore, you should guard against drifting away from the treatment program by continuously assessing for fidelity.

To determine if you have delivered the treatment specified in the treatment manual begin by asking yourself "Did I deliver the treatment interventions set out by the manual?" To answer this question you will first need to know the treatment well enough to understand which interventions are unique to the treatment and are essential to it, which features of the treatment are held in common with other treatments but are still essential, and which interventions are considered as not helpful or even harmful and therefore should be avoided (Blow, Sprenkle, & Davis, 2007; Borrelli et al., 2005; Margison et al., 2000; Moncher & Prinz, 1991; Waltz et al., 1993). You will also need to know and follow the sequence of the interventions dictated by the treatment manual. Finally, you will need to ensure that the clients have participated in treatment long enough to receive the full effects (Howard et al., 1996).

Many treatment manuals provide an adherence checklist that you can use to help you maintain treatment integrity. After each session use the checklist to evaluate your adherence to the manual. Consider the intervention you planned for the session as specified by the manual. How successful were you in delivering the planned intervention? Did you deliver the unique and essential elements of the intervention? Did you deliver the elements which are held in common with other treatments but are still essential? Did you include any elements which are deemed as not helpful or even harmful? If you delivered harmful elements what was the ratio of both the unique and essential interventions to the interventions that are contraindicated? For example, McMahon and Forehand's (2003) treatment manual for helping noncompliant children specifies that the treatment requires the interaction of the parents and the child. Some parents want the therapist to treat the child alone and not involve them. Working with the child alone would be considered a harmful intervention from the point of view of McMahon and Forehand. Therefore, if you are using this treatment you should review each session to determine that you did not slip into therapist-to-child treatment rather than teaching the parents how to interact with their child.

As you evaluate your adherence to the manual for completeness be aware of the stage of therapy you have reached. The stage of the therapy is determined by the sequence of the interventions and the number of sessions completed. For example, Gottman (1999) suggests that you start marital therapy with interventions to re-establish the clients' friendship and affection followed by working on solvable problems and then working on gridlocked or perpetual problems. This sequence is recommended although in some cases he suggests starting with an extended session to work on a specific gridlocked issue. Once past the gridlocked issue it is important to return to the regular sequence as the changes made by the clients in the extended session are often only temporary (Gottman, 1999). Gottman sees the sequences as unique and essential to the treatment program. The sequencing of interventions is also important in many other models (Alexander & Sexton, 2002; Beach, Sandeen, & O'Leary, 1990; Johnson, 2004; McMahon & Forehand, 2003).

Completeness of treatment delivery is also a function of the number of sessions in which all the family members participated in the treatment. Full participation by all the key family members in the majority of the sessions is seen as important for the therapy "dose." For example, successful marital therapy generally requires that both partners take part in the treatment in each session and for an extended number of sessions. For example Gottman (1999) recommends 14 weekly sessions and Johnson (2004) suggests 8 to 20 sessions.

However, rigidly adhering to the interventions prescribed by the treatment manual is not delivering the treatment competently. As discussed earlier delivering therapy based on a treatment manual can result in poor outcomes if the therapist does not attend to the factors which build and maintain a good alliance (Binder et al., 1993; Luborsky, 1994). How you deliver the treatment is as important or more so than what treatment you deliver. This is because 40 percent of the outcome variance is attributed to the client–therapist alliance and only 15 percent is attributed to the treatment model. Therefore, it is necessary to tailor the treatment to the needs of the clients. An extended discussion of tailoring the interventions to the clients' needs was presented in Chapter 4. It is recommended that you review the use of the Therapy Tailoring Skills rating form (TTS: Mead, 2007: Appendix I) to help you avoid over ridged administration of the treatment interventions.

Assessing treatment fidelity

Treatment program fidelity is specific to the treatment manual being used (Waltz et al., 1993). Most empirically-supported therapy models have an adherence rating form, which was used in the development of the model.[1] If the therapy model does not supply an adherence rating system then treatment fidelity can be assessed by self-report, by client reports, by structured interviews, and by observation and feedback. Assessment of treatment fidelity varies in reliability and validity just as do other assessments. More structured assessment methods result in greater reliability and validity.

Therapist self-reports of treatment adherence

Therapist self-reports of treatment fidelity are subject to a variety of biases but they have the benefits of convenience, low cost, and immediacy. Self-reports of treatment may take the form of case notes, checklists, and rating scales.

Wilkinson (2006) recommends the use of permanent products such as progress notes and outcome assessment scores as one method of assessing treatment adherence. For example, Dennehy and colleagues (2004) report development of a case progress form to facilitate computer data entry of case note material. The "Clinical Record Form" (CRF) developed by Dennehy and associates was used to evaluate compliance to a treatment protocol for bipolar disorder. The clinicians reported in a checklist format: patient visits, duration of the visits, and clinician recommendations about future visits. They also recorded patient symptoms, the clinicians' responses to the symptoms including medication strategies, followed by patient side effects, medication tolerance, and patient adherence to the treatment. The information from the CRF was entered into an electronic database to verify adherence to the treatment guidelines across clinicians and across treatment facilities. The authors reported that the CRF proved successful in improving reporting and assessment of treatment adherence. An interesting finding was that adherence was lower in the last 6 months of treatment than in the first 6 months. In a later paper Dennehy and colleagues (2005) found that clinicians with more experience using the treatment protocol tended to provide less adherent care over time. It should be noted that patients receiving adherent treatment and "average" (that is control) patients changed about equally over the first 3 months but that patients receiving adherent treatment made greater gains than average patients in months 3 to 12. Greater adherence was found to be significantly related to improvement in overall psychiatric symptoms over time compared to average patients. The authors speculated that some clinicians began to drift from the protocol when the patients did not show much improvement in the first 3 months. It may be that drifting from the protocols lead to less improvement over time, a finding consistent with the studies that recommend not changing from the manualized treatment without sufficient cause (Schulte & Eifert, 2002; Wilson, 1996). Dennehy concluded that "efforts should be directed at maintaining high levels of adherence and persistence with recommended treatments. Interventions [with clinicians] such as reminders, audit with feedback, and academic detailing ... may help improve or maintain provider adherence" (Dennehy et al., 2005, p. 23). Therapist drift has also been found in other studies (Bellg et al., 2004; Booth & Cottone, 2000; Borrelli et al., 2005; Henggeler et al., 1997).

Your progress notes are a type of "self-report" of treatment adherence. You may report adherence to the manualized treatment by entries to that effect in your progress notes. For example, if the manual recommends that a specific sequence of events occur in each session–such as asking the clients about their previous week, their homework assignments, or their outcome assessment scores–then recording compliance with those expectations in your progress notes is a record of treatment adherence. If the manualized treatment calls for a specific sequence of interventions, then recording the delivery of those interventions across sessions is an indication of treatment fidelity. In as much as common factors are a necessary although not unique part of every form of therapy then assessing the alliance and recording the alliance scores and describing any attempts to repair ruptures to the alliance is a mark of treatment integrity. However, unless a systematic format or checklist is established for progress notes there may be inconsistencies in the way the treatment interventions are recorded (Appendix D). Furthermore unless outside support is supplied in the form of supervisors or quality control officers (Booth & Cottone, 2000; Henggeler et al., 1997) then therapists may not fully comply with keeping accurate case notes as was reported by Dennehy and colleagues (2005). Inconsistent case notes may not be reliable. Case notes, which are not checked against another observer, such as the supervisor, may be questioned in terms of validity. Finally, case progress notes may be especially susceptible to personal and observer biases which may further invalidate the reports (see Box 5.1, p. 115).

Another important aspect of case progress notes is that they are considered as a permanent product. Case progress notes have a privileged ethical and legal status as a record of your professional conduct (Wilcoxon et al., 2007; Knapp & VandeCreek, 1997). Consequently, they may be reviewed for treatment adherence by supervisors, quality control officers, and lawyers. Therefore, anything you can do to improve the reliability and validity of your case progress notes will be of benefit to both you and to your clients.

The overall conclusion on therapist's self-reporting of adherence to the treatment protocols is that, while therapists' self-reports may be helpful as a reminder to the therapist to maintain treatment fidelity, the overall reliability and validity of this information must be viewed with caution. It is strongly recommended that methods to improve the reliability and validity of the therapists' case progress notes be used, especially for therapists in training. It appears that compliance to maintaining progress notes needs the support of supervisors' observations or auditing by quality control officers (Booth & Cottone, 2000; Dennehy et al., 2005; Henggeler et al., 1997; Noell et al., 2000; Wilkinson, 2006).

Client reports of therapist treatment adherence

Clients' self-reports are also subject to bias but have the advantage of providing the client's point of view as well as being convenient and relatively low cost. Lee, Emerson, and Kochka (1997) developed a list of seventy-four generic family therapy interventions from structural, strategic, brief, and transgenerational therapy models. The scale was used to provide feedback from clients to a therapist interns. Henggeler et al. (1997) used both parents' and adolescents' adherence reports in a treatment study of violent and chronic juvenile offenders. Henggeler and colleagues found a relationship between parents' and adolescents' adherence ratings of therapists' treatment fidelity and low rates of adolescents' re-arrest.

A novel way of collecting the clients' reports of therapist adherence to treatment protocols was developed by Essock, Covell, Shear, Donahue, and Felton (2006). Essock and associates reported the use of telephone interviews of clients receiving crisis counseling. Clients were asked to report on their clinicians use of six intervention components of a crisis counseling program. As reported by the clients, there was greater adherence with the delivery of the six interventions at treatment sites where all of the therapists were trained in the protocol than for sites where only some of the therapists were trained. The authors concluded that the telephone assessment strategy to determine therapist adherence was successful. No reliability or validity data was provided for the study but the process appears useful for assessing client reports of treatment fidelity by phone.

While client reports of therapist adherence to treatment protocols add a multiperson perspective to assessment of treatment fidelity only a limited amount of research to support this approach is currently available. Thus while the approach is recommended its empirical support is limited.

Using semistructured interviews to assess treatment adherence

Semi-structured interviews appear to have been less used to measure treatment fidelity than other methods. However, they have the potential to increase reliability and validity although at increased cost in terms of time required by therapists and supervisors. Wilkinson (2006) developed a semi-structured interview called the "Treatment Monitoring Interview" (TMI) to assess teacher adherence to a treatment program for student behavior problems. The goals of the interview were to (a) review fidelity to the treatment plan; (b) review teacher use of self-report checklists and permanent products; (c) provide for data-based feedback and support; and (d) determine the need for further training. Although Wilkinson provides no information on reliability or validity it may be assumed that a semi-structured interview will increase reliability and validity over unstructured interviews (Garb, 2005; MacLean, 2005; Westen & Weinberger, 2004; Widiger, 2002; Wilson, 1996). The TMI could be modified by supervisors to help monitor therapists' adherence to manualized treatments. Wilkinson concludes that "Consultee self-reports and permanent products combined with structured interviews and performance feedback are essential to monitoring and sustaining adequate treatment integrity" (Wilkinson, 2006, p. 433). Wilkinson appears to be advocating a multimethod, multiperson approach for determining adherence to treatment manuals.

Using observers to assess therapists' adherence to the treatment plan

Using trained observers to rate treatment fidelity has been widely employed in research studies (Codding et al., 2005; Falloon et al., 2005; Forgatch et al., 2005; Hogue, Liddle, Singer, & Leckrone, 2005; McIntosh et al., 2005; Milne and James, 2000). Observation is the gold standard for assessing treatment integrity but the costs are high and must be balanced against the training requirements for any given treatment program. Forgatch and colleagues reported that it required up to 40 hours to train competent observers to use their *Fidelity of Implementation* (FIMP) rating procedures (Forgatch et al., 2005). In 1993 Waltz reported that the cost in dollars for undergraduate coders was $1,890.00 and for expert raters the costs ran to $18,000.00 (Waltz et al., 1993). If the decision is to use trained observers to safeguard the integrity of the treatment delivery then the funds to train and employ observers will need to be budgeted into the training program (Miller, Moyers et al., 2005).

Supervisors as observers

Supervisors who are experts in the use of a particular treatment model may be considered to be expert observers. In fact, use of supervisors may have several advantages over the use of outside observers for training purposes. Feedback about therapist adherence can often be delivered more immediately by supervisors than by trained raters. In addition, supervisors will be in a position to deliver praise and encouragement for skillful delivery of the treatment interventions. They will also be able to provide directions for improvement when it is needed. For example, supervisors may observe that the therapist delivers the recommended interventions but fails to tailor them to the immediate needs of the clients. Supervisors may observe other incidences of less skillful delivery such as leaving out critical interventions or adding interventions which are contraindicated. The supervisor's early delivery of supportive and corrective feedback may help to increase the therapist's skill and competence.

Supervisors can help make the therapist-intern's use of accurate information more important by regularly inquiring about the intern's use of reliable and valid assessments of (a) the clients' therapy outcomes, (b) the clients' perception of the alliance, (c) administration of the interventions specified in the treatment manual, and (d) tailoring of the manual specified treatment interventions. To assist in this process supervisors may request therapists to complete a Preparation for Supervision Checklist (PSC) (Appendix K), which incorporates the TTS described in Chapter 4.

In some cases changes in administrative procedures may be necessary to establish a culture of providing therapists with accurate information about their performance (Arkes, 1991; Lambert et al., 2001). For example, McDonald (1991) found that law enforcement trainees' were more likely to continue to use new methods and techniques if the administration is committed to and provides follow-through for the new procedures. Similarly, Cukrowicz et al. (2005) reported that therapist-interns changed from the use of theory based treatments to the use of empirically-based treatments when the clinic administration made that change a matter of policy. Supervisors may need to educate administrators about the necessity of making assessment of therapy outcomes and processes standard procedure.

Once evidence-based practice becomes a part of administrative policy it will require supervisors to train therapist-interns in its use. In order, to prevent drift supervisors will need to support their therapist-interns continued adherence to evidence-based practice (Dennehy et al., 2005).

The problem is not limited to supervision in therapy. Codding et al. (2005) and others (Melde, Esbensen, & Tusinski, 2006; Noel et al., 2000; Wilkinson, 2006) found that supervision – in the form of performance feedback – increased teachers, treatment integrity for delivering planned teaching interventions. The conclusion appears to be that if there is no reinforcement supplied for using more accurate information then it appears likely that supervisors and therapists will fall back upon methods that are less costly to them, even if those methods provide less effective results (Arkes, 1991). For example, if there is no reinforcement for therapists and supervisors use of direct (live) supervision or video-recorded sessions then it appears likely that they will resort to methods with less response cost such as the therapist's self-reports. Similarly, if there is no support and reinforcement for therapists' use of assessment instruments and structured self-rating forms to (a) evaluate adherence to the manualized treatment, (b) evaluation of the treatment alliance, and (c) evaluation of client progress and outcomes, then therapist-interns are likely to simply use their best guess about how well they are delivering the planned treatment. Supervisors will need to remain diligent in providing support and guidance throughout the intern's training. Competent therapists will continue to use those procedures into their practices to protect their clients and to prevent against treatment drift.

In summary, the real measure of your competence as a therapist is your clients' successful outcomes. You can increase the probability of successful outcomes by: (1) using empirically-supported treatments, which have been fitted to your clients' needs and goals; (2) securing your clients' agreement on the goals and the treatment plan; (3) delivering the planned treatment by adherence to the treatment manual; (4) tailoring the interventions to your clients needs and goals; and (5) continuously using reliable and valid assessment instruments to monitoring (a) your treatment deliver, (b) the clients' outcomes, and (c) the client-therapist alliance. If you are successful in establishing and maintaining a therapeutic relationship and in delivering the planned treatment then the clients should be getting closer to their goals. Therefore, we turn next to ways you can evaluate your clients' treatment progress and outcomes.

Box 5.1 Improving Therapists' Cognitive Processes

There are two factors which complicate the therapist's cognitive processes. The first is the complexity of the therapy process. The second factor is the cognitive biases that plague all human decision making. The large number of variables requiring the therapist's attention and the complexity of the cognitive processing inherent in therapy sessions is difficult for experienced therapists and is sometimes overwhelming for beginners (Lambert & Hawkins, 2001). Therapy sessions are stressful because they demand that you pay attention to the clients' verbal, nonverbal, and affective responses for each individual in the session. In addition, in the case of couples and families, you must also attend to the family members' patterns of interpersonal relationships. Simultaneously you need to attend to your own personal cognitive, affective, and behavioral responses. Also vying for your attention is the requirement to deliver the planned treatment while building and maintaining an alliance with each family member. Consequently the complexity of the therapy process may exacerbate the problems of bias in clinical judgments.

Removing bias from your clinical judgments

All therapists' cognitive processes are fallible (Arkes, 1991). Therefore you will need to work to develop strategies designed to remove bias from your clinical judgments. There appear to be several steps you can take to improve the reliability and validity of your clinical judgments (Arkes, 1991; Garb, 2005; Schulte & Eifert, 2002; Westen & Weinberger, 2004; Wilson, 1996). Reliability and validity of clinical judgments can be improved by making use of multiple informants, by increasing the accuracy of the information used to make clinical judgments, by using checklists to prompt consideration of alternative solutions and methods, and by learning to consider both the gains and the losses associated with any given decision (Arkes, 1991).

Use of multiple informants to reduce bias in therapists' clinical judgments

One step in debiasing clinical judgments is to use multiple informants. Attempt to gain information from those who are best positioned to supply the needed information (Westen & Weinberger, 2004). For example, clients are best positioned to report their perceptions of their psychological symptoms and their marital relationships. Reliability of client information goes up when you use rating scales and standardized assessment instruments. For example, clients are best positioned to report on their marital relationships by use of the assessment instruments in the Standard Assessment Battery (Appendix C). Clients are also best positioned to report on their perception of treatment progress by use of outcome rating scales (Chapter 3, note 1). They are also able to report on their perception of the client–therapist alliance by use of alliance rating scales (Chapter 1, note 1). On the other hand you, as a therapist, may be best positioned to observe and report on the clients' in-session clinically relevant behavior and their interpersonal relationship patterns using observation ratings scales (Appendix E).

You are also in a position to report on your behavior in the therapy session. You can report on your use of (a) outcome assessment instruments to evaluate client progress (Appendix K) and (b) assessment instruments to evaluate clients' therapeutic alliance. You can document all of this information in your case progress notes (Appendix D). Finally, you can bring all of this information to your supervisor for feedback and planning (Appendix K).

Supervisors are best positioned to observe and report to you in your efforts to become a competent therapist by:

- Helping you use the manual to prepare for sessions.
- Observing your efforts to adhere to the manualized interventions in-sessions and providing feedback on your performance.
- Observing your efforts to build and maintain the therapeutic alliance and providing feedback on your performance.
- Providing reinforcement for your successes.

To summarize you will reduce bias in your clinical judgments by use of multiple respondents and multiple methods to obtain information. The more reliable and valid your sources of information the more likely you are to avoid bias. As you gain experience you will increase your skill in blending these various sources of information to evaluate your delivery of the treatment protocols.

Experience and clinical judgments

Experience alone does not improve clinical judgment. Experience generally leads to more conviction that one's opinions are right but does not necessarily lead to more accuracy in clinical judgments (Garb, 2005; Wilson, 1996). For example, researchers have found that experience alone does not increase therapist's accuracy in predicting the client's alliance (Hilsenroth, Ackerman, Clemence, Strassle, & Handler, 2002). Experience may lead therapists to drift from the planned treatment (Dane & Schneider, 1998; Dennehy et al., 2005; Margison et al., 2000), which often leads to poor outcomes (Henggeler et al., 1997; Schulte & Eifert, 2002; Wilson, 1996). However, experience based on specific training and feedback may help you improve your clinical judgment. The secret to becoming successful at any skill is first to get the best instruction available, second practice to improve your performance, and third receive feedback on your performance. The feedback may come from supervisors, colleagues, and from your systematic use of structured interviews, rating scales, and reliable and valid assessment instruments.

Evaluating the Clients' Treatment Outcomes

The purpose of evaluating treatment outcomes is to arrive at a decision about the future course of the treatment. Decisions about treatment outcomes can range from (a) continue the planned treatment, (b) intensify treatment, (c) change the treatment, or (d) terminate treatment (Lambert & Hawkins, 2004; Mullin et al., 2006). These decisions should be made based on the best information available. They should be made in collaboration with your clients and in consultation with your supervisor.

The best information available for making decisions about the future course of the treatment will be made by the use of assessment instruments that are valid, reliable, and feasible. For continuous assessment to be feasible the instruments must be brief enough to be administered and scored by you in session. In addition they must have sufficient face validity to appear meaningful and useful to the clients. The measures used should help you determine how to answer the questions of whether to continue, intensify, change, or terminate the treatment. Evaluation of client progress and satisfaction should be made continuously over the course of treatment. Continuous assessment will allow you to detect and correct lack of progress and potential breaches in the alliance before they disrupt the treatment.

Therapy outcome should be assessed at the beginning of each session. Outcome is assessed at the beginning of each session because we are measuring the impact of previous interventions. The Outcome Rating Scale (ORS: Miller & Duncan, 2004; Chapter 3, note 1) is a valid and reliable measure of psychological distress and it is brief and easily scored in session. When treating marital couples the Revised Dyadic Adjustment Scale (RDAS: Busby et al., 1995) is a reliable and valid instrument to assess the outcome variable of marital adjustment or satisfaction. To assess the client–therapist alliance the Session Rating Scale (SRS: Miller & Duncan, 2004, Chapter 1, note 1) meets the criterion of valid, reliable, and feasible.

Each partner's perceptions of their psychological distress may be assessed by the Outcome Rating Scale (Miller & Duncan, 2004). The ORS consists of 4 items, which can be easily administered and scored in session. Administration and scoring takes about 1 minute. The authors designed the ORS to measure the same variables as the OQ45 (Lambert et al., 1996). A correlation of .59 indicates a moderate concurrent validity. The correlation is respectable and supports the use of the ORS as a brief alternative to the OQ-45. The brief nature of the ORS makes it feasible to use as a continuous measure of treatment outcome.

When performing marital therapy the RDAS may be used to determine each partner's perception of the marital relationship. However, the RDAS may be difficult to use as a continuous measure as it contains 12 items and requires about 10 to 15 minutes to administer and score. One solution to this problem is to ask the clients to come 10 minutes early for their appointment to allow time to take the RDAS. If the RDAS can be administered by the receptionist in the waiting room then the RDAS will serve very well as a continuous measure. The receptionist could hand each partner the RDAS to be administered by a handheld computer. When they return it the receptionist could initiate the scoring program and hand the results to you when you come to the waiting room for the clients. If it is not possible to have the receptionist administer the RDAS every session then it can be administered by you at the initial assessment session and at the third and sixth treatment sessions as those are critical sessions for decision making. The RDAS should also be administered at termination to document progress made during the therapy.

Outcome scores should be reviewed in the third and sixth sessions. Clinical lore in the past has suggested that clients always get worse before they get better. However, this appears to be largely a myth. While it is true that some clients show deterioration after entering therapy most show improvement in their psychological symptoms (Lambert et al., 2002). In fact, Lambert et al. state that early improvement is a sign of potentially good therapy outcomes. Clients who have not made a statistically reliable gain by the third treatment session are at risk of a poor outcome. If your clients have not achieved a statistically reliable improvement by six sessions it is recommended that you consult with your clients about the possible causes for a lack of progress. Consult with your supervisor and discuss the options of intensifying the treatment, changing treatment, and referring the clients to another therapist. Your goal should be to help your clients have a successful outcome.

Statistical versus clinically significant outcomes

Statistically significant results are changes in the clients' outcome scores, which are greater than chance. Clinically significant outcomes are changes that signify that the clients' outcome assessment scores have moved from the clinical range to the nonclinical range. As stated earlier Lambert and Ogles (2004) found that for individual therapy it typically requires seven sessions for 50 percent of the clients to have statistically significant changes in outcome scores. Seventy-five percent of individual clients improved to the level of statistical significance following fourteen sessions. However, clinically significant changes generally require twenty-one sessions for 50 percent of the clients and forty-five sessions for 75 percent of the clients to reach a clinically significant change.

Administering, Scoring, and Interpreting the Outcome Rating Scale and the Revised Dyadic Adjustment Scale

When your clients come for a therapy session meet them in the reception area and escort them to the consulting room while carrying on a social conversation. Once in the consulting room see that they are seated comfortably and their coats and other gear are out of the way. Hand them each copies of the Outcome Rating Scale (Miller & Duncan, 2004) and a pencil. Ask them to complete the ORS and when they are done ask them to return them to you. Using a 10 cm ruler score each ORS item and sum the results. Item scores range from 0 to 10 and the total score ranges from 0 to 40. Next review their RDAS scores or if it was not administered by the receptionist then administer and score it at this time. Add their ORS and RDAS scores to their charts. Scan the graphs for changes in level, trend, and variation. Share the charts with your clients and discuss the outcomes. When you have finished the discussion of the ORS and RDAS charts ask if anything has changed since the last session. After you have listened to the clients' description of their recent complaints make a decision about the agenda for this session. Ask yourself, should the agenda focus on crisis issues such as family violence or suicide? Should the agenda be to continue the planned treatment? Intensify the treatment? Change to another treatment? Refer the clients to another therapist? Your decision should be based on your clients needs and your interpretation of the assessment scores.

A discussion of the interpretation of assessment scores and of combinations of assessment scores related to these decisions follows.

Interpreting the results of the outcome assessments

To illustrate the process of evaluating clients' outcome scores this chapter will focus on evaluating outcomes for a hypothetical marital couple. Similar procedures would be used for families and for individual clients. In this illustration each partner's perceptions of their psychological distress is assessed by the Outcome Rating Scale (Miller & Duncan, 2004) and their perceptions of their marital distress is measured by the Revised Dyadic Adjustment Scale (Busby et al., 1995).

Evaluating outcome scores presented in charts

The clients' outcome scores should be displayed in a graph, which can be analyzed to determine if clients are improving, staying the same, or deteriorating (Whipple et al., 2003). Graphic analysis of changes following treatment have traditionally been accomplished by inspecting the chart for changes in level, trend, and variability (Hayes et al., 1999; Parsonson & Baer, 1986). However, analysis may be improved if we have empirically derived reliable change index scores and established normative cutoff scores that can be used to determine the clients' status relative to known groups (Lambert et al., 2001).

Reliable change index scores

Reliable change index (RCI) scores are derived by a formula established by Jacobson and Truax (1991). A RCI score for an instrument indicates when the change is greater than chance. The RCI score for the ORS is reported to be ± 5 (Anker et al., 2010). Thurber and Mead (2002) used Jacobson and Truax's procedures and found the RCI score for the RDAS to be ± 5. After you have determined if there is a reliable change in the clients' scores look to determine if there has been a clinically significant change.

Clinically significant changes

Changes in ORS and RDAS scores of ± 5 or more points indicate a statistically reliable change. However, while a statistically reliable change is important it may not make a meaningful difference. If the clients' scores remain in the clinical range they may continue to experience disturbing psychological symptoms. ORS scores can range from 0–40 with lower scores indicating greater psychological distress. Miller, Duncan et al. (2005) found that a cutoff score of 25 separates clinical from nonclinical ORS scores. Scores of 25 and above are typical of individuals not in treatment. Therefore a client who scores 23 at time one and 29 at time 2 has made both a statically significant and a clinically significant change. A clinically significant change is defined as a change which crosses the cutoff score into the nonclinical range.

Clinically significant changes in RDAS (Busby et al., 1995) scores are somewhat more complicated. RDAS scores range from 0–69. Higher RDAS scores signify less marital distress. The cutoff line has been found to be 48 (Crane, Middleton, & Bean, 2000; Thurber & Mead, 2002). However, Thurber and Mead found a band of uncertainty of ± 5 points which surrounds the cutoff. Consequently, scores which fall within the band of 43 to 53 points can not be reliably determined to be either distressed or nondistressed. Therefore, a clinically significant change in RDAS scores would be a change to 54 or above.

One indication of the severity of the client's psychological symptoms and marital distress are determined by their initial ORS and RDAS scores. The clients' initial scores are considered to be their baseline scores. It is possible to use a single observation as a baseline score due to the known psychometric qualities of the two instruments (Hayes et al., 1999). Changes over the course of therapy are assessed as differences from the baseline scores.

Determining level scores

Three or more contiguous scores which are observed to be within the RCI range of each other can be considered level or no change. Therefore three or more ORS scores that remain within ± 5 points of each other are considered level. Similarly, three or more contiguous RDAS scores which are within ± 5 points of each other are consider to be level. When ORS scores are level and below the cutoff score of 25 they may be interpreted as indicting that the clients psychological symptoms are stable in the clinical range. ORS scores which are level at 26 or above are stable in the nonclinical range. Similarly, if the clients' RDAS scores are level at 54 or above then you may interpret that as stable in the maritally nondistressed range. RDAS scores level and below 43 are determined to be stable in the maritally distressed range.

Determining trends

Observed changes in ORS or RDAS scores may trend up or down over a series of sessions. By convention, a trend is established by three contiguous data points (Hayes et al., 1999; Parsonson & Baer, 1986). Of course the more data points we have the more confidence we have that a trend has been established. ORS scores that trend upward suggest improvement in the clients' psychological status whereas downward trends suggest that the clients' psychological status is deteriorating. Similarly increasing trends in RDAS scores suggest improvement while decreasing trends suggest greater marital distress.

Deteriorating trends in outcome scores should be investigated by the therapist in collaboration with the clients. The same is true if the outcome scores are level in the clinical range. According to the findings by Lunnen and Ogles (1998) level scores in the clinical range should be considered as no different from deteriorating scores. Both signal potentially unsatisfactory outcomes.

Determining variation in outcome scores

Variation can be large or small. Small variations in change scores are defined here as changes which exceed the RCI scores for the assessment instrument being evaluated. Changes that fall within the range of the RCI for an instrument are level by definition. Therefore, variation is defined here as changes greater than the RCI score for the assessment instrument and which are not part of a discernable trend. An example of variation in ORS scores might be: a score of 21 followed one week later with a score of 15 (−6) and the next week the score is 23 (+8). An example of variation in RDAS scores might be a baseline score of 43 followed by a score of 49 and then a score of 39. When there is considerable variation in the scores for either instrument the therapist should, in collaboration with the clients, look for the cause of this variation. If the cause of the variation can be discovered and removed then trends or levels will be more easily interpreted and treated. For example, if the ORS scores are showing variability and the downward spikes are determined to be related to negative events at the client's workplace then the client might consider alternatives such as seeking a change of job responsibilities or finding another job.

Interpreting sudden changes in level

If a therapy intervention is initiated and there is an immediate change in level, then you should investigate the relationship between the intervention and the observed change (Hayes et al.,

1999). If, following a specific intervention, there is a change of level from the clinical to the nonclinical range or from the distressed to the nondistressed range for the ORS and the RDAS scores respectively then there is evidence for the effectiveness of the intervention. Of course, care must be taken to determine that other variables do not systematically correlate with the change. For example, a planned intervention may correlate with a member of the family leaving home. Your treatment adherence evaluations should be of help in determining if other variables may have attributed to the change. Review your adherence assessments to attempt to determine if important elements of the treatment were left out or if proscribed elements were included. If after you have reviewed the treatment fidelity assessments you find that the treatment was delivered fully and fairly then there is support for the treatment as the cause of the successful changes. If the scores remain level in the nonclinical and nondistressed ranges following a therapy intervention then you should begin to discuss termination with the clients.

Helping clients terminate as soon as their goals have been met is an ethical requirement (AAMFT, 2001; Wilcoxon et al., 2007). It is unethical to continue treatment beyond the point where the clients are benefitting from the therapy (AAMFT, 2007). There are also legal implications related to terminating when clients have reached their goals. It would be illegal to charge clients for services they do not need. Timely termination will be cost effective for clients and for the agencies which serve them (Hayes, Barlow, & Nelson-Gray, 1999). Timely termination is cost effective for clinics as it frees clinic resources for clients who need more intensive or longer term treatment (Lambert & Hawkins, 2001). See Chapter 6 for an extended discussion of termination.

If there is a sudden change of scores into the clinical range or into the marital distressed range for the ORS and for the RDAS respectively then the client is deteriorating and this should be investigated. Sudden changes into the clinical or distressed ranges should be investigated without waiting for three data points to define a change in level.

A good place to start your investigation into the observed deterioration of the clients' outcome scores is by sharing the information from the charts. Ask your clients what they believe are the factors that are contributing to the current change scores. Use your best attending and listening skills. After listening to your clients explanations try to determine the best course of action.

Interpreting patterns in combined sets of couple outcome charted scores

The partners' individual graphs may be interpreted as above. That is, an individual's score may be trending up trending down, or staying level. These trends may be interpreted in relation to the cutoff line. For example, staying level or trending upward are interpreted positively. Level scores below the cutoff or scores trending down are interpreted as indicating the probability of poor outcomes unless changes are made to the treatment. However, the interpretation of the couples combined set of scores is a little more difficult.

Each couple will have two sets of charted outcome scores, one from the ORS and one from the RDAS. Statistical treatment of paired couple scores has been demonstrated by Anker et al. (2010). However, a visual model to facilitate your in-session use of the couple's combined charted ORS and RDAS information is useful. Each of the marital partners' paired sets of ORS and RDAS data may be represented graphically. This results in 24 sets of paired outcome combinations. Figure 5.1 illustrates each of the sets and suggests the action to be taken. It should be recalled that for ORS scores the cutoff is 25. ORS scores of 24 and below fall in the clinical range and scores of 25 and above are in the nonclinical range.

Recall that the RDAS (Busby et al., 1995) scores have a cutoff of 48 with an indeterminate zone of ± 5 (Thurber & Mead, 2003). Because of this RDAS scores of 54 and above are in the nondistressed range and scores of 43 and below are in the distressed range. Scores between 43 and 54 are not interpretable. RDAS graph lines which are trending up suggest that the client's

Figure 5.1 Some combinations of husband's and wives' outcome rating scale and revised dyadic adjustment scale scores in terms of levels and trends indicating successful, improving, deteriorating, and extremely distressed client outcomes

1. Successful Outcomes
All level scores are in the nonclinical and nondistressed ranges.

	Wife	Husband
ORS *Nonclinical*	⇒	⇒
RDAS *Nondistressed*	⇒	⇒

Action: Termination

2. Improving Outcomes
All level scores are in the nonclinical and nondistressed ranges.

	Wife	Husband	:	Wife	Husband	:	Wife	Husband
ORS *Nonclinical*	⇑	⇑	:	⇑	⇑	:	⇑	⇑
RDAS *Nondistressed*	⇑	⇑	:	⇑	⇒	:	⇒	⇑

	Wife	Husband	:	Wife	Husband	:	Wife	Husband
ORS *Nonclinical*	⇑	⇑	:	⇑	⇒	:	⇒	⇑
RDAS *Nondistressed*	⇒	⇒	:	⇒	⇑	:	⇑	⇒

	Wife	Husband	:	Wife	Husband	:	Wife	Husband
ORS *Nonclinical*	⇒	⇒	:	⇒	⇒	:	⇒	⇒
RDAS *Nondistressed*	⇑	⇑	:	⇑	⇒	:	⇒	⇑

	Wife	Husband	:	Wife	Husband
ORS *Nonclinical*	⇑	⇒	:	⇒	⇑
RDAS *Nondistressed*	⇑	⇑	:	⇑	⇑

Action: Continue Treatment

3. Deteriorating Outcomes
All level scores are in the clinical and distressed ranges.

	Wife	Husband	:	Wife	Husband	:	Wife	Husband
ORS *Clinical*	⇓	⇓	:	⇓	⇓	:	⇓	⇓
RDAS *Distressed*	⇓	⇓	:	⇓	⇒	:	⇒	⇓

	Wife	Husband	:	Wife	Husband	:	Wife	Husband
ORS *Clinical*	⇓	⇓	:	⇓	⇒	:	⇒	⇓
RDAS *Distressed*	⇒	⇒	:	⇒	⇓	:	⇓	⇒

	Wife	Husband	:	Wife	Husband	:	Wife	Husband
ORS *Clinical*	⇒	⇒	:	⇒	⇒	:	⇒	⇒
RDAS *Distressed*	⇓	⇓	:	⇓	⇒	:	⇒	⇓

	Wife	Husband	:	Wife	Husband
ORS *Clinical*	⇓	⇒	:	⇒	⇓
RDAS *Distressed*	⇓	⇓	:	⇓	⇓

Action: Intensify Treatment. Consult Family Therapy Decision Tree

4. Extremely Distressed
All level scores are in the clinical and distressed ranges.

	Wife	Husband
OQ-45 *Clinical*	⇒	⇒
RDAS *Distressed*	⇒	⇒

Action: Intensify Treatment. Consult Family Therapy Decision Tree

A level arrow (⇒) indicates that scores on the chart are level. An up arrow (⇑) indicates an improving trend and a down arrow (⇓) indicates a deteriorating trend.

perception of their marital satisfaction is improving and RDAS graph lines which are trending down suggest that they see their marital satisfaction is worsening. Various combinations of ORS and RDAS graph lines may result in what may be described as successful outcomes, improving outcomes, deteriorating outcomes, and extremely distressed couples (Figure 5.1).

Combinations indicating successful outcomes

If both spouses' ORS and RDAS graph lines are level in the nonclinical and nondistressed ranges then the therapy should be considered successful (Panel 1 of Figure 5.1). The action recommended is termination. This is truly time for an in-session celebration with your clients. Termination is discussed at length in Chapter 6.

Combinations indicating improving outcomes

When investigating the impact of treatment with clients, improvement should be remarked and celebrated. Trends in graph lines of the ORS scores that indicate movement toward fewer symptom behaviors (upward trends) and trends in the RDAS graph lines that suggest reduced marital distress (upward trends) should be celebrated in session with the clients as signs that they are meeting their goals. The combinations of levels and trends in the graph lines which suggest improvement are described in Panel 2 of Figure 5.1. Note that level trends in ORS scores in the nonclinical range and level trends in RDAS scores in the nondistressed range are considered as a positive sign. Therefore, if either of an individual's outcome scores, the ORS or RDAS, is level in the nonclinical or nondistressed range and their other outcome score shows an improving trend, then the combination suggests improvement. Similar combinations in partners sets also signal improvement. (Panel 2, Figure 5.1). When the combination of graph lines suggesting improved outcomes are found for both partners then both you and your clients should begin looking forward to successful completion of the treatment.

Combinations indicating deteriorating outcomes

Panel 3 of Figure 5.1 provides a description of the various charted combinations of ORS and RDAS scores that indicate deterioration in the partner's scores. Note that in cases where either partner's scores are level in the clinical range of the ORS or in the distressed range of the RDAS it is taken as an unsatisfactory situation. If the partner's scores are level in the clinical or distressed range and their partner's score in the set is deteriorating (Panel 3, Figure 5.1) this suggests that the couple may have poor outcomes unless remedial action is taken. The remedial action suggested is either to intensify the treatment or take a decision to change the treatment, change the therapist, or terminate therapy to protect the welfare of the clients. The Family Therapy Decision Tree (Figure 5.2, p. 127) should assist in making these decisions.

Combinations indicating extremely distressed couples

Extremely distressed couples have ORS scores and RDAS scores that are level in the clinical and distressed range (Panel 4 of Figure 5.1). Unless remedial action is taken it is very likely that these couples will have unsuccessful outcomes. The action to be considered should be to immediately move to intensify the treatment or consider changing treatment, changing the therapist, or terminating therapy for the good of the clients.

Session Rating Scale: Administering, scoring, and interpreting

As stated earlier the Session Rating Scale (SRS: Miller & Duncan, 2004) is designed to assess the client's perception of the client–therapist alliance in the current session. Consequently the SRS should be administered, scored, and interpreted to the clients toward the end of every session. The SRS consists of 4 items. The clients respond by putting a vertical mark on a horizontal 10 cm line. Score each item using a 10 cm rule and sum the scores. Enter the total score on a graph. If the total score is below 36 or if one of the items is at or below 9 cm then you should discuss the low scores with the clients. The cutoff on the SRS is 36. Scores of 36 and above are generally attained by individuals who are not seeking psychotherapy. Scores which are level below 36 or are trending down below 36 indicate potentially poor outcomes.

Level scores in the nonclinical range or positive changes from the clients' baseline SRS scores should be celebrated and the planned treatment should be continued. If the SRS scores are level in the clinical range or are deteriorating then you should discuss this with your clients. This discussion should be aimed at answering the questions which follow. The primary criterion for these decisions is the welfare of the clients.

- Should changes be made in how the treatment is being delivered?
- Is it the wrong treatment and should you change treatments?
- Would it be best to recommend transferring the clients to another therapist?

Establishing the agenda for the session

When you meet with clients and have administered the ORS then ask them how their week went. It is a good idea to ask them to report on their week before you share the information from the assessment instruments to avoid biasing their responses. Many clients will see the information from the assessment instruments as more authoritative than what they have to say. Determine if the clients are in crisis and if so shift to the appropriate crisis treatment. If they are not in crisis you can start the interview by saying something like, "Sorry that scoring the assessments took a minute or two but it will help me to help you in the rest of the session. I'll share the information right after I hear how your week went. Which one of you would like to start telling me how things went this week?" Elicit a response from both if possible. Use your best attending and listening skills then summarize their comments (Hill, 2004). After the clients describe their week share the information from the charts with them (Harmon et al., 2005). Harmon and colleagues found that 98 percent of the clients they studied wanted feedback on the assessments they had taken. They found that out of 201 cases only in one situation did a therapist withhold information out of concern for its effects on the client. They also found that feeding the assessment scores back to the clients appeared to improve outcomes.

You should interpret the outcome scores to the clients using only nontechnical terms. Improvement in any of the outcome scores should be celebrated. Follow up the clients discussion of their time since the last session with a summery of their statements. Then you can say something like,

> I'm pleased that your week went so well and (if they had a homework assignment) that you had a lot of success with the homework assignment (identify specific examples from their report). The outcome assessments pretty much agree with what you said, they both stayed about the same or showed improvement for each of you. In fact, Cosby, your marital adjustment score moved into the nondistressed range. That calls for a party. Your scores are so good that since we didn't have any carry over business from last session we should go right ahead and work on the next step in the treatment. Today we are going to work on . . .

If the clients outcome assessment scores stayed in the distressed or clinical range or showed a deteriorating trend then you should discuss this with them. As with the discussion of positive results start by summarizing their week. If it went poorly it will be possible to draw their attention to the fact that the outcome scores uphold their description. You can say something like, "It sounds like you had a rough week. I'm sorry about the fight you had last night. You know the outcome scores sort of reflect that you both remain unhappy. They stayed about the same or worsened a bit. Let's see if we can put our heads together and find out what needs to be done to get things moving forward. First, I'd like to hear more about what got in the way of your completing the homework assignment." Use your best attending and listening skills. If it appears that they did not understand the assignment then accept the responsibility by saying something like, "It sounds like I really didn't explain that very well. Let me try again and then we can practice it. Here is how I think it should go." Consider going back to an earlier step where they were previously successful and have them practice it. That way they will start with some success. Then try again to present the current intervention from the treatment manual using slightly different words. Help them to practice the procedure successfully. Then when you are 80 to 90 percent sure they will have success performing the intervention at home reassign the homework using the successful homework procedures (Appendix J). If you are not sure they will have success at home them tell them not to try it out until they have had more time to practice in session next week.

On the other hand, if they report a satisfactory week and the outcome scores suggest no change or deterioration you will want to share this with them in an effort to understand the difference. You can say something like, "It sounds as if your week went fairly well. I'm pleased that you had relatively good success with the homework. I'm surprised, however, that the outcome scores aren't keeping up with the success you reported. In fact, one of your marital distress scores got noticeably worse [referring to a score which exceeded the RCI in the wrong direction. You do not need to give the score just point out the trend]. What do you suppose caused that?" Use your good active listening skills to try to understand what is happening. Consider administering the Session Relationship Scale (SRS: Duncan et al., 2003; Miller & Duncan, 2004) at this point to evaluate the strength of the alliance. If you detect an alliance rupture attempt to repair it (Safran et al., 2002). If you are at an impasse use the therapist self-soothing procedures (Appendix B) and tell the clients you would like to think about the case some more and perhaps consult with your supervisor to see what you might do to be more helpful to them. It is okay to end a session short of the full 50 minutes so close the session at this point and set a new appointment.

In summary, when you establish the agenda for the session consider the clients self-reports about the previous week along with the information from ORS and the RDAS assessments. Determine if the clients are in crisis or not. If not in crisis then you should consider the clients' progress to date and their goals. If the clients are making satisfactory progress then the decision should be to continue with the planned treatment. This information may be shared and the decisions about the agenda should be made in collaboration with your clients. If the clients are not making satisfactory progress then the *Family Therapy Decision Tree* described below may help in making decisions about possible next steps to take.

The Family Therapy Decision Tree

Decisions about therapy outcomes and about changing treatments are some of the most important decisions you will make as a therapist. Therapists appear most likely to change treatments when they perceive that the current treatment is not working or when they have strong feelings about their clients (Ruscio & Holohan, 2006; Schulte & Eifert, 2002). Therefore, before you make a decision to change the treatment consider your affective, behavioral, and cognitive responses to the clients. What part are your responses to the clients playing in the decision to change or not change the treatment? The "Person of the Therapist Checklist" (Appendix A) may help you consider a range of responses you may be experiencing. If you are having strong personal responses to the clients consult with your supervisor.

It takes a great deal of courage to tell your supervisor about the responses you are experiencing toward your clients. Therapists have been known not to disclose what they perceive to be clinical mistakes, negative and positive reactions to clients, client attraction to the therapist, and therapist countertransference (Ladany et al., 1996). It appears that problems in the therapist–supervisor relationship are often the cause of the intern's failure to disclose to their supervisors issues related to clients. Therapists often report that they did not disclose events in the therapy session to their supervisors based on their perception of the issue as (a) unimportant, (b) fear of evaluation, (c) the personal nature of the event, and (d) negative feelings toward their supervisors. Although you may feel that there are good reasons for not sharing with your supervisor the research suggests that the benefits generally out weigh the downside (Ellis, 2002; Gray et al., 2001; Magnuson et al., 2000; Moskowitz & Rupert, 1983; Nelson & Friedlander, 2001; Wetchler et al., 1989).

After you have considered how your personal responses to the clients are effecting your decision to change or not change treatments consider the rest of the information you have available. Evidence-based practice requires that you consider all of the best available information before you take a decision to change treatments. Start with the outcome assessment scores. Ask yourself, according to the outcome scores are the clients making progress, staying about the same, or deteriorating? If they are making progress then the decision should be to continue the current treatment program. If the clients are staying the same or deteriorating then there is a chance of a poor outcome. If there is a chance of a poor outcome you will need to make a decision about how to improve the treatment to help your clients achieve their goals. The options appear to be:

- Intensify the current treatment.
- Change the treatment.
- Change the therapist.
- Terminate treatment to protect the clients.

Intensifying the treatment

Before you decide to change the treatment you should consider intensifying the treatment. Treatment may be intensified by increasing the number of sessions per week or by increasing the length of each treatment session. Increasing the sessions or extending the length of the sessions may provide more time for the clients to practice the interventions during the session. If intensifying the treatment does not result in improved outcome scores then consider the other factors in the *Family Therapy Decision Tree.*

The *Family Therapy Decision Tree* (Figure 5.2) presents several of the most common factors related to lack of treatment progress (Nezu & Nezu, 1989; Whipple et al., 2003). The following questions should be considered. First, is the therapy alliance between the clients and the therapist sufficient for successful treatment outcomes? Second, has the treatment been fully and fairly delivered? Third, are the clients sufficiently motivated for change at this time? Fourth, are the clients coping skills adequate for their current life stresses? Fifth, should alternative treatments be considered including the possibility of changing to another therapist? Finally, should referral for medication be recommended? The *Family Therapy Decision Tree* raises these questions, provides some methods to assess them, and provides some suggestions for intervention.

The first question in the *Family Therapy Decision Tree* is "Are the clients' perceptions of the therapeutic alliance sufficient for treatment progress?" If you are considering changing the treatment plan then it is appropriate to review your clients' perception of the alliance. Consult with your clients to attempt to determine if you and they still agree on their goals for therapy.

Figure 5.2 Family therapy decision tree

Are the clients' therapeutic alliances sufficient for treatment progress? Use Session Rating Scale .	No →	Review the therapeutic alliance interventions and repair material.
Yes ⇓		
Has the planned treatment been delivered fully and fairly? Use the protocol adherence checklist appropriate for the treatment manual being used.	No →	Review the appropriate treatment manual.
Yes ⇓		
Are the clients sufficiently motivated to change? Use the *Stages of Change Scale.*	No →	Review the readiness to change interventions material.
Yes ⇓		
Are the clients' social support resources adequate for coping with their current life stresses? Use *Coping Responses Inventory* or *Multidimensional Scale of Perceived Social Support.*	No →	Review the coping and social support interventions material.
Yes ⇓		
Are there alternative treatment plans which might be more efficacious?	No →	Would medication augment or be a more effective treatment option?

Source: Based on Whipple et al., 2003.

Inquire again about the clients' agreement on the treatment methods. Consider any changes in how they feel about you as their therapist. To help explore these issues think about assessing the alliance with an instrument other than the one you have used previously. If you have been using the Session Rating Scale (Miller & Duncan, 2004) it might be appropriate to re-evaluate the alliance using the "System for Observing Family Therapy Alliances" (SOFTA: Freidlander, Escudero, & Heatherington, 2006), the "Couple Therapy Alliance Scale" (CTAS: Pinsof 1995), or the "Revised Helping Alliance Questionnaire" (Haq-II: Luborsky et al., 1996). The SOFTA scales and the CTAS may be especially helpful with marital and family cases. Use of one of these instruments may provide additional information about your clients' perceptions of the alliance at this time.

Intervening to improve the therapy alliance

If you determine that the alliance has been damaged or ruptured then review the literature on repairing alliances and consult with your supervisor (see Chapter 1; Pinsof, 1995; Safran et al., 2002). Attempt to repair the alliance. If your repair attempts are successful return to the treatment plan and continue to tailor it to the clients' needs. If your repair attempts are unsuccessful then talk to your clients about what they perceive to be the problem. Consider again the fit of the treatment and your fit as a therapist and make a decision, in collaboration with your clients, about alternative treatment plans.

Treatment fidelity

The second question to consider is, "Has treatment been delivered fairly and fully?" Review your evaluation of the treatment fidelity. Have you missed a step or delivered a step out of sequence? Left out a critical intervention? Added an intervention that is contraindicated? Have you become absorbed in the therapy process at the expense of staying with the manualized treatment? In short, has an adequate "dose" of therapy been administered? As discussed above "dose" in psychotherapy generally refers to the number of sessions of the planned treatment actively participated in by the clients (Lambert et al., 2001; Ward & McCollum, 2005; Whipple et al., 2003). Active participation should take into account whether or not the clients understood the interventions and were able to perform them in the session and in their home or other environments. "Dose" can also refer to the question of whether the therapist-intern was competent and whether she or he adhered to the planned treatment (Addis & Cardemil, 2006; Codding et al., 2005; Dane & Schneider, 1998; Howard et al., 1995; Waltz et al., 1993). If the treatment plan was not adhered to it may be irrelevant how many sessions have been held. Dane and Schneider (1998) and others (Eifert et al., 1997) found that lowered adherence to protocol was frequently associated with poorer outcomes. However, it should be noted that one of the complaints about the use of treatment manuals is that when some therapists focus on the delivery of the technical aspects of the treatment they failed to use their basic therapy skills. Therefore, "dose" may be defined as competent delivery of the manualized treatment, including use of basic therapy skills, for a sufficient number of sessions (Waltz et al., 1993).

Intervening to improve treatment fidelity

If it is determined that the planned treatment was not delivered then review the relevant chapters in the treatment manual. After reviewing the manual review the procedures with your supervisor and practice delivering them in a behavior rehearsal. Then make another attempt to deliver the appropriate interventions (Waltz et al., 1993). Continue to monitor your delivery using the adherence scales for the treatment. Continue to monitor the outcome and the alliance scores.

On the other hand, if you and your supervisor determine that you have delivered the treatment as set out in the treatment manual, including use of your basic therapy skills, then move on to the next question in the Family Therapy Decision Tree.

Motivation to Change

The common factors research suggests that 40 percent of the outcome variance is accounted for by what the clients bring to therapy (Asay & Lambert, 1999; Sprenkle, et al., 1999). The most frequently mentioned extra-therapeutic client variables are the severity of clients' disturbances, their physical symptoms, their motivation for change, and their skills at using social support systems to cope with stress. As you consider treatment changes you may wish to review the clients' motivation for change.

Assessing readiness to change

If the clients do not seem to be making progress toward their goals then assess each of your clients' readiness to change and not assume that all clients are in the action stage. You can assess their readiness to change using a structured interview (Prochaska & Norcross, 2001). In addition, you can assess each client's current stage by administering the *Stages of Change Scale* (SCS: McConnaughy, Prochaska, & Velicer, 1983). Clients scoring in the Precontemplation and Contemplation stages of the SCS are identified as having unfavorable readiness for change (Whipple et al., 2003).

It is not at all unusual for couples to have a split in their motivation for change. When one member of the dyad appears to lack motivation to change then you will need to have a conversation with the clients about their differences before marital therapy can proceed (Gottman, 1999). Clarify with the couple their desire to maintain the relationship. If they both want to continue the relationship then decide with the clients if it is necessary to change the current treatment plan to a treatment plan designed to increase their motivation for change.

If the decision is to change the treatment plan return to the procedures described in Chapter 4 and establish a new treatment plan designed to increase the clients motivation to change (DiClimente, 1991). Follow the procedures in Chapter 4 to get the clients agreement to the plan and to the proposed treatment. Then follow the procedures in this chapter to establish treatment adherence and treatment outcomes for the new treatment plan.

If motivation for change is not an issue or if motivation has been restored then considering the clients' ability to cope with stress. Their ability to cope is often a function of their social support systems.

Social Support for Coping With Life Stress

If your clients are having difficulty achieving their therapy goals it may be due to their inability to deal with the stressful events in their lives. If stressful events appear to be blocking your clients progress consider changing the treatment plan to focus on the stress inducing context and their coping skills. The fourth question on the *Family Therapy Decision Tree* (Figure 5.2) asks, "Are the clients' social support resources adequate for coping with their current life stresses?" As you consider this question with your clients you will first need to determine the context of the stress the clients are encountering. Second, you will need to consider with your clients their resources for dealing with the stressors.

Defining stress

Stress is defined broadly as traumatic events that involve threat to the personal integrity of the person or others. Stress may result from exposure to natural or accidental disasters such as floods, large fires, automobile accidents, and health issues. Events which induce stress may include direct personal experience of actual or threatened death or injury. Stress symptoms may also follow difficult events such as loss of a job, legal action, failure to get a promotion, or failure to be admitted to an educational program.

Stress reactions include fear, anxiety, and feelings of helplessness. Other symptoms include frequent rehearsal of negative perceptions about the event. Stress responses include intense distress at exposure to stimuli that resemble the original stressful event and this often leads to avoidance of such events. Frequently there is increased arousal leading to difficulty falling asleep or staying asleep, increased irritability, or poor concentration.

When exposed to stressful life events people often seek social support. Social support may be defined as the assistance of others when coping with stress (Cutrona, 1996; Cutrona, Russell, & Gardner, 2005). Social support for stressful life events can be assessed by interview and by assessment instruments (Almeida, Stawski, & Cichy, 2011).

Interviewing to determine your clients social support needs

When interviewing your clients to determine their social support needs you may attempt to determine first, what is the context of the clients' stressful life events? Second, which of your clients is most concerned about social support resources? Third, how do your clients conceptualize the nature of social support? Fourth, what types of support are involved? Finally, what is the source of the social support being provided? Figure 5.3 will help you organize your investigation into your clients' perceptions of their social support needs.

What is the context of your clients' significant life stressors?

The context of marital stress may be defined as the influences on the relationship which are outside of the couple and their relationship (Karney et al., 2005). Some of the events, which potentially influence the relationship, are more proximal to the relationship than are others, for example, foreclosure on the mortgage is more proximal than family-of-origin variables. Some events are more controllable than others, such as failing an examination versus losing one's home in a flood.

Figure 5.3 Domains of social support used to cope with significant life stressors

1 Is the context of the stressful life event:
   A proximal or distal?
   B controllable or not controllable?
   C current or historical?
   D does the stressor affect both partners or just one?
2 Is the concern with the coping resources of:
   A the recipient?
   B the provider?
   C both recipient and provider?
3 How is social support conceptualized?
   A as utilization of the social network?
   B as perceived social support?
   C as enacted social support?
   D as cognitive appraisal of the stressor as threatening or solvable?
4 Types of social support.
   A Emotional.
   B Instrumental.
   C Informational.
5 Source of social support.
   A Informal.
   B Formal.

Some events are current, such as receiving a pink slip at work today, while others are historical, such as having been turned down for a promotion a year ago. Some contextual stressors directly affect both partners, for example, the nature of the neighborhood, whereas others directly affect only one partner, such as an unpleasant boss. Contextual variables moderate marital satisfaction and distress. Contextual variables may be open to manipulation and therefore may be changed to relieve stress.

What are the concerns about the coping resources of the recipient and the provider?

As you attempt to help clients who are coping with stressful situations you may need to determine if the concern is with the family member who is the recipient of the social support, the member of the family acting as provider, or both? The demands for coping skills vary whether one is the recipient or the provider.

Clients vary in their ability to make use of social support just as they vary in their readiness to change in therapy. How your clients respond to life stressors and social support from others may be a function of their attitudes and behaviors. For example, optimists are reported to receive more social support than do pessimists (Bissette, Scheier, & Carver, 2002; Zellers & Perrewé, 2001). Perfectionists experience more frequent daily durations of stress than do less perfectionistic individuals. Miczo (2004) found that self-criticism was negatively related to perceived social support and with willingness to accept medical help. Zellers and Perrewé (2001) found that conversations with a positive content were significantly correlated with fewer symptoms of job burnout. They reported greater rates of burnout when persons experiencing job stress took part in conversations with negative content. Couples who take part in negative conversations in marriage are associated with greater probabilities of divorce (Gottman, 1994). Individuals who have greater affective reactivity to daily stressors are more prone to have depressive symptoms (O'Neill, Cohen, Tolpin, & Gunthert, 2004). Clearly, clients' attitudes and behaviors shape how they will respond to social support.

The social skills of the recipient appear to play a part in how and when social support is sought and received. Folkman et al. (1991) suggest that "Overall the more socially skillful a person is, the more problem-focused the person is, and the more positive his or her outlook, the more effective he or she is in obtaining social support" (pp. 249–250). However, social support is only one strategy for coping with life stressors. Wethington and Kessler (1991) and others (Cheng, 2003; Moos, 2004; Moos & Schaefer, 1993) suggest a range of coping strategies including: (a) avoidance; (b) positive reappraisal by refocusing thinking to avoid being upset; (c) religion; (d) active cognition, that is thinking of ways to improve the situation; (e) active behavioral, such as doing things to improve the situation; and (f) social support by consulting with others. It may be necessary for you to help your clients develop a greater range of coping strategies to meet the stressors in their lives.

How is social support being conceptualized by your clients?

Streeter and Franklin (1992) suggest that social support may be conceptualized by the clients as help from a social network, as perceived social support, as enacted social support, and as cognitive appraisal of the stressor as either threatening or solvable. The effects of social support may be a function of the overall beneficial effect of support from the clients' social network or a function of protecting the clients from potentially adverse effects of stressful events. The latter has come to be know as the buffering effect (Cohen & Wills, 1985). When support is assessed from the point of view of the individual's emersion in a social network, such as the family, then an overall beneficial effect is found. Cohen and Wills conclude that, "Evidently, embeddedness in a social network is beneficial to well-being but not necessarily helpful in the face of stress" (Cohen & Wills, 1985, p. 348).

Perceived social support is the clients' view of the social environment and their confidence that support will be there when needed, will be sufficient to meet their needs, and will be offered in ways that will be acceptable and beneficial. The buffering effect appears to come into play when the focus is on the perceived availability of others to be responsive to the individual's needs such as loss of a job or dealing with an acute or chronic illness (Cohen & Wills, 1985).

Enacted social support is defined as the actual behaviors or actions performed by others for example, through:

- Material aid: Providing money or physical objects.
- Behavioral assistance: Assisting physically with tasks.
- Intimate interaction: Listening and expressions of care, respect, and understanding.
- Guidance: Giving information, instruction, or advice.
- Feedback: Providing feedback about behavior, thoughts, or feelings.
- Positive social interaction: Taking part in social interactions for recreation, fun, and relaxation.

The clients' cognitive appraisal of the stressor as either threatening or as a controllable problem may determine how they respond (Streeter & Franklin, 1992). Hudek-Knežević and Kardum (2000) found that the immediate response to stressful events is emotional. Following the emotional response the client may make a cognitive appraisal in which the stress is perceived as either a threat to their well being or as controllable. If the stressful event is perceived of as a threat this increases the use of both emotion-focused (venting and seeking emotional support) and avoidance coping strategies. On the other hand, the appraisal of the stressor as controllable has a significant effect only on problem-focused coping such as seeking support and taking rational action. McCrae and Costa (1986) report problem-focused and some emotion-focused strategies, such as expression of emotion, turning to religion, and humor, were seen by their respondents as most effective. Wishful thinking, self-blame, avoidance, limiting affect, and passivity were seen as less effective. Wethington and Kessler (1991) reported that positive reappraisal without taking action appears ineffective at reducing stress. Similarly active cognitive coping, that is thinking of ways to make things better, without taking action is also ineffective. Religion was found to be helpful for coping with death of a loved one and other events associated with long-term loss. Overall it appears that the most effective response to stressful events is to take action to correct the situation.

What types of social support are needed?

The types of support provided by others can be emotional, instrumental, or informational (Milne, 1999; Taylor et al., 2004). According to Taylor and colleagues emotional support includes expressions of warmth, caring, and nurturing. Instrumental support includes such tangible assistance as providing goods, services, or financial aid. Informational support includes communications that help the recipient understand the stressful situation and determine what resources and coping strategies may be needed and used to deal with it.

What sources of social support are available to your clients?

Based on evidence from surveys and epidemiological studies people turn first to informal helpers for everyday emotional problems (Barker & Pistrang, 2002). Milne (1999) reports that according to a large national sample in the United Kingdom the majority of people go to their spouse for social support (Barker et al., 1990 cited in Milne, 1999). Similar results were found in the United States (Lin & Westcott, 1991) and Switzerland (Bodenmann, 2005).

Social support can range from support supplied informally by ordinary people in everyday settings to formal support supplied by people with special training such as psychologists and marriage and family therapists (Barker & Pistrang, 2002; Bodenmann, 2005; Coyne & DeLongis, 1986; Milne, 1999). Spouses and partners, family, friends, co-workers, neighbors, hairdressers, and fellow hospital patients are sources of informal social support (Barker & Pistrang, 2002; Bowing et al., 2004; Cowen, 1982; Milne et al., 1992). The role of the therapist, with regards to social support, may range from helping the client make full use of the support provided by others in the community to actively providing emotional, instrumental, or informational support (Milne, 1999).

Couples with mismatched perceptions of social support

Couples may have mismatched perceptions of their levels of social support needs just as they may have mismatches with the therapeutic alliance or with their readiness to change (Revenson et al., 2005a). Mismatches about support can come from couple differences on, for example, whether the stressful life event is controllable, who in the family should be the recipient and who should be the provider, on whether their informal support systems will provide sufficient help or whether they need to take their issues to a professional, and so on. As with other couple mismatches the therapist should promote a dialogue between the spouses first about the mismatch and then about possible solutions.

As discussed before if the decision is to change the treatment plan return to the procedures described in Chapter 4 and establish a new treatment plan. Develop a plan to help the clients improve their coping skills. Follow the procedures in Chapter 4 to get the clients agreement to the plan and to the proposed treatment. Then follow the procedures in this chapter to establish treatment adherence and treatment outcomes for the new treatment plan.

Alternative Diagnoses and Treatments

Question 5 in the *Family Therapy Decision Tree* asks, "Are there alternative treatment plans which might be more efficacious?" In considering alternative diagnoses and treatments you are returning to Therapy Task 1: Assessment. You can start by reviewing the intake information, your initial assessments, your observations of the clients affective, cognitive, and behavioral processes, which you recorded in the case notes. To this you can add your recent assessments and your recent observations. Review your assessment of the severity of the clients' problems as determined by the baseline ORS and RDAS scores and the scores on the standard assessment battery instruments. At this point if you followed the steps in the *Family Therapy Decision Tree* you will have considered some of the principle types of difficulties encountered by clients such as the therapeutic alliance, their motivation for change, and their social support coping skills. You will also need to consider your affective, behavioral, and cognitive responses related to this case. If you have not already been consulting with your supervisor on this case now would a good time to do so.

As part of your review of the case you might ask yourself a series of problem-solving questions (Mead, 1990; Polya, 1971) such as: "Have I seen information like this before?" "Are some parts of this information similar to other cases I have seen?" "How can I better order the data?" "What information appears to be missing?" "Is there too much information?" "Can I simplify the problem in some way?" "What have we done so far that appears successful?" "Is there some part of the problem we can tackle that appears promising and might prove helpful?" Included in your deliberation may be a questions about the use of medication. First, "Is the client currently on medication?" "If 'yes' is the dosage appropriate?" Second, "Should medication be tried?" "Should another medication be tried?" If medication appears to be a good option then refer your client to his or her primary care physician or to a psychiatrist.

When treating couples and families consider the possibility of split-alliances (Friedlander et al., 2006; Pinsof & Catherall, 1986), split motivation for change (Prochasca & Norcross, 2001), splits in the partners attitudes toward marital therapy (Doss, Atkins, & Christensen, 2003), and splits in their coping skills. Any split issues may need to be resolved before further progress can be made in delivering the treatment. With marital couples, where there has been no progress, the therapist may want to inquire about the possibility of other stressors, which may have been unreported. The therapist might inquire privately of each partner again about the possibility of an affair outside of the current couple relationship including Internet affairs, pornography, or about domestic violence that has not been discussed. The question you need to ask yourself and the clients is, "Are there other traumas and stressors which have been overlooked?"

Once these questions have been answered by yourself, in consultation with your clients, and in consultation with your supervisor you will need to make a decision about the next step. As stated often above the alternatives appear to be: (a) Continue the current treatment; (b) Change to a new diagnosis and treatment plan; (c) Refer to another therapist; or (d) Discontinue therapy until a suitable treatment is available. Whatever your decision some clear, specific, and timely action should be taken to safeguard the welfare of the clients.

What You Should Take Away from Chapter 5

1 Competent therapists have successful client outcomes (Wampold, 2001). Supervisors are charged with the responsibility to safeguard the welfare of clients while increasing the competence of therapist-interns.

2 Successful client outcomes are a function of the client–therapist alliance and the therapist's adherence to an empirically support treatment matched to the clients' needs and goals (Waltz et al., 1993).

3 To ensure successful outcomes you should assess continuously the therapy outcomes, the client–therapist alliance, and your adherence to the planned treatment.

4 Continuous measurement will provide you with feedback about the clients' status and your competence as a therapist.

5 Use of continuous measurement of client progress will help you identify clients in need of additional treatment, a change of treatment, or termination. This leads to a more cost-effective use of your time and better outcomes for clients (Lambert et al., 2001; Whipple et al., 2003).

6 When clients' outcome scores suggest that they are making no improvement or are deteriorating a search may be initiated for possible causes. The *Family Therapy Decision Tree* (Figure 5.3) provides suggestions about possible areas to be investigated.
Consider:
- The client–therapist alliance.
- Your adherence to the planned treatment.
- The clients' motivation to change.
- The clients' social support for coping with stress.
- The case difficulty and the possible necessity to change the treatment plan and/or change the therapist.
- Supplementing the treatment with medication.

Chapter 6

Terminating Therapy

Introduction

The goal of therapy is to help clients meet their needs and reach their goals. When clients have achieved their goals it is time to terminate treatment. The purpose of termination is to bring therapy to an orderly close. Therapy Task 5 is Termination. Termination is a natural part of therapy, which follows logically from the therapy tasks of establishing the clients' needs and goals, gaining their agreement on the treatment plan, delivery of the planned treatment, and continuous assessment of the treatment outcomes. Once the clients have achieved their goals the termination processes help the clients (a) consolidate their new skills and behavior changes, (b) prepare for the possibility of relapse, and (c) look forward to life after therapy.

Defining Termination

There is no single definition of termination (Joyce, Piper, Ogrodniczuk, & Klein, 2007). Some argue that termination is simply a transition between the work of therapy and getting on with life. Others suggest that termination is a basic element of treatment that requires significant time for completion (Lamb, 1985). Definitions vary based upon: (a) the therapy model employed by the therapist or researcher; (b) who initiated the termination; (c) when termination was initiated; and (d) reasons for termination. Although there continues to be some disagreement about how to conceptualize the termination process some criteria may be suggested (Hatchett & Park, 2003; Joyce et al., 2007; Wierzbicki & Pekarik, 1993). Termination may be defined as any act which brings therapy to a close. Successful terminations occur when the clients have successfully achieved their goals. Termination may occur after one or after any number of therapy sessions. The action to terminate may be taken by either the clients, the therapist, or by mutual agreement.

There are questions related to each of the criteria for termination. One question is how to determine if treatment has been successful and who should make that decision? For example, should treatment success be determined by the achievement of predetermined criteria established from the beginning or by the completion a specific number of sessions? The question about who should make the decision to terminate treatment is another important element in the decision to

Becoming a Marriage and Family Therapist: From Classroom to Consulting Room, First Edition. D. Eugene Mead.

terminate. Would the treatment be considered successful if the either the client or the therapist made the decision unilaterally, or must successful termination always be by mutual agreement? How you answer these questions will determine if you consider the treatment to have been completed satisfactorily or if you consider the termination to be premature. There is reason to believe that termination based upon these various definitions are significantly different events and should not be treated as the same (Hatchett & Park, 2003).

Therapy models and termination

Most therapy models would agree on the following statements (Joyce et al., 2007). First, that termination serves to bring treatment to an orderly close. Second, you should attempt to make termination as clear and specific an event as possible. Third, whenever possible termination should be a mutual decision between therapist and clients. Termination should be discussed clearly and specifically in at least one session. Finally, the termination session should include discussion of potential separation anxiety and permission for the clients to return for additional treatment if needed.

Psychoanalytic and object relations models tend to recommend several sessions to achieve the termination tasks (Curtis, 2002; Kramer, 1990; Lamb, 1985) while behavioral models either build in termination steps from the beginning or use one or more sessions to terminate depending on the length of treatment delivered (Goldfried, 2002; Ledley, Marx, & Heimberg, 2005). Short-term therapy uses a limited number of sessions (10 to 20) but need not specify the number of treatment sessions required for successful termination. Brief Therapy generally specifies the number of sessions from the beginning thus fixing the date for termination (Nelson & Politano, 1993).

Issues related to early termination

Early termination has been taken to indicate that therapy ended before the clients reached appropriate levels of improvement or before they achieved their therapy goals (Hatchett & Park, 2003). One explanation for client initiated early terminations may be a function of how early terminations are determined. Studies in which early termination was defined as clients not returning after the intake but before a session is held account for 17.6 percent of terminations (Hatchett & Park, 2003). It has been reported that in university counseling centers 19–25 percent of terminations occur after the intake (Epperson, Bushway, & Warman, 1983). In one study at a university clinic 50 percent of the clients who were assigned to a therapist other than the intake therapist did not return (Nielsen et al., 2009). Garfield (1994) argues that terminations that follow intake but occurred before treatment has begun should not be considered early terminations as, according to Garfield, therapy has not begun. Clients, on the other hand, often perceive the assessment session to be part of therapy and changes in behavior have been observed following the assessment session (Hatchett & Park, 2003). One study found that 14 percent of clients reported improvement before attending the initial session (Kopta, Howard, Lowry, & Beutler, 1994). Therefore, client decisions not to begin therapy after the intake interview could be taken as an informed decision not to enter therapy, or it could be taken, as will be discussed later, that the decision is due to the client's dissatisfaction with clinic procedures or with the therapist.

Early termination has been a major concern of the mental health fields. Early termination has received many labels such as premature termination, unilateral termination, discontinuing, drop outs, no shows, or defections (Joyce et al., 2007; Reis & Brown, 1999). Many of these labels have a pejorative flavor and may be a form of blaming the victim, that is, blaming the clients. On the other hand the use of pejorative terms may reflect therapists' anxiety about clients' early withdrawal. Therapists' anxiety may be a function of concern about the clients' welfare or it may be a function of therapists' feelings of personal or professional rejection and/or failure (Brogan, Prochaska, & Prochaska, 1999).

Clients' early withdrawal from therapy may be demoralizing to therapists and especially to beginning therapists (Garfield, 1994). This may lead to painful affective reactions on the part of the therapist. These powerful affective responses can interfere with the therapist's ability to perform with other clients and it may even disrupt the therapist's personal life.

You should not assume, however, that all client initiated early exits are treatment failures. You can develop faster as a therapist if you take each termination as a chance to learn how to improve your skills and procedures. Sincere investigation with the clients of what led to their decision to terminate can be an important step toward increasing your competence.

Clients signal readiness to terminate treatment in a number of ways. Some clients indicate readiness to end therapy by missing scheduled appointments or by failure to complete a prescribed number of appointments. When determining termination by the number of missed appointments the number of missed sessions may be established arbitrarily by the therapist. For example, some believe that early termination occurs when a client fails to return for any scheduled appointment (Hatchett & Park, 2003). Others have suggested that early termination occurs only when clients miss three appointments in a row (Tryon & Kane, 1995).

The number of sessions established as the criteria for treatment success may be established arbitrarily or it may be a function of the research that established the efficacy of the treatment model. For example, Brogan et al. (1999) report that in one study if the client discontinued treatment before completing an arbitrarily established ten sessions it was considered early termination. Termination may be established as completion of a set number of sessions as prescribed by the studies that established treatment efficacy for a particular model. Many treatment models specify a course of treatment requiring a given number of sessions for treatment success. Many of these treatments also specify criterion for success. Hansen, Lambert and Foreman (2002) found that sixteen to eighteen sessions are required for successful outcomes with many therapy models. However, if the therapist is assessing the treatment continuously and finds that the client has crossed the cutoff line for successful treatment before a specific number of sessions then termination at that point would not be considered early termination. For example, Gottman (1999) recommends fourteen sessions and also establishes criteria for successful completion. Therefore, if a marital couple achieves the criteria for successful treatment before fourteen sessions and terminates then they would not be considered early terminators.

Lambert and Ogles (2004) report that if a successful outcome is defined as the clients' achieving a clinically significant change in their outcome assessments, then 50 percent will require twenty-one weekly sessions. An additional 25 percent of clients will require approximately fifty sessions to reach clinically significant scores. If the standard for success is set at the less stringent level of a statistically reliable change then it requires seven sessions for 50 percent of the clients to reach criterion and fourteen sessions for 75 percent to reach that criterion.

As discussed earlier the clients' expectations for length of treatment is another variable related to early termination. Wierzbicki and Pekarik (1993) state that the clients' expected treatment duration in terms of number of sessions predicted actual treatment duration better than any of the other variables examined. Typically clients expect to attend fewer sessions than the number of sessions expected by therapists. Pekarik (1985) reports that 70 percent of clients expect to attend ten sessions or less and 75 percent expect improvement in five sessions. Pekarik stated that in routine practice the number of sessions completed was three to five. This appears to conform to client expectations. Termination after three to five sessions may be a function of the fact that rapid change often occurs early in treatment and is followed by smaller incremental changes in subsequent sessions (Anderson & Lambert, 2001; Howard et al., 1986; Kadera et al., 1996). It may be that when clients perceive change in the early sessions they believe they should terminate.

The discrepancy between client's and therapist's expectations for the duration of treatment may be a source of disagreement about when therapy should be terminated. This suggests that you should enter into a discussion about expectations for number of sessions required for treatment success early in the treatment process, perhaps as a part of your discussion about the treatment plan. Reducing the discrepancies between client's and therapist's perspectives on when treatment should end may increase the probability that termination will be by mutual agreement (Corning, Malofeeva, Bucchianeri, 2007; Reis & Brown, 1999).

Issues concerned with who initiates termination

There appears to be three ways that clients and therapists terminate therapy, client initiated termination, therapist initiated termination, and mutually agreed upon termination. Client initiated termination has received the most attention in the literature because client initiated terminations occur at high frequencies. Wierzbicki and Pekarik (1993) completed a meta-analysis of 125 studies across different models of therapy and found an average rate of 46.8 percent of the terminations were client initiated. Hatchett and Park (2003) estimated that the range is between 17 and 53 percent depending on how you define termination.

Client-initiated terminations

Many factors control clients' decisions to terminate therapy. As stated earlier, for some clients the act of initiating therapy by a call or by taking part in the intake session may be a sufficient behavior change to constitute a successful outcome (Hatchett & Park, 2003).

Termination by clients may be for good reasons (Hunsley, Aubry, Verstervelt, & Vito, 1999; Ledley et al., 2005; Pekarik, 1992). Research has found that some terminating clients report that they have accomplished their goals and that the problem has improved (Hunsley et al., 1999; Pekarik, 1992). Geographical moves, physical illness or incapacity, and practical constraints such as lack of transportation may be cause for not returning for therapy (Beckham, 1992; Joyce et al., 2007; Pekarik, 1985). For others money may be an issue. The client may find that therapy will be more expensive than they had assumed, or that their insurance will not cover the treatment, or that their insurance coverage has run out (Greenberg, 2002; Hunsley et al., 1999). Client motivation for therapy may be lacking, for example, clients may be disinclined to continue therapy if the treatment is required by parents, clergy, or the courts (Ledley et al., 2005). Others may lack motivation for change as they are in the pre-contemplative stage of motivation and have not yet reached the action stage (Brogan et al., 1999; McConnaughy et al., 1983; Prochaska & Norcross, 2001). Clients' unilateral decision to terminate therapy may be idiosyncratic or it may be due to interaction with the clinic and/or the therapist.

The client's decision to terminate early may be a function of client variables interacting with therapist variables. In one study 30 percent of the clients reported dissatisfaction with the therapist or the treatment as the reason they withdrew from therapy (Hunsley et al., 1999). When clients report that concerns about the therapist resulted in their decision to terminate the issues were generally negative. For example, negative first impressions of the therapist are reported to lead to early termination (Beckham, 1992; Joyce et al., 2007). Hunsley et al. found that when clients report a loss of interest in therapy they were not reporting a lack of motivation for treatment. Rather they were more often expressing lack of confidence in the therapist (Beckham, 1992; Joyce et al., 2007). Clients reported that the therapist communicated a lack of respect, warmth, and empathy, which they saw as a lack of competence (Hunsley et al., 1999; Joyce et al., 2007). As a result they were uncomfortable talking to the therapist and they lost confidence in the therapist's ability to be helpful.

When therapists report on clients' reasons for termination they often state that the clients had reached their goals (Hunsley et al., 1999). However, therapists rarely gave as a reason for termination that clients were dissatisfied with the therapist or the treatment. This appears to be true for experienced as well for beginning therapists. This may be similar to the difficulties therapists have in detecting breaches in the alliance (Safran et al., 2002). One way to avoid overlooking client dissatisfaction is to measure the alliance continuously at the end of each session with a reliable and valid assessment instrument. This will help you to catch alliance breaches and dissatisfaction with the treatment early and allow you to make repairs which may prevent early termination.

Therapist-initiated terminations

Therapist-initiated terminations appear to come about in one of two ways (Joyce et al., 2007). The most common reason for therapist initiated termination is that the therapist is about to change her or his status such as ending training, moving out of the community, or when a school semester ends. Therapist initiated terminations also occur when the therapist has made a unilateral decision that the treatment has accomplished the goals of therapy or accomplished as much as is possible at this time. According to Joyce and colleagues therapist initiated terminations are often seen by clients as the therapist having put her or his personal needs over the needs of the client. Therefore, therapist- initiated termination should be avoided if possible.

The action therapists take to terminate treatment may be in the form of a suggestion that therapy is not appropriate at this time (Joyce et al., 2007). Another action to terminate therapy taken by therapists is to suggest a referral. If the clients agree to a referral then termination is by mutual agreement. If the clients do not agree then the termination is due to therapist action.

Mutually agreed upon terminations

Mutually agreed terminations are the results of the clients' and therapist's collaborative decision that the goals of therapy have been achieved. The goal to achieve a mutually agreed upon termination starts during the assessment and feedback sessions. In the assessment sessions you should initiate a discussion with your clients about their expectations for the goals of therapy and the methods to achieve those goals. Along with the discussion of goals and methods you should initiate a discussion of the number of sessions your clients expect will be needed to achieve their therapy goals. A discussion of the number of sessions necessary fits nicely in the feedback session. Establishing mutually agreeable goals and treatment methods and an understanding of the number of sessions needed appears to have several beneficial outcomes. First, it is likely to improve the client–therapist alliance and second, it is likely to reduce the probability of client initiated early terminations. It also appears helpful to clarify, in the initial sessions, any discrepancies between you and the client concerning the severity of the client's problem. Research has found that discrepancies between the client's and the therapist's perceptions of the severity of the problems reduces the probability of reaching a mutually agreed upon termination (Croning et al., 2007).

Termination by mutual agreement may occur even when the clients have not achieved their therapy goals. If the goals have not been achieved but the therapist recommends termination because therapy seems inappropriate or because the clients are not motivated and if the clients concur, than the termination is by mutual agreement (Corning et al., 2007).

Research has found that the client's initial impressions of the therapist have a significant effect on mutually agreed upon terminations (Beckham, 1992; Hynan, 1990). When clients perceived their therapists as lacking empathy, warmth, and respect they viewed the therapist as less competent. This resulted in greater frequencies of client initiated early terminations. Similarly, therapists' negative responses to clients are associated with higher frequencies of client initiated early terminations (Joyce et al., 2007). Therefore, if you are having personal negative responses to the clients it would be well to consider transferring the clients to another therapist.

It seems clear that the beginning predicts the end in terms of mutually agreed upon terminations. You can increase the probability of mutually agreed upon terminations by (1) establishing agreement on the severity of the problem, (2) establishing mutually agreed upon goals and treatment methods, and (3) establishing agreement on the number of sessions required to achieve their goals. You will also increase the probability of mutually agreed upon terminations if you continuously assess the impact of the treatment on the clients and continuously assess the client–therapist alliance. It will help to establish the impact of the treatment if you continuously evaluate your treatment adherence. By systematically monitoring your therapy processes and procedures you will increase your competence as a therapist.

Fitting Termination Processes to the Needs of the Clients

Termination procedures need to be tailored to the needs of the clients just as do other therapy interventions. Tailoring termination to the needs of the clients begins with you recognizing when the clients are ready to terminate. When you recognize that clients are nearing termination you can help them learn to deal with relapses. Still another aspect of tailoring the termination processes to the needs of the clients is helping them deal with any separation and dependency issues.

Recognizing clients' readiness to terminate therapy

Three ways to recognize that your clients are ready to terminate are (1) positive changes in their outcome assessment scores, (2) your observations of changes in their family process behaviors, and (3) your clients' subjective reports of readiness to terminate therapy.

When you begin to observe that your clients' outcome assessment scores are approaching or have reached statistically and/or clinically significant cutoff levels then your clients are approaching time to terminate therapy. To help clients be aware of the changes they have made over the course of therapy begin by asking them to repeat the Standard Assessment Battery (Appendix C). Compare their scores at the beginning of treatment with their current scores. In addition, review with them the graphs of the outcome assessment instruments. Note the changes in trends and levels and discuss the meaning of these changes. When clients come to have a clear understanding of the changes they have made and how they have made them they are more likely to feel empowered to continue on their own after therapy terminates (Wetchler & Ofte-Atha, 1993). Give the credit for the changes they have made to the clients while minimizing your role will further empower them. Celebrate their progress and begin to talk about termination.

Another way to determine your clients' readiness to terminate therapy is to determine whether or not they are actually behaving differently (Nelson & Politano, 1993). You may observe increased frequencies of adaptive behaviors such as more efficient family processes. More efficient family processes include: (a) more equal talk time, (b) more participation in conflict resolution and problem solving, (c) increased expressions of humor, (d) more acceptance of personal responsibility; (e) lowered frequencies of statements blaming others, (f) evidence of ability to generalize family coping skills to other problem areas, and (g) existence of mutual payoffs for each family member in which change has become a function of reciprocal reinforcement rather than punishment or removal of aversive stimuli as in negative reinforcement. When you observe such changes in their behavior you should initiate a conversation about termination.

The third indication that your clients are becoming ready for termination is their self-reports. In the therapy sessions clients will begin to report to you, in one way or another, that they are experiencing relief from distress, mastery of the problems related to their symptomatic behaviors, and the ability to function without your assistance (Goldfried, 2002; Joyce et al., 2007). Some clients are able to orally articulate their subjective readiness for termination. Other clients less able to orally communicate their needs may signal that they are ready to terminate by coming late to sessions or by missing sessions. When your clients are sending messages that they are ready to terminate therapy you should open a conversation with them to explore their thoughts and feelings about termination.

Review of Your Clients' Gains in Therapy and Practicing for a Relapse

When you open a conversation with your clients about termination you will want to discuss the gains they have made in therapy, the possibility of a relapse, their feelings about terminating, and their plans for life after therapy. Use of your basic therapist skills as you discuss each of these topics with your clients will provide you with opportunities to tailor the termination process to their needs.

Another way to help clients see how they have changed over the course of therapy is to point out that slip ups and relapses are to be expected in life. Although the goal is to terminate with the clients in control of their lives you should point out that there are many external events that influence their behavior. Change in life is universal. Events in their natural and social environments may cause conflicts in their relationships, which they may find difficult to overcome. For example, the events that caused their previous difficulties may return in some surprising new form. Should a relapse happen they should attempt to use their skills to deal with it. Tell them that it is a good idea to practice a relapse before ending treatment.

Ask them to imagine a scene in which a relapse occurs and help them to rehearse the event and how they might use their skills to overcome it. Christensen, Jacobson, and Babcock (1995) have suggested several ways to initiate such a conversation. For example, they might have a conversation about some basic differences between them and to try to experience their typical reaction to those differences. They might have a conversation about an upcoming event which might trigger the problem. Yet another way to have a conversation about a relapse would be to discuss a recent negative or positive event in which the problem occurred. Encourage them to have a relapse discussion and then review the conversation with them. Ask them to remark about how they handled the problem differently now from what they did in the past. Celebrate their changes and encourage them to continue to use their skills when they encounter actual relapses after termination. Remember the goal is to put the control over their behavior in their hands. Therefore, as stated earlier, be sure to credit their use of their new skills to their behavior and down play your role in the changes they have made.

Dealing with dependency and separation anxiety at termination of therapy

Discussion of termination may raise anxiety in both you and in your clients. Therefore, if you discuss your anxiety concerning the forthcoming separation with your clients you will be modeling effective ways to cope. Help your clients see that the decision to terminate is a healthy part of the therapy process and that anxiety about separation is a natural process in relationships. Share your concerns and encourage them to share theirs. One way to deal with separation anxiety is to discuss the ups and downs of the therapy relationship you may have had with them over the course of the treatment. This conversation will serve to clarify the nature of the therapy both you and they have experienced. Point out that these experiences are a part of relationships in general. Point out to them that your goal as a therapist has been to work yourself out of a job by teaching them how to recognize their problem behaviors and how to use their skills to handle their own problems. As another defense against anxiety related to terminating treatment keep the decision to terminate therapy in the hands of your clients. For example, let them set the date for the last session.

Client dependency on the therapist appears to be a function of the clients perceiving that you are empathic to their needs and that you have the resources needed to help them relieve their distress and achieve their goals (Strong, Welsh, Corcoran, & Hoyt, 1992). The resources you have as a therapist appear to be your expertness, your trustworthiness, and your attractiveness – as perceived by your clients (Heppner & Claiborn, 1989). When the clients perceive that these conditions exist they respond with dependency behaviors, that is, they are more responsive to your guidance. When clients are responsive they are more likely to accept your ideas and to perform behaviors you suggest. Client dependency appears to be greatest at the beginning of therapy but diminishes when clients believe you do not have the resources they need or that their distress is not so great as to necessitate the effort to attend sessions. The clients' responsiveness also wanes when they begin to perceive that their needs have been met and that their goals have been achieved. As noted above when this happens it is time for the therapy to be terminated. Therefore, if the clients remain dependent beyond what appears to be time for termination it would be a good idea to explore changes in their needs and goals. If the clients' needs and goals have not changed then you should take action to resolve their dependency behaviors.

One way to shift the clients' dependent behaviors is to change the relationship from client dependence on you to interdependence. You can begin to shift the power to the clients. Empowering the clients can be accomplished by identifying that it is they who have changed their behavior to the more adaptive behaviors. A key element in empowering the clients is to reduce your power in the relationship and to increase the emphasis on the clients' ability to be in control of their own lives. This can be accomplished by shifting from you directing the activities in the sessions to helping the clients to take charge of the direction of the sessions. For example, asking the clients to determine the need for and the timing of termination is one step in this direction. You can also shift your clients' dependency on you by shifting their focus from your support to their community support systems.

After recognizing your clients' readiness to terminate, helping them consolidate their therapy gains, preparing them to deal with relapses, and helping them resolve their separation and dependency issues it is time to take the final step in termination. The final step is giving your clients permission to return to therapy in the future should the need arise.

Leaving the door open for clients to return to therapy as needed

Some clients feel that once they have been to therapy they should never need to return. Therefore, it is important to educate the clients about the nature of family behavior problems. Family behavior is strongly influenced by any number of contextual variables. For example, developmental changes in family members occurring as the result of aging, changes in the family economic conditions, and changes in the community are just some of the contextual variables influencing family behavior. Therefore, clients should not expect that they will never encounter problems again. When family behavior problems occur then they should attempt to handle them using their new skills. However, just as they would return to their family physician for the recurrence of an infectious illness they should feel free to return for therapy if their behavior problems become too difficult for them to handle. In this way you can leave the door open for the clients to return to therapy if needed in the future.

In your final session with the clients you should congratulate them on their efforts on behalf of their marriage or family. If there is unfinished business share that with them and suggest actions they can take to deal with it. Finally, you should also point out their progress, highlight their gains, and wish them well in their life after therapy.

The Written Treatment Summary

After you have completed your last session you will need to write up your case notes and also complete a written treatment summary. The treatment summary should contain the clients' demographic information, a description of the initial presenting problem, a summary of the treatment provided and the results, reasons for termination, conditions at termination, and any final recommendations you had for the clients (Appendix H). When you have completed your treatment summary take a moment to review your gains in therapist skills and competence. You are then ready to move on to another case.

What Should You Take Away from Chapter 6?

1 Termination is a natural part of therapy that follows from the therapy tasks of establishing the clients' needs and goals, establishing the treatment plan, delivering the planned treatment, and continuously assessing the outcomes.
2 After the clients have achieved their goals the termination process helps the clients consolidate their new skills, prepare for the possibility of relapse, and begin life after therapy.
3 Termination may be defined as any act which brings therapy to a close. Successful terminations occur when the clients have successfully achieved their goals. Termination may occur after one or after any number of therapy sessions.
4 The action to terminate may be taken by either the clients, the therapist, or by mutual agreement. Early termination has been a major concern of the mental health fields.
5 Mutually agreed upon termination starts in your initial sessions. Mutually agreed upon terminations are more likely when you establish agreement on: (a) the severity of the problem; (b) the therapy goals; (c) the methods to achieve the goals; and (d) the expected duration of treatment.
6 You can determine your clients readiness for termination by continuous assessment of the clients' outcome assessment scores and continuous assessment of the client–therapist alliance. Client outcome scores are a function of treatment delivery so it is important to continuously evaluate your treatment deliver.
7 You will recognize your clients' readiness to terminate when their outcome scores reach statistical and/or clinical significance. You will also determine that they are ready for termination when they have changed from dysfunctional to functional family behaviors such as more equal talk time, more participation in conflict resolution, and problem solving.
8 Orderly terminations consist of a review of the clients gains in interpersonal skills, a discussion of relapse, a conversation about separation and dependence, and permission to return to therapy should the need arise.
9 The case is not complete until you have completed your written Treatment Summary.

Part II

Protocols for Selected Models of Marriage and Family Therapy

Delivering Evidence-Based Treatments

Introduction to Part II

The advantages of evidence-based practice are first the increased probability of more successful outcomes for clients (Dane & Schneider, 1998; Kazdin, 2008) and second growing confidence and competence for you as a therapist (Margison et al., 2000; Moncher & Prinz, 1991; Waltz et al., 1993). Your skills as a therapist will increase as you seek the best instruction available from teachers and treatment manuals. Once you have mastered the cognitive skills related to the treatment you will need to practice those skills under expert supervision. The protocols provided in Part II will serve as examples of carrying out evidence-based treatments using the treatment manuals. By following the protocols you will increase the probability of helping your clients achieve successful outcomes.

Part II contains two protocols for treating marital discord, Gottman Method Couples Therapy (Gottman, 1999) and Emotionally Focused Therapy with Couples (Johnson, 2004).

Protocols are guidelines for carrying out evidence-based treatments or what is coming to be called evidence-based practice (Kazdin, 2008). The protocols presented here were developed using two criteria. First, the protocol should be based on careful consideration of the scientific evidence of the "efficacy" of the treatment (American Psychological Association, 1995). The second criterion is that the treatment should be applicable and feasible in the therapeutic setting where the therapist practices. This criterion is known as "effectiveness" or "clinical utility" (American Psychological Association, 1995).

Competent therapists have successful client outcomes. You will be more successful if you continuously assess your clients' treatment alliance and then move to correct any breaches in the alliance as soon as they occur. By continuously assessing your clients' progress on relevant outcome variables you will be better able to tailor the treatment to your clients' needs. Continuous assessment of outcome variables will also help you determine when it is time to terminate therapy. You will also increase the probability of successful outcomes by adherence to the treatment manual. Continuously assess your adherence to the treatment manual and get feedback from your supervisor on your adherence. Finally keep your treatment focused on your clients by continuous application of the common factors skills of active empathic listening and the general helping skills (Hill, 2004). The protocols presented in Part II are designed to help you learn to apply these principles.

It should be noted that the protocols presented in Part II are only guidelines and you should carefully study the treatment manual associated with the model before beginning to practice.

Becoming a Marriage and Family Therapist: From Classroom to Consulting Room, First Edition. D. Eugene Mead.

Care should be taken to study the manual designed for training professional therapists and not the manuals designed to educate the lay public. For example, if you are preparing to practice Gottman's treatment for marital discord you should Study *The Marriage Clinic: A Scientifically-based Marital Therapy* (1999) rather than Gottman and Silver's (1999) *The Seven Principles for Making Marriage Work*. As a further caveat you should not undertake to practice any of the models without the guidance of a supervisor who is qualified to practice with the model of choice.

Outline of Protocol Chapters

The goal for each protocol chapter is to provide a guide to help you deliver an evidence-based therapy model to achieve successful client outcomes. The protocols outline the procedures to follow the treatment manual step by step based. The protocols will prompt you for the equipment needed for each session. They will indicate where to administer assessments to (a) assess the clients' problems, (b) monitor the alliance, and (c) to monitor their progress. In addition, you will be prompted to monitor your treatment deliver to ensure that the full treatment "dose" is administered.

Each protocol chapter will provide the following information:

1 The bibliographic information about the treatment manual and any other textual material related to treatment delivery.
2 A description of the treatment.
3 Prescribed and proscribed treatment elements.
4 Treatment delivery.
5 Evaluating treatment delivery and outcomes.
6 Treatment termination.
7 Where to go for additional help.

Finally, all therapy sessions have a beginning, a middle, and an end. Good beginnings tie the particular session to the treatment as a whole and set the stage for the work of the session. The primary work of the session takes place in the middle of the session. In the middle of the session you will help the clients acquire the skills they need to achieve satisfactory outcomes. The end of the session reviews the skills the clients are working on and sends them home to practice. The protocols outlined in Part II make the beginnings, middles, and endings of each session clear to help you structure the session for maximum success.

Chapter 7

Protocol for Conducting Gottman Method Couple Therapy

Introduction

The goals of Gottman Method Couple Therapy (Gottman, 1999) are to rebuild and strengthen the couples' marital friendship, to help them learn to manage disagreements, and to help them build a sense of shared meaning in their relationship. First sessions are usually scheduled for two hours. Later sessions may be for one to one-and-a-half hours in duration. The full treatment is for fourteen sessions but if clients reach the criteria for success prior to fourteen sessions then treatment may be terminated. Each session begins with evaluation and understanding of the clients' current needs, an explanation of the intervention to be practiced in this session, and opportunities to practice with feedback. The clients are frequently asked to complete at home additional practice of the skills acquired in the session.

Theory and Research

Based on fourteen years of research into the causes of divorce Gottman (1994) inductively developed a theory of marital therapy. In science, the inductive method starts with the "facts" determined by research and then builds a theory to explain those facts. In contrast Johnson and Greenberg's (1985) emotionally focused couples therapy (EFT) was developed deductively from Bowlby's attachment theory (Bowlby, 1969, 1988), which in turn was derived from the works of Sigmund Freud. The inductive and deductive methods are simply two different methods of developing scientific theory. Therefore, Gottman's (1999) model, now referred to as Gottman Method Couple Therapy (GMCT: Gottman, 2004), is a science-based model designed to reduce the probability of divorce.

Gottman's (1999) theory of marital therapy focuses on three basic findings from the divorce research (Gottman, 1994). First, it was found that couples with successful marriages kept up their friendship and the romantic quality of their relationship. Second, they managed their conflicts in such a way that their disagreements did not spiral out of control. Third, they created their own personal world of shared meaning that served to separate their marital system from other systems in the community. Consequently, as stated above, the goals of Gottman's marital

Becoming a Marriage and Family Therapist: From Classroom to Consulting Room, First Edition. D. Eugene Mead.

therapy are, first to help couples rebuild and strengthen their marital friendship. Second, to help them to learn to manage conflict by changing the balance between positive and negative exchanges before, during, and after marital conflict. In addition, GMCT attempts to help couples overcome the especially negative influences created by the exchange of criticism, defensiveness, contempt, and stonewalling. Third, GMCT helps couples manage conflict by learning that there are differences between them that are not going to go away. Therefore, they need to learn to adapt to these "perpetual problems." Finally, GMCT attempts to help couples build and strengthen their sense of shared meaning. The couples shared meaning makes their marital relationship special and unique.

Preparation to practice Gottman Method Couples Therapy

As you prepare to deliver Gottman Method Couples Therapy (GMCT) you should carefully study Gottman's (1999) treatment manual. In addition you will want to read *The Marriage Clinic Casebook*, Julie S. Gottman (2004). Before attempting treatment arrange for a qualified supervisor.[1] After you have read the manual discuss the theory and research with your colleagues and your supervisor. Under the direction of your supervisor observe and discuss the training videos found on the Gottman Institute website. Rehearse the procedures from the manual before each session and be prepared to execute them in the session. To become a competent Gottman Method Couple therapist follow the manual closely. To ensure that you are following the manual observe your sessions and rate your adherence to the planned interventions[2] (see Chapter 5 this volume). Ask your supervisor to observe your sessions and to provide you with feedback concerning your adherence to the manual and to your use of your basic therapist skills. You will need to complete all three of the Gottman professional training levels in addition to three or four cases under close supervision before you will be considered a proficient entry level GMCT therapist.

The Gottman Method Couples Therapy Treatment Protocol

The interventions which are unique to Gottman Method Couples Therapy

The interventions that are unique to this theory are: interventions to build and maintain the couples' friendship, interventions to help them manage conflict, and interventions to help them build shared meanings into their relationship (Gottman, 1999; J. S. Gottman, 2004). Unique to this model is the focus on reducing or eliminating the use of criticism, defensiveness, contempt, and stonewalling, known collectively as the "four horsemen of the apocalypse" (Gottman, 1999). Also unique to this model is the use of "soft startups" in communications about couple differences. Soft startups avoid the use of the four horsemen when beginning problem-solving discussions of sensitive issues. The model also recognizes that many problems are unsolvable. These problems are labeled "perpetual" or "gridlocked" problems. Perpetual problems stem from each partner's personal history, values, and lifestyle. A key element in solving solvable problems, according to Gottman, is repair attempts. Finally, rather than try to solve perpetual problems by attempting to change each other, the couple is better served if they learn to understand each other, understand where the differences come from, and understand the importance of the issues to the other person. They can then learn to accept these perpetual problems, make compromises in their adjustment to them, and help each other realize the dreams and hopes behind their differences.

Some Gottman Method interventions that are common with other models

Gottman (1999) method therapists make use of the basic therapy skills such as empathic listening, reframing, and building goal consensus and collaboration.

Interventions which are proscribed as harmful or unsafe in Gottman Method Couples Therapy

Gottman (1999) states that it is not helpful or may even be harmful for therapists to attempt to get clients who are in conflict situations to focus on changing their inappropriate negative behaviors to more positive behaviors. Expression of anger is not contraindicated because it is associated with increased marital satisfaction over time, whereas expressions of contempt and defensiveness are reliable predictors of divorce. Therefore expressions of contempt and defensiveness are discourage and should be replaced with clear, specific requests for change followed by attempts at understanding and accepting their partner's differences.

Initial phone contact

To begin GMCT make the initial phone contact with the clients using the procedures described in Chapter 3. In the initial phone call you will make an appointment for an initial 2-hour assessment session unless they are in crisis over a gridlocked problem. In the latter case schedule a 3-hour "Dreams-Within-Conflict" session (See Sessions 9 and 10 below).

Crisis management

In applying any model of therapy you must be prepared to manage clients in crises. You need to be prepared to intervene with crisis management any time there is evidence of suicidal ideation or family violence (see Chapter 2).

Another form of crisis that marital therapists need to be prepared to treat is the couple who comes to therapy in an intense fight and apparently gridlocked over some perpetual issue. One or both spouses may present as feeling criticized, unappreciated, and unaccepted by the other (Gottman, 1999). One or both may be below the cutoff of 43 on the Revised Dyadic Adjustment Scale (RDAS: Busby et al., 1995; Thurber & Mead 2002; Appendix C). RDAS scores of 43 and below signify marital distress. They may be at serious risk for divorce with the wife's Marital Status Inventory-Revised (MSI-R: Jamieson, 2007; Appendix C) score of 7 or greater (Crane et al., 1984; Crane et al., 1995). As a couple they may be rated by you at 53 or greater on the Oral History Rating Scale (Brewer, 2004; Brewer & Mead, 2008) further indicating that the couple is at risk for divorce. To intervene in such a crisis Gottman recommends what he calls the "Dreams-Within-Conflict" 3-hour interview (See Sessions 9 and 10 below). This intervention is designed to provide the couple with "initial, rapid, dramatic change" (Gottman, 1999). Following the "Dreams-Within-Conflict" session a regular course of GMCT will be needed to effect long-term structural changes.

The Sessions

Session 1: Initial interview

1 The assessment sessions

A careful assessment will prepare you to understand the needs of the clients. Understanding what the clients bring to therapy is important because individual client characteristics have been estimated to account for approximately 40 percent of the outcome variance (Lambert & Barley 2002). Schedule two assessment sessions. The first is a two-hour conjoint session to assess their relationship variables. The second assessment session is a one-hour session with each spouse individually to determine their views of the marriage and their contributions to it.

The specific purposes of the assessment sessions are to (a) establish a therapist–client working relationship by joining with each spouse, (b) establish a client database from which to determine the clients' problems and goals, and (c) establish a treatment plan using an evidence-based therapy matched to the clients' problems and goals.

1 Assessment

Specific goals. By the end of the assessment sessions, including the return of the Standard Test Battery (SAB: Appendix C), you should be able to answer the following questions (Gottman, 1999):

1. How distressed is this couple? How do they feel about the marriage?
2. How committed is this couple to the relationship? What is their marital friendship like?
3. What are the issues that divide them? How do they regulate conflict?
4. Why are these issues such a problem for them? What is the balance between Positive and Negative Sentiment Override?
5. What are the strengths holding them together? What are their shared interests and values? How do they support each other's life dreams?
6. What can treatment do to help them? What are the potential areas of resistance?
7. Is marital therapy contraindicated?

1 Therapist's cognitive knowledge

You should read the following texts as part of your preparation:

a Gottman (1999) pp. 113–160, 396–405.
b Oral History Interview Gottman (1999) pp. 398–401.
c Oral History Rating Scale (Brewer, 2004; Brewer & Mead, 2008).
d Administering the CAC Item Ranking Scales (Appendix C).
e Observing the Clients Interaction (Appendix E).
f Marital Standard Assessment Battery (Appendix C).
g Homework Success. (Appendix J).

1 Equipment needed for the session

a Two sets of the Standard Assessment Battery in separate envelopes (Appendix C).
b Three copies (1 for you and 1 for each of the clients) of the CAC Item Ranking Scales (Appendix C).
c One copy of the Observation Rating Form (Appendix E).

d A small kitchen timer, preferably one that can be worn around your neck to free your hands.
e Two copies of the Outcome Rating Scale (Chapter 3, note 1, p. 217).
f Two copies of the Session Rating Scale (Chapter 1, note 1, p. 217).

1 Pre-session preparations

a Call the clients 24 hours before the session. Re-establish the appointment or set a new appointment. Remind them to come 15 minutes before the session to complete the ORS and RDAS.
b Before the conjoint session begins review the case file to determine how much of the following information is available. Plan to obtain the missing information.
  1 Demographic data for each partner.
  2 Medical history for each partner and current medications.
  3 Presenting complaints from each partner.
c Alert the receptionist at least 1 hour prior to the clients arrival that you will be seeing Mr. and Mrs. ______ and ask the receptionist to administer the Outcome Rating Scale (ORS: Miller & Duncan, 2004) and the RDAS (Busby et al., 1995). If the receptionist in your clinic is not able to do this then you will need to administer the ORS and RDAS at the beginning of the session.
d You will need to arrive 10 minutes before the hour to set up seating and to arrange the video cameras if videotaping is available in your clinic.

1 Beginning

a Meet the clients in the reception area and walk them to the consulting room while engaging in social conversation. Help them remove their coats and be seated comfortably.
b If the receptionist is unable to administer the ORS and RDAS then administer them at this time.
c Review your clinic's "Authorization for Clinical Services" form briefly to determine that they have completely understood it. Give special attention to issues of confidentiality and the necessity to report child abuse and elder maltreatment (see Chapters 2 and 3). Discuss with the clients the necessity for the video and the one-way screens for your supervision. Get their signatures giving permission for videotaping and/or observation on the "Authorization for Clinical Services" form. Introduce and negotiate the Fee Agreement. Get their signatures on the fee agreement.
d Crisis assessment. At any time in the initial interview or in subsequent interviews when there is reason to suspect suicidal ideation, family violence, or marital crisis switch to the appropriate interview for that crisis (see Chapter 2 of this text).
e Next, explain to the clients that the first sessions are for assessment. Tell them that the assessment sessions are used to help you find out what the issues are so you can determine what treatment is needed, if any. Explain that the third session is a feedback session in which you will share your understanding of their marital strengths and any areas that might need improvement. Then you and they will decide together if marital therapy is recommended. Point out that it may be determined that: (a) no treatment is necessary, (b) a specific treatment is recommended, or (c) the recommended treatment is not available here in which case a referral will be made. If therapy is needed then it will begin after the feedback session. Determine their concerns and questions and attempt to answer them.
f Transition to the work of the session by presenting the agenda for this session which is:
  1 To understand what brings them to marital therapy at this time.
  2 To take a history of their marital relationship.

3 To observe their communication and problem-solving skills.
4 To gather additional information by use of several assessment instruments.

1 Middle

a Begin the work of the session by asking about the clients' presenting problems. Explain that you want to hear both their stories. Ask who would like to start.
 1 Ask them "What specific issues do you have at this time?"
 2 Ask about the history of their complaints. "How long has this been going on?" or "When did it start?"
 3 Ask what they have attempted to do about this? What was successful? What was not successful?
b Take a health history. If the following information is available in the case file then proceed to the Oral History. Otherwise, ask:
 1 Is the partner currently pregnant?
 2 Do either have a history of heart problems or high blood pressure?
 3 Are there any other health issues?
 4 Is either one currently depressed or do they have a past history of depression?
 5 Is either one currently on medications?
 6 Is there currently any drug or alcohol abuse? Is there a history of drug or alcohol abuse?
c Administer a standard Oral History (Gottman, 1999, pp. 398–401).
d Take a 5-minute brake, tell everyone how to find the restrooms and the water fountain.
e The observation session. Explain the use of the CAC Item Ranking form (Chapter 3) and help them arrive at a ranking of things they want to discuss with their partner (Appendix C).
f Complete two 6-minute observation sessions from behind the one-way screen (Chapter 3).
g Ask about pleasant Rituals, Roles, Goals, Symbols, and Spirituality that they have developed in their marriage (Gottman, 1999, "Meanings Interview," pp. 403–405).
h Assign homework: Assign the Standard Assessment Battery (Appendix C).
 a Provide your clients with a rationale for the SAB. For example, tell them that information from the SAB will help you get a complete picture of their marital relations. The battery gives information that you need to help them decide what treatment is needed if any. Briefly explain, in nontechnical language, each instrument to the clients. (Information about the instruments in the standard assessment battery is found in Appendix C).
 b Get them each to commit to complete the SAB independently. Apply the steps of the Homework Success routine (Appendix J).
 c Establish a day for them to return the SABs.

1 Ending

a At approximately 40 minutes past the hour ask clients to summarize the session.
b Administer and score the SRS (Chapter 1 note 1, p. 217) and discuss a total score of 36 and below and any item score of 9 or lower.
c Thank the clients for their efforts and praise them for looking at their marriage at this time.
d Remind them of the necessity of returning the assessment materials prior to scheduling an appointment for the feedback session.
e Set a time for their individual interviews. *Important*: If you have not already done so discuss your rules for confidentiality in individual interviews with both spouses present. For an extended discussion of these issues see Chapter 3.
f Close session on time (10 minutes before the hour).
g Walk them to the reception area while engaging in social conversation.

1 Reporting/recording

a Prepare written case notes within 24 hours (Appendix D).
b Score the Oral History Rating Scale (Brewer, 2004; Brewer & Mead, 2008).
c Secure any loose materials from the session in the Case Notes Folder, for example, the SRSs, ORSs, and so on.

Session 2: Commitment to the marriage

2 Individual interviews

The purposes of the individual interviews are to determine each spouse's commitment to the marriage, their expectations for the marriage, and their expectations of therapy. In addition, the individual interviews are used to screen for family violence, ongoing affairs, and individual mental health issues.

2 The specific goals

a Continue joining with the individual spouses to build and maintain the alliance.
b Determine the individual spouses' commitment to and expectations for the marital relationship.
c Determine the individual's expectations for therapy.
d Determine if there is family violence occurring in any of the three domains in the relationship.
e Determine if there is an ongoing extramarital relationship.
f Determine if there are individual mental health issues, which may impact the relationship.
g Determine if there are other sources of stress on the relationship.

2 Therapist's cognitive knowledge

You should read the following texts as part of your preparation:

a Gottman (1999) pp. 117–118.
b Review Chapter 2 of this text for family violence issues.
c Review Chapter 5 of this text for issues related to stress.

2 Equipment needed for the session

a One copy each of the ORS and the SRS.

2 Pre-session preparations

a Call the clients 24 hours before the session. Re-establish the appointment or set a new appointment. Remind them to come 15 minutes before the session to complete the ORS and RDAS.
b Alert the receptionist at least one hour prior to the client's arrival to inform the receptionist that you will be seeing (Mr. or Ms. _______) and to ask the receptionist to administer the ORS and RDAS to her or him.
c You will need to arrive 10 minutes before the hour to set up seating and to arrange the video cameras.

2 Beginning

a Meet the client in the reception area and walk her or him to the consulting room while engaging in social conversation. Help your client remove her/his coat and be seated comfortably.
b If the receptionist is not able to administer the ORS and RDAS administer them now.
c Ask if anything has changed since last session. Listen and observe. Determine any concerns and use clinical judgment to determine if you should alter the agenda for crises related to suicide or family violence.
d Transition to the work of the session by presenting the agenda for this session. Tell them something like "In this session I want to learn from you how you are feeling about your marriage and any issues related to it. Remember that my rules for confidentially are (restate your rules, see for example Chapter 3)."

2 Middle

Begin the work of the session by asking the client about her/his specific problems. These questions do not need to be asked in any specific order but be sure to cover all the topics. If you do not ask specifically many clients will not volunteer the information. Ask something like the following questions, then listen empathically to their answers, and where appropriate follow up to get the specific details about antecedents, the specific behavior in question, and what happens after.

1 "Tell me about any concerns you might be having about the marriage."
2 "In this session I would like to hear from you about your commitment to the marriage. For example, on a scale of 1 to 10 where 10 is high how committed are you to staying in this marriage?"
3 "Have you considered divorce or separation?"
4 "How do you expect therapy to help? What would the final outcome look like for you?"
5 "How is your sexual adjustment?"
6 "In all marriages there are disagreements. Have any of the disagreements in your marriage lead to pushing, shoving, or hitting?" Follow up using questions as recommended in Chapter 2. Get information about both partner's involvement and ask about hitting, shoving, and so on with children and elders.
7 "Are you or your partner seeing someone else outside the marriage in a romantic or intimate way including Internet relationships?" If they talk about their partner listen to the story then be sure to ask about their behavior. For example, "I think I get the picture about (use partner's name) behavior. What about you? Have you ever been involved in this way with others?"
8 "Are you or your partner engaged in the use of pornography?"
9 "Have you or your partner experienced any mental health problems, either now or in the past?" Follow up about both individuals.
10 "Are there other sources of stress in your marriage? For example,
   a "Do either of you have alcohol or drug abuse problems?"
   b "Are either of you having trouble at work or in school?"
   c "Are their money problems?"
   d "How are things with your in-laws?"
11 "Have I left anything out?"

2 Ending

a Ask the client to summarize the session.
b Administer and score the SRS and discuss a total score of 36 and below and any item score of 9 or lower.

c Thank her or him for their efforts on behalf of their marriage at this time.
d If they have not already returned the assessment instruments remind them of the necessity of returning them prior to scheduling an appointment for the feedback session.
e Close session on time (10 minutes before the hour).
f Walk your client to the reception area while engaging in social conversation.

2 Reporting/recording

a Record your case notes in a timely fashion including your graph of the ORS and RDAS data. Begin graphing the ORS, RDAS, and SRS data.
b Be sure to include the report from the SRS.

Session 3: The treatment plan

The purpose of Session 3 is to present the treatment plan to the clients and to secure their permission to do therapy.

3 Specific goals

a Present the clients with your understanding of their problems and get their agreement.
b Present your proposed treatment plan.
  1 If therapy is not appropriate then terminate the case.
  2 If the needed therapy is not available at this clinic, such as treatment for drug addiction, then refer the clients elsewhere for help.
  3 If marital therapy is appropriate then describe the proposed treatment.
  4 Ask the clients' for their consent to do therapy.

3 Therapist's cognitive knowledge

You should read the following texts as part of your preparation:

a Gottman (1999), Chapter 6, pp. 179–200).
b Review Chapter 4 of this text.

3 Equipment needed

a Your Written Treatment Plan (Appendix G).
b If the decision is that no treatment is needed at this time then no other equipment is needed.
c If the decision is for referral then have the names, addresses, and phone numbers of the referral agency or therapist(s) written out and available for the clients.
d Two copies of the ORS and the SRS.

3 Pre-session preparations

a Prepare a written treatment plan (see Chapter 4).
b Call the clients 24 hours before the session. Re-establish the appointment or set a new appointment. Remind them to come 15 minutes before the session to complete the ORS and RDAS.

c Call the receptionist at least one hour prior to the clients arrival to inform the receptionist that you will be seeing Mr. and Mrs. ______ and to ask the receptionist to administer the ORS and RDAS to them.
d You will need to arrive 10 minutes before the hour to set up seating and to arrange the video cameras.

3 Beginning

a Meet the clients in the reception area and walk them to the consulting room while engaging in social conversation. Help them remove their coats and be seated comfortably.
b If the receptionist is unable to administer the ORS and the RDAS then administer them at this time. Administer the ORS at the beginning of every session. If it is not feasible to administer the RDAS at the beginning of every session then administer it at the third, sixth, last treatment session.
c Ask if anything has changed since last session. Listen and observe. Determine any concerns and use clinical judgment to determine if you should alter the agenda for crises related to suicide, family violence, or the marriage.
d If they have had an argument between sessions listen to each side briefly, making notes. Then explain that this is a feedback session and that you have taken notes and will take up this problem in the next session, which is a treatment session.
e Transition to session Middle by discussing the agenda. The agenda is to present your understanding of the problem and potential solutions. "In this session I want to share back what you have shared with me. Together we will look at all the information I have and we will consider what it suggests. After that we will decide together if therapy is needed."

3 Middle

a Review very briefly your understanding of their relationship history. Check with them for agreement.
b Present a summary of the Standard Assessment Battery information in nontechnical terms. Actual scores should not be presented but rather report in general terms such as "You scored in the moderate range for marital satisfaction which suggests that you are somewhat dissatisfied with your marriage. Does that fit with how you see things?" Check with them to see if they generally understand the findings.
c Describe your general observations of the strengths and deficits in their relationship as assessed by the Oral History Rating Scale (Brewer, 2004; Brewer & Mead, 2008) and your observations of their communication and problem-solving skills. Check with them to determine if your observations agree with theirs.
d Describe your observations of any major relationship themes and associated controlling variables. Check with them to determine if their observations agree with yours.
e Present your assessment.
   1 If your assessment suggests that no treatment is needed at this time inform them of your decision and the rationale behind it then praise them for their efforts and go to Session 3 "Ending 'A'" below.
   2 If your decision is to refer to another agency or therapist then inform them of the decision and your rationale and present them with the referral reference(s). Then go to "Ending 'A'" below.
   3 If your assessment is for GMCT then present a treatment plan which corresponds with your assessment of the problem.
      a Describe the proposed therapy model.
      b Describe the potential benefits and side effects.

c Discuss your expectations for the number of treatment sessions.
d Share their rights, right of refusal, right to request another treatment model, right to request another therapist, and right to return to the clinic without prejudice.

4 A suggested treatment plan for GMCT is presented in Box 7.1.

Box 7.1 Presenting the Gottman Method Couple Therapy Treatment Plan

A Give a brief description of Moderate and Severe Marital Relationship Problems (MRPs).
1 Couples experiencing moderate MRPs find that communication and problem-solving difficulties occur about once a week and with moderate intensity (Gottman, 1994; Jacobson and Christensen, 1996). The partners are generally willing to work together and appear moderately willing to express acceptance and tolerance of each others' differences. Their leanings toward separation or divorce are only moderate or less.
2 Severe MRPs are defined as communication and problem-solving difficulties occurring with high frequency, say, more than once a week, and with high intensity. Couples with severe MRP find it difficult to work together to solve their problems. They have difficulty accepting and tolerating each others' differences. They may have come to fear that their problems are irreconcilable and unsolvable. One or both may be thinking strongly about separation or divorce.

B You should suggest which of these two definitions you think fits this couple and then determine if they agree. If they disagree attempt to reconcile the differences. If they agree then present your treatment plan.

C Present your treatment plan.
Briefly describe the Gottman Method Couple Therapy. You need not go into much detail as this is an overview. However, do elicit their concerns and attempt to answer them. Practice the following presentation so that you can give it without leaving out any of the important details.

> GMCT will be aimed at: (a) increasing your marital friendship, (b) reducing exchanges of negative behavior, (c) increasing exchanges of positive behavior, (d) improving your skill in resolving solvable problems and learning to talk to each other about perpetual problems, and (e) increasing your bonding through shared rituals and traditions.
>
> The goal is to understand how your differences cause the distress you are feeling in your marriage and to understand that your distress is a response to the differences and not to your partner. It is the process not the people which is the problem.
>
> None of this will be easy. Because you will be confronting your basic differences there will be emotional stress. It will take real effort to overcome old patterns and acquire new ones. However, 75–85 percent of the couples who stay with the treatment find their marriages to be more rewarding and less stressful.
>
> Should you choose not to accept this treatment I can transfer you to another therapist who may offer another form of treatment. Of course, you always have the option of not entering treatment at this time and you may drop out of treatment at any time without penalty. However, in cases of moderate and severe marital relational

problems the research suggests that these problems will not get better on their own. They either stay the same or get worse.

Therefore, I am recommending that we treat your problem with GMCT which is the treatment I just described. Are you willing to accept this treatment?

D If they agree then determine their commitment to work together for 10 to 14 sessions of about 1 hour each. Tell them they may be able to end with fewer sessions if they really work hard both in the therapy sessions and at home.

Ask, "How much are you personally committed to work on strengthening this marriage? Rank your commitment to personally work to strengthen this marriage on a scale of 1 to 10 where 1 is hardly willing to work at all and 10 is totally committed. Remember, this is your personal commitment."

Get a ranking from each partner and write it down to be entered in the case notes.

E If the clients' agree to GMCT set an appointment for the first treatment session. If they do not agree then according to their desires: (a) refer, or (b) no treatment.

F If you wish to use Gottman and Silver's text *The Seven Principles for Making Marriage Work* as a workbook then recommend that they check it out from their local library or purchase a copy.

G Begin closing the session about 20 minutes before the hour.

H Go to Session 3 "Ending 'B'" below.

3 Ending 'A'

a Ask the clients to summarize the session.

b Administer and score the SRS and discuss a total score of 36 and below and any item score of 9 or lower.

c Thank the clients for their efforts and ask if there is anything else you can do for them. Remind them that they may return to the clinic at any time.

d Close the session on time (10 minutes before the hour).

e Walk them back to the reception area while engaging in social conversation.

3 Ending 'B'

a If treatment is recommended and accepted then establish a time and date for the next session.

b Ask them to come 15 minutes early to complete the ORS and the RDAS. Ask them to each bring a spiral bound notebook or electronic device to the next session so that they can keep track of homework assignments.

c Administer and score the SRS and discuss a total score of 36 and below and any item score of 9 or lower.

d Close the session on time (10 minutes before the hour).

e Thank them for their efforts to strengthen their marriage.

f Walk them back to the reception area while engaging in social conversation.

3 Reporting/recording

Record your case notes in a timely fashion including your graph of the ORS and RDAS data.

Session 4: Marital friendship

4 Specific goal

The specific goal for Session 4 is to increase the couple's marital friendship by beginning to change the balance from negative sentiment override to positive sentiment override. This is accomplished by reducing the exchange of negative behavior, which leads to negative sentiment override and increasing the exchange of positive behavior to increase the probability of positive sentiment override.

4 Therapist's cognitive knowledge

You should read the following texts as part of your session preparation:

a Review the treatment manual Gottman (1999) pp. 191–193, 201–217, 379.
b Review "Delivering the Planned Treatment" in Chapter 4 of this text.
c Read the material on: "Four Horsemen Defined" (Gottman, 1999, pp. 41–48; Gottman & Silver, 1999, pp. 26–34).

4 Equipment needed

As a general rule have enough copies so you can give one to each of the clients and have one for yourself to read as you are instructing them in its use.

a Gottman's Appendix B, "Love Maps Questionnaire Gottman" (1999, p. 379).
b "Love Maps 20 Questions Game," (Gottman 1999, pp. 203–204; Gottman & Silver, 1999, pp. 52–54).
c "Real Map of Your Partner's Everyday Life," (Gottman, 1999, Table 7.2, p. 205; Gottman & Silver, 1999, pp. 55–56).
d Two copies each of the ORS and the SRS.
e Your timer.

4 Pre-session preparations

a Make a pre-session phone call, to the clients, 24 hours before the appointment. Re-establish the appointment or reset the appointment. Remind them to come in 15 minutes early to complete the ORS and the RDAS.
b Call the receptionist at least one hour prior to the clients' arrival to inform the receptionist that you will be seeing Mr. and Mrs. _______ and to ask the receptionist to please administer the ORS and RDAS to them.
c You will need to arrive 10 minutes before the hour to set up seating and to arrange the video cameras.

4 Beginnings

a Meet the clients in the reception area and walk them to the consulting room while engaging in social conversation. Help them remove their coats and be seated comfortably.
b If the ORS and RDAS were not administered by the receptionist then administer them at this time. Score the ORS and RDAS and add the scores to the graph on their chart.
c Ask if anything has changed since last session. Listen and observe.
d Review the ORS and RDAS graphs briefly with your clients.

e Based on the clients' responses to the "Has anything changed?" question and the ORS and RDAS information determine if there are any concerns and use clinical judgment to determine if you should alter the agenda for crisis related interventions such as suicide, dangerousness, or marital crisis. If the clients are not in crisis then continue with the planned interventions for this session.
f Transition to Session 4 Middle by discussing the agenda. The agenda is to increase their marital friendship by increasing their understanding of each other's personal world , what Gottman calls "love maps," and by reducing exchanges of negative behavior.

4 Middle

a Present the clients with the "Love Maps Questionnaire" (Gottman, p. 379). If you are using Gottman and Silver's text *The Seven Principles for Making Marriage Work* as a workbook then point out that they can read about love maps on pp. 47–56.
b Read the instructions with them or ask them to read the instructions for themselves. Ask if they have any questions.
c Ask them to take the "Love Map Questionnaire" and score it.
d Point out that it is not unusual for individuals experiencing marital distress to score below 10. Even if they score above 10 they can always improve their love maps scores in the future. One way to do that is to play the "Love Maps Twenty Questions Game."
e Hand out copies of the "Love Maps Twenty Questions Game" (pp. 203–204; Gottman & Silver, 1999, pp. 52–54).
  1 Ask them to write down a column of twenty numbers between 1 and 60 in their notebooks.
  2 Ask who would like to go first. Ask [use their name] to ask their partner their first question.
  3 If the partner is correct then she or he gets the points assigned for the question and the person asking the question gets 1 point. If the answer is not correct then no one gets any points.
  4 They are to proceed taking turns until each have asked all 20 questions.
  5 Explain that although the person who gets the most points after 20 questions "wins" they both win by getting to know each other better.
f Assign homework
  Point out that they can repeat this game often, and they should. Assign the game to be played at least once in the coming week as their homework assignment.
g Go to Session 4 Ending.

4 Ending

a At approximately 40 minutes past the hour begin ending the session.
b Ask the clients to summarize the session. Reinforce the parts they got correct and provide tentative corrective feedback for parts that appear to be off track.
c Administer and score the SRS (Chapter 1 note 1, p. 217) and discuss a total score of 36 and below and any item score of 9 or lower.
d Assign homework. Ask them to play the "Love Maps Twenty Questions Game" at least once during the week. If they are using Gottman and Silver (1999) assign pp. 1–60 and especially pp. 47–56. Use the Homework Success routine (Appendix J).
e They should be instructed not to try to resolve their difficulties at home. If issues arise they should "save" them for the next session.
f Thank them for their efforts on behalf of their marriage. Set an appointment for the next session then walk them to the reception area.

4 Reporting/recording

A Session 4: Reporting/Recording. Within 24 hours:
  1 Secure any loose materials from the session in the Case Notes Folder.
  2 Record your case notes in a timely fashion including your graph of the ORS and RDAS data.

Session 5: Increasing marital fondness and admiration

The goal for Session 5 is to increase the clients' feelings of fondness and admiration for each other by presenting Gottman's Intervention Sets 2 to 10. You will help your clients learn to increase their appreciation for each other's good qualities and to focus on what they admire in the present rather than on what is missing.

Tailor your interventions to the needs of your clients by selecting from the Fondness and Admiration Systems Interventions to increase their exchange of positive behaviors.

5 Therapist's cognitive knowledge

The following texts should be read as part of your preparation:

a Review Gottman (1999) pp. 203–213, 191–193.
b Review Chapter 5.

5 Equipment requirements

a Three copies of Gottman's "I Appreciate . . ." Adjective Checklist (Gottman, 1999, p. 207 or Gottman and Silver, 1999, pp. 68–69).
b Three copies of Gottman's Thanksgiving List (p. 208)
c Three copies of Gottman's Table 7.8 Building the Fondness and Admiration System (7-week Program).
d Two copies each of the ORS and the SRS.
e Your timer.

5 Pre-session preparations

Repeat the Pre-session Preparations from Session 4.

5 Beginnings

a–c As per session 4 pre-session preparations.
d After determining that the clients are not in crisis ask about the homework assignment which was to play the Love Maps Twenty Questions Game at least once. If they were successful celebrate with them. If they forgot or were unsuccessful explore what got in the way or what went badly. Help them to analyze the problem and to plan to carry it out successfully in the coming week (Appendix J, Homework Success). Remind them that the goal is to increase their marital friendship as a basis for the later exercises in the treatment program. Your stance should be one of acceptance using your basic therapy skills. Avoid blaming by focusing on process rather than people. Validate their difficulties, reinforce with praise their efforts, and encourage further attempts.
e Transition to Session 5 Middle by discussing the agenda. The agenda is to increase their marital friendship, fondness, and appreciation.

5 Middle

a *Appreciation exercise* Present your clients with Gottman's "I Appreciate . . ." Adjective Checklist (p. 207 or Gottman and Silver, 1999, pp. 68–69).
 1 Instruct them using Gottman's (1999) instructions on p. 206, Intervention 4. If they need help getting started ask what others appreciate about their partner, for example, mother, father, brothers and sisters, friends, teachers, and so on.
 2 Listen and comment on their use of positive statements.

b *Thanksgiving exercise* Present them with the Thanksgiving Checklist and instruct them to select three qualities they really appreciate about their spouse (Gottman, pp. 206–207, Intervention 5). They are then to take turns sharing the items they have selected along with their reasons they are thankful for that quality in their spouse.

c Assign homework.
 1 *Building fondness.* Share copies of Gottman's Table 7.8 Building the Fondness and Admiration System (7-week Program) or if they are using Gottman & Silver (1999) assign them to use pp. 72–77.
 2 Ask them to read the instructions. Ask for any questions or concerns. Attempt to respond to their questions and concerns.
 3 Ask them to read Week 1 and ask for any questions or concerns. Ask if they foresee any difficulties in the assignment. Attempt to help them plan to carry out the homework assignment (Appendix J).

d Go to Session 5 Ending.

5 Ending

a Begin ending the session at 40 minutes after the hour. Ask the clients to summarize the session. Provide reinforcement and corrective feedback as needed.

b Begin by asking them to perform the following as assignments at home:
 1 Ask them to tell their partner about the things they appreciate at least once a day.
 2 Whenever they feel distressed by their partner they should review the Thanksgiving List (see Gottman, 1999, Intervention 6, pp. 208–209).
 3 Begin Week 1 of the Seven-Week Fondness and Admiration program. Ask them to bring their homework and their copies of Gottman's Table 7.8 to the next session.
 4 Commiserate with them about the amount of homework this week. Point out that the goal is to increase their marital friendship, fondness, and appreciation before starting on somewhat more difficult exercises.
 5 Administer and score the SRS. Discuss a total score of 36 or lower or any items which are 9 or lower.
 6 Thank them for their efforts on behalf of their marriage. Set an appointment for the next session then walk them to the reception area.

5 Reporting/recording

Record your case notes in a timely fashion including your graph of the ORS and RDAS data.

Session 6: Increasing marital fondness and admiration

The goal for Session 6, Gottman's "Intervention Sets 11–14," is to increase the positive sentiment override by learning how to reduce stresses in their daily lives and how to sooth themselves and each other. The purpose is to help them make their home a haven from stress by teaching them how to receive support from each other (Gottman, 1999, pp. 213–217). Intervention Sets 11 to 14 may require several sessions to allow the clients to practice the skills to criterion prior to practicing at home.

Tailor the order and number of these exercises to the needs of the clients.

6 Specific goals

6A Learning to identify the strengths in their relationship.
6B Learning to use stress-reducing conversations.
6C Learning to communicate their needs for their partner's support, that is learning to turn toward one another rather than turning away.
6D Learning to sooth themselves and each other by:
  1 Learning to relax through relaxation training.
  2 Learning to sooth each other.

6 Therapist's cognitive knowledge for Sessions 6A, 6B, 6C and 6D

Read the following in preparation:

a Review Gottman (1999), pp. 201–217, 380–386.
b For 6A review Intervention 11, p. 213.
c Review "Social Support" in Chapter 5.

6A Equipment needed

a Three copies of Gottman's (1999) Areas of Strength Checklist p. 373.
b Two copies of Gottman's Table 7.8, pp. 212–213 in case they forget theirs.
c Two copies each of the ORS and SRS.
d Your timer.

6A Pre-session preparations

Repeat the pre-session preparations from session 4.

6A Beginnings

a–c Repeat steps A–C from Session 4 then go to D as follows.
d After determining that the clients are not in crisis ask about the homework assignment which was:
  1 To do Week 1 of the Seven-Week Course in Fondness and Admiration (Gottman & Silver, 1999, pp. 72–77). Ask them to report on their progress by sharing some of the following:
    a A loveable or endearing characteristic of their partner.
    b Their good time paragraph.
    c Their recall of a romantic moment.
    d A physical attribute they like about their partner.
    e A quality about their partner that makes them proud.

2 Celebrate success in their homework assignments be supportive and validate any difficulties.
   a Share one and only one suggestion for improvement where appropriate.
   b If they forgot or were unsuccessful explore what got in the way or what went badly. Help them to analyze the problem and to plan to carry it out successfully in the coming week (Appendix J, Homework Success). Remind them that the goal is to increase their marital friendship as a basis for the later exercises in the treatment program.
   c Your stance should be one of acceptance using your basic therapy skills. Avoid blaming by focusing on process rather than people. Validate their difficulties, reinforce with praise their efforts, and encourage further attempts.
   d Remember that if you do not follow up on homework assignments they will soon cease to carry them out.

e Transition to the middle of the session by setting the agenda. The agenda for Session 6A is to evaluate the strengths in their marriage.

6A Middle

a *Building marital strengths.* Provide each spouse with a copy of Gottman "Areas of Strengths Checklist".
   1 Tell them something like, "This is a list of things that some couples have wished to strengthen in their relationship. Please look at the list independently and do the following. If the item is already a strength in your marriage circle the item number and then go on to the next item. If an item is not a strength in your marriage but you believe it would be good to build strength in that area then indicate how important you think it is by circling 1 to 5 where 1 = important but not very important and 5 = very important.
   2 After they have both independently completed the checklist ask them to face each other and to go over the list together.
   3 Tell them that they are to jointly decide which areas are strengths and which might take some improvement. Be prepared to intervene when there is criticism, defensiveness, contempt, or stonewalling (Gottman, 1999, pp. 91–193).
      a Set your timer for 6 minutes and ask them to complete the exercise above. When time is up help them celebrate their strengths and tell them that they will be finding ways to build more strengths over the course of therapy.
      b If time permits ask them to repeat the exercise making it better.

b Assign homework.
   1 For homework assign them to notice their partners strengths and tell the other person about at least one strength they notice daily. They can use the same strength on more than one day but to keep looking for other strengths as well.
   2 Determine which week of the Seven-Week course they have completed and ask them to go on to the next week.
   3 If they are using Gottman and Silver ask them to read pp. 79–86 together as preparation for the next session.

c Go to Session 6A Ending.

Session 6B: Stress reducing conversations

6B Therapist's cognitive knowledge

The following should be read in preparation Gottman (1999) "Intervention 12" (pp. 213–214).

6B Equipment needed

a Three copies of Gottman's Table 7.9, p. 215 "Deposits to Your Emotional Bank Account" (1999).
b Two copies each of the ORS and SRS.
c Your timer.

6B Pre-session preparations

Use the Pre-session Preparations from Session 4.

6B Beginnings

a–c Use the Beginnings steps A–C from Session 4
d After determining that the clients are not in crisis ask about the homework assignment.
  1 Determine which week of the Seven-Week program they are on and review the specific assignments for that week with them (Gottman, 1999, pp. 212–213).
  2 Celebrate success in their homework assignments be supportive and validate any difficulties.
    a Share one and only one suggestion for improvement where appropriate.
    b If they forgot or were unsuccessful explore what got in the way or what went badly. Help them to analyze the problem and to plan to carry it out successfully in the coming week (Appendix J, Homework Success in this text). Remind them that the goal is to increase their marital friendship as a basis for the exercises which are to come later in the treatment program.
    c Your stance should be one of acceptance using your basic therapy skills. Avoid blaming by focusing on process rather than people. Validate their difficulties, reinforce their efforts with praise, and encourage further attempts.
    d Remember that if you do not follow up on homework assignments they will soon cease to carry them out.
e Transition to the middle of the session by setting the agenda. The agenda for Sessions 6B is: Learning to have stress-reducing conversations on a daily basis.

6B Middle

a Tell them that the purpose of stress-reducing conversations is to help them deal with the stresses of everyday life such as job stress, issues with the neighbors, car repairs, and so on. The issues should not be directly related to their marital issues. Couples who regularly take time for stress-reducing conversations at the end of each day are much less likely to end up in divorce.
b Give them each a copy of Gottman's Table 7.9: "Deposits to Your Emotional Bank Account." Ask them to read each bulleted item and ask questions. Answer their questions and resolve any concerns. Emphasize the item on "Listening and not giving advice."
c Point out that the purpose of Stress-reducing Conversations is to help with day to day external stresses such as occur on the job, at home, or at school. Ask them to "*discuss a recent or upcoming stress in each of their lives that is not related directly to a marital issue (like an upcoming visit to in-laws or a business venture)*" (Gottman, 1999, p. 214, italics in original).
d Remind them that the goal of the stress-reducing conversations is to listen to their partner, not to solve the problem for them. At the end if your partner wants advice or a solution they can ask for it. So wait to give advice until asked. As Gottman says, "*Understanding must precede advice*" (p. 214, italics in original).

e Point out to both that it is important to separate themselves from the stresses that their partner is describing. They should attempt not to see this stress as a marital problem. Be especially careful not to respond with complaints and criticisms of your own as you will have your turn (see also Social Support in Chapter 5 in this text).
   1 Ask who would like to go first, set your timer for 6 minutes and start. Note: tell them that 6 minutes is the interval for practice in the session. At home they should allow about 15 minutes each.
   2 Process the conversation with them to eliminate the Four Horsemen. Provide support and encouragement pointing up all the things they did right. Make one correction if needed.
   3 Then set your timer for 6 minutes and ask the other partner to take a turn sharing a stressful event. Ask the first partner to take the role of listener following the procedures outlined above.
   4 After the second partner has shared a stressful event ask them to process the conversation. Provide support and encouragement pointing up all the things they did right. Make one correction if needed.
   5 Next ask them to have a conversation about how they can build this kind of a conversation into each day. Use the Homework Success procedures (Appendix J).

f Assign homework
   1 Determine which week of the Seven-Week program they have completed and assign the next week.
   2 If you are using Gottman and Silver (1999) recommend they read pp. 87–92 to prepared for Session 6C.

g Go to session 6B Ending.

Session 6C: Communicating needs and learning to turn towards each other

6C Therapist's cognitive knowledge

Read the following in preparation: Gottman (1999) "Intervention" 13, p. 214.

6C Equipment needed

a Three copies of Gottman's "Turning Toward During Everyday Events Checklist" pp. 370–372.
b Two copies each of the ORS and SRS.
c Your timer.

6C Pre-session preparations

Use the pre-session Preparations from Session 4.

6C Beginnings

a–c A–C from Session 4
d After determining that the clients are not in crisis ask about the homework assignment:
   1 Determine which week of the Seven-Week program they are on and review the specific assignments for that week with them (Gottman, 1999, pp. 212–213).
   2 Celebrate success in their homework assignments be supportive and validate any difficulties.

e Transition to Session 6C Middle by sharing the agenda which is "Learning to communicate their needs for their partner's support, that is learning to turn toward one another rather than turning away."

6C Middle

a Provide them each with a copy of Gottman's "Turning Toward During Everyday Events Checklist" (pp. 370–372). If you are using Gottman and Silver (1999) suggest that they read pp. 79–97 at home.
   1 Ask them to read the instructions and ask any questions as they go. Answer their questions and then ask them to complete the checklist independently.
   2 Once they have completed the checklist ask them to turn toward each other and discuss their responses. They should attempt to understand the other's desires and point of view. Set your timer for 6 minutes. Ask them to discuss ways they can be more supportive around each other's desires. Remind them to avoid use of the Four Horsemen.
   3 When they have finished their conversation have them process the conversation. If they have not finished the Checklist ask them to do so at home.
   4 Next ask them to have a conversation about how they can build a "Turning Toward During Everyday Events" conversation into each day.

b Assign homework
   1 Ask them to have a conversation about "Turning Toward During Everyday Events" conversation each day. Use the Homework Success procedures (Appendix J).
   2 Determine which week of the Seven-Week program they have completed and assign the next week.
   3 If you are using Gottman and Silver (1999) recommend they read pp. 172–182 to prepared for Session 6D.

c Go to Session 6C Ending.

Session 6D: "Learning to sooth themselves and each other."

6D Therapist's cognitive knowledge

In preparation read: Gottman (1999) "Intervention 14," p. 215, 231–233.

6D Equipment needed

a Three copies of Gottman's Relaxation Instructions pp. 216–217.
b Two copies each of the ORS and SRS.

6D Pre-session preparations

Use the pre-session preparations from session 4.

6D Beginnings

a–c Steps A–C from Session 4 beginnings.

d After determining that the clients are not in crisis ask about the homework assignment.
   1 Determine which week of the Seven-Week program they are on and review the specific assignments for that week with them (Gottman, 1999, pp. 212–213).
   2 Celebrate success in their homework assignments be supportive and validate any difficulties.

      Share one and only one suggestion for improvement where appropriate.

e Transition to Session 6D Middle by sharing the agenda. The agenda is to learn to sooth themselves and each other.

6D Middle

a Provide them with copies of Gottman's (1999) Relaxation Instructions pp. 216–217.
b Give a rationale for relaxation training.
  1 The goal of relaxation training is to prepare you to self-sooth and to sooth each other whenever you become emotionally aroused in your discussions of your marital differences. The idea is to make your marriage a place to go for refuge from the stresses and storms of life. Relaxation is useful in any stressful or anxiety provoking situation. For some couples this proves to be the best method of soothing during a time out in their conflict discussions.
  2 Use time out when one or both begin to be flooded with emotion as evidenced by a racing heart, shallow breathing, and a pulse rate of 95 bpm or greater. Take a minute to teach them how to take their pulse rate with fingers on the artery in their throat for 30 seconds then multiply by 2. Explain that one of the most effective means to combat flooding is by relaxing. Therefore, the goal should be to learn to relax completely wherever and whenever one begins to feel flooded with emotion.
  3 Ask which one wants to be first at helping their partner relax. This person will be the reader or you may be the reader. The other partner gets into a reclining chair, if available, and if they choose to do so they may loosen any tight clothing and removes their glasses preparing to relax completely.
    a The reader instructs their partner to lean back in the chair and close their eyes.
    b The reader then reads the script in a quiet, soft, soothing voice. Do not hurry the presentation.
    c After the script ask how they responded to the relaxation training. Answer any questions and respond to their concerns.
  4 Ask them to switch places and repeat the steps in 3 above.
c Go to Session 6D Ending.

6A Ending

a Ask the clients to summarize the session. Provide reinforcement and corrective feedback as appropriate.
b Remind them of the homework assignments.
  1 Determine which week of the Seven-Week program they are on. Ask them to continue the Seven-Week course by going to the next week's exercises. Determine if there are any issues (Appendix J, Homework Success).
  2 For homework assign them to notice their partners strengths and tell the other person about at least one strength they noticed daily. They can use the same strength on more than one day but to keep looking for other strengths as well.
c See "Generic ending" below (p. 171).

6B Ending

a Ask the clients to summarize the session. Provide reinforcement and corrective feedback as appropriate.
b Remind them of the homework assignments.
  1 Determine which week of the Seven-Week program they are on. Ask them to continue the Seven-Week course by going to the next week's exercises. Determine if there are any issues (Appendix H, Homework Success).

   2 For homework ask them to have a stress-reducing conversation each day for the coming week. Tell them "This may be some of the best 20 to 30 minutes they spend on behalf of their marriage."
c See "Generic ending" below.

6C Ending

a Ask the clients to summarize the session. Provide reinforcement and corrective feedback as appropriate.
b Remind them of the homework assignments.
   1 Determine which week of the Seven-Week program they are on. Ask them to continue the Seven-Week course by going to the next week's exercises. Determine if there are any issues (Appendix J, Homework Success).
   2 For homework ask them to have a conversation about "Turning Toward During Everyday Events" conversation into each day. Use the Homework Success procedures (Appendix J).
c See "Generic ending" below.

6D Ending

a Ask the clients to summarize the session. Provide reinforcement and corrective feedback as appropriate.
b Remind them of the homework assignments.
   1 Determine which week of the Seven-Week program they are on. Ask them to continue the Seven-Week course by going to the next week's exercises. Determine if there are any issues (Appendix J, Homework Success).
   2 For homework ask them to practice relaxation with each other at least two times in the coming week, more if they like!
c See "Generic ending" below.

Generic ending for 6A to 6D

a Administer and score the SRS. Discuss a total score of 36 or lower or any items which are 9 or lower.
b Thank them for their efforts on behalf of their marriage. Set an appointment for the next session then walk them to the reception area.

6A to 6D Reporting/recording

Record your case notes in a timely fashion including your graph of the ORS and RDAS data.

Session 7: Solving solvable problems

The goal for Session 7 is to help the clients learn to determine which are solvable problems and which are gridlocked or perpetual problems. In this session they will work on solving a solvable problem. To solve problems they will learn to use four basic skills: soft startups; repair and de-escalation; accepting influence and compromise; and soothing. It may require more than one session for the clients to practice the skills to criterion prior to practicing at home.

Tailor the order and number of these exercises to the needs of the clients. The sessions are as follows:

7A Soft startups.
7B Repair and de-escalation.
7C Accepting influence and compromise.
7D Soothing.

Session 7A: Soft startups

7A Therapist's cognitive knowledge

You should read:

a For Session 7 review Gottman (1999) pp. 41–56, 74–85, 218–233, 281–287, 383–387.
b Review Chapter 5 in this text
c Specific for Session 7A read Gottman pp. 220, 224–225.

7A Equipment needed

a Three copies of the following:
 1 Gottman (1999) Solvable Problems Intervention 1. Copy the "Examples" (p. 224) and p. 225 the first three paragraphs down to "Exercise."
 2 Rules for Softened Startup (Gottman, Table 8.3, pp. 226–227).
 3 Exercises on Softened Startup (Table 8.4, pp. 228–229).
b Case notes with their CAC Item Ranking forms which you obtained following Session 2 above as part of the Standard Assessment Battery (Appendix C). Alternatively you could use the "Gottman Areas of Change Checklist: Solvable Problems" (pp. 361–362).
c Two copies each of the ORS and SRS.
d Your timer.

7A Pre-session preparations

Repeat the Pre-session Preparations from Session 4.

7A Beginnings

a–c Repeat steps A to C from Session 4 then go to D as follows.
d After determining that the clients are not in crisis ask about the homework assignment.
 1 Determine which week of the Seven-Week program they are on and review the specific assignments for that week with them (Gottman, 1999, pp. 212–213).
 2 Celebrate success in their homework assignments, be supportive and validate any difficulties.
 Share one and only one suggestion for improvement where appropriate.
e Transition to Session 7A by setting the agenda which is to teach soft startups.

7A Middle

a Present the clients with Gottman (1999) Table 8.3 "Rules for Softened Startup" (pp. 226–227). Ask them to individually read over the rules for soft startups one rule at a time. After each bullet point ask if they have any questions or concerns. Attempt to answer their questions and concerns.

Point up the difference between complaints and criticisms.
   a Complaints are generally "I" statements.
   b Complaints do not blame the other partner.
   c Complaints do not put the other person down.
   d Complaints do not use the words *always* and *never.*
   e A list of multiple complaints becomes criticism.

b Hand them their CAC items and ask them to each pick an easy item. Alternatively use the "Gottman Areas of Change Checklist" (pp. 361–362). Take turns starting a conversation about an easy item using soft startups.
   1 After each discussion ask them to point out all the soft startup things they did right.
   2 Provide feedback on the things they did right. Provide one, and only one, area for improvement.

c Ask them to try again making their soft startup even better.
   1 After each discussion ask them to point out all the soft startup things they did right.
   2 Provide feedback on the things they did right. Provide one, and only one, area for improvement.

d Caution them not to try this at home unless they are 80 to 90 percent sure they can do soft startups successfully.

e Assign homework
   1 Hand them copies of the Exercises on Soft Startups (Gottman, pp. 228-229). Ask them to do this exercise at home. They are to do this exercise individually. Suggest that they cover the answers with a sheet of paper and then do each topic. After they have done the topic they should look at the answer. When they have completed the exercise they can talk it over with each other.
   2 Determine which week of the Seven-Week program they are on. Ask them to continue the Seven-Week course by going to the next week's exercises. Determine if there are any issues and attempt to resolve them.

f Go to Session 7 Ending.

Session 7B: Repair and de-escalation

7B Specific goals

a Teach the couple to repair negative communications and de-escalate conflict situations.
b Gottman regards Repair Attempts as a critical element in GMCT.

7B Therapist's cognitive knowledge

The following should be read in preparation:

a Gottman (1999) p. 218, 220, 224, 225, 227. Note that the narrative on these pages is interrupted by tables of various kinds.
b Review your case notes with attention to the clients' CAC Item Ranking forms. The CAC rankings were obtained following Session 2 above as part of the Standard Assessment Battery.

7B Equipment needed

a Three copies of the following:
   1 Gottman (1999) Table 8.5 "Gottman Repair Checklist" (p. 230).
   2 Gottman (1999) Table 8.2 "Solvable Problems Checklist" (pp. 221–223).
   3 Gottman (1999) Table 8.1 "Perpetual Issues" (pp. 219–220).

4 From your case notes three copies of the clients' CAC Item Ranking forms which you obtained following Session 2 above as part of the Standard Assessment Battery. Alternatively you could use the "Gottman Areas of Change Checklist: Solvable Problems" (Gottman (1999) pp. 361–362).

b Two copies each of the ORS and SRS.

c Your timer.

7B Pre-session preparations

Repeat the Pre-session Preparations from Session 4.

7B Beginnings

a–c Repeat steps A to C from Session 4.

d After determining that the clients are not in crisis ask about the homework assignment which was

1 Ask about their practicing soft startups at home.

2 Determine which week of the Seven-Week program they are on and review the specific assignments for that week with them (Gottman, 1999, pp. 212–213).

e Transition to the middle of Session 7B by setting the agenda. The agenda for Session 7B is to teach repair and de-escalation.

7B Middle

a Explain that when couples are discussing a point of disagreement or conflict they just naturally make bids for repair. Hand them each a copy of "Gottman Repair Checklist 5" (Gottman, 1999, Table 8.5, p. 230). Ask them to read over the entire list and ask any questions they may have.

b Next hand them copies of their CAC Item Ranking forms from their case file. Alternatively you could use the "Gottman Areas of Change Checklist: Solvable Problems" or Gottman (1999) Table 8.5 "Gottman Repair Checklist." The goal here is to provide the clients with material to prompt them in picking a solvable problem.

c Ask them to select an easy problem to discuss. Ask them to choose a problem that is solvable. If they appear to pick a perpetual issue you may share copies of Table 8.1 "Perpetual Issues" (Gottman, pp. 219–220) with them to help distinguish between solvable and perpetual problems.

d After they have selected a solvable problem ask them to have a discussion about the issue for 6 minutes.

1 Ask them to start this discussion with a soft startup.

2 While having a discussion about a solvable problem they are to avoid use of the Four Horsemen (Gottman, 1999, p. 68). If one of the Four Horsemen occurs they are to stop and announce that they are attempting to offer a Repair Attempt. They then select one of the repair attempt procedures from the Gottman Repair Checklist.

3 The person receiving the Repair Attempt makes an effort to find some part of the repair attempt that she or he can agree with. This is also known as accepting influence. Suggest that they keep in mind that Repair Attempts are an effort to make things better.

e Set your timer for 6 minutes. And ask them to start the discussion.

f After the exercise get them to debrief their efforts.

1 They should identify all the things they did well.

2 You should point out what they did well and offer one, and only one, suggestion for improvement.

g Set you timer for 6 minutes and ask them to repeat the exercise attempting to make the conversation even better.
h After the timer sounds once again debrief the session with them.
i Assign homework.
  1 If you and they are 80 to 90 percent sure that they can have conversations about solvable problems successfully then ask them to have practice conversations at home each day on easy problems using soft startups and repair attempts. If a fight occurs stop the discussion and bring it to the next session.
  2 Determine which week of the Seven-Week program they are on. Ask them to continue the Seven-Week course by going to the next week's exercises. Determine if there are any issues and attempt to resolve them.
j Congratulate the couple on their efforts and go to Session 7 Ending.

Session 7C: Learning to accept influence and to compromise

7C Specific goals

The goal for Session 7C is to help the clients learn to accept influence and compromise.

7C Therapist's cognitive knowledge

The following should be read in preparation: Gottman (1999) "Intervention 4," p. 233.

7C Equipment needed

a Three copies of their CAC Item Ranking forms from their case file. Alternatively you could use the Gottman Areas of Change Checklist: Solvable Problems or Gottman (1999) Table 8.5 Gottman Repair Checklist.
b Two copies each of the ORS and SRS.
c Your timer.

7C Pre-session preparations

Repeat the Pre-session Preparations from Session 4.

7C Beginnings

a–c Repeat steps A to C from Session 4.
d After determining that the clients are not in crisis ask about the homework assignment which was:
  1 Ask about conversations they had about solvable problems using soft startups and repair attempts. Empathize with any problems they may have had and attempt to resolve the issues. Repeat Session 7B if needed.
  2 Determine which week of the Seven-Week program they are on and review the specific assignments for that week with them (Gottman, 1999, pp. 212–213).
  3 Celebrate success in their homework assignments be supportive and validate any difficulties.

  Share one and only one suggestion for improvement where appropriate.

e Transition to Session 7C. The agenda for Session 7C is to teach couples how to learn to seek common ground, to find areas they can both agree on related to the disagreement, and to learn to let go of the need to hold on to their position (Gottman, 1999, p. 233).

7C Middle

a Tell them something like, "The cost of holding to their position at all costs may be the loss of the relationship. Accepting influence means learning to win by letting go of a firm position and making the attempt to find a position in which both partners get some of what they want or feel they need."
b Tell them that they should ask each other:
  1 How can we better understand this issue?
  2 What are our common feelings or what are the most important feelings we have about this issue?
  3 What goals do we have in common about this issue?
  4 What ways can we agree upon to accomplish our goals?
c Hand them copies of their CAC Item Ranking forms from their case file. Alternatively you could use the "Gottman Areas of Change Checklist: Solvable Problems" or Gottman (1999) Table 8.5 "Gottman Repair Checklist". The goal here is to provide the clients with material to prompt them in picking a solvable problem.
d Ask them to select an easy problem to discuss, one that is a solvable problem. If they appear to pick a perpetual issue you may share copies of Table 8.1 "Perpetual Issues" (Gottman, 1999, pp. 219–220) with them to help distinguish between solvable and perpetual problems.
e After they have selected a solvable problem ask them to have a discussion about the issue for 6 minutes.
  1 Ask them to start this discussion with a soft startup and to use repair attempts as needed. Ask them to seek common ground, to find areas they can both agree on related to the disagreement, and to learn to let go of the need to hold on to their position.
  2 When the timer sounds ask them to debrief the session starting by asking them to discuss:
    a How they sought common ground?
    b How they found areas they could both agree on related to the disagreement?
    c How they were able to let go of their position and to affect compromises.
  3 Tell them what they did right and make one, and only one, suggestion for improvement.
f Set the timer for 6 minutes and ask them to have the conversation again only make it better.
  1 When the timer sounds ask them to debrief the session starting by asking them to discuss the questions in E2 above.
  2 Provide feedback about what they did right and make one, and only one, suggestion for improvement.
g Assign homework
  1 If you and they are 80 to 90 percent sure that they successfully have conversations about solvable problems ask them to have practice conversations on easy problems using soft startups, repair attempts, seeking common ground, finding areas they can both agree on related to the disagreement, and letting go of the need to hold on to their position at all costs. Practice daily. If a fight occurs stop the discussion and bring it to the next session.
  2 Determine which week of the Seven-Week program they are on. Ask them to continue the Seven-Week Course by going to the next week's exercises. Determine if there are any issues and help them resolve the issues.
h Congratulate the couple on their efforts and go to Session 7 Ending.

Session 7D: Learning to recognize flooding and to self-sooth

7D Therapist's cognitive knowledge

The following should be read in preparation: Gottman (1999) "Intervention 3," pp. 227, 229, 231–233. See also pp. 74–85.

7D Equipment needed

a Three copies of the "Innocent Victim and Righteous Indignation Scale" (Gottman, 1999) p. 392.
b Two copies each of the ORS and SRS.
c Your timer.

7D Pre-session preparations

Repeat the pre-session preparations from session 4.

7D Beginnings

a–c Repeat steps A to C from Session 4.
d After determining that the clients are not in crisis ask about the homework assignment which was:
  1 To have practice conversations on easy problems using soft startups repair attempts, seeking common ground, finding areas they can both agree on related to the disagreement, and letting go of the need to hold on to their position at all costs.
  2 Determine which week of the Seven-Week program they are on and review the specific assignments for that week with them (Gottman, 1999, pp. 212–213).
  3 Celebrate success in their homework assignments be supportive and validate any difficulties.
e Transition to the agenda for Session 7D. The agenda is to teach couples how to recognize when one of them is flooded during conflict discussions and how to take a break to self-sooth.

7D Middle

a Describe the nature of flooding to the couple (Gottman, 1999, pp. 74–85, 227, 229, 231). If you are using Gottman and Silver (1999) recommend that they read pp. 34–39. You can tell your clients something like this.
  1 You can recognize when you are getting emotionally flooded when your heart begins to race. If you take your pulse you may find it to be at 95 bpm or greater.
  2 Your stomach may get tight.
  3 Breathing may become shallow.
  4 The palms of your hands and your feet may get sweaty.
b Tell them that some results of flooding are:
  1 You may notice that when you are flooded it influences your ability to listen, it also influences recent learning, thinking, and creative problem-solving abilities.
  2 Flooding leads to reliance on old over-learned behaviors and fight-or-flight behaviors.

3 It also begins the "Distance and Isolation Cascade" (Gottman, 1999, pp. 72–73) in which problems are seen as severe, one or both partners become convinced it is best to work out the problems on their own which leads to the couple leading parallel lives and eventually they come to feel alone and lonely.
4 Flooding may be more pronounced in the husband as there appears to be gender differences in flooding. Males find it harder to self-sooth and require longer times to sooth.
5 Flooding is often associated with the pursuer-distancer or demand-withdraw pattern of couple interaction. The demand-withdraw pattern is found in all marriages. In this pattern it is often the woman who starts the conversation with a harsh startup, most likely because the couple has a history of not resolving their difficulties. The man begins to feel flooded and in an effort to avoid the unpleasant physiological reactions associated with emotions he begins to attempt to withdraw from the conversation. Gottman (1999) points out that these patterns may be a function of how well the couple connects when they are not in a conflict conversation rather than a gender difference. Therefore, the goal of therapy is not to learn to solve problems so much as it is to learn to build a strong marital relationship which will not be devastated by the inevitable marital conflict.

c Flooding Intervention A: Taking a break.
1 Ask each partner to describe to the other:
a What makes them feel flooded? What they feel inside. What are they thinking?
b How they bring up issues or complaints.
c If they store things up rather than bringing them up when they happen.
2 Ask them to tell each other what the other can do that will sooth them in a disagreement.
3 Ask them to describe what they can do to sooth themselves.
4 Ask them to discuss with each other what signals they can develop to let the other know when they are getting flooded and they need to take a break. They need to establish a ritual for taking a break and coming back together to discuss the issue. Breaks need to be for about 20 minutes and should be truly relaxing without rehearsing distress-maintaining thoughts such as "I don't have to take this," "I'm going to get even," "Innocent victim," and "Righteous Indignation." If "Innocent victim" and "Righteous Indignation" appear to be a problem consider administering the scale found in Gottman (1999) p. 392.

d Flooding Intervention B. Imagining and Self-Soothing.
1 Ask the clients to imagine feeling tense, anxious, and getting flooded. They are then to signal to their partner that they need to take time out.
2 While in "time out" start by taking long slow breaths and letting it out slowly. Do this about six times per minute.
3 Next ask them to notice the areas of their body which are tense. Intentionally contract and relax the muscle groups which are tense. Intensify the tension, then let it flow out.
4 Suggest that they let the tense regions grow heavy, as if weighted down and leaden.
5 Imagine the tense regions getting comfortably warm to allow deep relaxation.
6 Suggest that they imagine themselves to be in a place where they are completely relaxed such as on a calm comfortably warm ocean shore or near a lake or river, where ever they would feel completely peaceful and comfortable. Ask them to go there in their imagination and let themselves become completely relaxed.
7 Ask them to discuss a recent solvable issue they have disagreed about in the past week or two. Set your timer for 15 minutes. Even if the issue does not cause flooding ask them to practice taking a time out using their choice of the procedures described above.
8 Coach their time out practice, providing support and praise for the parts they do well and provide corrective feedback. If time permits have them practice returning to the conversation after the time out.

e Assign homework
   1 Ask them to practice time out at home at least once a day.
   2 Determine which week of the Seven-Week program they are on. Ask them to continue the Seven-Week course by going to the next week's exercises. Determine if there are any issues and attempt to resolve them.
   3 Go to Session 7 Ending.

7 Ending

a Ask the clients to summarize the session. Provide reinforcement and corrective feedback as needed.
b Review the homework assignments.
c Administer and score the SRS. Discuss a total score of 36 or lower or any items which are 9 or lower.
d Thank them for their efforts on behalf of their marriage. Set an appointment for the next session then walk them to the reception area.

7 Reporting/recording

Record your case notes in a timely fashion including your graphs of the ORS and RDAS data.

Session 8: Establishing a dialogue about perpetual problems

The goal for Session 8 is to help clients learn to carry on a dialogue about their perpetual problems. Perpetual problems are issues that the couple may have been coping with for many years. They often appear to be centered in basic differences between the partners' personal traits, needs, and values. The goal is not to attempt to resolve the issue as it will probably never be fully resolved. The goal is to change the emotional behaviors associated with the issue. The goal is to change the prevailing negative sentiment override to more positive sentiment override. Often their differences are perceived of as badness and as a result they attempt to change the other by use of criticism and blaming. Therefore, they need to learn to be more accepting of each other's differences and they need to learn to communicate their acceptance. Gottman (1999) suggests that this can be accomplished by uncovering the meanings or dreams that give rise to their current behavior. Therefore, Gottman asserts that the primary intervention for gridlocked problems is the "Dreams Within Conflict Interview."

This intervention may require more than one session for the clients to practice the skills to success criterion before practicing at home. If they are gridlocked over a perpetual issue it may be helpful to schedule a two- or three-hour session. Tailor the order and number of these exercises to the needs of the clients.

Couples whose initial issue when they come to therapy is a gridlocked conflict are often started on Session 8 and 9 interventions (Gottman, 1999, pp. 186–189). Gottman points out after completing Sessions 8 and 9 they will need to work on the full treatment as removal of the gridlocked problem is rarely a permanent solution to their marital disagreements.

8A Specific goals

a Teach the clients to:
   1 Recognize their strengths.
   2 Imagine each other's dreams.

3 Establish each other's dreams within conflict.
4 Honor one another's dreams.
5 Handle the most common resistance to this intervention.

8A Therapist's cognitive knowledge

The following should be read in preparation:

a Review the treatment manual Gottman (1999) pp. 186–189, 219–220, 234–259, 269–271, 273, 303. See also Gottman and Silver (1999) pp. 217–241.
b Review Chapter 5 in this text.

8A Equipment needed

a Three copies of
 1 Gottman Areas of Strengths Checklist (p. 373).
 2 Strengths Discussion Questions (p. 236).
 3 Imagining Others' Dreams (pp. 238–247).
b Two copies each of the ORS and SRS.
c Your timer.

8A Pre-session preparations

Repeat the pre-session preparations from Session 4.

8A Beginnings

a–c Repeat steps A to C from Session 4.
d After determining that the clients are not in crisis ask about the homework assignment.
 1 Ask how the relaxation training is progressing.
 2 Ask about their progress in the Seven-Week course in Fondness and Admiration. If they have completed it congratulate them. Otherwise determine which week of the Seven-Week program they are on and review the specific assignments for that week with them (Gottman, 1999, pp. 212–213).
 3 Transition to Session 8A. The agenda is to recognize each other's strengths, learn to be able to imagine their partner's dreams, establish each other's dreams within the conflict and learn to honor one another's dreams.

8A Middle

a **Important**. As stated earlier Gottman (1999) believes that it is not helpful, and may even be harmful, for therapists to attempt to get clients into conflict situations in order to focus on changing their negative behavior to more positive behavior. Instead you should help the clients search for the dreams behind the conflict. They should not focus on the conflict but instead seek out the hidden meanings. If the couple attempts to understand each others' dreams then the conflict may vanish.
b Provide each partner with a copy or Gottman's "Areas of Strengths Checklist" (p. 373) and ask them to complete it.
c Share the list of "Strengths Discussion Questions" from Gottman page 236. Ask them to have a conversation with each other to specify and clarify the strengths in their relationship (Gottman, pp. 236–238).

d Ask them to discuss their gridlocked or perpetual problem:
   1 What has each already done to adapt to this issue?
   2 What are their underlying emotions related to this issue?
   3 What would be the possible trade-offs with perhaps one person "winning" on one issue and the other "winning' on another issue?
   4 How they might further adapt to this issue?
   5 While they look for common ground they should ask themselves how importance is this issue? To themselves? To their partner?
   6 How they might accept each other's minor flaws and defects related to the issue.
   7 Can they see the humor in the situation?
e Ask them to summarize the strengths they have related to this problem area.
f Assign homework: Ask them to continue to search for strengths during the next week.
g Present the couple with copies of "Imagining Other's Dreams" (pp. 238–247). Have each read one example. Ask one of them to take the even numbered exercises and the other to take the odd numbered exercises. Take turns sharing and discussing their responses to any of the items they find interesting. Hint: Gottman gives responses to the items on pages 243–247.
h Assign homework: Ask them to think about their dreams related to their marital issues during the week and to come prepared to share them in the next session.
i Go to Session 8 Ending.

Session 8B: Helping couples explore their dreams within a conflict area

8B Therapist's cognitive knowledge

The following should be read in preparation:

a Review the treatment manual Gottman (1999) pp. 186–189, 219–220, 234–259, 269–271, 273, 303. See also Gottman and Silver (1999) pp. 217–241.
b Review Chapter 5 in this text.

8B Equipment needed

a Have three copies of each of the following available:
   1 "Dreams Within Conflict–Sample Dreams" (p. 248).
   2 Bulleted questions on page 248.
b Two copies each of the ORS and SRS.
c Your timer.

8B Pre-session preparations

Repeat the pre-session preparations from Session 4.

8B Beginnings

a–c Repeat steps A to C from Session 4.
d After determining that the clients are not in crisis ask about the homework assignment.
   1 Ask each partner to describe strengths they discovered in their partner during the week.
   2 Ask them to share their dreams about the marital relationship that they thought about during the week.

3 Ask about their progress in the Seven-Week course in Fondness and Admiration. If they have completed it congratulate them. Otherwise determine which week of the Seven-Week program they are on and review the specific assignments for that week with them (Gottman, 1999, pp. 212–213).
4 Transition to Session 8B: Middle. The agenda for Session 8B is to explore their dreams within their conflicts.

8B Middle

a Structure this session carefully. You might say something like: "Today we will be discussing one of your hot topics. I want to start by laying down some ground rules" (see Gottman, pp. 247–250).
  1 First, and foremost, *you are not to try to solve this problem.*
  2 You will each have 6 minutes to share your dream related to this problem or the dream which you have lost related to this issue.
  3 *Speaker's guidelines:* Tell honestly, without the four horsemen, what the position you have taken on this issue means to you. Try to describe the dream behind your position. Tell the story behind this dream. Where does it come from? What does it symbolize? Be as clear and specific as possible so that your partner can really understand your position.
  4 *Listener's guidelines:* The listener's job is to just listen, the way a good friend would listen. The listener is not to try to offer ideas for solving the problem. Just suspend judgment. Just listen and do not judge. Listen and attempt to understand the meaning of your partner's dream. You may ask questions which convey genuine interest. For example, you might ask:
    a What are your thoughts and beliefs about this issue?
    b What are your feelings about it?
    c What would you like most to happen?
    d How can your dream goals be accomplished?
    e Does this dream have symbolic meaning for you?
    f What part would you like me to play in your dream? How can I help or contribute?
  5 *The bottom line about life dreams:* Neither one of "you want to have the kind of marriage in which you win and are influential in the marriage but wind up crushing your partner's dream. You want the kind of marriage in which you are supporting one another's dreams. If your dreams connect, so much the better" (Gottman, 1999, p. 249).

b *Instructions to the therapist.* The implicit reframe in this exercise is that they may be able to resolve the conflict related to this issue if each person were to understand what their partner's position means symbolically. Therefore, instruct them as often as necessary to: "Search for the dream behind the conflict. Forget about the conflict, go after the hidden dream. Then try to understand and to support your partner's dream. The conflict then vanishes. Discuss all the feelings that surrounding this issue. Don't let the dream stay hidden" (Gottman, 1999, p. 250). Because this is generally harder for males than for females let's have you start first [use husband's name].
  1 Hand them each a copy of "Dreams Within Conflict – Sample Dreams" (p. 248). They may use this list to prompt their thinking about the dreams they may have within the conflict issue.
  2 Hand them copies of the bulleted questions on page 248.

c Remind them that they should use soft startups, repair attempts, compromise, accepting influence, and time out for soothing to make the dreams conversation go better.
  1 Set your timer for 6 minutes and invite the husband to start.
  2 When the timer sounds ask them to debrief the discussion. They should attend to the things they did right.

3. Reinforce the things they did right and suggest one, and only one, area for improvement.
4. Reset your timer for 6 minutes and invite the wife to start.
5. When the timer sounds ask them to debrief the discussion. They should attend to the things they did right.
6. Reinforce the things they did right and suggest one, and only one, area for improvement.
7. Should they reach a sticking point ask them to stop and take a time out for self-soothing. Caution them about rehearsing negative thoughts.
8. Validate their efforts in the session and point out that one goal of this exercise is to help them learn to make the next conversation about this and other hot topics better. Remind them that they can do this by using soft startups, repair attempts, compromise, accepting influence, and time out for soothing.

d Assign homework: If they and you believe they are able to do this assignment at home with 80 to 90 percent success then ask them to practice having conversations at home about their dreams for the marriage. Otherwise return next week to practice in-session.

e Go to Session 8. Ending.

Session 8C: Honoring each other's dreams

8C Therapist's cognitive knowledge

The following should be read in preparation:

a Review the treatment manual Gottman (1999) pp. 186–189, 219–220, 234–259, 269–271, 273, 303. See also Gottman and Silver (1999) pp. 217–241.

b Review Chapter 5 in this text.

8C Equipment needed

a Have three copies of each of the following available.
  1. Dreams Within Conflict – Sample Dreams (p. 248).
  2. The bulleted questions on page 248.

b Two copies each of the ORS and SRS.

c Your timer.

8C Pre-session preparations

Repeat the pre-session preparations from Session 4.

8C Beginnings

a–c Repeat steps A to C from Session 4.

d After determining that the clients are not in crisis ask about the homework assignment.
  1. Ask how the practice conversations about their dreams for the marriage went. If they had difficulties ask them to replay the session for you this time making it better by using soft startups, repair attempts, compromise, accepting influence, and time out for soothing.
  2. Ask about their progress in the Seven-Week course in Fondness and Admiration. If they have completed it congratulate them. Otherwise determine which week of the Seven-Week program they are on and review the specific assignments for that week with them (Gottman, 1999, pp. 212–213).
  3. Transition to session 8C Middle. The agenda is to learn to honor each other's dreams.

8C Middle

a Ask them to briefly review their recall of:
   1 Soft startups.
   2 Repair attempts for failed bids.
   3 Accepting influence.
   4 Compromise.
   5 Time out with relaxation.

b Then guide them in carrying on a discussion of a gridlocked issue.
   1 Start by structuring the session with a discussion of honoring each other's dreams. Point out that honoring may be done in many ways but it always means supporting and respecting the other's dreams and needs. The goal is to move from gridlock to dialogue.
   2 Ask one of them to start a conversation about their differences with a soft startup.
   3 Coach them in the process by reinforcing their correct performance and stopping them briefly when they stray or bring in the four horseman.
   4 When they reach a sticking point ask them to stop and take a time out for self-soothing. Caution them about rehearsing negative thoughts.
   5 Ask them to start a search with each other for their strengths related to this issue. Use any of the following open questions which seem to pertain to their dialogue.
      a Ask them to discuss what each has already done to adapt to this issue.
      b Ask them about their underlying emotions related to this issue.
      c Ask them to explore possible trade-offs with perhaps one person "winning" on one issue and the other "winning' on another issue.
      d Ask them to talk about how they might further adapt to this issue.
      e Ask them to review the importance of this issue by looking for common ground.
      f Ask them to accept each other's minor flaws and defects related to the issue.
      g Ask them to attempt to see the humor in the situation.
   6 Next ask them to define the minimal core areas that they cannot yield on: Use soft startups, repair attempts, and time out for soothing.
   7 Next ask them to determine areas of the problem which are not so hot and were they can be more flexible in their positions.
   8 Finally, ask them to come up with a temporary compromise and a plan to implement it.

c Help them see that this problem may never go away in their marriage but that they can continue their dialogue about it without punishment and coercion.

d Assign homework: If you and they are 80 to 90 percent sure they can have this conversation without getting into a fight then ask them to continue practicing conversations about their dreams for the marriage at home.

e Go to Session 8 Ending

Session 8D: Helping couples overcome their fears about accepting or honoring their partner's dream

8D Therapist's cognitive knowledge

The following should be reviewed in preparation: Gottman (1999) pp. 251, 266–291, 307–321.

8D Equipment needed

a Two copies each of the ORS and SRS.

b Your timer.

8D Pre-session preparations

Repeat the pre-session preparations from Session 4.

8D Beginnings

a–c Repeat steps A to C from Session 4.

d After determining that the clients are not in crisis ask about the homework assignment.
  1 Ask them to share the conversations about their dreams for their marital relationship that they talked about during the week.
  2 Ask about their progress in the Seven-Week course in Fondness and Admiration. If they have completed it congratulate them. Otherwise determine which week of the Seven-Week program they are on and review the specific assignments for that week with them (Gottman, 1999, pp. 212–213).
  3 Transition to Session 8D, Middle. The agenda for Session 8D is to help the couple deal with the major sources of resistance to the "Dreams Within Conflict" exercises.

8D Middle

a Explain that sometimes we have catastrophic expectations about what will happen if we give in to our partner's dreams and needs. Sometime this is a fear of accepting influence, sometimes it is a fear of sharing power, and sometimes it is a fear of the other person's intense emotional response to the issue. All of these types of fears, and others, are perfectly understandable given the couple's personal and marital histories. In this exercise I want you to take the time to explore your fears together concerning this issue.

b Ask the couple to discuss a gridlocked issue. Remind them of soft startups, and the Four Horsemen.

c Each is to share the dreams she/he has behind their position for 6 minutes. While advocating for their position each is to attempt to accept the other's point of view on small points but to stay with their dream and not give it up for the sake of "peace" or to "end the discussion." Instruct them to share their fears about the issue. Tell them that some common fears are: (a) fears of accepting influence from their partners, (b) fears of truly sharing power, and (c) fears of losing control in the relationship. Ask them to consider where these fears come from in their personal histories, perhaps from their families of origin.

d The speaker is to talk to their partner about their partner's dream and to be genuine about what she or he fears about helping their partner to reach their dream. Listeners should try to accept all of their partner's ideas that they can live with. Above all do not be mean spirited. You will gain the most by allowing your partner to influence you. You will have your turn next.

e Listeners should ask about their partner's fears. Try to learn what the other sees as the worst thing that could happen if you were to realize your dream. Try to sooth their fears about that outcome. Help your partner feel good about sharing her or his dream by helping to make plans to make it come true. In this conversation, the more you give the more you are likely to get when it is your turn.
  1 Set your timer for 6 minutes and ask the husband to go first. Coach expressions of soft startups, expressions of fears, and the use of the Four Horsemen.
  2 Help them process the conversation at the end of 6 minutes looking for all the things they did well.
  3 Give the other person the floor for 6 minutes and follow the instructions in C, D, and E above.
  4 Process the conversation looking for all the things they did well.

f Go to 8 Ending.

8 Ending

a Ask the clients to summarize the session. Provide reinforcement and corrective feedback as needed.

b Review homework

  1 Review the homework for the intervention you are applying, that is for Session 8A, 8B, 8C, or 8D.

  2 Recommend that they continue the Seven-Week course in Fondness and Admiration if they have not completed it.

c Administer and score the SRS. Discuss a total score of 36 or lower or any items which are 9 or lower.

d Thank them for their efforts on behalf of their marriage. Set an appointment for the next session then walk them to the reception area.

8 Reporting/Recording

Record your case notes in a timely fashion including your graph of the ORS and RDAS data.

Session 9: Building shared meanings and life dreams

The specific goals

The goals for Session 9 are to help the couple explore the roles, values, and symbols that gives their marriage meaning and helps them build their family culture. To accomplish this the couple will need to explore the meanings behind several areas in life such as shared rituals, roles, goals, symbols, spirituality, and family histories. This can be accomplished by use of the "Shared Meanings Questionnaire" as a precursor to a conversation they can have on these topics. It can also be accomplished by use of the "Meanings Interview," which is a structured interview.

Session 9 may require more than one session. Tailor the order and number of these exercises to the needs of the clients. The specific goals are outlined thus:

a The goals for Session 9 are to help the couple:

  1 Establish a dialogue about family rituals.

  2 Establish a dialogue about family roles.

  3 Establish a dialogue about family goals.

  4 Establish a dialogue about family symbols.

b **Important**

  1 Before you begin Session 9 you will need to decide whether the "Shared Meanings Questionnaire" or the "Meanings Interview" approach will fit best with your clients. The "Shared Meanings Questionnaire" approach will be presented as Session 9A and the Meanings Interview approach will be Session 9B.

  2 If you are going to use the "Shared Meanings Questionnaire" it would be helpful if you could send home the questionnaire the week before and ask them to complete it independently and bring it to the next session.

9A Therapist's cognitive knowledge

The following should be read in preparation: Gottman (1999) pp. 108–109, 186–189, 260–265, 288–291.

9A Equipment needed

a Three copies of the following from Gottman (1999).
   1 "Shared Meanings Questionnaire," pp. 393–395.
   2 Table 10.1 "Family Rituals," p. 261.
   3 Table 10.2 "Family Roles," p. 262.
   4 Table 10.3 "Goals," p. 262.
   5 Table 10.4 "Symbols," p. 263.
b Two copies each of the ORS and SRS.
c Your timer.

9A Pre-session preparations

Repeat the pre-session preparations from Session 4.

9A Beginnings

a–c Repeat steps A to C from Session 4.
d After determining that the clients are not in crisis ask about the homework assignment.
   1 What additional strengths have they identified in their relationship and in each other?
   2 What are the outcomes of their Seven-Week course in Fondness and Admiration?
e Transition to the middle of the session by setting the agenda.
   1 The agenda for both Sessions 9A and 9B is to help the couple dialogue about the meanings behind the rituals, symbols, metaphors, and family stories that bind them together in a shared family culture and to explore any discrepancies between their ideal values for their relationship and the actuality of their relationship.
   2 Tailor the interventions by selecting the section or sections from the "Shared Meanings Questionnaire" which are most appropriate for your clients.

9A "Shared Meanings Questionnaire" approach to building shared meaning

a If they did not do the questionnaire at home then hand them copies of the "Shared Meanings Questionnaire" (p. 393) and ask them to do the section that best fits their perpetual or gridlocked problem.
   If they did the questionnaire at home proceed directly to the section which appears to best represent their gridlocked problem.
b Have them share and compare their results and discuss areas of agreement and then discuss areas where they differ and how they can respect, honor, and support each other's values, philosophies, and dreams. Set your timer for 6 minutes. Debrief the discussion for use of soft startups, repair attempts, time out, and use of the Four Horsemen.
c If this session was used in conjunction with a marital crisis then consider with your clients returning to specific content areas as presented in Sessions 4 through 7 if they have already been through the assessment sessions. If they have not been through the assessment sessions return them to Session 1.
d Go to Session 9 Ending.

Session 9B: Shared meanings interview approach to building shared meaning in family rituals

9B Therapist's cognitive knowledge

The following should be read in preparation: Gottman (1999), pp. 263–265, 403–405.

9B Equipment needed

a “Meanings Interview” pp. 403–405.
b Two copies each of the ORS and SRS.
c Your timer.

9B Pre-session preparations

Repeat the pre-session preparations from Session 4.

9B Beginnings

a–c Repeat steps A to C from Session 4.
d After determining that the clients are not in crisis ask about the homework assignment.
  1 What additional strengths have they identified in their relationship and in each other?
  2 What are the outcomes of their Seven-Week course in Fondness and Admiration?
e Transition to the agenda for Session 9B which is to help them to begin a dialogue about their shared rituals, roles, goals, and symbols.

9B Middle

a Begin with the rationale given in the instructions to the couple on page 403.
b If you know which section – rituals, roles, goals, symbols, or spirituality – frames their gridlocked position then begin the interview with that section of the interview.
c If you do not know which section includes their perpetual problem then hand them copies of the “Shared Meanings Questionnaire” (pp. 393–394) and ask them to complete it.
d Have them share their results with each other and attempt to determine the areas of their gridlock.
e Start with the section of the “Meanings Interview” that best frames their area of conflict. Conduct the interview in the manner of the Oral History Interview.
  1 Use your best therapy skills to help them each discuss their position.
  2 Follow the guidelines for the Dreams Within Conflict interventions on pp. 247–251.
f Have them share and compare their results and discuss areas of agreement and then discuss areas where they differ and how they can respect, honor, and support each other’s values, philosophies, and dreams.
  Debrief the discussion for use of soft startups, repair attempts, time out, and the Four Horsemen.
g If this session was used in conjunction with a marital crisis then consider with your clients returning to specific content areas as presented in Sessions 4 through 7 if they have already been through the assessment sessions (see Gottman, 1999, pp. 188–189). If they have not been through the assessment sessions return them to Session 1.
h Go to Session 9 Ending.

9 Ending

a Ask the clients to summarize the session. Provide reinforcement and corrective feedback as needed.
b Administer and score the SRS. Discuss a total score of 36 or lower or any items which are 9 or lower.
c Thank them for their efforts on behalf of their marriage. Set an appointment for the next session then walk them to the reception area.

9 Reporting/recording

Within 24 hours record your case notes in a timely fashion including your graph of the ORS and RDAS data

Session 10: Preparing for possible relapses

The goal for Session 10 is to prepare the couple for a possible relapse.

10 The specific goals

The specific goals are to teach the couple to use:

1 Aftermath of a marital argument.
2 Building rituals of connection.
3 Early detection of emotional distress.

10 Therapist's cognitive knowledge

The following should be read in preparation:

a Gottman (1999) pp. 281 skips to 287–291.
b For those using Gottman and Silver (1999), pp. 148–155, 243–258, 259–266).

10 Equipment needed

a Three copies of the following from Gottman (1999):
   1 "Aftermath of a Marital Argument Questionnaire" (pp. 282–285).
   2 "Admitting Your Role" (pp. 285–286).
   3 "Failed Marital Argument Interview." Begins at the bottom of p. 281 and continues on p. 287.
   4 "Building Rituals of Connection" (pp. 289–290).
   5 "Marital Poop Detector" (p. 301).
b One copy of Appendix E, Observations of the Couples' Communication and Problem-solving Behaviors Therapist's Rating Form in this text.
c Two copies each of the ORS and SRS.
d Your timer.

10 Pre-session preparations

Repeat the pre-session preparations from Session 4.

10 Beginnings

a–c Repeat steps A to C from Session 4.
d After determining that the clients are not in crisis ask about the homework assignment: Follow up on any previously assigned homework.
e Transition to Session 10 Middle by discussing the agenda. The agenda for session !0 is to prepare the couple for relapses, and to generalize their skills in preparation for termination.

10 Middle

a Explain to the couple that they are to pick a topic that is a perpetual problem, perhaps one they had a disagreement about in the previous week. They are to discuss this topic for 6 minutes with you out of the room if you have a one-way screen or with you in a corner of the room. You will tap on the window to start and stop their conversation. They are to use all of the skills they have learned. Ask if there are any questions. Answer their questions and allay their concerns.
   1 Step out of the room to the observation booth. Set your timer for 6 minutes and tap on the widow.
   2 Observe and rate their dialogue for: (a) Soft startups; (b) Repair attempts for failed bids; (c) Accepting influence; (d) Compromise; and (e) Time out with relaxation. Use the observation rating form (Appendix E of this text).
   3 After the 6 minutes are over tap on the window and return to the room.

b Return to the room and ask them to process their conversation. Remind them that they are to discuss the argument, not to start it again. They are to take the point-of-view of scientists making detached and objective observations about the event.

c Set your timer for 6 minutes and remain silent while they process their discussion.
   1 Observe their interaction to determine if they discuss: (a) Any feelings they had during the discussion; (b) Any attacking or blaming and defensiveness, i.e., the Four Horsemen; (c) Their two subjective realities; (d) The triggers they experienced; (e) Admitting their responsibility for the argument; (f) Their dreams and needs; (g) Responding with old patterns; (h) The conversation they would have liked to have had; and (I) At least one idea for making the next conversation better.
   2 After they have processed their discussion provide them each with copies of the "Aftermath of a Marital Argument Questionnaire" (pp. 282–285).
   3 Ask them each to complete the questionnaire independently.
   4 When they have completed the questionnaire ask them to discuss their answers with each other. Point out that there is no such thing as "absolute reality." They each have their own subjective and legitimate view of things. While they have different views of the event they should remember that difference is only difference it isn't badness.

d Go to Session 10 Ending

10 Ending

a Ask the clients to summarize the session. Provide reinforcement and corrective feedback as needed.

b Administer and score the SRS. Discuss a total score of 36 or lower or any items which are 9 or lower.

c Thank them for their efforts on behalf of their marriage. Set an appointment for the next session then walk them to the reception area.

10 Reporting/recording

Record your case notes in a timely fashion including your graph of the ORS and RDAS data.

Session 11: Terminating Gottman Method Couple Therapy

The goal for Session 11 is to determine the clients' readiness to terminate therapy. The decision should be made using the best available information. You should review with the clients the graphs of the outcome scores to determine if they have reached their therapy goals as indicated by statistically reliable and/or clinically reliable scores (Chapters 5 and 6). In addition, you should discuss their subjective evaluations of their progress. Gottman (1999) suggests that clients are ready to terminate when they have established reliable love maps, activated their fondness and admiration system, and moved from negative to positive sentiment override. They are moving toward termination when the markers of negative sentiment override such as the Four Horsemen, or emotional disengagement, have been significantly reduced. When nearing termination couples should be dealing effectively with solvable problems by the use of softened startups, accepting influence through compromise, and are able to de-escalate arguments by use of repair, soothing, and time outs. They will also be able to deal with perpetual problems by communicating respect and acceptance of each other's dreams and values. Finally, couples are ready for termination when they have the tools to avoid relapse without the therapist's assistance. They can avoid relapse by early detection of signs of discord or emotional distance and by the use of rituals of emotional connection. When couples are able to meet these criteria they will be ready to terminate.

11 Specific goals

- a Review and consolidate the new knowledge and skills the clients have gained specifically their ability to regulate conflict and marital friendship.
- b Assess the couple's readiness for termination.
  - 1 Review the ORS and RDAS graphs and scores to determine if the clients have made statistical and/or clinically significant improvements (Chapter 5).
  - 2 Re-administer the Marital Standard Assessment Battery.
  - 3 Evaluate your clients' progress against the Gottman criteria (pp. 302–304).
  - 4 Review your adherence to Gottman Method Couples Therapy (Chapter 5) and Gottman's Adherence rating materials.[2]
- c Evaluate with your clients their readiness to terminate
  - 1 Assess together the nature and extent of any dependency and separation issues you and they may be experiencing.
  - 2 Empower your clients by attributing the changes they have made to their efforts and by devaluing the contributions you have made thus equalizing the relationship.
  - 3 Predict and practicing relapses.
  - 4 Give permission to the clients to return for treatment for this or any other problems.

11 Therapist's cognitive knowledge

The following should be read in preparation:

- a Gottman (1999) pp. 292–306.
- b Gottman and Silver (1999, pp. 259–266).
- c Review Chapters 5 and 6 in this text.

11 Equipment needed

- a Three copies, from Gottmann (1999) of
  - 1 Paper tower instructions (pp. 293–294).
  - 2 "Gottman Mountain Survival Problem," Table 13.1 (p. 295).
  - 3 "Gottman Island Survival Problem," Table 13.2 (pp. 296–297).
  - 4 "Who Does What in the Marriage?" Table 13.4 (pp. 298–300).
  - 5 "Marital Poop Detector," Table 13.5 (p. 301).
  - 6 "The Five Magic Hours," (p. 304).
- b Two copies each of the ORS and SRS.
- c Two copies of the Standard Assessment Instruments (Appendix C).

11 Pre-session preparations

a Repeat the pre-session preparations from Session 4.
b In addition you will need to review your case progress notes for evidence of your clients' readiness to terminate:
   1 Clients' self-reports (See Chapter 6 in this text).
   2 Clients' match to the Gottman criteria for termination.
   3 ORS and SRS charts and scores for statistical and clinical significant changes.

11 Beginnings

a–c Use the Beginnings steps a–c from Session 4.
d After determining that the clients are not in crisis ask about the homework assignment:
   1 Review any outstanding homework assignments.
   2 Review the information you have about the clients' readiness to terminate.
e Transition to Session 11 middle. The agenda for Session 11 middle is to tailor this session to the needs of your clients by deciding if they will benefit from the team building exercise(s) or from discussing gender roles. Provide couples with the capacity to take over their lives by reviewing skills which they can use to resolve conflicts and to maintain their marital friendship. Seek closure by dealing with separation issues and giving permission to return as needed.

11 Middle

a Determine if the clients will benefit from the team-building exercise. If they will benefit then:
   1 Select the intervention (1–3) and provide the required materials.
   2 Follow the instructions for intervention.
b Determine if the clients will benefit from the gender roles intervention. If so, provide the clients with Table 13.4 and conduct Intervention 4.
c Teach the couple to monitor the occurrence of emotional distance and to resolve it early.
   1 Provide the clients with Table 13.5. Ask them to read and discuss it.
   2 Recommend that they use it frequently in the months to come to monitor a drift into emotional distance and to correct any drift by bringing up the issue using soft startups (Appendix J, Homework Success).
d Provide them with copies of "Five Magic Hours."
   1 Ask them to read this handout and discuss it with each other.
   2 Ask them to commit to performing the Five Magic Hours for one month and to then assess its impact on their relationship (Appendix J, Homework Success).
e Present the clients with a rationale for termination procedures including dealing with concerns, assessment of progress, and permission to return to therapy (see Chapter 6). Be especially attentive for dependency behaviors on the part of the clients. Respond as needed.
   1 Permission to Return to Therapy. Some clients feel that once they have been to therapy they should never need to return. Therefore, it is important to educate the clients to the nature of family behavior problems.
      a Family behavior is strongly influenced by family members' developmental changes such as the birth of a child or a child becoming a teenager. Family behavior is also influenced by changes in the community and other contextual variables. Therefore, clients should expect that they will encounter problems again. If family behavior problems recur and become too difficult for them to handle they should feel free to return for therapy just as they would return to their family physician for the recurrence of a physical illness.
      b Always leave the door open for the clients to return to therapy in the future if needed.

f Provide them with copies of the Standard Assessment Batteries. Ask them to stay and complete them or to take them home and complete them for your final assessment of their progress.
g Administer and score the SRS. Discuss a total score of 36 or lower or any items which are 9 or lower.

11 Ending

a Ask the clients to summarize the treatment they have received.
b Thank them for their efforts on behalf of their marriage and celebrate their successes.

11 Reporting/recording

a Record your case progress notes in a timely fashion including graphing their ORS and RDAS data.
b Write your Treatment Summary (Appendix H). Indicate the clients' progress from pre- and post-treatment SAB scores. Summarize the treatment and the clients' response to it. Make recommendations for further treatment as needed.

Epilogue

Therapists who desire to become Gottman Method Couples Therapy therapists will find guidelines in J. M. Gottman (1999) and J. S. Gottman (2004). In addition, there are training opportunities through the Gottman Institute on the Internet at www.gottman.com. You will also find additional readings plus audio and visual training materials on the website. In addition, you will find information about how to find supervision and training by qualified Gottman Method Couples Therapy supervisors and trainers.

Chapter 8

Protocol for Conducting Emotionally-Focused Therapy with Couples

Introduction

Emotionally-Focused Therapy (EFT: Johnson, 2004) is a treatment program for couples experiencing fears of psychological, emotional, or physical separation, and/or loss of one's intimate partner. These fears and concerns result in marital distress. The goal of EFT is to help couples create secure attachment bonds between intimate partners.

The EFT model is comprised of three stages: de-escalation of negative cycles of interaction; changing interactional positions; and consolidation and integration. Within these stages there are 9 steps.

Stage 1 De-escalation:

Step 1. Creating an alliance and assessing the conflict issues.
Step 2. Identifying the negative interaction cycle.
Step 3. Assessing the unacknowledged emotions.
Step 4. Reframing the problem.

Stage 2 Changing interactional positions:

Step 5. Promoting interaction with one's own attachment and emotional needs.
Step 6. Promoting acceptance of experience.
Step 7. Facilitating the expression of needs and wants.

Stage 3 Consolidation and integration:

Step 8. Facilitating new solutions.
Step 9. Consolidating new attachment behaviors.

Becoming a Marriage and Family Therapist: From Classroom to Consulting Room, First Edition. D. Eugene Mead.

Theory and Research

Emotionally-Focused Therapy is based on Bowlby's (1969, 1988) theory of adult attachment (Johnson, 2004). The model assumes that children have an innate need for attachment. The child's need for attachment is based on survival needs shaped in the human evolutionary process. Because infants cannot survive without a nurturing and care-giving adult the infant is said to form an attachment bond to the adult caregiver. It is hypothesized that if caregivers are sensitive and responsive to children's needs then the child comes to experience others as trustworthy. The child also comes to perceive of herself or himself as worthy of others' responsiveness and love (Meyer & Pilkonis, 2002). If, on the other hand, caregivers respond to the child's needs inconsistently then the child comes to perceive relationships with others as unpredictable, unstable, and in need of constant monitoring. If the child perceives the caregiver's behavior to be consistently unresponsive then she/he may come to respond with distancing behavior and attempts to be self-sufficient. As a result, adult spouses may fear the loss of their intimate partner and that results in constricted patterns of behavioral and emotional responses (Johnson, Hunsley, Greenberg, & Schindler, 1999). These constricted behavior patterns may result in marital distress and conflict. The nature of the adult–child relationship experienced in early childhood is believed to form an attachment style manifest by adults which lasts throughout their lifetimes. Although the attachment style is relatively stable it can be modified by sustained contextual changes in interaction with significant others. EFT theorists state that the best way to treat these dysfunctional emotional and behavioral patterns is to intervene while the couple is engaged in the process of emotional interaction. The goal is to change the processes to help each spouse achieve their basic emotional attachment needs.

Research

Meyer and Pilkonis (2002) reviewed the research on attachment theory. They report that there is evidence for the hypothesis that humans appear to be motivated to form lasting affectional bonds. They also found evidence that children's emotional attachment styles can be distinguished reliably. The research reviewed by Meyer and Pilkonis shows that attachment styles formed in childhood are relatively stable into adulthood. It has also been found that negative interpersonal experiences such as depression can cause lasting changes in attachment. On the other hand it has also been shown that greater attachment security can be achieved in the course of the child's development. Finally, they found that adult attachment styles can be reliably discriminated.

The clinical efficacy of EFT has been studied extensively. A number of randomized controlled trials (RCTs) have been conducted (Goldman & Greenberg, 1992; James, 1991; Johnson & Greenberg, 1995; Walker, Johnson, Manion, & Cloutier, 1996) as well as two studies in which the respondents acted as their own controls (Johnson & Greenberg, 1995; Johnson & Talitman, 1997). These studies have found that EFT reduces marital distress both statistically (Dandeneau & Johnson, 1994; Goldman & Greenberg, 1992; James, 1991; MacPhee, Johnson, & Van Der Veer, 1995) and clinically (Goldman & Greenberg, 1992; James, 1991; MacPhee, Johnson, & Van Der Veer, 1995; Walker et al., 1996). A meta-analysis (Johnson et al., 1999) was made across the four RCT studies with an overall mean effect size of 1.28, which was statistically significant. This is a large effect size especially when compared with other studies of marital therapy which found an average effect size of $d = .84$ (Shadish & Baldwin, 2002). It is fair to conclude that EFT is an empirically-supported treatment that has been found efficacious for treatment of marital distress which stems from attachment disorders.

Preparation to practice Emotionally-Focused Therapy

Prepare to practice Emotionally-Focused Therapy by carefully studying Susan M. Johnson's (2004) *The Practice of Emotionally-Focused Marital Therapy: Creating Connection* (2nd ed.). In addition you will want to study *Becoming an Emotionally-Focused Couple Therapist: The Workbook* (Johnson et al., 2005). Before attempting treatment arrange for a qualified supervisor (see the Epilogue). After you have read the manual discuss the theory and the research with your colleagues and your supervisor. Under the direction of your supervisor observe and discuss the training videos listed in the EFT website (see Epilogue). Rehearse the procedures from the manual before each session and be prepared to execute them in the session.

Therapists who follow treatment manuals have been found to have successful client outcomes (Bellg et al., 2004; Dane & Schneider, 1998; Waltz et al., 1993). Observe your sessions and rate your adherence to the planned interventions described in the treatment manuals using the Emotion-Focused Therapy-Therapist Fidelity Scale (Denton, Johnson, & Burleson, 2009) (see also Chapter 5 in this text). Ask your supervisor to observe your sessions and to provide you with feedback concerning your adherence to the manual. You will need to complete three or four cases under close supervision before you will be considered proficient in EFT at an entry level.

Protocol for Emotionally-Focused Therapy for Couples

The interventions that are unique to Emotionally-Focused Therapy for couples

As an EFT therapist you should structure the sessions to help each member of the couple discover new aspects of her/his emotional experiences or responses (Johnson et al., 2005). You should track and reflect the sequences and patterns of emotional interaction as they occur in the session. Focus on each partner's moves in the cycle which are a function of their relationship and which highlight the clients' primary emotions. Their primary emotions underlie their interaction pattern. This allows you to identify and specify the clients' attachment needs and fears. Understanding the clients' attachment needs and fears will allow you to create enactments where partners share these responses with each other.

Enactments are defined as therapist-facilitated and coached-couple interaction episodes (Butler, Davis, & Seedall, 2008). The goal of enactments is to have couples interact with each other rather than with you. Johnson et al. (2005) provides excellent guidelines on enactments (see pp. 90-96). The interested therapist will also find the work of Butler and his colleagues helpful (Butler et al., 2008; Butler & Gardner, 2003; Davis & Butler, 2004). Butler et al. (2008) developed the Observational Assessment of Enactment Proficiency (OAEP) rating scale, which you can use to determine enactment coherence. This will contribute to your assessment of your treatment integrity. The OAEP may also be used by your supervisor for supervision. The focus on expression and expansion of emotional experience in enactments is key to restructuring the couple's relationship patterns (Johnson et al., 2005).

Some Emotionally-Focused Therapy interventions that are common with other models

Johnson and Talitman (1997) reported that the client–therapist alliance was related to successful EFT outcomes. As a therapist your empathic stance along with acceptance and genuineness (Rogers, 1961) will communicate understanding of each partner's goals and expectations for therapy and this will contribute markedly to the development of the alliance (for an extended discussion of the alliance see Chapter 1).

Another area in which EFT is similar to other approaches to marital therapy is the attention paid to the destructive effects of the partner's expressions of negative affect (see for example Gottman, 1999). Changing the couple's expression of negative affect for higher rates of expression of positive affect is seen as a move toward secure attachment (Johnson, 2003).

EFT also draws heavily on systems theory (Minuchin & Fishman, 1981). The couple's interactional patterns structure and maintain their emotional cycles and patterns. These patterns are predictable in the couple's interaction with each other (Johnson et al., 2005). As a therapist you must intervene in these emotionally laden interaction cycles to help them restructure the negative patterns into new more functional positive emotional attachment forms.

What interventions are proscribed as harmful or unsafe in Emotionally-Focused Therapy?

Teaching specific communication and problem-solving skills is generally proscribed in EFT. EFT therapists are encouraged to focus on the emotional exchanges related to attachment and safety in the couple's interaction rather than on the couple's communication and problem solving skills (Johnson et al., 2005).

Focusing on past emotional experiences is not part of EFT because focusing on past emotional experiences of the relationship often leads to blaming one's partner or justifying one's own behavior (Johnson, 2004). Ventilating negative emotions is also discouraged as is labeling one partner's behavior in an attempt to get the other partner to change behavior. Instead, EFT focuses on the here and now behavior in order to clarify, reframe, and revise their perceptions of their behavior and the behavior of their partner.

Initial phone contact

EFT begins with the initial phone contact using the procedures described in Chapter 3. Call your clients to make an appointment for an initial assessment session. Schedule two assessment sessions. The first is a one-hour conjoint session to assess their relationship variables. The second assessment session is a one-hour individual session with each spouse to determine their individual views of the marriage and their contributions to it.

Crisis management

Whenever you meet with clients you must be prepared to manage crises. You should be prepared to intervene with crisis management whenever there is evidence of suicidal ideation or family violence (see Chapter 2).

The Sessions

Session 1

Initial interview: The assessment sessions

In EFT assessment is seen as an ongoing process. However, sessions 1 and 2 focus on assessing how the partners experience each other emotionally and how they emotionally respond to their relationship. In addition you will need to determine the negative interaction cycle which defines their relationship. Because therapy is conceived as starting from the beginning of the first session you will begin to intervene by reflecting back the cycle to the clients, validating their associated feelings, and specifying their distress. Part of the assessment comes in observing their response to your interventions.

The specific goals of the assessment sessions are (a) to connect with both partners and establish a working alliance, (b) to determine the nature of their problem and the nature of their relationship, (c) to ascertain each partner's goals for therapy, and (d) to establish a treatment plan.

1 Specific goals

The goals for the assessment sessions are to continue joining with the individual spouses to build and maintain the alliance. By the end of the assessment sessions both partners should feel understood and validated. In addition you should be able to answer the following questions (Johnson, 2004; Johnson et al., 2005).

a How did their marital relationship evolve? Why are they seeking therapy at this time?
b What is the nature of their relationship history in terms of emotional attachment issues and vulnerabilities?
c What are their blocks to secure attachment and emotional engagement?
d What are the recurring sequences of interaction that maintain their distress?
e What are the focus points where you should intervene?
f How do they respond when you intervene to access their primary emotions?
g What are their positive strengths in the relationship?
h Is marital therapy contraindicated?

1 Therapist's cognitive knowledge

Read the following in preparation for the session:

a Review Johnson (2004) pp. 113–130; Johnson et al. (2005) pp. 105–139.
b Review also basic EFT skills (Johnson, 2004, pp. 53–112; Johnson et al., 2005, 41–104).
c Review Chapter 2 in this text for suicidal ideation and family violence issues.
d Review the Assessment Battery (Appendix C).
e Review "Homework Success." (Appendix J).

Equipment needed for the session

a Two copies each of the Session Rating Scale (SRS: Chapter 1, note 1, p. 217) and the Outcome Rating Scale (ORS: Chapter 3, note 1, p. 217).
b Two copies each of the RDAS (Appendix C).
c Two sets of the Standard Assessment Batteries in separate envelopes (Appendix C).

Pre-session preparations

a *Pre-session phone call.* Call the clients 24 hours before the appointment. Re-establish the appointment or reset the appointment. Remind them to come in 15 minutes early to complete the ORS and the RDAS.
b Before the conjoint session begins review the case file to determine how much of the following information is available. Plan to obtain any missing information.
  a Demographic Data for Each Partner.
  b Medical History for Each Partner and Current Medications.

- c Alert the receptionist at least 1 hour prior to the clients' arrival that you will be seeing Mr. and Mrs. _______ and to ask the receptionist to administer the ORS, and the RDAS. If the receptionist in your clinic is not able to do this then you will need to administer them at the beginning of the session.
- d You will need to arrive 10 minutes before the hour to set up seating and to arrange the video cameras if videotaping is available in your clinic.

1 Beginning

- a Meet the clients in the reception area and walk them to the consulting room while engaging in social conversation. Help them remove their coats and be seated comfortably.
- b If the receptionist is unable to administer the ORS and the RDAS then administer them now.
- c Review your clinic's "Authorization for Clinical Services" form with the clients and determine that they have completely understood it. Give special attention to issues of confidentiality and the necessity to report child abuse and elder maltreatment (see Chapter 2). As appropriate discuss with the clients the necessity for the video and the one-way screens for your supervision. Get their signatures giving permission for videotaping and/or observation on the "Authorization for Clinical Services" form. Introduce and negotiate the Fee Agreement. Get their signatures on the fee agreement.
- d *Crisis assessment.* At any time in the initial interview or in subsequent interviews when there is reason to suspect suicidal ideation or family violence switch to the appropriate interview for that crisis (see Chapter 2).
- e Next, explain to the clients that the first sessions are for assessment. The assessment sessions are used to help you find out what the issues are so you can determine what treatment is needed, if any. Explain that the third session is a feedback session where you will share your understanding of their marital strengths and any areas that might need improvement. Then you and they will decide together if marital therapy is recommended. Point out that it may be determined that (a) no treatment is necessary, (b) a specific treatment is recommended, or (c) the recommended treatment is not available here in which case a referral will be made. If therapy is needed then it will begin after the feedback session. Determine their concerns and questions and attempt to answer them.
- f Transition to the work of the session by presenting the agenda for this session which is:
  - 1 To understand what brings them to marital therapy at this time.
  - 2 To take a history of their marital relationship.
  - 3 To observe their attachment needs, their areas of vulnerability, and their negative relationship interaction cycle.
  - 4 To gather additional information by use of several assessment instruments.

1 Middle

- a Begin the work of the session by asking about the clients' presenting problems. During this session you should listen empathically and encourage them each to tell their story. Attempt to elicit their issues concerning how they experience each other. Attempt to determine their feelings of acceptance, connection, rejection, and vulnerability in the relationship. Look for patterns of negativity in the cycle of their interaction. Explain that you want to hear both their stories. Ask who would like to start. Be sure to elicit the same information from each partner.
  - 1 Ask them "What specific issues do you have at this time?"
  - 2 Ask about the history of their complaints. "How long has this be going on?" "When did it start?"
  - 3 Ask what they have attempted to do about this? What was successful? What was not successful?

4 Take a health history. If the following information is available in the case file then proceed to the discussion of the Standard Assessment Battery. If the information is not available then ask:
   a Is the wife currently pregnant?
   b Do either have a history of heart problems or high blood pressure?
   c Are there any other health issues?
   d Is either one currently depressed or do they have a past history of depression?
   e Is either one currently on medications?
   f Is there currently any drug or alcohol abuse? Is there a history of drug or alcohol abuse?

b Assign the Standard Assessment Battery (SAB).
   1 Provide your clients with a rationale for the SAB (Chapter 3 in this text; Johnson et al., 2005, p. 136). For example, tell them that information from the SAB will help you get a complete picture of their marital relations. The battery gives information that you need to help them decide what treatment is needed if any. Briefly explain, in nontechnical language, each instrument to the clients. (Information about the instruments in the standard assessment battery is found in Appendix C).
   2 Get them each to commit to complete the SAB independently. Apply the steps of the Homework Success routine (Appendix J).
   3 Establish a specific date for them to return the SABs.

1 Ending

a Ask clients to summarize the session.
b Administer and score the SRS (Chapter 1 note 1, p. 217) and discuss a total score of 36 and below and any item score of 9 or lower (see Chapter 3).
c Thank clients for their efforts and praise them for looking at their marriage at this time.
d Remind them of the necessity of returning the assessment materials prior to scheduling an appointment for the feedback session.
e Set a time for their individual interviews. *Important*: If you have not already done so discuss your rules for confidentiality in individual interviews with both spouses present (Johnson, 2004, p. 122; Johnson et al., 2005, pp 136–137). For an extended discussion of these issues see Chapter 3 in this text.
f Close session on time (10 minutes before the hour).
g Walk them to the reception area while engaging in social conversation.

1 Reporting/recording

Prepare written case notes within 24 hours (Appendix D).

1 Secure any loose materials from the session in the Case Notes Folder, for example, the SRS, ORS, and the RDAS reports.
2 Begin graphing ORS, RDAS, and SRS scores.

Session 2

2 Individual assessment interview

The purpose of the individual assessment interview is to determine each spouse's commitment to the marriage, their expectations for the marriage, and their expectations for therapy (Johnson,

2004, pp. 121–122; Johnson et al., 2005, p. 136). In addition, the individual interviews are used to screen for family violence, ongoing affairs, and individual mental health issues.

2 *Specific goals*

a Continue joining with the individual spouses to build and maintain the alliance.
b Determine the individual spouses' commitment to and expectations for the marital relationship.
c Determine the individual's expectations for therapy.
d Determine if there is family violence occurring in the relationship.
e Determine if there is an ongoing extramarital relationship.
f Determine if there are individual mental health issues which may impact the relationship.
g Determine if there are other sources of stress impacting the relationship.

Therapist's cognitive knowledge

Read the following in preparation for the session:

a Review Johnson (2004) pp. 121–122; Johnson et al. (2005) pp. 136–138.
b Review also basic EFT skills (Johnson, 2004, pp. 53–112; Johnson et al., 2005, 41–104).
c Review Chapter 5 in this text, concerning issues related to stress.

Equipment needed for the individual sessions

Two copies each of the Session Rating Scale (SRS: Chapter 1, note 1, p. 217), Outcome Rating Scale (ORS: Chapter 3, note 1, p. 217), and the RDAS (Appendix C).

Pre-session preparations

a *Pre-session phone call.* Call the clients 24 hours before the appointment. Re-establish the appointment or reset the appointment. Remind them to come in 15 minutes early to complete the ORS and the RDAS.
b Alert the receptionist at least 1 hour prior to the clients arrival to inform the receptionist that you will be seeing Mr. or Mrs. _______ and to ask the receptionist to administer the ORS and RDAS to them.
c You will need to arrive 10 minutes before the hour to set up seating and to arrange the video cameras.

2 *Beginning*

a Meet the client in the reception area and walk her or him to the consulting room while engaging in social conversation. Help your client remove her/his coat and be seated comfortably.
b If the receptionist is not able to administer the ORS and RDAS then administer them at this time.
c Transition to the work of the session by presenting the agenda for this session. Tell them something like "In this session I want to learn from you how you are feeling about your

marriage and any issues related to it. Remember that my rules for confidentially are . . . ." (see Chapter 3).

2 *Middle*

Begin the work of the session by asking the client about her/his specific problems. These questions do not need to be asked in any specific order but be sure to cover all the topics. If you do not ask specifically many clients will not volunteer the information. Ask something like the following, then listen empathically to their answers, and where appropriate follow up to get the specific details about antecedents, the specific behavior in question, and what happens after.

1. "Tell me about any concerns you might be having about the marriage."
2. "In this session I would like to hear from you about your commitment to the marriage. For example, on a scale of 1 to 10 where 10 is high and 1 is low rank how committed are you to staying in this marriage?"
3. "Have you considered divorce or separation?"
4. "How do you expect therapy to help? What would the final outcome look like for you?"
5. "How is your sexual adjustment?"
6. "In all marriages there are disagreements. Have any of the disagreements in your marriage led to pushing, shoving, or hitting?" Follow up using questions as recommended in Chapter 2. Get information about both partner's involvement and ask about hitting, shoving, and so on with children and elders.
7. "Are you or your partner seeing someone else outside of the marriage in a romantic or intimate way in person or on the Internet?" If they talk about their partner listen to the story then be sure to ask about their behavior. For example, "I think I get the picture about [use partner's name] behavior. What about you? Have you ever been involved in this way with others?"
8. "Have you or your partner experienced any mental health problems, either now or in the past?" Follow up about both individuals.
9. "Are there other sources of stress in your marriage? For example, do either of you have alcohol or drug abuse problems?" "Are either of you having trouble at work or in school?" "Are their money problems?" "How are things with your in-laws?"
10. "Have I left anything out?"

2 *Ending*

a Ask the client to summarize the session.
b Administer and score the SRS (Chapter 1, note 1, p. 217) and discuss a total score of 36 and below and any item score of 9 or lower.
c Thank her or him for their efforts on behalf of their marriage at this time.
d If they have not already returned the assessment instruments remind them of the necessity of returning them prior to scheduling an appointment for the feedback session.
e Close session on time (10 minutes before the hour).
f Walk your client to the reception area while engaging in social conversation.

2 *Reporting/recording*

a Record your case notes in a timely fashion including your graph of the ORS and RDAS data
b Be sure to include the report from the SRS.

Session 3

Purpose

The purpose of Session 3 is to present the treatment plan to the clients and to secure their permission to do therapy.

3 *Specific goals*

a Continue joining with the both spouses to build and maintain the alliance.
b Present the clients with your understanding of their problems and get their agreement.
c Present your proposed treatment plan.
 1 If therapy is not appropriate or if the needed therapy is not available at this clinic then refer the clients elsewhere for help.
 2 If therapy is appropriate then describe the proposed treatment.
d Ask the clients' for their consent to do therapy.

3 *Therapist's cognitive knowledge*

Read the following in preparation for the session:

a Johnson (2004) pp. 129–130; Johnson et al. (2005) pp. 137–139.
b Review also basic EFT skills (Johnson, 2004, pp. 53–112; Johnson et al., 2005, 41–104).
c Review Chapter 4 "Establishing a Treatment Plan" in this text.

3 *Equipment needed*

a Your Written Treatment Plan (Appendix G).
b If the treatment plan decision is "no treatment" then no other equipment is needed.
c If the decision is for referral have the names, addresses, and phone numbers of the referral agency or therapist(s) written out and available for the clients.
d Two copies each of the ORS, the RDAS, and the SRS.

3 *Pre-session preparations*

a Prepare a written treatment plan (see Chapter 4).
b Call the clients 24 hours before the session. Re-establish the appointment or set a new appointment. Remind them to come 15 minutes before the session to complete the ORS, and RDAS.
c Call the receptionist at least 1 hour prior to the clients arrival to inform the receptionist that you will be seeing Mr. and Mrs. _______ and to ask the receptionist to administer the ORS and RDAS to them.
d You will need to arrive 10 minutes before the hour to set up seating and to arrange the video cameras.

3 *Beginning*

a Meet the clients in the reception area and walk them to the consulting room while engaging in social conversation. Help them remove their coats and be seated comfortably.
b If the receptionist is not able to administer the ORS and RDAS then administer them at this time.

c Ask if anything has changed since last session. Listen and observe. Determine any concerns and use clinical judgment to determine if you should alter the agenda for crises related to suicide or dangerousness.
   1 If they have had an argument between sessions listen to each side briefly, making notes. Then explain that this is a feedback session and that you have taken notes and will take up this problem in the next session which is a treatment session.
   2 Transition to session Middle by discussing the agenda, which is: To present your understanding of the problem and potential solutions, e.g., "In this session I want to share back what you have shared with me. Together we will look at all the information I have and we will consider what it suggests. After that we will decide together if therapy is needed."

3 *Middle*

a Review very briefly their relationship history. Check with them for agreement.
b Present a summary of the Standard Assessment Battery information in non-technical terms. Actual scores should not be presented but rather report in general terms such as "You scored in the moderate range for marital satisfaction which suggests that you are somewhat dissatisfied with your marriage. Does that fit with how you see things?" Check with them to see if they generally understand the findings.
c Describe your general observations of the struggles they have had in their marriage and any successes they have had in overcoming them. Describe their interaction pattern and how they each appear to experience their relationship. Check with them to determine if your observations agree with theirs.
d Present your assessment.
   1 If your assessment suggests that no treatment is needed at this time inform them of your decision and the rationale behind it then praise them for their efforts and go to Session 3 Ending A below.
   2 If your decision is to refer to another agency or therapist then inform them of the decision and your rationale and present them with the referral reference(s). Then go Session 3 Ending A below.
   3 If your assessment is for EFT then present a treatment plan which corresponds with your assessment of the problem.
      a Describe the proposed therapy model.
      b Describe the potential benefits and side effects.
      c Discuss expectations for number of treatment sessions.
      d Share their rights, right of refusal, right to request another treatment model, right to request another therapist, and right to return to the clinic without prejudice.
   4 Secure their permission to continue therapy.
e Go to session 3 Ending B.

3 *Ending A*

a Ask the clients to summarize the session.
b Administer and score the SRS and discuss a total score of 36 and below and any item score of 9 or lower.
c Thank the clients for their efforts and ask if there is anything else you can do for them. Tell them that they may return to the clinic at any time.
d Close the session on time (10 minutes before the hour). It is okay to close the session early if you have concluded the goals of the session.
e Walk them back to the reception area while engaging in social conversation.

3 *Ending B*

a If treatment is recommended and accepted then establish a time and date for the next session.
If they are going to return for treatment ask them to come 15 minutes early to complete the ORS and the RDAS. Ask them to each bring a spiral bound notebook or electronic device to the next session that they can use to keep track of homework assignments.
b Administer and score the SRS and discuss a total score of 36 and below and any item score of 9 or lower.
c Close the session on time (10 minutes before the hour).
d Thank them for their efforts to strengthen their marriage.
e Walk them back to the reception area while engaging in social conversation.

3 *Reporting/recording*

Record your case notes in a timely fashion including your graph of the ORS and RDAS data.

Session 4

Emotionally-Focused Therapy Stage 1: De-escalation

The goals for Session 4, EFT Stage 1 De-escalation Steps 1 to 4, are to further determine with your clients the recurring positions they take in response to each other in their negative cycle. Achieving the goals of Session 4 may require more than one session. If additional sessions are required consider them to be Sessions 4A, 4B, and so on.

4 *Specific goals*

a Step 1. Continue joining with both spouses to build and maintain the alliance.
b Step 2. Help the couple identify their negative cycle.
c Step 3. Help them identify their unacknowledged secondary and primary affective responses in the cycle.
d Step 4. Begin to reframe each partner's position in attachment terms.
e The end point of the de-escalation process is to refocus the couple on their negative cycle as the target for their change attempts rather than on attempting to change their partner's behavior.

4 *Therapist's cognitive knowledge*

Read the following in preparation for the session:

a Review Johnson (2004) pp. 131–145 and Johnson et al. (2005) pp. 141–164.
b Review also basic EFT therapist skills (Johnson, 2004, pp. 53–112; Johnson et al., 2005, 41–104).
c Review "Delivering the Planned Treatment" in Chapter 5 of this text.

4 *Equipment needed*

Two copies each of the ORS, the RDAS, and the SRS.

4 *Pre-session preparations*

a *Pre-session phone call* Call the clients 24 hours before the appointment. Re-establish the appointment or reset the appointment. Remind them to come in 15 minutes early to complete the ORS and the RDAS.

b Call the receptionist at least one hour prior to the clients arrival to inform the receptionist that you will be seeing Mr. and Mrs. ______ and to ask the receptionist to please administer the ORS and RDAS to them.

c You will need to arrive 10 minutes before the hour to set up seating and to arrange the video cameras.

4 *Beginnings*

a Meet the clients in the reception area and walk them to the consulting room while engaging in social conversation. Help them remove their coats and be seated comfortably.

b If the receptionist is not able to administer the ORS and RDAS then administer them at this time.

c Ask if anything has changed since last session. Listen and observe.

d Review the ORS and RDAS information with the clients.

e Based on the clients' responses to the "Has anything changed?" question and the ORS and RDAS information determine if there are any concerns and use clinical judgment to determine if you should alter the agenda for crisis related to suicide or domestic violence (see Chapter 2). If the clients are not in crisis then continue with the planned interventions for this session.

f Ask about the homework assignment as appropriate. If they were successful celebrate with them. If they forgot or were unsuccessful explore what got in the way or what went badly. Help them to analyze the problem and to plan to carry it out successfully in the coming week. Your stance should be one of acceptance using your basic therapy skills. Avoid blaming by focusing on process rather than people. Validate their difficulties, reinforce with praise their efforts, and encourage further attempts.

g Transition to session 4 Middle by discussing the agenda.

h The agenda for session 4 is to determine the pattern of their negative interaction cycle and the unacknowledged emotions underlying their interactions in the cycle. Your goal will be to carefully track and focus on the negative pattern and point out the nature of each partner's impact on the other partner's behavior. It is important that each partner becomes aware of their secondary and primary emotions. The cycle is identified as "external" to the couple's relationship and is labeled as the "enemy" of the couple's relationship.

4 *Middle*

a Setting the agenda. You might say something like, "The agenda for this and the next session is to more fully identify the negative cycle that has taken over your relationship. When you are caught in this cycle you are experiencing emotions that prevent you from feeling close and safe with each other. We will identify those emotions and see how they work to separate you from each other. Let's start by asking: What happens when you two have a fight?" See follow up questions in the Workbook (Johnson et al., 2005) p. 145–149.

b Use your basic empathic listening and RISSSC skills (Johnson, 2004, pp. 109–110, 240, 307; Johnson et al., 2005, pp. 52–102).

c Point out the elements of the cycle and label the pattern. See Johnson (2004), pp. 19–20; Johnson et al. (2005) pp. 145–147.

d Help each partner identify their secondary and primary emotions (Johnson (2004) pp. 63–90; Johnson et al. (2005) pp. 45–53, 165–191.
e Help them understand their emotional experiences in attachment terms.

4 Endings

a At approximately 40 minutes past the hour begin ending the session.
b Ask the clients to summarize the session. Reinforce the parts they got correct and provide tentative corrective feedback for parts that appear to be off track.
c Administer and score the SRS and discuss a total score of 36 and below and any item score of 9 or lower.
d Assign homework as appropriate (Appendix J).
e Thank them for their efforts on behalf of their marriage. Set an appointment for the next session then walk them to the reception area.

4 Reporting/recording

Within 24 hours record your case notes in a timely fashion including your graph of the ORS and of the RDAS data.

Session 5

EFT Stage 1 Step 4 De-escalation

The goal for Session 5, EFT Stage 1 De-escalation Step 4, is to complete the de-escalation process by helping the couple to learn to identify their negative cycle and the secondary and primary affective responses that sustain it. In Step 4 they will learn to describe their positions in attachment terms. In EFT Step 4 you will help them to define the problem as external to their relationship. You will also help them to see that the problem is exacerbated by each partner's emotional responses and attachment needs. The end point of the de-escalation process is for the couple to be able to refocus on their negative cycle as the target for their change attempts and not on changing their partner's behavior.

5 Therapist's cognitive knowledge

Read the following in preparation for the session:

a Review Johnson (2004) pp. 131–145 and Johnson et al. (2005) pp. 141–164.
b Review "Delivering the Planned Treatment" in Chapter 5.

5 Equipment needed

Two copies of the ORS, the RDAS, and the SRS.

5 Pre-session preparations

Follow the "Pre-session preparations" outlined in Session 4 above.

5 Beginning

a–f Follow the "Beginning" procedures A to F found in Session 4.
g Transition to session 5 Middle by discussing the agenda.
h The agenda for session 5 is to de-escalate the negative cycle by increasing their understanding of the cycle and how their emotions and attachment needs contribute to it.

5 Middle

a You might say something like: "The agenda for today's session is to help you learn to de-escalate your negative cycle by clarifying how your emotional responses and attachment needs contribute to the cycle. If you had a fight or disagreement this week how did it go? If you did not have a fight or disagreement how did you avoid it?" After they have described their week follow up with something like: "What part did your cycle contribute to how the week went?" "What part did your emotions and attachment needs contribute to the cycle?"
b Listen empathically and use your RISSSC skills of validation, evocative responding, heightening, empathic conjecturing, and reframing to help them identify the cycle and the part their emotions and attachment needs played in the process (Johnson et al., 2005, p. 154).
c Help each partner identify their secondary and primary emotions that were evoked by the context and the partner. Help them identify how this contributed to the cycle.
d When the partners are able to identify their pattern of interaction and how it defines their cycle they will be on the way to de-escalation and ready to move on to EFT Stage 2 Changing Interactional patterns, Steps 5, 6, and 7.

5 Ending

Begin ending the session at forty minutes after the hour.

1 Ask the clients to summarize the session. Provide reinforcement and corrective feedback as needed.
2 Administer and score the SRS and discuss a total score of 36 and below and any item score of 9 or lower.
3 Thank them for their efforts on behalf of their marriage. Set an appointment for the next session then walk them to the reception area.

5 Reporting/recording

Record your case notes in a timely fashion including your graph of the ORS and RDAS data.

Session 6A

EFT Stage 2, Steps 5 and 6: Deepening engagement by expanding and heightening emotion

The goals for Session 6, EFT Stage 2, Steps 5 and 6, are to help your clients identify disowned attachment needs and other disowned aspects of their self-concept. Step 5 is the most intensely intrapsychic step of EFT. Step 5 focuses on one of the partner's – known as the experiencing partner (EP). Step 5 focuses on the EP's attachment needs and fears associated with the marital relationship. Step 5 leads to Step 6 in which the other partner (OP) is helped to hear, process, and respond positively to the EP's sharing. The goal is to restructure the marital relationship by reshaping the EP's perception of self in the relationship and her or his perception of how the OP responds to her or him in the relationship. At the same time the OP's behavior in the relationship is changed by her or his new perception of the EP and the EP's changed responses. The shift in focus from the EP's to the OP's understanding and acceptance of the EP's attachment needs and feelings is Step 6. It will be necessary to repeat Steps 5 and 6 with the partners switching roles. Therefore in Session 6B the partners will switch roles and repeat the processes of Session 6A

6 *Therapist's cognitive knowledge*

Read the following in preparation for the session:

a Review the treatment manual Johnson (2004) pp. 147–169 and workbook Johnson et al. (2005) pp. 165–191.
b Review also basic EFT skills (Johnson, 2004, pp. 53–112; Johnson et al., 2005, 41–104).
c Review "Delivering the Planned Treatment" in Chapter 5 .

6 *Equipment needed*

Two copies of the ORS, the RDAS, and the SRS.

6 *Pre-session preparations*

Follow the "Pre-session Preparations" outlined in Session 4 above.

6A *Beginning*

a–f Follow the "Beginning" procedures A to F found in Session 4.
g Transition to Session 6A Middle by discussing the agenda.
h The agenda for Session 6A, Step 5, is to help one of the partners, usually the withdrawing partner, fully experience her or his disowned attachment needs and reformulate them into the relationship (Johnson, 2004; Johnson et al., 2005).

6A *Middle*

a You might say something like: "The agenda for today's session is to help you experience your attachment responses related to the attachment needs and feelings you have been experiencing in relationship to your partner and your marriage. Since it would be difficult for you both to engage in this process at the same time we will take one partner at a time. It may take us several sessions to get through this entire process for both of you. Why don't we start with [name the more withdrawing partner]. Tell us, what has been happening with you in this relationship?"
b Follow up using your RISSSC skills of validation, evocative responding, heightening, empathic conjecturing, and reframing to help them identify the cycle and the part their emotions and attachment needs played in the process (Johnson et al., 2005, p. 154). Help your client become aware of and own, their feelings of vulnerability, hurt, and fear. Help them recognize these feelings more deeply. This means they will increase their engagement with their attachment needs and feelings. Help them distill, that is to be more specific and clear about, these feelings. Finally, help them disclose these feelings to their partner in a nonthreatening way (Johnson et al., 2005, pp. 169–184).
c Help the OP listen and accept their partner's fears and hurt feelings. This is EFT Step 6. The goal in Step 6 is for the OP to validate their partner's feelings by acknowledging and accepting the EP's right to have those feelings (Johnson et al., 2005, pp. 185–191). Help the OP

avoid punishment in the form of criticism, defensiveness, contempt, and stonewalling, known collectively as the "four horsemen of the apocalypse" (Gottman, 1999).

d Session 7 will shift focus from the withdrawn partner as the EP to the blaming partner who will become the EP. In Session 7 you will need to repeat A, B, and C above for the blaming partner as EP.

6A Endings

a Ask the clients to summarize the session. Provide reinforcement and corrective feedback as appropriate.
b Administer and score the SRS and discuss a total score of 36 and below and any item score of 9 or lower.
c Thank them for their efforts on behalf of their marriage. Set an appointment for the next session then walk them to the reception area.

6A Reporting/recording

Record your case notes in a timely fashion including your graph of the ORS and RDAS data.

Session 6B

EFT Stage 2, Steps 5 and 6: Deepening engagement by expanding and heightening emotion

The goals for Session 6B, EFT Stage 2, Steps 5 and 6, are to help your clients switch roles and identify disowned attachment needs and other disowned aspects of the second partner as in Session 6A above. Therefore Session 6B repeats Session 6A above with the partners roles reversed.

Session 7

EFT Stage 2, Step 7 Emotional engagement: Enactments and bonding

The goals for Session 7 EFT Stage 2, Step 7 are to further process and expand the emotional experiences of Steps 5 and 6 and to increase each client's awareness and ownership of their attachment fears, longings, and needs. The goals of Step 7 also include helping the EP clarify their attachment-related views of themselves and their spouse. In Step 7 the OP is guided to listen to and respond with empathy and acceptance to the EP's expressions of attachment needs and emotions. Additionally, the goal is to help the couple restructure their relationship in terms of more secure bonds.

7 Therapist's Cognitive Knowledge

Read the following in preparation for the session:

a Review the treatment manual (Johnson, 2004) pp. 171–186; Workbook (Johnson et al., 2005) pp. 193–237.
b Review also basic EFT skills (Johnson, 2004, pp. 53–112; Johnson et al., 2005, 41–104).
c Review "Delivering the Planned Treatment" in Chapter 5.

7 Equipment needed

Two copies of the ORS, the RDAS, and the SRS.

Pre-session preparations

Follow the "Pre-session Preparations" outlined in Session 4 above.

7 Beginning

a–f Follow the "Beginning" procedures A to F found in Session 4.

g The agenda for Session 7, Stage 2, Step 7, is:

1. To help the couple use their new emotional experiences from Steps 5 and 6 to change their relationship positions and interaction patterns.
2. To help them become more engaged by owning and sharing their attachment needs and wants.
3. To help them soften their relationship positions.
4. As they come to own these new positions and as they can begin to practice more positive interaction cycles they may come to experience a powerful new bonding experience.

7 Middle

a You might start Session 7 by saying something to the more withdrawing partner like: "Why don't we start by your telling us about your emotional experiences in the previous sessions?"

b Help the EP expand and clarify to their partner their attachment fears, needs, and wants. Use your basic empathic listening and RISSSC skills (Johnson, 2004, pp. 109–110, 240, 307; Johnson et al., 2005, pp. 52–102).

c Help the OP listen and accept their partner's expressions of attachment fears, needs, and wants. Reframe any statements by the OP that discount or negate the EP's statements. When the OP responds positively reinforce this behavior by reflecting and/or heightening their comments (See Johnson et al., 2005, pp. 218–221).

d If the EP gets side tracked help them refocus back on their attachment needs, wants, and fears.

e Reverse the partner's roles so that both have the opportunity to share their attachment needs, fears, and desires.

f Repeat these processes as needed to help them through the softening process as they move toward renewed bonding. Renewed bonding is signaled by their ability to ask for comfort, reassurance, and soothing (see also Gottman, 1999).

7 Ending

a Ask the clients to summarize the session. Provide reinforcement and corrective feedback as needed.

b Assign homework as appropriate.

c Administer and score the SRS and discuss a total score of 36 and below and any item score of 9 or lower.

d Thank them for their efforts on behalf of their marriage. Set an appointment for the next session then walk them to the reception area.

7 Reporting/recording

Record your case notes in a timely fashion including your graph of the ORS and RDAS data.

Session 8

EFT Stage 3, Step 8: Consolidation of a secure base

The goals for Session 8, EFT Stage 3, Step 8 are to facilitate the couple's development of their new relationship skills and the use of the new relationship as a foundation for solving problems and issues.

8 Therapist's cognitive knowledge

Read the following in preparation for the session:

a Review the treatment manual Johnson (2004) pp. 187–200; Workbook Johnson et al. (2005) pp. 239–255).
b Review also basic EFT skills (Johnson, 2004, pp. 53–112; Johnson et al., 2005, 41–104).
c Review "Delivering the Planned Treatment" in Chapter 5.

8 Equipment needed

Two copies of the ORS, the RDAS, and the SRS.

Pre-session preparations

Follow the "Pre-session Preparations" outlined in Session 4 above.

8 Beginning

a–f Follow the "Beginning" procedures A to F found in Session 4.
g The agenda for Session 8, EFT Stage 3, Step 8 is to help the couple use their new positive relationship skills to deal with problems and issues of a more practical nature such as sexual relations, finances, and in-laws.

8 Middle

a You might start with something like: "Tell me how you two are handling some of the long term issues in your relationship, such as [tailor this to the couple, for example for one couple it may be finances, for another it may be child rearing, and so on]."
b Use your basic empathic listening and RISSSC skills (Johnson, 2004, pp. 109–110, 240, 307; Johnson et al., 2005, pp. 52–102).
c Help each partner accept and own her or his part in the discussion of the issue.
d Help the couple explore and discuss the issue but take care to let them find their own solutions.
e Point out how this process can be a source of intimacy and contact even while they are confronting obstacles.
f Go to session 8 Ending.

8 Ending

a Ask the clients to summarize the session. Provide reinforcement and corrective feedback as needed.
b Assign homework as appropriate.
c Administer and score the SRS and discuss a total score of 36 and below and any item score of 9 or lower.
d Thank them for their efforts on behalf of their marriage. Set an appointment for the next session then walk them to the reception area.

8 Reporting/recording

Record your case notes in a timely fashion including your graph of the ORS and RDAS data.

Session 9

EFT Stage 3, Steps 8 and 9: Consolidation and termination

This session begins the termination phase of EFT. The goal for Session 9, which is EFT Stage 3, Steps 8 and 9, is to further consolidate the partner's new emotional attachments and bonding. As with other EFT steps, it make take several sessions to achieve the goals of Session 9. During these sessions the clients may indicate that they are ready to leave therapy. You should determine the clients' readiness to terminate therapy using the best available information. You should review the graphs of the outcome scores with the clients to determine if they have reached their therapy goals (Chapters 5 and 6). In addition, you should discuss their subjective evaluations of their progress and you should help them create their own story of the therapy process. Be sure to emphasize that the changes in their relationship are a function of their efforts while down playing your role in the process. They are ready for termination when they can respond to their problems and issues from a secure base of emotional attachment. This means they deal with negative issues in a new nondefensive way. They are able to move from the negative responses to more constructive patterns such as stating their needs and recognizing their emotional responses as well as those of their partner. Finally, couples should be prepared for termination by helping them prepare for relapses without your assistance. They can avoid relapse by recognizing signs of slipping back into the negative cycle. When they recognize that they are returning to the negative cycle they should turn to each other rather than to the therapist (see also Gottman, 1999). In addition, they construct new positive rituals which strengthen their relationship (again see Gottman, 1999). When couples are able to meet these criteria they will be ready to terminate.

9 Specific goals

a Help the couple construct a story of their experiences in therapy.
b Help them articulate how they exit from their negative cycle and turn to their new positive cycle to resolve issues.
c The goal is for the couple to be able to resolve the negative issues which have caused their distress and to shift to maintaining a level of emotional engagement that builds and strengthens the bond between them. This includes developing positive rituals that build and strengthen their emotional attachments to each other and their relationship.
d Assess the couple's readiness for termination.
   1 Review and consolidate the new knowledge and skills the clients have gained.

2 Assess together the nature and extent of any dependency and separation issues you and they may be experiencing related to terminating therapy.
3 Empower your clients by attributing the changes they have made to their efforts and by devaluing the contributions you have made thus equalizing the relationship.
4 Predict and practice relapses.
5 Give permission to the clients to return for treatment for this or any other problems.

e Review the ORS and RDAS scores to determine if the clients have made statistical and/or clinically significant improvements and have achieved their goals (Chapter 5).
f Review your delivery of EFT (Chapter 5).
g Be prepared to discuss your recommendations for termination with your clients.

9 Therapist's cognitive knowledge

Read the following in preparation for the session:

a Review Johnson (2004) pp. 187–200, 254; Johnson et al. (2005) pp. 239, 247–255.
b Review also basic EFT skills (Johnson, 2004, pp. 53–112; Johnson et al., 2005, 41–104).
c Review Chapter 6, "Termination of Therapy."

9 Equipment needed

Copies of the graphs of the ORS and RDAS scores to share with the clients to demonstrate the progress they have made in terms of statistical and/or clinically significant improvements (Chapter 5).

9 Pre-session preparations

Follow the "Pre-session preparations" outlined in session 4 above.

9 Beginning

a–f Follow the "Beginning" procedures A to F found in session 4.
g The agenda for session 9 is to help the couple build a narrative about how they were and how they are now in their relationship. This will include:
1 An awareness and understanding of how they handle negative affect.
2 The ability to express the value they place on the other and their relationship.
3 A discussion of how they avoid defensiveness.
4 A discussion about how they have each personally grown as a result of the changes in their relationship.

9 Middle

a You might begin by asking something like, "When you two look back on what you have learned in therapy what has changed in your relationship?" Follow up with questions such as;
1 "What changes have you each made?"
2 "What part has your emotions played in these changes?"
3 "What have you learned about how to get out of your negative cycle?"
4 "What have you learned about how important it is to take some risks in expressing your wants and needs?"
5 "What are you each doing to protect and support each other?"

b Another goal for Session 9 is to initiate termination. It is time to initiate termination when your clients and/or your charts indicate that therapy has been successful. Readiness to terminate is indicated by their ability to do the things outlined in (A) above. Readiness to terminate is also indicated when they have achieved statistical and clinical changes from clinical to nonclinical levels in their ORS and the RDAS charts. When your clients have achieved their goals it is time to imitate termination (see Chapter 6).
 1 Discuss their success and indicate their readiness to terminate.
 2 Discuss the nature and extent of any dependency and separation issues you and they may be experiencing related to terminating therapy.
 3 As stated earlier empower your clients by attributing the changes they have made to their efforts and by devaluing the contributions you have made thus equalizing the relationship.
 4 Talk about the possibility of relapses and practice what they can do should a relapse occur.
 5 Finally give your clients permission to return for treatment for this or any other problem in the future.

9 *Ending*

a Ask the clients to summarize the session. Provide reinforcement and corrective feedback as needed.
b Administer and score the SRS and discuss a total score of 36 and below and any item score of 9 or lower).
c Administer the post-treatment SAB assessments (Appendix C).
d If they have not completed the consolidation of their relationship or the termination steps then schedule additional sessions. When consolidation and termination are complete then congratulate them on their success, indicate areas for further improvement, repeat your invitation to return in the future if necessary, and say your goodbyes.

9 *Reporting/recording*

a Record your case notes in a timely fashion including your graph of the ORS and RDAS data.
b Write your Treatment Summary (Appendix H). Indicate the clients' progress using pre- and post-treatment SAB scores. Summarize the treatment and the clients' response to it. Make recommendations for further treatment as needed.

Epilogue

Therapists who desire to become emotionally-focused therapists will find guidelines in Johnson (2004) and Johnson et al. (2005). In addition, there are training opportunities through the International Centre for Excellence in Emotionally-Focused Therapy online at www.iceeft.com. There you will also find audio and visual training materials. Also, you will find information about how to find supervision and training by qualified EFT supervisors and trainers.

Notes

Chapter 1

1 The Session Rating Scale and the Outcome Rating Scale are available free by going to the website http:// Scottdmiller.com and looking under the Performance Metrics tab.
2 The SOFTA-o is available at http://www.softa-soatif.net.
3 Efficacious treatments are those that have been found to work under controlled conditions. Effective treatments are those that have been shown to work in everyday clinical practice (see Chapter 4).

Chapter 3

1 The Outcome Rating Scale (ORS) is available free by going to http://Scottdmiller.com and looking under the Performance Metrics tab.

Chapter 5

Adherence rating scales are available for:

- Emotionally Focused Therapy: Emotion-Focused Therapy-Therapist Fidelity Scale (EFT-TFS): Conceptual development and content validity. *Journal of Couple and Relationship Therapy*, 8, 226–246.
- Functional Family Therapy: Alexander, J. F., Pugh, C., Parsons, B., & Sexton, T. (2000). *Blueprints for violence prevention: Book Three: Functional family therapy* (Appendix B). Boulder, CO: Center for the Study and Prevention of Violence, Institute of Behavioral Science University of Colorado. See also http://www.colorado.edu/cspv/ blueprints/modelprograms/FFT.html
- Gottman Method Couples Therapy: Available at http://www.gottman.com go to the Professional Training & Events tab. The adherence rating material is part of Level 3.

Becoming a Marriage and Family Therapist: From Classroom to Consulting Room, First Edition. D. Eugene Mead.

- Helping the Noncompliant Child: Long, N. & Forehand, R. (2007). Fidelity checklist for Helping the Noncompliant child. Unpublished manuscript. Available from R. Forehand, University of Vermont, Department of Psychology, Burlington, VT. See also Jones, D. J. (2010). HNC fidelity checklist (R-34). Unpublished document. Available from D. J. Jones, University of North Carolina, Department of Psychology, Chapel Hill, NC.
- Integrative Behavioral Marital Therapy: For adherence rating scales for Integrative Behavioral Couple Therapy contact Andrew Christensen at http://christensenresearch .psych.ucla.edu/ or http://ibct.psych.ucla.edu/

Chapter 7

1 To find a supervisor go to The Gottman Relationship Institute website http://www.gottman.com and go to the Professional training tab.

2 An adherence rating scale for Gottman Couples Therapy may be found at http://www.gottman.com under the Level Three, Certification Track, Appendix A.

Appendix A

Person of the Therapist Checklist

D. Eugene Mead, August 2007

Ask yourself which of the following responses you experienced during the session. Begin by asking yourself "Am I experiencing feeling stuck, frustrated, ambivalent, anxious, angry, fearful, panic, rage, disgust, passion, sexual arousal, guilt/shame, depression, grief, optimism, or mirth?" Determine if the response was appropriate for the context and if your behavior related to the affective response was therapeutic or not therapeutic. Similar questions should be raised about your behavior and your cognitive thoughts. Ask yourself, "Is my behavior congruent with the treatment being delivered?" "Are my thoughts centered on the clients and their behavior or am I "out of the room" some of the time?"

RESPONSE	Did this response occur in this session? In any previous sessions?	Was my AFFECTIVE response appropriate/ congruent for the context?	Was my COGNITIVE response client centered?	Was my BEHAVIOR therapeutic/ client centered?
Feeling stuck				
Frustrated				
Ambivalent				
Anxious				
Angry				
Fear				
Panic				
Rage				
Disgust				

RESPONSE	Did this response occur in this session? In any previous sessions?	Was my AFFECTIVE response appropriate/ congruent for the context?	Was my COGNITIVE response client centered?	Was my BEHAVIOR therapeutic/ client centered?
Passion				
Sexual arousal				
Guilt				
Shame				
Depression				
Grief				
Optimism				
Mirth				
Joy				
Elation				
Other				

Appendix B

Therapist Self-Soothing Procedures

D. Eugene Mead

The purpose of this appendix is to provide the therapist with some techniques for self-soothing. Therapist self-soothing should occur whenever the therapist's affective arousal in the session becomes great enough to interfere with effective performance of therapy. To be able to determine when affect arousal is occurring first establish your resting pulse rate outside therapy.

Determining When to Apply Therapist Self-Soothing Techniques

During therapy take your pulse when you recognize: (a) Changes in your smooth muscles and glands, such as sweaty palms and feet, dry mouth, tears, and/or tight stomach muscles; (b) That you have tense large muscles such as neck, jaw, forehead, and back muscles; or (c) That you have reason to ask yourself, "Am I experiencing feeling: stuck, frustrated, ambivalent, anxious, angry, fearful, panic, rage, disgust, passion, sexual arousal, guilt/shame, depression, grief, optimism, or mirth?" If your pulse is 10-12 beats per minute above your resting pulse rate you are becoming emotionally aroused and self-soothing is recommended.

Here are some techniques to use to self-sooth to reduce affective arousal in sessions.

1. Slowly take three deep breaths.
2. Ask yourself what the therapy task is for this session. Give yourself an answer.
3. Review the things you have done right so far in this session relevant to the therapy task. There are sure to be many things you have done correctly so don't give up, keep digging them out. They do not need to be big things.
4. The cognitive behavior required to complete this step is part of the self-soothing process so it is not intended as a self-blame, shame, and guilt game. Just recall all the things you have done well so far.

Becoming a Marriage and Family Therapist: From Classroom to Consulting Room, First Edition. D. Eugene Mead.

5 Ask yourself what you need to do next to be therapeutic for these clients. Give yourself several alternatives such as:
   a Using "I" statements to reflect your feelings to the clients.
   b Reflecting and restating the clients' behavior clearly and specifically in a nonblaming way and then asking the clients for their interpretation.
   c Asking the clients to describe the recent events in therapy to each other or to you.
   d If necessary, excuse yourself, step out, walk around, get a drink, before returning to the session
   e If necessary seek out a supervisor or peer for consultation.
6 Once you have determined what you can do to be therapeutic for these clients at this time implement your intervention.
7 Then tell yourself to stop, listen, and observe the client responses.
8 If possible, once you have clarified the issues, return to the treatment plan and the task for this session. Otherwise, take what ever action you feel is necessary using your best clinical reasoning. Remember you do not need to use all 50 minutes of the session. When it is time to terminate the session do so.
9 Terminate the session as usual with a summary and some positive statements to your clients for support and encouragement.
10 Review the session with your supervisor.

Appendix C

Standard Assessment Battery for Marital Relational Problems

Appendix C contains a brief review of each of the following instruments.

Assessment Instrument	*Purpose*
Revised Dyadic Adjustment Scale (RDAS: Busby, Crane, Larson, & Christensen, 1995).	Assess Marital Satisfaction
Marital Status Inventory -Revised (MSI-R: Jamieson, 2007)	Assess Marital Stability (Divorce Potential)
Brief Screen for Depression (Hakstian, & McLean, 1989)	Screen for Depression
Conflict Tactics Scale 2 (CTS2: Straus, Hamby, Boney-McCoy, & Sugarman, 1996).	Screen for Family Violence
Comprehensive Areas of Change Item Ranking Form. (Mead, 2006)	Complaints and issues to be discussed in later sessions.
Outcome Rating Scales (ORS: Miller & Duncan, 2004)	Assesses individual partner's subjective distress. It is designed to measure the client's progress in the course of therapy.
The Alcohol Use Disorders Identification Test (AUDIT). Babor, de la Fuente, Saunders, & Grant, 1992)	Assesses alcohol abuse.

Becoming a Marriage and Family Therapist: From Classroom to Consulting Room, First Edition. D. Eugene Mead.

Revised Dyadic Adjustment Scale (RDAS)

D. M. Busby, C. Christensen, D. R. Crane, and J. H. Larson

Purpose: Assesses marital adjustment or satisfaction.

Range of Scores: The scale overall scores can range from 0 to 69. The RDAS provides an overall score and three subscales, Consensus, Satisfaction, and Cohesion.

Reliability: The RDAS appears to have excellent test-retest reliability. For the Total RDAS Chronbach's Alpha was reported to be .90, Guttman Split-Half = .94 and Spearman-Brown Split-Half was found to be .95.

Validity: The RDAS is reported to distinguish reliably between distressed and nondistressed samples (Busby et al, 1995).

Reliable Change Index Scores. Reliable change index (RCI) scores are derived by a formula established by Jacobson and Truax (1991). A RCI score for an instrument indicates that the change is greater than chance. Thurber and Mead (2002) following Jacobson and Truax found the RCI score for the RDAS (Busby 1995) to be ±5.

Cutoff Scores: The cutoff line for nondistressed and distressed marital satisfaction has been found to be 48 (Crane, et al. 2000; Thurber & Mead 2002). However, Thurber and Mead found a band of uncertainty of ±5 points surrounding the cutoff. Consequently, scores that fall within the band of 43 to 53 points can not be reliably determined to be either distressed or nondistressed. Therefore, a *clinically significant change* in RDAS scores would be a change from 43 or below to 53 or above. Changes of that magnitude will exceed the RCI for the RDAS of ±5.

Availability: In the public domain.

Marital Status Inventory-Revised

Rachel V. Jamieson and D. Eugene Mead

Name____________________

Male________ Female________

Date____________________

We would like to get an idea of how your marriage stands *right now.* Please answer the following by circling true or false for each item.

T	F	1	I have occasionally thought of divorce or wished that we were separated, usually after an argument or other incident.
T	F	2	I have considered divorce or separation a few times other than during or shortly after a fight, although only in vague terms.
T	F	3	I have thought specifically about separation or divorce. I have considered who would get the kids, how things would be divided, pros and cons of such actions, etc.
T	F	4	I have discussed the question of my divorce or separation with someone other than my spouse (Trusted friend, therapist, minister, etc.)
T	F	5	I have suggested to my spouse that I wished to be divorced, separated, or rid of him/her.
T	F	6	I have made specific plans to discuss separation or divorce with my spouse. I have considered what I would say, etc.
T	F	7	I have discussed the issue seriously or at length with my spouse.
T	F	8	My spouse and I have separated. [This is a (a) trial separation or (b) permanent separation; circle one.]
T	F	9	Thoughts of separation or divorce occur to me very frequently, as often as once a week or more.
T	F	10	I have made inquiries from nonprofessionals as to how long it takes to get a divorce, grounds for divorce, costs involved in such actions, etc.
T	F	11	I have consulted a lawyer or other legal aide about the matter.
T	F	12	I have set up an independent bank account in my name as a measure of protecting my own interests.
T	F	13	I have contacted a lawyer to make preliminary plans for a divorce.
T	F	14	I have filed for divorce or we are divorced.

Scoring

Score one point for each item marked "T" for True. Wife's score of 8 and above indicates increased probability of divorce within the next two years.

References

Crane, D. R., & Mead, D. E. (1980). The Marital Status Inventory: Some preliminary data on an instrument to measure marital dissolution potential. *The American Journal of Family Therapy, 8*, 31–35.

Crane, D. R., Newfield, N., & Armstrong, D. (1984). Predicting divorce at marital therapy intake: Wives' distress and the Marital Status Inventory. *Journal of Marital and Family Therapy, 10*, 305–312.

Crane, D. R., Soderquist, J. N., & Gardner, M. D. (1995). Gender differences in cognitive and behavioral steps toward divorce. *The American Journal of Family Therapy, 23*, 99–105.

Jamieson, R. V. (2007). *A revision of the marital status inventory: Reliability and validity with marital and remarital couples.* Unpublished Thesis, Marriage and Family Therapy Programs, School of Family Life, College of Family, Home, and Social Sciences, Provo, Utah.

Weiss, R. L., & Cerreto, M. (1980). The Marital Status Inventory: Development of a measure of dissolution potential. *The American Journal of Family Therapy, 8*(2), 80–86.

Brief Screen for Depression (BSD)

A. R. Hakstian and P. D. McLean

Purpose: A brief screen for indications of depression.
Range of Scores: The Brief Screen for Depression (BSD) is a four item assessment with scores ranging from 0 to 35.
Reliability: Alpha = .65. Test Re-test = .54
Validity: Correlates .58 with Beck Depression Inventory (Beck, Steer, & Brown, 1996). Classification efficiency 95.8% between depressed and normal subjects and 85.8% between depressed and nondepressed psychiatric control subjects.
Clinical Cutoff Score: Cutoff score of 21 yielded a depression hit rate of 95.8% with 3.6% false positives and 0.6% false negatives. Total score Depressed $M = 33.88$ $SD = 6.61$; Normal $M =$ 13-27 $SD = 5.22$.
Availability: In the public domain.

References

Beck, A. T., Steer, R. A., & Brown, G. (1996). *Beck Depression Inventory (2nd ed.).* San Antonio, TX: The Psychological Corporation.

Hakstian, A. R., & McLean, P. D. (1989). Brief Screen for Depression. *Psychological Assessment, 1,* 139–141.

Conflict Tactics Scale 2 (CTS2)

M. A. Straus, S. L. Hamby, S. Boney-McCoy, and D. B. Sugarman

Purpose: Assesses for domestic violence in the form of psychological aggression, physical assault, sexual coercion, and inflicted injury.

Range of Scores: The Conflict Tactics Scale 2 (Straus, Hamby, Boney-McCoy, & Sugarman, 1996) contains 39 items scored for first the respondent's behavior and second for the behavior of the respondent's spouse for a total of 78 items. Scores are established by the midpoints of the frequency of an event. For example "I called my partner fat or ugly" is scored 0 for the answer "this never happened" 1 for "once in the past year" 2 for "twice in the past year" 4 for "3–5 times in the past year" 8 for "6–10 times" 15 for "11–20 times" and 25 for "more than 20 times." Therefore scores can range from 0 to 1950. The CTS2 contains 5 subscales: (a) Negotiation; (b) Psychological aggression; (c) Physical assault; (d) Sexual coercion; and (e) Injury.

Reliability: The authors report that the alpha reliability coefficients of the subscales were found to be (a) Negotiation (alpha = .86); (b) Psychological aggression (alpha = .79); (c) Physical assault (alpha = .86); (d) Sexual coercion (alpha = .87); and (e) Injury (alpha = .95).

Validity: The authors present evidence for construct and discriminant validity. Discriminate validity is based on comparison of the correlation between the subscales "negotiation" and "sexual coercion" and "negotiation" and "injury." The assumption was that there should be no theoretical reason for correlation between these sets of subscales. The findings were that there are only nonsignificant or low correlations for these pairs. The authors caution that the findings are based on college student couples.

Clinical Cutoff Scores: Prevalence percentages and Chronicity means for each of the subscales may be found in Straus et al. (2003 Table 12, p. 48). Prevalence score is the percentage of the sample that reported 1 or more instances of the acts in a subscale. Chronicity indicates how often the set of acts assessed by each subscale among those who engaged in one or more instances of the acts.

Administration Time: The authors report that administration time for the CTS2 is 10 to 15 minutes.

Availability: CTS-2 is available from Western Psychological Services, 12031 Wilshire Blvd. Los Angeles, CA 90025-1251, Telephone: (800) 648-8857 - FAX: (310) 478-7838, www.wpspublish.com

References

Straus, M. A., Hamby, S. L., Boney-McCoy, S. B., & Sugarman, D. B. (1996). The revised Conflict Tactics Scales (CTS2): Development and preliminary psychometric data. *Journal of Family Issues*, 17, 283–316.

Straus, M. A., Hamby, S. L., & Warren, W. L. (2003). *The Conflict Tactics Scales Handbook: Revised Conflict tactics Scales (CTS2): CTS: Parent-Child Version (CTSPC)*. Western Psychological Services.

Comprehensive Areas of Change Questionnaire (CAC) Item Ranking Form

Purpose: Inventory of the couples' complaints and serves to generate items for discussion in observation assessment and in treatment. The CAC Item Ranking Form replaces The Comprehensive Areas of Change Questionnaire (Mead, Vatcher, Wyne, & Roberts, 1990).

Range of Scores: The CAC Item Ranking Form (Mead, 2006) consists of 71 items. The respondents are asked to place an "X" in the left column to indicate items they feel they need to talk about. Following this they review the items they have selected to talk about and rank them from easiest to hardest to talk about. The therapist can then ask them to discuss the items and while they are discussing them the therapist may observe their communication and problem-solving skills. In treatment the therapist may ask the couple to select items for discussion and use them to practice improving their communication and problem-solving skills.

Reliability and Validity: No reliability or validity information is supplied as these items are used for client discussion followed by therapist observation and instruction and not for formal assessment.

Availability: This material is in the public domain.

Comprehensive Areas of Change Questionnaire (CAC)

Item Ranking Form

D. Eugene Mead, revised August 2006

Name: ____________________ Date: ____________________

Below is a list of things some couples try to change in each other. Please review this list and for each of the items you and your partner have differences over mark an "X" in the column on the left labeled "We need to talk about."

Next, rank all the items you put an "X" in front of . Start by finding the *easiest* item for you to talk about and problem solve about. Write a "1" in the "Rank" column behind the easiest item. Find the next easiest item and mark a "2". Find the third easiest item and write "3" in the Rank column. Note that each item is becoming more difficult for you and your partner to talk about. Continue in this way until you have ranked all the items you marked with an "X".

We need to talk about	*Item*	*Rank*
	1. Conforming to proper social behavior	
	2. Hitting the children	
	3. Drinking	
	4. Preparing interesting meals	
	5. Going to church	
	6. Agreeing on values	
	7. Paying attention to my sexual needs	
	8. Holding my hand	
	9. Spending money	
	10. Leaving me time to myself	
	11. Speaking for me	
	12. Getting together with our friends	
	13. Solving problems without fighting	
	14. Helping plan our free time	
	15. Using street drugs	
	16. Spending time in outside activities	
	17. Assuming responsibility for finances	
	18. Working late	
	19. Showing me that he/she cares about me	
	20. Being concerned about my wish to die	
	21. Acting "crazy"	
	22. Discussing our marital problems with his/her relatives	
	23. Spending time alone with his/her friends	
	24. Talking about his/her physical illnesses	
	25. Trying to change my values	
	26. Getting together with my relatives	
	27. Taking over my jobs	
	28. Starting interesting conversations with me	
	29. Being jealous	
	30. Making decisions together	

We need to talk about	Item	Rank
	31. Allowing others to make sexual advances toward him/her	
	32. Playing with our children	
	33. Wasting time worrying about nonexistent physical problems	
	34. Being "depressed"	
	35. Initiating sexual relations with me	
	36. Having the final say so on making decisions	
	37. Hitting me	
	38. Looking for different work	
	39. Having good personal hygiene	
	40. Being involved with his/her previous spouse	
	41. Being "anxious"	
	42. Trying to control me	
	43. Worrying about his/her job	
	44. Expressing his/her emotions clearly	
	45. Being the "boss"	
	46. Fulfilling my expectations for marriage	
	47. Touching the children in a sexual way	
	48. Worrying about doing better on the job or in school	
	49. Paying attention to his/her appearance	
	50. Making me feel like he/she loves me	
	51. Getting together with my friends	
	52. Complaining about problems that do not seem to exist	
	53. Helping with housework when asked	
	54. Expressing loving feelings	
	55. Comparing me to his/her previous spouse	
	56. Disciplining the children	
	57. Assuming he/she knows what I am thinking without asking me	
	58. Being moody	
	59. Giving me hugs	
	60. Spending time keeping the house clean	
	61. Making decisions without consulting me	
	62. Being caring	
	63. Listening to me	
	64. Engaging in extra-marital sexual relationships	
	65. Talking in a socially acceptable way	
	66. Trying to make me jealous	
	67. Paying the bills on time	
	68. Having meals ready on time	
	69. Time spent playing computer games	
	70. Involvement with pornographic material including computer, television, magazines, books, and so on	
	71. Gambling	

Notes: Adapted from Mead, D. E., Vatcher, G. M., Wyne, B. A., & Roberts, S. L. (1990). The Comprehensive Areas of Change Questionnaire: Assessing marital couples' presenting complaints. *The American Journal of Family Therapy, 18*(1), 65–79.

Outcome Rating Scale

S. D. Miller and B. L. Duncan

Purpose: The Outcome Rating Scale (ORS) was designed to be administered at the beginning of each session as a continuous measure of progress. The Outcome Rating Scale is a four-item visual analogue scale. Clients respond by placing a hash mark nearest the pole on the line which best describes their experience. It was designed to measure the same variables as the OQ-45® (a) subjective discomfort or symptom distress, (b) interpersonal relationships, and (c) social role performance.

Range of Scores: The line for each item is 10 cm long and therefore scores can range from 0 to 10 for each item, total scores range from 0 to 40.

Validity: Concurrent validity was assessed by use of a Pearson product moment correlation between the ORS and the OQ-45®. The correlation was found to be $r = .58$. The authors believe this is adequate given the brevity of the ORS.

Reliability: Reliability was assessed by use of Cronbach's alpha ($r, = .93$). Test-retest reliability at the second session was found to be $r = .66$.

Sensitivity to Change: As the ORS was designed to measure change over time. Pre- and post-test scores for a clinical group and a nonclinical group were compared. Scores for the clinical group were significantly different while scores for the nonclinical group were relatively stable.

Cutoff Scores: Based on a large sample (n = 34,790) and using procedures established by Jacobson and Truax (1991) the clinical cutoff for the ORS was found to be 24. Scores of 25 and above were found to be in the non-clinical range.

Reliable Change Index (RCI): The RCI for the ORS was found to be a 5-point change. A change of 5 or more points indicates a statistically reliable change.

Accessibility: The Outcome Rating Scale (ORS) is available free by going to http://Scottdmiller.com and looking under the Performance Metrics tab.

References

Miller, S. D. & Duncan, B. L. (2004). *The outcome and session rating scales: Administration and scoring manual* (Rev.). Chicago IL: Scott D Millar.

Jacobson, N. S. and Truax, P. (1991). Clinical significance: A statistical approach to defining meaningful change in psychotherapy research. *Journal of Consulting and Clinical*, 59, 12–19.

The Alcohol Use Disorders Identification Test (AUDIT)

T. F. Babor, J. R. de la Fuente, J. Saunders, and M. Grant (1992)

Purpose: The Alcohol Use Disorders Identification Test (AUDIT: Babor, de la Fuente, Saunders, & Grant, 1992) was developed to identify individuals with early alcohol problems. Specifically the AUDIT is used to detect harmful and hazardous alcohol consumption. The AUDIT is a ten-item questionnaire developed for the World Health Organization (WHO: Babor et al, 1992) as a cross-national clinical screening instrument.

Range of Scores: The AUDIT is a ten-item questionnaire with a range of scores from 0–40. Symptom. Distress scores range from 0–100, Interpersonal Relations scores range from 0–44, and Social Role scores range from 0–36.

Reliability: The AUDIT is a ten-item questionnaire and scores can rang from 0 to 40. Among the drinking clients the drinking behavior and the adverse psychological reactions domains had high alpha coefficient 0.93 and 0.81 respectively (Saunders, Aasland, Babor, de la Fuente, & Grant (1993). There was little variation across national samples.

Validity: Validity was determined in five ways:

> Based on the sample of 913 drinking patients, Saunders et al. . . . evaluated the accuracy of AUDIT in detecting harmful and hazardous alcohol consumption by comparing the sensitivity and specificity for five different "gold standards": 1. hazardous alcohol consumption (defined as a typical daily intake exceeding 60g for a man and 40g for a woman) or recurrent intoxication; 2. dependence symptoms (a positive response to at least one feature of the alcohol dependence syndrome); 3. alcohol problems in the last year/a positive response to any of five questions on physical and psychosocial consequences); 4. a combined index (which was a summation of all the evidence of harmful of hazardous alcohol consumption from the data set); and 5. positive classification within groups of known alcoholics or abstainers (Babor et al., 1992, p. 21).

Cutoff Scores: The cutoff points for the screening instrument were determined by examining the relationship between sensitivity and specificity for the first four conditions [hazardous alcohol consumption or recurrent intoxication, dependence symptoms, alcohol problems in the last year, and a combined index which is the sum of all harmful alcohol consumption]. Two cutoff points were determined, 8+ and 10+ . Using the lower cutoff point the sensitivity for hazardous consumption and/or recurrent intoxication ranged from 95% to 100%. For dependence symptoms it varied from 93% to 100%, and for the problems in the last year from 91% to 100%. The sensitivity using the combined index ranged from 87% to 96%, with the overall value being 92%. The specificity of AUDIT with respect to the combined index ranged from 81% to 98%, with an overall value of 93%. When the cutoff point of 10 was taken, the sensitivities were lower, with an overall value of 80% for the combined index. The specificities were correspondingly higher: for the combined index values ranged from 95% to 100%, with an overall value of 98%.

Among the drinking patients, all those who had three or more dependence criteria had a score of 10 or more.

Of the known alcoholics, 99% had a score of 10 or more. Less than 2% of the nondrinkers had a score of 8 or more.

Using a score of 5 or more as indicating a "positive" case, the sensitivity and specificity of the clinical procedure were also examined, again using hazardous alcohol consumption" as the reference standard. The sensitivity varied from a low of 13% in Bulgaria to 67% in Norway with a mean value of 41%. The specificity was better, ranging from 81% to 97% with a mean of 92%. It performed poorly in comparison with the core instrument in all centers except Norway, where it was superior. The marketed center-to-center variation in validity suggests that disguised screening procedures may be feasible but that country-specific tests may need to be devised. Sensitivity was also calculated using the alcoholics as the criterion group. The results averaging 74% across centers indicate that the clinical procedure may have limited utility even for the detection of alcoholics (Babor et al., 1992, p. 21).

Scoring: The AUDIT is hand scored.

Availability: The AUDIT is in the public domain.

Appendix D

Written Case Progress Notes

D. Eugene Mead, November 2006

Outline for case progress notes

Session Information

Date seen. Date notes made. Session number.
Clients in attendance this session.

Session Summary

Therapy task planned for this session.
Therapy task that was delivered in this session.
Impact of the therapy task on the clients.

Observations

Review of the homework.
Discussion of the events in the client's life since the previous session.
Outcome assessment scores.
Other assessment and rating scores.
Client's clinically relevant behaviors observed in the session.
Therapist's therapeutic interventions.
Client's alliance ratings.

Conceptualizations

What are your hypotheses about the etiology of the client's behavior?
What information is missing?

Becoming a Marriage and Family Therapist: From Classroom to Consulting Room, First Edition. D. Eugene Mead.

How do your interventions fit or not fit with the observations described above?
How do the observations fit or not fit with the therapy model you are applying?

Assignments and Future Plans

Homework assigned or not assigned.
Plans to collect missing information.
Rationale for continuing the current treatment task or moving to a new task (Therapy tasks are: assessment, feedback, treatment delivery and evaluation, and termination).

Appendix E

Observations of the Couples' Communication and Problem-solving Behaviors Therapist's Rating Form Based on Gottman (1999)

D. Eugene Mead, Rev. October 2006

Couple Name:____________________ Therapist's Name:__________________ Date:__________

	EASY PROBLEM		HARD PROBLEM	
	Partner 1	Partner 2	Partner 1	Partner 2
Soft start up				
Harsh start up				
Bids				
Repair attempt				
Accept influence				
Time out				
Solutions				
Complaints				
Criticism				
Defensiveness				
Contempt				
Stonewalling				

Comments:

Source: Based on Gottman, J. M. (1999). *The marriage clinic: A scientifically-based marital therapy*. New York: Norton.

Appendix F

Clinical Experience Log

Name: ______________________________

Therapy Hours

<table>
<tr><td rowspan="2"></td><td rowspan="2">Mode of therapy performed by the therapist</td><td colspan="4">Unit/System participating in treatment</td></tr>
<tr><td>Individual</td><td>Couple</td><td>Family</td><td>TOTAL</td></tr>
<tr><td rowspan="6">Beginning/ ending dates:
____
to
________</td><td>Therapist solo</td><td></td><td></td><td></td><td></td></tr>
<tr><td>Group therapy</td><td></td><td></td><td></td><td></td></tr>
<tr><td>Psychoeducational</td><td></td><td></td><td></td><td></td></tr>
<tr><td>TOTAL</td><td></td><td></td><td></td><td>Grand total =</td></tr>
<tr><td></td><td>% of total = col tot/grand tot
Indiv. =</td><td>% of total = col tot/ grand tot
Cpl. =</td><td>% of total = col tot/ grand tot
Fam. =</td><td rowspan="2"></td></tr>
<tr><td>Relationship hours % of total hours</td><td></td><td colspan="2">% relationship therapy is sum of % couple + % family =</td></tr>
</table>

(*continued*)

Becoming a Marriage and Family Therapist: From Classroom to Consulting Room, First Edition. D. Eugene Mead.

Supervision Hours

	Mode of supervision received by the therapist	Unit/System participating in treatment			
		Direct (live) Supervision	Recorded video supervision	Case report	TOTAL
Beginning/ ending dates:	Individual supervision				
	Group supervision				
______	TOTAL				Grand total
to	% of total	% of total = col tot/grand tot =	% of total = col tot/grand tot =	% of total = col tot/ grand tot =	
______		Supervision using raw data % = Total sum of direct + video =			

Appendix G

Preparing a Written Treatment Plan

Preparing the treatment plan requires significant
amounts of work prior to the feedback session

Some suggestions for writing treatment plans

Purpose

The purpose of a Treatment Plan is to provide the information required to describe:

a The family members' complaints and goals.
b The specific empirically supported treatment proposed to reduce or eliminate the complaints and achieve the goals.
c The criteria which will be used to determine when therapy is to be terminated.

The amount of detail required may depend upon the nature of the treatment model;

a If an empirically-supported treatment manual is to be used then a note to that effect along with any details about how the standard treatment is to be tailored to fit this specific couple should be satisfactory.
b If a theory-based treatment is to be used then careful specification of the treatment in considerable detail is recommended. If the treatment lacks empirical support for efficacy then the clients' written informed consent for taking part in an experimental treatment is needed. Enough detail must be supplied so that another competent therapist could carry out the treatment.

Expectations for the written treatment plan

A reasonably complete treatment plan will contain the following sections: (a) description of the clients; (b) discussion of the presenting problem(s); (c) the data upon which the decisions about the treatment plan will be made; (d) the therapist's assessment of the problem; (e) any clinical diagnoses if applicable; (f) the treatment goals; (g) the estimated number of sessions; and (h) the criteria for termination.

Becoming a Marriage and Family Therapist: From Classroom to Consulting Room, First Edition. D. Eugene Mead.

Who are the clients?

Demographics for each person in treatment

Describe each of the family member involved in therapy. Give their name, age, gender, race or ethnic background, religious affiliation, and relationship to the other family members. For example, "John Klient is a white male student, aged 35, member of the Church of Jesus Christ, Latter-day Saints (LDS or "Mormon"), married for 5 years to Mary Klient. John has two children by a previous marriage, John Jr, and Sariah. John does not appear suicidal or dangerous at this time. Mary Klient is a 33 year old white female, a member of the LDS Church, homemaker, working part time in a bank. This is her first marriage and they have no children of their own. Mary does not appear suicidal or dangerous at this time. John Jr. is a white 13 year old boy attending Wabash Middle School in the 7th grade and he is active in the LDS Church. Sariah is a 12 year old white female in the 6th grade at Bowler Elementary School. She is also active in the LDS Church. Neither child appears suicidal or dangerous at this time."

What is the problem?

Presenting problem as seen by each person in treatment

Presenting complaints A statement of the presenting complaints for each family member in the family member's words. Example: "Mrs. Klient stated, 'We just don't seem to communicate like we did when we were dating.'" "Mr. Klient said, 'We argue all the time.'"

What is the data?

Tabulate and describe the assessment information

Include a table (Table G.1) and a verbal discussion of the assessment information. The table should stand alone, that is one should be able to read the table and understand the case without reading the discussion. The discussion in the body of the Treatment Plan should also stand alone, although it may refer to information in the table.

An example of the discussion of the assessment instruments and therapist observations

Mrs. Klient's Outcome Questionnaire (OQ-45) score of 77 suggests that she is clinically distressed while Mr. Klient's OQ-45 score of 35 indicates he is functioning in the nonclinical range at this time. Mrs. Klient scored 40 on the Revised Dyadic Adjustment (RDAS) and Mr. Klient scored 44, which suggests that both are maritally distressed. Mrs. Klient's Marital Status Inventory (MSI) score was 3 and her Oral History Rating was 49. Mr. Klient scored 0 on the MSI and 28 on the Oral History Rating. These scores suggest that neither Mrs. Klient nor Mr. Klient appear divorce prone at this time. No evidence for depression for either spouse was found in the Brief Screen for Depression (BSD) with scores of 9 for Mrs. Klient and 7 for Mr. Klient Based on the BSD scores. The Beck Depression Inventory (BDI) was not administered. Physical Violence, as assessed by the Revised Conflict Tactics Scales (CTS2) does appear to be a factor at this time as Mrs. and Mr. Klient scored: Negotiation 33 and 25, Psychological Aggression 12 and 17, Physical Assault (pushing and shoving) 1 and 2, respectively, and Sexual Coercion and Injury were 0 for both. Pushing and shoving, while classified as minor physical aggression by Straus et al. (1996) should be investigated further. Mr. and Mrs. Klient's marital distress and Mrs. Klient's clinical distress suggests that treatment for marital relational problems may be appropriate.

Table G.1 Example of an assessment table in a treatment plan

Assessment Instrument	*Wife*	*Husband*
OQ45		
Symptom Distress (SD)	40	33
Interpersonal Relationships (IR)	37	02
Social Role (SR)	00	00
TOTAL	77	35
Revised Dyadic Adjustment Scale	40	44
Marital Status Inventory	3	0
Oral History Divorce Potential Rating	49	28
Brief Screen for Depression	9	7
The Revised Conflict Tactics Scales (CTS2)		
Negotiation	33	25
Psychological Aggression	12	17
Physical Assault	1	2
Sexual Coercion	0	0
Injury	0	0
The Alcohol Use Disorders Identification Test (AUDIT)		
Recent Alcohol Consumption	0	1
Dependence Symptoms		0
Alcohol Related Problems		0
Total Score	0	1
Others as Needed		

Scoring the Oral History Rating Scale, Revised For Divorce Potential

Wife We-Ness	Score	9
Husband We-Ness	Score	7
Couple Glorifying the Struggle	Score	8
Husband's Fondness	Score	9
Husband's Negativity	Score	9
Husband's Expansiveness	Score	7
Couple Chaos	Score	8
Wife Disappointment/Disillusionment	Score	8
Husband Disappointment/Disillusionment	Score	10
	TOTAL DIVORCE POTENTIAL SCORE	75

Alcohol abuse does not appear to be a problem for either spouse at this time as assessed by AUDIT.

The couple's Oral History Rating Scale score of 75 suggests that the couple may be experiencing elevated divorce potential at this time. However the results are mixed as indicated by the MSI subclinical scores.

The Observation Session ratings suggest that the couple used high rates of criticism and defensiveness. Their responses on the "difficult" problem did reveal a tendency for the husband to withdraw from or "stonewall" emotional issues. This suggests that they need to improve their communication skills. They did not provide many solutions and did not seem to follow up on those that were suggested. Therefore, it appears that they also need to improve their problem-solving skills.

Ask yourself as a therapist

Are there any initiation (resistance) problems (Nezu & Nezu, 1989)? For example, emotional acceptance issues (Jacobson & Christensen, 1996), sharply differing concepts of marriage or individual psychological distress such as depression (Gottman, 1999). If so, can they be resolved well enough to carry out marital therapy? If one or both clients assess with depression behaviors did the depression precede the marriage or did it follow the marriage date? If the former then consider Beach, Sandeen, and O'Leary's (1990) behavioral marital therapy for depression.

Describe your assessment of the problems

Describe your assessment of the problems as perceived by each family member in therapy (Kohlenberg & Tsai, 1991; Nezu & Nezu, 1989).

a What data has been collected related to the family members' strengths and problems (Kohlenberg & Tsai, 1991; Nezu & Nezu, 1989)? Indicate the source of the data:
   1 Oral History Interview Report. Specific complaints and themes. Couple conflict style.
   2 Observation Report. Specific complaints, themes, strengths.

b Summarize what is known about the problem in clear, specific, operational terms. Be sure to separate inferences, hypotheses, and conjectures from what is known. Be sure to consider the client's (insider) and the therapist's and others' (outsiders) points of view. Describe the clinically relevant behaviors you have observed in specific and concrete terms. Describe the marital strengths you have observed in specific and concrete words. Also consider the history (development) of each of these variables as well as the current controlling variables. Be sure to consider hypotheses which pertain to each of the following domains: (1) Biomedical (genetics, surgeries, medication, alcohol, drugs); (2) Cognitive; (3) Family relational patterns; (4) Physical environment; (5) External systems (Police, courts, school, work, Church).

Goals

What are each family member's expectations and goals for therapy in their words? Example: "Mrs. Klient would prefer to, 'be able to talk and not get in fights.'" Mr. Klient stated that he would like it if, "we could just get some of our problems resolved with out all this fuss and emotion."

What is the diagnosis?

1 <u>Relational diagnosis</u> This establishes the system functions as related to the DSM-IV (American Psychiatric Association, 2000) diagnostic behaviors (Kaslow, 1996). System variables may be a response by family members to the behavior of the identified patient (IP). The symptom pattern behaviors of the IP may be due to: (a) genetically inherited characteristic; (b) induced by medical procedures, trauma, or drugs, and/or; (c) structured, and/or maintained by interaction patterns which are characteristic of this family.

2 <u>Provisional diagnosis</u> A provisional DSM-IV-TR (APA, 2000) diagnosis may be needed to establish a clinical case for treatment. Be sure to include a "Global Assessment of Relational Functioning (GARF) Scale" in your diagnosis (DSM-IV-TR, APA, 2000) to help establish the need for family therapy.

3 <u>Functional analysis of the specific complaints</u>
   a Most complaints are likely to be descriptions of behaviors which are too much, too little, or missing and which are aversive to the client or to others.

b These behaviors typically evoke any combination of emotional, escape, avoidance, counter-attack, or actively doing something else (e.g. stonewalling) responses from those who find the behavior aversive.

c After ruling out genetic, trauma, or drug induced behavior you may begin to consider the following. Behavior which is missing altogether will require a training program for the affected family members. Behavior which is too frequent or not frequent enough is often a function of the client's motivation, where motivation can be described as a function of the three term contingencies of reinforcement, that is the context or antecedents, the behavior, the consequences. Phobias and other forms of anxiety may be a function of conditioned aversive behavior.

Therapy goals

Therapist specified short and long term goals for therapy

a How will progress be determined for both short and long term goals?
b How will outcome be determined for both short and long term goals?
c Identify any potential blocks to attainment of the family members' goals.

Treatment plan

Describe the treatment to be applied to help the family members attain their goals.

Specifying the treatment design

Describe treatment alternatives (Nezu & Nezu, 1989).

1 Specify treatment alternatives for each goal.
2 Describe likely consequences of each alternative for each family member.
3 Rate the likely effects of each alternative for each family member. What is the likelihood that:
   a This treatment will achieve the specified goals?
   b You can optimally implement this particular treatment approach?
   c That others could carry out this treatment more effectively?
   d These family members will be able to perform the behaviors required for this treatment?
   e That this treatment approach will contribute to each family member's ability to cope more effectively with future problems?
4 Rate value effects for each alternative. What will be the personal consequences for each family member in terms of
   a Effort, time, money, or other resources required to achieve these goals with this treatment?
   b Emotional costs and gains?
   c The family members' morals, values, and ethics?
   d Physical side effects?
   e Related problem areas?
5 Recommend treatment which rates highest for likelihood and for value effects.

Estimated number of sessions

Give a reasonable estimate of the number of sessions required to deliver the treatment successfully. Base your estimate on the information found in the treatment manual for empirically-tested treatments, or on clinical reports for theory-based treatments.

What are the criteria for terminating therapy?

1. Will statistically significant changes as indicated by RCI scores on assessment scores be considered satisfactory for termination?
2. Will clinically relevant scores on the assessment instruments be required for satisfactory termination?
3. Who will determine when to terminate? Clients? Therapist? Mutual agreement?

In preparing a treatment plan you will need to do the following:

1. Review the Intake Interview notes and the case notes for the assessment session(s). Look for major themes and their controlling variables (Jacobson & Christensen, 1996; Christensen et al., 1995). Write down a range of examples for each major theme (Engelmann & Carnine, 1991). Write down the connection between these response classes and your hypothesized controlling variables.
2. Score and order in a table the paper and pencil assessment instruments and your observation rating scores. Write a brief narrative description of the results of the assessments.
3. Rate the couple's relationship using the Global Assessment of Relationship Functioning Scale (GARF: American Psychiatric Association, 2000).
4. Determine the relational diagnosis . The following questions follow Polya (1971). Ask yourself, is there a pattern in this data? Have I seen this before? Have I seen parts of this before? What is missing? What other hypotheses does this information suggest? Is a Relational Diagnosis appropriate for this couple? If so what is/are the relational diagnosis(es)?
5. Review the data to determine if a DSM-IV-TR (APA, 2000) diagnosis is appropriate for the IP or other family members.
6. Your decision to treat or not treat should be based on the information above. Your options are:
   a. No treatment needed at this time.
   b. An empirically-supported treatment is available and you would recommend treatment "X". Determine possible benefits, possible risks, possible outcomes if left untreated, and discuss other available treatments.
   c. No empirically-supported treatment is available but treatment based on theory "Y" may prove beneficial. Determine possible benefits, possible risks, possible outcomes if left untreated, and other theoretical approaches.
   d. Treatment is recommended but the needed treatment is not available in this clinic. Recommend referral to an appropriate agency or therapist.
   e. No empirically-supported treatment and no sound theory available. Therefore, recommend no treatment at this time.
7. If therapy is appropriate:
   a. Use clinical reasoning to connect the clients' complaints and goals to a treatment plan.
   b. Consider how this treatment plan can be specifically tailored to these clients.
8. Write up the treatment plan as outlined above.
9. The therapist reports the Treatment Plan to her/his supervisor or case manager and records her/his treatment plan in the file.
10. After completing the above the therapist is prepared to schedule a Feedback Session and present his/her evaluation of the problem and the proposed treatment to the clients.

Appendix H

Written Treatment Summary

D. Eugene Mead, Fall 2006

Please enter the following headings and subheadings in your Treatment Summary and enter the information. Where applicable you may cut and paste material from the Case Notes and/or the Treatment Plan and enter the information under the appropriate subheadings.

Type of Therapy:

Description of the Clients:
Client's Names and Demographics:

Initial Presenting Problems:
Client(s) Statements of the Problems:
Initial Outcome Assessment Scores (*e.g.* OQ 45© & RDAS):
Initial Standard Assessment Battery Scores:
Other assessments for example, the observational assessment of enactment proficiency.

Treatment Summary:
Total number of sessions you met with the client(s):
Treatment(s) delivered:

Reasons for Termination:
Indicate whether termination was initiated by the clients, by the therapist, mutually:
Provide reason(s) for termination:

Conditions at Termination:
Final Outcome Assessment Scores:
Final Standard Assessment Battery Scores:
Therapist's evaluation of the treatment outcome(s):

Post-Termination Recommendations:
Therapist's recommendations for further treatment or follow-up:

Becoming a Marriage and Family Therapist: From Classroom to Consulting Room, First Edition. D. Eugene Mead.

Appendix I

Therapy Tailoring Skills Rating Form

D. Eugene Mead, 2007

Therapist's Name: __________ Date: ________ Case No. ________ Session No. ____________

Alliance		
I did not measure the alliance in this session.	1 2 3 4 5	I measured the alliance in this session. I discussed any breaches in the alliance with the clients.
Empathy		
During the session I was unable to understand each client's thoughts, feelings, and struggles.	1 2 3 4 5	During the session I attempted to understand each client's thoughts, feelings, and struggles.
Goal Consensus		
I did not check with each client to determine if they understood how each intervention pertained to their goals. I did not attempt to tailor the treatment to the clients.	1 2 3 4 5	I checked with each client to determine if they understood how each intervention pertained to their goals. I tailored the treatment to the clients.
Collaborative Involvement		
I was unable to get the clients to cooperate and to take an active role in the treatment. I was unable to get them to accept the homework assignment or they failed to complete the homework assignment.	1 2 3 4 5	I was able to get the clients to cooperate and to take an active role in the treatment. They accepted and/or completed the homework assignment(s).
Family Cohesion		
I did not recognize and reinforce family members' expressions of acceptance and support for each other. I did not observe and reframe their expressions of negativity.	1 2 3 4 5	I recognized and reinforced family members' expressions of acceptance and support for each other. I observed and reframed their expressions of negativity.
Structuring the Session		
In this session I did not state clearly and specifically the expectations for the treatment intervention(s). I did not define or redefine therapy rules.	1 2 3 4 5	In this session I stated clearly and specifically the expectations for the treatment intervention(s). I defined or redefined the therapy rules.

Source: Based on Horvath and Bedi (2002) pp. 37–69; Bohart et al. (2002) pp. 89–108; Tryon and Winograd (2002) pp. 109–125; Burlingame, Fuhriman, and Johnson (2002) pp. 71–87 in Norcross, J. C. (Ed.) (2002b).

Appendix J

Homework Success: Therapist Guidelines

Homework success

1 The clients' success or failure with homework assignments is a function of the therapist's behavior (Jacobson & Christensen, 1996, pp. 162–169). If the clients are willing to work together, cooperate, compromise, and accommodate to each other reasonably well they are probably ready for homework assignments.

2 Helping clients prepare for homework assignments.

A Exaggerate the difficulty of the task.

a Warn them about the difficulty. Some commonly heard difficulties (i) there is no time in their busy schedules; (ii) it is hard to remember; (iii) it is hard to keep it all straight; (iv) it is hard to do when one is upset with their partner; and (v) other things in their lives may get in the way.

b Apologize and commiserate with them about going through this.

B Anticipate and head off reasons for non-compliance (Jacobson & Christensen, 1996).

i *Reason number 1. No time*

a If they are committed to their marriage will it be worth it to set some time aside each day to make their marriage better? Will marital therapy be less expensive than a divorce lawyer?

b Help them plan a time they can set aside daily to add to their list.

c Get them to commit to doing it at the time they have planned.

ii *Reason number 2. Forgetting to do the assignment*

a Help them plan personal reminders, for example, note on the refrigerator, bathroom mirror, or by the door they use most often when they leave home.

b Handouts and written descriptions help keep the assignments straight.

iii *Reason number 3. Getting upset with each other*

a The homework assignments require considerable effort. Therefore, it is hard to do when you are upset with each other or are fighting about something. Nonetheless, that simply indicates how important it is to do the homework. They need to work on the assignments even if their partner is not doing so at the present time. Remember

Becoming a Marriage and Family Therapist: From Classroom to Consulting Room, First Edition. D. Eugene Mead.

Virginia Satir's statement "You have to give to get." The more positive and loving things you do for your partner the more you love will get back. It may not be returned immediately but over time it generally evens out. Remember too that Gottman (1994) suggested a 5:1 or greater ratio of positive to negative exchanges is one factor that insulates against divorce. Of course 5 boxes of candy or 5 bouquets of flowers do not make up for one act of infidelity. The exchanges need to be of about equal in value.

iv *Reason number 4. What else might get in the way?* Ask them if they are aware of anything else that might get in the way of the homework assignment? What can be done to plan around this obstacle?

Therapists who consistently prepare clients for therapy homework in this way have highly successful clients. Most homework failure is therapist failure, "the fault, dear therapist, is in us, not in the clients" (with apologies to Shakespear).

Source: Based on Jacobson and Christensen (1996) pp. 162–169.

Appendix K

Preparation for Supervision Checklist: Couples

D. Eugene Mead, September 2007

THERAPIST:__________________________ DATE:______________________

CASE NUMBER:____________________ SESSION NUMBER:___________

THERAPY TASK: ☐ Assessment ☐ Treatment Plan ☐ Treatment Delivery ☐ Termination

TREATMENT MANUAL:______________________________

OUTCOME ASSESSMENTS:

Wife Outcome Score:______ Difference Score:______ ☐ Statistically Sign. Change? ☐ Clinically Sign. Change?

Husband Outcome Score:______ Difference Score:______ ☐ Statistically Sign. Change? ☐ Clinically Sign. Change?

INTERPRETATION: Wife ☐ Improving ☐ Staying the Same ☐ Deteriorating

Husband ☐ Improving ☐ Staying the Same ☐ Deteriorating

Wife RDAS Score:______ Difference Score:______ ☐ Statistically Sign. Change? ☐ Clinically Sign. Change?

Husband RDAS Score:______ Difference Score:______ ☐ Statistically Sign. Change? ☐ Clinically Sign. Change?

INTERPRETATION: Wife ☐ Improving ☐ Staying the Same ☐ Deteriorating

Husband ☐ Improving ☐ Staying the Same ☐ Deteriorating

Other Assessments:__________ Score:______ ☐ Statistically Sign. Change? ☐ Clinically Sign. Change?

INTERPRETATION: ☐ Improving ☐ Staying the Same ☐ Deteriorating

Becoming a Marriage and Family Therapist: From Classroom to Consulting Room, First Edition. D. Eugene Mead.

ALLIANCE ASSESSMENT: SRS Administered? ☐ No ☐ Yes

Wife SRS: Relationship______cm Goals & Topics______cm Method______cm Overall______cm

Husband SRS: Relationship________cm Goals & Topics________cm Method________cm Overall______cm

Discussed SRS Responses of 9 or less with the clients? ☐ No ☐ Yes

TREATMENT INTERVENTION EMPLOYED THIS SESSION

CRISIS? ☐ No ☐ Yes If Yes how assessed?____________ How managed?______________

INTERVENTION PLANNED FOR THIS SESSION:________________________________

____

Required elements of the intervention:______________________________________

Acceptable common elements:____

Proscribed, harmful, or unhelpful elements:__________________________________

Adherence to the Manualized Intervention

In this session I did not deliver all of the required elements of the intervention and the acceptable common elements. I included proscribed, harmful or unhelpful elements.	☐ 1 ☐ 2 ☐ 3 ☐ 4 ☐ 5	In this session I delivered all of the required elements of the intervention and the acceptable common elements. I did not include proscribed, harmful or unhelpful elements.

Structuring the Session

In this session I did not state clearly and specifically the expectations for the treatment intervention(s). I did not define or redefine therapy rules. I did not specify roles and skills needed for effective performance of the skills.	☐ 1 ☐ 2 ☐ 3 ☐ 4 ☐ 5	In this session I stated clearly and specifically the expectations for the treatment intervention(s). I defined or redefined the therapy rules. I specified the roles and skills needed for effective performance of the skills.

Collaborative Involvement

I was unable to get the clients to cooperate and to take an active role in the treatment. I was unable to get them to accept the homework assignment or they failed to complete the homework assignment.	☐ 1 ☐ 2 ☐ 3 ☐ 4 ☐ 5	I was able to get the clients to cooperate and to take an active role in the treatment. They accepted and/or completed the homework assignment(s).

Empathy

During the session I was unable to understand each client's thoughts, feelings, and struggles.	☐ 1 ☐ 2 ☐ 3 ☐ 4 ☐ 5	During the session I was able to understand each client's thoughts, feelings, and struggles.

Goal Consensus

I did not check with each client to determine if they agreed with each intervention. I did not attempt to tailor the treatment to the clients.	☐ 1 ☐ 2 ☐ 3 ☐ 4 ☐ 5	I checked with each client to determine if they agreed with each intervention. I tailored the treatment to the clients.

Couple Cohesion and Processes

I did not recognize and reinforce couple expressions of acceptance and support of each other. I did not observe and reframe their expressions of negativity.	☐ 1 ☐ 2 ☐ 3 ☐ 4 ☐ 5	I recognized and reinforced couple expressions of acceptance and support of each other. I observed and reframed their expressions of negativity.

Supervisors Comments:____

Source: Based on Horvath and Bedi (2002) pp. 37–69; Bohart et al. (2002) p. 89–108; Tryon & Winograd (2002) pp. 109–125; Burlingame et al. (2002) pp.71–87 in Norcross, J. C. (Ed.) (2002b).

References

Achenbach, T. M. (1994). Child behavior checklist and related instruments. In M. E. Maruish (Ed.), *The use of psychological testing for treatment planning and outcome assessment.* (pp. 517–549). Hillsdale, NJ: Lawrence Erlbaum Associates.

Addis, M. E., & Cardemil, E. V. (2006). Psychotherapy manuals can improve outcomes. In J. C. Norcross, L. E. Beutler & R. F. Levant (Eds.), *Evidence-based practices in mental health: Debate and dialogue on the fundamental questions.* (pp. 131–140). Washington, DC: American Psychological Association.

Administration on Aging. (2007). *2007 World Elder Abuse Awareness Day.* Retrieved 13 March 2008, from http://www.aoa.gov/eldfam/Elder_abuse/Elder_abuse.asp.

Agar, K., & Read, J. (2002). What happens when people disclose sexual or physical abuse to staff at a community mental health centre? *International Journal of Mental Health Nursing, 11*(2), 70–79.

Alexander, J. F., & Sexton, T. L. (2002). Functional family therapy: A model for treating high risk, acting out youth. In J. Lebow (Ed.), *Comprehensive handbook of psychotherapy, volume IV: Integrative/Eclectic.* (pp. 111–132). New York: Wiley.

Alexander, J. F., Pugh, C., Parsons, B., & Sexton, T. (2000a). *Blueprints for violence prevention: Book three: Functional family therapy.* Boulder, CO: Center for the Study and Prevention of Violence, Institute of Behavioral Science, University of Colorado.

Alexander, J. F., Waldron, H. B., Barton, C., & Mas, C. H. (1989). The minimizing of blaming attributions and behaviors in delinquent families. *Journal of Consulting and Clinical Psychology, 57,* 19–24.

Almeida, D. M., Stawski, R. S., & Cichy, K. E. (2011). Combining checklist and interview approaches for assessing daily stressors: The Daily Inventory of Stressful Events. In R. J. Contrada & A. Baum (Eds.), *The handbook of stress science: Biology, psychology, and health.* (pp. 583–595). New York: Springer.

American Association for Marriage and Family Therapy (AAMFT) (1998). *AAMFT Code of Ethics.* Washington, DC: Author.

American Association for Marriage and Family Therapy (AAMFT) (2001). *AAMFT Code of Ethics.* Washington, DC: Author.

American Association for Marriage and Family Therapy (AAMFT) (2004, December). *Marriage and family therapy core competencies.* Retrieved 26 May 2005, from American Association for Marriage and Family Therapy: www.aamft.org.

Becoming a Marriage and Family Therapist: From Classroom to Consulting Room, First Edition. D. Eugene Mead.

American Association for Marriage and Family Therapy (AAMFT) (2007). *Legal guidelines for family therapists with selected ethical opinions.* Alexandria, VA: Author.

American Psychiatric Association. (2000). *Diagnostic and Statistical Manual of Mental Disorders, 4th ed., Text Revision.* Washington, DC: American Psychiatric Pub.

American Psychological Association. (1995). *Template for developing guidelines: Interventions for mental disorders and psychosocial aspects of physical disorders.* Washington, DC: Author.

American Psychological Association. (2002). *Ethical principles of psychologists and code of conduct 2002.* Washington, DC: Author.

American Psychological Association. (2006). Evidence-based practice in psychology. *American Psychologist, 61*(4), 271–285.

Anderson, E. M., & Lambert, M. J. (2001). A survival analysis of clinically significant change in outpatient psychotherapy. *Journal of Clinical Psychology, 57,* 875–888.

Anderson, S. A., Schlossberg, M., & Rigazio-DiGilio, S. (2000). Family therapy trainees' evaluations of their best and worst supervision experiences. *Journal of Marital and Family Therapy, 26,* 79–91.

Anker, M. G., Duncan, B. L., & Sparks, J. A. (2009). Using client feedback to improve couple therapy outcome: A randomized clinical trial in a naturalistic setting. *Journal of Consulting and Clinical Psychology, 77,* 693–704.

Anker, M. G., Owen, J., Cuncan, B. L., & Sparks, J. A. (2010). The alliance in couple therapy: Partner influence, early change, and alliance patterns in a naturalistic sample. *Journal of Consulting and Clinical Psychology, 78*(5), 635–645.

Ansbacher, H. L., & Ansbacher, R. R. (1956). *The individual psychology of Alfred Adler: A systematic presentation in selections from his writings.* New York: Harper & Row.

Appel, A. E., & Holden, G. W. (1998). The co-occurrence of spouse and physical child abuse: A review and appraisal. *Journal of Family Psychology, 12,* 578–599.

Arai, M. (2004). Japan. In K. Malley-Morrison (Ed.), *International perspectives on family violence and abuse: A cognitive ecological approach.* (pp. 283–299). Mahwah, NJ: Lawrence Erlbaum Associates.

Archer, J. (2000). Sex differences in aggression between heterosexual partners: A meta-analytic review. *Psychological Bulletin, 126,* 651–680.

Arkes, H. R. (1991). Costs and benefits of judgment errors: Implications for debasing. *Psychological Bulletin, 110,* 486–498.

Arnkoff, D. B., Glass, C. R., & Shapiro, S. J. (2006). Expectations and preferences. In J. C. Norcross, L. E. Beutler & R. F. Levant (Eds.), *Evidence-based practices in mental health: Debate and dialogue on the fundamental questions.* (pp. 335–356). Washington, DC: American Psychological Association.

Asay, T. P., & Lambert, M. J. (1999). The empirical case for the common factors in therapy: Quantitative findings. In M. A. Hubble, B. L. Duncan & S. D. Miller (Eds.), *The heart & soul of change: What works in therapy.* (pp. 23–55.). Washington DC: American Psychological Association.

Attride-Sterling, J., Davis, H., Farrell, L., Groark, C., & Day, C. (2004). Factors influencing parental engagement in a community child and adolescent mental health service: A qualitative comparison of completers and non-completers. *Clinical Child Psychology and Psychiatry, 9*(3), 347–361.

Avis, J. M. (1988). Deepening awareness: A private study guide to feminism and family therapy. In L. Braverman (Ed.), *A guide to feminist family therapy.* (pp. 15–46.). New York: Harrington Park Press.

Babcock, J. C., Jacobson, N. S., Gottman, J. M., & Cordova, J. V. (1994, Nov.). *Predictors of battered women leaving abusive relationships.* Paper presented in J. C. Babcock, (Chair) symposium entitled "Longitudinal perspectives on domestic violence: Predicting changes in relationship status, satisfaction and aggressive behavior." Association for the Advancement of Behavior Therapy Annual Convention, San Diego.

Babor, T. F., de la Fuente, J. R., Saunders, J., & Grant, M. (1992). *AUDIT The Alcohol Use Disorders Identification Test: Guidelines for use in primary health care.* New York: World Health Organization.

Barker, C., & Pistrang, N. (2002). Psychotherapy and social support: Integrating research on psychological helping. *Clinical Psychology Review, 22*(3), 361–379.

Barnett, J. E. (2004). Skimping on records is bad advice. *The National Psychologist, March/April ed.*, sec. Ethics for Psychologists, p. 10.

Baucom, D. H., Shoham, V., Mueser, K. T., Daiuto, A. D., & Stickle, T. R. (1998). Empirically supported couple and family interventions for marital distress and adult mental health problems. *Journal of Consulting and Clinical Psychology, 66*, 53–88.

Bauman, W. F. (1972). Games counselor trainees play: Dealing with trainee resistance. *Counselor Education and Supervision, 11*(4), 251–256.

Beach, S. R. H., Sandeen, E. E., & O'Leary, K. D. (1990). *Depression in marriage.* New York: Guilford Press.

Beach, S. R. H., Sandeen, E., O'Leary, K. D. & Barlow, D. H. (1990). *Depression in marriage: A model for etiology and treatment.* New York: Guilford Press.

Beck, A. T., & Steer, R. A. (1993). *Beck anxiety inventory manual.* San Antonio: The Psychological Corporation.

Beck, A. T., Brown, G., & Steer, R. A. (1997). Psychometric characteristics of the Scale for Suicide Ideation with psychiatric outpatients. *Behaviour Research and Therapy, 35*, 1039–1046.

Beck, M., Friedlander, M. L., & Escudero, V. (2006). Three perspectives on clients' experiences of the therapeutic alliance: A discovery-oriented investigation. *Journal of Marital and Family Therapy, 32*(3), 355–368.

Beck, A. T., Steer, R. A., & Brown, G. (1996). *Beck Depression Inventory* (*2nd ed.*). San Antonio, TX: The Psychological Corporation.

Beck, A. T., Rush, A. J., Shaw, B. F., & Emery, G. (1979). *Cognitive therapy of depression.* New York: Guilford Press.

Beckham, E. E. (1992). Predicting patient dropout in psychotherapy. *Psychotherapy: Theory, Research and Practice, 29*, 177–182.

Becvar, D. S. (2003). Eras of epistemology: A survey of family therapy thinking and theorizing. In T. L. Sexton, G. R. Weeks & M. S. Robbins (Eds.), *Handbook of family therapy: The science and practice of working with families and couples.* (pp. 3–20.). New York: Brunner-Routledge.

Bellg, A., Borrelli, B., Resnick, B., Hecht, J., Minicucci, D. S., & Ory, M., et al. (2004). Enhancing treatment fidelity in health behavior change studies: Best practices and recommendations from the Behavior Change Consortium. *Health Psychology, 23*, 443–451.

Berger, T. (2004). Computer-based technological applications in psychotherapy training. *Journal of Clinical Psychology, 60*(3), 301–315.

Berman, A. (2006, July/August). Risk assessment, treatment planning, and management of the at-risk-for-suicide client. *Family Therapy Magazine (Alexandria, VA), 5*(4), 13–15.

Bernard, J. M. (1988). Receiving and using supervision. In H. Hackney & L. S. Cormier (Eds.), *Counseling strategies and interventions* (*3rd ed.*). (pp. 153–169). Englewood Cliffs, NJ: Prentice Hall.

Beutler, L. E. (1998). Identifying empirically supported treatments: What if we didn't? *Journal of Consulting and Clinical Psychology, 66*, 113–120.

Binder, J. L., Strupp, H. H., Bongar, B., Lee, S. S., Messer, S., & Peake, T. H. (1993). Recommendations for improving psychotherapy training based on experiences with manual-guided training and research: Epilogue. *Psychotherapy, 30*, 599–600.

Bissette, I., Scheier, M. F., & Carver, C. S. (2002). The role of optimism in social network development, coping, and psychological adjustment during a life transition. *Journal of Personality and Social Psychology, 82*(1), 102–111.

Blow, A. J., Sprenkle, D. H., & Davis, S. D. (2007). Is who delivers the treatment more important than the treatment itself? *Journal of Marital and Family Therapy, 33*(3), 298–317.

Bodenmann, G. (2005). Dyadic coping and its significance for marital functioning. In T. A. Revenson, K. Kayser & G. Bodenmann (Eds.), *Couples coping with stress: Emerging perspectives on dyadic coping.* (pp. 33–49). Washington, DC: American Psychological Association.

Bograd, M., & Mederos, F. (1999). Battering and couples therapy. Universal screening and selections of treatment modality. *Journal of Marital and Family Therapy, 25,* 291–312.

Bohart, A. C., Elliott, R., Greenberg, L. S., & Watson, J. C. (2002). Empathy. In J. C. Norcross (Ed.), *Psychotherapy relationships that work: Therapist contributions and responsiveness to patients.* (pp. 89–108). Oxford: Oxford University Press.

Bomba, P. A. (2006). Use of a single page elder abuse assessment and management tool: A practical clinician's approach to identifying elder mistreatment. *Journal of Gerontological Social Work, 46*(3–4), 103–122.

Bongar, B. (2002). *The suicidal patient: Clinical and legal standards of care* (*2nd ed.*). Washington, DC: American Psychological Association.

Bonomo, J., Ostron, N., & Sexton, T. L. (2001, October). *Integrating the principles of evidence-based family intervention (FFT) with effective supervision practices.* PowerPoint handout presented at the American Association for Marriage and Family Therapy, Nashville, TN.

Booth, T. J., & Cottone, R. R. (2000). Measurement, classification, and prediction of paradigm adherence of marriage and family therapists. *American Journal of Family Therapy, 28*(4), 329–346.

Borders, L. D., & Brown, L. L. (2005). *The new handbook of counseling supervision.* Mahwah, NJ: Lawrence Erlbaum Associates.

Bordin, E. S. (1979, Fall). The generalizability of the psychoanalytic concept of the working alliance. *Psychotherapy: Theory, Research and Practice, 16*(3), 252–260.

Borkovec, T. D., & Castonguay, L. G. (2006). Effectiveness research. In J. C. Norcrorss, L. E. Beutler & R. F. Levant (Eds.), *Evidence-based practices in mental health: Debate and dialogue on the fundamental questions.* (pp. 89–96). Washington, DC: American Psychological Association.

Bornstein, R. F. (2006). The complex relationship between dependency and domestic violence: Converging psychological factors and social forces. *American Psychologist, 61*(6), 595–606.

Borrelli, B., Sepinwall, D., Ernst, D., Belig, A. J., Czajkowski, S. B., R., DeFancesco, C. et al. (2005). A new tool to assess treatment fidelity and evaluation of treatment fidelity across 10 years of health behavior research. *Journal of Consulting and Clinical Psychology, 73*(5), 852–860.

Boughner, S. R., Hayes, S. F., Bubenzer, D. L., & West, J. D. (1994). Use of standardized assessment instruments by marital and family therapists: A survey. *Journal of Marital and Family Therapy, 20,* 69–75.

Bowen, M. (1978). *Family theory in clinical practice.* New York: Aronson.

Bowing, N. A., Beehr, T. A., Johnson, A. L., Semmer, N. K., Henricks, E. A., & Webster, H. A. (2004). Explaining potential antecedents of workplace social support: Reciprocity or attractiveness? *Journal of Occupational Health Psychology, 9*(4), 339–350.

Bowlby, J. (1969). *Attachment and loss:* Vol. 1. *Attachment.* New York: Basic Books.

Bowlby, J. (1988). *A secure base.* New York: Basic Books.

Boylin, W., & Briggie, C. R. (1986). The battle for structure in family psychotherapy. *International Journal of Family Psychiatry, 7,* 149–156.

Bradbury, T. N., & Fincham, F. D. (1990). Attributions in marriage: Review and critique. *Psychological Bulletin, 107,* 3–33.

Bragg, H. L. (2003). *Child protection in families experiencing domestic violence.* Washington, DC: US Department of Health and Human Services (HHS), Administration for Children and Families (ACF), Administration on Children, Youth and Families, Children's Bureau, Office of Child Abuse and Neglect (108).

Brewer, A. L. (2004). *A preliminary study of the reliability and concurrent validity of the Marital Oral History Rating Scale-Revised.* Unpublished Thesis, Brigham Young University, Marriage and Family Therapy Programs, School of Family Life (p. 122).

Brewer, A. L., & Mead, D. E. (2008). The Oral History Rating Scale-Revised: Preliminary evaluation of a clinician-rated measure of divorce potential. *Journal of Divorce & Remarriage, 49*(1/2), 110–130.

Brock, R. L., & Lawrence, E. (2008). A longitudinal investigation of stress spillover in marriage: Does spousal support adequacy buffer the effects? *Journal of Family Psychology, 22*(1), 11–20.

Brody, E. M., & Farber, B. A. (1989). Effects of psychotherapy on significant others. *Professional Psychology: Research and Practice, 20,* 116–122.

Brogan, M. M., Prochaska, J., & Prochaska, J. M. (1999). Predicting termination and continuation status in psychotherapy using the transtheoretical model. *Psychotherapy, 36*(2nd ed.), 105–112.

Bromley, D. B. (1977). *Personality description in ordinary language.* New York: Wiley.

Buehlman, K., & Gottman, J. (1996). The Oral History Interview and The Oral History Coding System. In J. M. Gottman (Ed.), *What predicts divorce? The measures.* (pp. OHI - 1 - OHI - 118). Mahwah, NJ: Lawrence Erlbaum Associates.

Buehlman, K., Gottman, J. M., & Katz, L. (1992). How a couple views their past predicts their future: Predicting divorce from an oral history interview. *Journal of Family Psychology, 5,* 295–318.

Burger, J. M. (1986). Increasing compliance by improving the deal: The that's-not-all technique. *Journal of Personality and Social Psychology, 51,* 277–283.

Burisch, M. (2002). A longitudinal study of burnout: The relative importance or dispositions and experiences. *Work & Stress, 16*(1), 1–17.

Burke, B. L., Vassilev, G., Kantchelov, A., & Zweben, A. (2002). Motivational interviewing with couples. In W. R. Miller & S. Rollnick (Eds.), *Motivational interviewing (2nd ed.)* (pp. 347–361). New York: Guilford Press.

Burlingame, G. M., Fuhriman, A., & Johnson, J. E. (2002). Cohesion in group psychotherapy. In J. C. Norcross (Ed.), *Psychotherapy relationships that work: Therapist contributions and responsiveness to patients.* (pp. 71–87). Oxford: Oxford University Press.

Burns, D. D. (1980). *Feeling good: The new mood therapy.* New York: Morrow.

Busby, D. M., Crane, D. R., Larson, J. H., & Christensen, C. (1995). A revision of the Dyadic Adjustment Scale for use with distressed and non distressed couples: Construct hierarchy and multidimensional scales. *Journal of Marital and Family Therapy, 21,* 289–308.

Butler, M. H., & Bird, M. H. (2000). Narrative and interactional process for preventing harmful struggle in therapy: An integrative empirical model. *Journal of Marital and Family Therapy, 26*(2), 123–142.

Butler, M. H., Davis, S. D., & Seedall, R. B. (2008). Common pitfalls of beginning therapists using enactments. *Journal of Marital and Family Therapy, 34*(3), 329–352.

Butler, M. H., & Gardner, B. C. (2003). Adapting enactments to couple reactivity: Five developmental stages. *Journal of Marital and Family Therapy, 29,* 311–327.

Butler, M. H., & Wampler, K. (1999). Couple-responsible therapy process: Positive proximal outcomes. *Family Process, 38,* 27–54.

Calhoun, K. S., Moras, K., Pilkonis, P. A., & Rehm, L. P. (1998). Empirically supported treatments: Implications for training. *Journal of Consulting and Clinical Psychology, 66,* 151–162.

Campbell, T. L. (2006). Improving health through family interventions. In D. R. Crane & E. S. Marxhall (Eds.), *Handbook of families & Health: Interdisciplinary perspectives.* (pp. 379–395). Thousand Oaks, CA: Sage.

Carr, A. (2000). Evidence-based practice in family therapy and systemic consultation II Adult-focused problems. *Journal of Family Therapy, 22,* 273–295.

Catania, C., Shimoff, E., & Matthews, B. A. (1989). An experimental analysis of rule-governed behavior. In S. C. Hayes (Ed.), *Rule-governed behavior: Cognition, contingencies, and instructional control.* (pp. 119–150). New York: Plenum Press.

Chambless, D. L., & Hollon, S. D. (1998). Defining empirically supported therapies. *Journal of Consulting and Clinical Psychology, 66,* 7–18.

Charles, L. L., Ticheli-Kallikas, M., Tyner, K., & Barber-Stephens, B. (2005). Crisis management during "live" supervision: Clinical and instructional matters. *Journal of Marital and Family Therapy, 31*(3), 207–219.

Chemtob, C. M., Bauer, G. B., Hamada, R. S., Pelowski, S. R., & Muraoka, M. Y. (1989). Patient suicide: Occupational hazard for psychologists and psychiatrists. *Professional Psychology: Research and Practice, 20,* 294–300.

Cheng, C. (2003). Cognitive and motivational processes underlying coping flexibility: A dual-process model. *Journal of Personality and Social Psychology, 84*(2), 435–438.

Chiles, J. A., & Strosahl, K. D. (2005). *Clinical manual for assessment and treatment of suicidal patients.* Washington, DC: American Psychiatric Pub.

Choi, N. G., & Mayer, J. (2000). Elder abuse, neglect, and exploitation: Risk factors and prevention strategies. *Journal of Gerontological Social Work, 33*(2), 5–25.

Chou, K., & Chi, I. (2001). Stressful life events and depressive symptoms: Social support and sense of control as mediators or moderators? *International Journal of Aging & Human Development, 52,* 155–171.

Christensen, A., & Jacobson, N. S. (1998). Acceptance and change in couples therapy. In K. S. Dobson & K. D. Craig (Eds.), *Empirically supported therapies: Best practice in professional psychology.* (pp. 133–156). Thousand Oaks, CA: Sage.

Christensen, A., Jacobson, N. S., & Babcock, J. C. (1995). Integrative behavioral couple therapy. In N. S. Jacobson & A. S. Gurman (Eds.), *Clinical handbook of couple therapy.* (pp. 31–64.). New York: Guilford Press.

Christophersen, E. R., & Mortweet, S. L. (2001). *Treatments that work with children: Empirically supported strategies for managing childhood problems.* Washington DC: American Psychological Association.

Clark, D. A., Beck, A. T., and Alford, B. A. (1999). *Scientific foundations of cognitive theory and therapy of depression.* New York: John Wiley & Sons.

Clarke, G., DeBar, L., Ludman, E., Asamow, J., & Jaycox, L. (2002). *Study Project: Intervention Manual* (Therapist Treatment Manual and Workbook for Adolescents). Retrieved 15 November 2008, from http:/www.kpchr.org/public/acwd/acwd.html.

Cleghorn, J. M., & Levin, S. (1973). Training family therapists by setting learning objectives. *American Journal of Orthopsychiatry, 43,* 439–446.

Codding, R. S., Feinberg, A. B., Dunn, E. K., & Pace, G. M. (2005). Effects of immediate performance feedback on implementation of behavior support plans. *Journal of Applied Behavior Analysis, 38*(2), 205–219.

Cohen, M., Halevi-Levin, S., Gagin II, R., & Friedman, G. (2006). Development of a screening tool for identifying elderly people at risk of abuse by their caregivers. *Journal of Aging and Health, 18*(5), 660–685.

Cohen, S., & Syme, S. L. E. (1985). *Social support and health.* Orlando, FL: Academic Press.

Cohen, S., & Wills, T. A. (1985). Stress, social support, and the buffering hypothesis. *Psychological Bulletin, 98*(2nd ed.), 310–357.

Comijs, H. C., Pot, A. M., Smit, J. H., Bouter, L. M., & Jonker, C. (1998). Elder abuse in the community: Prevalence and consequences. *Journal of the American Geriatrics Society, 46*(7), 885–888.

Comtois, K. A., & Linehan, M. M. (2006). Psychosocial treatments of suicidal behaviors: A practice-friendly review. *Journal of Clinical Psychology, 62*(2), 161–170.

Cordova, J. V., Warren, L. Z., & Gee, C. B. (2001). Motivational interviewing as an intervention for at-risk couples. *Journal of Marital and Family Therapy, 27,* 315–326.

Corning, A. F., Malofeeva, E. V., & Bucchianeri, M. M. (2007). Predicting termination type from client-therapist agreement on the severity of the presenting problem. *Psychotherapy: Theory, Research, Practice, Training, 44*(2), 193–204.

Coulter, M. L., & Chez, R. A. (1997). Domestic violence victims support mandatory reporting: For others. *Journal of Family Violence, 12*(3), 349–356.

Cowen, E. L. (1982). Help is where you find it: Four informal helping groups. *American Psychologist, 37,* 385–395.

Coyne, J. C., & DeLongis, A. M. (1986). Going beyond social support: The role of social relationships in adaptation. *Journal of Consulting and Clinical Psychology, 54,* 454–460.

Coyne, J. C., Rohrbaugh, M. J., Shoham, V., Sonnega, J. S., Nicklas, J. M., & Cranford, J. A. (2001). Prognostic importance of marital quality for survival of congestive heart failure. *American Journal of Cardiology, 88,* 526–529.

Crane, D. R. (1995). Health care reform in the United States: Implications for training and practice in marriage and family therapy. *Journal of Marital and Family Therapy, 21,* 115–125.

Crane, D. R., & Hafen, M. J. (2002). Meeting the needs of evidence-based practice in family therapy: Developing the scientist-practitioner model. *Journal of Family Therapy, 24,* 113–124.

Crane, D. R., Hillin, H. H., & Jakubowski, S. F. (2005). Costs of treating conduct disordered Medicaid youth with and without family therapy. *The American Journal of Family Therapy, 33,* 403–413.

Crane, D. R., Newfield, N., & Armstrong, D. (1984). Predicting divorce at marital therapy intake: Wives' distress and the Marital Status Inventory. *Journal of Marital and Family Therapy, 10,* 305–312.

Crane, D. R., Middleton, K. C., & Bean, R. A. (2000). Establishing criterion scores for the Kansas Marital Satisfaction Scale and the Revised Dyadic Adjustment Scale. *The American Journal of Family Therapy, 28,* 53–60.

Crane, D. R., Soderquist, J. N., & Gardner, M. D. (1995). Gender differences in cognitive and behavioral steps toward divorce. *The American Journal of Family Therapy, 23,* 99–105.

Craske, M. G. (1999). *Anxiety disorders: Psychological approaches to theory and treatment.* Boulder, CO: Westview Press.

Craske, M. G., Barlow, D. H., & O'Leary, T. A. (1992). *Mastery of your anxiety and worry: Client workbook.* New York: The Psychological Corporation.

Craske, M. G., & Zoellner, L. A. (1995). Anxiety disorders: The role of marital therapy. In N. S. Jacobson & A. S. Gurman (Eds.), *Clinical handbook of couple therapy.* (pp. 394–410). New York: Guilford Press.

Crews, J. A., & Hill, N. R. (2005). Diagnosis in marriage and family counseling: An ethical double bind. *Family Journal: Counseling & Therapy for Couples & Families, 13*(1), 63–66.

Crits-Christoph, P., & Gibbons, M. B. C. (2002). Relational interpretations. In J. C. Norcross (Ed.), *Psychotherapy relationships that work: Therapist contributions and responsiveness to patients.* (pp. 285–300). Oxford: Oxford University Press.

Croning, A. F., Malofeeva, E. V., & Bucchianeri, M. M. (2007). Predicting termination type from client-therapist agreement on the severity of the presenting problem. *Psychotherapy: Theory, Research and Practice, Training, 44*(2), 193–204.

Cukrowicz, K. C., White, B. A., Reitzel, L. R., Burns, A. B., Driscoll, K. A., Kemper, T. S. et al. (2005). Improved treatment outcome associated with the shift to empirically supported treatments in a graduate training clinic. *Professional Psychology: Research and Practice, 36*(32), 330–337.

Curtis, R. (2002). Termination from a psychoanalytic perspective. *Journal of Psychotherapy Integration, 12*(3), 350–357.

Cutrona, C. E. (1996). *Social support in couples.* London: Sage.

Cutrona, C. E., Russell, D. W., & Gardner, K. A. (2005). The relationship enhancement model of social support. In T. A. Revenson, K. Kayser & G. Bodenmann (Eds.), *Couples coping with stress: Emerging perspectives on dyadic coping.* (pp. 73–95). Washington, DC: American Psychological Association.

Dadds, M. R., and McHugh, T. A. (1992). Social support and treatment outcome in behavioral family therapy for child conduct problems. *Journal of Consulting and Clinical Psychology, 60,* 252–259.

Dandeneau, M. L., & Johnson, S. M. (1994). Facilitating intimacy: Interventions and effects. *Journal of Marital and Family Therapy, 20*(1), 17–33.

Dane, A. V., & Schneider, B. H. (1998). Program integrity in primary and early secondary prevention: Are implementation effects out of control? *Clinical Psychology Review, 18,* 23–45.

Davidson, G. N. S., & Horvath, A. O. (1997). Three sessions of brief couples therapy: A clinical trial. *Journal of Family Psychology, 11,* 422–435.

Davis, S. D., & Butler, M. H. (2004). Enacting relationships in marriage and family therapy: A conceptual and operational definition of enactment. *Journal of Marital and Family Therapy, 30*, 319–333.

Deacon, S. A., Kirkpatrick, D. R., Wetchler, J. L., & Niedner, D. (1999). Marriage and family therapists' problems and utilization of personal therapy. *American Journal of Family Therapy, 27*(1), 73–93.

Dennehy, E. B., Suppes, T., Rush, A. J., Crismon, M. L., Witte, B., & Webster, J. (2004). Development of a computerized assessment of clinician adherence to a treatment guideline for patients with bipolar disorder. *Journal of Psychiatric Research, 38*, 285–294.

Dennehy, E. B., Suppes, T., Rush, A. J., Miller, A. L., Grivedi, M. H., Crismon, M. L. et al. (2005). Does provider adherence to a treatment guideline change clinical outcomes for patients with bipolar disorder? Results from the Texas Medication Algorithm Project. *Psychological Medicine, 35*(12), 1695–1706.

Denton, W. H., Johnson, S., & Burleson, B. (2009). Emotion focused therapy-therapist fidelity scale (EFT-TFS): Conceptual development and content validity. *Journal of Couple & Relationship Therapy, 8*(3), 226–246.

Denton, W. H., Walsh, S. R., & Daniel, S. S. (2002). Evidence-based practice in family therapy: Adolescent depression as an example. *Journal of Marital and Family Therapy, 29*(3), 39–45.

DiClemente, C. C. (1991). Motivational interviewing and stages of change. In W. R. Miller & S. Rollnick (Eds.), *Motivational interviewing: Preparing people for change.* New York: Guilford.

Dobson, K. S., & Craig, K. D. (1998). *Empirically supported therapies: Best practice in professional psychology.* Thousand Oaks, CA: Sage.

Doherty, W. J. (1981). Cognitive processes in intimate conflict: I. Extending attribution theory. *The American Journal of Family Therapy, 9*(1), 3–13.

Doss, B. D., Atkins, D. C., & Christensen, A. (2003). Who's dragging their feet? Husbands and wives seeking marital therapy. *Journal of Marital and Family Therapy, 29*, 165–176.

Dozier, R. M., Hicks, M. W., Cornille, T. A., & Peterson, G. W. (1998). The effect of Tomm's therapeutic questioning styles on therapeutic alliance: A clinical analog study. *Family Process, 37*, 189–200.

Drye, R. C., Goulding, R. L., & Goulding, M. E. (1973). No-suicide decisions: Patient monitoring of suicidal risk. *American Journal of Psychiatry, 130*, 171–174.

Duncan, B. L., & Miller, S. D. (2006). Treatment manuals do not improve outcomes. In J. C. Norcross, L. E. Beutler & R. F. Levant (Eds.), *Evidence-based practices in mental health: Debate and dialogue on the fundamental questions.* (pp. 140–149). Washington, DC: American Psychological Association.

Duncan, B. L., Miller, S. D., Sparks, J. A., Claud, D. A., Reynolds, L. R., Brown, J. et al. (2003). The Session Rating Scale: Preliminary psychometric properties of a "working" alliance measure. *Journal of Brief Therapy, 3*(1), 3–12.

Duncan, E. A. S., Nicol, M. M., & Ager, A. (2004). Factors that constitute a good cognitive behavioural treatment manual: A Delphi study. *Behavioural and Cognitive Psychotherapy, 32*(2), 199–213.

Dutton, D. G. (2007, October). The complexities of domestic violence. *American Psychologist, 62*, 708–709.

Earp, J. L., Ory, M. G., & Strogatz, D. S. (1982). The effects of family involvement and practitioner home visits on the control of hypertension. *American Journal of Public Health, 72*, 1146–1154.

Edin, K. E., & Hogberg, U. (2002). Violence against pregnant women will remain hidden as long as no direct questions are asked. *Midwifery, 19*, 268–278.

Egan, M. P. (1997). Contracting for safety: A concept analysis. *Crisis: The Journal of Crisis Intervention and Suicide Prevention, 18*(1), 17–23.

Eifert, G. H., Evans, I. M., & McKendrick, V. G. (1990). Matching treatments to client problems but not diagnostic labels: A case for paradigmatic behavior therapy. *Journal of Behaviour Therapy and Experimental Psychiatry, 21*, 163–172.

Eifert, G. H., Schulte, D., Zvolensky, M. J., Lejuez, C. W., & Lau, A. W. (1997). Manualized behavior therapy: Merits and challenges. *Behavior Therapy, 28*, 499–509.

Ellis, A. (2002). *Overcoming resistance: A Rational Emotive Behavior Therapy integrated approach (2nd ed.)*. New York: Springer.

Engelmann, S., & Carnine, D. (1991). *Theory of instruction: Principles and applications.* Eugene, OR: ADI Press.

Epperson, D. L., Bushway, D. J., & Warman, R. E. (1983). Client self-terminations after one counseling session: Effects of problem recognition, counselor gender, and counselor experience. *Journal of Counseling Psychology, 30,* 307–315.

Epstein, N. B., & Baucom, D. H. (2003). Couple therapy. In R. L. Leahy (Ed.), *Roadblocks in cognitive-behavioral therapy.* (pp. 217–235). New York: Guilford Press.

Essock, S. M., Covell, N. H., Shear, K. M., Donahue, S. A., & Felton, C. J. (2006). Use of clients' self-reports to monitor Project Liberty clinicians' fidelity to a cognitive-behavioral intervention. *Psychiatric Services, 57*(9), 1320–1323.

Falender, C. A., & Shafranske, E. P. (2004). *Clinical supervision: A competency-based approach.* Washington DC: American Psychological Association.

Falloon, I. R. H., Economou, M., Palli, A., Maim, U., & Mizuno, M. M., M. (2005). The Clinical Strategies Implementation Scale to measure implementation of treatment in mental health services. *Psychiatric Services, 56*(12), 1584–1590.

Family Violence Prevention Fund. (2008). *National Consensus Guidelines on Identifying and Responding to Domestic Violence Victimization in Health Care Settings.* Washington DC: Author.

Farber, B. A. (1983). The effects of psychotherapeutic practice upon psychotherapists. *Psychotherapy: Theory, Research and Practice, 20,* 174–182.

Felson, R. B. (2002). *Violence and gender reexamined.* Washington, DC: American Psychological Association.

Fincham, F. D., Garnier, P. C., Gano-Phillips, S., & Osborne, L. N. (1995). Pre-interaction expectations, marital satisfaction, and accessibility: A new look at sentiment override. *Journal of Family Psychology, 9*(1), 3–14.

Fleming, M. F. (1991). The Alcohol Use Disorders Identification Test (AUDIT) in a college sample. *International Journal of the Addictions, 26*(11), 1173–1185.

Folkman, S., Chesney, M., McKusick, L., Ironson, G., Johnson, D. S., & Coates, T. J. (1991). Translating coping theory into an intervention. In J. Eckenrode (Ed.), *The social context of coping* (pp. 239–260). New York: Plenum Press.

Fonagy, P., Target, M., Cottrell, D., Phillips, J., & Kurtz, Z. (2002). *What works for whom? A critical review of treatments for children.* New York: Guilford Press.

Forgatch, M. S., Patterson, G. R., & DeGarmo, D. S. (2005). Evaluating fidelity: Predictive validity for a measure of competent adherence to the Oregon Model of Parent Management Training. *Behavior Therapy, 36*(1), 3–13.

Foulkes, P. (2003). Trainee perceptions of teaching of different psychotherapies. *Australasian Psychiatry, 11*(2), 209–214.

Frank, J. D., & Frank, J. B. (1991). *Persuasion and healing: A comparative study of psychotherapy (3rd ed.)*. Baltimore, MA: Johns Hopkins University Press.

Frank, J. D., & Frank, J. B. (2004). Therapeutic components shared by all psychotherapies. In A. Freeman, M. J. Mahoney, P. Devito & D. Martin (Eds.), *Cognition and psychotherapy. (2nd ed.)*. (pp. 45–76). Springer.

Friedlander, M. L., Escudero, V., & Heatherington, L. (2006). *Therapeutic alliances in couple and family therapy: An empirically informed guide to practice.* Washington, DC: American Psychological Association.

Friedlander, M. L., Escudero, V., Horvath, A. O., Heatherington, L., Cabero, A., & Martens, M. P. (2006). System for observing family therapy alliance: A tool for research and practice. *Journal of Counseling Psychology, 53,* 214–225.

Friedrich, W. N., Olafson, E., & Connelly, L. (2004). Child abuse and family assessment: Strategies and inventories. In L. Sperry (Ed.), *Assessment of couples and families: Contemporary and cutting-edge strategies.* (pp. 207–247). New York: Brunner-Routledge.

Garb, H. N. (2005). Clinical judgment and decision making. In S. Nolan-Hoeksema (Ed.), *Annual Review of Clinical Psychology, Vol. 1.* Palo Alto, CA: Annual Reviews Inc.

Garfield, R. (2004). The therapeutic alliance in couples therapy. *Family Process, 43*(4), 457–465.

Garfield, S. (1998). Some comments on empirically supported treatments. *Journal of Consulting and Clinical Psychology, 66,* 121–125.

Garfield, S. L. (1994). Research on client variables in psychotherapy. In A. E. Bergin & S. L. Garfield (Eds.), *Handbook of psychotherapy and behavior change.* (pp. 190–228). New York: Wiley.

Gelso, C. J., & Hayes, J. A. (2002). The management of counter transference. In J. C. Norcross (Ed.), *Psychotherapy relationships that work: Therapist contributions and responsiveness to patients.* (pp. 267–283). Oxford: Oxford University Press.

Gershoff, E. T. (2002). Corporal punishment by parents and associated child behaviors and experiences: A meta-analytic and theoretical review. *Psychological Bulletin, 128,* 539–579.

Gielen, A. C., Campbell, J., Garza, M. A., O'Campo, P., Dienemann, J., Kub, J. et al. (2006). Domestic violence in the military: Women's policy preferences and beliefs concerning routine screening and mandatory reporting. *Military Medicine, 17*(8), 729–735.

Gielen, A. C., O'Campo, P. J., Campbell, J. C., Schollenberger, J., Woods, A. B., Jones, A. S. et al. (2000). Women's opinions about domestic violence screening and mandatory reporting. *American Journal of Preventive Medicine, 19*(4), 279–285.

Gladding, S. T., Remley, T. P., Jr., & Huber, C. H. (2001). *Ethical, legal, and professional issues in the practice of marriage and family therapy.* (*3rd ed.*). Upper Saddle River, NJ: Merrill Prentice Hall.

Goff, H. W., Shelton, A. J., Byrd, T. L., & Parcel, G. S. (2003). Preparedness of health care practitioners to screen women for domestic violence in a border community. *Health Care for Women International, 24*(2), 135–148.

Goldfried, M. R. (2002). A cognitive-behavioral perspective on termination. *Journal of Psychotherapy Integration, 12,* 364–372.

Goldman, A., & Greenberg, L. (1992). Comparison of integrated systemic and emotionally focused approaches to couples therapy. *Journal of Consulting and Clinical Psychology, 60,* 962–969.

Goldstein, A. P. (2001). *Reducing resistance: Methods for enhancing openness to change.* Champaign, IL: Research Press.

Gollan, J. K., Gortner, E. T., & Jacobson, N. S. (1996). Partner relational problems and affective disorders. In F. W. Kaslow (Ed.), *Handbook of relational diagnosis and dysfunctional family patterns.* (pp. 322–337). New York: Wiley.

Gottman, J. M. (1994). *What predicts divorce? The relationship between marital processes and marital outcomes.* Hillsdale, NJ: Lawrence Erlbaum Associates.

Gottman, J. M. (1999). *The marriage clinic: A scientifically-based marital therapy.* New York: Norton.

Gottman, J. M., & Silver, N. (1999). *The seven principles for making marriage work.* New York: Crown Publishers.

Gottman, J. S. (2004). *The marriage clinic casebook.* New York: Norton.

Gray, L. A., Ladany, N., Walker, J. A., & Ancis, J. R. (2001). Psychotherapy trainees' experience of counterproductive events in supervision. *Journal of Counseling Psychology, 48,* 371–383.

Greenberg, L. S. (2002). Termination of experiential therapy. *Journal of Psychotherapy Integration, 12*(3), 358–363.

Greene, K., & Bogo, M. (2002). The different faces of intimate violence: Implications for assessment and treatment. *Journal of Marital and Family Therapy, 28*(4), 455–466.

Greenson, R. R., & Jaffe, L. (2004). How to handle the initial phone call. In L. Jaffe (Ed.), *The technique and practice of psychoanalysis, Vol. III.* (pp. 77–86). New York: International Universities Press.

Gresham, F. M., & Gansel, K. A., & Noell, G. H. (1993). Treatment integrity in applied behavior analysis with children. *Journal of Applied Behavior Analysis, 26*(2), 257–263.

Guerin, B. (1994). *Analyzing social behavior: Behavior analysis and the social sciences.* Reno, NV: Context Press.

Haddock, S. A. (2002). Training family therapists to assess for and intervene in partner abuse: A curriculum for graduated courses, professional workshops, and self-study. *Journal of Marital and Family Therapy, 28*(2), 193–202.

Hakstian, A. R., & McLean, P. D. (1989). Brief Screen for Depression. *Psychological Assessment, 1*, 139–141.

Haley, J. (1987). *Problem solving therapy (2nd ed.).* San Francisco: Jossey Bass.

Hansen, N. B., Lambert, M. J., & Foreman, E. M. (2002). The psychotherapy dose-response effect and its implications for treatment delivery services. *Clinical Psychology: Science & Practice, 9*, 329–343.

Harris, J. M., Kutob, R. M., Surprenant, Z. J., Maiuro, R. D., & Delate, T. A. (2002). Can Internet-based education improve physician confidence in dealing with domestic violence. *Family Medicine, 34*, 287–292.

Harwood, M. D., & Eyberg, S. M. (2004). Therapist verbal behavior early in treatment: Relation to successful completion of parent-child interaction therapy. *Journal of Clinical Child and Adolescent Psychology, 33*(3), 601–612.

Hastings, R. P. (2003). Behavioral adjustment of siblings of children with autism engaged in applied behavior analysis early intervention programs: The moderating role of social support. *Journal of Autism & Developmental Disorders, 32*(2), 141–150.

Hatchett, G. T., & Park, H. L. (2003). Comparison of four operational definitions of premature termination. *Psychotherapy: Theory, Research and Practice, Training, 40*(3), 226–231.

Hayes, S. C., Barlow, D. H., & Nelson-Gray, R. O. (1999). *The scientist practitioner: Research and accountability in the age of managed care (2nd ed.).* Boston: Allyn and Bacon.

Heatherington, L., & Friedlander, M. L. (1990). Couple and family therapy alliance scales: Empirical considerations. *Journal of Marital and Family Therapy, 16*, 299–306.

Henggeler, S. W., Melton, G. B., Brondino, M. J., Scherer, D. G., & Hanley, J. H. (1997). Multisystem therapy with violent and chronic juvenile offenders and their families: The role of treatment fidelity in successful dissemination. *Journal of Consulting and Clinical Psychology, 65*, 821–833.

Henry, W. P., Schacht, T. E., Strupp, H. H., Butler, S. F., & Binder, J. L. (1993). Effects of training in time-limited psychotherapy: Mediators of therapists' response to training. *Journal of Consulting and Clinical Psychology, 61*, 441–447.

Heppner, P. P., & Claiborn, C. D. (1989). Social influence research in counseling: A review and critique. *Journal of Counseling Psychology, 36*(3), 365–387.

Herron, W. G., & Sitkowski, S. (1986). Effect of fees on psychotherapy: What is the evidence? *Professional Psychology: Research and Practice, 171*(4157), 347–351.

Hersen, M., & Turner, S. M. (1985). *Diagnostic interviewing.* New York: Plenum Press.

Heyman, R. E., & Slep, A. M. S. (2006). Creating and field-testing diagnostic criteria for partner and child maltreatment. *Journal of Family Psychology, 20*(3), 397–408.

Hiebert, W. J., & Gillespie, J. P. (1984). The initial interview. In R. F. Stahmann & W. J. Hiebert (Eds.), *Counseling in marital and sexual problems (3rd ed.).* (pp. 17–33). Lexington, MA: Lexington Books.

Hill, C. E. (2004). *Helping skills: Facilitating exploration, insight, and Action (2nd ed.).* Washington DC: American Psychological Association.

Hilsenroth, M. J., Ackerman, S. J., Clemence, A. J., Strassle, C. G., & Handler, L. (2002). Effects of structured clinician training on patient and therapist perspectives of alliance early in psychotherapy. *Psychotherapy: Theory/Research/Practice/Training, 39*(4), 309–323.

Hilton, N. Z., & Harris, G. T. (2005). Predicting wife assault: A critical review and implications for policy and practice. *Trauma, Violence, & Abuse, 6*(1), 3–23.

Hilton, N. Z., Harris, G. T., & Rice, M. E. (2009). *Risk assessment for domestically violent men: Tools for criminal justice, offender intervention, and victim services.* Washington, DC: American Psychological Association.

Hipple, J. L., & Hipple, L. B. (1983). *Diagnosis and management of psychological emergencies: A manual for hospitalization.* Springfield, IL: C. C. Thomas.

Hogue, A., Liddle, H. A., Singer, A., & Leckrone, J. (2005). Intervention fidelity in family-based prevention counseling for adolescent problem behaviors. *Journal of Community Psychology, 33*(2), 191–211.

Holtzworth-Munroe, A., Clements, K., & Farris, C. (2005). Working with couples who have experienced physical aggression. In M. Harway (Ed.), *Handbook of couples therapy.* (pp. 289–312). New York: Wiley.

Holtzworth-Munroe, A., Meehan, J. C., Rehman, U., & Marshall, A. D. (2002). Intimate partner violence: An introduction for couple therapists. In A. S. Gurman & N. S. Jacobson (Eds.), *Clinical handbook of couple therapy* (*3rd ed.*). (pp. 441–465). New York: Guilford Press.

Holtzworth-Munroe, A., Meehan, J. C., Stuart, G. L., Herron, K., & Rehman, U. (2003). Do subtypes of maritally violent men continue to differ over time? *Journal of Consulting and Clinical Psychology, 71*(4), 728–740.

Holtzworth-Munroe, A., Stuart, G. L., & Hutchinson, G. (1997). Violent versus nonviolent husbands: Differences in attachment patterns, dependency, and jealousy. *Journal of Family Psychology, 11*, 314–331.

Horvath, A. O., & Bedi, R. P. (2002). The alliance. In J. C. Norcross (Ed.), *Psychotherapy relationships that work: Therapist contributions and responsiveness to patients.* (pp. 37–69). Oxford: Oxford University Press.

Horwitz, A. V., White, H. R., & Howell-White, S. (1996). Becoming married and mental health: A longitudinal study of a cohort of young adults. *Journal of Marriage and the Family, 58*, 895–907.

Howard, K. I., Kopta, S. M., Krause, M. S., Merton, S., & Orlinsky, D. E. (1986). The dose-effect relationship in psychotherapy. *American Psychologist, 41*(2), 159–164.

Howard, K. I., Moras, K., Brill, P. L., Martinovich, Z., & Lutz, W. (1996). Evaluation of psychotherapy: Efficacy, effectiveness, and patient progress. *American Psychologist, 51*(10), 1059–1064.

Hubble, M. A., Duncan, B. L., & Miller, S. D. (1999). *The heart & soul of change: What works in therapy.* Washington, DC: American Psychological Association.

Hudek- Knežević, J., & Kardum, I. (2000). The effects of dispositional and situational coping, perceived social support, and cognitive appraisal on immediate outcome. *European Journal of Psychological Assessment, 16*(3), 190–201.

Hunsley, J., Aubry, T. D., Verstervelt, C. M., & Vito, D. (1999). Comparing therapist and client perspectives on reasons for psychotherapy termination. *Psychotherapy, 36*(4), 380–388.

Huppert, J. D., & Abramowitz, J. S. (2003). Special series. Going beyond the manual: Insights from experienced clinicians. *Cognitive and Behavioral Practice, 10*(1), 1–2.

Hutt, C. H., Scott, J., & King, M. (1983). A phenomenological study of supervisees' positive and negative experiences in supervision. *Psychotherapy: Theory, Research and Practice, 20*, 118–123.

Hynan, D. J. (1990). Client reasons and experiences in treatment that influence termination of psychotherapy. *Journal of Clinical Psychology, 46*, 891–895.

Jacob, T., & Seilhamer, R. (1985). Adaption of the Areas of Change Questionnaire for parent-child relationship assessment. *American Journal of Family Therapy, 13*(2), 28–38.

Jacobs, D. G. (1999). *The Harvard Medical School guide to suicide assessment and intervention.* San Francisco: Jossey-Bass.

Jacobs, D. G., Brewer, M., & Klein-Benheim, M. (1999). Suicide assessment. In D. G. Jacobs (Ed.), *The Harvard Medical School guide to suicide assessment and intervention.* (pp. 3–39.). San Francisco: Jossey-Bass.

Jacobs, D. G., Gutheil, T. G., Harburger, J., Kelly, M. J., Maltsberger, J. T., Miller, M. C. et al. (1999). Guidelines for identification, assessment, and treatment planning for suicidality. In D. G. Jacobs (Ed.), *The Harvard Medical School guide for suicide* (pp. 579–591). San Francisco: Jossey-Bass.

Jacobson, N. S. (1984). A component analysis of behavioral marital therapy: The relative effectiveness of behavior exchange and problem-solving training. *Journal of Consulting and Clinical Psychology, 52*, 295–305.

Jacobson, N. S., & Christensen, A. (1996). *Integrative couple therapy: Promoting acceptance and change.* New York: W. W. Norton.

Jacobson, N. S., & Christensen, A. (1998). *Acceptance and change in couple therapy: A therapist's guide to transforming relationships.* New York: Norton.

Jacobson, N. S., & Margolin, G. (1979). *Marital therapy: Strategies based on social learning and behavior exchange principles.* New York: Brunner/Mazel.

Jacobson, N. S., & Truax, P. (1991). Clinical significance: A statistical approach to defining meaningful change in psychotherapy research. *Journal of Consulting and Clinical Psychology, 59*, 12–19.

James, P. S. (1991). Effects of a communication training component added to an emotionally focused couples therapy. *Journal of Marital and Family Therapy, 17*, 263–275.

Jamieson, R. V. (2007). A revision of the marital status inventory: Reliability and validity with marital and remarital couples. Unpublished master's thesis, Brigham Young University, Provo, Utah.

Johnson, L. N., Wright, D. W., & Ketring, S. A. (2002). The therapeutic alliance in home-based family therapy: Is it predictive of outcome? *Journal of Marital and Family Therapy, 284*(1), 93–102.

Johnson, S. M. (1996). *The practice of emotionally focused marital therapy: Creating connection.* New York: Brunner/Mazel.

Johnson, S. M. (2003). The revolution in couple therapy: A practitioner-scientist perspective. *Journal of Marital and Family Therapy, 29*(3), 365–384.

Johnson, S. M. (2004). *The practice of emotionally focused marital therapy: Creating connection (2nd ed.).* New York: Brunner-Routledge.

Johnson, S. M., Bradley, B., Furrow, J., Lee, A., Palmer, G., Tilley, D. et al. (2005). *Becoming an emotionally focused couple therapist: The workbook.* New York: Routledge.

Johnson, S. M., & Greenberg, L. S. (1985). Emotionally focused couples therapy: An outcome study. *Journal of Marital and Family Therapy, 11*, 313–317.

Johnson, S. M., & Greenberg, L. S. (1995). The emotionally focused approach to problems in adult attachment. In N. S. Jacobson & A. S. Gurman (Eds.), *Clinical handbook of couple therapy.* (pp. 121–141). New York: Guilford.

Johnson, S. M., Hunsley, J., Greenberg, L., & Schindler, D. (1999). Emotionally focused couples therapy: Status and challenges. *Clinical Psychology: Science & Practice, 6*, 67–79.

Johnson, S. M., & Talitman, E. (1997). Predictors of success in emotionally focused marital therapy. *Journal of Marital and Family Therapy, 23*, 135–152.

Johnston, C. (1996). Addressing parent cognitions in interventions with families of children with disruptive disorders. In K. S. Dobson & K. D. Craig (Eds.), *State of the art in cognitive-behavioral therapy.* (pp. 193–209). Beverly Hills, CA: Sage.

Joiner, T. E., Jr., Pettit, J. W., & Rudd, M. D. (2004). Is there a window of heightened suicide risk if patients gain energy in the context of continued depressive symptoms? *Professional Psychology: Research and Practice, 35*(1), 84–89.

Joiner, T. E., Jr., Pfaff, J., & Acres, J. G. (2002). A brief screening tool for suicidal symptoms in adolescents and young adults in general health settings: Reliability and validity data from the Australian National General Practice Youth Suicide Prevention Project. *Behaviour Research and Therapy, 40*, 471–481.

Joiner, T. E., Jr., Rudd, D. M., & Rajab, M. H. (1999). Agreement between self- and clinician-rated suicidal symptoms in a clinical sample of young adults: Explaining discrepancies. *Journal of Consulting and Clinical Psychology, 67*(2), 171–176.

Joiner, T. E., Steer, R. A., Brown, G., Beck, A. T. P., & Rudd, M. D. (2003). Worst-point suicidal plans: A dimension of suicidality predative of past suicide attempts and eventual death by suicide. *Behaviour Research and Therapy, 41*, 1469–1480.

Joiner, T. E., Jr., Walker, R., Rudd, M. D., & Jobes, D. (1999). Scientizing and routinizing the outpatient assessment of suicidality. *Professional Psychology: Research and Practice, 30*, 447–453.

Jones, D. J. (2010). *HNC fidelity checklist (R–34)*. Chapel Hill, NC: Department of Psychology.

Jouriles, E. N., McDonald, R., Norwood, W. D., & Ezell, E. (2001). Issues and controversies in documenting the prevalence of children's exposure to domestic violence. In S. A. Graham-Bermann & J. L. Edleson (Eds.), *Domestic violence in the lives of children: The future of research, intervention, and social policy*. (pp. 12–34). Washington, DC: American Psychological Association.

Joyce, A. S., Piper, W. E., Ogrodniczuk, J. S., & Klein, R. H. (2007). *Termination in psychotherapy: A psychodynamic model of processes and outcomes*. Washington, DC: American Psychological Association.

Kadera, S. W., Lambert, M. J., & Andrews, A. A. (1996). How much therapy is really enough? A session-by-session analysis of the psychotherapy dose-effect relationship. *Journal of Psychotherapy Practice and Research, 5*, 132–151.

Karam, E., & Sprenkle, D. H. (2010). The research informed clinician: A guide to training the next generation MFT. *Journal of Marital and Family Therapy, 36*, 3, 307–319.

Karney, B. R., Story, L. B., & Bradbury, T. N. (2005). Marriages in context: Interactions between chronic and acute stress among newlyweds. In T. A. Revenson, K. Kayser & G. Bodenmann (Eds.), *Couples coping with stress: Emerging perspectives on dyadic coping*. (pp. 13–32). Washington, DC: American Psychological Association.

Kaslow, F. W. (1996). *Handbook of relational diagnosis and dysfunctional family patterns*. New York: Wiley.

Katz, J., Beach, S. R. H., & Anderson, P. (1996). Self-enhancement versus self-verification: Does spousal support always help? *Cognitive Therapy and Research, 20*, 345–360.

Kazdin, A. E. (2008). Evidence-based treatment and practice. *American Psychologist, 63*(3), 146–159.

Kiecolt-Glaser, J. K., & Newton, T. L. (2001). Marriage and health: His and hers. *Psychological Bulletin, 127*, 472–503.

Kihlstrom, J. F. (2006). Scientific research. In J. C. Norcross, L. E. Beutler & R. F. Levant (Eds.), *Evidence-based practices in mental health: Debate and dialogue on the fundamental questions*. (pp. 23–30). Washington, DC: American Psychological Association.

Kisch, J., Leino, E. V., & Silverman, M. M. (2005). Aspects of suicidal behavior, depression, and treatment in college students: Results from the Spring 2000 National College Health Assessment Survey. *Suicide and Life-Threatening Behavior, 35*(1), 3–13.

Kluger, A. N., & DeNisi, A. (1998). Feedback interventions: Toward the understanding of a double-edged sword. *Current Directions in Psychological Science, 7*, 67–72.

Knapp, S., & VandeCreek, L. (1997). Ethical and legal aspects of clinical supervision. In C. E. Watkins, Jr. (Ed.), *Handbook of psychotherapy supervision* (pp. 589–599). New York: Wiley.

Knickerbocker, L., Heyman, R. E., Slep, A. M. S., Jouriles, E. N., & McDonald, R. (2007). Co-occurence of child and partner maltreatment: Definitions, prevalence, theory, and implications for assessment. *European Psychologist, 12*(1), 36–44.

Knobloch-Fedders, L. M., Pinsof, W. M., & Mann, B. J. (2004). The formation of the therapeutic alliance in couple therapy. *Family Process, 43*(4), 425–442.

Kohlenberg, R. J., & Tsai, M. (1991). *Functional analytic psychotherapy: Creating intense and curative therapeutic relationships*. New York: Plenum Press.

Kopta, S. M., Howard, K. I., & Lowry, J. L., Beutler. (1994). Patterns of symptomatic recovery in psychotherapy. *Journal of Consulting and Clinical Psychology, 62*, 1009–1016.

Kozlowska, K., Nunn, K., & Cousens, P. (1997). Adverse experiences in psychiatric training. Part 2. *Australian and New Zealand Journal of Psychiatry, 31*, 641–652.

Kramer, S. A. (1990). *Positive endings in psychotherapy: Bringing meaningful closure to therapeutic relationships.* San Francisco: Jossey-Bass.

Kurrle, S. E., Sadler, P. M., & Cameron, I. (1992). Patterns of elder abuse. *Medical Journal of Australia, 157*, 673–676.

Kyriacou, D. N., Anglin, D., Taliaferro, E., Stone, S., Tubb, T., Linden, J. A. et al. (1999). Risk factors for injury to women from domestic violence. *New England Journal of Medicine, 341*, 1892–1898.

Lachs, M. S., & Pillemer, K. (1995). Abuse and neglect of elderly persons. *New England Journal of Medicine, 332*(7), 437–443.

Lachs, M. S., Williams, C., O'Brien, S., Hurst, L., & Horwitz, R. (1997). Risk factors for reported elder abuse and neglect: A nine-year observational cohort study. *The Gerontologist, 37*(4), 469–474.

Ladany, N., Hill, C. E., Corbett, M. M., & Nutt, E. A. (1996). Nature, extent, and importance of what psychotherapy trainees do not disclose to their supervisors. *Journal of Counseling Psychology, 43*, 10–24.

Ladany, N., Lehrman-Waterman, D., Molinaro, M., & Wolgast, B. (1999). Psychotherapy supervisor ethical practice: Adherence to guidelines, the supervisory working alliance, and supervisee satisfaction. *The Counseling Psychologist, 27*, 443–475.

Lafferty, P., Beutler, L. E., & Crago, M. (1991). Differences between more and less effective-psychotherapists: A study of selected therapist variables. *Journal of Consulting and Clinical Psychology, 57*, 76–80.

Laireiter, A., & Willutzki, U. (2003). Self-reflection and self-practice in training of cognitive behavior therapy: An overview. *Clinical Psychology & Psychotherapy, 10*(1), 19–30.

Lamb, D. H. (1985). A time-frame model of termination in psychotherapy. *Psychotherapy, 22*(3), 604–609.

Lambert, M. J. (1992). Psychotherapy outcome research: Implications for integrative and eclectic therapists. In J. C. Norcross & M. R. Goldfried (Eds.), *Handbook of psychotherapy integration.* (pp. 94–129). New York: Basic Books.

Lambert, M. J., & Barley, D. E. (2002). Research summary on the therapeutic relationship and psychotherapy outcome. In J. C. Norcross (Ed.), *Psychotherapy relationships that work: Therapist contributions and responsiveness to patients.* (pp. 17–32). Oxford: Oxford University Press.

Lambert, M. J., Hansen, N. B., & Finch, A. E. (2001). Patient-focused research: Using patient outcome data to enhance treatment effects. *Journal of Consulting and Clinical Psychology, 69*, 159–172.

Lambert, M. J., Hansen, N. B., Umphress, V., Lunnen, K., Okiishi, & Heufner, J. C., & Reisinger. (1996). *Administration and scoring manual for the Outcome Questionnaire (OQ–45.2).* Wilmington, DE: American Professional Credentialing Services.

Lambert, M. J., Harmon, C., Slade, K., Whipple, J. L., & Hawkins, E. J. (2005). Providing feedback to psychotherapists on their patients' progress: Clinical results and practice suggestions. *Journal of Clinical Psychology/In Session, 61*(2), 165–174.

Lambert, M. J., & Hawkins, E. J. (2001). Using information about patient progress in supervision: Are outcomes enhanced? *Australian Psychologist, 36*(2), 131–138.

Lambert, M. J., & Ogles, B. M. (2004). The efficacy and effectiveness of psychotherapy. In M. J. Lambert (Ed.), *Bergin and Garfield's handbook of psychotherapy and behavior change. Fifth edition.* (pp. 139–193). New York: Wiley.

Lambert, M. J., Whipple, J. L., Vermeersch, D. A., Smart, D. W., Hawkins, E. J., Nielsen, S. L. et al. (2002). Enhancing psychotherapy outcomes via providing feedback on client progress: A replication. *Clinical Psychology and Psychotherapy, 9*, 91–103.

Laszloffy, T. A. (2007, May/June). The hidden effects of family violence on children. *Family Therapy Magazine (Alexandria, Virginia), 6*(3), 16–19.

Lavee, Y., & Avisar, Y. (2006). Use of standardized assessment instruments in couple therapy: The role of attitudes and professional factors. *Journal of Marital and Family Therapy, 32*(2), 233–244.

Ledley, D. R., Marx, B. P., & Heimberg, R. G. (2005). *Making cognitive-behavioral therapy work: Clinical process for new practitioners.* New York: Guilford Press.

Lee, J. B., & Bartlett, M. L. (2005). Suicide prevention: Critical elements for managing suicidal clients and counselor liability without the use of no-suicide contract. *Death Studies, 29*(9), 847–865.

Lee, R. E., Emerson, S., & Kochka, P. B. (1997). Using the Michigan State University family therapy questionnaire for training. *Contemporary Family Therapy: An International Journal, 19*(2), 289–303.

Lee, R. E., & Everett, C. A. (2004). *The integrative family therapy supervisor: A primer.* New York: Brunner-Routledge.

Levendosky, A. A., & Graham-Bermann, S. A. (2001). Parenting in battered women: The effects of domestic violence on women and their children. *Journal of Family Violence, 16*, 171–191.

Levendosky, A. A., Leahy, K. L., Bogat, G. A., Davidson, W. S., & von Eye, A. (2006). Domestic violence, maternal parenting, maternal mental health, and infant externalizing behavior. *Journal of Family Psychology, 20*(4), 544–552.

Lewinsohn, P. M., Clarke, G. N., Rohde, P., Hops, H., & Seeley, J. R. (1996). A course in coping: A cognitive-behavioral approach to the treatment of adolescent depression. In E. D. Hibbs & P. S. Jensen (Eds.), *Psychosocial treatments for child and adolescent disorders: Empirically based strategies for clinical practice.* (pp. 109–135). Washington DC: American Psychological Association.

Liddle, B. J. (1986). Resistance in supervision: A response to perceived threat. *Counselor Education and Supervision, 26*(26), 2.

Liddle, H. A. (1991a). Empirical values and the culture of family therapy. *Journal of Marital and Family Therapy, 17*, 327–348.

Liddle, H. A. (1991b). Training and supervision in family therapy: A comprehensive and critical analysis. In A. S. Gurman & D. P. Kniskern (Eds.), *Handbook of family therapy, Vol. II* (pp. 638–697). New York: Brunner/Mazel.

Liddle, H. A., Becker, D., & Diamond, G. M. (1997). Family therapy supervision. In J. C. E. Watkins (Ed.), *Handbook of psychotherapy supervision.* (pp. 400–418). New York: Wiley.

Lin, N., & Westcott, J. (1991). Marital engagement/disengagement, social networks, and mental health. In J. Eckenrode (Ed.), *The social context of coping.* (pp. 213–237). New York: Plenum Press.

Linehan, M. M. (1999). Standard protocol for assessing and treating suicidal behaviors for patients in treatment. In D. G. Jacobs (Ed.), *The Harvard Medical School guide to suicide assessment and intervention.* (pp. 146–187). San Francisco: Jossey-Bass.

Linehan, M. M., Goodstein, J. L., Nielsen, S. L., & Chiles, J. A. (1983). Reasons for staying alive when you are thinking of killing yourself: The Reasons for Living Inventory. *Journal of Consulting and Clinical Psychology, 51*, 276–286.

Lock, J., & Le Grange, D. (2001). Can family based treatment of anorexia nervosa be manualized? *Journal of Psychotherapy Practice and Research, 10*(4), 253–261.

Lock, J., Le Grange, D., Agras, W. S., & Dare, C. (2001). *Treatment manual for anorexia nervosa. A family based approach.* New York: Guilford Press.

Lohr, J. M., Hamberger, L. K., Witte, T. H., & Parker, L. M. (2006). Scientific evidence for domestic violence treatment. In J. E. Fisher & O'Donohue W. T. (Eds.), *Practitioner's guide to evidence-based psychotherapy.* (pp. 258–265). New York: Springer.

Long, N., & Forehand, R. (2007). *Fidelity checklist for helping the noncompliant child.* Unpublished manuscript., University of Vermont, Department of Psychology, Burlington, VT.

Lowe, R. (2005). Negotiating goals in conjoint therapy: From virtual to actual practice. *Journal of Family Psychotherapy, 16*(1–2), 43–49.

Luborsky, L. (1990). Theory and technique in dynamic psychotherapy – Curative factors and training therapists to maximize them. *Psychotherapy and Psychosomatics, 53*, 50–57.

Luborsky, L. (1994). Therapeutic alliances as predictors of psychotherapy outcomes: Factors explaining the predictive success. In A. Horvarth & L. Greenberg (Eds.), *The working alliance – Theory, research, and practice.* (pp. 38–50). New York: Wiley.

Luborsky, L., Barber, J. P., Siqueland, L., Johnson, S., Najavits, L. M., Frank, A. et al. (1996). The revised Helping Alliance Questionnaire (HAq-II). *Journal of Psychotherapy Practice and Research, 3*, 260–271.

Luborsky, L., Crits-Christoph, P., McLellan, A. T., Woody, G., Piper, W., Liberman, B. et al. (1986). Do therapists vary much in their success? Findings from four outcome studies. *American Journal of Orthopsychiatry, 56*, 501–512.

Luborsky, L., McLellan, A. T., Diguer, L., Woody, G., & Seligman, D. A. (1997). The psychotherapist matters: Comparison of outcomes across twenty-two therapists and seven patient samples. *Clinical Psychology: Science and Practice, 4*, 53–65.

Lunnen, K. M., & Ogles, B. M. (1998). A multiperspective, multivariable evaluation of reliable change. *Journal of Consulting and Clinical Psychology, 66*(3), 400–410.

MacLean, A. P. (2005). A problem well stated is a problem half solved. In M. Cierpka, V. Thomas & D. H. Sprenkle (Eds.), *Family assessment: Integrating multiple perspectives.* (pp. 53–80). Kirkland, WA/Gottingen, Germany: Hogrefe & Huber.

MacPhee, D. C., Johnson, S. M., & Van Der Veer, M. M. C. (1995). Low sexual desire in women: The effects of marital therapy. *Journal of Sex & Marital Therapy, 21*, 159–182.

Magnuson, S., Wilcoxon, S. A., & Norem, K. (2000). A profile of a lousy supervision: Experienced counselors' perspectives. *Counselor Education and Supervision, 39*, 189–202.

Mamodhoussen, S., Wright, J., Tremblay, N., & Poitras-Wright, H. (2005). Impact of marital and psychological distress on therapeutic alliance in couples undergoing couple therapy. *Journal of Marital and Family Therapy, 31*(2), 159–169.

Margison, F. R., Barkham, M., Evans, C., McGrath, G., Mellor-Clark, J., Audin, K. et al. (2000). Evidence-based practice and practice-based evidence. *British Journal of Psychiatry, 177*, 123–130.

Margolin, G. (1982). Ethical and legal considerations in marital and family therapy. *American Psychologist, 37*, 788–801.

Margolin, G., & Gordis, E. B. (2003). Co-occurrence between marital aggression and parents' child abuse potential: The impact of cumulative stress. *Violence and Victims, 18*, 243–258.

Margolin, G., Gordis, E. B., Medina, A. M., & Oliver, P. H. (2003). The co-occurrence of husband-to-wife aggression, family-of-origin aggression, and child abuse potential in a community sample. *Journal of Interpersonal Violence, 18*, 413–440.

Margolin, G., John, R. S., & Gleberman, L. (1988). Affective responses to conflictual discussions in violent and nonviolent couples. *Journal of Consulting and Clinical Psychology, 56*, 24–33.

Maslach, C., & Jackson, S. E. (1981). *The Maslach Burnout Inventory (Research ed.).* Palo Alto, CA: Consulting Psychologists Press.

McCloskey, K., & Grigsby, N. (2005). The ubiquitous clinical problem of adult intimate partner violence: The need for routine assessment. *Professional Psychology: Research and Practice, 36*(3), 264–275.

McConnaughy, E. A., Prochaska, J. O., & Velicer, W. F. (1983). Stages of change in psychotherapy: Measurement and sample profiles. *Psychotherapy: Theory, Research and Practice, 20*, 368–375.

McCrady, B. S., & Epstein, E. E. (1995). Marital therapy in the treatment of alcohol problems. In N. S. Jacobson & A. S. Gurman (Eds.), *Clinical handbook of couple therapy* (pp. 369–393). New York: Guilford Press.

McCrae, R. R., & Costa, P. T. (1986). Personality, coping, and coping effectiveness in an adult sample. *Journal of Personality, 54*, 385–405.

McDonald, R. M. (1991). Assessment of organisational context: A missing component in evaluations of training programmes. *Evaluation and Programme Planning, 14*, 273–279.

McIntosh, V. V. W., Jordan, J., McKenzie, J. M., Luty, S. E., Carter, F. A. C., Frampton, C. M. A. et al. (2005). Measuring therapist adherence in psychotherapy for anorexia nervosa: Scale adaptation, psychometric properties, and distinguishing psychotherapies. *Psychotherapy Research, 15*(3), 339–344.

McMahon, R. J., & Forehand, R. L. (2003). *Helping the noncompliant child: Family-based treatment for oppositional behavior (2nd ed.).* New York: Guilford Press.

Mead, D. E. (1990). *Effective supervision: A task-oriented model for the mental health professions.* New York: Brunner/Mazel.

Mead, D. E. (2006). *The Comprehensive Areas of Change Questionnaire Item Ranking Form.* Unpublished ranking form, Marriage and Family Therapy Programs, School of Family Life, College of Family, Home & Social Sciences, Brigham Young University, Provo, Utah.

Mead, D. E. (2007). *Therapy Tailoring Skills Rating Form* (Assessment Instrument). Brigham Young University, Provo. UT: Marriage and Family Therapy Programs.

Mead, D. E., Thurber, S. L., & Crane, B. E. (2003). Spanish translations of a standard assessment battery for marital distress. *The American Journal of Family Therapy, 31,* 409–412.

Mead, D. E., Vatcher, G. M., Wyne, B. A., & Roberts, S. L. (1990). The Comprehensive Areas of Change Questionnaire: Assessing marital couples' presenting complaints. *The American Journal of Family Therapy, 18*(1), 65–79.

Meichenbaum, D. (2005). 35 years of working with suicidal patients: Lessons learned. *Canadian Psychology, 46*(2), 64–72.

Melde, C. E., Ebensen, F., & Tusinski, K. (2006). Addressing program fidelity using onsite observations and program provider descriptions of program delivery. *Evaluation Review, 30*(6), 714–740.

Messer, S. B. (2006). Patient values and preferences. In J. C. Norcross, L. E. Beutler & R. F. Levant (Eds.), *Evidence-based practices in mental health: Debate and dialogue on the fundamental questions.* (pp. 31–40). Washington, DC: American Psychological Association.

Meyer, B., & Pilconis, P. A. (2002). Attachment style. In J. C. Norcross (Ed.), *Psychotherapy relationships that work: Therapist contributions and responsiveness to patients.* (pp. 367–382). Oxford: Oxford University Press.

Michelson, L. K., & Marchione, K. (1991). Behavioral, cognitive, and pharmacological treatments of panic disorders with agoraphobia: Critique and synthesis. *Journal of Consulting and Clinical Psychology, 59,* 100–114.

Miczo, N. (2004). Stressors and social support perceptions predict illness attitudes and care-seeking intentions. *Health Communication, 16*(3), 347–361.

Miller, G. E., & Prinz, R. J. (2003). Engagement of families in treatment for childhood conduct problems. *Behavior Therapy, 34*(4), 517–534.

Miller, M. C., Jacobs, D. G., & Gutheil, T. G. (1998). Talisman or taboo: The controversy of the suicide prevention contract. *Harvard Review of Psychiatry, 6,* 78–87.

Miller, R. B., Johnson, L. N., Sandberg, J. G., Stringer-Seibold, T. A., & Gfeller-Strouts, L. (2000). An addendum to the 1997 outcome research chart. *American Journal of Family Therapy, 28*(4), 347–354.

Miller, S. D., & Duncan, B. L. (2004). *The Outcome and Session Rating Scales: Administration and Scoring Manual (Rev. ed.).* Chicago: Institute for the Study of Therapeutic Change.

Miller, S. D., Duncan, B. L., & Hubble, M. A. (2004). Beyond integration: The triumph of outcome over process in clinical practice. *Psychotherapy in Australia, 101*(2nd ed.), 2–19.

Miller, S. D., Duncan, B. L., Sorrell, R., & Brown, G. S. (2005). The partners for change outcome management system. *Journal of Clinical Psychology/In Session, 61*(2), 199–208.

Miller, T. R., & Taylor, D. M. (2005). Adolescent suicidality: Who will ideate, who will act? *Suicide and Life-Threatening Behavior, 35*(4), 425–435.

Miller, W. R., Moyers, T. B., Arciniega, L., Ernst, D., & Forcehimes, A. (2005). Training, supervision and quality monitoring of the COMBINE study behavioral interventions. *Journal of Studies on Alcohol, 66*(suppl 15), 188–195.

Miller, W. R., & Rollnick, S. (2002). *Motivational interviewing: Preparing people for change* (2nd ed.). New York: Guilford Press.

Milne, D. L. (1992). *Assessment: A mental health portfolio.* Reading: NFER-Nelson.

Milne, D. L. (1999). *Social therapy: A guide to social support interventions for mental health practitioners.* New York: Wiley.

Milne, D. L., Baker, C., Blackburn, I. M., James, I., & Reichelt, K. (1999). Effectiveness of cognitive therapy training. *Journal of Behavior Therapy & Experimental Psychiatry, 30,* 81–92.

Milne, D., Cowie, I., Gormly, A., White, C., & Harley, J. (1992). Social supporters and behaviour therapists: Three studies on the form and function of their help. *Behavioural Psychotherapy, 20,* 343–354.

Milne, D., & James, I. (2000). A systematic review of effective cognitive-behavioral supervision. *British Journal of Clinical Psychology, 39*(2), 111–127.

Milne, D. L., & James, I. A. (2002). The observed impact of training on competence in clinical supervision. *British Journal of Clinical Psychology, 41,* 55–72.

Milne, D. L., James, I., Keegan, D., & Dudley, M. (2002). Teachers' PETS: A new observational measure of experiential training interactions. *Clinical Psychology and Psychotherapy, 9,* 187–199.

Minuchin, S., & Fishman, H. C. (1981). *Family therapy techniques.* Cambridge, MA: Harvard University Press.

Minuchin, S., Montalvo, B., Guerney, B. G., Rosman, B. L., & Schumer, F. (1967). *Families of the slums.* New York: Basic Books.

Moncher, F. J., & Prinz, F. J. (1991). Treatment fidelity in outcome studies. *Clinical Psychology Review, 11,* 247–266.

Moos, R. H. (2004). *Coping responses inventory: An update on research applications and validity.* Lutz, FL: Psychological Assessment Resources.

Moos, R. H., & Schaefer, J. A. (1993). Coping resources & processes: Current concepts & measures. In L. Goldberger & S. Brezniz (Eds.), *Handbook of stress: Theoretical & Clinical Aspects* (*2nd ed.*). New York: Free Press.

Moras, K. (1993). The use of treatment manuals to train psychotherapists: Observations and recommendations. *Psychotherapy, 30,* 581–586.

Morgan, H., Jones, H., & Owen, J. (1993). Secondary prevention of nonfatal deliberate self-harm: The green card study. *British Journal of Psychiatry, 163,* 111–112.

Morrissey-Kane, R., & Prinz, R. J. (1999). Engagement in child and adolescent treatment: The role of parental cognitions and attributions. *Clinical Child and Family Psychology Review, 2,* 183–198.

Moskowitz, S. A., & Rupert, P. A. (1983). Conflict resolution within the supervisory relationship. *Professional Psychology: Research and Practice, 14,* 632–641.

Mothersole, G. (1996). Existential realities and no-suicide contracts. *Transactional Analysis Journal, 26*(2), 151–159.

Mueser, K. T. (2006). Families and major mental illness. In D. R. Crane & E. S. Marxhall (Eds.), *Handbook of families & Health: Interdisciplinary perspectives.* (pp. 126–144). Thousand Oaks, CA: Sage.

Mullin, T., Barkham, M., Mothersole, G., Bewick, B. M., & Kinder, A. (2006). Recovery and improvement benchmarks for counselling and psychological therapies in routine primary care. *Counselling & Pschotherapy Research, 6*(1), 68–80.

Murphy, C. M., & Eckhardt, C. I. (2005). *Treating the abusive partner: An individualized cognitive-behavioral approach.* New York: Guilford Press.

Najavits, L. M., & Strupp, H. H. (1994). Differences in the effectiveness of psychodynamic therapists: A process-outcome study. *Pschotherapy, 31*(1), 114–123.

Nathan, P. E. (1998). Practice guidelines: Not yet ideal. *American Psychologist, 53,* 290–299.

National Association of Social Workers. (1996). *Code of Ethics of the National Association of Social Workers.* Washington, DC: Author.

National Center on Elder Abuse (2011) Retrieved 26 December 2011, from www.ncea.aoa.gov/Manin_site/pdf/publication/FinalStaitstics050331.pdf.

Neill, J. R., & Kniskern, D. P. (1982). *From psyche to system: The evolving therapy of Carl Whitaker.* New York: Guilford Press.

Nelson, M. L., & Friedlander, M. L. (2001). A close look at conflictual supervisory relationships: The trainee's perspective. *Journal of Counseling Psychology, 48*, 384–395.

Nelson, W. M., & Politano, P. M. (1993). The goal is to say "goodbye" and have the treatment effects generalize and maintain: A cognitive-behavioral view of termination. *Journal of Cognitive Psychotherapy, 7*(4), 251–263.

Nezu, A. M., & Nezu, C. M. (1989). *Clinical decision making in behavior therapy: A problem-solving perspective.* Champaign, IL: Research Press.

Nielsen, S. L., Okiishi, J., Nielsen, D. L., Hawkins, E. J., Harmon, S. C., Pedersen, T. et al. (2009). Termination, appointment use, and outcome patterns associated with intake therapist discontinuity. *Professional Psychology: Research and Practice, 40*(3), 272–278.

Nock, M. K., & Kazdin, A. B. (2001). Parent expectancies for child therapy: Assessment and relation to participation in treatment. *Journal of Child and Family Studies, 10*, 155–180.

Noell, G. H., Witt, J. C., LaFleur, L. H., Mortenson, B. P., Ranier, D. D., & LeVelle, J. (2000). Increasing intervention implementation in general education following consultation: A comparison of two follow-up strategies. *Journal of Applied Behavior Analysis, 33*, 271–284.

Noonan, J. R. (1973). A follow-up of pre-therapy dropouts. *Journal of Community Psychology, 1*, 43–44.

Norcross, J. C. (2002). *Psychotherapy relationships that work: Therapist contributions and responsiveness to patient needs.* New York: Oxford University Press.

Norcross, J. C. (2005). The psychotherapist's own psychotherapy: Educating and developing psychologists. *American Psychologist, 60*(8), 840–850.

Norcross, J. C., Beutler, L. E., & Levant, R. F. (2006). *Evidence-based practices in mental health: Debate and dialogue on the fundamental questions.* Washington, DC: American Psychological Association.

O'Dell, S. L. (1982). Enhancing parent involvement in training: A discussion. *Behavior Therapist, 5*(1), 9–13.

Odell, M., & Campbell, C. E. (1998). *The practical practice of marriage and family therapy: Things my training supervisor never told me.* New York: Haworth Press.

Odell, M., & Campbell, C. E. (2001). The practical practice of marriage and family therapy: Things my training supervisor never told me. *Family Therapy, 28*(2), 120–121.

Ogg, J., & Bennett, G. (1992). Elder abuse in Britain. *British Medical Journal, 305*, 998–999.

O'Leary, K. D. (1999). Developmental and affective issues in assessing and treating partner aggression. *Clinical Psychology: Science & Practice, 6*, 400–414.

O'Leary, K. D., Slep, A. M. S., & O'Leary, S. G. (2000). Co-occurrence of partner and parent aggression: Research and treatment implications. *Behavior Therapy, 31*, 631–648.

O'Leary, K. D., Vivian, D., & Malone, J. (1992). Assessment of physical aggression against women in marriage: The need for multimodal assessment. *Behavioral Assessment, 14*(1), 5–14.

O'Neill, S. C., Cohen, L. H., Tolpin, L. H., & Gunthert, K. C. (2004). Affective reactivity to daily interpersonal stressors as a prospective predictor of depressive symptoms. *Journal of Social and Clinical Psychology, 23*(2), 172–194.

Parsonson, B. S., & Baer, D. M. (1986). The graphic analysis of data. In A. D. Poling & R. W. Fuqua (Eds.), *Research methods in applied behavior analysis: Issues and advances.* (pp. 157–186). New York: Plenum Press.

Patterson, G. R., & Forgatch, M. S. (1985). Therapist behavior as a determinant for client noncompliance: A paradox for the behavior modifier. *Journal of Consulting and Clinical Psychology, 53*, 846–851.

Patterson, J. E., Miller, R. B., Carnes, S., & Wilson, S. (2004). Evidence-based practice for marriage and family therapists. *Journal of Marital and Family Therapy, 30*(2), 183–195.

Patterson, J., Williams, L., Grauf-Grounds, C., & Chamow, L. (1998). *Essential skills in family therapy: From the first interview to termination.* New York: Guilford Press.

Pekarik, G. (1985). Coping with dropouts. *Professional Psychology: Research and Practice, 16,* 114–123.

Pekarik, G. (1992). Relationship of client's reasons for dropping out of treatment to outcome and satisfaction. *Journal of Clinical Psychology, 48,* 91–98.

Penhale, B. (2007). Elder abuse in Europe: An overview of recent developments. *Journal of Elder Abuse and Neglect, 18*(1), 107–116.

Persons, J. B., & Silberschatz, G. (1998). Are results of randomized controlled trials useful to psychotherapists? *Journal of Consulting and Clinical Psychology, 66,* 126–135.

Phillips, J. B. (1983). Some ethical concerns regarding the individual psychotherapy of the married client. *Canadian Psychology, 24*(1), 8–13.

Pillemer, K., & Finkelhor, D. (1988). The prevalence of elder abuse: A random sample survey. *The Gerontologist, 28*(1), 51–57.

Pinsof, W. M. (1994). An integrative systems perspective on the therapeutic alliance: Theoretical, clinical, and research implications. In A. O. Horvath & L. S. Greenberg (Eds.), *The working alliance: Theory, research and practice.* (pp. 173–195). New York: Wiley.

Pinsof, W. M. (1995). *Integrative problem-centered therapy: A synthesis of family, individual, and biological therapies.* New York: Basic Books.

Pinsof, W. M., & Catherall, D. R. (1986). The integrative psychotherapy alliance: Family, couple and individual therapy scales. *Journal of Marital and Family Therapy, 12,* 137–151.

Pinsof, W. M., & Wynne, L. C. (1995a). The effectiveness and efficacy of marital and family therapy: Introduction to the special issue. *Journal of Marital and Family Therapy, 21,* 341–344.

Pinsof, W. M., & Wynne, L. C. (1995b). The efficacy of marital and family therapy: An empirical overview, conclusions, and recommendations. *Journal of Marital and Family Therapy, 21,* 585–613.

Pinsof, W. M., & Wynne, L. C. (2000). Toward progress research: Closing the gap between family therapy practice and research. *Journal of Marital and Family Therapy, 26,* 1–8.

Pistrang, N., & Barker, C. (2005). How partners talk in times of stress: A process analysis approach. In T. A. Revenson, K. Kayser & G. Bodenmann (Eds.), *Couples coping with stress: Emerging perspectives on dyadic coping.* (pp. 97–119). Washington, DC: American Psychological Association.

Pittaway, E. D., Westhues, A., & Peressini, T. (1995). Risk factors for abuse and neglect among older adults. *Canadian Journal of Aging, 14*(2), 20–44.

Podnieks, E. (1992). National survey on abuse of the elderly in Canada. *Journal of Elder Abuse and Neglect, 4,* 5–58.

Polya, G. (1971). *How to solve it: A new aspect of mathematical method.* Princeton, NJ: Princeton University Press.

Polya, G. (1954). *Induction and analogy in mathematics.* Princeton, NJ: Princeton University Press.

Prinz, R. J., & Miller, G. E. (1994). Family-based treatment for childhood antisocial behavior: Experimental influences on dropout and engagement. *Journal of Consulting and Clinical Psychology, 62,* 645–650.

Prochaska, J. O. (1994). Strong and weak principles for progressing from precontemplation to action on the basis of twelve problem behaviors. *Health Psychology, 13*(1), 47–51.

Prochaska, J. O., DiClemente, C. C., & Norcross, J. C. (1992). In search of how people change. *American Psychologist, 47*(9), 1102–1114.

Prochaska, J. O., & Norcross, J. C. (2001). Stages of change. *Psychotherapy, 38,* 443–448.

Prochaska, J. O., Velicer, W. F., Rossi, J. S., Goldstein, M. G., Marcus, B. H., Rakowski, W. et al. (1994). Stages of change and decisional balance for 12 problem behaviors. *Health Psychology, 13*(1), 39–46.

Quinn, W. H., Dotson, D., & Jordan, K. (1997). Dimensions of therapeutic alliance and their association with outcome in family therapy. *Psychotherapy Research, 7,* 429–438.

Quinnsey, V. L., Harris, G. T., Rice, M. E., & Cormier, C. A. (2006). *Violent offenders: Appraising and managing risk. (2nd ed.).* Washington, DC: American Psychological Association.

Rait, D. S. (1998). Perspectives on the therapeutic alliance in brief couples and family therapy. In J. D. Safran & J. C. Muran (Eds.), *The therapeutic alliance in brief psychotherapy.* (pp. 171–191). Washington, DC: American Psychological Association.

Reed, G. M. (2006). Clinical expertise. In J. C. Norcross, L. E. Beutler & R. F. Levant (Eds.), *Evidence-based practices in mental health: Debate and dialogue on the fundamental questions.* (pp. 13–23). Washington, DC: American Psychological Association.

Reis, B. F., & Brown, L. G. (1999). Reducing psychotherapy dropouts: Maximizing perspective convergence in the psychotherapy dyad. *Psychotherapy: Theory, Research, Practice, Training, 36,* 123–136.

Reis, M., & Nahmiash, D. (1995). Validation of the Caregiver Abuse Screen (CASE). *Canadian Journal of Aging, 14*(2, Suppl 2), 45–60.

Reis, M., & Nahmiash, D. (1998). Validation of the indicators of abuse (IOA) screen. *The Gerontologist, 38,* 471–480.

Revenson, T. A., Kayser, K., & Bodenmann, G. (2005a). Introduction. In T. A. Revenson, K. Kayser & G. Bodenmann (Eds.), *Couples coping with stress: Emerging perspectives on dyadic coping.* (pp. 3–10). Washington, DC: American Psychological Association.

Revenson, T. A., Kayser, K., & Bodenmann, G. (2005b). *Couples coping with stress: Emerging perspectives on dyadic coping.* Washington, DC: American Psychological Association.

Richards, K., & Range, L. M. (2001). Is training in psychology associated with increased responsiveness to suicidality? *Death Studies, 25*(3), 265–279.

Roberts, L. J., & McCrady, B. S. (2002). *Alcohol problems in intimate relationships: Identification and intervention: A guide for marriage and family therapists.* Washington, DC: American Association for Marriage and Family Therapy, National Institute on Alcohol Abuse and Alcoholism.

Rodriguez, M. A., McLoughlin, E., Nah, G., & Campbell, J. C. (2001). Mandatory reporting of domestic violence injuries to the police: What do emergency department patients think? *JAMA: Journal of the American Medical Association, 286*(5), 580–583.

Rodriguez, M. A., Sheldon, W. R., & Rao, N. (2002). Abused patient's attitudes about mandatory reporting of intimate partner abuse injuries to police. *Women & Health, 35*(2–3), 135–147.

Rogers, C. (1961). *On becoming a person.* Boston, MA: Houghton-Mifflin.

Rosenberg, T., & Pace, M. (2006). Burnout among mental health professionals: Special considerations for the marriage and family therapist. *Journal of Marital and Family Therapy, 32*(1), 87–99.

Ross, L. V., Friman, P. C., & Christophersen, E. R. (1993). An appointment-keeping improvement package for outpatient pediatrics: Systematic replication and component analysis. *Journal of Applied Behavior Analysis, 26,* 461–467.

Rounsaville, B. J., O'Malley, S. O., Foley, S., & Weissman, M. M. (1988). Role of manual-guided training in the conduct and efficacy of Interpersonal Psychotherapy for Depression. *Journal of Consulting and Clinical Psychology, 56,* 681–688.

Ruscio, A. M., & Holohan, D. R. (2006). Applying empirically supported treatments to complex cases: Ethical, empirical, and practical considerations. *Clinical Psychology: Science & Practice, 13*(2), 146–162.

Ryan, D., & Carr, A. (2001). A study of the differential effects of Tomm's questioning styles on the therapeutic alliance. *Family Process, 40,* 67–77.

Sachs, C. J., Koziol-McLain, J., Glass, N., Webster, D., & Campbell, J. (2002). A population-based survey assessing support for mandatory domestic violence reporting by health care personnel. *Women & Health, 35*(2–3), 121–133.

Safran, J. D., & Muran, J. C. (1996). The resolution of ruptures in the therapeutic alliance. *Journal of Consulting and Clinical Psychology, 64,* 447–458.

Safran, J. D., Muran, J. C., Samstag, L. W., & Stevens, C. (2002). Repairing alliance ruptures. In J. C. Norcross (Ed.), *Psychotherapy relationships that work: Therapist contributions and responsiveness to patients.* (pp. 235–254). Oxford: Oxford University Press.

Sandberg, J. G., Johnson, L. N., Dermer, S. B., Gfeller-Strouts, L. L., Seibold, J. M., Stringer-Seibold, T. A. et al. (1997). Demonstrated efficacy of models of marriage and family therapy: An update of Gurman, Kniskern, and Pinsof's chart. *American Journal of Family Therapy, 25*(2), 121–137.

Saunders, J. B., Aasland, O. G., Babor, T. F., De La Fuente, J. R., & Grant, M. (1993). Development of the Alcohol Use Disorders Identification Test (AUDIT). *Addiction, 88*, 791–804.

Schulte, D., & Eifert, G. H. (2002). What to do when manuals fail? The dual model of psychotherapy. *Clinical Psychology: Science & Practice, 9*, 312–328.

Schulte, D., Kunzel, R., Pepping, G., & Schulte-Bahrenberg, T. (1992). Tailor-made versus standardized therapy of phobic patients. *Advances in Behavioral Research and Therapy, 14*, 67–92.

Schwartz, G. S., Friedlander, M. L., & Tedeschi, J. T. (1986). Effects of clients' attributional explanations and reasons for seeking help on counselor impressions. *Journal of Counseling Psychology, 33*, 90–93.

Segrin, C., Badger, T. A., Meek, P., Lopez, A. M., Bonham, E., & Sieger, A. (2005). Dyadic interdependence on affect and quality-of-life trajectories among women with breast cancer and their partners. *Journal of Social and Personal Relationships, 22*(5), 673–689.

Sexton, T. L., Weeks, G. R., & Robbins, M. S. (2003). *Handbook of family therapy: The science and practice of working with families and couples.* New York: Brunner-Routledge.

Shadish, W. R., & Baldwin, S. A. (2002). Meta-analysis of MFT interventions. In D. H. Sprenkle (Ed.), *Effectiveness research in marriage and family therapy* (pp. 339–370). Alexandria, VA: American Association for Marriage and Family Therapy.

Shadish, W. R., & Baldwin, S. A. (2003). Meta-analysis of MFT interventions. *Journal of Marital and Family Therapy, 29*, 547–570.

Shadish, W. R., & Baldwin, S. A. (2005). Effects of behavioral marital therapy: A meta-analysis of randomized controlled trials. *Journal of Consulting and Clinical Psychology, 73*(1), 6–14.

Shadish, W. R., Matt, G. E., Navarro, A. M., & Phillips, G. (2000). The effects of psychological therapies under clinically representative conditions: A meta-analysis. *Psychological Bulletin, 126*, 512–529.

Shadish, W. R., Ragsdale, K., Glaser, R. R., & Montgomery, L. M. (1995). The efficacy and effectiveness of marital and family therapy: A perspective from meta-analysis. *Journal of Marital and Family Therapy, 21*, 345–360.

Shepherd, M. (2007). Domestic violence and AVOs: A legal guide for doctors, psychologists, counsellors, and other healthcare professionals. *Australian Journal of Clinical Hypnotherapy and Hypnosis, 28*(2), 34–44.

Shields, C. G. (1986). Critiquing the new epistemologies: Toward minimum requirements for a scientific theory of family therapy. *Journal of Marital and Family Therapy, 12*, 359–372.

Shields, C. G., Sprenkle, D. H., & Constantine, J. A. (1991). Anatomy of an initial interview: The importance of joining and structuring skills. *The American Journal of Family Therapy, 19*, 3–18.

Shields, C. G., Wynne, L., McDaniel, S. H., & Gawinski, B. A. (1994). The marginalization of family therapy: A historical and continuing problem. *Journal of Marital and Family Therapy, 20*(1), 117–138.

Sidman, M. (1989). *Coercion and its fallout.* Boston, MA: Authors Cooperative.

Simmons, D. S., & Doherty, W. J. (1995). Defining who we are and what we do: Clinical practice patterns of marriage and family therapists in Minnesota. *Journal of Marital and Family Therapy, 21*(1), 3–16.

Simon, R. I. (2004). *Assessing and managing suicide risk: Guidelines for clinically based risk management.* Washington, DC: American Psychiatric Pub.

Simon, R. I., & Gutheil, T. G. (2002). A recurrent pattern of suicide risk factors observed in litigated cases: Lessons in risk management. *Psychiatric Annals, 32*(7), 384–387.

Simone, S., & Fulero, S. M. (2005). Tarasoff and the Duty to Protect. *Journal of Aggression, Maltreatment & Trauma, 11*(1–2), 145–168.

Skinner, B. F. (1953). *Science and human behavior.* New York: The Free Press.

Skinner, B. F. (1969). *Contingencies of reinforcement: A theoretical analysis.* New York: Appleton-Century-Crofts.

Skinner, B. F. (1974). *About behaviorism.* New York: Alfred A. Knopf.

Slep, A. M. S., & Heyman, R. E. (2006). Creating and field-testing child maltreatment definitions: Improving the reliability of substantiation determinations. *Child Maltreatment, 11*, 217–236.

Slep, A. M. S., & O'Leary, S. G. (2001). Examining partner and child abuse: Are we ready for an integrated theory of family violence? *Child and Family Psychology Review, 4*, 87–108.

Slep, A. M. S., & O'Leary, S. G. (2005). Parent and partner violence in families with young children: Rates, patterns, and connections. *Journal of Consulting and Clinical Psychology, 74*, 435–444.

Slovenko, R. (1980). Legal issues in psychotherapy supervision. In A. K. Hess (Ed.), *Psychotherapy supervision: Theory, research and practice.* (pp. 453–473). New York: Wiley.

Smith, A. (2001). Domestic violence laws: The voices of battered women. *Violence and Victims, 16*(1), 91–111.

Smith, A., & Winokur, K. P. (2004). What doctors and policymakers should know: Battered women's views about mandatory medical reporting. *Journal of Criminal Justice, 32*(3), 207–221.

Smith, R. C., Mead, D. E., & Kinsella, J. A. (1998). Direct supervision: Adding computer-assisted feedback and data capture to live supervision. *Journal of Marital and Family Therapy, 24*, 113–125.

Sperry, L. (2004). *Assessment of couples and families: Contemporary and cutting-edge strategies.* New York: Brunner-Routledge.

Spirito, A., & Overholser, J. (2003). Child and adolescent psychiatric emergencies: Family psychodynamic issues. *Child and Adolescent Psychiatric Clinics of North America, 12*(4), 649–665.

Spitzer, R. L., Skodol, A. E., Williams, J. B. W., Gibbon, M., & Kass, F. (1982). Supervising intake diagnosis. *Archives of General Psychiatry, 39*, 1299–1305.

Sprenkle, D. H. (2002). *Effectiveness research in marriage and family therapy.* Alexandria, VA: The American Association for Marriage and Family Therapy.

Sprenkle, D. H., & Blow, A. J. (2004). Common factors and our scared models. *Journal of Marital and Family Therapy, 30*, 113–129.

Sprenkle, D. H., Blow, A. J., & Dickey, M. H. (1999). Common factors and other nontechnique variables in marriage and family therapy. In M. A. Hubble, B. L. Duncan & S. D. Miller (Eds.), *The heart & soul of change: What works in therapy.* (pp. 329–359). Washington, DC: American Psychological Association.

Sprenkle, D., H., Davis, S., & Lebow, J. (2009). *Common factors in couple and family therapy: The overlooked foundation for effective practice.* New York: Guilford Press.

Stack, S., & Eshleman, J. (1998). Marital status and happiness: A 17-nation study. *Journal of Marriage and the Family, 60*, 527–536.

Stanford, E. J., Goetz, R. R., & Bloom, J. D. (1994). The no harm contract in the emergency assessment of suicide risk. *Journal of Clinical Psychiatry, 55*, 344–348.

Stets, J., & Straus, M. A. (1992). The marriage license as a hitting license. In M. A. Straus & R. J. Gelles (Eds.), *Physical violence in American families: Risk factors and adaptations to violence in 8,145 families.* (pp. 227–244). New Brunswick, NJ: Transaction.

Stirman, S. W., & DeRubeis, R. J. (2006). Research patients and clinical trials are frequently representative of clinical practice. In J. C. Norcross, L. E. Beutler & R. F. Levant (Eds.), *Evidence-based practices in mental health: Debate and dialogue on the fundamental questions.* (pp. 171–179). Washington, DC: American Psychological Association.

Stith, S. M., Rosen, K. H., & McCollum, E. E. (2002). Domestic violence. In D. H. Sprenkle (Ed.), *Effectiveness research in marriage and family therapy.* (pp. 223–254). Alexandria, VA: The American Association for Marriage and Family Therapy.

Stolk, Y., & Perlesz, A. J. (1990). Do better trainees make worse therapists? A follow-up study of client families. *Family Process, 29*, 45–58.

Stoltenberg, C. D. (2005). Enhancing professional competence through developmental approaches to supervision. *American Psychologist, 60*(8), 857–864.

Stoltenberg, C. D., & Delworth, U. (1987). *Supervising counselors and therapists: A developmental approach.* San Francisco: Jossey-Bass.

Straus, M. A. (1994). *Beating the devil out of them: Corporal punishment in American families.* Lexington, MA: Lexington/Macmillan Books.

Straus, M. A., & Douglas, E. M. (2008, Winter). Research on spanking by parents: Implications for public policy. *The Family Psychologist (Washington, DC), 24,* 18–20.

Straus, M. A., & Gelles, R. J. (1990). *Physical violence in American families: Risk factors and adaptations to violence in 8,145 families.* New Brunswick, NJ: Transaction Books.

Straus, M. A., Gelles, R. J., & Steinmetz, S. K. (1980). *Behind closed doors: Violence in the American family.* Garden City, NJ: Anchor Press.

Straus, M. A., Hamby, S. L., Boney-McCoy, S. B., & Sugarman, D. B. (1996). The revised Conflict Tactics Scales (CTS2): Development and preliminary psychometric data. *Journal of Family Issues, 17,* 283–316.

Straus, M. A., Hamby, S. L., Finkelhor, D., Moore, D. W., & Runyan, D. (1998). Identification of child maltreatment with the parent-child conflict scales. Development of psychometric data for a national sample of American parents. *Child Abuse and Neglect, 22,* 249–270.

Straus, M. A., & Stewart, J. H. (1999). Corporal punishment by American parents: National data on prevalence, chronicity, severity, and duration, in relation to child and family characteristics. *Clinical Child and Family Psychological Review, 2*(2), 55–70.

Streeter, C. L., & Franklin, C. (1992). Defining and measuring social support: Guidelines for social work practitioners. *Research on Social Work Practice, 2*(1), 81–98.

Stroebe, W., Stroebe, M., Abakoumkin, G., & Schut, H. (1996). The role of loneliness and social support in adjustment to loss: A test of attachment versus stress theory. *Journal of Personality and Social Psychology, 70,* 1241–1249.

Strong, S. R., Welsh, J. A., Corcoran, J. L., & Hoyt, W. T. (1992). Social psychology and counseling psychology: History, products, and promise of an interface. *Journal of Counseling Psychology, 39*(2), 139–157.

Symonds, D., & Horvath, A. O. (2004). Optimizing the alliance in couple therapy. *Family Process, 43*(4), 443–455.

Tarrier, N., & Humphreys, A. (2003). PTSD and the social support of the interpersonal environment: The development of social cognitive behavior therapy. *Journal of Cognitive Psychotherapy, 17*(2), 187–198.

Taylor, S. E., Sherman, D. K., Kim, H. S., Jarcho, J., Takagi, K., & Dunagan, M. S. (2004). Culture and social support: Who seeks it and why? *Journal of Personality and Social Psychology, 87*(32), 354–362.

Thomas, S. E. G., Werner-Wilson, R. J., & Murphy, M. J. (2005). Influence of therapist and client behaviors on therapy alliance. *Contemporary Family Therapy: An International Journal, 27*(1), 19–35.

Thurber, S. L., & Mead, D. E. (2002). *Reliable change scores and clinically significant change cutoff scores for the Revised Dyadic Adjustment Scale: Establishing criteria for client improvement or deterioration.* Provo, UT: Brigham Young University, Marriage and Family Therapy Programs.

Todahl, J. L., Linville, D., Chou, L., & Maher-Cosenza, P. (2008). A qualitative study of intimate partner violence universal screening by family therapy interns: Implications for practice, research, training, and supervision. *Journal of Marital and Family Therapy, 34*(1), 28–43.

Tolan, P., Gorman-Smith, D., & Henry, D. (2006). Family violence. *Annual Review of Psychology, 57,* 557–583.

Tryon, G. S., & Kane, A. S. (1995). Client involvement, working alliance, and type of therapy termination. *Psychotherapy Research, 5*(3), 189–198.

Tryon, G. S., & Winograd, G. (2002). Goal consensus and collaboration. In J. C. Norcross (Ed.), *Psychotherapy relationships that work: Therapist contributions and responsiveness to patients.* (pp. 109–125). Oxford: Oxford University Press.

Turkus, J. A. (1995). Crisis intervention. In C. Classen & I. D. Yalom (Eds.), *Treating women molested in childhood.* (pp. 35–61). San Francisco, CA: Jossey Bass.

Turner, A. J., & Vernon, J. C. (1976). Prompts to increase attendance in a community mental-health center. *Journal of Applied Behaviour Analysis, 9*(2), 141–145.

Uchino, B. N., Cacioppo, J. T., & Kiecolt-Glaser, J. K. (1996). The relationship between social support and physiological processes: A review with emphasis on underlying mechanisms and implications for health. *Psychological Bulletin, 119*, 488–531.

Walker, J. G., Johnson, S., Manion, I., & Cloutier, P. (1996). Emotionally focused marital intervention for couples with chronically ill children. *Journal of Consulting and Clinical Psychology, 64*(5), 1029–1036.

Waltz, J., Addis, M. E., Koerner, K., & Jacobson, N. S. (1993). Testing the integrity of a psychotherapy protocol: Assessment of adherence and competence. *Journal of Consulting and Clinical Psychology, 61*, 620–630.

Wampold, B. E. (2001). *The great psychotherapy debate: Models, methods, and findings.* Mahwah, NJ: Lawrence Erlbaum Associates.

Wampold, B. E. (2006). The psychotherapist. In J. C. Norcross, L. E. Beutler & R. F. Levant (Eds.), *Evidence-based practices in mental health: Debate and dialogue on the fundamental questions.* (pp. 200–208). Washington, DC: American Psychological Association.

Ward, D. B., & McCollum, E. E. (2005). Treatment effectiveness and its correlates in a marriage and family therapy training clinic. *American Journal of Family Therapy, 33*(32), 207–223.

Watkins, C. E., Jr. (1997). *Handbook of psychotherapy supervision.* New York: Wiley.

Watzlawick, P. (1972). A structured family interview. In G. D. Erickson & T. P. Hogan (Eds.), *Family therapy: An introduction to theory and technique.* (pp. 265–278). Monterey, CA: Brooks/Cole.

Weiss, A. (2001). The no suicide contract: Possibilities and pitfalls. *American Journal of Psychotherapy, 55*(3), 414–419.

Weiss, L. (2004). *The therapist's guide to self-care.* New York: Brunner-Routledge.

Weiss, R. L., & Cerreto, M. (1980). The Marital Status Inventory: Development of a measure of dissolution potential. *The American Journal of Family Therapy, 8*(2), 80–86.

Weisz, J. R., Jensen-Doss, A., & Hawley, K. M. (2006, October). Evidence-based youth psychotherapies versus usual clinical care. *American Psychologist, 61*(7), 671–689.

Welfel, E. R., Danzinger, P. R., & Santoro, S. (2000). Mandated reporting of abuse/maltreatment of older adults: A primer for counselors. *Journal of Counseling & Development, 78*(3), 284–292.

Wells, M. G., Burlingame, G. M., Lambert, M. J., Hoag, M. J., & Hope, C. A. (1996). Conceptualization and measurement of patient change during psychotherapy: Development of the Outcome Questionnaire and Youth Outcome Questionnaire. *Psychotherapy, 33*, 275–283.

Westen, D. I. (2006). Patients and treatments in clinical trials are not adequately representative of clinical practice. In J. C. Norcross, L. E. Beutler & R. F. Levant (Eds.), *Evidence-based practices in mental health: Debate and dialogue on the fundamental questions.* (pp. 161–171). Washington, DC: American Psychological Association.

Westen, D., & Weinberger, J. (2004). When clinical description becomes statistical prediction. *American Psychologist, 59*(7), 595–613.

Wetchler, J. L., & Gutenkunst, G. (2005). First contact and preconditions for the initial interview: Conducting the first interview. In M. Cierpka, T. Volker & D. H. Sprenkle (Eds.), *Family assessment: Integrating multiple perspectives.* (pp. 35–52). Kirkland, WA/ Gottingen, Germany: Hogrefe & Huber.

Wetchler, J. L., & Ofte-Atha, G. R. (1993). Empowering families at termination: A structural/strategic orientation. *Journal of Family Psychotherapy, 4*(1), 33–44.

Wetchler, J., Piercy, F., & Sprenkle, D. (1989). Supervisors' and supervisees' perceptions of the effectiveness of family therapy supervisory techniques. *The American Journal of Family Therapy, 17*, 35–47.

Wethington, E., & Kessler, R. C. (1991). Situations and processes of coping. In J. Eckenrode (Ed.), *The social context of coping* (pp. 13–29). New York: Plenum Press.

Whipple, J. L., Lambert, M. J., Vermeersch, D. A., Smart, D. W., Nielsen, S. L., & Hawkins, E. J. (2003). *Clinical Support Tools Decision Tree.* Brigham Young University, Provo, UT.

Widiger, T. A. (2002). Personality disorders. In M. M. Antony & D. H. Barlow (Eds.), *Handbook of assessment and treatment planning for psychological disorders* (pp. 453–480). New York: Guilford Press.

Wierzbicki, M., & Pekarik, G. (1993). A meta-analysis of psychotherapy dropout. *Professional Psychology: Research and Practice, 29,* 190–195.

Wilcoxon, A., & Fenell, D. (1983). Engaging the non-attending spouse in marital therapy through the use of therapist-initiated written communication. *Journal of Marital and Family Therapy, 9*(2), 199–203.

Wilcoxon, S. A., Remley, T. P., Jr., Gadding, S. T., & Huber, C. H. (2007). *Ethical, legal, and professional issues in the practice of marriage and family therapy, 4th ed.* Upper Saddle River, NJ: Pearson, Merrill, Prentice Hall.

Wilkinson, L. A. (2006). Monitoring treatment integrity: An alternative to the 'Consult and Hope' strategy in school-based behavioural consultation. *School Psychology International, 27*(4), 426–438.

Wilson, G. T. (1996). Manual-based treatments: The clinical application of research findings. *Behavior Research and Therapy, 34,* 295–314.

Wingate, L. R., Joiner, T. E., Walker, R. L., Rudd, M. D., & Jobes, D. A. (2004). Empirically informed approaches to topics in suicide risk assessment. *Behavioral Sciences & the Law, 22*(5), 651–665.

Worthen, V., & McNeill, B. W. (1996). A phenomenological investigation of "good" supervision events. *Journal of Counseling Psychology, 43,* 25–34.

Worthington, E. L., Jr., McCullough, M. E., Shortz, J. L., Mindes, E. J., Sandage, S. J., & Chartrand, J. M. (1995). Can couples assessment and feedback improve relationships? Assessment as a brief relationship enrichment procedure. *Journal of Counseling Psychology, 42,* 466–475.

Wulfert, E., Greenway, D. E., Farkas, P., Hayes, S., & Dougher, M. J. (1994). Correlation between self-reported rigidity and rule-governed insensitivity to operant contingencies. *Journal of Applied Behavior Analysis, 27,* 659–671.

Zellars, K. L., & Perrewé, P. L. (2001). Affective personality and the content of emotional social support: Coping in organizations. *Journal of Applied Psychology, 86*(32), 459–467.

Zinbarg, R. E., Craske, M. G., & Barlow, D. H. (1993). *Mastery of your anxiety and worry: Therapist guide.* New York: Graywind Publications.

Zuroff, D. C., & Blatt, S. J. (2002). Vicissitudes of life after the short-term treatment of depression: Roles of stress, social support, and personality. *Journal of Social and Clinical Psychology, 21*(5), 473–496.

Index

AAMFT *see* American Association for Marriage and Family Therapy
abandonment 43
abuse
  child 41, 48
  emotional 43
  indicators of 57
  physical 41, 43, 48
  sexual 45, 71
abusive males 44
abusive relationships 48
acceptance 105, 179, 191
active behavioral coping 131
active cognitive coping 131, 132
adolescents
  and adherence to treatment reports 113
  and family violence 57
  and therapeutic alliance 6, 7
  initial interviews 79
  motivational issues 88
  observational procedures 80
  parental control and guidance 48
  parental engagement in treatment of 65
  suicidal ideation among 27
  violence among 45
  see also adult-to-child maltreatment; children
Adult Protective Services (APS) 42, 43, 57, 76
adult-to-child maltreatment 39
  and corporal punishment 48–9, 56
  and partner-to-partner maltreatment 40, 43, 50
  assessing 56
  definitions 41
  mild 50, 56
  prevalence 39, 48, 52
  reporting of 41–2, 76
  risk factors 48, 49–50
  screening for 53
  severe 48, 50, 56
  sexual 41, 44, 49
  "spillover effect" 50
adversarial tone 29
affairs 66, 92, 134, 155
age
  and adult-to-child mistreatment 49
  and aggressive behavior in males 44
  and elder mistreatment 50–1
  and partner-to-partner aggression 45
  of therapists 21
aggression
  acts of 44
  mild forms of 40
  physical 6, 42, 44, 45, 47
  psychological 6, 45
  see also aggressive behavior; family violence
aggressive behavior 45
  and age 44
  and suicide risk 33, 34
  personal history of 47, 50, 51
  see also aggression; behavior; family violence
agoraphobia 4
alcohol problems 45, 66, 82, 88
Alcohol Use Disorders Identification Test (AUDIT) 83, 233–4
American Association for Marriage and Family Therapy (AAMFT) 63, 81
anger, expression of 151
anorexia nervosa 68, 89
antidepressant medication 37
antisocial behavior 44, 65
  and corporal punishment 49
  see also behavior
antisocial personality disorders 33, 34

Becoming a Marriage and Family Therapist: From Classroom to Consulting Room, First Edition. D. Eugene Mead.

anxiety 4, 245
  and corporal punishment 49
  and suicide risk 34, 35, 36
  and supervision 23
  disorders 33, 34
  of therapists 23, 27, 29, 136–7
  treatments for 4, 35–6
  see also performance anxiety; separation anxiety
appreciation exercise 164
Areas of Strengths Checklist 166
ASP *see* Adult Protective Services
assessment 73–83
  authorization for services form 74–5, 77
  confidentiality issues 75–7
  initial interview 78–9
  instruments 81–3
  observations 79–81
  purpose of 73, 84
  structuring expectations for therapy 77
  see also diagnosis
attachment injury xiv, 89
attachment styles 196
attachment theory 149, 196
AUDIT *see* Alcohol Use Disorders Identification Test
Australia 39, 42, 50, 76
authorization for services form 74–5, 77
autism 68
availability heuristic 89
avoidance
  as coping strategy 130, 131, 132
  treatments for 4

basic therapy skills 17, 128
Beck Anxiety Inventory 86
Beck Depression Inventory 86
Becoming an Emotionally-Focused Couple Therapist 197
behavior
  assessing children's 83
  clinically relevant 25–6, 79–80
  cognitive 25
  defined 25
  dysfunctional 25, 26, 73–4, 79
  emotional 25, 26, 44
  fight-or-flight 19, 177
  functional 25, 26, 79
  "here and now" 25, 196
  impulsive 33, 34
  irresponsible 34
  therapists' 19, 253
  over-learned 177
  relational patterns 74, 79–80, 86–8
  verbal 25
  see also aggressive behavior; antisocial behavior
bereavement 68
bipolar disorder 99, 112
Blueprints for Violence Prevention 217
brainstorming techniques 23
breaks 178
breast cancer 68
Brief Screen for Depression (BSD) 83, 227
BSD *see* Brief Screen for Depression
buffering effect 131–2

CAC *see* Comprehensive Areas of Change (CAC) Item Ranking Form
Canada 39, 41, 42, 43, 50, 76
Caregiver Abuse Screen (CASE) 57
caregiver neglect 43
caregivers
  risk factors for child mistreatment 49–50
  risk factors for elder mistreatment 51
  screening for elder mistreatment 57
  see also caregiver neglect
CASE *see* Caregiver Abuse Screen
case progress notes 57–61, 235–6
  assessment 83
  initial phone call 72
  missing information 60
  treatment adherence 112–13
  treatment plan 93
  interventions 59–60
CBT, *see* cognitive behavioral therapy
chance meetings, rule for 75–6
change, motivation for 128–9, 134
child abuse 41, 48
  see also adult-to-child maltreatment
Child Behavior Checklist 83
child neglect 48
Child Protective Services (CPS) 41–2, 48
child rearing
  arguments over 52
  stress over 50
children
  and attachment 196
  and authorization for services form 77
  assessment of psychological distress 83
  attending marital therapy 77
  behavior problems 68
  corporal punishment 40, 48–9, 56
  exposure to domestic violence 50, 51
  noncompliant 57, 79, 111, 218
  physical abuse of 41, 48
  psychological distress in 83
  sexual mistreatment of 41, 44, 49
  witnessing partner-to-partner violence 50, 51
  see also adolescents; adult-to-child maltreatment; child abuse; child neglect; child rearing
circular questions 69
client-focused approach 12–13, 99
client–therapist alliance *see* therapeutic alliance
clinical experience log 83, 239–40
clinical judgment
  and experience 116–17
  removing bias from 86, 115–16
clinically relevant behavior (CRB) 25–6, 79–80

clinically significant changes 101, 118, 119–20
Clinical Record Form (CRF) 112
cognitive behavior 25
cognitive behavioral therapy (CBT) 4
collaborative involvement 105
commitment 155–7
communication problems 45, 159
comorbidity 100–1
competence 13–14, 90
Comprehensive Areas of Change (CAC) Item Ranking Form 80, 96, 229–31
compromise 175–6
conceptualizations 59, 235–6
confidentiality 21–2, 66, 71, 75–6
  and reporting of child abuse 41–2, 76
  legal limits to 76–7
Conflict Tactics Scale, Parent-Child (CTSPC) 56
Conflict Tactics Scale 2 (CTS2) 56–7, 83, 228
confrontation 7
conjoint therapy
  exceptions to recommending 71, 92
  motivation for attending 69–70
  pros and cons for attending 70–1
  resistance to 67–8
  supporting reasons for 68–9
contempt 44, 150, 151
contextual variables 74
  and emotional responses 25
  and family behavior 142, 192
  and family mistreatment 52
  and marital stress 130–1
control issues 45
coping skills 126, 129, 131, 134
coping strategies 131, 132
corporal punishment 40, 48–9, 56
  and parental physical mistreatment 49
  defined 48
countertransference 19, 24, 126
Couple Therapy Alliance Scale (CTAS) 127
court referred cases 88
CPS *see* Child Protective Services
CRB *see* clinically relevant behavior
CRF *see* Clinical Record Form
crisis management 26–7, 151
  see also family violence; suicidal ideation; suicide risk assessment
criticism 44, 150
crying 25
CTAS *see* Couple Therapy Alliance Scale
CTS2 *see* Conflict Tactics Scale 2
CTSPC *see* Conflict Tactics Scale, Parent-Child

damage 28
deadlines 23
de-escalation 173
defensiveness 7, 9, 44, 150, 151
delinquent behavior 49
  see also juvenile offenders
demand–withdraw pattern 178
dementia 50, 51
dependency
  and abusive relationships 48
  and family mistreatment 51, 52
  on the therapist 141–2
depression
  and affective reactivity to daily stressors 131
  and attachment 196
  and CBT 4
  and corporal punishment 49
  and family support 68
  and suicide 27, 35–7
  treatments for 35–6
Depression in Marriage 59, 88, 101
Depressive Symptoms Index 31
diagnosis
  provisional 244
  relational 86, 244
  single versus multiple 100–1
  using DSM-IV-TR 81–2, 88, 244–5
  see also assessment
Diagnostic and Statistical Manual of Mental Disorders (DSM-IV-TR) 81–2, 88, 244–5
direct causation 28
disability
  and adult-to-child mistreatment 49
  and elder mistreatment 51
Distance and Isolation Cascade 178
divorce
  and contempt 151
  and defensiveness 151
  and harsh startups 107
  and individual therapy 70–1
  and negative conversations 131
  and stress-reducing conversations 167
  research on causes 149
  see also divorce potential; marital stability
divorce potential 56, 59, 82
  see also marital stability
domestic violence
  and conjoint therapy 71
  children's exposure to 50, 51
  screening for 52
  see also family violence; partner-to-partner maltreatment
dreams
  honoring each other's 183–6
  within conflict area 181–3
Dreams Within Conflict 151, 179
dropouts 65, 67, 105, 136
  see also early termination
drug abuse 66, 88
DSM Axis I disorders 33
DSM Axis II disorders 34
DSM-IV-TR *see* Diagnostic and Statistical Manual of Mental Disorders
duty of care 28

dysfunctional behavior 25, 26, 73–4, 79
dysfunctional families 50

early childhood 196
early termination 136–8
  and agreement on therapy goals and methods 92
  and clients' expectations 92
  and clients' participation 65
  defined 136
  see also dropouts
economic dependency 51, 52
educational background 49, 51
EFT *see* Emotionally-Focused Therapy
elder maltreatment 39
  assessing 56–7
  by grown-up children 43, 50, 51, 56–7
  legal definitions 43
  partner-to-partner 50, 56
  prevalence 39, 50, 52
  reporting 43, 76
  risk factors 50–1
  screening for 53
emotional abuse 43
emotional behavior 25–6
  changing 179
  withholding of 44
  see also behavior
emotional dependency 52
emotional distance 192
Emotionally-Focused Therapy (EFT) 89, 149, 195–216
  adherence rating scales 197, 217
  assessment 198–203
  consolidation 213–16
  crisis management 198
  de-escalation 206–9
  emotional engagement 209–13
  harmful/unsafe interventions 198
  initial interview 198–201
  initial phone contact 198
  preparation to practice 197
  protocol for 197–216
  termination 214–16
  theory and research 196
  treatment plan 204–6
  unique interventions 197
emotional triangles 6
Emotion-Focused Therapy-Therapist Fidelity Scale
    (EFT-TFS) 197, 217
empathic listening 18–19
empathic responding 18–19
  and treatment manuals 102
empathic statements 18
empathy 18, 24, 104
  and therapist self-reflection 21
  lack of in caregivers 50
  perceived lack of in therapists 138, 140
  see also empathic listening; empathic responding;
    empathic statements
empowering clients 140, 142
enactments 197
Europe
  child abuse 41
  children's exposure to domestic violence 51
  corporal punishment 38
  elder mistreatment 43, 50
  partner-to-partner maltreatment 42
  prevalence of family violence 39
  reporting laws 41, 43, 76
  therapists' personal therapy 24
evidence-based practice 10–11, 114, 126, 147
evidence-based therapy 10–11, 103–4, 108
  selecting 11–13, 89
experience
  and clinical judgment 116–17
  and treatment adherence 110, 117
exposure treatments 4
extremely distressed couples 123

facilitative conditions 18, 61
family
  allegiances 5, 9
  cohesion 105
  conflict 43–5
  history interview 78–9
  loyalty 5
  processes 140–1
  secrets 6, 66
  subunits 9
  support 68, 70
  see also family violence
Family Therapy Decision Tree 123, 125–34
family violence 39, 44–7
  and gender 44–5, 47
  and therapist stress 20
  assessing 56–7
  co-occurrence 39, 40, 43–4, 51–2
  definitions 40
  goals in treatment of 39
  prevalence 39–40, 52
  risk factors 47–52, 51–2
  screening for 52–5
  treatment plan 57
  see also adult-to-child maltreatment; elder
    maltreatment; partner-to-partner maltreatment
feedback session 91–3
fees 71, 72, 77–8
feminist theory 10
Fidelity of Implementation (FIMP) 114
fight-or-flight behavior 19, 177
FIMP *see* Fidelity of Implementation
financial exploitation 43, 44, 51
financial struggles 48
Five Magic Hours 192
flooding 177–9
Fondness and Admiration 163–6
"four Ds" 28

"four horsemen of the apocalypse" 150, 174
see also contempt; criticism; defensiveness; stonewalling
Freud, Sigmund 149
functional behavior 25, 26, 79
functional family therapy 217

GARF *see* Global Assessment of Relational Functioning (GARF) Scale
gender
and adult-to-child maltreatment 49
and elder maltreatment 51
and family violence 44–5, 47
and flooding 178
and partner-to-partner maltreatment 44–5, 47
and therapeutic alliance 6
and therapist job burnout 21
roles 192
genuineness 18, 24, 61, 197
Global Assessment of Relational Functioning (GARF) Scale 244, 246
GMCT *see* Gottman Method Couple Therapy
goal consensus 105
Gottman Method Couple Therapy (GMCT) 149–93
accepting influence and compromise 174–6
adherence rating scales for 217
commitment to the marriage 155–7
communicating needs 168–9
crisis management 151
flooding and self-sooth 177–9
fondness and admiration 163–6
goals of 149
initial interview 152–5
initial phone call 151
interventions common with other methods 151
interventions that are harmful/unsafe 151, 180
interventions unique to 150–93
marital friendship 161–3
perpetual problems 179–86
preparation to practice 150
preparing for possible relapse 189–90
protocol 150–93
repair and de-escalation 173–5
shared meanings 186–9
soft startups 172–3
solvable problems 171–9
soothing 169–70, 178
termination 190–3
theory and research 149–50
treatment plan 157–60
Gottman Relationship Institute 218
gridlocked problems *see* perpetual problems
grievances 45

Haq-II, *see* Revised Helping Alliance Questionnaire-II
harsh startups 107
heart disease 68
Helping the Noncompliant Child 218
helplessness 22, 23
homework assignments 60, 107, 125
Homework Success procedures 253–4
hopelessness 33, 34, 48
humor 54, 132, 140
hypertension 68

IBCT, *see* Integrative Behavioral Couples Therapy
illness 51, 138
see also comorbidity; mental health problems
imagining 178
"I'm no good" strategy 22
impulse control 31, 47, 50
impulsive behavior 33, 34
see also behavior
incest 71
indicators of abuse (IOA) 57
individual interviews 52–3
individual therapy
and divorce 70–1
role of therapeutic alliance 3, 6
influence, accepting 174–6
initial interview 78–9
Emotionally-Focused Therapy 198–201
Gottman Method Couple Therapy 152–5
reporting and confidentiality issues 41
screening for domestic violence 52–3
initial phone call 63–73
clarifying clients' problems and goals 65
clarifying clinic procedures 71–2
clarifying expectations for therapy 65
closing the initial interview 72
conjoint versus individual therapy 67–71
deciding who should attend 66–7
Gottman Method Couple Therapy 151
initiating contact 64–5
purposes of 63–4, 67, 83
reconfirming sessions 72–3
setting safety needs 65–6
see also telephone interviews
Integrative Behavioral Couples Therapy (IBCT) xiv, 89
adherence rating scales 218
intergenerational therapy model 10
Internet affairs 134
see also affairs
interpersonal variables 52
intimate partner violence *see* partner-to-partner maltreatment
intrapersonal variables 51–2
IOA *see* indicators of abuse
irresponsible behavior 34
see also behavior

Japan 39
jealousy 45

job burnout 20–1
  and negative conversations 131
juvenile offenders 113
  see also delinquent behavior 49

labeling 54, 81
legal issues 28–9
  see also reporting
life stressors 52
  affective reactivity to 131
  and social support 130–3
  and suicide 34
  cognitive appraisal of 132
  context of 130–1
  effect on the individual's social network 68
  see also coping skills; coping strategies
limiting affect 132
love maps 162, 191
Love Maps Questionnaire 162
Love Maps Twenty Questions Game 162, 163
love triangles 45

malpractice litigation 28
marital adjustment 6, 82, 117
  see also marital satisfaction
marital conflict 47, 89, 149–50
marital distress
  and Emotionally-Focused Therapy 196
  and family support 68
  and partner-to-partner aggression 56
  and therapeutic alliance 6
  assessing 56, 151
  assessment of therapy outcomes 13, 90, 119
marital friendship 149–50, 161–3
marital history interview 78–9
marital relationship problems (MRPs) 159–60
marital satisfaction 47
  and expression of anger 151
  assessment of 82, 83, 117
  see also marital adjustment
marital stability 82, 83
  see also divorce potential
marital status 49
Marital Status Inventory 83
Marital Status Inventory-Revised (MSI-R) 151, 225–6
Marriage Clinic, The 11, 89, 148
Marriage Clinic Casebook, The 150
Maslach Burnout Inventory 21
Meanings Interview 186–8
medication 133
mental health problems
  and child mistreatment 50
  and corporal punishment 49
  and elder mistreatment 51
  see also psychiatric symptoms
mental health workers 24
  ethical codes for 66
  see also therapists
mental status 83
missed appointments 137
Modified Scale for Suicidal Ideation 32
mood disorders 33, 34
moral internalization 49
mother-child mistreatment 50
MRPs *see* marital relationship problems
MSI-R *see* Marital Status Inventory-Revised
multiple informants 116
multiple problems 88, 100–1

needs, communicating 168–9
negative affect 198
negative conversations 131
negativity
  and family cohesion 105
  and marital conflict 47
  and therapeutic alliance 7, 9
  see also negative affect; negative conversations
Netherlands, the 40
noncompliant children 57, 79, 111, 218

OAEP *see* Observational Assessment of Enactment Proficiency
Observational Assessment of Enactment Proficiency (OAEP) 197
observations 75
  case progress notes 59
  during assessment sessions 79–81
  to assess treatment fidelity 114
Observations of the Couples' Communication and Problem-Solving Behaviors Therapist's Rating Form 237
one-way screens 37, 75
open questions 104
optimism 131
OQ-45 *see* Outcome Questionnaire
Oral History Interview 78
Oral History Rating Scale 59, 96, 97
ORS, *see* Outcome Rating Scale
Outcome Questionnaire (OQ-45) 117
Outcome Rating Scale (ORS) 13, 74, 82–3, 90, 217, 232
  administering 117–18
  clinically significant changes 119–20
  interpretation of assessment scores 119–23, 151

panic disorder 4
Parent-adolescent Areas of Change Questionnaire 80
parental stress 50, 52
partner-to-partner maltreatment 39
  and adult-to-child maltreatment 40, 43, 50
  and age 45
  and gender 44–5, 47
  and other forms of family violence 40, 43–4, 50–2
  legal definitions 42
  prevalence 52
  reporting 42, 76
  risk factors 47–8

screening for 53–5
self-report instruments 56
see also domestic violence; family violence
passivity 132
perfectionism 131
performance anxiety 23
see also anxiety
perpetual problems 150–1
Gottman Method Couple Therapy 179–86
personal therapy, for therapists 24–5
Person of the Therapist Checklist 19, 22, 126, 219–20
pessimism 131
phobias 99, 245
physical abuse
of children 41, 48
of elders 43
physical aggression 6, 42, 47
and age 45
and child mistreatment 52
and psychological aggression 45
to coerce sexual behavior 44, 45
physical conflict 44
see also physical aggression
placebo effect 4
pornography 66, 134
positive reappraisal 131, 132
positive statements 18
post-crisis risk assessment 36–7
post-traumatic stress disorder 68
poverty 48
power issues
and family conflict 45
and therapeutic alliance 5–6
practice guidelines 11, 28
Practice of Emotionally-Focused Marital Therapy, The 197
Preparation for Supervision Checklist (PSC) 114, 255–7
privacy
fears about invasion of 66
right to 21–2, 75
see also confidentiality
privately shared confidences 76
private practice 21
problem-solving 31, 36, 74, 80–1, 198
process-focused treatment 37
projection 23
protocols
defined 147
for conducting Emotionally-Focused Therapy 197–216
for conducting Gottman Method Couple Therapy 150–93
provisional diagnosis 244
PSC *see* Preparation for Supervision Checklist
psychiatric hospitalization 35–6
psychiatric symptoms 6, 112
see also mental health problems
psychological aggression 45
psychological distress
assessment of 83, 117, 119
in children 83
in parents 83
pulse rate 170, 177

questions
circular 69
open 104
reflexive 69

randomized controlled trials (RCT) 100
RCI *see* reliable change index
RCT *see* randomized controlled trials
RDAS, *see* Revised Dyadic Adjustment Scale
reactance 68, 105
referrals 90–1, 139
reflections 104
reflexive questions 69
reframing xiv, 105, 151
relational behavior patterns 74, 79–80, 86–8
relational diagnosis 86, 244
relationship skills 17, 50
relaxation training 170
reliable change index (RCI) 119, 120
religion
and elder mistreatment 51
as coping strategy 131, 132
Repair Attempts 173–5
reporting
of child maltreatment 41–2, 76
of elder maltreatment 43, 76
of partner-to-partner maltreatment 42
resistance 68, 105
resources, withholding of 44
respect 104, 106
perceived lack of 138, 140
Revised Dyadic Adjustment Scale (RDAS) 13, 74, 82–3, 91, 97, 224
administering 117–18
clinically significant changes 119–20
interpretation of assessment scores 119–23, 151
Revised Helping Alliance Questionnaire-II (Haq-II) 7, 104, 127
rigidity 102–3
rituals 4
role strain 47–8

SAB *see* Standard Assessment Battery
safety needs 65–6
safety plan 26
SCS *see* Stages of Change Scale
self-blame 132
self-criticism 131
self-esteem 24, 47, 50
self-help 21, 35
self-neglect 51, 57

self-practice 21
self-reflection 21
self-report instruments
for assessing family violence 56–7
for suicide risk assessment 31–2
self-reports
and readiness to terminate therapy 140
of adherence to treatment 112–13
self-soothing 20, 178, 221–2
semi-structured interviews
assessing treatment fidelity 113–14
initial interview 78–9
initial phone call 63–73
screening for family violence 53–5
suicide risk assessment 30–2
sentiment override 161, 164, 179, 191
separation anxiety 136, 141–2
see also anxiety
Session Rating Scale (SRS) 83, 93, 124, 217
detecting split alliances 7–8, 10, 125
sessions, structure of 105–6
Seven Principles for Making Marriage Work, The 107, 148, 162
sexual abuse 45, 71
see also sexual mistreatment
sexual conflict 44, 45
sexual mistreatment
of children 41, 44, 49
of elders 43
see also sexual abuse
shared meanings 149, 150, 186–9
Shared Meanings Questionnaire 186, 187
sibling conflict 45
sibling rivalry 40
social isolation 34, 51
social networks 68, 131
social reinforcement 105, 106, 107
social skills 131
social support 129–33
ability to use 131
as help for therapist stress 21–2
conceptualization of 131–2
defined 130
determining needs 130
enacted 132
lack of 52
low 50
perception of 131, 132, 133
sources of 132–3
types of 132
socioeconomic status 50
SOFTA *see* System for Observing Family Therapy Alliances
soft startups 107, 150, 172–3
solvable problems 150, 171–9
soothing 169–70, 178
spanking 49
"spillover effect" 50
split alliance 5, 134
causes of 5–7
detecting 7–8
strength of 7
supervision in 9–10
see also therapeutic alliance
SRS, *see* Session Rating Scale
Stages of Change Scale (SCS) 129
Standard Assessment Battery (SAB) 56, 82–3, 87, 94–6, 140, 223
standard of care 28
statistically significant changes 101, 118
stigma 66
stonewalling 44, 150
strategic therapy model 11
strengths 88, 166
stress
defined 129–30
in therapists 20–5, 27
reactions 129
reducing 164–5
responses 129–30
see also life stressors; stress-reducing conversations
stress-reducing conversations 166–8
structural therapy model 10
Structured Family Interview 80
submission 22
substance abuse 51
suicidal ideation
and hospitalization 35–6
assessment of 31
prevalence 27
treatment of 35–7
see also suicide; suicide risk assessment
suicide
and depression 27, 35–7
categories of risk 34
higher risk following treatment 36–7
prevalence 27
prevention contracts 29
protective factors 31
risk factors 32
see also suicidal ideation; suicide risk assessment
suicide risk assessment 27–32
additional assessment domains 34
classifying the risk 32–5
legal issues 28–9
"resolved plans and preparations" 32–3, 36
role of supervisors 27–8, 29, 37–8
"suicidal desire and ideation" 32–3, 36
use of self-report instruments 31–2
use of semi-structured interview 30–2
Suicide Risk Checklist 32
supervision
and bias in clinical judgment 116
and crisis management 26–7
and split alliances 9–10
and suicide risk assessment/intervention 27–9, 37–8

and treatment plan 91
as help for therapist stress 22–4
as source of anxiety 23
resistance to 22–3
see also supervisors; therapist–supervisor relationship
supervisors 75, 126
as observers assessing treatment fidelity 114–15
responsibility for errors of trainees 37
see also supervision; therapist–supervisor relationship
Switzerland 132
System for Observing Family Therapy Alliances (SOFTA) 7–8, 10, 104, 127, 217
systems theory 10, 198

team-building exercises 192
telephone interviews 28, 113
see also initial phone call
tentative restatements 104
termination 135–43
and open door for returning 142–3
and therapy models 136
client-initiated 138–9
clients' readiness for 137, 140
criteria for 135–6, 246
defined 135–6
Gottman Method Couple Therapy 190–3
legal implications 121
mutually agreed upon 139–40
preparing for possible relapses 141
tailoring to the needs of clients 140–1
therapist-initiated 139
see also dropouts; early termination
thanksgiving exercise 164
theory-based therapy 10, 11
therapeutic alliance 5–10, 18
and duty of care 28
and family power issues 5–6
and family secrets 6
and gender 6
and no-suicide contracts 29
and therapy outcomes 4, 6, 111
and treatment manuals 85, 99
assessing 102–3, 104, 116, 117, 124, 139
detecting ruptures in 7
measuring 104
repairing raptures 8–10, 128
see also split alliance
therapeutic contract 109, 110
therapist–client relationship 19, 28, 37, 99, 152
see also split alliance; therapeutic alliance
therapists
and anxiety 23, 136–7
and job burnout 20–1
and stress 20–5, 27
and therapy outcomes 17
and treatment delivery 19–20
behavior of 19, 253
clients' dependency on 141–2
clients' initial impressions of 138, 140
cognitive processes of 115–17
competence of 13–14, 90
personal history 19
personal responses to clients 19–20, 22, 125–6, 140
personal therapy for 24–5
self-help 21
self-soothing 20, 221–2
social support 21–2
see also Person of the Therapist Checklist; split alliance; supervision; supervisors; therapeutic alliance; therapist–client relationship; therapist–supervisor relationship
therapist–supervisor relationship 22, 23, 126
therapy goals 5
determining clients' 65, 78, 86–9
difficulties achieving 129
disagreement on 6, 92
therapy models 10
and termination 136
see also evidence-based therapy; theory-based therapy
therapy outcomes
and focus on planned treatment 38
and respect for clients 104
and therapists' personal therapy 24
and treatment adherence 110
clinically significant changes 101, 118–20
deteriorating 123
evaluation of 13, 117–34
improving 123
interpretation of scores 118–124
role of common factors 3–5
role of therapist 17
statistically significant changes 101, 118
successful 101, 104, 115, 123, 134, 137
see also Family Therapy Decision Tree; treatment efficacy
therapy research 103–4
Therapy Tailoring Skills (TTS) rating form 104–6, 251
therapy tasks 63
see also assessment; termination; therapy outcomes; treatment delivery; treatment fidelity; treatment plan
thoughts 25
threats 42, 44
TMI *see* Treatment Monitoring Interview
transference 19
treatment adherence *see* treatment fidelity
treatment delivery 98–108
and person of the therapist 19–20
combining treatments 102, 103
general procedures 106–8
tailoring the treatment 12–13, 104–6
using clients' ideas 106–7
treatment effectiveness 147, 217

treatment efficacy 100–1, 147, 217
absolute xiv
relative xiv
see also therapy outcomes
treatment fidelity 109–15, 128
and therapist's experience 110, 117
clients' self-reports of 113
therapist self-reports of 112–13
using observers for assessing 114
using semi-structured interviews for assessing 113–14
using treatment manuals for assessing 110–11
treatment guidelines 11
treatment length 101–2
clients' expectations for 92, 102, 137–8
see also termination
treatment manuals 12, 85, 98–100, 107
benefits of use 99–100
criticism of 102–3
for assessing treatment adherence 110–11
use in training 99
Treatment Monitoring Interview (TMI) 113
treatment plan 85–98, 245
and therapist competence 90
establishing clients' problems and goals 86–9
evaluating outcome progress 90
example of 93–8
Gottman Method Couple Therapy 157–60
organizing assessment information 86
preparing written 241–6
presenting 92–3
selection of 89
sharing 91–3
see also treatment fidelity
treatment strategy 89, 90
treatment summary 93, 143, 249
treatment techniques 3–5
TTS *see* Therapy Tailoring Skills (TTS) rating form
"turning the tables" 22

United Kingdom
elder mistreatment 39, 50
evidence-based practice 10
reporting laws 76
sources of social support 132
United States
child mistreatment 52
corporal punishment 48–9
elder mistreatment 43, 50, 52
prevalence of family violence 39, 40, 52
reporting laws 41
sources of social support 132
therapists' personal therapy 24

verbal behavior 25
verbal conflict 44
vicarious traumatization 20
see also job burnout
videotaping 75

warmth 18, 24
"we-ness" 105
widowhood 31, 51
wishful thinking 132
withdrawal 7
workplace issues 68

Youth Outcome Questionnaire 83

Printed and bound by CPI Group (UK) Ltd, Croydon, CR0 4YY
16/09/2026
14963381-0001

Springer-Verlag Berlin Heidelberg GmbH

Engineering ONLINE LIBRARY

http://www.springer.de/engine/

Cesarettin Alasalvar
Tony Taylor (Eds.)

Seafoods – Quality, Technology and Nutraceutical Applications

With 56 Figures and 38 Tables

Springer

Dr. Cesarettin Alasalvar
Professor Tony Taylor
University of Lincoln
Faculty of Health and Life Sciences
Food Research Centre
Brayford Pool
Lincoln, LN6 7TS
United Kingdom

ISBN 978-3-642-07635-0

Die Deutsche Bibliothek – CIP-Einheitsaufnahme

Alasalvar, Cesarettin:
Seafoods – Quality, Technology and Nutraceutical Applications : With 56 Figures and 38 Tables / Cesarettin Alasalvar ; Tony Taylor.
ISBN 978-3-642-07635-0 ISBN 978-3-662-09836-3 (eBook)
DOI 10.1007/978-3-662-09836-3

http://www.springer.de

Originally published by Springer-Verlag Berlin Heidelberg New York in 2002
Softcover reprint of the hardcover 1st edition 2002

Typesetting: Fotosatz-Service Köhler GmbH, Würzburg
Cover Design: Design & Production, Heidelberg

Printed on acid-free paper SPIN: 10762086 51/3020/kk – 5 4 3 2 1 0

Preface

This book was developed mainly from the selected presentations and contributions made during the 3rd Biennual European Conference on Fish Processing in Grimsby, UK, 29th June–1st July 1999, which was sponsored by the Society of Chemical Industry, University of Lincoln, and North East Lincolnshire Council.

The book is divided into three sections preceded by an introductory chapter providing an overview of seafood quality, technology and nutraceutical applications. The first section (Chaps 2–10) describes a range of aspects of seafood quality from the impact of slaughter procedures, practical evaluation, texture, measuring fish content, protein functionality, histamine toxicity and flavour; the second section (Chaps 11–13) covers value-added waste products, automation in fish processing and water treatment; the final section (Chaps 14–16) discusses food and health applications of marine nutraceuticals/functional foods. Contributing to this volume are researchers from different countries who are well recognised in their respective areas of expertise, providing a diverse and global perspective of the issue of seafood quality, technology and nutraceutical applications.

This book will be a resource for those interested in the potential application of new developments in marine nutraceuticals/functional foods, quality and technology as well as the role of science and technology in ensuring safety and quality. Biochemists, chemists, food scientists/technologists, fish technologists, working in academia, government laboratories and industry will benefit from this publication. Although this book is intended primarily as a reference book, it also summarises the current state of knowledge in key research areas and contains ideas for future work. In addition, it provides easy to read text suitable for teaching undergraduate and post-graduate students.

We are particularly grateful to Professor Fereidoon Shahidi (Memorial University of Newfoundland-Canada) for his valuable advice during preparation of this book. Finally, we wish to extend our sincere thanks and gratitude to all authors for co-operative efforts and commendable contributions.

Lincoln, November 2001

Cesarettin Alasalvar
Tony Taylor

Contents

1 **Seafoods: Quality, Technology and Nutraceutical Applications – an Overview** . . . 1
CESARETTIN ALASALVAR

2 **The Killing of Quality: The Impact of Slaughter Procedures on Fish Flesh** . . . 7
DAVE ROBB

2.1 Introduction . . . 7
2.2 What is Quality? . . . 7
2.3 Fish Muscle Structure and Physiology . . . 8
2.4 Slaughter Procedures . . . 10
2.5 Effects of Slaughter Activity and Stress on the Quality of the Fish 11
2.6 Conclusions . . . 14
References . . . 15

3 **Practical Evaluation of Fish Quality** . . . 17
CESARETTIN ALASALVAR, TONY GARTHWAITE, ABDULLAH ÖKSÜZ

3.1 Introduction . . . 17
3.2 Extended Shelf Life . . . 18
3.3 Evaluation of Fish Freshness and Quality . . . 20
3.3.1 Sensory Methods . . . 20
3.3.2 Non-Sensory Methods . . . 22
3.3.3 Systematic Methods . . . 22
3.4 Practical Methods of Evaluation of Fish Freshness . . . 22
3.4.1 Materials and Methods . . . 22
3.4.2 Freshness Assessment of Cultured Sea Bream Stored in Ice . . . 23
3.4.2.1 TFRU Sensory Assessment Scheme . . . 23
3.4.2.2 K Value Assessment . . . 24
3.4.2.3 Texture Assessment . . . 26
3.4.3 Freshness Assessment of Cultured Rainbow Trout Stored in Ice . 27
3.5 Conclusions . . . 29
References . . . 29

4 Eating Quality of Deep-Water Fish Species and their Products . . 33
Martine Brennan, Ronan Gormley

4.1 Introduction 33
4.2 Materials and Methods 34
4.2.1 Catching and Storage of the Fish 34
4.2.2 Concentrations of Heavy Metals and Micro-Organisms 34
4.2.3 Colour and Toughness of Flesh 34
4.2.4 Sensory Evaluation 35
4.2.5 Preparation of Fish Products 35
4.2.5.1 Nuggets 35
4.2.5.2 Fish-Cakes 35
4.3 Results and Discussion 36
4.3.1 Concentrations of Heavy Metals and Micro-Organisms 36
4.3.2 Fish Appearance 37
4.3.3 Fish Texture 37
4.3.4 Sensory Analysis of Fillets 38
4.3.5 Sensory Analysis of Fish Products 38
4.3.6 Problems for Processors 40
4.4 Conclusions 40
References 41

5 Quality Control by Instrumental Texture Measurements 43
Paul Nesvadba

5.1 Introduction 43
5.2 Difficulties in Measuring Texture of Fish 44
5.3 Sensory and Instrumental Tests for Texture of Fish 45
5.3.1 Sensory Tests of Texture as an Attribute of Quality 45
5.3.2 Instrumental Tests for Texture of Fish and Fish Products 46
5.3.3 Connection Between Sensory and Instrumental Tests 49
5.4 Modelling of Viscoelastic Properties in Terms of Lumped Parameters 49
5.4.1 Oscillatory Measurements 51
5.4.2 Creep and Relaxation Measurements 52
5.5 Instrumental Texture Measurements of the Quality of Fish 53
5.6 Conclusions 56
References 56

6 Measurement of the Fish Content in Fish Products 59
Kevin D. Hargin

6.1 Introduction 59
6.2 Legislative Position 60
6.3 Problems in Measuring Fish Content 61
6.3.1 Total protein content 63
6.4 Code of Practice 67
6.5 Conclusions 70
References 71

7	**Functional Properties of Fish Proteins**	73
	RACHEL GOODBAND	
7.1	Introduction	73
7.2	Proteins of Fish Muscle	73
7.3	Supply Chain and Protein Functionality	75
7.4	Effect of Freezing	76
7.5	Use of High Pressure to Prevent Frozen Deterioration	78
7.5.1	Principles of High Hydrostatic Pressure Processing	79
7.5.2	Effect of Hydrostatic Pressure on Myofibrillar Proteins	79
7.5.3	Stabilisation of Cod Muscle Against Frozen Deterioration by the Application of High Hydrostatic Pressure	79
7.6	Conclusions	82
	References	82
8	**Binding and Texture Modification Using Transglutaminase**	83
	ANGELA MUMBY	
8.1	Introduction	83
8.2	Properties of Transglutaminase	83
8.3	Activa EB for Binding	84
8.4	Activa WM for Texture	86
8.5	Conclusions	87
9	**Histamine Toxicity and Scombroid Fish Poisoning: a Review**	89
	PANOS MAVROMATIS, PETER QUANTICK	
9.1	Introduction	89
9.2	What is Histamine?	90
9.3	Health Aspects of Histamine	90
9.3.1	Allergic Reactions and Role of Histamine	90
9.3.2	Histamine in Humans	91
9.3.2.1	Symptoms	91
9.3.3	Mechanism of Toxicity	92
9.3.4	Synthesis of Indigenous Histamine	93
9.3.5	Histamine Receptors and Their Role	93
9.3.6	Role of Histamine Receptors and their Agonists and Antagonists	94
9.3.6.1	Histamine Agonists	94
9.3.6.2	Histamine Antagonists	94
9.3.7	Antihistamines	95
9.4	Scombroid Poisoning and Histamine in Fish	95
9.4.1	Controlling Histamine Formation	97
9.4.2	Permissible Limits for Histamine in Fish	98
9.4.3	Outbreaks and Epidemiology	98
9.5	Conclusions	99
	References	99

10 **Analysis of Seafood Aroma/Odour by Electronic Nose Technology and Direct Analysis** . . . 105
John M. Grigor, Brenden J. Theaker, Cesarettin Alasalvar, William T. O'Hare, Zulfiqur Ali

10.1 Introduction . . . 105
10.2 Flavour Active Compounds . . . 106
10.2.1 Development of Desirable Fresh Flavour . . . 106
10.2.2 Loss of Freshness and Spoilage . . . 107
10.2.3 Pre and Post Harvest Taints . . . 107
10.3 Analysis of Seafood Aroma by Sensor Array Technology . . . 108
10.3.1 High Temperature Sensors . . . 109
10.3.1.1 MOS Sensors . . . 109
10.3.1.2 MOSFET Sensors . . . 109
10.3.2 Ambient Temperature Sensors . . . 109
10.3.2.1 Conducting Polymer Sensors . . . 109
10.3.2.2 BAW and SAW Sensors . . . 110
10.3.3 Pattern Recognition . . . 110
10.3.4 Applications . . . 112
10.3.5 Advantages and Disadvantages of Electronic Nose Technology . . 114
10.4 Direct Approach to the Analysis of Seafood Aroma . . . 114
10.4.1 Identification and Quantitation of Aroma Compounds . . . 114
10.4.2 Extraction and Concentration of Important Aroma Compounds 115
10.4.2.1 Traditional Extraction Techniques (Distillation and Solvent Extraction) . . . 116
10.4.2.2 Headspace Sampling Techniques . . . 116
10.4.2.3 Model Systems and Direct Sampling . . . 118
10.5 Conclusions . . . 118
References . . . 118

11 **Improved Utilisation of Fish and Shellfish Waste** . . . 123
Tony Taylor, Cesarettin Alasalvar

11.1 Introduction . . . 123
11.2 Recovery of Fish Flesh . . . 125
11.2.1 Whitening of Mince Using Titanium Dioxide . . . 126
11.2.2 Whitening of Flaps Using Hydrogen Peroxide . . . 128
11.3 Extraction and Purification of Enzymes . . . 129
11.3.1 Extraction of Enzymes from Shellfish Waste . . . 130
11.3.2 Extraction and Purification of Hyalurunoglucosidase (EC 3.2.1.35) . . . 131
11.4 Intermediate Moisture Animal Feed (Pig Feed) . . . 133
11.4.1 Product Development . . . 133
11.5 Conclusions . . . 135
References . . . 135

12 **The Icelandic Way Towards Automation in Fish Processing** . . . 137
KRISTINN ANDERSEN, HALLDOR MAGNUSSON
12.1 Introduction 137
12.2 New Technology: Flowlines and Intelligent Portioning Machines 138
12.3 New Fish Processing Concepts 140
12.4 Results and Further Development 141
References 142

13 **Reducing Water and Trade Effluent Costs in Fish Processing** . . . 143
RICHARD B. WATSON
13.1 Introduction 143
13.2 Effluent Disposal Options 143
13.3 Mogden Calculated Trade Effluent Charges 144
13.4 Seafish Work 144
13.5 Waste Minimisation 145
13.5.1 Benefits of Waste Minimisation 145
13.5.2 Principles of Water Use Minimisation 145
13.5.3 Principles of Effluent Strength Minimisation 146
13.6 Typical Processing Problems and Solutions 146
13.6.1 Defrosting 146
13.6.2 Manual Filleting 148
13.6.3 Skinning 150
13.6.4 Secondary Processing 152
13.6.5 Cleaning 152
13.6.6 Drainage System 153
13.6.6.1 Drain Covers 153
13.6.6.2 Drain Catch Baskets 154
13.7 End of Pipe Treatment Equipment 155
13.8 Conclusions 155

14 **Omega-3 Fatty Acid Concentrates:**
a Review of Production Technologies 157
UDAYA N. WANASUNDARA, JANITHA WANASUNDARA,
FEREIDOON SHAHIDI
14.1 Introduction 157
14.2 Methods of Concentration of ω3-PUFA 158
14.2.1 Chromatographic Methods 159
14.2.2 Distillation Method 160
14.2.3 Enzymatic Methods 161
14.2.3.1 Lipase-Catalysed Hydrolysis 161
14.2.3.2 Lipase-Catalysed Esterification 164
14.2.4 Low Temperature Crystallisation 165
14.2.5 Solubility Differences of Fatty Acid Salts 166
14.2.6 Supercritical Fluid Extraction 166
14.2.7 Urea Complexation 167
14.3 Conclusions 170
References 170

15 **Food and Health Applications of Marine Nutraceuticals: a Review** . . . 175
Cesarettin Alasalvar, Fereidoon Shahidi, Peter Quantick

15.1 Introduction . . . 175
15.2 Marine Lipids . . . 176
15.2.1 Nutritional Aspects and Dietary Intake of ω3-PUFA . . . 176
15.2.2 The Health Benefits of ω3-PUFA . . . 177
15.2.3 Essentiality of ω3-PUFA . . . 178
15.3 Food Application of Marine Nutraceuticals . . . 179
15.3.1 Fish Oil . . . 179
15.3.2 Seal Blubber Oil . . . 181
15.3.3 Microalgae . . . 182
15.3.3.1 Microalgae Oil . . . 182
15.3.3.2 Carotenoids . . . 184
15.3.3.3 Phycobilins . . . 184
15.3.3.4 Polysaccharides . . . 185
15.3.3.5 Sterols . . . 185
15.3.3.6 Other Bioactive Compounds . . . 185
15.3.4 Shark Cartilage and Shark Liver Oil . . . 185
15.3.5 Chitin, Chitosan and Related Products . . . 186
15.3.5.1 Food Application of Chitinous Materials . . . 186
15.3.6 Enzymes . . . 189
15.3.7 Peptides and Related Compounds . . . 190
15.3.8 Vitamins . . . 190
15.3.9 Seaweeds (Macroalgae), Sea Cucumbers and Sea Mussels . . . 192
15.3.10 Protein Hydrolysates . . . 192
15.4 Regulatory Aspects of Marine Nutraceuticals . . . 193
15.5 Conclusions . . . 194
References . . . 195

16 **Marine Nutraceuticals and Functional Foods in Japan** . . . 205
Toshiaki Ohshima

16.1 Introduction . . . 205
16.2 Fish Oils with Omega-3 Polyunsaturated Fatty Acids (ω3-PUFA) 205
16.3 Effects of Marine Lipids on Taste . . . 209
16.4 Application of Marine Nutraceuticals and Functional Foods . . . 210
16.4.1 Chitin and Chitosan . . . 210
16.4.2 Chondroitin Sulphate . . . 213
16.4.3 Milt Proteins as Food Preservatives . . . 213
16.4.4 Carbohydrates . . . 213
16.4.5 Enzymes . . . 214
16.4.6 Others . . . 214
16.5 Bioactive Reagents . . . 217
16.6 Conclusions . . . 217
References . . . 218

Contributors

Cesarettin Alasalvar
Faculty of Health and Life Sciences,
Food Research Centre,
University of Lincoln,
Brayford Pool,
Lincoln, LN6 7TS, UK
e-mail: calasalvar@lincoln.ac.uk

Zulfiqur Ali
School of Science and Technology,
University of Teesside, Middlesborough,
TS1 3BA, UK

Kristinn Andersen
Marel hf., Reykjavik, Iceland
e-mail: kiddi@marel.is

Martine Brennan
Teagasc, The National Food Centre,
Castleknock, Dublin 15, Ireland
e-mail: m.brennan@nfc.teagasc.ie

Tony Garthwaite
Faculty of Health and Life Sciences,
Food Research Centre,
University of Lincoln,
Brayford Pool,
Lincoln, LN6 7TS, UK

Rachel Goodband
Unilever Research Colworth House,
Sharnbrook, Bedford, MK44 1LQ, UK
e-mail: rachel.goodband@unilever.com

Ronan Gormley
Teagasc, The National Food Centre,
Castleknock, Dublin 15, Ireland

John M. Grigor
School of Science and Technology,
University of Teesside,
Middlesborough, TS1 3BA, UK
e-mail: j.grigor@tees.ac.uk

Kevin D. Hargin
Food Labelling and Standards Division,
Joint Food Safety and Standards Group,
Ministry of Agriculture,
Fisheries and Food,
PO Box 31037, Ergon House,
17 Smith Square, London, SW1P 3WG, UK
e-mail:
kavin.hargin@foodstandards.gsi.gov.uk

Halldor Magnusson
Marel hf., Reykjavik, Iceland

Panos Mavromatis
Faculty of Health and Life Sciences,
University of Lincoln,
Brayford Pool,
Lincoln, LN6 7TS, UK
e-mail: pmavromatis@lincoln.ac.uk

Angela Mumby
Forum Products Limited, 41 – 51
Brighton Road, Redhill, Surrey,
RH1 6YS, UK
e-mail: angela.mumby@forumgroup.co.uk

Paul Nesvadba
Food Science and Technology
Research Centre,
The Robert Gordon University,
St Andrews Street, Aberdeen,
AB25 1HG, UK
e-mail: p.nesvadba@rgu.ac.uk

Abdullah Öksüz
Faculty of Health and Life Sciences,
Food Research Centre,
University of Lincoln,
Brayford Pool, Lincoln, LN6 7TS, UK

William T. O'Hare
School of Science and Technology,
University of Teesside, Middlesborough,
TS1 3BA, UK

Toshiaki Ohshima
Department of Food Science and Technology, Tokyo University of Fisheries,
Konan 4, Minato-ku, Tokyo 108-8477, Japan
e-mail: tohshima@tokyo-u-fish.ac.jp

Peter Quantick
Faculty of Health and Life Sciences,
Food Research Centre,
University of Lincoln, Brayford Pool,
Lincoln, LN6 7TS, UK

Dave Robb
EWOS Innovation
N-4335 Dirdal
Norway
e-mail: Dave.Robb@ewos.com

Fereidoon Shahidi
Department of Biochemistry, Memorial University of Newfoundland, St. John's,
NF, A1B 3X9 Canada

Tony Taylor
Faculty of Health and Life Sciences,
Food Research Centre,
University of Lincoln, Brayford Pool,
Lincoln, LN6 7TS, UK
e-mail: ttaylor@lincoln.ac.uk

Brenden J. Theaker
School of Science and Technology,
University of Teesside, Middlesborough,
TS1 3BA, UK

Udaya N. Wanasundara
POS Pilot Plant Corporation,
118 Veterinary Road, Saskatoon,
SK, S7N 2R4 Canada
e-mail: udaya@pos.ca

Janitha Wanasundara
Department of Applied Microbiology and Food Science, University of Saskatchewan,
Saskatoon, SK, S7N 5A8 Canada

Richard B. Watson
Seafish Industry Authority,
St Andrew's Quay, Hull, HU3 4QE, UK
e-mail: r-watson@seafish.co.uk

1 Seafoods: Quality, Technology and Nutraceutical Applications – an Overview

Cesarettin Alasalvar

This introductory chapter provides an overview of the topics covered in this book. It introduces the evaluation of seafood quality, safety, processing technology, and nutraceutical applications and sets them in the overall context of the fish processing industry. It also highlights some of the important advances in these fields.

The consumption and popularity of seafoods has consistently increased during recent years since seafoods are increasingly recognised as important sources of nutrients for human health [1]. Protein, lipids and bioactive components from seafoods have unique features that differ from those of land animals [2]. Some important factors such as quality, safety and technology as well as nutraceuticals are considered in this book. These factors contribute to optimal utilisation of the marine resources together with the consequent maximisation of health benefits.

Quality is one of the most abused words in seafoods research. It has been used to describe a wide range of characteristics of the fish, from the flesh and skin, to how well it can be processed to the impact of the fish on the environment. Quality deterioration of seafoods may originate from poor slaughter process, handling of raw materials during processing and post-harvest periods. The stress around slaughter has been shown to result in an increase in muscle activity and this activity can affect the quality attributes of the fish in two ways: physically and biochemically [3, 4]. The impact of slaughter procedures, activity and stress on the quality of the fish is described in Chap. 2.

Freshness makes a major contribution to the quality of seafoods. Despite all beneficial health effects of seafoods, it is imperative to assure that the fresh quality of products is preserved. Both objective and subjective methods of analysis are used for this purpose. Although a variety of objective (chemical/biochemical, physical and microbiological) methods have been used to assess the quality of fish during the chill storage, the main quality parameters for fresh fish are the sensory responses (appearance, aroma, taste and texture) [5]. When objective methods are being used for assessing the quality of fish, subjective evaluation (Tasmanian Food Research Unit schemes, or Torry schemes or European Union Grading schemes) should be conducted to ensure that those results show good agreement with the objective tests [5–9]. Detailed information on different aspects of seafood quality are discussed in Chaps 3–6.

For the consumers, the principle attributes determining the quality of frozen seafood products are the flavour and texture. Although the enzymes in fish may contribute to flavour changes that take place during frozen storage, fish proteins impact primarily on the sensory attributes relating to the texture of products. For frozen fish and seafoods, the freezing process, and storage in the frozen state, are important determinants of product quality [10–13]. For gadoid species in particular, significant deterioration in texture can occur during frozen storage. These changes, although not fully understood, involve aggregation of the myofibrillar proteins. The supply chain and protein functionality, and a patented process for the use of ultra high-pressure to control frozen deterioration, are described in Chap. 7.

Transglutaminase (TG) is a unique enzyme that acts by cross linking the proteins glutamine and lysine widely found in fish. There are many areas where TG as a binding and texture modifying enzyme (Chap. 8) can be used to produce innovative meat, fish, pasta, deserts, yoghurt and vegetarian food products, etc.

Scombrotoxin formation as a results of time/temperature abuse of certain species of fish can cause consumer illness known as histamine or scombroid poisoning. This poisoning accounts for more than 50% of the food poisoning incidents and outbreaks associated with the consumption of seafoods [14]. Scombroid poisoning has been a food safety concern despite the high hygienic standards imposed by new legislation and guidelines. Although well investigated, the issue of whether histamine is indeed the causative agent of scombroid fish poisoning is still a matter of controversy as many investigators have presented opposing arguments [15, 16]. Health aspects of histamine and scombroid poisoning have been reviewed in detail and this is described in Chap. 9.

Finally, with reference to quality, seafoods are appreciated worldwide for their distinct and delicate flavours. The flavour of seafoods is comprised of both volatile aroma-active and non-volatile taste-active components [1]. Isolation and identification of volatile aroma-active compounds has been an important area of research. Isolation or sampling of volatiles prior to gas chromatographic analysis can be conducted in a number of ways. Each isolation technique has its strengths and weaknesses and each will give somewhat biased results since it selects for certain groups of compounds over others. Identification of characteristic and important aroma compounds in seafoods has been challenging due to presence of these compounds at extremely low levels, often at sub part-per-billion (ppb) concentrations [1, 24, 25]. Therefore, an increasing emphasis has been placed on developing instrumentation and methods which can reliably identify and rapidly quantify key odorants in seafoods (Chap. 10). Use of an electronic aroma sensor for the analysis of seafoods odour is a recent development [26].

In the preparation of fish for today's consumer market up to 50% of the whole fish is commonly discarded as waste [38]. There are many ways in which the fish and shellfish waste could be better utilised (Chap. 11). Full utilisation of the harvest, especially for production of value-added products for direct human use, is encouraged. In addition, processing discards from many species of fish and shellfish could be successfully processed to produce enzymes, chitin/chitosan, pigments, gelation, fish leather, manufacture of aquaculture and other animal feed, and speciality products [17–23].

The competitive environment of the fish processing industry and challenges it created gives rise to new technology. The development of flow lines has been successfully used in fish processing to improve quality, productivity and to increase both yield and production of value-added products. Latest technology and automation in fish processing is covered in Chap. 12.

Coastal fish processors face a dramatic increase in trade effluent charges as a results of tightening environmental legislation. In the near future new environmental legislation will add greatly to the cost and difficulty of disposing of waste water, which will present a significant problem to the fish industry. Therefore, reducing the cost associated with water usage and trade effluent disposal in fish processing is reviewed in Chap. 13.

With the growing public awareness of the nutritional, diet and health benefits of seafoods, the stage is now to set for the development of mainstream nutraceutical products. Marine nutraceuticals are food or dietary supplements that contain bioactive components (oils mainly EPA, DPA and DHA, shark cartilage, chitin, chitosan and associated products, enzymes, peptides, vitamins, seaweeds, sea cucumbers, sea mussels, protein hydrolysates and other products) from marine resources [27, 29–32, 34, 35]. Among these bioactives, fish oils and their long-chain omega-3 polyunsaturated fatty acids (LC ω3-PUFA) components have received much attention in recent years, due to their potential beneficial health effects in curing or treatment of certain cardiovascular diseases (CVD) by lowering serum triacylglycerol and cholesterol [33, 36] and playing an important role in the prevention and treatment of a variety diseases [28, 33, 36, 37]. Resources, food and health applications of marine nutraceuticals/functional foods are reviewed in detail in Chaps 15 and 16. One of the best ways to obtain these important fatty acids is to incorporate them into common foods as well as infant formulas. To meet the demand for nutritionally and pharmaceutically valuable LC ω3-PUFA, they must be extracted, isolated or concentrated from the source materials. Numerous methods have been established to concentrate and recover specific fatty acids and their derivatives (i.e. esters, free fatty acids, triacylglycerols, etc.) from various naturally occurring sources, but only few are suitable for large-scale production [39, 40]. The production technologies of marine oils are also extensively reviewed in Chap. 14.

References

1. Shahidi F, Cadwallader KR (1997) Flavour and lipid chemistry of seafoods: an overview. In: Shahidi F, Cadwallader KR (eds) Flavor and lipid chemistry of seafoods. American Chemical Society, Washington, DC (ACS Symposium Series 674), pp 1–8
2. Shahidi F (1997) Seafood safety, processing and biotechnology: an overview. In: Shahidi F, Jones Y, Kitts DD (eds) Seafood safety, processing, and biotechnology. Technomic Publishing, Lancaster, USA, pp 1–3
3. Robb DHF (1998) Some factors affecting the flesh quality of salmonids: pigmentation, composition and eating quality. PhD thesis, University of Bristol, UK
4. Robb DHF, Kestin SC, Warriss PD (2000) Muscle activity at slaughter: I. Changes in flesh colour and gaping in rainbow trout. Aquaculture 182: 261–269
5. Alasalvar C, Taylor KDA, Öksüz A, Garthwaite T, Alexis MN, Grigorakis K (2001) Freshness assessment of cultured sea bream (*Sparus aurata*) by chemical, physical and sensory methods. Food Chem 72: 33–40
6. Botta JR (1995) Sensory evaluation: freshness quality grading. In: Botta JR (ed) Evaluation of seafood freshness quality. VCH Publishers, New York, pp 65–97

7. Gormley R (2000) Freshness, quality and safety in seafoods. Flair-Flow Europe Technical Manual (F-FE 380A/00), [ISBN 1 84170 110 6]
8. Ólafsdóttir G, Martinsdóttir E, Oehlenschläger J, Dalgaard P, Jensen B, Undeland I, Mackie IM, Henehan G, Nielsen J, Nilsen H (1997) Methods to evaluate fish freshness in research and industry. Trends Food Sci Technol 8: 258–265
9. Sørensen NK (1992) Physical and instrumental methods for assessing seafood quality. In: Huss HH (ed) Quality assurance in the fish industry. Elsevier Science Publishers, Amsterdam, pp 321–332
10. Mackie IM (1993) The effects of freezing on flesh proteins. Food Rev Int 9: 575–610
11. Goodband RM, Hedges ND, Wilding P (1999) Process for providing a frozen fish product. US Pat 6,007: 864
12. Wright DJ, Wilding P (1984) Differential scanning calorimetric study of muscle and its proteins – myosin and its subfragments. J Sci Food Agric 35: 357–372
13. Yamamoto K, Hayashi S, Yasui T (1983) Hydrostatic pressure-induced aggregation of myosin molecules in 0.5 m KCl at pH 6.0. Biosci Biotechnol Biochem 57: 383–388
14. Bean NH, Goulding JS, Lao C, Angulo FJ (1997) Surveillance for foodborne-disease outbreaks-CDSC. Scombrotoxic fish poisoning and imported tuna steaks. Communicable Disease Rep CDR Weekly 7: 1
15. Clifford MN, Walker R, Wright J, Hardy R, Murray CK (1989) Studies with volunteers on the role of histamine in suspected scombrotoxicosis. J Sci Food Agric 47: 365–375
16. Ijomah P, Clifford MN, Walker R, Wright J, Hardy R, Murray CK (1991) The importance of endogenous histamine relative to dietary histamine in the aetiology of scombrotoxicosis. Food Add Contam 8: 531–542
17. Brezeski MM (1987) Chitin and chitosan – putting waste to good use. Infofish Int 5: 31–33
18. Krishnapillai AM, Taylor KDA, Morris AEJ, Quantick PC (1999) Extraction and purification of hyaluronoglucosidase (EC 3.2.1.35) from Norway lobster (*Nephrops norvegicus*) Food Chem 65: 359–365
19. Meyers SP (1986) Utilisation of shrimp processing waste. Infofish Marketing Dig 4: 18–19
20. Nair KGR, Madhavan P, Gopakumar K (1986) Novel use of chitinous waste from crustacean processing plants. Infofish Marketing Dig 4: 20
21. Olsen RL, Johansen A, Myrnes B (1990) Recovery of enzymes from shrimp waste. Process Biochem 25: 67–68
22. Shahidi F, Synowiecki J (1992) Quality and compositional characteristics of Newfoundland shellfish processing discards. In: Brine CJ, Sanford PA, Zikakis JP (eds) Advances in chitin and chitosan. Elsevier Applied Science, London, pp 617–626
23. Simpson BK, Haard NF (1985) The use of proteolytic enzymes to extract carotenoproteins from shrimp wastes. J Appl Biochem 7: 212–222
24. Cadwallader KR, Macleod AJ (1998) Instrumental methods for analysing the flavour of muscle foods. In: Shahidi F (ed) Flavour of meat, meat products and seafoods. Blackie Academic and Professional, London, pp 355–372
25. Wampler TP (1997) Analysis of food volatiles using headspace-gas chromatographic techniques. In: Marsili R (ed) Techniques for analysing food aroma. Marcel Dekker, New York, pp 27–58
26. Luzuriaga DA, Balaban MO (1999) Evaluation of the odour of decomposition in raw and cooked shrimp: correlation of electronic nose readings, odour sensory evaluation and ammonia levels. In: Hurst WJ (ed) Electronic noses and sensor array based systems-design and applications. Technomic Publishing Company, Lancaster, pp 177–184
27. Boudreau J (2000). Marine nutraceuticals: opportunities and challenges. In: Shahidi F (ed) Seafood in health and nutrition: transformation in fisheries and aquaculture: global perspectives. Science Tech Publishing, St. John's, Canada, pp 7–14
28. Dehmer GJ (1988) Reduction in the rate of early restenosis after coronary angioplasty by a diet supplemented with n-3 fatty acids. N Engl J Med 319: 733–740
29. Fleurence J (1999) Seaweed proteins: biochemical, nutritional aspects and potential uses, a review. Trends Food Sci Technol 10: 25–28
30. Garcia DJ (1998) Omega-3 long chain PUFA nutraceuticals. Food Technol 52: 44–49

31. Haard NF, Simpson BK (2000) Seafood enzymes: utilization and influence on postharvest seafood quality. Marcel Dekker, New York
32. Kristinsson HG, Rasco BA (2000) Fish protein hydrolysates: production, biochemical and functional properties. Crit Rev Food Sci Nutr 40: 43–81
33. Lees RS, Karel M (1990) Omega-3 fatty acids in health and disease. Marcel Dekker, New York
34. Ohshima T (1998) Recovery and use of nutraceutical products from marine resources. Food Technol 52: 50–54
35. Shahidi F, Arachchi JKV, Jeon YJ (1999) Food applications of chitin and chitosan, a review. Trends Food Sci Technol 10: 37–51
36. Simopoulos AP (1991) Omega-3 fatty acids in health and disease and in growth and development, a review. Am J Clin Nutr 54: 438–463
37. Siscovick DS (1995) Dietary intake and cell membrane levels of long-chain n-3 polyunsaturated fatty acids and the risk of primary cardiac arrest. J Am Med Assoc 274: 1363–1367
38. Windsor M, Barlow S (1981) Introduction to fishery by-products. Fishing News Books, Surrey, UK
39. Wanasundara UN (1966) Marine oils: stabilization, structural characterization and omega-3 fatty acid concentration. PhD thesis, Memorial University of Newfoundland, St. John's, Canada
40. Wanasundara UN, Shahidi F (1998) Lipase assisted concentration of ω3-polyunsaturated fatty acids in acylglycerols form from marine oils. J Am Oil Chem Soc 75: 945–951

2 The Killing of Quality: The Impact of Slaughter Procedures on Fish Flesh

Dave Robb

Live fish have a certain level of intrinsic 'quality'. From the point of slaughter onwards this quality cannot be improved, but tends to be lost due to the natural degradation of the flesh. Slaughter and the procedures immediately prior to this point can have a large impact on the intrinsic 'quality' attributes and these impacts are all negative. By minimising the levels of stress and activity at slaughter it is possible to keep the fish closer to their intrinsic levels of 'quality', but highly stressful slaughter procedures result in a big reduction in 'quality' at an early stage in the processing line. Improvements in slaughter methods give the chance of improving final product quality.

2.1 Introduction

Live fish will have a certain level of intrinsic characteristics which will depend on their life history. The introduction of aquaculture as a method of producing fish for food has led to greater control over the life cycle of the fish and thus the characteristics of the final product. The ability to regulate the food and control disease in certain species of fish has allowed greater uniformity of the product. Such control is not possible with the wild caught fisheries, where the fish are influenced by their surrounding environment. However, from the point of slaughter onwards everything that is done to the fish will impinge on some of these intrinsic characteristics and so it is important to understand what are the mechanisms influencing them.

This chapter is dedicated to the immediate pre-slaughter handling and slaughter procedures imposed on fish and how these affect 'quality' characteristics of the fish flesh. Quality is many things to many people and as such this chapter will first start with a description of the form of quality which will be discussed. A brief introduction to fish muscle structure and physiology together with the responses of fish to slaughter processes will lead to the discussion of how the slaughter processes will impact on the quality characteristics of fish.

2.2 What is Quality?

Quality is one of the most abused words in food science and especially fisheries and aquaculture research [3]. It has been used to describe a wide range of characteristics of the fish, from the flesh and the skin, to how well it can be processed to the impact of the fish on the environment. For the purposes of this chapter, I will for the most part try to avoid the word quality. If the word is used, for the sake of simplicity, it will refer to attributes of the flesh (muscle) which are considered to increase the attraction of the product to the consumer.

Studies of fish flesh have shown that consumer preference for products was found to depend on the visual impression (40%), previous impression of flavour (40%) and the texture (20%) [23]. The flavour of fish has been shown to be heavily affected by dietary factors [14, 15] and fat levels within the flesh [16, 24] and not by stress [17]. Therefore flavour lies outside the effects under investigation in this chapter. However, both texture and appearance are affected by pre-slaughter handling and slaughter methods and will be discussed below. Areas of particular interest to the visual appearance are 'gaping', colour and opacity, each of which will be discussed separately.

2.3 Fish Muscle Structure and Physiology

The muscle of vertebrates falls into two basic categories, smooth and striated. This chapter concerns only the striated muscle, of which two types are recognised – red and white. Red muscle is used for routine movements and white muscle for faster or burst actions. The faster the movements required, the greater the degree of use of white muscle [5]. Striated muscle blocks are formed from many cells called muscle fibres. The cells are arranged in blocks called myotomes, separated by connective tissue (myosepta). The cells contain many parallel myofibrils which contain contractile units called sarcomeres. The sarcomeres are made from two types of protein myofilaments: actin monomers and myosin molecules. The myosin molecules are arranged so that the heads of the molecules are free (and can potentially form crosslinks between myofilaments) and the tails are bound together to form the myofilament. The actin myofilaments have tropomyosin and troponin complexes associated with them.

When the muscle is at rest the tropomyosin blocks any links between the actin and the myosin myofilaments. However, when the muscle cells are stimulated by motor neurons the tropomyosin-troponin complexes are pulled away from active sites on the actin. The heads of the myosin molecules then bind to these sites. As the myosin heads bend they expose sites which have (adenosine triphosphate) ATPase activity, breaking down ATP to adenosine diphosphate (ADP) and releasing energy. This energy causes the myosin heads to release from the actin, straighten and reattach to the next actin binding site. Thus the actin myofilament is pulled over the myosin filament using a series of ratchet-like movements. When the muscle stimulation by the motor neuron ceases, further ATP is required to release the myosin heads and allow the tropomyosin-troponin complexes to cover the receptor sites on the actin myofilaments.

The ATP molecules required for the processes are supplied by respiration. This uses energy derived from the oxidation of glycogen to synthesise ATP from ADP (Fig. 2.1). Respiration can be aerobic or anaerobic. In white muscle the res-

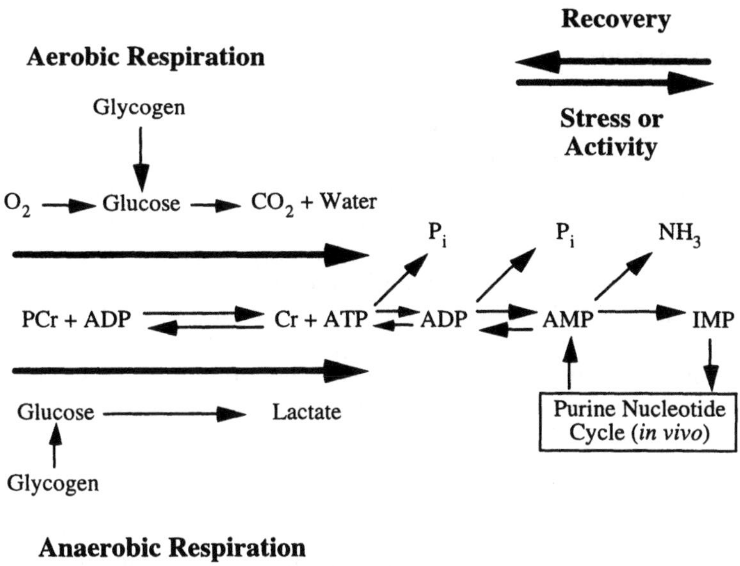

PCr: phosphocreatine, Cr: creatine, ATP: adenosine triphosphate, ADP: adenosine diphosphate, AMP: adenosine monophosphate, IMP: inosine monophosphate, P_i: inorganic phosphate.

Fig. 2.1. Energy metabolism in fish white muscle during rest (aerobic), stress or activity (anaerobic) and recovery

piration is predominantly anaerobic, but is predominantly aerobic in red muscle. The products of aerobic respiration are carbon dioxide and water, compared to the lactic acid produced from anaerobic respiration. Under normal conditions the lactic acid is later oxidised when aerobic conditions return. For instance, when a fish has to move quickly white muscle is used, producing lactic acid. When the muscle stops moving oxygen can be transported to that muscle and the lactic acid oxidised.

During normal swimming at slow speeds fish predominantly use red muscle for movement. However, as the level of activity increases white muscle is used more, so that at very high levels of activity white muscle will be predominantly used. This results in a large amount of anaerobic respiration, resulting in the production of large amounts of lactic acid. If the animal is allowed to recover from the activity the lactic acid will be cleared from the blood and muscle [20]. However, if the animal is killed immediately after the activity this will not happen and the pH of the flesh will remain low. This could have effects on the characteristics of the flesh.

The production of the acid can be simply measured by a drop in the muscle pH or by an increase in muscle and blood lactate levels. The acid remains in the body until it can be oxidised while the muscle is resting and oxygen can diffuse into the area. When the fish is killed immediately after activity, the acid is not cleared and thus a low muscle pH, or a high muscle or blood lactate content is a very good indicator of preslaughter muscle activity.

2.4 Slaughter Procedures

During the slaughter process the fish are rounded up from a large area, removed from water and killed in some way. The processes vary between wild fisheries and aquaculture, with the former being far more stressful to the fish. In aquaculture the fish are already confined in a small area and the crowding process need only take a few minutes. As crowding is highly stressful to the fish, increasing interactions between individuals and increasing the level of activity [8], they show an increase in the level of cortisol (a stress hormone) and lactate (an indicator of muscle activity) in their blood (Figs. 2.2 and 2.3, respectively). The fish are then removed from the water by pumps or nets and killed. This may occur in a variety of ways, from simply allowing the fish to die of anoxia by leaving it in air or on ice to physically causing its death by a blow to the head or by cutting major blood vessels resulting in exsanguination. Once the fish is dead the carcass is then placed on ice.

In wild fisheries, trawled fish are chased by the nets until they are exhausted, falling into the back of the net. Fish caught in gill nets and on longlines make re-

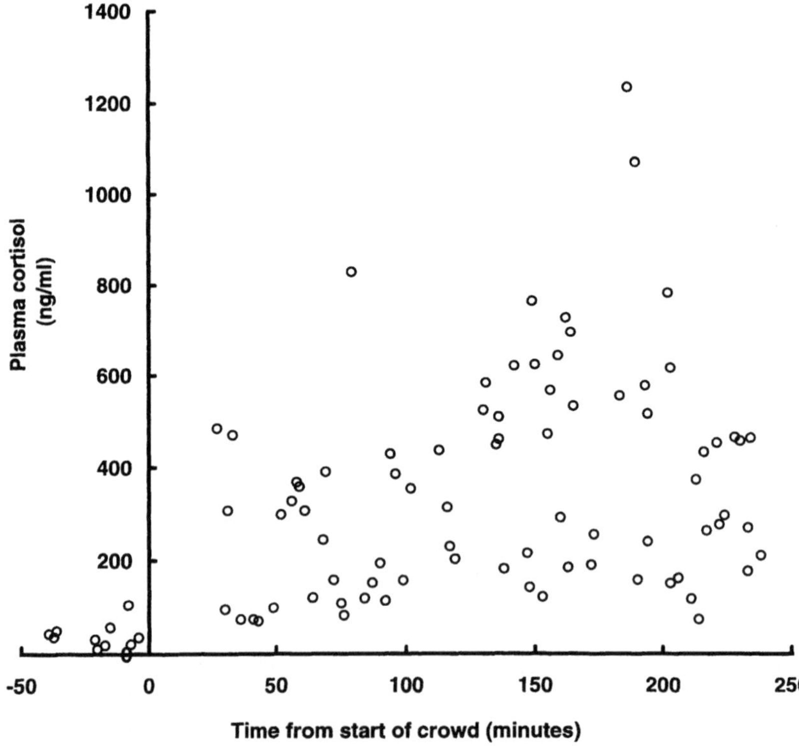

Fig. 2.2. Increasing plasma cortisol with time after the start of crowding of caged Atlantic salmon prior to slaughter. Controls (fish with negative times) show the resting level of cortisol

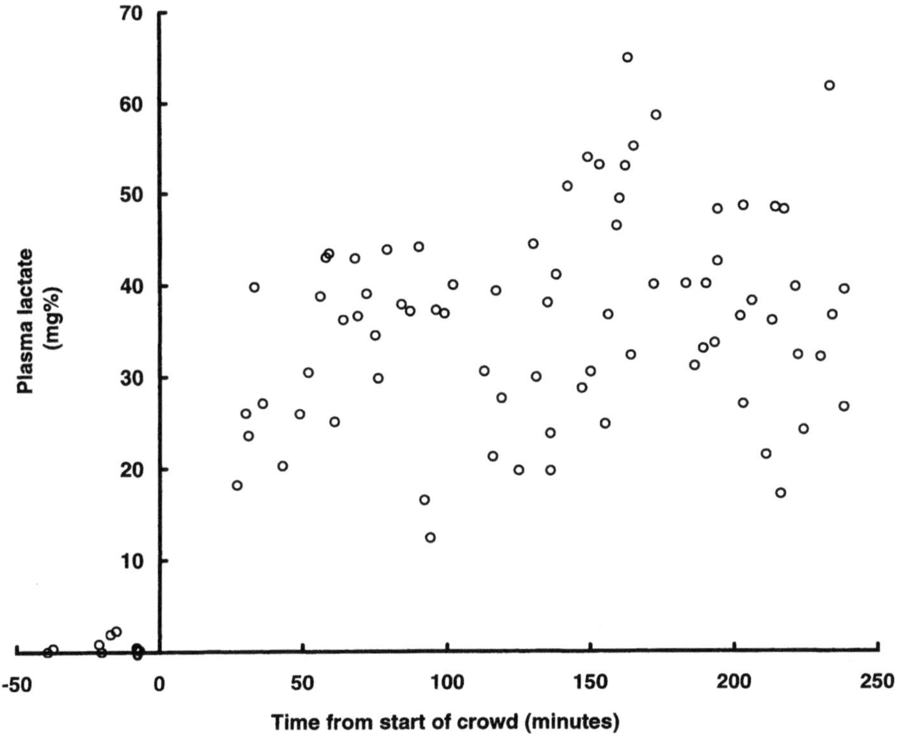

Fig. 2.3. Increasing plasma lactate with time after the start of crowding of caged Atlantic salmon prior to slaughter. Controls (fish with negative times) show the resting level of lactate

peated escape attempts until death. The more strenuous or prolonged the activity, the greater the lactic acid concentration [19]. Both of these methods are stressful to the fish and result in prolonged levels of muscular activity. Often the fish are brought up dead, death having resulted from exhaustion. However, some individuals and indeed some species are able to survive the catching process (S. Kestin 2000, personal communication). Following capture and landing, they are placed on ice, possibly eviscerated, and left until death. Research has shown that death may not occur until 6 h after evisceration in some cases, during which time the fish would make repeated movements.

2.5 Effects of Slaughter Activity and Stress on the Quality of the Fish

The stress around slaughter has been shown to result in an increase in muscle activity and this activity can affect the 'quality' attributes of the fish in two ways: physically and biochemically. When the fish are swimming vigorously from the start of the crowd or netting to the point of death and the cessation of movement they are likely to hit into other fish or solid objects. This can cause them to lose scales, become cut or bruised. Such problems are particularly encountered with species with sharp spines, such as gilthead seabream (*Sparus aurata*) and seabass (*Dicentrarchus labrax*), where the external appearance of the fish can be seriously affected [29]. Long periods of contact with nets, as will often occur in long trawl durations, also cause damage to fish, normally manifested by scale loss, the impact of which will vary with species. Rough handling also causes physical damage which cannot be repaired and excellent pictorial examples of such physical damage are given by Doyle [4].

When the fish is considered dead, which can be defined clinically as the point when brain activity has ceased and will not return, and blood circulation ceases, individual cells within the fish may still be alive and will continue to respire. Initially they will use up any remaining oxygen within the flesh and then will respire anaerobically, with the associated production of lactic acid and drop in pH [12]. This results in a characteristic drop in muscle pH post-slaughter, from a 'resting' (i.e. from muscle which has not shown any recent activity) pH of about 7.5 to an 'ultimate' (lowest level affected after death) pH of about 6.4 in salmonids [13, 25].

As the pH of the flesh drops it interferes with enzymatic reactions until it eventually prevents the synthesis of ATP, the molecule required to allow movement of muscle myofilaments. Without ATP, the myofilaments are unable to slide over each other, and thus lock resulting in *rigor mortis*. This occurs on an individual cell level, but acts over the whole fish, making the carcass stiffer as rigor develops.

Fish that showed muscle activity prior to slaughter already have a high lactic acid content and so are closer to the pH which prevents ATP synthesis. Further, the muscle will already be depleted of oxygen, so they will continue to respire anaerobically post-slaughter, producing more lactic acid. This reduces the time to the onset of rigor compared to 'rested' fish [18, 25] and also results in a much stiffer fish during rigor, as more cells enter rigor at the same time [1, 25]. This is supported by investigations which have shown that comparatively 'rested' fish contain ATP even when they are in peak rigor, while stressed fish have no ATP at peak rigor [7]. These results indicate that some cells had not entered rigor in the 'rested' fish, although the majority of cells had, resulting in the fish being as stiff as it would become during the rigor process.

Boyd et al. [2] showed that the time to the onset of rigor could also be affected post-catching by the killing method employed. Complete and immediate destruction of the brain of fish caught on a line resulted in a longer time to rigor onset as there were no muscular movements following this process. Even following the stress and activity of a short period of being caught on a trolled lure, the instant killing process resulted in a significant difference in the time to the onset of rigor compared to fish allowed to die in ice slurry, which takes considerably longer. As would be expected, the spiked fish had higher levels of muscle ATP and lower lactic acid concentrations than the unspiked control fish, showing that the employment of the killing method, as opposed to just leaving the fish to die, had reduced the amount of activity at slaughter.

Having induced activity in the fish at slaughter, the rate of onset of rigor cannot be reduced by reducing the temperature of the fish. Watabe et al. [31] found the rate of the onset of rigor of plaice (*Paralichthys olicaceus*) to be temperature dependent as would be expected, as temperature controls the enzymatic rate. However, the rate of reduction in ATPase activity (the enzyme which breaks down ATP) with temperature is slower than the rate of reduction of uptake of Ca^{2+} ions from the myofibrils of the muscle at 0 °C than at 10 °C. The Ca^{2+} ions trigger the ATPase action within the myofibrils and, as they are not removed rapidly at low temperature, the breakdown of ATP is actually faster at lower temperatures according to Watabe et al. [31], although this differs with the results of Mochizuki and Sato [21] who found almost no difference in the rate of progress of rigor at 0 °C and 8 °C in horse mackerel.

The more rapid breakdown of ATP in fish which show a high level of activity immediately prior to slaughter results in an increase in the concentration of its metabolites [1, 18, 21]. This affects the so-called indicator of freshness, the *K* value of the fish. Fish with a lower *K* value are regarded as more 'fresh', as this indicates a higher concentration of ATP relative to its metabolites [27]. However, it has been shown above that stress and activity at slaughter lead to a rapid loss of ATP, and this has been shown to lead to a rapid increase in the *K* values [9, 10, 19]. Thus, using traditional nomenclature, fish which have been stressed at slaughter are actually less 'fresh' than 'rested' fish, although they will have been killed at the same time.

The impact of preslaughter stress and activity on the attributes of the fish thus immediately manifests in two ways. First, exposure to a period of stress gives rise to fish which are 'less fresh' immediately after slaughter. Second, these fish enter rigor more rapidly and are stiffer when in rigor. This rapid onset of rigor may lead to the fish being eviscerated while in rigor, causing damage to the muscle blocks which are already very stiff and so susceptible to breakage when handled. By reducing pre-slaughter stress and activity the fish will take longer to go into rigor and this will allow more time to process and pack the fish on ice before they enter rigor, reducing the possibility of damage to the flesh.

Reducing the 'strength' of the rigor may also affect the degree of muscle damage observed in the flesh. 'Gaping' within the flesh occurs when the myotomes separate at the myosepta. Although Fletcher et al. [11] found no effect of preslaughter activity, Robb et al. [25] showed that fish subjected to high levels of muscle activity had a higher degree of 'gaping'. This was postulated to be caused by stronger rigor tensions pulling the tissues apart and there is some supporting evidence for this theory. Muscle fibre strength is directly affected by the degree of muscle activity pre-slaughter. Increasing the activity results in greatly decreased strength of the individual fibres [13, 21]. The whole fillets of stressed fish were also weaker than rested fish [28]. Thus, it seems possible that the 'gaping' could arise from the strong rigor tensions pulling the myotomes apart.

The colour attributes of the flesh are also affected by preslaughter stress and activity. Colour is a very important determinant of the consumer's opinion of a product, but the effects of highly stressful preslaughter conditions cause a reduction in the positive attributes. The clearest example of such changes are observed in tuna and salmonids. High levels of activity prior to slaughter result in lighter, less red and more translucent flesh (A. Smart, 2000, personal communication) [25]. The more rapid pH drop immediately post-slaughter associated with high activity preslaughter results in an increased lightness (L* value from the Minolta chromameter) in salmonids [25] and hybrid striped bass [6].

Investigation into the cause of the loss of colour has shown that fish showing a high level of muscle activity at slaughter have a significantly lower soluble muscle protein content [26]. This is very similar to an effect which occurs in pigs which are acutely stressed at slaughter, which results in similarly pale flesh [30]. Known as Pale, Soft and Exudative (P. S. E.) flesh, the muscle of such animals has lower levels of soluble muscle proteins. The rapid change in the muscle pH post-slaughter causes the soluble muscle proteins to denature, becoming insoluble and releasing water [22]. This change in conformation of the muscle results in a change in the reflection of incident light shone onto the surface of the flesh. The light becomes scattered, causing interference and thus making the flesh appear whiter or lighter to an observer. The pigments within the flesh are masked by the interference and the flesh appears more opaque. This is very similar to the results of Robb [24] (unpublished work) and it therefore appears probable that P.S.E. can occur in fish, certainly salmonids.

2.6 Conclusions

From the review of studies on the effects of preslaughter stress and activity on the characteristics of the flesh of fish, it is becoming clear that activity reduces the number of positive attributes (Table 2.1). As more carefully controlled experiments allow a detailed description of the effects of muscle activity to be studied, it can be seen high levels of muscle activity are responsible for many downgrading conditions.

The degree of physical damage to the exterior of the fish is an obvious result of poor handling during the catching. Less obvious, until the publication of recent studies, were the effects on rigor onset, 'gaping', texture and colour. These show how traditional methods could impinge on the flesh characteristics and how by reducing preslaughter stresses these affects could be reduced.

Table 2.1. Summary of the effects of preslaughter stress and activity on fish attributes, compared to 'rested' fish

External	Scale loss Bruising Cuts to the skin
Internal	Decreased time to rigor Stronger rigor tension Increased gaping Decreased muscle fibre strength Decreased 'freshness' Lighter/paler flesh Less red flesh (salmonids) More opaque flesh

With the growing demand from retailers for products which are reproducible in characteristics, there is a need for the reduction in the degree of variability between fish. By reducing the levels of activity at slaughter, the variability can be reduced, leading to improved overall 'product quality'. However, it would appear difficult to reduce the activity levels of wild caught fish, due to the methods of catching and the conditions associated with the industry. By using aquaculture, where there is much more control over the conditions at slaughter, it is possible to reduce dramatically the levels of activity at slaughter and so improve the attributes of the flesh. Using this knowledge, research is being carried out to trap fish from the wild, allow them to recover from this stress in net cages and then kill them under the same controlled conditions. If this is feasible it may open the way for much less product variability and great improvements in the 'quality' of fish flesh.

References

1. Berg T, Erikson U, Nordtvedt TS (1997) Rigor mortis assessment of Atlantic salmon (*Salmo salar*) and effects of stress. J Food Sci 62: 439–446
2. Boyd NS, Wilson ND, Jerrett AR, Hall BI (1984) Effects of brain destruction on post harvest muscle metabolism in the fish kahawai (*Arripis trutta*). J Food Sci 49: 177–179
3. Bremner HA (2000) Toward practical definitions of quality for food science. Crit Rev Food Sci Nutr 40: 83–90
4. Doyle JP (1995) Care and handling of salmon: the key to quality. Marine Advisory Bull No.45, School of Fisheries and Ocean Sciences, University of Alaska Fairbanks, USA
5. Driedzic WR, Hochachka PW (1978) Metabolism in fish during exercise. In: Hoar WS, Randall DJ (eds) Fish physiology, vol 8: Locomotion. Academic Press, London, pp 503–543
6. Eifert JD, Hackney CR, Libey GS, Flick GJ Jr (1992) Aquacultured hybrid striped bass fillet quality resulting from post-harvest cooling or CO_2 treatments. J Food Sci 57: 1099–1102
7. Erikson U (1997) Muscle quality of Atlantic salmon (*Salmo salar*) as affected by handling stress. PhD thesis, Norwegian University of Science and Technology, Trondheim, Norway
8. Erikson U (2000) Potential effects of pre-slaughter fasting, handling and transport. In: Kestin SC, Warriss PD (eds) Farmed fish quality. Blackwell Science, Oxford, UK, pp 202–219
9. Erikson U, Beyer AR, Sigholt T, Jørgensen L (1995) Effect of handling stress on the phosphate metabolites and K-value of Atlantic salmon. In: Scheire K, Aspeslangh L, Joncheere H (compilers) Quality in aquaculture. Special Publication 23, European Aquaculture Society, Gent, Belgium, pp 376–377
10. Erikson U, Beyer AR, Sigholt T (1997) Muscle high-energy phosphates and stress affect *K*-values during ice storage of Atlantic salmon (*Salmo salar*). J Food Sci 62: 43–47
11. Fletcher GC, Hallett IC, Jerrett AR, Holland AJ (1997) Changes in the fine structure of the myocommata-muscle fibre junction related to gaping in rested and exercised muscle from king salmon (*Oncorhynchus tshawytscha*). Lebensm Wiss Technol 30: 246–252
12. Jeacocke RE (1996) The control of post-mortem metabolism and the onset of *rigor mortis*. In: Bailey AJ (ed) Recent advances in the chemistry of meat. Special Publication 47, The Royal Society of Chemistry, London, pp 41–57
13. Jerrett AJ, Stevens J, Holland AJ (1996) Tensile properties of white muscle in rested and exhausted king salmon (*Oncorhynchus tshawytscha*). J Food Sci 61: 527–532
14. Johansson L (1992) Eating quality of rainbow trout. PhD thesis, University of Uppsala, Sweden

15. Johansson L, Kiessling A, Kiessling KH, Berglund L (2000) Effects of altered ration levels on sensory characteristics, lipid content and fatty acid composition of rainbow trout (*Oncorhynchus mykiss*). Food Qual Pref 11: 247–254
16. Kestin S, Nute G, Read N, Warriss P (1995) The effect of muscle fat content of rainbow trout (*Oncorhynchus mykiss*) on texture, flavour and acceptability. Paper presented at the Aquaculture Europe '95. European Aquaculture Society Special Publication 23, pp 184–185
17. Kestin S, Warriss P, Nute G, Wiseman G (1995) The effect of fasting or exercise in rainbow trout (*Oncorhynchus mykiss*) on blood chemistry, meat and eating quality. Paper presented at the Aquaculture '95. World Aquaculture Society Conference, Book of Abstracts, San Diego, USA, February 1–4, pp 153–154
18. Korhonen RW, Lanier TC, Giesbrecht F (1990) An evaluation of simple methods for following rigor development in fish. J Food Sci 55: 346–348, 368
19. Lowe TE, Ryder JM, Carragher JF, Wells RMG (1993) Flesh quality in snapper, *Pagrus auratus*, affected by capture stress. J Food Sci 58: 770–773, 796
20. Milligan CL (1996) Metabolic recovery from exhaustive exercise in rainbow trout. Comp Biochem Physiol 113A: 51–60
21. Mochizuki S, Sato A (1994) Effects of various killing procedures and storage temperatures on post-mortem changes in the muscle of horse mackerel. Nippon Suisan Gakkaishi 60: 125–130
22. Penny IF (1977) The effect of temperature on the drip, denaturation and extracellular space of pork *Longissimus dorsi*, muscle. J Sci Food Agric 28: 329–338
23. Rasekh J, Kramer A, Finch R (1970) Objective evaluation of canned tuna sensory quality. J Food Sci 35: 417–423
24. Robb DHF (1998) Some factors affecting the flesh quality of salmonids: pigmentation, composition and eating quality. PhD thesis, University of Bristol, UK
25. Robb DHF, Kestin SC, Warriss PD (2000) Muscle activity at slaughter: I. Changes in flesh colour and gaping in rainbow trout. Aquaculture 182: 261–269
26. Rustad T, Løken JT (1995) Effect of handling on the muscle chemistry and quality of salmon. In: Scheire K, Aspeslangh L, Joncheere H (compilers). Quality in aquaculture. Special Publication 23, European Aquaculture Society, Gent, Belgium, pp 385–386
27. Saito T, Arai K, Matsuyoshi M (1959) A new method for estimating the freshness of fish. Bull Japan Soc Sci Fish 24: 749–750
28. Sigholt T, Erikson U, Rustad T, Johansen S, Nordvedt T, Seland A (1997) Handling stress and storage temperature affect meat quality of farmed-raised Atlantic salmon (*Salmo salar*). J Food Sci 62: 898–905
29. Smart G (2000) Problems of seabass and sea bream quality in the Mediterranean. In: Kestin SC, Warriss PD (eds) Farmed fish quality. Blackwell Science, Oxford, UK, pp 120–128
30. Warriss PD (2000) Meat science: an introductory text. CABI Publishing, Oxford, UK
31. Watabe S, Ushio H, Iwamoto M, Yamanaka H, Hashimotot K (1989) Temperature-dependency of rigor-mortis of fish muscle: myofibrillar Mg^{2+}-ATPase activity and Ca^{2+} uptake by sarcoplasmic reticulum. J Food Sci 54: 1107–1110, 1115

3 Practical Evaluation of Fish Quality

Cesarettin Alasalvar, Tony Garthwaite, Abdullah Öksüz

The quality of raw material arriving at the processor's door is of vital importance to the quality perception by the consumer of the product when eaten. Fish are a highly perishable food due to their biological composition. Therefore, they should be handled at all times with great care and in such a way as to extend the shelf life. This gives more time for retailers and processors to sell their products at full price and better quality. Both retailers and processors want the fish to reach the consumer and be eaten at the highest level of quality possible. In practice, the dates printed on the packs of pre-packed foods ("Sell by" and "Consume by") are well within the safety limits for consumption of those products. This chapter provides information on supermarket demands, the shelf life extension of fresh fish, evaluation of freshness and quality and practical applications. Sensory and non-sensory assessments are also discussed. The importance and usefulness of modification of a particular sensory scheme for the processors needs is stressed.

3.1 Introduction

During the last two decades of the twentieth century we have seen the fish species consumed in Northern Europe changing. The demand for fish has increased partly due to changing eating habits as the public look for healthier food, and partly due to increased travel to other parts of the world where the native fish species on offer are different.

The increasing demand for fish and fishery products during the 1980s and 1990s has placed an increasing pressure on the fisheries resources of the European coastal waters. This has not been solely a European problem. As the colder water fishing grounds of the temperate regions become less productive because of over-fishing or other reasons, the fish traders and fish processing factories look to other parts of the world to fill the shortfall between supply and demand for their products.

Improved preservation techniques and developments in packaging together with faster and more effective distribution have given impetus to new fishery products. The main drive has been in chilled and frozen distribution, which are highly developed in parts of Europe. The sale of chilled products has increased considerably with the improved road networks and the technological improvements that have made the increase in the production and distribution of chilled fresh fish and ready meals possible.

Competition between the various supermarkets means that they are looking to achieve 'better value for money' and 'higher profits for shareholders'. Virtually all the retail packs of chilled products are sold through the supermarket chains and the supermarkets are looking to achieve the highest possible return on the shelf space allocated to each product. Products with a short shelf life are the most difficult items to keep in stock at levels that ensure a continuous supply of high quality produce. Fish products are extremely difficult to control, as supplies of many of the fish are dependent upon fishing conditions, seasons and quotas. It is sometimes difficult to find fresh fish which has the potential shelf life required for distribution in the supermarket chains. Short shelf life products are often sold at a discount near the end of their shelf life and this reduces the profit to the retailer. In order to avoid such losses the retailers are always looking to extend the shelf life of their products, giving them more time to sell the products at full price, thus maximising profits.

This chapter summarises the shelf life extension of fresh fish, evaluation of freshness and quality and practical applications.

3.2 Extended Shelf Life

The increased focus on the safety of foods has meant that the processor and retailer must consider the safe shelf life of the food and set a time limit for each foodstuff after which the risk of the consumer getting food poisoning from that product becomes unacceptable. In practice, the dates printed on the packs of pre-packed foods ("Sell by" and "Consume by") are well within the safety limits for consumption of those products. This allows for consumer abuse of the product by inadvertent warming for short periods during transport by the purchaser or by storing in a refrigerator operating at too high a temperature. Generally we are concerned with microbiological hazards when considering the safety of the product for human consumption but hazards may also be chemical in nature or a combination of the two, as is the case with histamine. In these cases the maintenance of low temperatures is essential in extending the shelf life of the product.

However, the safety of the fish to the consumer is not the only issue at stake here. The quality of the fish as perceived by the prospective purchaser and the eating qualities of the cooked product are also important factors. Both the producer and the retailer want the fish to reach the consumer and be eaten at the highest level of quality possible. There is a point on this quality scale below which the retailer does not wish to market the product. This is to ensure that the retailer is associated with high quality produce. It is also because the technologists know that below this point the taste of the cooked product may be affected in a way that makes it less acceptable or, in the extreme case, rejected by the consumer. The "Sell by" and "Consume by" dates are calculated to avoid the risk of such an occurrence. It is the job of the fish technologist to set the "Sell by" and "Consume by" dates for the various species and products produced. The technologist calculates this based on fish that is the best quality available.

Let us consider the change in quality of fresh fish represented in Fig. 3.1. We may assume that this fish is kept chilled (on ice) after catching or removal from the water and handled correctly. For the purposes of this example, we may as-

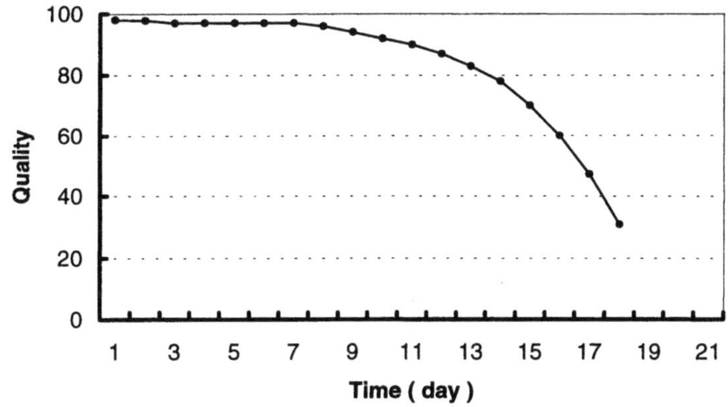

Fig. 3.1. Fresh fish quality with respect to time after catching

sume that as long as the fish quality score is above 80 then the fish is of a high enough quality to sell in the retail store. Also, for the purposes of this example, below a score of 60, the fish will have unacceptable characteristics when consumed. It is possible to see that the supermarket has 15 days from catching to sell the fish and at approximately 17 days after capture the fish will be unacceptable to the consumer. If the retail organisation wants a shelf life 'in store' of 8 days, then the fish must be caught, landed, processed and delivered to the retailer by day 8 after catching.

If we consider the fish buyer on the market who purchases Fish A and Fish B illustrated in Fig. 3.2, the organoleptic quality scores are the same at day 1 when the fish is bought. However, the fish are already "catching + 2 days" for Fish A and "catching + 5" days for Fish B. If we assume that it takes 48 h to transport the fish to the processor, process and re-pack the fish and transport to the retail organisation, it is possible to see that Fish A has a remaining shelf life of 10 days, whilst Fish B has a remaining shelf life of only 7 days. Thus, it is clear that Fish B will be below the standard required by the retailer for sale to the consumer if it is sold

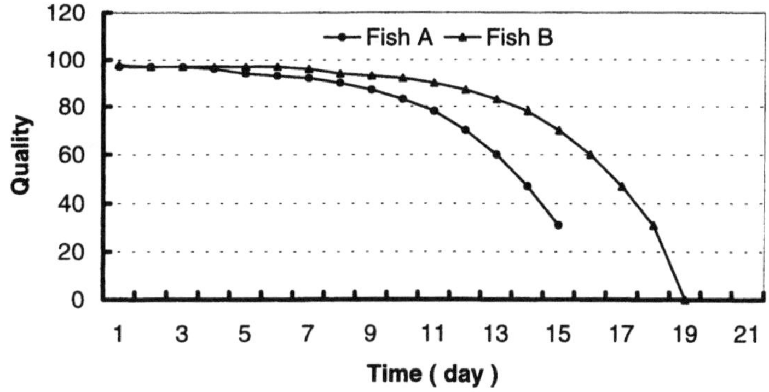

Fig. 3.2. Fresh fish quality for two fish with respect to time after purchase on the market

on day 8 after arriving in the store. The pressures on the fish buyer and the Quality Assurance team are therefore becoming much greater as the retailer looks for longer shelf life in order to maximise profitability. Knowledge of spoilage patterns becomes even more essential to the buying team.

3.3 Evaluation of Fish Freshness and Quality

Freshness makes a major contribution to the quality of fish or fishery products. For all kinds of products, freshness is essential for the quality of the final product. It has been frequently stated that no single method is generally reliable for assessment of freshness and quality of fish. Therefore a range of methods have been proposed for evaluation of freshness and quality (Fig. 3.3). Each method has its particular advantages and disadvantages [19].

Generally there are two main methods available for assessing fish freshness and quality, namely sensory (subjective) and non-sensory (objective). To these, the systematic approach of hazard analysis critical control point (HACCP) can also be added. There are a number of books, book chapters and articles published in discussing the advantages and disadvantaged of each method [3, 7, 10, 17–19, 24, 25, 31, 32]. Here sensory, non-sensory and systematic methods are briefly discussed.

3.3.1 Sensory Methods

Sensory methods are still the most satisfactory way of assessing the freshness of fish and fishery products. They can be applied to all fish species, need no laboratory facilities and are quick and non-destructive unless the sample is being cooked. Sensory methods depend upon human senses, with the exception of hearing, and are used in the fishing industry to judge quality by sight, touch (texture), odour and flavour. Sensory tests can be divided into three groups: discriminate, descriptive and affective [23]. The choice of the method depends on the purpose of the application of the sensory evaluation and whether it is used in product development, quality control and consumer studies or research [24].

The Tasmanian Food Research Unit (TFRU) [12] and European Union (EU) [15, 20] schemes are the most commonly used methods for the quality assessment of raw fish in the inspection service and fishing industry. However, it is more common to cook fillets before carrying out sensory evaluation, and the Torry scheme [28] is the most commonly used scale for the freshness evaluation of cooked fish. These methods, as opposed to non-sensory, offer the best opportunity of getting a valid idea of what the consumer wants because they provide immediate quality information [11].

Although the sensory methods are still the most satisfactory way of assessing the freshness of fish, they have limitations and therefore their uses are potentially limited in fish processing and technology sites. However, most trade is based on sensory assessments, although measurements are not always objective and documented. Thus, when non-sensory methods are being used for assessing

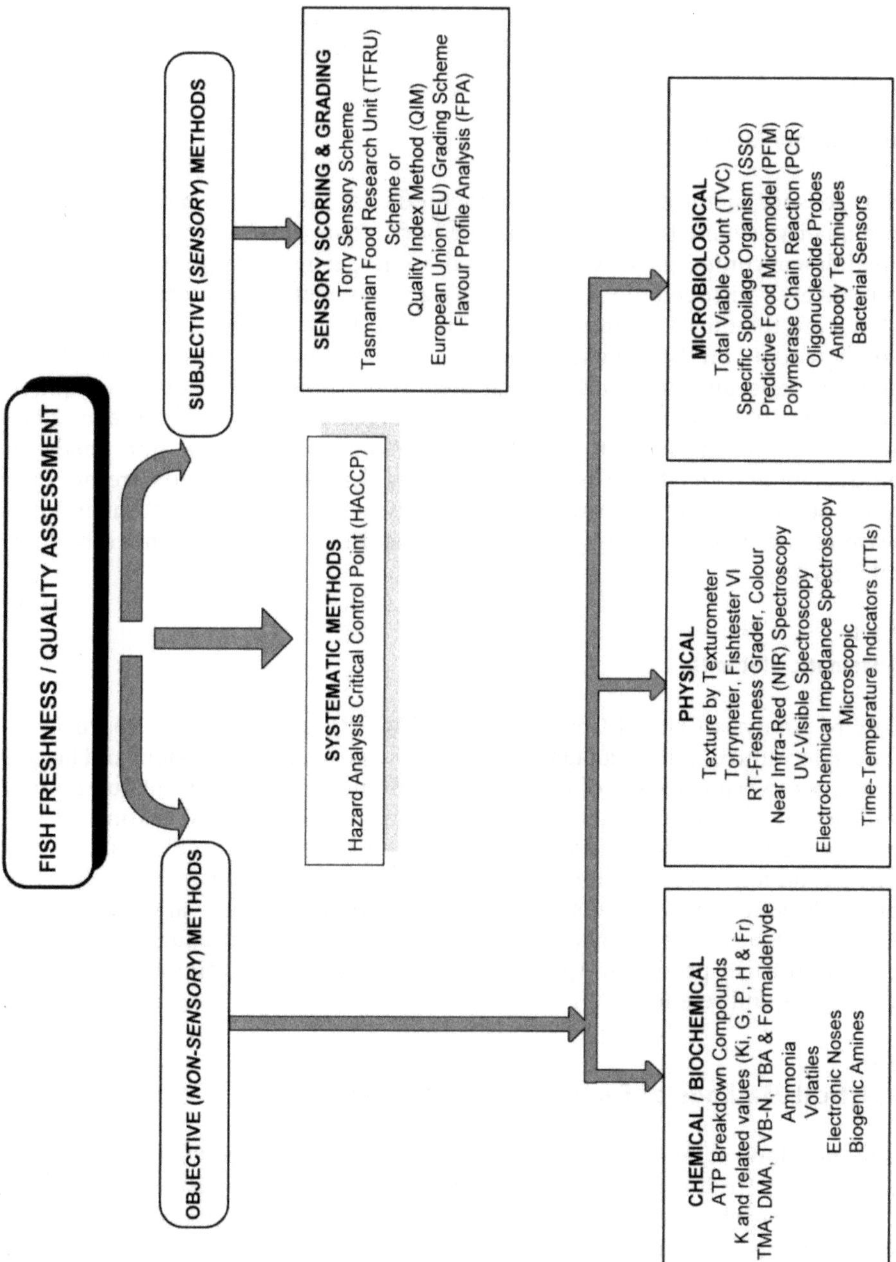

Fig. 3.3. Methods of fish freshness and quality assessment

the quality of fish, sensory evaluation should be conducted to ensure that those results show good agreement with the objective methods [2].

3.3.2
Non-Sensory Methods

Non-sensory methods are objective methods used to determine fish freshness and quality. Among the non-sensory methods, adenosine 5′-triphosphate (ATP) breakdown compounds, *K* and related values, trimethylamine (TMA), total volatile base-nitrogen (TVB-N), biogenic amines, texture and total viable count (TVC) are the most commonly used (Fig. 3.3). These are analytical techniques not dependant on the human senses for evaluation, but are produced by instruments or laboratory methods so that there is no subjective evaluation required on the part of the person conducting the test. The advantages of these methods are that the results are not subject to human variation and are more easily reproducible and reliable. The disadvantage is that these methods are not currently suitable for all types of quality attributes [4]. There are a number of assessment methods including chemical/biochemical, physical and microbiological (Fig. 3.3).

3.3.3
Systematic Methods

Hazard Analysis Critical Control Point (HACCP) is a systematic approach to food safety and quality management [13]. It is a cost-effective system and targets resources to critical areas of processing, so reducing the risk of manufacturing and selling unsafe products [1]. Traditional microbiological testing system methods are often slow, laborious and provide only retrospective data on finished product. There is, therefore, a need for quick, reliable and cost-effective methods to control organisms at the point of production and prevention. HACCP can be used systematically for assessing the freshness, quality and safety of fish and fish products. Application of HACCP is now compulsory for fish processors and retailers.

3.4
Practical Methods of Evaluation of Fish Freshness

If we now look at two examples of fish that have been studied with respect to assessment of freshness using different techniques, we can illustrate the advantages and problems of the various methods used. The first fish, sea bream, is a saltwater species, whilst the second species, rainbow trout, is freshwater.

3.4.1
Materials and Methods

Cultured sea bream (*Sparus aurata*) and rainbow trout (*Onchorynchus mykiss*) used in this study were obtained from Greek and English farms, respectively.

Sea bream and rainbow trout were stored inside polystyrene boxes with ice at surrounding temperature of 2 ± 2 °C, for a period of 23 and 14 days, respectively.

The sensory assessment of sea bream and rainbow trout were conducted using the modified TFRU scoring scheme [2] and EU grading scheme [15, 20], respectively. ATP-related compounds were determined using the HPLC technique, according to Ryder [26]. The K, K_i, G, H and Fr (or the IMP ratio) values were calculated according to Saito et al. [27], Karube et al. [21], Burns et al. [8], Luong et al. [22] and Gill et al. [16], respectively. Texture measurement was carried out to Sigurgisladottir et al. [29], modified by Alasalvar et al. [2].

3.4.2 Freshness Assessment of Cultured Sea Bream Stored in Ice

In this experimental work, K value was compared with those of TFRU sensory scoring system and texture over the storage period in ice. Time-independent relationship between the TFRU, K value and hardness over the storage period were also assessed.

3.4.2.1 *TFRU Sensory Assessment Scheme*

As illustrated in Fig. 3.3, although there are many methods of assessing the freshness of fish by subjective methods, the TFRU scheme seems to be superior to others in terms of its speed and reliability. Also, minor variations in scoring individual attributes have little influence on the overall score.

Botta [7] said that whenever one intends to use the TFRU system for a "new" species, preliminary studies must be conducted to ensure that all the criteria and their corresponding defined characteristics incorporated in the grade standards are appropriate and will actually be used. The TFRU system has already been modified for iced anchovy, Atlantic cod, Atlantic herring, plaice, red fish, saithe and sardine [7].

Some of the descriptors on the original score sheet of the TFRU system [12] were not related to the cultured sea bream. Therefore, Alasalvar et al. [2] modified this scheme to be appropriate for this fish according to the panellists' perceptions obtained during the storage period in ice (Table 3.1). The developers of the original TFRU system observed that it was necessary to modify the general TFRU system for a "new" species [7].

Some of the descriptions such as "skin", "eyes shape", "gills colour", "mucus", "smell", "belly discoloration", "firmness", and "vent condition" were modified. However, "eyes shape" and "gills colour", which changed unevenly during the storage period, were found not to be good indicators of freshness for this fish. "Rigor mortis", "very bright appearance", "dark red gills", "possessing seaweedy odour" and "possessing shell-fish odour" should be considered as attributes of extreme freshness, whereas "loss of brilliance", "sunken and bloody eyes", "dark brown or grey gills colour", "spoilt smell" and "excessive discoloration in belly area" would indicate stale fish. A table of descriptive terms obtained from the

Table 3.1. Modified Tasmanian Food Research Unit (TFRU) sensory assessment scheme for cultured sea bream

Parameters being assessed		Demerit points			
		0	1	2	3
Appearance		Very bright	Bright	Slightly dull	Dull
Skin		Firm or elastic	Soft		
Slime		Absent	Slightly slimy	Slimy	Very slimy
Stiffness		Pre-rigor	Rigor	Post-rigor	
Eyes	Clarity	Clear	Slightly cloudy	Cloudy	
	Shape[a]	Normal	Flat sunken	Sunken or swollen	
	Iris	Visible	Slightly visible	Not visible	
	Blood	No blood	Slightly bloody	Bloody	Very bloody
Gills	Colour[a]	Dark red	Red	Brown	Dark brown or grey
	Mucus	Absent	Slight	Moderate	Excessive or sticky
	Smell	Neutral	Fishy	Stale	Spoilt
Belly	Discoloration	White iridescent	Some yellowish	Yellow	Excessive yellow
	Firmness	Firm	Soft	Sunken	Burst
Vent	Condition	Normal	Slight break and darkening	Excessive	
	Smell	Fresh	Neutral	Fishy	Spoilt

Total demerit points (0–38).
[a] Eyes shape and gills colour are not good indicators for cultured sea bream during storage period in ice.
Source: Adapted from Alasalvar et al. [2].

modified TFRU sensory assessment scheme for cultured sea bream stored in ice is shown in Table 3.2.

Panellists found that the limit for acceptability for cultured sea bream stored in ice was about 17–18 days (Table 3.3). However, the perceived level of acceptability of sea bream quality depends on the particular buyer, user or regulatory agency [2].

3.4.2.2
K Value Assessment

K value is gaining in popularity in certain parts of the world and relates freshness to the autolytic degradation of nucleotides in fish muscle after death [14]. There were good time-independent relationships between the sensory evaluation by the TFRU and the *K* value, with r^2 value of linear regression ($r^2 = 0.98$) over the storage period (Fig. 3.4). As the sensory quality of sea bream decreased, *K* value increased. When the fish was considered unacceptable by the members

Table 3.2. Table of descriptive terms obtained from Modified TFRU sensory assessment scheme for cultured sea bream stored in ice

Storage time (day)		1	6	10	14	17	21	23
Appearance		Very bright	Bright	Bright	Slightly dull	Slightly dull	Dull	Dull
Skin		Firm or elastic	Firm or elastic	Firm or elastic	Soft	Soft	Soft	Soft
Slime		Absent	Absent	Absent	Slightly slimy	Slightly slimy	Slimy	Very slimy
Stiffness		Rigor	Post-rigor	Post-rigor	Post-rigor	Post-rigor	Post-rigor	Post-rigor
Eyes	Clarity	Clear	Clear	Slightly cloudy	Slightly cloudy	Slightly cloudy	Cloudy	Cloudy
	Shape	Normal	Normal	Flat sunken	Flat sunken	Flat sunken	Sunken	Sunken
	Iris	Visible	Visible	Visible	Visible	Slightly visible	Slightly visible	Not visible
	Blood	No blood	No blood	Slightly bloody	Slightly bloody	Slightly bloody	Slightly bloody	Bloody
Gills	Colour	Red	Red	Red	Red	Brown	Dark brown	Dark brown
	Mucus	Absent	Slight	Slight	Moderate	Moderate	Moderate	Moderate
	Smell	Neutral	Fishy	Fishy	Stale	Spoilt	Spoilt	Spoilt
Belly	Discoloration	White iridescent	White iridescent	White iridescent	Some yellowish	Some yellowish	Some yellowish	Some yellowish
	Firmness	Firm	Firm	Soft	Soft	Soft	Soft	Sunken
Vent	Condition	Normal	Normal	Normal	Normal	Normal	Slight break	Slight break
	Smell	Fresh	Neutral	Neutral	Fishy	Fishy	Spoilt	Spoilt

Source: Adapted from Alasalvar et al. [2].

Table 3.3. Rejection point of *K* value of some fish

Fish species	Rejection day	Rejection value (%)
Cultured sea bream	17–18	35–40
Cultured sea bass	16–17	50–55
Cultured trout	9–12	75–80
Mackerel	7–12	73–80
Tilapia	12–14	65–70
Red snapper	8–10	90–94
Salmon	13–15	70–75
Tuna	14–15	55–60
Carp	14–15	80–85

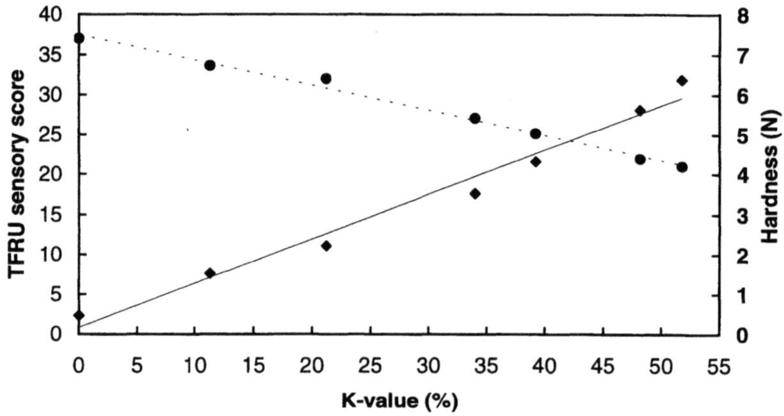

r^2 values of linear regressions are 0.98 (FTRU and K-value), and 0.99 (Hardness and K-value)
Maximum demerit points: 38
Unaccaptable limit: TFRU: 20-25; K-value: 35-40%; Hardness: 5-5.5N

Fig. 3.4. Time-independent relationship between the TFRU and *K* value and between the hardness and *K* value over the storage period

of the panel on day 17–18, the *K* value was 39%. This value differs among different species, as shown in Table 3.3.

3.4.2.3
Texture Assessment

Texture measurements can be used to determine structural changes. Texture of fish is commonly tested in the industry by the "finger method". A finger is pressed on the skin and firmness is evaluated as a combination of the hardness when pressed on fish and the mark or hole left in the fish after pressing. This technique is not desirable in the retail situation. This method depends to a large extent upon subjective evaluation of the person who is performing the measurements [30]. Texture of raw fish can be measured by different methods using mechanical food testing equipment. The main techniques applied for fish are puncture, compression, shear and tensile stress. Among them, the shearing force and compression methods are recommended to be used for fresh fish [29]. When the texture of raw fish is measured, hardness and springiness are often the major variables [6].

Hardness of cultured sea bream was measured for a period of up to 23 days. There was a good time-independent relationship between the hardness and the *K* value with r^2 value of linear regression ($r^2 = 0.99$) over the storage period (Fig. 3.4). There were statistically significant ($P < 0.05$) differences in hardness during the storage period. Initial hardness of fish was 7.4 N on day 1 and gradually decreased over the storage period. When the fish was considered unacceptable on day 17–18, the hardness of fish was just over 5 N. This value may differ between species. Measurement of hardness in fish can be used as a quality indicator and shows good correlation with sensory and chemical results. Borderias et al. [5] found that comparison of texture measurements of fish with sensory analysis have shown good correlation in some cases. Although the shearing force is recommended to be used for raw salmon fillets compared to the compression method [29], the later is less destructive than the shearing force.

3.4.3 Freshness Assessment of Cultured Rainbow Trout Stored in Ice

In this experimental work *K* and related values were compared with those of the EU grading system over the storage period in ice. *K* and related values of ice stored rainbow trout are shown in Table 3.4. The *K* value of rainbow trout was 19.1 ± 3.1% on day 1. In recently harvested rainbow trout this value is expected to be less than 20%.

Almost linear increases were found in *K* value up to day 11. It was observed, however, that the rate of increase in *K* value slowed down, producing a curve beyond the acceptable limit of the fish (i.e. *K* value > 80%). After 11 days, the ATP breakdown reaction [9] is almost complete and the levels of the last three components [inosine 5′-monophosphate (IMP), inosine (Ino) and hypoxanthine (Hx)] in the pathway are changing very slowly. This is due to the relatively low levels of IMP remaining. No significant differences ($P > 0.05$) were found be-

Table 3.4. Changes on *K* and related values of rainbow trout stored in ice

Day	Sensory grades	*K* value (%)	*Ki* value (%)	*G* value (%)	*H* value (%)	*Fr* value (%)
1	E	19.1 ± 3.1	20.2 ± 3.2	20.3 ± 3.2	2.0 ± 0.5	79.8 ± 3.2
2	E	27.0 ± 1.5	28.8 ± 0.6	29.2 ± 0.6	3.1 ± 0.8	71.2 ± 0.7
4	A	40.6 ± 3.7	42.0 ± 3.5	43.8 ± 3.8	5.0 ± 0.4	58.0 ± 3.5
7	A–B	59.6 ± 2.1	62.5 ± 2.5	66.8 ± 2.1	7.3 ± 1.0	37.5 ± 2.5
9	B	77.2 ± 2.7	83.2 ± 3.2	97.9 ± 4.8	15.9 ± 2.8	16.8 ± 3.2
11	B–C	88.1 ± 3.2	91.5 ± 1.3	121.7 ± 5.6	24.8 ± 3.3	8.5 ± 1.3
14	C	90.3 ± 3.3	98.2 ± 1.3	141.4 ± 2.8	31.4 ± 1.4	1.8 ± 1.4

tween *K* and *Ki* values of rainbow trout during the 14 days of storage period; thus both values could be used a freshness indicators.

The *G* value followed a trend similar to the *K* value up to 7 days after harvesting, then rose to its maximum level (141 %) on day 14. The *G* value measures the ratio of Ino and Hx to the AMP, IMP and Ino concentrations [8]; thus the *G* value may be more useful for the fish species that accumulate Ino rather than Hx. However, in rainbow trout both Ino and Hx were accumulated. This was the reason why the *G* value exceeds the 100 % level.

The *H* value is expressed as the ratio of Hx to total concentrations of IMP, Ino and Hx [22]. Since the accumulation of Hx was very small up to 7 days, and then showed gradual increases with rest of the storage period, highly significant differences ($P < 0.01$) were observed between the *H* value and the rest of them (*K*, *Ki*, *G* and *Fr*) over the storage period.

The EU sensory grading system for cultured rainbow trout was modified (Table 3.5) and used for sensory assessment. Fish were graded as follows: Extra

Table 3.5. Modified EU sensory grading scheme for cultured rainbow trout

Parameters being assessed	Grade			
	E	A	B	C
Skin	Green/grey colours; iridescent over all body; well defined lateral line with pink colouration; spots on upper surface; clear mucus developing over all surface	Green/grey colours; iridescent over all body; lateral line pink colouration fading slightly; clear mucus over all surface	Loss of bright colours; no iridescence; washed out appearance of colours; patchy iridescence	Dull/greyish colour
Texture	Stiff	Firm	Slight softening	Limp and floppy, finger impression remains
Eyes	Bulging with protruding lens; shiny jet black/blue pupil with metallic brown iris; transparent eye cup	Convex; no no clouding of lens	Plain; slight clouding of lens and wrinkling of iris; clouding of eye cap	Sunken eye and cloudy lens
Gills appearance	Uniformly pink with free blood and water clear slime	Loss of colour with pale margins to gills	Further loss of colour with patchy bleaching; increase in slime	Bleached; fading to yellow/brown; thick slime
Gills odour	Fresh neutral; fresh-cut grass; earthy	Fresh-cut grass; earthy; muddy	Bready malty; musty slightly sour; caprylic; old grass cuttings: strong oily	Composted grass; ammonia; slightly sweet/fruity; chloroform like; slight rancid oil

(E), A, B or Unfit (C) [10, 20]. Rainbow trout which were up to 2 days old in ice without any temperature abuse or delayed icing and had an average *K* value of 27.0% were assessed as E grade (Table 3.4). The fish were assessed grade A on day 4. On day 7, when the *K* value was almost 60%, they were graded lower grade A and upper grade B. This point may be considered as the beginning of grade B. On day 9, the fish were on the acceptability limit (grade B), with *K* value of 78%. Therefore, rainbow trout with *K* value beyond 80% may be considered inappropriate for consumption.

K and *Ki* values were well correlated with the EU grading system, showing a linear relationship with time of storage, enabling prediction of shelf life, whereas *H* value did not followed a linear increase. This value was low, and therefore the *H* value may not be considered as a good indicator of freshness for rainbow trout. *Fr* value also shows a potential freshness index (as does *K* value) with values greater than 20% indicating the acceptability of trout. However, in contrast to the *K* value, a high *Fr* value will be considered as premium freshness of fish and a low *Fr* value will represent poor quality fish.

3.5 Conclusions

Freshness, quality and safety are the three important words in seafoods to be considered. The selection of rapid, simple and reliable methods for assessing freshness and quality of fish is important for fish retailers and processors. Whatever non-sensory methods are being used for assessing the quality of fish, sensory evaluation should be conducted to ensure that those results show good agreement with the objective sensory methods.

Generally, *K*, *Ki* and *G* values for cultured sea bream and *K* and *Ki* values for cultured rainbow trout showed good correlation with the degree of freshness and can be used as freshness indictors for both fish. These values were also correlated well with modified TFRU scoring schemes (sea bream) and EU grading schemes (rainbow trout) over the storage period.

References

1. Alasalvar C, Quantick PC (1997) Temperature modelling and relationships in fish transportation. In: Hall GM (ed) Fish processing technology, 2nd edn. Blackie Academic and Professional, London, pp 249–288
2. Alasalvar C, Taylor KDA, Öksüz A, Garthwaite T, Alexis MN, Grigorakis K (2001) Freshness assessment of cultured sea bream (*Sparus aurata*) by chemical, physical and sensory methods. Food Chem 72: 33–40
3. Ashie INA, Smith JP, Simpson BK (1996) Spoilage and shelf-life extension of fresh fish and shellfish. Crit Rev Food Sci Nutr 36: 87–121
4. Bonnel AD (1994) Quality assurance in seafood processing: a practical guide. Chapman and Hall, London
5. Borderias AJ, Lamua M, Tejada M (1983) Texture analysis of fish fillets and minced fish by both sensory and instrumental methods. Food Technol 18: 85–95
6. Botta JR (1991) Instrument for non-destructive texture measurement of raw Atlantic cod *(Gadus morhua)*. J Food Sci 65: 962–968

7. Botta JR (1995) Sensory evaluation: freshness quality grading. In: Botta JR (ed) Evaluation of seafood freshness quality. VCH Publishers, New York, pp 65–97
8. Burns GB, Kee PJ, Irvine BB (1985) Objective procedure for fish freshness evaluation based on nucleotide changes using a HPLC system. Canadian Technical Report of Fisheries and Aquatic Science No 1373
9. Chiba A, Hamaguchi M, Kosaka M, Tokuno T, Asai T, Chichibu S (1991) Quality evaluation of fish meat by ^{31} phosphorus. J Food Sci 56: 660–664
10. Connell JJ, Shewan JM (1980) Sensory and non-sensory assessment of fish. In: Connell JJ (ed) Advances in fish science and technology. Fishing News Book, London, pp 56–65
11. Connell JJ (1975) Control of fish quality. Fishing News Books, London
12. CSIRO (1984) CSIRO Division of Food Research, Annual Report. CSIRO Division of Food Research, Canberra, Australia
13. Dillon M, McEachern V (1997) HACCP and quality assurance of seafood. In: Hall GM (ed) Fish processing technology. Blackie Academic and Professional, London, pp 224–248
14. Ehira S, Uchiyama H (1987) Determination of fish freshness using the *K* value and comments on some other biochemical changes in relation to freshness In: Kramer DE, Liston J (eds) Seafood quality determination. Elsevier Science Publishers, Amsterdam, pp 185–207
15. European Union (1996) Council Regulations (EC) No 2406/96 of 26 November 1996. Laying down common marketing standards for certain fishery products. Official Journal of the European Communities 1996, No L-334/2
16. Gill TA, Thompson JW, Gould S, Sherwood D (1987) Characterisation of quality deterioration of yellowfin tuna. J Food Sci 52: 580–583
17. Gormley R (2000) Freshness, quality and safety in seafoods. Flair-Flow Europe Technical Manual (F-FE 380A/00) [ISBN 1 84170 110 6], May 2000
18. Hanna J (1992) Rapid microbial methods and fresh fish quality assessment. In: Hall GM (ed) Fish processing technology, 1st edn. Blackie Academic and Professional, London, pp 275–305
19. Howgate PF (1982) Quality assessment and quality control. In: Aitken A, Mackie IM, Merrit JH, Windsor ML (eds) Fish handling and processing. HMSO Press, Edinburgh, pp 177–186
20. Howgate P, Johnston A, Whittle KJ (1992) Multilingual guide to EC freshness grades for fishery products. Torry Research Station and MAFF, Aberdeen, Scotland
21. Karube I, Matsuoka H, Suzuki S, Watanabe E, Toyama K (1984) Determination of fish freshness with an enzyme sensor system. J Agric Food Chem 32: 314–319
22. Luong JHT, Male KB, Masson C, Nguyen AL (1992) Hypoxanthine ratio determination in fish extract using capillary electrophoresis and immobilised enzymes. J Food Sci 57: 77–81
23. Meilgaard G, Civille V, Carr BT (1991) Sensory evaluation techniques, 2nd edn. CRC Press, Boca Raton, USA
24. Ólafsdóttir G, Martinsdóttir E, Oehlenschläger J, Dalgaard P, Jensen B, Undeland I, Mackie IM, Henehan G, Nielsen J, Nilsen H (1997) Methods to evaluate fish freshness in research and industry. Trends Food Sci Technol 8: 258–265
25. Pedrosa-Menabrito A, Regenstein JM (1990) Shelf-life extension of fresh fish – a review. Part III – fish quality and methods of assessment. J Food Qual 13: 209–223
26. Ryder JM (1985) Determination of adenosine triphosphate and its breakdown products in fish muscle by high-performance liquid chromatography. J Agric Food Chem 33: 678–680
27. Saito T, Arai K, Matsuyoshi M (1959) A new method for estimating the freshness of fish. Bull Japan Soc Sci Fish 24: 749–750
28. Shewan JM, Mackintosh RG, Tucker CG, Ehrenberg ASC (1953) The development of a numerical scoring system for the sensory assessment of the spoilage of wet white fish stored in ice. J Sci Food Agric 6: 183–189
29. Sigurgisladottir S, Hafsteinsson H, Jonsson A, Lie O, Nortvedt R, Thomassen M, Torrissen O (1999) Textural properties of raw salmon fillets as related to sampling method. J Food Sci 64: 99–104

30. Sigurgisladottir S, Torrissen O, Lie O, Thomassen M, Hafsteinsson H (1997) Salmon quality: methods to determine the quality parameters. Rev Fish Sci 5: 1–30
31. Sørensen NK (1992) Physical and instrumental methods for assessing seafood quality. In: Huss HH (ed) Quality assurance in the fish industry. Elsevier Science Publishers, Amsterdam, pp 321–332
32. Storey RM, Mills A (1976) Instrumental techniques applied to the measurement of fish quality. Process Biochem 11: 25–28

4 Eating Quality of Deep-Water Fish Species and their Products

MARTINE BRENNAN, RONAN GORMLEY

The quality of 23 frozen under-utilised fish species was examined. The species were spot samples of deep-water fish caught near the Rockall Trough. Lead, cadmium and mercury concentrations were determined for six species and were much lower than the maximum levels set in 1992. Ammonia levels were unacceptably high in three shark species. Some of the fish species had very high levels of drip loss on thawing, indicative of freezing damage; others were potentially difficult to fillet automatically. Sensory analysis showed that, as fillets, taste panellists preferred six species to cod, while, presented as nuggets and fish-cakes, ten and eight species, respectively, were preferred to cod. Orange roughy, black scabbard, morid cod and Portuguese dogfish scored particularly well for acceptability. Some of the species that were very tough or soft as fillets, scored much better as nuggets, perhaps because their texture was improved by mincing. Skinless deep-water flying squid was preferred to commercially sourced squid (*Illex coindetti*), due to its texture and flavour. This study has highlighted that many under-utilised deep-water fish species are highly acceptable. If deep-water fishing gear is not prohibitively expensive and marketing is managed well, then there will be good potential for commercial gain from deep-water fishing.

4.1 Introduction

Cod has been popular for many years but recently there have been major concerns that the stocks of cod and other popular species around Ireland and the UK are in decline. To reduce the risk of extinction of the species, quotas are in place to restrict over-fishing and catching of immature fish. This has led to the exploitation of deep-water fish species. This fishery developed in the late 1980s and the main countries fishing the North-East Atlantic deep-water are Iceland, The Faroes, France, The Netherlands and Norway. Markets have been developed in France, Spain and the USA [1–3], but deep-water fish are still relatively unknown to Irish and British consumers.

Deep-water fish are nominally those found deeper than 500 m. The Fisheries Research Centre of the Irish Marine Institute and An Bord Iaschaigh Mhara (Irish Sea Fisheries Board) have been carrying out surveys of North Atlantic deep-water fish since the late 1980s [4–6]. They have been assessing the slopes of the continental shelf and, in particular, the slopes of the Rockall Trough which lie to the west of Scotland and Ireland. Their aim was to obtain information on the age of deep-water fish populations, their maturity and reproduction. This is important because many deep-water fish are vulnerable to over-fishing due to their longevity (more than 80 years for orange roughy [7]) and slow sexual maturity (about 25 years for orange roughy). Part of the attraction of these species is that catch sizes are unrestricted by quotas, but careful management is recommended to avoid over-exploitation.

Some of the species that were caught in these surveys are already used commercially. For example, black scabbard is popular in Portugal, there is a large orange roughy fishery in New Zealand [7], and argentines were heavily fished in the late 1980s [4]. However, the aim of the research program at The National Food Centre was to quantify the acceptability of a large number of deep-water fish species and assess which species were suited to the manufacture of fish products.

4.2 Materials and Methods

4.2.1 Catching and Storage of the Fish

Fish were caught by personnel from the Fisheries Research Centre (FRC) during two deep-water surveys in August and October/November 1997 [5, 6]. The fish were from hauls and longline catches from depths of 500 to 1400 m on the eastern slopes of the Rockall Trough. The fish were identified, gutted, filleted (most species) and frozen at sea, then stored frozen at the FRC and the National Food Centre at –25 °C until required. Twenty-two species were obtained in quantities varying from 1 to 42 kg. There were 7 species of shark (5 dogfish sharks and two rabbitfish), 14 bony fish (including tusk, ling and greater argentine) and a cephalopod (flying squid). Cod was used as a control species: fresh fillets were purchased, then blast frozen (–30 °C) and stored at –25 °C until required.

4.2.2 Concentrations of Heavy Metals and Micro-Organisms

Samples of six species were freeze-dried and analysed for heavy metals. Lead and cadmium were determined by digestion and atomic absorption, while mercury was analysed by oxidation and atomic fluorescence [8].

Thawed fish samples of 10 g were stomached with 90 ml diluent and tested by pour plate method to determine the total viable plate count. Incubation was at 30 °C for 72 h.

4.2.3 Colour and Toughness of Flesh

Portions (approximately 200 g) of each fish species were thawed overnight at 4 °C. Flesh colour was measured using a calibrated Minolta Chroma Meter (CR-331) using CIE illuminant D65 as the light source and a 5 cm^2 aperture. For each species five measurements were taken, evenly spaced over the entire flesh surface. The mean values of each species were recorded in the Hunter Lab colour space. The fish were placed in plastic containers, covered in perforated cling film (to reduce water loss) and cooked in a microwave oven (850 W for 2 min). They were cooled at room temperature to about 20 °C. The colour was re-measured, as above, then shear values were determined for 50 g portions of the cooled flesh using a calibrated Kramer design T-2000 Texture Test System with a standard shear compression cell (model CS-1). The mean shear value for duplicate samples was calculated for each species.

4.2.4 Sensory Evaluation

A pool of 20 tasters was formed from work colleagues who liked fish. Fillets of four deep-water species plus cod were thawed overnight at 4 °C, then portioned into pieces of approximately 2 × 2 × 1 cm which were cooked in plastic trays covered with perforated cling film in a microwave oven (850 W for 2 min). They were presented anonymously to twelve taste panellists who were asked to score each species for acceptability by marking a 6 cm line on which 0 cm represented least acceptable and 6 cm represented most acceptable. The acceptability scores were measured and the mean score of all the taste panellists for each species was calculated. The panellists were also invited to add comments about each fish. The panel (four deep-water species plus cod) was repeated on different days until all the fish species were scored. All of the tasters were from the pool of 20 and, where possible, the same 12 tasters were used each time. The same method of evaluation was followed for the nuggets and fish-cakes using the appropriate product made from cod as an unlabelled control.

4.2.5 Preparation of Fish Products

4.2.5.1 *Nuggets*

Fish pieces were thawed overnight at 4 °C. The skin and bones (or cartilage) were removed and the flesh was processed through the grating disk (5 mm diameter holes) of a food processor. Ice cube trays were filled with grated flesh to form nuggets of approximately 2 × 3 × 2 cm. The trays of nuggets were frozen in an air-blast freezer at −30 °C, then bagged and stored at −25 °C for 1–4 days. The nuggets were individually coated in lemon crisp pre-dust, soft batter and crumb, then flash-fried in vegetable oil at 190 °C for 20 s. They were refrozen at −30 °C, as above, then stored at −25 °C. When required, final cooking involved deep-frying in vegetable oil for 8 min at 160 °C which allowed the centre of the nuggets to reach >70 °C.

4.2.5.2 *Fish-Cakes*

Each fish sample was thawed and cooked in a microwave oven (1000 W for 2–4 min). The flesh was flaked and 200 g were mixed with 36 g potato flakes, 144 g water, 20 g binder and 0.4 ml liquid smoke. The mixtures were each shaped into six fish-cakes then coated with crumbs, blast-frozen at −30 °C and stored at −25 °C. When required, the fish-cakes were deep-fried in vegetable oil at 170 °C for 6 min.

4.3 Results and Discussion

4.3.1 Concentrations of Heavy Metals and Micro-Organisms

Examination of trace metals in the deep sea is not widely reported because the deep-waters are subjected to less human pollution than coastal waters, and because the fish stocks are less exploited [9]. However, the long-life of some deep-water species poses the concern that, with time, metals could accumulate to unacceptably high levels.

Mercury is the only heavy metal for which there is an EC maximum limit for fishery products (0.5 µg/g, wet weight). For physiological reasons, some species (including Portuguese dogfish) accumulate mercury more readily than others and so have a higher EC acceptable limit of 1.0 µg/g, wet weight. There are no EC standards for lead and cadmium in fish; however, some countries have developed standards or guidelines and the strictest of these are included Table 4.1. The values obtained from the current study were well within the strictest standards in Europe (Table 4.1).

It should be noted that this was a very small study of only six fish of unspecified age. The concentration of mercury in orange roughy caught near New Zealand increased with fish length and thus, presumably age [10]. Evidence of homeostasis of some trace metals [9] and excretion of cadmium [11] have been observed in deep-water shark, suggesting that accumulation of metals to high levels might not be a problem in some species. More detailed studies are underway at the FRC.

Table 4.1. Lead, cadmium and mercury concentrations of selected fish species

Species	Concentration (µg/g)		
	Lead	Cadmium	Mercury
Black scabbard	0.0058 ± 0.0003	0.0043 ± 0.0005	0.0002 ± 0.00006
Greater argentine	0.0146 ± 0.0003	0.0034 ± 0.0004	0.0001 ± 0.00006
Portuguese dogfish	0.0101 ± 0.0004	0.0056 ± 0.0005	0.0024 ± 0.00007
Roundnose grenadier	0.0050 ± 0.0004	0.0069 ± 0.0005	0.0001 ± 0.00006
Orange roughy	0.0039 ± 0.0003	0.0034 ± 0.0004	0.0002 ± 0.00007
Morid cod	0.0060 ± 0.0004	0.0018 ± 0.0005	0.0005 ± 0.00007
Standard	0.5[a]	0.1[a]	0.5[b]

Data are expressed as mean±SD (n: 2), on a fresh weight basis.

[a] Dutch standard, which is the strictest maximum limit used by countries participating in the Oslo and Paris Conventions.

[b] EC maximum limit, but a higher value of 1.0 is set for some species including black scabbard and Portuguese dogfish.

Microbial loads were within acceptable limits for raw fish, with only five species having more than 1×10^5 colony forming units (cfu)/g but none with more than 6×10^5 cfu/g. The species with very low microbial counts (10^1–10^2 cfu/g) were sharks and ling. These species received less handling before freezing because they were not filleted.

4.3.2 Fish Appearance

Many of the deep-water fish are somewhat ugly. Some of the fish have characteristics suited to the low light intensity and high pressures associated with deep-waters, such as large eyes and tough scales; others have long tapering bodies. For successful marketing of these fish species, it may be necessary to sell them only as fillets, steaks and in products to avoid the consumer from being put off by the appearance. For fillets and steaks the colour of the flesh is important; ideally it should be very white, not very yellow, and not grey. Raw and cooked flesh colours are both important as they influence the purchaser and consumer, respectively. Colour measurements showed that raw and cooked leafscale gulper shark, Baird's smoothead and Portuguese dogfish had the highest white:yellow ratio, and were considerably whiter than cod. Table 4.2 shows the species with the highest and lowest white:yellow ratio values, together with cod.

4.3.3 Fish Texture

The texture of fish can have a big influence on its acceptability. Table 4.3 shows the species with the lowest and highest shear values, together with cod as a comparison. The three least tough species were all sharks, but the most tough species was also a shark. It should be noted that all the fish had been frozen and thawed and this can change fish texture.

Table 4.2. Colour (white to yellow ratio) of raw and cooked fish flesh

Species [a]	L/b raw [b]	L/b cooked [b]
Leafscale gulper shark	52 ± 3.1	19 ± 2.1
Baird's smoothead	40 ± 3.4	10 ± 3.1
Portuguese dogfish	22 ± 2.0	16 ± 1.4
Cod	13 ± 1.2	11 ± 1.5
Bluemouth rockfish	8 ± 1.0	7 ± 1.7
Snake mackerel	6 ± 1.3	7 ± 2.6
Spotted wolf-fish	7 ± 2.0	6 ± 1.7

Data are expressed as mean±SD (n: 5).

[a] The three most and three least white species are listed, together with cod.

[b] Hunter Lab scale; L: whiteness, b: yellowness.

Table 4.3. Shear values of cooked fish flesh

Species[a]	Shear value (N/50 g)
Rabbitfish	426 ± 0.5
Leafscale gulper shark	474 ± 52
Birdbeak dogfish	539 ± 7
Cod	800 ± 28
Blue ling	1551 ± 77
Tusk	1607 ± 82
Small-eyed rabbitfish	2372 ± 95

Data are expressed as mean ± SD (n: 2)
[a] The three least and three most tough species are listed, together with cod.

4.3.4 Sensory Analysis of Fillets

The mean score for each species (Table 4.4) showed that six species were preferred to cod. Orange roughy, black scabbard, morid cod and greater argentine scored 3.9, while snake mackerel and Portuguese dogfish scored 3.8 and cod scored 3.6. Ten other species scored at least 3.0, i.e. at least 50% along the score line. Two species scored less than 2.0; these were rabbitfish and flying squid (see below). Leafscale gulper shark, ling and cod were frequently described as bland while some of the sharks had a sweetish flavour.

Deep-water flying squid was also compared to commercially available frozen squid species. The squid pieces were thawed overnight at 4°C and boiled in a tomato sauce. A taste panel found no significant ($P > 0.05$) difference in preference between flying squid, long finned squid (*Lologo vulgaris*) and squid from Taiwan (*Illex coindetti*). However, when a layer of skin was removed from the squid prior to cooking, the toughness was reduced and the flying squid was preferred over skinless squid from Taiwan. Based on flavour alone, the flying squid was preferred due to its savoury, less salty taste.

4.3.5 Sensory Analysis of Fish Products

Processing has the potential to change or disguise fish appearance, flavour or texture. An assessment of the eating quality of fish nuggets and fish-cakes was carried out to see if processing had the potential to increase acceptability of species which were less desirable as fillets.

As nuggets, ten species were preferred to cod (Table 4.4) and a further five species had mean scores of ≥3.0 (on a scale of 0 to 6). Most species received higher scores as nuggets than as fillets; for example, orange roughy scored 4.7 and 3.9, respectively, and leafscale gulper shark, 4.1 and 2.8. Mincing the flesh may have improved the texture. Processing in this way increased the number of species which have potential for exploitation. Fish nuggets should also be con-

Table 4.4. Mean acceptability scores from twelve taste panellists for fish and fish products

Species		Acceptability scores[a]		
English name	Latin name	Fillet	Nugget	Cake
Orange roughy	*Hoplostethus atlanticus*	**3.9 ± 1.9**	**4.7 ± 1.1**	2.7 ± 1.4
Morid cod	*Mora moro*	**3.9 ± 1.3**	**4.2 ± 1.3**	**3.7 ± 1.7**
Black scabbard	*Aphanopus carbo*	**3.9 ± 1.5**	**3.8 ± 1.2**	**3.6 ± 1.5**
Greater argentine	*Argentina silus*	**3.9 ± 1.5**	nd	**3.4 ± 1.8**
Portuguese dogfish	*Centroscymnus coelolepis*	**3.8 ± 1.0**	**4.1 ± 1.3**	2.8 ± 1.3
Snake mackerel	*Nessiarchus nassutus*	**3.8 ± 1.2**	nd	2.7 ± 1.2
Cod	*Gadus morhua*	3.6 ± 1.3	3.7 ± 1.3	3.0 ± 1.5
Roundnose grenadier	*Coryphaenoides rupestris*	3.5 ± 1.5	**4.0 ± 1.3**	nd
Baird's smoothead	*Alepocephalus bairdii*	3.4 ± 1.4	**4.1 ± 0.9**	2.3 ± 1.7
Wolf-fish	*Anarhichas lupus*	3.4 ± 1.3	**4.1 ± 1.0**	**3.4 ± 1.3**
Bluemouth rockfish	*Helicolenus dactylopterus*	3.3 ± 1.7	3.4 ± 1.1	**3.5 ± 1.6**
Redfish	*Sebastes mentella*	3.3 ± 1.0	nd	nd
Greater lantern shark	*Etmopterus princeps*	3.2 ± 1.3	3.1 ± 1.7	3.0 ± 1.3
Ling	*Molva molva*	3.1 ± 1.4	**4.0 ± 1.2**	**3.3 ± 1.4**
Tusk	*Brosme brosme*	3.0 ± 1.3	**4.0 ± 1.5**	**3.3 ± 1.5**
Forkbeard	*Phycis blennoides*	3.0 ± 1.6	3.0 ± 1.1	2.5 ± 1.6
Blue whiting	*Micromesistius poutassou*	3.0 ± 1.0	nd	**3.2 ± 1.3**
Leafscale gulper shark	*Centrophorus squamosus*	2.8 ± 1.3	**4.1 ± 1.3**	2.7 ± 1.2
Blue ling	*Molva dipterygia*	2.8 ± 1.3	3.7 ± 1.4	2.9 ± 1.6
Longnose velvet dogfish	*Centroscymnus crepidater*	2.7 ± 1.5	3.2 ± 1.2	2.8 ± 1.4
Birdbeak dogfish	*Deania calceus*	2.6 ± 1.8	1.8 ± 1.5	-
Small-eyed rabbitfish	*Hydrolagus affinis*	2.3 ± 1.4	1.4 ± 0.7	-
Flying squid	*Todarodes sagittatus*	1.7 ± 1.4	1.9 ± 1.3	-
Rabbitfish	*Chimaera monstrosa*	1.6 ± 1.5	1.0 ± 0.9	-
	No. of species tasted[b]	24	20	18
	No. of species preferred to cod	6	10	8

Data are expressed as mean ± SD (n: 12).
[a] 0: Least acceptable; 6: most acceptable.
[b] Including cod.
nd: not determined due to lack of sample.
-: Not determined.
Scores in **bold** are those greater than the corresponding score for cod.

sidered for species which were highly acceptable as fillets but still scored better as nuggets. The three species which scored at least 0.5 units lower as nuggets than as fillets were those which had high concentrations of free ammonia (mg N/100 g): birdbeak dogfish 76, small-eyed rabbitfish 98 and rabbitfish 207 (other species had 7–30 mg N/100 g). Unless the ammonia level can be controlled [12, 13], these species are not suitable for use in products.

The mean acceptability scores for fish-cakes showed that eight species were preferred to cod (Table 4.4). Orange roughy was not well suited to the fish-cake recipe because of its stringy texture and Baird's smoothead was too soggy.

4.3.6
Problems for Processors

Differences between some deep-water and highly utilised species may create problems for fish processors. For example, bones may be a problem in manufacturing nuggets and fish-cakes which, ideally, should be boneless. Greater argentine, which has many small bones, and Baird's smoothead, with many long bones, were particularly difficult to de-bone. The possibility of scales getting mixed with flesh may also be a problem. In the laboratory, tiny black scales from the longnose velvet dogfish and large tough pink scales from the bluemouth rockfish were particularly noticeable. Similar problems have been reported for grenadiers while staining of flesh with a black inky substance is a problem with black scabbard [14].

The shape of the fish can pose problems where automatic processing equipment has not been designed to cope with large heads and long, tapering bodies. If automation is impossible, then the cost of processing these fish may be prohibitive.

Drip loss on thawing was very high for some of the species: 40 wt% (of frozen fish) for spotted wolf-fish and Baird's smoothead, 25% for leafscale gulper shark and 20% for longnose velvet dogfish and roundnose grenadier. This represents a loss in money for processors. The effect of drip loss on the texture of the fish has not been assessed because fresh fish samples were unavailable. For some species it is likely that high drip loss is linked to deleterious effects of freeze-thawing on structure, such as toughening or over-drying. However, for other species the drip loss may have beneficial effects, such as firming the flesh.

4.4
Conclusions

The results reported here indicate that many deep-water species are of acceptable eating quality. Of the 23 species examined in the current tests, 14 were preferred to cod as either fillets, nuggets or fish-cakes. Processing the fish into nuggets and other added-value products increased the number of acceptable species. Orange roughy, black scabbard, morid cod and Portuguese dogfish were the most acceptable species. Five others scored at least 3.0 (scale: 0–6) and flying squid was preferred to commercialised squid species. Thus, it is concluded that 20 of the species in the current study have potential value.

Acknowledgements. We acknowledge, with gratitude, grant aid under the Marine Research Measure of the Operational Programmed for Fisheries. The programme is administered by the Marine Institute and is part-financed by the EU European Regional Development Fund. The results presented here and at the 3rd Biannual European Conference on Fish Processing highlight the deep-water fish programme carried out at the National Food Centre. Other work includes: composition, polyunsaturated fatty acids, smoked fish, the effect of freeze-thaw cycles on quality, and the use of cryoprotectants to reduce freeze-thaw damage. Details are available from the authors.

References

1. Gregory H (1995) Deepwater species offer resource hope. Seafood Int 10: 30–31
2. Monfort MC (1992) New species to the rescue. Seafood Int 7: 33–35
3. Moustgaard P (1992) An industry under reconstruction. Seafood Int 7: 31–35
4. McCormick R (1995) The Irish experience of deep-water fishing in the North East Atlantic. In: Hopper AG (ed) Deep-water fisheries of the North Atlantic oceanic slope. Kluwer Academic Publishers, Dordrecht, pp 297–305
5. Clarke M, Kelly CJ, Connolly PL (1999) Preliminary catch, discards and selectivity results of a trawl survey in the deep water slopes of the Rockall Trough in 1997. Fishery Leaflet 178. Marine Institute, Dublin
6. Connolly PL, Kelly CJ, Clarke M, Haredie NR (1999) Deep water longline survey on the eastern slopes of the Rockall Trough in 1997. Fishery Leaflet 180. Marine Institute, Dublin
7. Clark M (1995) Experience with management of orange roughy (*Hoplostethus atlanticus*) in New Zealand waters, and the effects of commercial fishing on stocks over the period 1980–1993. In: Hopper AG (ed) Deep-water fisheries of the North Atlantic oceanic slope. Kluwer Academic Publishers, Dordrecht, pp 251–266
8. Brennan MH, Gormley TR (1999) Quality and safety evaluation of non-quota/under-utilised fish species and their related products. The National Food Centre, Dublin
9. Vas P, Gordon JD, Fielden PR, Overnell J (1993) The trace metal ecology of ichthyofauna in the Rockall Trough, North-eastern Atlantic. Mar Pollut Bull 26: 607–612
10. Van den Broek WLF, Tracey DM (1981) Concentration and distribution of mercury in flesh of orange roughy (*Hoplostethus atlanticus*). N Z J Mar Freshwater Res 15: 244–260
11. Vas P, Gordon JDM (1988) Trace metals in deep-sea sharks from the Rockall Trough. Mar Pollut Bull 26: 400–402
12. Kailasapathy K, Salmampessy J (1999) Suitability of shark flesh for surimi production. Food Aust 51: 110–115
13. Anon (1987) Seafood deodorizing. Seafood Int 2: 48
14. MacNamara JP (1996) The handling, processing, storage and eating qualities of deep water fish. Seafish Report, SR453, Sea Fish Industry Authority, Hull, UK

5 Quality Control by Instrumental Texture Measurements

PAUL NESVADBA

Texture is an important attribute of the quality of fresh and frozen fish and fish products. After reviewing the scenarios for measurements of texture and types of texture measurement relating to the fish processing industry, the discussion focuses on physical instrumental methods of rapid non-destructive measurements of mechanical properties of fish muscle tissue. Lumped parameter mathematical models of dynamic viscoelastic behaviour are presented. These theoretical models, albeit very simplified in relation to the very complex behaviour of fish as a biomaterial, assist in modelling, analysis and interpretation of data. The concepts are illustrated by results for transient and oscillatory measurements obtained in the course of an European Union (EU) project CT98–4076 with both large commercial laboratory instruments and portable hand-held sensors and probes suitable for industrial fish processing scenarios. The results agree with sensory evaluation by the Quality Index Method (QIM).

5.1 Introduction

Quality of any product is judged by its fitness for a particular purpose. In the fish production and processing path there are various critical points where quality needs to be quantified. For example a fish buyer at fish market needs to assess the quality of fresh fish. A fish processor assesses the quality of imported frozen fish. A fish product developer monitors the various attributes of a newly formulated product to ensure its acceptance by the consumer. The consumer judges the quality of the fish product by several attributes such as appearance, colour, smell and feel. The fish product is ultimately eaten and therefore the sensations during chewing and swallowing are important as well. These sensory attributes depend on the textural properties of the product. Therefore there is a need to characterise and quantify these properties. Much effort has been devoted over many years to relating the textural properties to mechanical behaviour of foods measured by universal testing machines such as the Instron. However, the most reliable method is still a sensory panel in conjunction with an appropriate set of criteria for judging the quality. Bourne [4] concludes that there is generally a poor correlation between fundamental and sensory measurements.

The term 'texture' was initially used to describe the feel of surfaces, in particular textiles and is also used in computer analysis of images [6]. In food science and technology 'texture' is used to describe the mouth-feel of foods and even drinks. In this context 'texture' refers to mechanical properties of foods and is an important attribute of the quality of foods such as fresh and frozen fish and fish products. ISO [12] defines texture as a collection of all the rheological and structural (shape and surface) attributes of a food product. These are perceptible by mechanical, tactile and possibly also visual and even auditory receptors.

With instrumental methods becoming available, attempts started to correlate texture of foods with physical instrumental measurements of deformations resulting from applied forces. This task is fraught with difficulties because of the subjective nature of the sensory evaluation. The instrumental measurements in turn are affected by the inhomogeneity and variability of fish as any biological material. Therefore achieving the goal of obtaining a complete correlation between mouth-feel and instrumental measurements is very difficult.

5.2 Difficulties in Measuring Texture of Fish

The main problem is the complex and variable structure of fish. For whole fish the compression properties are influenced by the presence of the skin layer. For fillets the discrete nature of muscle blocks means that the scale of compression must be carefully chosen to give a meaningful representation of the average mechanical properties of the muscle. In this sense measurements of texture through the skin may be more robust as the skin acts as an envelope and provides a degree of spatial averaging. The muscle blocks themselves have complex structure of actomyosin fibres arranged in bundles [7, 11]. A large proportion (about 80%) of the muscle is water held by capillary forces between the bundles. Compression of the muscle leads to hydrodynamic effects of water displacement. The bundles are further assembled into skewed blocks (myotomes) measuring typically several millimetres and held together by connective tissue. Thus, except for very homogeneous muscles such as the adductor muscle in scallops, it is generally very difficult to excise samples with a uniform orientation of fibres and a reasonably isotropic structure. In addition, the structure is inhomogeneous on a medium scale (centimetres) because of the presence of skeletal bones. On the scale comparable with the dimensions of the fish, the presence of fish organs and the irregular geometry of the body of the fish may affect a compression test. These difficulties are common for all biological materials from the plant and animal kingdoms, including the human body. There is a high value in effective techniques for diagnosis of cancer and other diseases, conventionally based on palpation but increasingly being superseded by non-invasive imaging techniques [15]. Thus there is hope for a synergy between the developments of tissue characterisation in medical, plant and food sciences. With rapid progress in measurement technology we can be looking forward to solving hitherto intractable problems of structure and texture characterisation.

In spite of these difficulties, the value of instrumental measurements is in quantitative, objective determination of a number of mechanical properties. Second, interpretation of the results in terms of mechanical models allows an understanding of the mechanisms of deformation and fracture of muscle fibres. Such understanding and insight then allows prediction from a more theoretical basis than is possible from empirical sensory evaluations.

5.3
Sensory and Instrumental Tests for Texture of Fish

5.3.1
Sensory Tests of Texture as an Attribute of Quality

Trained (expert) or untrained (consumer, hedonic) panels can perform sensory tests. There are several scoring systems for expert panels and various methods for the untrained panel (for example the triangular test in which one sample is different from the other two). Increasingly the Quality Index Method (QIM), developed for some fish in recent years, is used in which various attributes of quality of fish (appearance, smell and texture) are assessed against set criteria and a demerit score is awarded for each attribute. The assessment can be carried out on raw fish. This obviates the need for cooking it and serving it warm to the sensory panel and feeling it in the mouth. The individual scores are then added together to obtain the total score. Thus a top quality fish scores 0 whilst spoiled fish has a high score (typically 15 or so). A somewhat easier task may be correlating instrumental readings with sensory observations when the surface of the food is felt with a finger under a moderate pressure. In this way raw fish can be evaluated without the need for cooking it.

The test for texture within assessment by the QIM takes into account the elasticity, firmness, plasticity, softness and the speed with which the indentation made by the finger disappears or any residual deformation that does not disappear. The human observer seems able to integrate these aspects and the resulting score is surprisingly consistent and repeatable (Fig. 5.1).

The QIM has been used as the reference method throughout the work. The QIM attribute relating to texture was "stiffness", scored on a scale 0–3, with 0 indicating firm elastic fish and 3 extremely soft fish. The scores were averaged over assessors and fish in a daily batch. Figure 5.1 clearly shows that QIM detected fish softening with storage time in ice, indicating that texture measurements are relevant for determination of fish freshness. As discussed later, this softening is also detectable by instrumental measurements that remove the subjective component of the QIM tests.

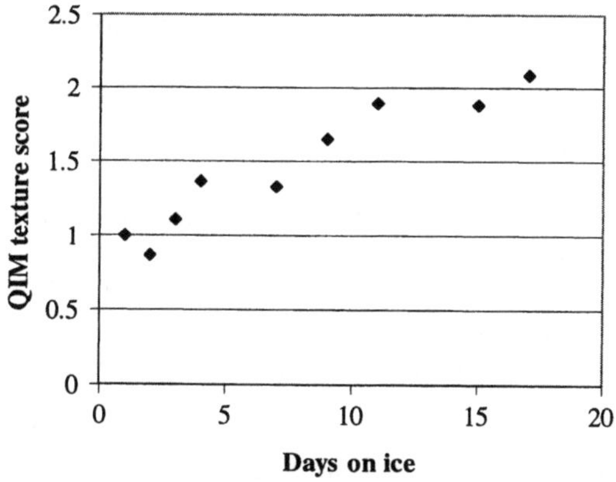

Fig. 5.1. QIM scores (0: firm, elastic; 3: soft, plastic) for the texture attribute only, for Atlantic cod (*Gadus morhua*) as a function of the days of chilled storage. The assessments were on five fish by nine assessors at the Icelandic Fisheries Laboratory in December 1999

Subjectivity in sensory tests such as the QIM is minimised by careful design of the quality criteria. The assessors have to be trained or at least briefed before the tests. It is also desirable to use several (six or more) panellists to obtain a robust estimate by averaging out the subjective variation between the judges. For all these reasons, constituting sensory assessment panels is expensive. This is why for many years there has been a search for rapid instrumental methods that could be easily used in the industry. Chemical methods of quality assessment are well established. However, physical methods are preferred whenever possible as they are generally faster and more convenient than chemical analyses [9].

5.3.2 Instrumental Tests for Texture of Fish and Fish Products

There are many instrumental methods that have been developed for measuring the mechanical properties of foods in general [4, 17, 22] and fish products in particular [2, 21]. These reviews classify tests according to whether they are destructive or non-destructive, fundamental or empirical (penetration, extrusion, cutting, flow or mixing), sensory or instrumental or imitative (attempt to simulate the action of the mouth), tests performed on large immobile laboratory instruments or portable hand-held instruments [3].

Many tests have been developed specifically for quantifying the quality or assisting in product development of specific products such as surimi gels and monitoring their gelling and storage performance. These tests help in understanding how texture is affected by microstructure such as the protein fibre matrix. This matrix is modified by the biochemical reactions of the autolytic and externally driven spoilage processes.

All tests can be divided into two groups depending on whether they are destructive or non-destructive. The applied force can be a shear force (Warner-Bratzler arrangement) or a compression or, less usually, a tensile force. It is possible also to use a mixture of shear and tensile forces (Kramer cell); this leads back to empirical correlation with sensory assessments.

Lewis [17] divides methods of texture determination into:

- *Imitative* – attempt to simulate mouth-feel
- *Empirical* – for example penetration by a punch or a cutter or extrusion or mixing – having the disadvantage that the pattern of forces is difficult to establish, and results are dependent on the particular conditions during experiment
- *Chemical and microscopic* examinations that relate texture to chemical composition that in turn determines the physical structure and texture – pectins in fruit are an example
- *Fundamental* in which the geometry of the sample is regular and permits the results to be given in universal physical units that are well established in the physics of deformation of materials

Two properties completely describe the behaviour of a purely elastic body – the Young's modulus, E, and the Poisson ratio, σ. The former is the ratio between the applied stress, F/A and the resulting strain, $\Delta y/y$, where F is the applied force acting over area A, and $\Delta y/y$ is the fractional change in the dimension y of the sample. If E does not change with varying F, then the material obeys Hooke's law. Since strain is a dimensionless number, the units of Young's modulus are the same as those of pressure (force per unit area). Tabulated values are normally in kPa or MPa (Pa = Pascal).

The Poisson ratio is a measure of compressibility of the material with values ranging between 0.5 (incompressible, for example fish muscle) and 0 (completely compressible, for example powders such as breadcrumbs). For materials that are viscoelastic (this means they return to their original shape after some relaxation time and therefore dissipate heat during deformation), the Young's modulus becomes a complex quantity $G^* = G' + iG''$. G' corresponds to the Young's modulus (representing stored and recoverable energy) whilst G'' represents the energy dissipation component. The physical dimension of these quantities is Pascal (Pa). G^* is conveniently determined from deformation y caused by a force F varying as a sine wave. Then $G' = \Delta y/\Delta F \cos\delta$, $G'' = \Delta y/\Delta F \sin\delta$, where δ is the amount (in radians) by which y lags behind F.

Food engineers require these and other mechanical properties for designing and monitoring food processing operations. A database described by Houška and Nesvadba [10] provides numerical values of properties derived from both sensory and instrumental measurements.

Figure 5.2 shows the most frequently used test for the mechanical properties of fish. This involves indentation of the surface of fish by a cylindrical indenter. The force and displacement of the indenter are measured and recorded as a function of time. The depth of indentation depends on whether the test is to be destructive or non-destructive (as far as practicable). Opinions vary as to what depth of indentation should be used if the measurement on fish is to be non-destructive. Some researchers indent by a fixed percentage of the thickness of the fish, others deform the fish by a small absolute amount unrelated to the thickness of the fish (assuming that the fish is sufficiently thick as to have no influence on the test).

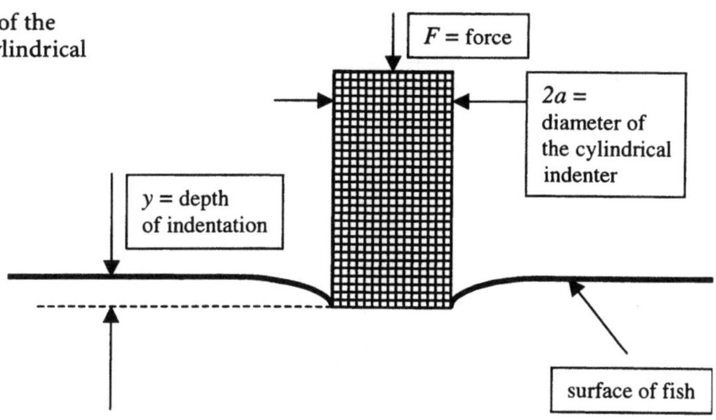

Fig. 5.2. Indentation of the surface of fish by a cylindrical indenter of radius a

If the depth of indentation y_C is small in comparison with the overall thickness of the sample (assumed to be elastic half-space), the classical solution of Boussinesq (1885) applies [13]:

$$y_C = \frac{(1-\sigma^2)}{2E}\,\frac{F}{a} \tag{5.1}$$

where y is the deformation, a is the radius of the indenter, F is the applied force, σ is the Poisson's ratio and E is the Young's modulus. As explained below, fish muscle is viscoelastic, interpreted in terms of the model shown in Fig. 5.3. Therefore two stages of indentation have to be distinguished. In the first stage there is a relatively rapid elastic compression by the amount y_{C1} (see Fig. 5.3 for definition). The fish is not changing its volume (water in the tissue has no time to be squeezed out sideways). The Poisson's ratio, σ, for an incompressible material is 0.5 and therefore Eq. (5.1) gives

$$E = \frac{3F}{8ay_{C1}} \tag{5.2}$$

For typical measurements on cod muscle [8] $a = 2$ mm, $F = 0.1$ N and $y_{C1} = 0.4$ mm, giving $E = 47$ kPa. This is of the same order as values of E obtained for

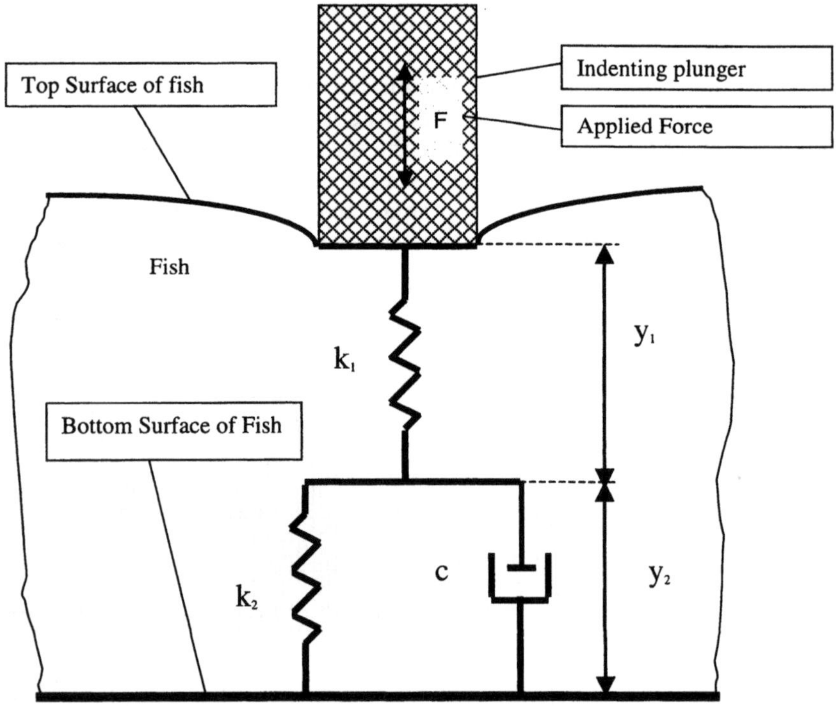

Fig. 5.3. A lumped parameter viscoelastic model of fish muscle

food gels [19]. Zheng et al. [26] report values of 14 kPa and 59 kPa for relaxed and contracted human forearm muscle, respectively. The advantage of the fundamental physical measurements is that the properties of the sample are given in terms of recognised physical properties (such as E and σ), independent of the experimental set up (sample geometry) used. Since in practice it is difficult to control the geometry of the sample, some degree of dependence of the experimental results on the experimental set up always persists.

5.3.3 Connection Between Sensory and Instrumental Tests

The connection between instrumental and sensory evaluations of texture is very important in view of the food being of necessity mechanically modified (normally by mastication) before it is consumed. Establishing this connection has become a quest extending over several decades of research leading to involvement of the psychology of human perception of food [23, 25]. The current state of the art is not satisfactory as there is no general model that would establish the connection. Nevertheless, some manufacturers of texture analysers have championed the use of terms such as firmness, cohesiveness, crispness, stickiness, chewiness and so on. These quantities are derived from various features of graphs of deformation vs applied force, for example ratios of slopes, areas and peak forces entering into empirical formulae. Such an approach is usually termed texture profiling [5] and can provide a close correlation with sensory assessment for some foods especially when used in conjunction with powerful statistical projection methods such as principal component analysis [16].

5.4 Modelling of Viscoelastic Properties in Terms of Lumped Parameters

Due to the polymeric structure of fish muscle and the presence of water, there are definite time-dependent effects where the observed properties depend on the rate of deformation. The simplest model is to view these viscoelastic phenomena as flow of water along the fibres. Creep and relaxation tests can quantify the viscoelastic behaviour. In a creep test the sample is subjected to a constant force (stress) and the displacement is measured as a function of time. In a relaxation test the sample is compressed (or elongated or expanded) by a fixed amount of strain. This leads to a peak force that then decreases due to the structure of the sample relaxing to accommodate partially the applied strain.

A general time-varying force $F(t)$ produces a time varying deformation $y(t)$. In principle it should be possible to derive all viscoelastic properties from such an experiment. However, in practice it is much easier to use $F(t)$ that is either a step or a sinusoidal function. Oscillatory measurements use the sinusoidal dependence whilst creep and relaxation experiments correspond to $F(t)$ being a step function. The resulting displacements are exponentials of the type $y = y_0 \exp(-t/\tau)$ and are easy to analyse. An oscillating force gives rise to oscillating displacement from which the ratio G''/G' can be obtained easily.

Although the fish muscle is a complex three-dimensional structure, the simplest approach to modelling its mechanical properties is to use a lumped parameter model. This is an arrangement of springs (totally elastic, non-dissipative elements) and dashpots (totally plastic, viscous dissipative elements). The simplest such arrangement consists of just one spring and one dashpot in parallel (Kelvin-Voigt element) or in series (Maxwell element). Figure 5.3 shows a three-element model (a Kelvin-Voigt element in series with a spring). This model is the simplest lumped parameter model that is able to capture the viscoelastic behaviour of fish muscle with any degree of realism.

There are other combination and parallel or series arrangements of springs and dashpots. These models originated in studies of polymers [1] and as most foods include high molecular weight biopolymers, these concepts are equally applicable to foods. Alfrey [1] employs a four-element (Burger's) model. Experiments suggest that the behaviour of fish muscle requires at least three elements and as many as seven have been employed [24]. The springs are assumed to deform in proportion with applied force. This assumption is reasonable if the strains do not exceed about 2 mm in fish muscle. However, there is some evidence that even such small deformations of fish muscle lead to a small amount of irreversible (plastic) deformation and departure from linearity. Non-linear elasticity models are much more difficult to use and their development is in a tentative stage.

A linear viscoelastic system can be described by a first-order differential equation:

$$a\frac{dF}{dt} + bF = c\frac{dy}{dt} + dy \tag{5.3}$$

where F is the applied force, y is the resulting displacement and a, b, c and d are non-negative parameters characterising the material.

Equation (5.3) shows that the way in which a viscoelastic system responds to an applied force depends on the speed of deformation. For very small speeds of deformation y is proportional to bF/d and Eq. (5.3) reduces to Hooke's law, d/b corresponding to the Young's modulus. For oscillatory force the complex modulus is $G^* = (d + i\omega c)/(b + i\omega a)$.

For the system in Fig. 5.3, Eq. (5.3) assumes the form

$$ck_1k_2\frac{dF}{dt} + (k_1 + k_2)F = k_2c\frac{dy}{dt} + y - yo \tag{5.4}$$

where y_0 is the thickness of the fish when there is no applied force (the springs have their equilibrium length). It can be shown that with a general applied force $F = F(t)$ the change in the lengths of the springs, $y - y_0$, and therefore the deflection of the top surface of the fish is given by Eq. (5.5):

$$y - y_0 = k_1F + \frac{1}{c}\exp\left(-\frac{t}{k_2c}\right)\int \exp\left(\frac{t}{k_2c}\right)Fdt \tag{5.5}$$

This equation can be used to model the deformation of the fish subjected to any time varying force F. In practice, three particular time variations of F are used: oscillatory, a step-wise increase (creep) and a step-wise decrease (relaxation). The corresponding mathematical models are described in the following sections.

5.4.1 Oscillatory Measurements

A harmonically varying force, $F = F_0 \sin(\omega.t)$ results in the displacement

$$y - y_0 = rF_0 \sin(\omega[t - \tau]) \tag{5.6}$$

where r and τ are given by Eqs. (5.7) and (5.8):

$$r = \sqrt{\left(k_1 + \frac{k_2}{1 + k_2^2c^2\omega^2}\right)^2 + \left(\frac{k_2^2 c\omega}{1 + k_2^2c^2\omega^2}\right)^2} \tag{5.7}$$

$$\tau = \frac{1}{\omega} \arctan \frac{k_2^2 c\omega}{k_1(1 + k_2^2c^2\omega^2) + k_2} \tag{5.8}$$

Equation (5.6) predicts that the deflection of the top surface of the fish, $y - y_0$, lags behind the applied sinusoidal force by the time τ, independent of the magnitude of the force (within the limits of linear viscoelastic behaviour). Since time is easier to measure than the absolute value of the stress, measuring the delay time is a convenient way of following changes in viscoelastic properties of the food material. The modulus r tends to increase with frequency in the range from 0 to 800 Hz, whilst the delay time τ decreases with increasing frequency ω [18].

The time delay can be measured directly from the difference on the time axis between the positions of the minima or maxima of $F(t)$ and $y(t)$. Figure 5.4 shows a convenient method based on plotting $y(t)$ against $F(t)$ in the form of an elliptical limit cycle (a special case of a Lissajous figure) to which the oscillations settle after the initial transient after applying the sinusoidal force. Equations (5.9) and (5.10) give the values of the loss angle $\omega\tau$ and the complex modulus G^* as functions of the parameters of the ellipse:

$$\omega\tau = \arctan \frac{y_4 - y_3}{y_2 - y_1} \tag{5.9}$$

$$|G^*| = \frac{y_{max} - y_{min}}{F_{max} - F_{min}} \quad G' = |G^*| \cos \omega\tau \quad G'' = |G^*| \sin \omega\tau \tag{5.10}$$

This method has the advantage that the settling period is more clearly visible from the limit cycle than from following the time records $F(t)$ and $y(t)$ in the time domain. The limit cycle provides a degree of averaging over a number of cycles and gives a more robust estimate of the loss angle and the complex modulus. All this assumes that the fish does not undergo a significant plastic deformation by the measuring indenter.

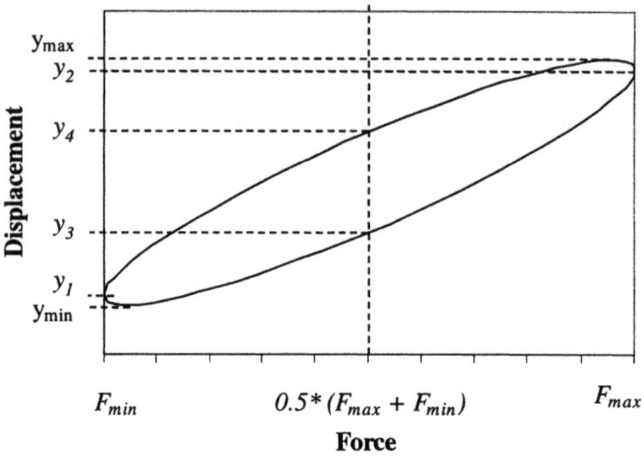

Fig. 5.4. A convenient way of estimating the viscoelastic loss angle $\omega\tau$ and the complex modulus G^*

5.4.2 Creep and Relaxation Measurements

During creep measurements a constant deforming force F_0 is applied to the sample.

If inertial forces are neglected, then the deformation of the top surface decreases instantaneously by the amount $y_C = k_1 F_0$ due to the spring k_1 getting compressed before the Kelvin-Voigt element has time to compress. When that happens the displacement is described by an exponential function of time as given in Eq. (5.11):

$$y_0 - y = F_0 \left[k_1 + k_2 + k_2 \exp\left(-\frac{t}{k_2 c} \right) \right] \tag{5.11}$$

Figure 5.5 shows schematically the displacement as a function of time during creep and subsequent relaxation. Relaxation commences when the applied force F_0 is removed. If the spring k_1 comes to its original length (which happens instantaneously except for inertial delay due to a finite mass in real experiments), the deflection of the top surface of the fish is given by

$$y_0 - y = F_0 k_2 \exp\left(-\frac{t}{k_2 c} \right) \tag{5.12}$$

Experiments show that the spring k_1 may not recover its original length after compression because it suffers a plastic deformation given by $y_D = y_{C1} - y_{R1}$. The viscoelastic model given by Eq. (5.3) does not take into account plastic deformation. In order to do that a dashpot would need to be included in series with the spring k_1 in Fig. 5.3, resulting in a four element Burger's model.

Identification of the lumped parameters k_1, k_2 and c (three unknowns) requires three independent equations to be used. Since the Eqs. (5.11) and (5.12) enable only $k_2 c$ to be identified, two further equations are needed if all of the pa-

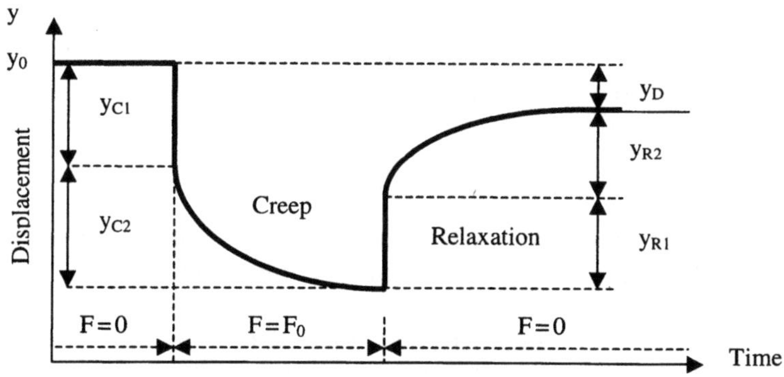

Fig. 5.5. A schematic graph of the deflection of fish surface during indentation

rameters in Fig. 5.3 are to be identified. These additional equations are probably most conveniently generated from Eqs. (5.7) or (5.8) by measuring τ at two different frequencies. In any case, if more than two parameters are to be identified, it is necessary to employ the frequency dependence of the viscoelastic behaviour.

5.5 Instrumental Texture Measurements of the Quality of Fish

Texture is one of the important indicators of the quality of fish. Soft texture in fresh (unfrozen) fish is indicative of spoilage, as shown in Fig. 5.1. Mechanical damage of fish, caused for example by stacking overfilled fish boxes on top of each other, also results in soft texture. In frozen fish tough texture indicates that the fish has been badly stored (too low or fluctuating storage temperature, too long storage time), resulting in denaturation and cross-linking of proteins.

Creep, relaxation and oscillation measurement were carried out in the frame of a larger EU project "Multisensor techniques for monitoring the quality of fish" (CT98-4076). The aim of the project was to apply instrumental measurements to improving the quality of fresh and frozen fish. Apart form the instruments measuring texture, instruments and sensors for electrical, optical and physico-chemical properties were used. The objectives of the work were (i) to assess the synergy in fusing the data from the various sensors and (ii) to provide a basis for introduction of portable instruments for rapid determination of quality in industry.

The work was started by a survey of the European fish processing industry. The view of the industry was that texture of fish is a very useful attribute of quality. The industry would also welcome the availability of portable texturometers that could be used on the factory processing floor and in fish market auctions [14].

Various prototypes were constructed, including portable texturometers. These were used in three 'work-ins' to measure the various properties of fish under the same and controlled conditions. In the first and second work-ins (Icelandic Fisheries Laboratory, Reykjavik, 1999 and Norwegian Fisheries Research Institute, Tromsø, 2000) wild Atlantic cod (*Gadus morhua*) caught by commercial fishermen was used. In the third work-in (CSIC Instituto del Frio, Madrid, 2000) frozen (–29 °C) defrosted cod and Atlantic hake (*Merluccius merluccius*) were investigated.

The instruments used for texture measurements were:

- A commercially produced texture analyser (Stable Microsystems TA.XT2 used by the Icelandic and Spanish teams in compression/shearing and oscillatory modes).
- A hand-held compression instrument measuring Shore hardness (Fischprüfgerät, Zwick Company, Germany, used by the German team).
- Hand-held pressure probes (both oscillatory and creep/relaxation type, constructed and used by the Scottish team).

The overall results from these instrumental texture measurements showed that the measured parameters characterising texture of fish (forces and deformation distances, creep/relaxation compliances and their characteristic times) were subject to large statistical variations. Therefore at least four measurements on each of five individual fish from each batch were taken in order to determine the inter-batch variations. The measurement method involved compression by a cylindrical indenter. The main general findings were as follows:

- For fresh fish kept in chilled storage the softness in any particular position on the fish increases (in agreement with the QIM results in Fig. 5.1) as seen in Table 5.1 (section a). For a constant force the deformation of fresh fish increases by a factor of about 2 over the chilled storage period of 17 days. However, the main increase in softness occurs during the first four days.
- For frozen/defrosted hake the instantaneous deformations y_{C1} and y_{R1} decrease during both chilled and frozen storage (Table 5.1, section b). This means that the fish muscle becomes harder during chilled storage.
- Hake taken out of frozen storage after 4 months and kept on ice for 9 days does not become significantly softer during this time (Table 5.1, section c). This is in variance with the results for fresh cod (Table 5.1, section a).
- The viscoelasticity of hake as quantified by the relaxation times associated with the Voigt decreases with increasing duration of frozen storage (Table 5.2, section a). (The creeptime constants do not decrease significantly).
- For hake kept for 4 months in frozen storage then defrosted and kept on ice for 9 days the Voigt relaxation times increase during the chilled storage (Table 5.2, section b).

These results show that, as expected from the QIM evaluation, fresh cod becomes softer in chilled storage due to autolytic changes in the muscle tissue. During frozen storage the protein matrix becomes tougher due to denaturation and cross-linking of protein molecules. Independent biochemical tests are needed to confirm this. Montero and Borderías [20] found that it is difficult to explain fully the changes in the texture of frozen fish muscle solely in terms of the aggregation of myofibrillar protein. Therefore they attempted to relate to such textural changes in frozen hake muscle to the modification that collagen

Table 5.1. Results of creep and relaxation tests: (a) Fresh (unfrozen) cod kept in chilled storage for up to 17 days; (b) Hake kept in frozen storage for 18 months; (c) Hake taken out of frozen storage after 4 months, defrosted and kept chilled on ice for 9 days[a]

(a)	Start of storage (day 1)	End of storage (day 17)
y_{C1} (mm)	1.2 ± 0.2	2.5 ± 0.7
y_{R1} (mm)	0.7 ± 0.2	1.5 ± 0.7
y_D (mm)	0.2 ± 0.1	0.2 ± 0.1
(b)	Start of storage (month 0)	End of storage (month 18)
y_{C1} (mm)	0.66 ± 0.25	0.52 ± 0.19
y_{R1} (mm)	0.50 ± 0.21	0.36 ± 0.05
y_D (mm)	0.18 ± 0.13	0.20 ± 0.12
(c)	Start of storage (day 0)	End of storage (day 9)
y_{C1} (mm)	0.51 ± 0.15	0.48 ± 0.10
y_{R1} (mm)	0.44 ± 0.11	0.36 ± 0.05
y_D (mm)	0.14 ± 0.11	0.14 ± 0.11

[a] Data are expressed as mean ± SD.

Table 5.2. Viscoelastic time constants for frozen/thawed hake: (a) Frozen storage; (b) Hake taken out of frozen storage after 4 months, defrosted and kept chilled on ice for 9 days[a]

(a)	Start of storage (month 0)	End of storage (month 18)
k_2c-creep (ms)	440 ± 110	420 ± 130
k_2c-relaxation (ms)	696 ± 95	536 ± 59
(b)	Start of storage (day 0)	End of storage (day 9)
k_2c-creep (ms)	438 ± 111	555 ± 217
k_2c-relaxation (ms)	450 ± 58	603 ± 134

[a] Data are expressed as mean ± SD.

undergoes during frozen storage. Any hardening of defrosted hake in chilled storage (not significant in Table 5.1, section c) could be due to drip loss and consequent dehydration of the tissue.

The plastic deformation y_D appears to be independent of the storage time. This means that fish muscle is affected by the measurement to the same degree regardless of its age. A possible interpretation is that the plastic deformation is confined to a region near the surface of the fish where the character of the tissue is different from that of the bulk (for example the presence of skin).

The retardation times k_2c associated with the Voigt element seem to decrease due to frozen storage but increase after chilled storage. Also, the retardation times k_2c are shorter for creep than for relaxation. This could be due to the time during which water is squeezed out from under the indenter being shorter than the time needed for the water to return back under capillary action.

5.6 Conclusions

Physical instrumental methods of determining the texture of fish are very demanding due to the inhomogeneous nature of the fish muscle. However, considerable progress has been made in recent years in developing both the experimental techniques and the underlying theoretical models. Large laboratory-based instruments produce results that correlate to a significant degree with sensory evaluations such as the QIM. With advances in sensors and information technology it is now possible to construct portable and hand-held instruments for determining texture of fish in industrial settings. A degree of success was obtained during the work of the EU project in correlating the descriptors of texture obtained by sensory evaluations, large commercial laboratory instruments and portable hand-held devices.

Acknowledgements. This work has been partly funded by a grant from the European Commission under the contract CT98-4076. The industrial survey was partly supported by the EU project CT97-4174. This assistance is gratefully acknowledged.

References

1. Alfrey T (1948) Mechanical behaviour of high polymers. Interscience Publishers, New York
2. Barroso M, Careche M, Borderias AJ (1999) Quality control of frozen fish using rheological techniques. Trends Food Sci Technol 9: 223-229
3. Botta JR (1991) Instrument of nondestructive texture measurement of raw Atlantic cod (*Gadus morhua*) fillets. J Food Sci 56: 962-964, 968
4. Bourne MC (1982) Food texture and viscosity: concept and measurement. Academic Press, New York
5. Brandt MA, Skinner EZ, Coleman JA (1963) Texture profile method. J Food Sci 28: 404-409
6. Dagnall H (1980) Exploring surface texture. Rank Taylor Hobson, Leicester, UK
7. Dunajski E (1979) Texture of fish muscle. J Texture Stud 10: 301-317
8. EU (1998) Development of multi-sensor techniques for monitoring the quality of fish. EU Project CT98-4076. Commission of the European Communities, Brussels
9. Heia K, Sigernes F, Nilsen H, Oehlenschläger J, Schubring K, Borderias J, Nilsson K, Jørgensen B, Nesvadba P (1997) Evaluation of fish freshness by physical measurement techniques. Proceedings of a Conference on Evaluation of Fish Freshness (AIR3 CT94-2283). International Institute of Refrigeration, Nantes, France, pp 347-354
10. Houška M, Nesvadba P (2000) Online database of rheological and mechanical properties of foods. Proceedings of the 13th International Congress on Rheology, August 20-25, 2000, Cambridge, UK
11. Huxley HE (1972) Molecular basis for contraction of cross-striated muscle. In: Bourne GH (ed) The structure and function of muscle, 2nd edn, vol 1. Academic Press, New York, pp 302-387
12. ISO (International Organisation for Standardisation) (1981) Sensory analysis vocabulary, part 4. Geneva, Switzerland
13. Johnson KL (1985) Contact mechanics. Cambridge University Press, Cambridge, UK

14. Ólafsdóttir G et al. (2002) A study of the views of the European fish sector on monitoring the quality and labelling of fish products. Trends Food Sci Technol (submitted)
15. Kruse SA, Smith JA, Lawrence AJ, Dresner MA, Manduca A, Greenleaf JF (2000) Tissue characterisation using magnetic resonance elastography: preliminary results. Phys Med Biol 45:1579–1590
16. Larmond E (1988) Beyond the texture profile. In: Blanshard JMV, Mitchel JR (eds) Food structure and its creation and evaluation. Butterworths, London, pp 449–463
17. Lewis MJ (1996) Physical properties of foods and food processing systems. Woodhead Publishing, Cambridge, UK
18. Lu R, Abbott JA (1996) A transient method for determining dynamic viscoelastic properties of solid foods. Trans ASAE 39: 1461–1467
19. Ma L, Barbosa-Canovas GV (1997) Viscosity of gels made with selected food gums. In: Jowitt R (ed) Proceedings of 12th International Congress on Engineering and Food (ICEF7). Sheffield Academic Press, Sheffield, UK, pp E76–E79
20. Montero P, Borderías J (1990) Behaviour of myofibrillar proteins and collagen in hake (*Merluccius merluccius* L.) muscle during frozen storage and its effect on texture. Z Lebensm Unters Forsch 190: 112–117
21. Ólafsdóttir G, Luten J, Dalgaard P, Careche M, Verres-Bagnis V, Martinsdóttir E, Heia K (1997) Methods to determine the fish freshness of fish in research and industry. International Institute of Refrigeration, Paris
22. Rao VNM, Skinner GE (1986) Rheological properties of solid foods. In: Rao MA, Rizvi SSH (eds) Engineering properties of foods. Marcel Dekker, New York, pp 215–254
23. Rosenthal AJ (1999) Food texture: measurement and perception. Aspen Publishers, Gaithersburg, USA
24. Sato Y, Nakayama T (1970) Discussion of the binding quality of minced meats based on their rheological properties before and after heating. J Texture Stud 1: 309–326
25. Szczesniak AS, Kramer A (1973) Texture measurements of food: psychophysical fundamentals, sensory, mechanical and chemical procedures and their relationships. Reidel Publishing, Dordrecht, Netherlands
26. Zheng Y, Mak AFT, Lue B (1999) Objective assessment of limb tissue elasticity: development of a manual indentation procedure. J Rehabil Res Dev 36: 71–85

6 Measurement of the Fish Content in Fish Products

Kevin D. Hargin

In an attempt to introduce product labels that better inform the consumer, recent amendments to European Food Labelling Regulations mean that most fish products will now be required to declare the percentage amount of fish contained within the product. This has led to great difficulties for enforcement officers who are charged with verifying product label declarations, since they do not always have immediate access to product recipe information. Within the UK this problem is largely overcome by advocating chemical analysis of the product to determine its nitrogen content as the first step in enforcement. Although the nitrogen content of fish can vary, depending on factors such as species, season and harvesting ground, by applying an appropriate nitrogen factor the amount of fish can be calculated.

A Code of Practice has been drawn up in agreement with enforcement, analytical and industrial representatives that outlines good manufacturing practices with respect to water uptake and soluble nitrogen losses during fish processing. Interim nitrogen factors have been agreed for the main commercial species of fish, and an undertaking that chemical analyses should be followed by in-factory inspection where the analytical result suggests that the label declaration is incorrect.

6.1 Introduction

The advent of the QUID (Quantitative Ingredient Declaration) amendment to the Food Labelling Regulations, and hence a requirement for fish content declaration in most fish products, cannot be ignored. Also, it must not be overlooked that the purpose of a fish content declaration is to inform the consumer as to the true nature of the product. With a fish fillet on a fishmonger's slab the consumer can visually inspect the product before it is bought and an assessment, perhaps subconsciously, can be made on the quality of the fillet being offered for sale. However, with a fish product the situation is different and the consumer is often not in a position to make the same sort of judgement before buying, because the product is coated, mixed with other ingredients and/or packaged. Hence the need for informative labelling. The information that the consumer needs is such as to be able to make a meaningful comparison between different fish products which can be related, albeit subliminally, to the fresh fish fillet. The main problem, however, remains in establishing on what basis the fish content of a product should be declared.

This chapter outlines the basics of new legislative requirements, discusses the problems in measuring the fish content of a product, and introduces the recent agreement reached in the UK between the enforcement authorities, public analysts and the fish industry on the measurement of the fish content in fish products.

6.2 Legislative Position

QUID is the term used to describe one element of the package of changes made to the EC Food Labelling Directive (79/112/EEC) [1] by directive 97/4/EC [2]. Directive 97/4/EC was adopted on 27 January 1997 and requires quantitative ingredient declarations to be given on food labels for certain ingredients or categories of ingredients used in foods. This is a horizontal measure and applies across all foodstuffs and not just to fish products. Within the UK, this Directive has been implemented by the Food Labelling (Amendment) Regulations 1998, though the changes did not become fully effective until 14 February 2000. This 'lead in' period was to allow for changes to be made to labels.

So what does it all mean in practice? It means that in a product declarations are *required* for those ingredients or categories of ingredients which:

- Appear in the name of the food or which are usually associated with that name by consumers
- Are emphasised on the label in either words, pictures or graphics
- Are essential to characterise a food and to distinguish it from products with which it might be confused because of its name or appearance

In other words, a *Salmon Mousse* or *Fish Cakes* would have to declare the amount of 'salmon' or 'fish' contained in these products, respectively. Also, for a product such as *Fisherman's Pie*, since this would be expected by the consumer to contain fish, e. g. cod and haddock, it would be necessary to give the percentage 'fish' in the product. For products where special emphasis is given to an ingredient, e. g. *Seafood Lasagne with Prawns* or where the packaging portrayed a particular ingredient, such as a picture of a casserole highlighting scallops, it would be necessary to 'QUID' the prawns and scallops, respectively, in these examples.

With regard to the third bullet point above, this is unlikely to be a problem for fish products made in the UK for the UK market. However, processors should be aware that things might not be quite so simple when making products in the UK for export to other Member States. However, it is worth pointing out that, in fact, the only examples of products in this category agreed at EU level to date are 'mayonnaise' and 'marzipan'.

There are, of course, some instances where declarations are *not* required:

- Where similar information is already required to be given by Community legislation. (For example, a 'drained weight' declaration would be required for *Canned Tuna in Brine*.)
- Where Community legislation stipulates precisely the quantities of ingredients or categories of ingredients which must be used without requiring any indication on the label. (This is probably a clause for the future – no category of fish product is yet affected by this.)
- Where the ingredients or category of ingredients has been used in small quantities to flavour a food. (Therefore, in *Salmon* and *Sorrel Fish Cakes*, it would not be required to 'QUID' the sorrel.)

Table 6.1. "Fish" in a fish finger

Ingredient	Weight (g)
Fish	70
Batter	20
Crumb	20
Total before frying	110
Frying oil taken up	7
Total mixing bowl	117
Water lost from batter during frying	-5
Total of ingredients	112

The quantity of an ingredient should generally be expressed as a percentage. The percentage may be rounded to the nearest whole number or to the nearest 0.5 decimal place in those cases where it is below 5%.

Care needs to be taken in calculating a 'QUID' declaration to ensure that the figure quoted is that which best represents the amount of the ingredient at the time of use in the preparation of the product. Processing variability should be taken into account in order that consumers are not misled. The percentage declaration should go in or next to the name of the food, or go in the ingredients list in connection with the ingredient in question.

The percentage should normally be calculated by using the same method as that used for determining the order in the list of ingredients (regulation 13(1) and (2) of the Food Labelling Regulations 1996, as amended). This means that the weight of an ingredient to be quantified would need to be divided by the total weight of all of the ingoing ingredients (except the weight of any added water or volatile ingredients lost in processing). Table 6.1 gives an example for a 'fish finger'.

As usual, there are some derogations to the way ingredients declarations are calculated, and these can be found in the Food Labelling (Amendment) (No. 2) Regulations 1999. Basically, there are two situations that require a different treatment:

1. For foodstuffs which have lost moisture during processing, calculate the quantity of raw ingredient as a percentage related to the finished product.
2. If the quantity exceeds 100%, replace by weight of ingredient of 100 g of finished product.

6.3 Problems in Measuring Fish Content

The enforcement of label claims for fish content can prove exceedingly difficult. When a product is sampled from a supermarket shelf by an enforcement officer and sent to the public analyst, currently the only real option open to the analyst is to measure the nitrogen content of the product, apply a factor to determine the protein content and then equate that to the fish content. The future may bring

Table 6.2. Nitrogen content of fish and shellfish

Species	Mean nitrogen (%)	Range nitrogen (%)
White fish		
Cod	2.87	2.21–3.20
	2.91	2.64–3.29
Coley/saithe	2.92	2.52–3.27
	2.93	2.54–3.32
European hake	2.87	2.52–3.28
Haddock	2.96	2.52–3.31
Ling	3.02	2.70–3.36
Plaice	2.67	1.91–3.19
Whiting	2.91	2.35–3.35
Oily fish		
Anchovy	2.45	–
Herring	–	2.56–3.41
Mackerel	–	2.57–3.66
Pilchard	–	2.45–3.20
Sardine	3.07	–
Shellfish		
Crab	2.4	–
Lobster	2.7	–
Prawn	–	2.38–2.86
Shrimp	–	1.68–3.78
Scampi		
Hand peeled, unwashed	–	3.00–3.06
Hand peeled, washed	–	2.64–2.83
Water blown, unwashed	–	2.77–2.86
Water blown, washed	–	2.59–2.71

more sophisticated and precise techniques, but for the time being we ultimately rely on a nitrogen determination and the application of a nitrogen factor.

However, one of the great problems with nitrogen factors for fish is the sheer number of fish available. Table 6.2 shows a small fraction of the species available with their nitrogen content ranges.

In comparison with red meat and poultry, fish products are prepared from a far greater number of species and from starting material that exhibits much wider compositional variation. 'Meat' or 'fish' basically comprises the muscle or flesh, though its definition may also include other edible tissues, and so protein is a vital component in determining actual meat or fish content. The protein content of a sample is normally calculated by determining the amount of nitrogen present using a recognised method (usually Kjeldahl) and applying a pre-determined factor to express the nitrogen in terms of fish content. Thus the distribution of nitrogen within muscle tissue and the degree of solubility of all nitrogen-containing compounds play an important role in the analytical determination of meat or fish.

Muscle contains hundreds of different proteins along with other nitrogen-containing molecules, referred to as non-protein nitrogen (NPN). The three principal groups of muscle protein are:

Table 6.3. Principal nitrogen components in fish and meat

	Fish (%)	Meat (%)
Myofibrillar protein	70–80	39–69
Stroma protein	2–3	16–28
Sarcoplasmic protein	18–28	21–26
NPN: consisting of (%):	2–9	11–12
Creatin+creatinine	40	33
Nucleotides	18	24
Amino acids	15	42
TMAO+volatile bases	22	–
Other	5	1

1. Sarcoplasmic proteins that are from the fluid within the muscle cells. They are mainly enzymes and are the only water-soluble proteins.
2. Myofibrillar proteins are the contractile proteins.
3. Stroma proteins (largely connective tissue) hold the muscle bundles together and to the skeleton. Other proteins are associated with cellular membranes.

NPN compounds originate mostly from the sarcoplasm and include peptides, amino acids, amines, amine oxides, guanidine compounds, quaternary ammonium compounds, purines and urea. A total 'crude protein' figure can be calculated by totalling the protein+NPN. Contrasting meat from land animals with finfish muscles highlights significant differences in the types of protein present. For example, fish contain less connective tissue protein (2–3% compared with 16–28%), more myofibrillar protein (70–80% compared with 39–68%) and more NPN (10–40% or more of the sarcoplasmic fraction in fishery products) [3]. White fish muscle tissue often contains more sarcoplasmic protein [4] and less NPN [5] than dark muscle. The variable occurrence and properties of specific protein or NPN components in fish are a major determinant of why different species are more or less suitable for dehydration, freezing, thermoprocessing and fermentation. The importance of habitat conditions is also reflected in findings that the amounts of free amino acids and other NPN compounds differ considerably in cultured and wild fish of the same species [5]. The principal differences in nitrogen compounds between meat and fish are highlighted in Table 6.3.

6.3.1 Total Protein Content

From a study of 540 species by Sidwell in 1981 [6] it was found that the crude protein content of seafoods ranged from less than 8% to more than 25% of fresh weight, shellfish generally being at the lower end of this scale. However, most finfish muscle tissue contains about 18–22% protein, with an average of about 18.5% [6]. Crustacean flesh tends to contain more crude protein than that of molluscs, and within species white flesh has more protein than dark flesh [4]. Although the fat content of muscle may vary considerably at different times of the year, the total protein content does not generally undergo large changes with fishing season [3]. However, maturation of the gonads and/or long periods of feed deprivation can result in tissue depletion with marked decreases in the muscle protein [7–12]. Protein depletion is normally associated with increased water in the muscle.

Fish muscle and skin collagens differ from bovine collagens in having a significantly higher content of essential amino acids and often contain a lower concentration of hydroxyproline [13], of the order of 1.5–10% compared with 10.9% in bovine collagen. Therefore, caution should be exercised if calculating the collagen content of fish on the basis of hydroxyproline content, as is usually the procedure for other meats.

Although manufacturers base their meat and fish contents on the basis of ingoing ingredients, these declarations have traditionally been checked and enforced using a chemical determination of meat and fish content in the final product. The standard method of determining nitrogen content is very precise, but the use of conversion, or nitrogen, factors to calculate the meat or fish content is very much less so.

Generally there has been agreement between industry and enforcement authorities on the nitrogen factors used for red meat and poultry. This is because the variability due to breed and different cuts is more or less known and accepted and the preparation of meat as an ingredient is normally by a "dry" process, so its composition remains relatively unchanged during primary processing.

There has never been a satisfactory agreement between industry and enforcement authorities for nitrogen factors to determine fish content. This is because there are a large number of fish species commercialised and the variability due to different fishing grounds, size, sex, spawning cycles, or even shell-moulting in the case of crustaceans, is known to have a very large effect on the nitrogen content of fish or shellfish (Table 6.2). These effects have not been fully quantified. Additionally, the preparation of fish or shellfish is normally a "wet" process, and hence a degree of water absorption and loss of soluble nitrogen is inevitable, especially in scampi when the tailmeat membrane is lost after removal from the shell. This mass balance is very complex and still there are insufficient corroborated data available to demonstrate satisfactorily on the extent of the transfer of nitrogen from, and water into, the fish flesh.

It would appear from the data in Table 6.3 that the total volatile bases do not account for a great deal of the total nitrogen within fish. However, perhaps the major difference between fish and meat is in the level of stroma proteins. These are responsible for the integrity of the muscle and whereas in meat the muscle fibres are surrounded by a connective tissue sheath this is not the case in fish. As such, fish muscle is more easily damaged and, coupled with the large surface area to volume in fish which is exposed during most processing, it is not unreasonable to expect that there would be proportionately larger losses of total nitrogen from fish flesh than from meat from the washing out of cell contents.

That fish meat is different in composition to meat from land animals, particularly with respect to the content of stroma proteins and NPN, is beyond dis-

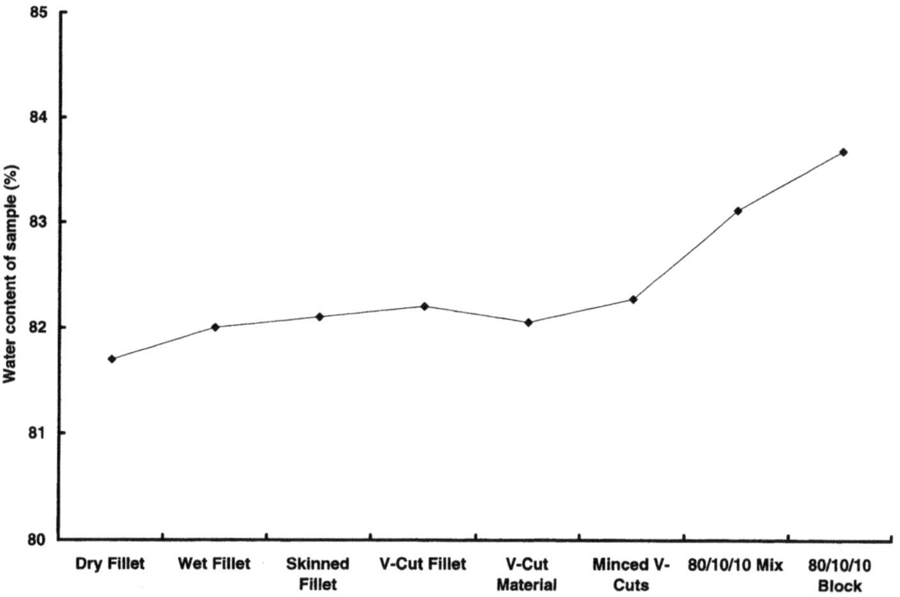

Fig. 6.1. Changes in water content during processing (white fish)

pute. The variety of species consumed and the compositional variability of the raw material ensures that a simple solution is far from likely. Further, the 'wet' nature of fish processing is inevitable and complicates the matter tremendously. Figure 6.1 illustrates the changes in water content of white fish during processing. Biochemical changes are quicker in fish than in meat and breakdown of structure leads to a muscle more vulnerable to water uptake, especially after filleting.

This, of course, has very practical implications for the processor and Fig. 6.2 shows how the fish content decreases, as measured by nitrogen content, throughout the process of fish block production. Such blocks will be used to make further processed fish products and it is important that the manufacturer is aware of the fish content of a block to enable full and proper product label declarations.

Changes in the nitrogen content, and therefore apparent fish content, can be further complicated by the differences within species due to the location or season of the catch. Differences in the nitrogen content due to fishing ground (Fig. 6.3) can be significant when related to the fish content of a product.

Data generated by Torry Research Station [14] and others have demonstrated that losses of nitrogen and uptake of water do occur during fish processing and after storage on ice. However, the degree of these nitrogen losses varies considerably from species to species, with groups such as molluscs and crustacea exhibiting the greatest losses since these contain the highest levels of water-extractable protein and NPN compounds. This is shown in Fig. 6.4 for scampi processing where more traditional waterblown peeling is compared to a mechanical

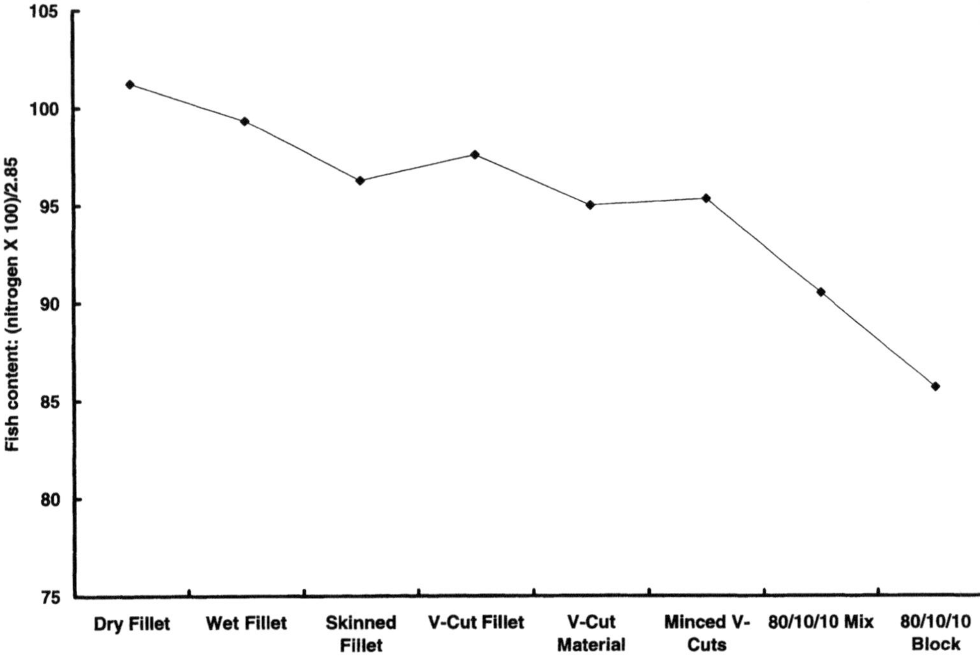

Fig. 6.2. Changes in fish content during processing (white fish)

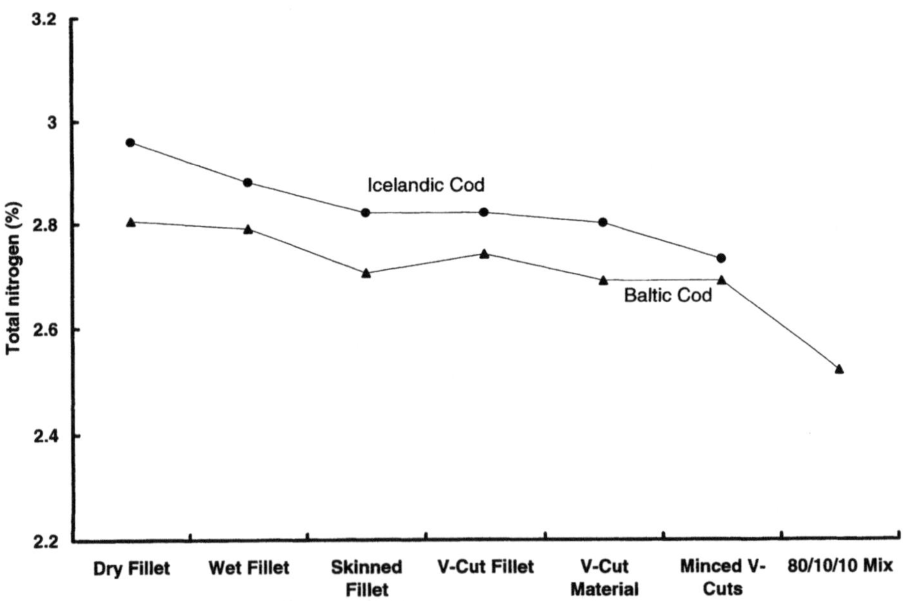

Fig. 6.3. Changes in nitrogen content during processing-origin differences

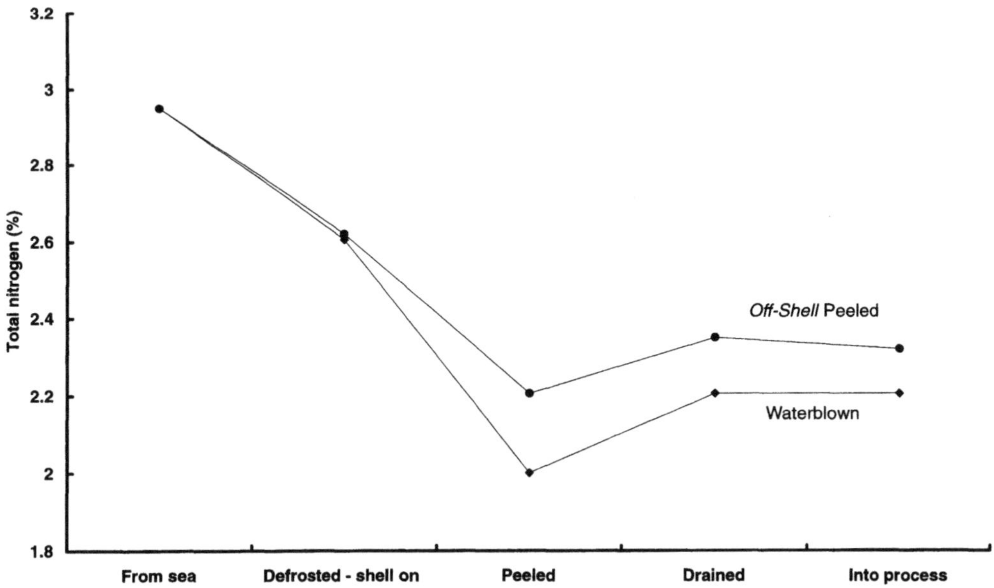

Fig. 6.4. Changes in nitrogen content during scampi peeling process

'dry' peeler. It is interesting to note that once the scampi membrane has been removed there is greater scope for nitrogen losses. Some more recent unpublished studies tend to suggest that the end-point difference shown in Fig. 6.4 is not quite so great between the waterblown and *Off-Shell* peeled samples. Therefore, it is probable that legislators and analysts will have to take into consideration that there is a technological minimum of added water and/or nitrogen loss associated with the processing of scampi and, in fact, with all fish.

6.4 Code of Practice

It was for this very reason that in 1998 the UK manufacturers got together with the enforcement authorities and public analysts to produce the *Code of Practice on the Declaration of Fish Content in Fish Products*. After many years of debate and disagreement, the parties finally settled on a code based around two important principles:

1. That fish treated in accordance with good manufacturing practice (GMP) is regarded as fish as an ingredient for fish products.
2. Fish content is determined initially by nitrogen content using an agreed nitrogen factor based on fish processed by GMP, followed by in-factory inspection.

This essentially recognises the nature of fish and the inevitable changes that occur post-harvest. It further recognises that fish is different to meat and is more susceptible to these changes, not least of all because of the methods needed to wash, de-head, gut and fillet fish. In terms of its nitrogen content, fish taken straight from the sea will be very different to the fish used to prepare a 'fish finger'.

For the Code to be successful, processors have to apply GMP. GMP are defined conditions and operating practices which do not debase the product unnecessarily in relation to composition, quality, form or texture. In relation to the Code, this is important with respect to the uptake of water and loss of soluble proteins. Thus, the Code defines *Defect Action Points (DAPs)* as "a point, step, or procedure in a process at which control can be applied and loss of soluble protein compounds reduced, or water uptake limited to the technologically unavoidable minimum".

Appendices in the Code provide flow diagrams for several different generic types of processes with DAPs listed against suggested steps. Figure 6.5 illustrates the process for fish block manufacture and Table 6.4 lists the DAPs. Importantly, within each of the diagrams, as appropriate, there is a dotted line. This signifies the point in the particular process at which the fish can be considered as a 'fish ingredient'; in other words, the nitrogen content of the fish fillet in Fig. 6.5 above the dotted line can be used in calculating the fish content of the block or subsequent products.

For many of the main commercial species in the UK, interim nitrogen factors have been agreed (Table 6.5). They have been agreed in order to get the Code off the ground but it is recognised by all sides that they need to be reviewed and

Table 6.4. Examples of defect action points for fish block manufacture

DAP 1/2	Fillets should be adequately drained[a]
DAP 3	Mince after bone extraction can occasionally be washed to improve colour. This process will lead to rapid loss of soluble nitrogen compounds and fish liquors along with uptake of wash water. Such processes cannot be recommended and would almost certainly result in the mince having a lower nitrogen content, which could lead to the eventual fish block having to be labelled 'fish with added water'
DAP 4	V cut material for 80:10:10 or other fish materials for bone extraction should be effectively drained prior to use and stored in chill after processing
DAP 5	Brine and or phosphate solution should be prepared and monitored to specified strength
DAP 6	80:10:10 blends and similar should be accurately weighed and blended through appropriate equipment to ensure uniformity of the mix and this should be used with minimum delay to prevent drip, or puddling
DAP 7	Allowance of extra weight of fish to achieve end-product weight will be required, according to condition of the fish
DAP 8	After packing fish into fish wraps and frames for block production, they should be plate frozen with minimum of delay to prevent drip and puddling to occur at block surfaces.[b]
DAP 9	Fish drip will be squeezed from the fish during expansion and freezing so that final block weight should be monitored

[a] Within the Code fillet production is covered separately.
[b] Blended blocks must be labelled appropriately.

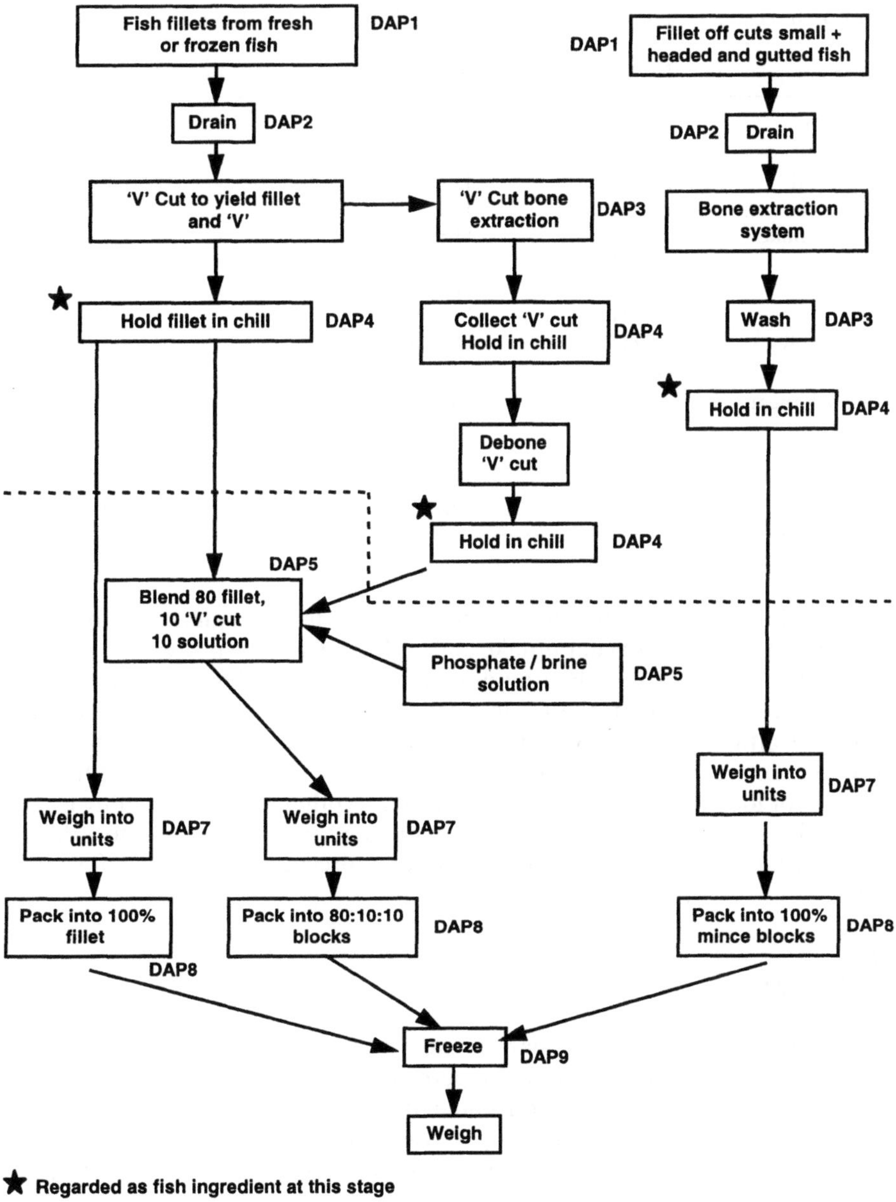

Fig. 6.5. Flow diagram of a typical fish block manufacturing process

Table 6.5. Interim nitrogen factors to be used for fish and shellfish ingredient

Species	Nitrogen (%)	Species	Nitrogen (%)
White fish		Shellfish	
Cod	2.66 [15, 16]	Crab	2.40 [17]
Minced cod	2.61 [18]	Lobster	2.70 [17]
Coley/saithe	2.69 [15, 16]	Prawn	2.62 [17]
European hake	2.64 [16]	Shrimp	2.73 [17]
Haddock	2.72 [16]	Scampi – from sea	3.05 [14]
Ling	2.78 [16]	Scampi – washed and peeled	2.33 [14]
Plaice	2.46 [16]	Scallops	2.64 [19]
Alaskan pollack	2.59 [18]	Queens	2.55 [19]
Whiting	2.68 [16]	Oily fish	
White fish mean	2.65	Anchovy	2.45 [17]
		Herring	2.99 [17]
		Mackerel	3.12 [17]
		Pilchard	2.83 [17]
		Sardine	3.07 [17]

amended in the light of further studies and any technological developments which affect the level of water uptake and/or loss of soluble proteins.

Nevertheless, this still only provides a guide to the analyst and enforcement officer. In cases of doubt, the Code requires in-factory inspection by the enforcement officer to assess whether GMP have been adhered to, or if there are any other factors, e.g. unusual nitrogen content for a particular batch of fish due to season or location, perhaps. The Code contains other relevant labelling issues, beyond the scope of this chapter, and provides a pragmatic solution to a thorny issue that has dogged the fish industry and enforcement authorities for many years.

6.5 Conclusions

Recent European legislative changes now require that many, if not most, fish products will have to declare the percentage quantity of fish they contain. While many people can recognise a whole fish it is not so easy to determine what is the fish in a fish product. Thus on-pack declarations will require careful monitoring and control of the production processes to ensure that consumers are not misled.

Within the UK, enforcement of such label claims will essentially take the form of determining the fish content of a product by chemical analysis. In cases where there is reasonable doubt about the declaration, this will be followed by in-factory inspection to check the recipe, processing records and processing conditions to determine whether GMP have been met.

References

1. EC (1979) OJ No. L33, 8.2.79, p 1
2. EC (1997) OJ No. L43, 14.2.97, p 21
3. Haard NF (1995) Composition and nutritive value of proteins and other nitrogen compounds. In: Ruiter A (ed) Fish and fishery products - composition, nutritive properties and stability. CAB International, Wallingford, UK, pp 77-116
4. Suzuki T (1981) Fish and krill processing technology. Applied Science Publishers, London
5. Haard NF (1992) Control of chemical composition and food quality attributes of cultured fish. Food Res Int 25: 289-307
6. Sidwell V (1981) Chemical and nutritional composition of finfishes, whales, crustaceans, molluscs, and their products. NOAA Technical Memorandum, NMFS F/SEC-11. United States Department of Commerce, Washington, DC
7. Bilinski E, Jonas REE, Peters MD, Choromanski EM (1984) Effects of sexual maturation on the quality of coho salmon (*Oncorhynchus kisutch*) flesh. Can Inst Food Sci Technol J 17: 271-273
8. Love RM (1988) The food fishes: their intrinsic variation and practical implications. Farrand Press, London, p 59
9. Hendrickson GL, Fritzsche RA, Fisher RA (1986) Histology and ultrastructure of the 'jellied' condition in Dover sole (*Microstomus pacificus*). California Sea Grant College Program, University of California, A-032, La Jolla, pp 230-234
10. Haard NF (1987) Protein and non-protein constituents in jellied American plaice, *Hippoglossoides platessoides*. Can Inst Food Sci Technol J 20: 98-101
11. Govindan TK (1987) Impact of Govindan effect on water extractable and non-protein nitrogen fractions in iced prawn muscle. Seafood Export J 19: 33-35, 37-40
12. Flick GJ, Lovell RT, Enriquez-Ibarra LG, Arganosa GC (1994) Changes in nitrogenous compounds in freshwater crayfish (*Procambarus clarkii*) tail meat stored in ice. J Muscle Foods 5: 105-118
13. Sikorski ZE, Kolakowska A, Pan PS (1990) The nutritive composition of the major groups of marine food organisms. In: Sikorski ZE (ed) Seafood resources, nutrition, composition and preservation. CRC Press, Boca Raton, Florida, pp 29-54
14. Early JC, Stroud GD, Smith GL (1983) Variations in the composition and yield of *Nephrops norvegicus*. 1. Nitrogen content. Project Report, Torry Research Station, Aberdeen, UK
15. Holland B, Brown J, Buss DH (1993) Fish and fish products. Third supplement to the 5th edn of McCance and Widdowson's The composition of foods. The Royal Society of Chemistry/Ministry of Agriculture, Fisheries and Food
16. Ministry of Agriculture, Fisheries and Food (1987) Food Advisory Committee report on coated and ice-glazed fish products. Fd AC/REP/3, HMSO
17. Pearson D (1976) The chemical analysis of foods, 7th edn. Churchill, Livingston, UK
18. Ross Youngs (1997) Unpublished data
19. Ministry of Agriculture, Fisheries and Food (1997) Unpublished data

References

[illegible]

7 Functional Properties of Fish Proteins

Rachel Goodband

Unilever's fish business is largely based on frozen fish products. For the consumer the principal attributes determining the quality of these products are the flavour and the texture. Fish proteins impact primarily on the sensory attributes relating to the texture of products. Fish fillet is composed of parallel muscle fibres arranged in blocks known as myotomes. The myotomes are separated by collagenous sheaths and form the flakes of the cooked fillet. The texture of fish is determined to a large extent by the myofibrillar proteins within the muscle fibres. The handling of fish, throughout the supply chain, impacts on the state of fish proteins and thereby influences the final textural quality. For frozen fish products, the freezing process, and storage in the frozen state are important determinants of product quality. For gadoid species in particular, significant deterioration in texture can occur during frozen storage. These changes, although not fully understood, involve aggregation of the myofibrillar proteins. A patented process for the use of ultra high-pressure to control some of the textural sensory attributes of cod during frozen storage is described.

7.1 Introduction

Unilever's fish business is largely based on frozen fish products, with products sold under well-known household brands in Europe and the Americas. For the consumer, the principle attributes determining the quality of frozen fish products are the flavour and the texture. Although the enzymes in fish may contribute to flavour changes that take place during frozen storage, the proteins impact primarily on the texture of fish products. This chapter briefly describes the proteins of fish muscle. The effects of freezing and frozen storage on fish muscle and the implications for fish texture are discussed. A patented technology involving the use of ultra high pressure to control some of the textural sensory attributes of cod during frozen storage is described.

7.2 Proteins of Fish Muscle

Figure 7.1 shows the hierarchical structure of fish. The fish fillet is divided into blocks of muscle known as myotomes which are separated by collagenous myocomata. On cooking the collagen of the myocomata is denatured and the myotomes may separate, forming the flakes of the cooked fish. The fish muscle fibres run between adjacent myocomata. Within the muscle fibres are the myofibrils, the contractile elements of the muscle. The myofibrils are made up of thick fila-

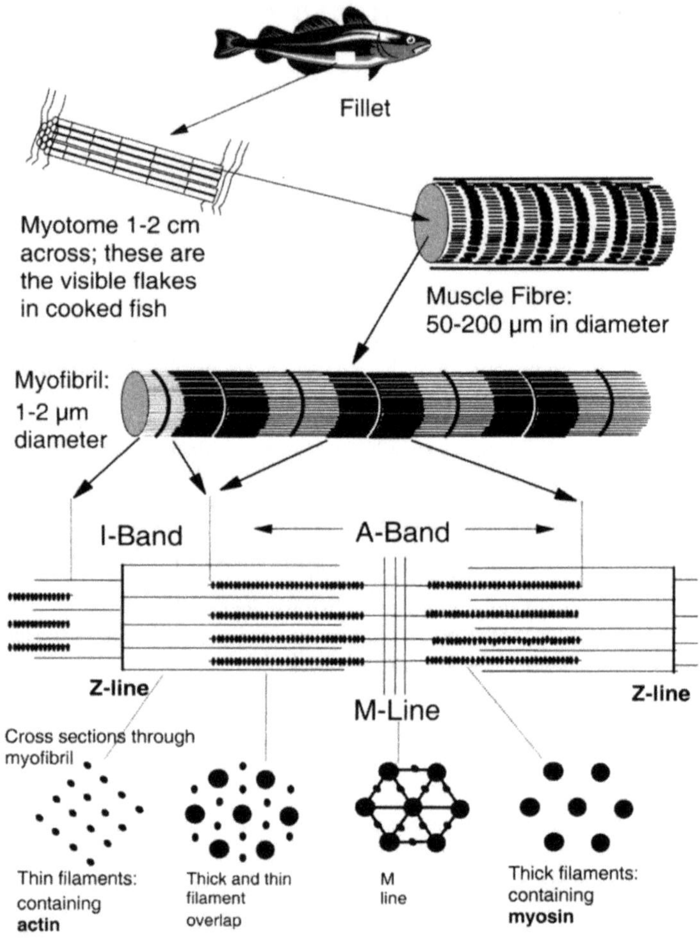

Fig. 7.1. The structural organisation of fish fillet

ments of myosin and thin filaments of actin. The arrangement of these filaments, shown in Fig. 7.1, gives muscle its characteristic banding pattern. The repeating unit of the myofibrils, the distance between two *Z* lines, is known as a sarcomere.

The proteins of fish muscle are usually considered as three main groups: the sarcoplasmic proteins, the myofibrillar proteins and the connective tissue. The sarcoplasmic proteins are water-soluble and consist mainly of enzymes that are involved in the metabolism of the cell. These proteins precipitate on cooking and do not contribute significantly to the texture of the fish. The connective tissue comprises mainly collagen. In mammalian muscle, the collagens are chemically crosslinked to varying degrees, sometimes necessitating extensive cooking to tenderise the muscle. In contrast the collagens of fish muscle have lower melting temperatures and are easily converted to gelatin on cooking.

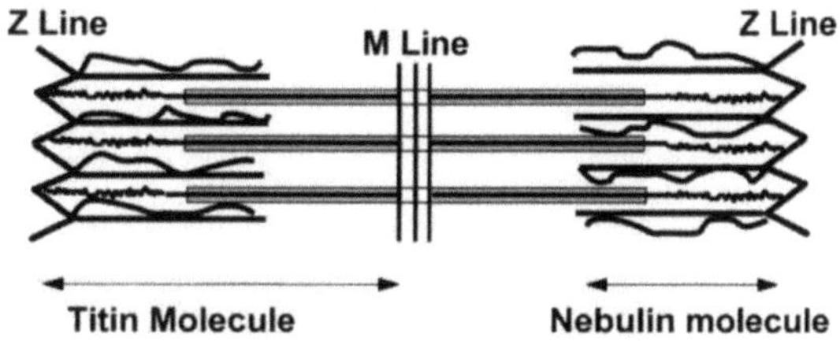

Fig. 7.2. Diagrammatic representation of the sarcomere showing some of the cytoskeletal elements

Depending on the fish species, the myofibrillar proteins, myosin and actin account for 65–75% of the total protein. The myofibrils occupy a substantial volume of the muscle and it has been shown that changes in the water holding capacity of whole muscle arise from changes in the water holding capacity of the myofibril [1]. The high water holding capacity of fish muscle proteins accounts for the juiciness and succulence of fish.

Associated with the myofibrillar proteins are the cytoskeletal proteins which form a three-dimensional network within and between the muscle cells. Figure 7.2 is a diagrammatic representation of a sarcomere showing the key elements of the cytoskeleton associated with the myofibrillar proteins. Connectin filaments are associated with the thick myosin filaments, linking them to the *Z* line. Nebulin filaments form the template for and are associated with the thin actin filaments.

Many groups are currently researching the role of the cytoskeletal proteins in determining the texture of fish. In particular several authors have attributed the post mortem softening of fish muscle to degradation of elements of the cytoskeleton.

7.3 Supply Chain and Protein Functionality

The textural quality of a frozen fish product, at the time of preparation by the consumer, is determined by many elements of the supply chain. As stated before, the myofibrillar proteins are the major determinants of texture and many effects of the supply chain can be interpreted in terms of their effects on these proteins.

After death, the circulation of blood ceases and as the muscle is no longer supplied with oxygen, the mitochondria are unable to produce ATP aerobically. ATP is then produced primarily anaerobically, from glycogen reserves, with the production of lactic acid. When the ATP level can no longer be maintained, the muscle stiffens as the interaction of the thick and thin filaments occurs. As a result of the bonding between the thick and thin filaments, the muscle becomes rigid, a state known as rigor mortis. Fish are normally allowed to pass through rigor before processing. If muscle is removed from the fish pre-rigor, an extreme contraction leading to an unacceptable toughness may result from rigor. Fish which is filleted and frozen pre-rigor can exhibit thaw rigor also leading to toughening and distortion of products.

The time which fish spends on ice prior to processing can have a significant effect on quality. The post mortem conditioning process leads to softening mus-

Fig. 7.3. Electron micrographs showing changes in the ultrastructure of cod during ice storage

cle tissue, and in mammalian muscle, a period of chill storage is often necessary to tenderise muscle. In fish tissue, in addition to characteristic flavour changes, the post mortem conditioning process can lead to excessive softening. Although the main myofibrillar proteins, actin and myosin are believed to remain largely intact during conditioning, many of the cytoskeletal proteins, for example connectin, nebulin and desmin, are believed to be degraded. There have been many recent studies of post mortem conditioning in fish and the consensus seems to be that the process may not be the same in all fish species. Certainly the rate at which the degradative changes and the associated softening occurs varies considerably between fish species. Figure 7.3 shows the nature of the ultrastructural changes that are observed during ice storage of cod.

After freezing, microbial degradation of fish ceases, but the flavour and texture of many fish species continue to change. In oily fish species the flavour changes resulting from lipid oxidation may limit the frozen shelf life. For fish products that are based on fish of the gadoid species such as cod, haddock and Alaskan pollock, the potential for loss of quality through textural changes is the prime concern. To understand the origin of the textural changes that can occur during frozen storage we need to consider what happens when fish is frozen.

7.4 Effect of Freezing

For a comprehensive review of the effect of freezing on flesh proteins with particular reference to problems associated with freezing fish, the reader is referred to Mackie [2]. Under normal commercial freezing regimes, ice nucleates not between the myofibrils but between the muscle cells. As these ice crystals grow, water is abstracted from the myofibrils and the cells become condensed. Figure 7.4 shows a longitudinal section of frozen fish showing large extracellular ice crystals between the muscle fibres.

The effect of this condensation of the muscle fibres on the myofibrillar lattice is shown in Fig. 7.5. Clearly as a result of the condensation of the fibres, the myofilaments are in closer proximity to each other. If fish is thawed soon after being frozen, the lattice recovers its original dimensions and a large proportion of the water returns to the muscle cells. In these circumstances the textural quality

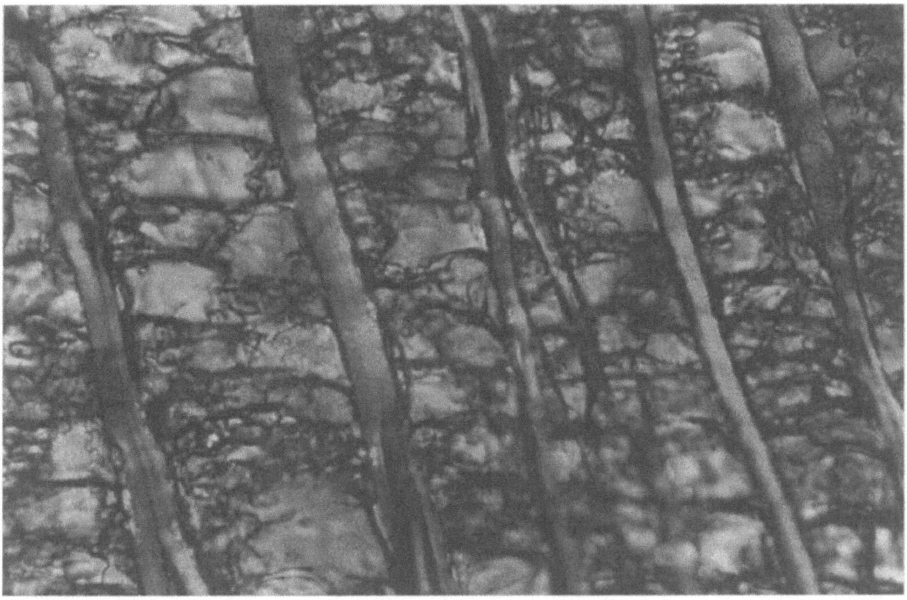

Fig. 7.4. Longitudinal section of frozen fish muscle showing large ice crystals between condensed muscle fibres

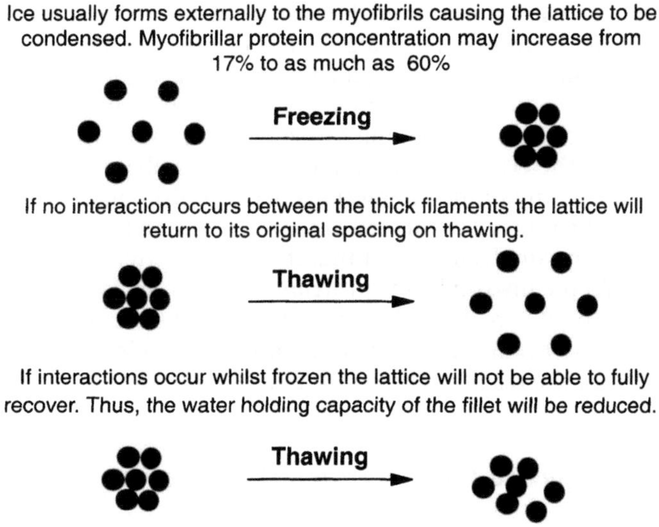

Fig. 7.5. Effect of freezing on the myofibrillar lattice

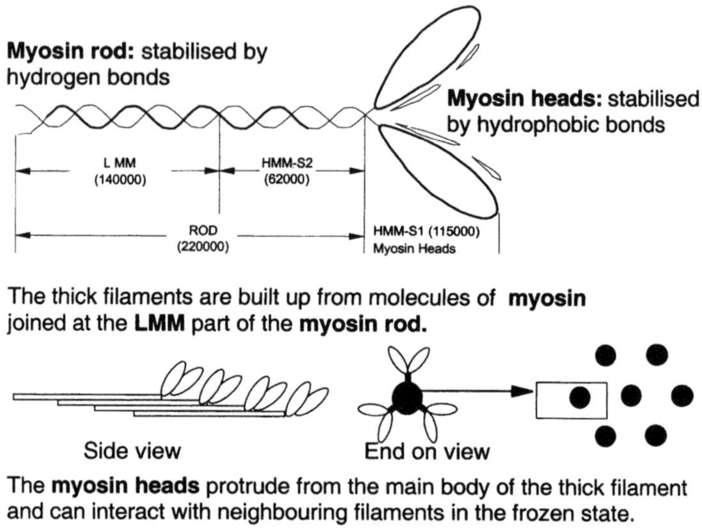

Fig. 7.6. The myosin molecule

of the fish is maintained. If however, fish is stored in the frozen state for a period of time, interactions between the myofilaments can occur. As a result, on thawing, the water is unable to return to the cells and remains in the extracellular spaces. Some of this water may be lost as drip and further water may be lost on cooking. This redistribution or loss of moisture can result in the sensory characteristics typical of frozen deteriorated fish. The fish may have a very high initial juiciness, but on further chewing the fish is tough, fibrous and dry.

The process of myofibrillar protein aggregation can be monitored by studying the decrease in protein salt solubility. Changes in the water distribution within the muscle and in the water holding capacity are also observed. Despite extensive research, the nature of the interactions between fish muscle proteins or the mechanism by which they are formed are not understood. It is known that the extractability of myosin declines and that its ATPase activity is reduced during frozen storage. As the myosin heads protrude from the surface of the thick filaments (see Fig. 7.6), it is reasonable to presume that interactions between thick filaments is likely to occur via the head regions of the molecules. This hypothesis is supported by the results of the work described below.

7.5 Use of High Pressure to Prevent Frozen Deterioration

The following section describes some patented work for preventing protein aggregation during on frozen storage of cod [3]. The technology is based on the known effects of ultra hydrostatic pressure on proteins.

7.5.1
Principles of High Hydrostatic Pressure Processing

A system at equilibrium will tend to minimise the effects of an external perturbant (Le Chatelier's Principle). Application of pressure will, therefore, favour changes that result in a reduction in volume. As a consequence, high hydrostatic pressure tends to stabilise hydrogen bonds since their formation results in a slight reduction in volume. Conversely, ionic bonds and hydrophobic interactions are broken since their disruption results in a decrease in volume. Covalent bonds tend to be unaffected by high hydrostatic pressure.

The stability of covalent bonds to high hydrostatic pressure offers clear advantages for food processing. Many important low molecular weight molecules such as flavours and vitamins will not be affected by hydrostatic pressure. Since pressure is transmitted in a uniform and instantaneous manner though food substances, the process is independent of sample volume or geometry.

7.5.2
Effect of Hydrostatic Pressure on Myofibrillar Proteins

Figure 7.6 shows a diagrammatic representation of the myosin molecule and the organisation of myosin molecules within the thick filaments. The myosin heads are stabilised by internal hydrophobic bonds and will tend to be denatured under ultra high pressure. Conversely, the myosin rod is stabilised, predominantly, by hydrogen bonding, and is likely to be stabilised by ultra high pressure. It is possible, therefore, to denature selectively the myosin head region without inducing large changes in the main body of the thick filament [4, 5], thus preserving most of the structure of the myofibrils.

The actin molecules of the thin filaments are globular in nature, and are joined together rather like two strings of pearls twisted together. The actin molecules are stabilised by hydrophobic bonds and will also be denatured by pressure [4].

7.5.3
Stabilisation of Cod Muscle Against Frozen Deterioration by the Application of High Hydrostatic Pressure

By application of ultra high hydrostatic pressure it may possible to denature selectively the myosin molecule. By selectively denaturing the myosin head regions, so rendering them "inert" prior to freezing, it ought to be possible to prevent/reduce thick filament associations during frozen storage. Reducing the extent of thick filament association in the frozen state will allow the myofibrillar lattice to recover on thawing, and water losses from the fillet will be reduced. If the pressure treatment can be tailored such that neither the helical regions of myosin nor the actin in the thin filaments are denatured, the myofibril structure will be largely preserved. Consequently, the water-holding capacity of the myofibril should not be reduced, and the fish will maintain a raw and unprocessed appearance.

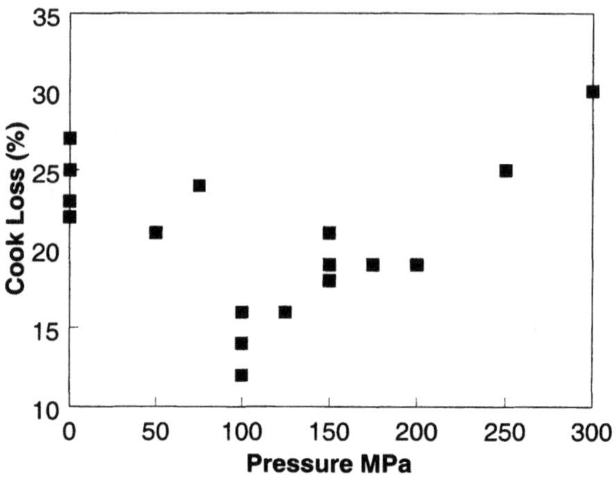

Fig. 7.7. The effect of high hydrostatic pressure on water loss of cod cooked at 85 °C

Selective denaturation of the myosin molecule by heat, although in principle possible, tends to cause some denaturation of the helical regions of myosin leading to water loss and a cooked appearance [6, 7].

It has now been shown that the application of ultra high pressure can reduce cooking loss from frozen cod fillets. For example, Fig. 7.8 shows the effect of increasing hydrostatic pressure on the thermal properties of cod fillet (as monitored by differential scanning calorimetry) and the ultra structure of the myofibril.

It can be seen that application of a pressure of 100 MPa to the cod fillet (prior to freezing) caused denaturation of parts of the myosin molecule, a slight change in the ultra structure of the myofibril. Figure 7.7 also shows that a reduction in cook loss is observed for this pressure treatment. On increasing the pressure treatment to 200 MPa denaturation of actin was observed. The denaturation of actin was coincident with a dramatic change in the myofibril structure and an increase in the amount of moisture lost on cooking. This suggests that denaturing the thin filament protein actin causes a dramatic drop in the water-holding capacity of the myofibrils. From these results, it is clear that by careful selection of pressurising conditions specific effects on the muscle proteins can be achieved.

Figure 7.7 shows the amount of water lost on cooking cod fillet which has been frozen and subjected to a short period of frozen storage as a function of applied hydrostatic pressure.

Results have also shown that increases in the water-holding capacity of cod fillet can be achieved by application of hydrostatic pressure. Data also suggest that these increases in water holding capacity can be maintained through freezing and frozen storage. Further work is required to investigate the impact that high hydrostatic processing has on the sensory properties of cod fillet, and to determine if the textural quality of pressure treated cod is preserved during frozen storage.

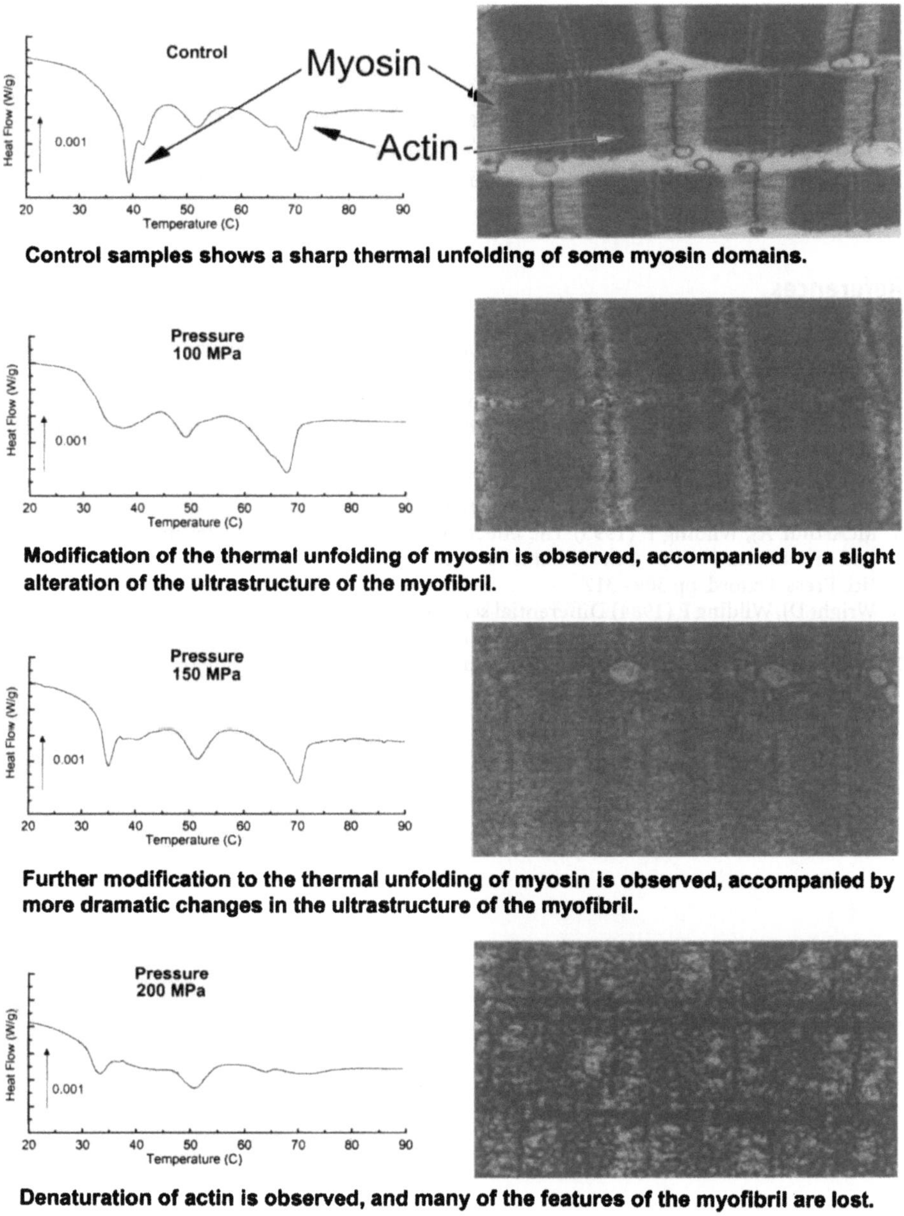

Fig. 7.8. The effects of ultra high pressure on the thermal properties and ultrastructure of cod

7.6 Conclusions

The myofibrillar proteins of fish to a large extent determine the textural quality of fish products. Control of the supply chain and the use of process regimes that influence the properties of these proteins can maximise the quality of fish products.

References

1. Offer G, Trinick J (1983) On the mechanism of water holding in meat – the swelling and shrinking of myofibrils. Meat Sci 8: 245–281
2. Mackie IM (1993) The effects of freezing on flesh proteins. Food Rev Int 9: 575–610
3. Goodband RM, Hedges ND, Wilding P (1999) Process for providing a frozen fish product. US Pat No 6,007,864
4. Yamamoto K, Hayashi S, Yasui T (1983) Hydrostatic pressure-induced aggregation of myosin molecules in 0.5 m KCl at pH 6.0. Biosci Biotechnol Biochem 57: 383–388
5. McArthur AJ, Wilding P (1995) The effect of high pressure on skeletal muscle myofibrils and myosin. In: Phillips GO, Williams PA (eds) Gums and stabilisers in the food industry. IRL Press, Oxford, pp 309–317
6. Wright DJ, Wilding P (1984) Differential scanning calorimetric study of muscle and its proteins – myosin and its subfragments. J Sci Food Agric 35: 357–372
7. Wright DJ, Leach LB, Wilding PJ (1977) Differential scanning calorimetric studies of muscle and its constituent proteins. J Sci Food Agric 28: 557–564

8 Binding and Texture Modification Using Transglutaminase

Angela Mumby

Transglutaminase (TG) is an enzyme that catalyses the cross-linking reaction between glutamine and lysine residues in protein molecules. TG has various effects on the physical properties of food proteins such as gelation capability, thermal stability, water-holding capacity, binding, viscosity modification, elasticity of protein gels, etc. This chapter summarises the use of TG and its application (properties and preparation).

8.1 Introduction

Over recent years in the UK food industry, a requirement has grown for an ingredient with:

- Superior binding qualities without loss of fish quality
- Excellent texture enhancement
- However, will also allow the removal of ingredients such as salt and phosphates to produce "healthier" foods

Transglutaminase (TG) is a unique enzyme commercialised by Ajinomoto which meets these other requirements.

Ajinomoto itself is a US$6.7 billion turnover company which is the world's leading manufacturer of amino acids. Forum Products are the U.K. agents for Ajinomoto as well as a number of key ingredients from around the world including Aspartame which has revolutionised the low calories/low sugar market soft drinks market.

The use of TG allows the production of new and innovative foods. The main usage of the enzyme is in meat and fish but there are many other applications for binding and texture modification in products such as pasta, pet food, croutons and bread crumbs, cooked meats, sauces, deserts, yoghurt and meat free or vegetarian foods.

8.2 Properties of Transglutaminase

TG acts on protein molecules both intermolecularly and intramolecularly, and cross links are formed between glutamine and lysine amino acids.

This reaction results in rheological changes in food proteins. So far most of the industrial enzymes such as amylases and proteases break down substrates into smaller molecules; however TG has the totally opposite function. It is a different kind of enzyme in that it creates larger molecules from small protein substrates through the cross linking reaction. This is extremely useful in food processing to aid with improving quality and adding value in various areas of food manufacture.

TG is widely found in nature and is found in the tissues of various mammals such as cows, sheep, pigs, fish (salmon and tuna), and birds such as chicken. It is also found in the growing shoots and leaves of plants, for example peas, broccoli and alfalfa. In addition, TG is frequently available in the livers and blood of mammals, and in fact in humans has been found in blood to be a contributory agent in blood coagulation and the terminating of bleeding and aiding of wound healing. The use of TG extracted from mammals has been too expensive to utilise; thus Ajinomoto's Research and Development Division developed TG, together with Amano Pharmaceutical Company Limited, from a micro-organism called *Streptoverticillium mobaraense* and have succeeded in mass production and commercialisation of TG by a patented fermentation method.

TG is produced in a similar way to alcohol production such as beer or wine by a simple fermentation process. The micro organism, *Streptoverticillium mobaraense,* grows on a nutrient broth producing TG. When the fermentation process is over, all the TG producing micro-organism is completed removed.

The TG manufactured by Ajinomoto also has the advantage of being calcium independent and is active over a wide pH and temperature range. TG reacts well between pH 5 and pH 8, which is the pH range of most foods. The optimum temperature for TG is 50–55 °C. During food processing the enzyme works in a variety of temperatures including chilled. At 0 °C binding will occur in a little over 2.5 h and at 10 °C within 1 h. Binding time depends on temperature and protein availability. Once the binding has occurred, food products using TG can then withstand further processing such as cooking, smoking, freezing, chilling, etc. Strong and irreversible binding is maintained in all these processes and there is no effect on the taste and flavour of the food.

The nutritional value of the food is not lost either since the cross linked proteins have no adverse effect and can be readily absorbed in the body as they are when found naturally in food. In Japan, TG is widely used in Surimi, a formed crab stick and Kamaboko which is a boiled fish paste to improve texture. The enzyme is also used in noodles, sausages, fresh and cooked meats, fish and soya products such as tofu.

There are various different preparations of TG the trade name of which is Activa. I will initially discuss Activa EB.

8.3 Activa EB for Binding

If strong binding is required between individual pieces of fish then Activa EB is used. Adding Activa EB allows the reduction of salt and phosphate addition since binding occurs because of the addition of the enzyme not due to salt and phosphate use or long tumbling times and extraction of protein on the muscle surface which would destroy the texture of the fish. Caseinate has a specific ef-

Table 8.1. Reactivity of Ajinomoto TG with various proteins

	Food protein	Reactivity[a]
Milk	Casein	1
	Na-casinate	1
	α-Lactalbumin	3
	β-Lactoglobulin	3
Eggs	Egg white protein (obalbumin)	3
	Egg yolk protein	2
Meats	Myoglobin	3
	Collagen	2
	Gelatin	1
	Myofibril: Myosin	1
	Myofibril: Actin	4
Soybean	11 S globulin	1
	7 S globulin	1
Wheat	Gliadin	2
	Glutenin	2

[a] 1 – reacts very well; 2 – reacts well; 3 – reacts depending on conditions; 4 – mostly does not react.

fect on improving the binding strength of TG thus explaining its use in Activa EB. Caseinate treated with TG becomes more viscose which acts as a stable sticky adhesive layer which can be used to hold together temporarily different food stuffs allowing the action of the enzyme to form strong cross links. TG enzyme is added as a powder or liquid usually at the mixing stage requiring only sufficient mixing to coat the surface area before forming into a shape or mould. Once binding has occurred the bound product can be further processed as required.

The most popular method is initially to rehydrate the enzyme with water to form a slurry or paste which is then added to fish prior to forming. The enzyme can also be added as a dry dusting powder before being pressed into a mould and compressed to eliminate air pockets. This dusting method is also suitable for rolled fillets such as plaice fillets rolled with a sauce or whole fish fillet "Kiev" style products.

TG can bind not only fresh but also cooked, cured and salted fish and meat as well as all types of shellfish and fish rich in fat such as fresh and smoked salmon.

TG is very reactive with myosin molecules which is the main component of myofibrillar protein. It is considered that TG promotes the formulation of cross links in the heavy chains of myosin found in muscle proteins. This results in strengthening of the protein network structure which means that various rheological and physical properties can be improved such as firmness, elasticity and cohesiveness. Here we can see how reactive TG is with different protein components of milk, eggs, meats, soybean or wheat (Table 8.1). A score of 1 is given to the most reactive protein.

8.4 Activa WM for Texture

A second and popular preparation of TG is Activa WM. Commonly Activa WM is specifically used to improve texture. The addition level, reaction time and temperature are important to obtain the required break strength or firmness of the product.

In the processing of prepared foods, especially meat and fish products, salt and/or phosphates are usually added to increase water holding capacity, improve binding and to improve the products texture. Recently, as health demands increase, prepared foods with reduced salt or reduced phosphates are widely on the market or are being currently developed. The texture and physical properties of these "healthier" products however can still be undesirable. In Japan and Europe, processors are already offering reduced salt or reduced phosphate products by using TG. In products such as sausages, the gel strengthened using Activa WM compensates for some gel weaknesses caused by low salt and lack of phosphates (Table 8.2).

A further use of the enzyme is to prevent the deterioration of texture and enhance the characteristics of the original product that is retorted. The glutamine and lysine covalent bonds that are formed are very strong compared to the normal sulphur bonds formed; thus the structure is resistant to the strain of heating and retorting. This attribute of Activa WM is particularly useful as well in canned pasta, pet food, fish and meat.

Figure 8.1 shows the results of adding Activa WM to a low protein sausage. The break strength was considerably increased by the addition of Activa WM significantly improving the texture compared to a rather "soft" standard. The use of Activa WM also increased juiciness through its water holding ability, reduced stickiness and chewiness, giving a product with improved snap or crispness referred to as break strength.

A further use of TG can be to improve the thermal stability of protein gels, a useful property in gelatine-based sauces which do not melt away on cooking. At 100°C with 5 units of TG per gram of protein, a gel is still formed even after 60 min, giving a very stable gelatine gel.

Concerning safety, TG has been through many detailed safety studies before the enzyme was marketed initially in Japan but is now widely sold in Europe and the U.K.

Table 8.2. Substitution of phosphates for Activa WM-sausage

	No phosphate	0.3% phosphate	0.25% Activa WM
Break strength (g/cm^2)	239	374	465
Strain (%)	13	15	18
Cooking loss (%)	8.5	3.1	2.2

Formulation: pork leg: 45%, fat: 25%; ice: 26%.
Cooking: smoke: 40°C for 45 min; boil: 80°C for 40 min.

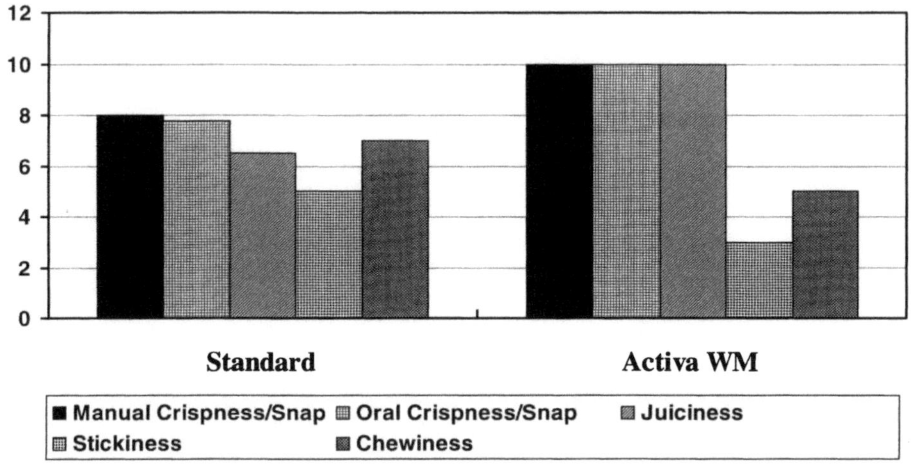

Fig. 8.1. Sensory analysis – Wiener sausage

8.5 Conclusions

In conclusion, there are many areas where TG as a binding and texture modifying enzyme can be used to produce innovative foods and we are constantly finding new applications for this unique and interesting enzyme.

To recap:

- TG is an enzyme already extensively found naturally.
- TG is a pure enzyme products by a patented fermentation reaction.
- TG acts by cross linking the proteins glutamine and lysine widely found in fish.
- TG reacts over a wide pH and temperature range and is easy to use in a variety of applications.
- MAFF have approved TG as a processing aid.
- TG has both excellent texture and binding benefits.

9 Histamine Toxicity and Scombroid Fish Poisoning: a Review

Panos Mavromatis, Peter Quantick

Histamine is a naturally occurring compound synthesised in the body. It has been identified as a toxic agent which causes allergic reactions. Histamine can be indigenous or dietary. Indigenous histamine is produced in the human body mainly in mast cells and is released as a result of responses to allergens. The mechanism of histamine toxicity involves mediators known as histamine receptors, which are responsible for the development of the various symptoms. Dietary histamine is produced in various foods the most important of which is fish of the scombroid family and is the result of microbial activity. Specific microbial strains are known to produce the enzyme *histidine decarboxylase*, which converts the amino acid histidine to histamine. Histamine (scombroid) poisoning is one of the commonest food intoxications associated with seafood in both the USA and England and Wales. Although detailed records are not available, the disease is of world-wide occurrence and there is a good evidence that the number of histamine poisoning cases is under reported. Histamine formation in fish can be controlled by proper handling and cold storage. The allergic response can be treated with antihistamines, drugs known to possess histamine antagonistic character. This chapter provides an insight into the issues related to histamine and scombroid poisoning.

9.1 Introduction

Histamine is reported to be the causative agent of histamine (scombroid) poisoning associated with the consumption of fish of the scombroid family such as tuna and mackerel [48]. Histamine can also be produced in a number of foods including cheese and sausages as well as drinks such as wine and beer [18]. Histamine is found in many plant and animal tissues [64] and is specifically important in human physiology because it is one of the chemicals released from certain cells (particularly mast cells) upon tissue injury or during the neutralisation of foreign material (antigens) by certain types of antibodies [40].

The aim of this literature survey is to investigate the allergenic character of histamine by looking at the mechanisms of its production and release in the body as well as in scombroid fish. The biochemical role of histamine in the body, the nature of the disease syndrome, the formation of histamine and other biogenic amines in fish and potential methods for the control of the syndrome including technological and medicinal approaches are analysed.

Table 9.1. Histamine in foods

Fish	Tuna Herring Mackerel Anchovies Sardines	Meats	Meats Processed meats Salami Sauerkraut Sausage
Beverages	Wines Beer Fermented beverages Vinegar	Vegetables	Spinach Tomatoes Avocados Eggplant
Dairy products	Cheeses Yoghurt Sour cream	Other foods	Canned foods Fermented foods Yeast extract Jams Some oriental foods

9.2 What is Histamine?

Histamine is a natural substance produced by the body and is also present in many foods, primarily fish but also beer, cheese, wine, etc. [18, 43, 59, 68, 78]. Table 9.1 shows foods reported to contain histamine.

Histamine is an organic compound produced from the amino acid histidine by the removal of a carboxyl group (COOH) [8]. This removal is achieved with the action of an enzyme called *histidine decarboxylase* [11, 54, 69]. Histamine is a small, polar, organic molecule of low molecular weight, which comprises an imidazole ring and an ethylamine side chain; it is water soluble and is a base. It is a biologically active amine which has important physiological effects in humans, either psychoactive or vasoactive. As a psychoactive amine, histamine affects the nervous system by acting on neural transmitters, and as a vasoactive amine it also acts on the vascular system [45, 64].

9.3 Health Aspects of Histamine

9.3.1 Allergic Reactions and Role of Histamine

Allergies are caused by an immune response to a normally innocuous substance (i. e. pollen, dust) that comes in contact with lymphocytes specific for that substance, or antigen. In many cases the lymphocyte triggered to respond is a mast cell. For this response to occur, a free-floating IgE (an immunoglobulin associated with allergic response) molecule specific to the antigen must first be attached to cell surface receptors on mast cells. The antigen binding to the mast cell-attached IgE then triggers the mast cell to respond. This response often includes the release of histamine [34].

An allergic reaction, then, is an immune response that should not be occurring because the substance that causes it should not exert any harmful effect [42]. Histamine is a chemical with an important role in many allergic reactions that is normally present in tissue mast cells and certain white blood cells (basophils) circulating in the body. Large amounts of histamine are released in response to an injury or in conjunction with an antigen-antibody reaction, such as an allergic reaction [30, 40]. The release of histamine can be induced by almost any allergen. Examples include inhalant allergens, drugs, chemicals, insect venoms and some foods. Because of its vasoactive character, histamine is able to create havoc with many body functions because it is contained in almost all body tissues. These main body tissues include the lungs, skin, intestinal mucosa, mast cells and basophils [70].

Anaphylaxis [30] and allergic responses due to antibody/antigen interactions are two important responses mediated in part by histamine. Major effects of histamine include arteriolar dilation and increased capillary permeability, a decrease in heart rate (H_2 receptor effect), bronchoconstriction (H_1 receptor effect), and gastric acid secretion (H_2 receptor effect) [61, 81].

9.3.2 Histamine in Humans

In humans it occurs mainly in an inactive bound form in most body tissues. When released, it interacts with specific macromolecules (histamine receptors) on the cell surface or within a target cell to elicit changes in many different bodily functions. As mentioned earlier, histamine is a powerful biologically active chemical and can exert many responses within the body. Although mast cells and blood basophils contain large amounts of histamine, which is stored in special granules (Fig. 9.1), harmful effects resulting from the consumption of foods rich in biogenic amines can be expected only when these amines gain access to the bloodstream [35, 40, 64].

Histamine can directly stimulate the heart as a result of its effect on the liberation of adrenaline and noradrenaline from the suprarenal gland and so can excite the smooth muscles of the uterus, the intestine and the respiratory tract, stimulate both sensory and motor neurons, and control gastric acid secretion [35, 64, 70].

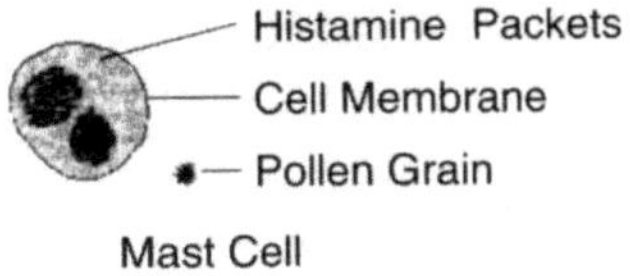

Fig. 9.1. Histamine granules in a mast cell

9.3.2.1 *Symptoms*

When histamine is released from the mast cells as a result of an allergic reaction or indeed ingested form a dietary source, it may cause one or more of the following symptoms [28, 30, 77]:

- Eyes itch, burn, or become watery
- Nose itches, sneeze, and produce more mucus
- Skin itches, develops rashes or hives
- Sinuses become congested and causes headaches
- Lungs wheeze or have spasms
- Stomach experiences cramps and diarrhoea
- Oedema (swelling) usually manifested as acute urticaria (rapidly appearing hives, accompanied by severe itching)
- Burning sensation or peppery taste in the mouth
- Facial flushing, tachycardia, pruritis, and asthma-like symptoms can also occur

Released histamine tends to dilate blood capillaries (causing the skin to appear red and feel warm) and makes the capillaries more permeable, allowing fluid to escape into the tissues (Fig. 9.2).

Histamine poisoning produces one or more of the above symptoms and is usually a mild illness with short duration, which makes treatment unnecessary [31]. For more severe cases or in patients with underlying medical conditions, oral antihistamines may be beneficial. Illness begins minutes to hours after ingestion of the toxic fish [31]. The lack of severity may be because histamine is absorbed very poorly from the gastrointestinal tract and because the liver and the intestinal mucosa have a great capacity to detoxify histamine [71]. Released histamine does not last long in the body. It is rapidly inactivated and disappears from the bloodstream within minutes. A fairly efficient detoxification system exists in the intestinal tract to metabolise ingested histamine and histamine which may be formed by intestinal bacteria. The detoxification system is composed of two distinct enzymes; *diamine oxidase* and *histamine-N-methyl transferase*. These enzymes convert histamine into non-toxic products. This detoxification system is adequate for handling normal dietary intakes of histamine. However, it apparently fails to detoxify the large amounts of histamine that can be ingested with spoiled scombroid fish [64].

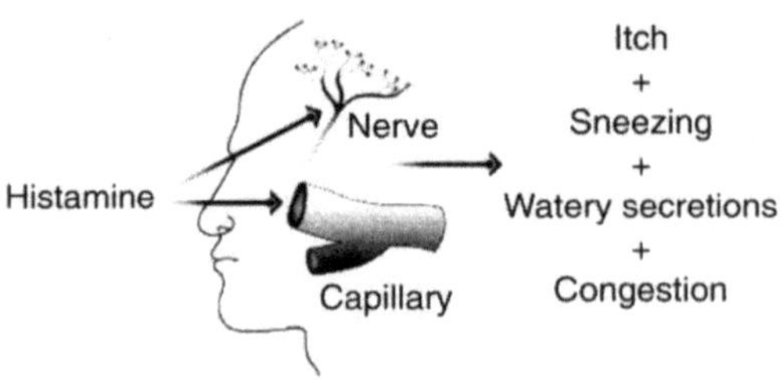

Fig. 9.2. Mechanism of histamine allergic reactions

9.3.3
Mechanism of Toxicity

Histamine is one of the aminergic neurotransmitters, playing an important role in the regulation of several (patho)physiological processes. In the mammalian brain, histamine is synthesised in a restricted population of neurons located in the tuberomammillary nucleus of the posterior hypothalamus [61]. These neurons project diffusely to most cerebral areas and have been implicated in several brain functions (e.g. sleep/wakefulness, hormonal secretion, cardiovascular control, thermoregulation, food intake and memory formation) [61]. Histamine is released by the body during times of stress and allergy and exerts its effects by binding to receptors on cellular membranes, which are found in the cardiovascular system and in various secretory glands [35, 64].

Histamine can be released by an allergic reaction but can also appear as a result of a non-allergic release. In the first case, sensitisation of the individual is necessary and there is an interaction of the antigen with divalent IgE class antibodies [30]. In the case of non-allergic release, the causative agent could be radio contrast media or plasma expander and pre-sensitisation of the individual is not required.

The release of histamine causes several allergic symptoms, as listed below [3, 47, 70]:

1. It contributes to an inflammatory response.
2. It causes contraction of pulmonary smooth muscle (bronchoconstriction) that results in an asthma-like disorder.
3. Histamine also dilates small blood vessels and increases their permeability.

Histamine allergic reactions can be treated with antihistamines, as will be discussed.

9.3.4
Synthesis of Indigenous Histamine

The chief sites of histamine in the body are the mast cells of connective tissue and their circulating counterparts in the blood, the basophils [10]. These cells synthesise histamine by the action of an enzyme that removes the carboxyl group from the amino acid L-histidine. Histamine is then stored in many tissues of the body [30, 40].

In peripheral tissues, histamine is stored in mast cells, basophils, enterochromaffin cells and granules with other mediators. Mast cell histamine plays an important role in the pathogenesis of various allergic conditions. In an allergic response, an allergen stimulates the release of antibodies, which attach themselves to mast cells [30]. After mast cell degranulation, release of histamine leads to various well-known symptoms of allergic conditions in the skin and the airway system [57]. Based on these observations, histamine is considered as one of the most important mediators of allergy and inflammation.

9.3.5
Histamine Receptors and Their Role

Histamine, like many other transmitters, mediates responses via receptors, which are divided into three subtypes H_1, H_2 and H_3. The H_1 receptors are found in the smooth muscle of the intestines, bronchi, and blood vessels [15]. The H_2 receptors are found in gastric parietal cells and in the vascular and central nervous systems. The H_3 receptors are found in brain and in the periphery and regulate histamine release [26, 74].

The concept of histamine receptors became broadly accepted through the subsequent development of substances such as metiamide and cimetidine, which demonstrated effective inhibitory effects on the action of histamine in the stomach and the heart [12]. Epinephrine and H_1 receptor blocking antihistamines reverse the actions of histamine on smooth muscles; H_2 receptor blocking antihistamines, such as cimetidine or ranitidine, reverse the gastric acid stimulant action of histamine. Both the histamine H_1 and H_2 receptors belong to the large family of G-protein coupled receptors (GPCRs) [6, 78]. Recent research has revealed that histamine also functions as a neurotransmitter [61], which means that there is a presynaptic receptor (H_3) for histamine as well [5]. The H_3 receptor controls the formation and release of histamine [60]. Although the genetic information for the H_1 and H_2 receptors has been available for some years now, as yet no information on the primary structure of the H_3 receptor is known.

9.3.6
Role of Histamine Receptors and their Agonists and Antagonists

9.3.6.1
Histamine Agonists

Agonists can be defined as chemical substances, for example, drugs, capable of combining with a receptor on a cell and initiating a reaction or activity. In the case of histamine and its receptors, selective agonists exist for H_1, H_2 and H_3 receptors. For H_1 receptor, imidazole-based compounds have been found to yield the most successful selective H_1 agonists. For example, 2 (meta-halogenated)phenylhistamines are relatively potent agonists in guinea pig ileum [82]. Dimaprit originally found in the search for H_2 receptor antagonists is a relatively selective H_2 agonist, almost as active as histamine itself at the H_2 receptors. Although it displays hardly any H_1 agonism, it is a moderate H_3 receptor agonist [41]. At the H_3 receptor, histamine itself is an active agonist. Imetit, also a potent agonist, is effectively a histamine molecule with the amine moiety replaced by a thiourea grouping [27].

9.3.6.2
Histamine Antagonists

Antagonists, by contrast, are agents, which operate in the body to reduce the physiological activity of another chemical substance. The action of H_1 antagonists is primarily on intestinal and bronchial smooth muscle, although some effects on the CNS also occur (including the CNS depressant effect) [26, 74]. Over the years, medicinal chemists have focused on developing H_1 antagonists with reduced CNS penetration, thereby limiting unwanted side-effects such as drowsiness. Terfenadine was one of the early H_1 antagonists with reduced CNS penetration. Unfortunately, it does produce cardiac arrhythmias. Astemizole is an effective H_1 antagonist with low CNS activity [27].

Histamine stimulates muscle contractions in the atrium and the uterus, as well as gastric acid secretion in the gut. These responses are mediated through H_2 receptors. Metiamide is an H_2 antagonist, which due to its chemical structure results in increased membrane permeability and greater oral absorption. Metiamide is not used clinically however, due to its renal toxicity. The peptic ulcer drug cimetidine is a prototypical H_2 antagonist derived from metiamide. Low toxicity is maintained by the modification of its chemical structure, a cyano substituent replaces a thio group as found in metiamide [74]. H_3 antagonists have been developed with potential application in enhancing alertness by elevating histamine release in the central nervous system. Thioperamide is a prototypical H_3 antagonist that can potentiate the release of histamine and reverse the action of R-α-methylhistamine at the autoreceptor [26, 74].

9.3.7 Antihistamines

Antihistamines are a group of synthetic drugs that can inhibit various actions of histamine. They have some chemical resemblance to histamine and act as antagonists by competing with histamine for occupation of its receptor sites, thereby preventing histamine from eliciting its usual responses. They are helpful therapeutically in preventing rather than in reversing histamine actions [65].

Research results in the past years led to the development of several potent "antihistamines" (e.g. mepyramine), which demonstrated efficiency in inhibiting certain symptoms of allergic conditions [81]. Antihistamines, due to their histamine receptor antagonistic character, inhibit the histamine-mediated release of inflammatory mediators by leukocytes [19], and they also cause neutralisation of histamine, preventing it from binding and activating immune-related cells in the area.

The most rapidly effective treatment is epinephrine (adrenaline), which is usually given by injection. Antihistamines are better at preventing reactions than treating them and are useful if an allergic reaction, such as hay fever, is expected. Additionally, histamine allergies are frequently treated by drugs such as Claritin and Allegra [20]. Intravenous cimetidine has also been found to exert antihistamine effects but its use requires further study [13]. The use of antihistamines allows us to live more safely and comfortably by counteracting the body's immunological mistakes.

9.4 Scombroid Poisoning and Histamine in Fish

Scombroid poisoning is named from the family *Scombroidae*, which includes tuna and mackerel, but this illness can occur after ingestion of any dark-fleshed non-scombroid species, such as herring, containing high levels of free histidine [21].

The formation of histamine is caused by bacteria possessing the enzyme *histidine decarboxylase*, which converts histidine to histamine [11, 54, 69, 79]. Histamine is reportedly produced by a wide range of micro-organisms, the vast majority of which are gram negative rods of the *Enterobacteriaceae* family [39, 51, 59]. However, it has been reported that only *Hafnia alvei, Morganella morganii* and *Klebsiella pneumoniae* are able to produce toxicologically significant amounts of histamine [11, 14, 16, 25, 33, 39, 44, 50, 52, 54, 69, 73, 80]. The kinds of bacteria that are associated with histamine development are commonly present in the salt-water environment. They naturally exist on the gills and in the gut of live fish, with no harm to the fish [38].

Histidine decarboxylase reacts with free histidine, a naturally occurring chemical that is present in larger quantities in some fish than in others. The result is the formation of histamine [71]. Once the enzyme *histidine decarboxylase* has been formed, it can continue to produce histamine in the fish even if the bacteria are not active. The enzyme can be active at or near refrigeration temperatures. *Histidine decarboxylase* is likely to be more stable than the bacteria in the frozen state and may be reactivated very rapidly after thawing. Recent studies suggest that if histamine production is advanced (i. e. high levels of *histidine decarboxylase*), histamine formation can continue even in frozen storage [40].

Scombrotoxin formation as a result of time/temperature abuse of certain species of fish can cause consumer illness known as histamine (scombroid) poisoning. Scombroid poisoning has primarily been associated with the consumption of tuna, mahi-mahi and blue fish. The illness is most closely linked to the development of histamine in these fish. In most cases, histamine levels in illness-causing fish have been above 200 ppm, often above 500 ppm [22]. The important factor with regards to the role of histamine in scombroid fish poisoning is that although it has been possible to produce mild symptoms of histamine excess after the oral administration of the substance in massive doses to humans it has not been possible to reproduce the illness with doses comparable to the quantities ingested in fish that have caused scombrotoxism [29, 49, 75]. Results by Taylor [71] and Hui and Taylor [32] have led to speculation that substances may be present in the spoiled fish that enhance the pharmacological activity of histamine, facilitate its absorption or inhibit its inactivation by *histamine N-methyltransferase, diamine oxidase* or both [48, 71].

There is strong evidence that the primary scombrotoxin is a mast cell degranulator which causes the release of indigenous histamine and other biologically active substances, which in turn are responsible for the gastrointestinal symptoms. Therefore, the toxic role of dietary histamine as posed by indigenous histamine is slight [17]. There are also indications that decomposition can result in the production of other toxins (e.g. biogenic amines, such as putrescine and cadaverine) that have the potential to cause illness, even in the absence of histamine formation. Such illnesses have been reported in a number of fish species [23].

There have been suggestions by several authors that histamine, by itself, may not be the principle causative agent of histamine poisoning in humans. Several authors have proposed that there is a requirement for potentiators of various types. Kim and Bjeldanes [37] reported that putrescine potentiates the peroral toxicity of subsequent doses of histamine in guinea pigs and that cadaverine causes a pronounced increase in the toxicity of histamine when the two compounds are administered simultaneously. They also report that histamine taken with a meal is absorbed to a greater extent than when consumed by itself.

Anecdotal information suggests that combinations of food are not recommended in certain parts of the world. For example, the consumption of fish and cheese, or other dairy products, is avoided in Greece. This may be because of the way in which these dietary constituents contain histamine and its potentiators. There has been little or no research undertaken in this area and, if it were demonstrated to be the case that these combined food effects exist, then it could have significance in epidemiological studies relating to histamine poisoning and be of importance to the food industry in general. A small study was undertaken within the Food Research Centre (University of Lincoln, UK) in which volunteers, within the same day, were fed with histamine containing fish (mackerel) and cheese (Smoked Austrian) separately and within 30 min of each other. Typical symptoms were only recorded when fish and cheese were consumed in close succession. It is known that tyramine is a prominent biogenic amine in cheeses, which also contain histamine, and it is possible that there is potentiating effect of these two, and possibly other amines.

However, Clifford and Walker [17] suggested that there is no compelling evidence for the potentiation of dietary histamine by other dietary amines. Additionally, Morrow et al. [48] concluded that histamine is the causative agent of scombrotoxicosis.

9.4.1 Controlling Histamine Formation

Soon after death the defence mechanisms of the fish no longer inhibit bacterial growth, and histamine-forming bacteria start to grow and produce the enzyme *histidine decarboxylase*, which attacks free histidine in the fish flesh. The enzyme converts free histidine to histamine, which has a more alkaline character. Once this enzyme is formed control of the hazard is unlikely. Histamine is more commonly the result of high temperature (>20 °C) spoilage than of long-term relatively low temperature spoilage. Rapid chilling or freezing of fish immediately after death is the most important element in any strategy for preventing the formation of scombrotoxin.

The potential for histamine formation is increased when the flesh of the fish is directly exposed to the enzyme-forming bacteria (EFB). This occurs when the fish are processed (e.g. butchering or filleting) [22]. Freezing for an extended period of time (e.g. 24 weeks) may inactivate the EFB and therefore almost eliminates the potential for further histamine development. Recent studies suggest that if histamine production is advanced, histamine formation can continue even in frozen storage.

Cooking can inactivate both the enzyme and the bacteria. However, once the toxin is formed it cannot be eliminated by heat (including retorting) or freezing. Because histamine is generally not uniformly distributed in a decomposed fish, a guidance level of 50 ppm has been set. If 50 ppm is found in one section, there is the possibility that other sections may exceed 500 ppm [24].

9.4.2
Permissible Limits for Histamine in Fish

Although in the USA histamine in canned sardines, mackerel and anchovies may not exceed 50 ppm, in the European Union (EU) up to 150 ppm of histamine in canned fish is permitted. The EU follows the guidelines of the United Nations' Food and Agriculture Organization's (FAO) *Codex Alimentarius*, or Food Code. The USA sets a lower limit based upon the presence in its population of individuals with a high sensitivity to histamines. Luten et al. [46] have reported that the EU has proposed that the average content of histamine in fish may not exceed a level of 10 mg/100 g. It is clear that quality criteria with respect to the presence of histamine in fishery products are necessary from a toxicological as well as from a technical point of view. Limits on the allowable levels of histamine in fish and fish products vary among countries. Additionally, some countries still do not have any regulatory limits.

9.4.3
Outbreaks and Epidemiology

Scombroid poisoning has been a significant food poisoning problem for many years and occurs world-wide [1, 2, 14, 33, 36, 48, 58, 63, 67, 72]. Many epidemiological surveys carried out in recent years have suggested that the number of histamine poisoning incidents has remained unchanged in spite of higher hygienic standards, the food regulations established in European countries and better education, which has resulted in increased public awareness [43]. It has also been reported that the annual number of histamine poisonings is under-estimated mainly due to inadequate record keeping and lack of an effective mechanism capable of collecting and efficiently analysing food poisoning outbreaks reports [9, 58, 62, 76].

Histamine poisoning accounts for more than 50% of the food poisoning incidents and outbreaks associated with the consumption of fish and seafood [9]. It is the most commonly reported illness associated with the consumption of fish in the UK [66]. In the vast majority of reported cases, scombrotoxin poisoning is associated with seafood and, more specifically, finfish of the scombroid type. Scombroid poisoning is diagnosed by history and clinical symptoms combined with the measurement of histamine levels in implicated fish. Fresh fish normally contains less than 1 mg/100 g of histamine; levels of 20 mg/100 g in some species have been reported to produce symptoms [7].

In the USA, between 1973 and 1986, around 178 outbreaks of scombrotoxin poisoning involving 1096 cases were reported to the CDC's Food Disease Outbreak Surveillance System [4]. Between 1988 and 1997, 145 outbreaks involving 811 cases were reported. Most commonly reported seafood outbreaks are associated with mahi-mahi, tuna and bluefish [53].

Overall, in the UK (between 1992 and 1996) scombrotoxin poisoning accounted for around 4% of outbreaks by aetiological agents. Seafood, in total, accounts for about 16% of all outbreaks in the UK by vehicle of transmission. This level is comparable to desserts.

In a large proportion of outbreaks associated with seafoods, aetiological agents are unknown (33 %). A similar situation is reported in the USA [53]. However, in England and Wales between 1992–96, scombrotoxin poisoning (26.5 %) was the most important, followed by bacteria such *Salmonella* spp. (18 %) and small round structured viruses (17 %). Therefore, in the UK, scombrotoxin poisoning is reportedly the most commonly recorded illness associated with eating fish (22 out of 32 fish-borne outbreaks). Panisello et al. [55] confirmed the results found by Sockett et al. [66] and Scoging [62]. Scombrotoxin poisoning in the UK has been mainly reported to be associated with tuna products, which are improperly stored (between 1992 and 1996, 12 % of cases fall into this category); however incidents have also been linked to non-scombroid fish [66]. More recent data, for 1997–98, indicate 11 outbreaks of scombrotoxin poisoning, which represents 3 % of all outbreaks where the aetiological agent is known. This level is higher than reported outbreaks for *Bacillus cereus* and *Bacillus subtilis* and comparable to numbers of outbreaks for *Cryptosporidium* [56]. Data are not freely available for many parts of the world, but the occurrence of scombrotoxin poisoning has been reported across the world [73].

9.5 Conclusions

Histamine in the body can be the product of either indigenous synthesis or dietary intake. Indigenous histamine can be released as an allergic response and produce clinical symptoms. Dietary histamine formed by decarboxylation of histidine is reported to play a role on the release of indigenous histamine. Scombroid fish as well as other foods are reported to contain histamine at levels capable of initiating allergic reactions. Histamine (scombroid) poisoning has been a food safety concern despite the high hygienic standards imposed by new legislation and guidelines. Although well investigated, the issue of whether histamine is indeed the causative agent of scombroid fish poisoning, is still a matter of controversy as many investigators have presented opposing arguments. However, it seems that histamine plays an important role, main or complementary, in the development of allergic symptoms after the consumption of foods containing high levels of histamine (> 500 ppm).

References

1. Ahmed FE (1992) Response. Int J Food Sci Technol 27: 725–726
2. Ahmed FE (1992) Review: assessing and managing risk due to consumption of seafood contaminated with micro-organisms, parasites and natural toxins in the US. Int J Food Sci Technol 27: 243–260
3. Andriopoulou P, Navarro P, Zanetti A, Lampugnani MG, Dejana E (1999) Histamine induces tyrosine phosphorylation of endothelial cell-to-cell adherens junctions. Arterioscler Thromb Vasc Biol 19: 2286–2297
4. Anonymous (1989) Epidemiologic notes and reports: scombroid fish poisoning. Morbid Mortal Wkly Rep 38: 140–142, 147
5. Arrang JM, Garbarg M, Schwarz (1983) Auto-inhibition of brain histamine release mediated by a novel class (H_3) of histamine receptors. Nature 302: 832–837

6. Ash AS, Schild HO (1966) Receptors mediating some actions of histamine. Br J Pharmacol 27: 427–439
7. Bartholomew BA, Berry PR, Rodhouse JC, Gilbert RJ, Murray CK (1987) Scombrotoxic fish poisoning in Britain: features of over 250 suspected incidents from 1976 to 1986. Epidemiol Infect 99: 775–782
8. Bauer F (1993) Histamine in fermented raw sausage. Meat Focus Int 2: 64–66
9. Bean NH, Goulding JS, Lao C, Angulo FJ (1997) Surveillance for foodborne-disease outbreaks – CDSC. Scombrotoxic fish poisoning and imported tuna steaks. Commun Dis Rep CDR Wkly 7: 1
10. Beaven MA (1978) Histamine: its role in physiological and pathological processes. Monogr Allergy 13: 1–5
11. Behling AR, Taylor SL (1982) Bacterial histamine production as function of temperature and time of incubation. J Food Sci 47: 1311–1314
12. Black JW, Duncan WAM, Durant CJ, Ganellin CR, Parsons EM (1972) Definition and antagonism of histamine H_2 receptors. Nature 236: 385–390
13. Blakesley ML (1983) Scombroid poisoning: prompt resolution of symptoms with cimetidine. Ann Emerging Med 12: 104–106
14. Bremer PJ, Osborne CM, Kemp RA, Van Veghel P, Fletcher GC (1998) Thermal death times of *Hafnia alvei* cells in a model suspension and in artificially contaminated hot-smoked khawai (*Arripis trutta*). J Food Prot 61: 1047–1051
15. Cavanah DK, Casale TB (1993) Histamine. In: Kaliner MA, Metcalfe DD (eds) The mast cell in health and disease. Marcel Dekker, New York, pp 321–342
16. Chen CM, Wei CI, Koburger JA, Marshall MR (1989) Comparison of four agar media for detection of histamine producing bacteria in tuna. J Food Prot 52: 808–813
17. Clifford MN, Walker R (1992) The aetiology of scombrotoxicosis. Int J Food Sci Technol 27: 721–724
18. Coutts RT, Baker GB, Pasutto FH (1986) Foodstuffs as sources of psychoactive amines and their precursors: content, significance and identification. Adv Drug Res 15: 169
19. Cuss FM (1999) Beyond the histamine receptor: effects of antihistamines on mast cells. Clin Exp Allergy 29: 54–59
20. Emanuel MB (1999) Histamine and the antiallergic antihistamine: a history of their discoveries. Clin Exp Allergy 29: 1–11
21. Etkind P, Wilson ME, Gallagher K, Cournoyer J (1987) Working group on foodborne illness control. Bluefish-associated scombroid poisoning: an example of the expanding spectrum of food poisoning from seafood. J Am Med Ass 258: 3409–3410
22. Food and Drug Administration (FDA) (1998) Scombrotoxin (histamine) formation. In: Fish and fishery products hazards and controls guide, 2nd edn. Department of Health and Human Services, Office of Seafood, Food and Drug Administration, Washington DC, pp 73–90
23. Food and Drug Administration (FDA) (1998) Other decomposition-related hazards. In: Fish and fishery products hazards and controls guide, 2nd edn. Department of Health and Human Services, Office of Seafood, Food and Drug Administration, Washington DC, pp 91–92
24. Food and Drug Administration (FDA) (1998) FDA and EPA guidance levels. In: Fish and fishery products hazards and controls guide, 2nd edn. Department of Health and Human Services, Office of Seafood, Food and Drug Administration, Washington DC, pp 245–248
25. Fletcher GC, Summers G, Van Veghel P (1998) Levels of histamine and histamine-producing bacteria in smoked fish from New Zealand markets. J Food Prot 61: 1064–1070
26. Foye WO, Lemke TL, Williams DA (1995) Principles of medicinal chemistry, 4th edn. Williams and Wilkins, Baltimore, USA
27. Garbarg M, Arrang JM, Rouleau A (1992) *S*-[2-(4-Imidazolyl)ethyl]isothiourea: a highly specific and potent histamine H_3 receptor agonist. J Pharmacol Exp Ther 263: 304–308
28. Gilbert RJ, Hobbs G, Murray CK (1980) Scombrotoxic fish poisoning: features of the first 50 incidents to be reported in Britain (1976–9). Br Med J 281: 71–72

29. Granerus G (1968) Effects of oral histamine, histidine and diet on urinary excretion of histamine, methyl-histamine and 1-methyl-4imidazoleacetic acid in man. Scand J Clin Lab Invest - Suppl 104: 49-58
30. Hefle SL (1996) The chemistry and biology of food allergens. Food Technol 3: 86-92
31. Hughes JM, Merson MH (1976) Fish and shellfish poisoning. N Engl J Med 295:1117-1120
32. Hui JU, Taylor SL (1985) Inhibition of in vitro histamine metabolism in rats by food borne and pharmacologic inhibitors of diamine oxidase, histamine *N*-methyltransferase and monoamine oxidase. Toxicol Appl Pharmacol 81: 241-249
33. Hwang DF, Chang SH, Shiau CY, Cheng CC (1995) Biogenic amines in the flesh of sailfish *(Istioforous platypterus)* responsible for scombroid poisoning. J Food Sci 60: 926-928
34. Janeway CA, Travers P, Walport M, Capra JD (1999) Immunobiology: the immune system in health and disease, 4th edn. Current Biology Publication, London
35. Joosten HMLG (1988) The biogenic amines content of Dutch cheese and their toxicological significance. Neth Milk Dairy J 42: 25-42
36. Kawabata T, Ishizaka K, Miura T, Sasaki T (1956) Studies on the food poisoning associated with putrefaction of marine products. An outbreak of allergy-like food poisoning caused by sahimi of *Parathunnus mabachi* and the isolation of the causative bacteria. Bull Japan Soc Sci Fish 22: 41-47
37. Kim IS, Bjeldanes LF (1979) Amino content of toxic and wholesome canned tuna fish. J Food Sci 44: 922-923
38. Kim S, An H, Price RJ (1999) Isolation and characterisation of histamine producing bacteria in albacore. Paper presented at the Annual Meeting of the Institute of Food Technologists, Chicago, USA, July 24-28, Book of Abstracts, pp 228-229
39. Klausen NK, Huss HH (1987) A rapid method for detection of histamine producing bacteria. Int J Food Microbiol 5: 137-146
40. Lehane L, Olley J (2000) Review: histamine fish poisoning revisited. Int J Food Microbiol 58: 1-37
41. Leurs R, Vollinga RC, Timmermann H (1995) The medicinal chemistry and therapeutic potential of ligands for the histamine H_3 receptor agonist In: Jucker E (ed) Progress in drug research. Birkhauser, Basel, Switzerland, pp 107-165
42. Lifshitz F (1998) Food intolerance. In: Chiaramonte LT, Shneider AT, Lifshitz F (eds) Food allergy. Marcel Dekker, New York, pp 3-21
43. Lopez-Sabater EI, Rodriguez-Jerez JJ, Hernadez-Herrero M, Roig-Sagues AX, Mora-Ventura MT (1996) Sensory quality and histamine formation during controlled decomposition of tuna (*Thunnus thynnus*). J Food Prot 59: 167-174
44. Lopez-Sabater EI, Rodriguez-Jerez JJ, Hernandez-Herrero M, Mora-Ventura MT (1996) Incidence of histamine forming bacteria and histamine content in scombroid fish species from retail markets in the Barcelona area. Int J Food Microbiol 24: 411-418
45. Lovenberg W (1974) Psycho- and vasoactive compounds in food substances. J Agric Food Chem 22: 23-26
46. Luten JB, Bouquet W, Seuren LAJ, Burggraff MM, Rieekwell BG, Duran P, Etienne M, Gouyou JP, Landrein A, Retchie A, Leclerg M, Guinet R (1992) Biogenic amines in fishery products. Standardisation methods within EC. In: Huss et al. (eds) Quality assurance in the fish industry. Elsevier Science Publishers, Amsterdam, pp 427-439
47. Marone G, Granata F, Spadaro G, Onorati AM, Triggiani M (1999) Antiinflammatory effects of oxatomide. J Invest Allergol Clin Immunol 9: 207-214
48. Morrow JD, Margolies GR, Rowland J, Roberts LJ (1991) Evidence that histamine is the causative toxin of scombroid fish poisoning. N Engl J Med 324: 716-720
49. Motil KJ, Scrimshaw NS (1979) The role of exogenous histamine in scombroid poisoning. Toxicol Lett 3: 219-223
50. Niven CF, Jeffrey MB, Corlett DA (1981) Differential plating medium for quantitative detection of histamine producing bacteria. Appl Environ Microbiol 41: 321-322
51. Okuzumi M, Hiraishi A, Kobayashi T, Fuji T (1994) *Photobacterium histaminum* sp. nov., a histamine producing marine bacterium. Int J Syst Bacteriol 44: 631-636

52. Okuzumi M, Okuda S, Awano M (1982). Occurrence of pshychrophilic and halophilic histamine-forming bacteria (N-Group Bacteria) on/in red meat fish. Bull Japan Soc Sci Fish 48: 799–804
53. Olsen SJ, MacKinnon LC, Goulding JS, Bean NH, Slutsker L (2000) Surveillance for foodborne-disease outbreaks-USA, 1993–1997. CDC surveillance summaries (March). Morbid Mortal Wkly Rep 49 (no. SS-1)
54. Omura Y, Price RJ, Olcott HS (1978) Histamine forming bacteria isolated from spoiled skipjack tuna and Jack mackerel. J Food Sci 43: 1779–1781
55. Panisello PJ, Rooney R, Quantick PC, Stanwell-Smith R (2000) Application of food borne disease data in the development and maintenance of HACCP systems. Int J Food Microbiol 59: 221–234
56. Public Health Laboratory Service (PHLS) (1999) Outbreak report data to Communicable Disease Surveillance Centre (CDSC). Web site address: http://www.phls.co.uk/facts/iid-t01.htm
57. Ring J, Rothenberger JH, Clauss W (1985) Histamine and allergic diseases. In: Ring J (ed) New trends in allergy. Springer, Berlin Heidelberg New York, pp 44–53
58. Chinese Department of Health (1992) Reports of the Chinese Department of Health. Annual report of food poisoning in Taiwan. Department of Health, Republic of China, Taipei, Taiwan
59. Roig-Sagues AX, Hernandez-Herrero MM, Lopez-Sabater EI, Rodriguez-Jerez JJ, Mora-Ventura MT (1997) Evaluation of three decarboxylating agar media to detect histamine and tyramine producing bacteria in ripened sausages. Lett Appl Microbiol 25: 309–312
60. Schlicker E, Malinowska B, Kathmann M (1994) Modulation of neurotransmitter release via histamine H_3 heteroreceptors. Fundam Clin Pharmacol 8: 128–137
61. Schwartz JC, Arrang JM, Garbarg M (1991) Histaminergic transmission in mammalian brain. Physiol Rev 71: 1–51
62. Scoging A (1998) Scombrotoxic (histamine) fish poisoning in the United Kingdom: 1987 to 1996. Commun Dis Public Health 1: 204–205
63. Serrar D, Brebant R, Bruneau S, Denoyel GA (1995) The development of a monoclonal antibody based ELISA for the determination of histamine in food: application to fishery products and comparison with the HPLC assay. Food Chem 54: 85–91
64. Shalaby AR (1997) Significance of biogenic amines to food safety and human health. Food Res Int 29: 675–690
65. Showalter CV (1980) T's and Blues: abuse of pentazocine and tripelennamine. J Am Med Ass 224: 1224–1225
66. Sockett PN, Cowden JM, Le Baigue S, Ross D, Adack GK, Evans H (1993) Foodborne disease surveillance in England and Wales: 1989–1991. Commun Dis Rep CDR Rev 3: 159–174
67. Straton EJ, Hutkins WR, Taylor SL (1991) Biogenic amines in cheese and other fermented foods. A review. J Food Prot 54: 460–470
68. Taylor SL, Ellen R, Lieber ER, Leatherwood M (1978) A simplified method for histamine analysis of foods. J Food Sci 43: 247–250
69. Taylor SL, Guthertz LS, Leatherwood M, Lieber ER (1979) Histamine production by *Klebsiella pneumonia* and an incident of scombroid fish poisoning. Appl Environ Microbiol 37: 274–278
70. Taylor SL, Hui JV, Lyons DE (1984) Toxicology of scombroid poisoning. In: Ragelish EP (ed) Sea food toxins. American Chemical Society, Washington DC, pp 417–430
71. Taylor SL (1986) Histamine food poisoning: toxicology and clinical aspects. CRC Crit Rev Toxicol 17: 91–128
72. Taylor SL (1985) Histamine poisoning associated with fish, cheese and other foods. Monograph. World Health Organisation, Geneva, Switzerland
73. Taylor SL (1983) Monograph on histamine poisoning. Codex Alimentarious Commission, FAO/WHO, Rome. 19th Session of the Codex Committee on Food Hygiene, Washington, DC, 26–30 September
74. Watling KJ (1998) The RBI handbook of receptor classification and signal transduction, 3rd edn. RBI Publisher, Natick, MA, USA

75. Weiss S, Robb GP, Ellis LB (1932) The systemic effects of histamine in man. Arch Int Med 49: 360–396
76. WHO (World Health Organisation) (1995) Surveillance programme for control of food-borne infections and intoxications in Europe. Sixth report 1990–1992. WHO, Berlin
77. Wu ML, Yang CC, Yang GY (1997) Scombroid fish poisoning: an overlooked marine food poisoning. Vet Hum Toxicol 39: 236–241
78. Yamashita M, Fukui H, Sugama K (1991) Expression cloning of a cDNA encoding the bovine histamine H_1 receptor. Proc Nat Acad Sci USA 88: 11,515–11,519
79. Yen GC, Hsien CL (1991) Simultaneous analysis of biogenic amines in canned fish by HPLC. J Food Sci 56: 158–160
80. Yoshinaga DH, Frank HA (1982) Histamine producing bacteria in decomposing skipjack tuna (*Katsuwonus pelamis*). Appl Environ Microbiol 44: 447–452
81. Zhang MQ, Timmermann H (1997) Histamine H_1-receptor antagonists. In: Wolff ME (ed) Burger's medicinal chemistry and drug discovery, 5th edn. Wiley, New York, pp 495–521
82. Zingel V, Leschke C, Schunack W (1995) Developments in histamine H_1-receptor agonists. In: Jucker E (ed) Progress in drug research. Birkhauser, Basel, Switzerland, pp 49–85

10 Analysis of Seafood Aroma/Odour by Electronic Nose Technology and Direct Analysis

John M. Grigor, Brenden J. Theaker, Cesarettin Alasalvar,
William T. O'Hare, Zulfiqur Ali

Volatile aroma compounds are generally regarded to be important parameters for determining the flavour quality and spoilage index in marine-based products. Although sensory assessment is desirable (provided it is carried out scientifically and correctly) it has limitations, including the study of flavour at the molecular level. Therefore an increasing emphasis has been placed on developing instrumentation and methods which can reliably identify and rapidly quantify key odourants in seafood, and studying how processing, abuse and storage can affect them. This chapter describes the major chemical classes of flavour compounds found in seafood and the methods available for their detection.

10.1 Introduction

Freshness, flavour and safety are the major factors which customers consider before purchasing fish [1]. Subjective flavour analysis and subjective grading by organoleptic means are by far the most popular techniques used in the Fish Industry. Freshness of fish can be analysed subjectively and rapidly by organoleptic means in the raw state by schemes such as the European Union and Tasmanian schemes [2, 3]. Subjective flavour analysis can be assessed qualitatively and quantitatively by using techniques such as quantitative descriptive analysis (QDA) and other flavour profile methods [4, 5]. The success of these subjective techniques are dependent upon the use of trained or expert panels which requires expense and time for proper motivation, training and maintenance. Recent developments have included the development of computerised sensory systems to help train assessors and improve the accuracy of sensory evaluation such as the WiseFresh system developed as part of a CRAFT-project within the FAIR-programme funded by the EC (QimIT, website communication). However subjective techniques are always likely to be associated with low precision, and can cause suspicion particularly when implemented in regulatory control. This major drawback, as well as other concerns such as the removal of morphological characteristics in fish block production, has led to a number of alternative chemical and physical methods being proposed [6–11]. This has included several techniques utilising volatile compounds as spoilage indicators. However bacteriological assessment and markers of microbiological deterioration ignore the loss of freshness caused by autolytic degradation shortly following death.

Therefore any objective measure should:

1. Take into consideration all the biochemical processes causing loss of fish freshness
2. Be as transportable as possible, enabling results to be obtained at sea, dockside and processing lines
3. Be robust and reliable enough to be incorporated within regulatory testing, giving satisfactory results in inter-laboratory testing amongst other validation requirements [12, 13]
4. Be responsive to post- and pre-harvest taints (as distinct from spoilage induced off-flavours)

These stringent criteria have therefore lead to a plethora of suggestions from academic and research institutions but as of yet the industry has not fully incorporated project developments.

The successful objective analysis of flavour requires the identification and quantification of all key aroma compounds. Alternatively electronic nose technology allows the possibility for the entire pattern of volatiles to be studied. This recently developed technique has been used to measure various aspects of fish freshness by utilising multivariate statistics to correlate sensor response with organoleptic measurements. Clearly the initial technological priming of these new techniques is high; however, once set up these instrumental techniques have the potential to provide rapid and reliable data.

The main aims of this chapter are to:

1. Review briefly the types of aroma active compounds which characterise the subjective quality levels of seafood
2. Review developments in sensor array technology and evaluate the transfer of this technology for the indirect object measure of freshness and flavour in seafoods
3. Describe the direct approach to objective aroma analysis in seafoods and indicate potential pitfalls and possible new areas for future research

10.2 Flavour Active Compounds

10.2.1 Development of Desirable Fresh Flavour

Characteristic fresh fish flavour aroma compounds are present during the first few days after harvest, and this aroma seems to be at least in part due to 6-, 8-, and 9-carbon carbonyls and alcohols. These compounds are generally found in the fish flesh at low levels (ppb), but due to their low threshold levels contribute significantly to the characteristic fresh fish flavour. It has been reported that lipoxygenase-mediated enzymatic reactions seem to play the most significant role in generating these fresh fish flavours by initiating lipid peroxidation to produce hydroperoxides which break down to produce aldehydes, ketones and alcohols [14, 15].

10.2.2
Loss of Freshness and Spoilage

Loss of freshness is associated with nucleotide catabolism. This biochemical process is linked to textural changes and flavour in seafood. Inosine monophosphate (IMP) which is reported to contribute to the fresh flavour is produced rapidly via endogenous enzyme catabolism of adenosine triphosphate (ATP). In turn IMP is broken down to inosine by endogenous and microbial enzymes [16]. This area has been well researched and is still currently on-going at the University of Lincoln, UK.

Spoiled fish flavour and aromas is characterised by rancid/fishy, strong sulphurous, ammoniacal and off-flavours [17–19] which are produced by S-containing compounds such as H_2S, $(CH_3)_2SH$, $(CH_3)_3S$ and N-containing compounds such as amines and NH_3. It is well known that trimethylamine oxide (TMAO) which is found in a large number of marine fish and shellfish is broken down to $(CH_3)_3N$ (TMA) by either endogenous or bacterial enzymes, which then consequently react with the lipids in fish muscle to contribute to the spoilt fish odour [20]. Certain aldehydes such as (*Z*)-4-heptenal (rancid odour) also contribute to spoilt fish flavour [17, 21, 22] as well as microbial breakdown products from protein such as indole (faecal odour). It has been suggested that while oxidation secondary products of ω3-polyunsaturated fatty acids (ω3-PUFA) may be important in fresh fish flavour at low concentrations; however, as oxidation proceeds during storage (via enzymatic and non-enzymatic catalysis) the concentration of these compounds will increase and may impart oxidative off-flavours [16]. Unlike loss of fresh fish flavour, which is at least in part determined by endogenous enzymatic activity, spoilt fish flavour is dominated by microbial activity. Bacteria present in the gills, gut and skin metabolise surrounding low-molecular weight compounds producing the characteristic spoilage odourants.

10.2.3
Pre and Post Harvest Taints

Off-flavours arising from environmental sources cannot be ruled out. Oil spills may produce kerosin-like flavours in fish; however, environmental tainting is produced naturally [23]. Off-odours such as (a) strong garlic flavours in prawns, (b) iodoform-like flavours in prawns, shrimps, *Nemadactylus douglasii* and *Acanthopagrus australis* fish species, (c) petroleum-like odours in canned chum salmon and (d) "blackberry-like" odours in North Atlantic cod have been reported to arise due to feeding on certain marine organisms known to contain highly odorous compounds. However, the occurrence of these type of off-flavours is sporadic, and is restricted to a specific coastline or even in some cases to a single day's catch [24]. Nevertheless, any objective test to analyse fish freshness will need to be sensitive enough to detect odourants with potentially very low thresholds such as 2,6 dibromophenol (with an observable threshold concentration of 5×10^{-4} ng/g in water), a compound reported to be responsible for the iodoform flavour in prawns [25].

10.3 Analysis of Seafood Aroma by Sensor Array Technology

The instrumental analysis of fish odour can be categorised into two main approaches – the direct approach and the indirect approach. The direct approach uses traditional chemistry techniques to study quantitatively and qualitatively the molecular basis of flavour, whilst the indirect approach is demonstrated by sensor array technology.

The concept of an electronic nose system was proposed by Persaud and Dodd [26]. An electronic nose comprises an array of electronic chemical sensors with partial specificity and an appropriate pattern-recognition system (Fig. 10.1). Since the sensor array has only partial specificity to the odour or volatile compounds, it has good reversibility. Selectivity for the analyte is achieved from the pattern of sensor array response which acts as a fingerprint for the analyte. When the volatiles sensed have an odour, these systems are referred to as an electronic nose [27].

The electronic nose and mammalian nose perform the same function but clearly have many differences in operating principle, type and number of sensors, sensitivity and selectivity. The biological mechanism for olfaction allows the recognition of a wide variety of compounds with high sensitivity and selectivity. Thousands of different odour active compounds can be discriminated at the parts per trillion level. When air is inhaled, the odourants traverse the mucus layer which covers the nasal epithelium. Odourant molecules are thought to be transferred to the receptor sites by odourant binding sites in the mucus layer. Interaction of ligands with specific receptor proteins in the ciliary membrane leads to a multi-step reaction cascade which amplifies the olfactory signal and ultimately leads to the electrical response of the sensory neurons. The strength and duration of odour stimuli are translated into distinct patterns of neuronal activity. Residual odourants in the mucus layer are eliminated by biotransformation enzymes to allow new incoming odourant molecules to be recognised.

Electronic nose systems can employ a variety of gas sensors. The gas sensors used can be divided into those that operate at high temperatures, e.g. the metal oxide semiconductors (MOS) and metal oxide field effect transistor (MOSFET) and those that operate at around room temperature such as conducting polymers, piezoelectric quartz crystals (also known as bulk acoustic wave or BAW) and surface acoustic wave sensors (SAW) [28]. Optical sensor arrays are also being investigated; these devices are often termed artificial noses [29]. A variety of gas sensors are discussed in more detail below.

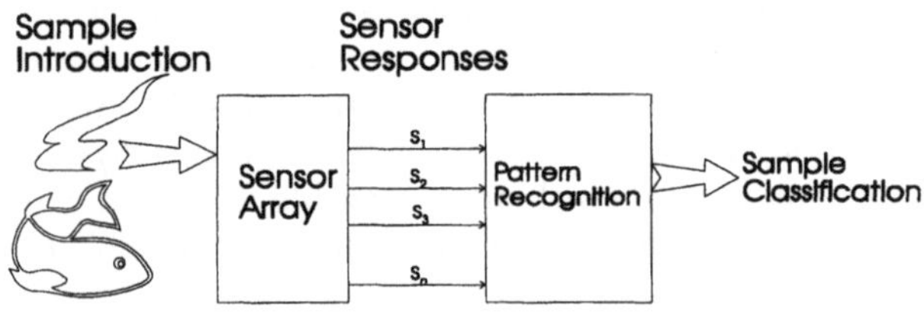

Fig. 10.1. A schematic diagram of an electronic nose

10.3.1 High Temperature Sensors

10.3.1.1 *MOS Sensors*

These consist of a ceramic substrate coated by a metal oxide semi-conducting film and heated by a wire. The metal oxide coating can be either of the *n*-type or *p*-type. Thermal or photolytic excitation of an *n*-type semiconductor leads to an excess of electrons in the conduction band which increases the reactivity with oxidising molecules. An excited *p*-type semiconductor is electron deficient in its valence band and promotes reactions with reducing compounds. MOS sensors are further sub-divided into thin (6–1000 nm) or thick (10–300 μM) film sensors. Thin film sensors are developed using physical or chemical vapour deposition, evaporation or spraying. Thick film sensors are produced by screen printing or painting. Thin film sensors have faster response and higher sensitivity but are more difficult to manufacture reproducibly. Selectivity of the devices can be altered by doping with noble catalytic metals or by altering the operating temperature.

The selectivity of MOS sensors is not as good as other sensor types and they also suffer from poisoning by sulphur compounds or weak acids. Their high operating temperature also means that they are not suitable in flammable environments. Taguchi sensors are commercially available doped metal oxide sensors.

10.3.1.2 *MOSFET Sensors*

These are composed of three layers; successively the three layers are: a silicon semiconductor layer, a silicon oxide insulator layer and finally a catalytic metal which acts as a gate. A normal transistor operates by three contacts on the source, drain and the gate. The potential on the gate determines the current that flows between the source and drain. In the MOSFET, the gate and drain contacts are shortcut. The applied voltage on the gate and drain contact creates an electric field which influences the conductivity of the transistor. When polar compounds interact with the gate the electric field and hence the current flowing through the sensor is modified. The response is recorded in terms of the change in voltage necessary to keep a constant preset drain current. MOSFET sensors, like MOS sensors, have relatively low sensitivity to moisture but their manufacture requires a high degree of expertise.

10.3.2 Ambient Temperature Sensors

10.3.2.1 *Conducting Polymer Sensors*

These are comprised of a substrate onto which are deposited a pair of gold-plated electrodes and a conducting polymer film. Electrochemical deposition of the films allows the spatial extent of the film to be controlled. The deposited film contains cation sites balanced by anions from the electrolyte. The cation sites consist of polarons or bi-polarons, which are small regions of positive charge in the polymer chain providing mobile holes for electron transport. When a voltage is applied across the electrodes, a current passes through the conducting polymer. The presence of volatile compounds at the surface alters the electron flow in the system and hence the resistance of the sensor. The volatiles may interact with the polymer or the counter-ion. Selectivity can be modified somewhat by altering the counter-ions present in the conducting polymer. Conducting polymers are most appropriate for polar compounds. They are, however, sensitive to moisture. More recently, sensor arrays have been developed using thin film carbon-black polymer composites. Absorption of the sample headspace into the polymer matrix leads to an increase in its volume and a concomitant increase in resistance due to conductive carbon-black pathways being broken [30]. This simple and low-cost sensor format is very attractive.

10.3.2.2
BAW and SAW Sensors

These are two of the most common mass sensors [31]. The two devices differ in that, in the former, an acoustic wave travels through the bulk of the material, while in the latter case the acoustic wave travels on the surface. A mathematical relationship between the mass of material on the piezoelectric quartz crystal and frequency shift was first derived by Sauerbrey [32] and is given in Eq. (10.1).

$$\Delta f = -2.3 \times 10^6 \cdot f_o^2 \cdot \frac{\Delta M_s}{A} \tag{10.1}$$

where Δf is the change in frequency of the quartz crystal (Hz), f_o is the resonant frequency of the quartz crystal (MHz), ΔM_s is the mass of the coating or substance sorbed (g) and A is the area coated (cm^2).

They are converted into chemical or biosensors by incorporation of a chemical or biochemical layer on the device surface, which will abstract the analyte from the sample stream. Since a wide range of coatings can be applied onto the device surface these sensors have very broad selectivity.

10.3.3
Pattern Recognition

The responses from the sensor array can be analysed by using pattern recognition methods [33]. These methods can be sub-divided into supervised or unsupervised techniques. Unsupervised methods such as principal component analysis (PCA) and cluster analysis are used in exploratory data analysis since they will attempt to identify a gas mixture without prior information. These techniques are most appropriate when no example of different sample groups is available or when hidden relationships between samples or variables is suspected. Supervised learning techniques such as canonical discriminant analysis

(CDA), feature weighting (FW), artificial neural network (ANN) and fuzzy logic classify a sample by developing a mathematical model relating training data to a set of descriptors. Test samples are then evaluated against a knowledge base and predicted class membership determined. ANN and fuzzy logic methods are attractive since they are able to deal with non-linear problems.

Artificial neural networks (ANNs) have been used in finding patterns in signals [34]. ANNs are a simplistic abstraction of the human brain; they are often referred to as connectionist networks when their computing ability is emphasised rather than biological fidelity. A neural network is a collection of units (neurons or nodes) that are connected in some pattern to allow communication between units. The node is a simple processor which has a rule for combining the inputs and an activation function to calculate an output. Output signals are sent to other units using connections known as weights which can either excite (increase) or inhibit (decrease) the signal. The task that a network is required to perform is coded in the weights that connect units. The weight values are learnt during a training phase. In many cases training is the only option for programming a network since we do not possess the task-solving knowledge required for conventional programs.

There are many different types of networks and they differ in terms of their pattern of connectivity, i.e. the way in which the units are connected. In some networks each unit may be connected to every other unit; in other models the units are ordered in a hierarchy of layers where connections are only allowed between units in immediately adjacent layers. The most widely used network is the back-propagation network. This is a fully connected feed-forward network with back-propagation. The back-propagation defines two sweeps of the network; first a forward sweep from the input layer to the hidden layer(s) to the output layer, and then a backward sweep from the output layer to the input layer. The forward sweep propagates the input vectors to provide outputs at the output layer. In the backward sweep, the error values are propagated back through the network to determine how the weights should be changed during training. In training, each input pattern has an associated target output pattern. Training is designed to determine the network weights which minimise the error between actual and target output.

Fuzzy logic, originally conceived by Zadeh [35], tries to deal with imprecise data and unlike traditional statistics it is based on possibility rather than probability. In standard statistical methods an object normally belongs to a discrete set (also known as a crisp set). In fuzzy logic an object has a degree of membership to a given set, information about a system is encoded using membership functions. A membership function is a function that maps one or more variables to a degree of membership. Figure 10.2 shows a crisp and Gaussian fuzzy membership function for the variable temperature about 25 °C. It is attractive in machine olfaction because it can deal with error and also sensor outputs can be related to linguistic variables such as 'good' and 'poor'. Two basic approaches have been taken in the use of fuzzy logic in electronic nose classification: (i) the sensor and or classification space are defined using fuzzy function and (ii) the pattern recognition algorithm is fuzzified. Yea et al. [36] have developed trapezoidal membership functions for different classes of compound and sensors based on

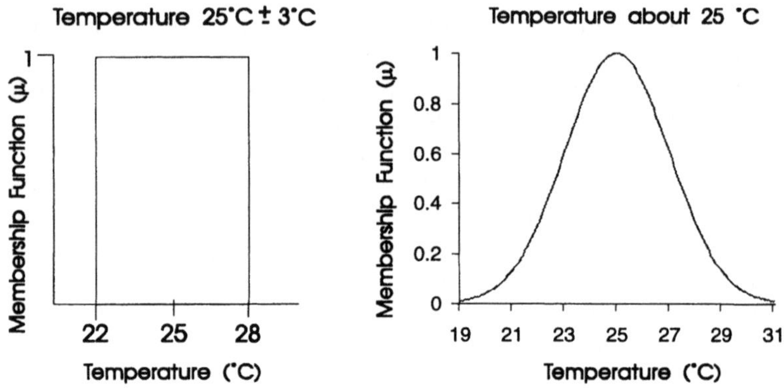

Fig. 10.2. Crisp and Gaussian membership functions for temperature

experience. The grade of membership of an unknown odour was classified by taking the supremum of the fuzzy group. A fuzzy cross-correlation method using Gaussian membership functions has been used for classification of model organic compounds [37]. A Simplified Fuzzy ARTMAP (SFAM) was found to be very effective in the classification of edible oils [38].

10.3.4 Applications

The quality of fish can be expressed in the chemical pattern of the volatile compounds evolving from the fish, with the dominant chemical classes being amines, alcohols and sulphides. An array of sensors with appropriate pattern classification can be used in assessment of fish quality.

Various types of metal oxide sensors have been utilised to monitor fish volatiles. A MOS (TiO_2) doped with 0.5% (w/w) ruthenium operating at 555 °C was used by Shimizu et al. [39] The optimum concentration of ruthenium and the operating temperature of the sensor were optimised using 300 ppm concentrations of TMA and ammonia. The sensor was exposed to a sample of saurel stored at room temperature over a period of 20 h. The resistance change of the sensor was related to the *K* value fish freshness indicator over this 20 h period.

Nanto et al. [40] used a MOS (zinc oxide) doped with 2% (w/w) aluminium oxide to monitor fish freshness. The sensor was shown to be sensitive to 1 ppm TMA concentration. The sensor was presented with varying sea-food samples stored at room temperature. Increased sensor responses were observed for samples of salmon, squid, oyster and sardine over storage periods of up to 75 h. In each case the sensor response showed a similar profile to the 1 ppm TMA samples suggesting that the odours were sensitive and selective for TMA which appeared to be the main odour from the stored fish.

Winquist et al. [41] used an electronic nose based on an array on ten MOSFETs, four Taguchi sensors and an infra red optical sensor to determine the age of cod samples over a period of three days. Samples of fish, stated to be less than 8 h old at time of purchase, were used to train the electronic nose. The training samples were stored at 4 °C during the 3-day measurement period, during which 30 measurements from each of 10 samples were taken. The data from the reference samples were split into two groups to train and test the neural networks (NN). A three-layer feed-forward with back-propagation network was used. The network had 15 input nodes, 10 nodes in the hidden layer and 1 output node relating to the storage of the cod fillets. After training the instrument, fresh unknown samples were analysed. The instrument predicted the age of the samples to be between 33 and 47 h.

Ólafsson et al. [42] used an array of four Taguchi sensors to sample haddock, which had been stored both at room temperature and under ice and cod samples stored under ice at 5 °C. The sensors showed linear responses for three compounds, propanone (0 – 5 ppm), butanol (0 – 10 ppm) and TMA (0 – 30 ppm), which are common indicators of fish freshness. The fish samples were also evaluated by an 8-members sensory panel, who scored the fish on a scale of 3 (very poor) to 10 (very fresh) where a score of below 5.5 would define a fish as too poor for human consumption. The sensor responses for the haddock samples stored at room temperature increased with time and this was used to test the actual sensitivity of the sensors. The sensor responses to the headspace above the haddock stored in ice showed non-linearity with a peak during the first few days. The authors link this to the high concentration of fresh fish aromas which has been demonstrated by a further group using sensory evaluation [43]. The Taguchi sensors had similar sensitivities to the change in headspace compared to the other methods of chemical and sensory evaluation. The authors suggest a possible advantage for Taguchi sensors by stating "the sensors had reasonable sensitivity during the first days of spoilage when chemical methods are least sensitive".

Di Natale et al. [44] used an array of four metalloporphyrin coated piezoelectric quartz crystal sensors to study the headspace volatiles evolved from samples of cod over a period of seven days. The responses of the sensors were shown to respond in predominantly linear fashions to thiophene (0 – 2500 ppm), triethylamine (0 – 3000 ppm) and methanol (0 – 4000 ppm), which were used by the group to represent typical compounds evolved from fish. The sensor array was used for the classification and for identification of the degree of freshness of stored cod fish. A key feature was an attempt to preserve information about the temporal succession amongst the classes.

Luzuriaga and Balaban [45] developed a predictive model of odour changes in salmon fillets stored at different temperatures using an electronic nose. Fresh Atlantic salmon fillets were stored at various temperatures and evaluated using an electronic nose composed of 12 conducting polymer sensors and also a 6-member trained sensory panel. The US Food and Drug Administration (FDA) evaluates the odour of fishery products on the basis of three categories. Discriminant Function Analysis (DFA) was used to develop a model from the sensor outputs to classify samples into three odour groups. The electronic nose was able to correlate the odour of salmon fillets with storage time and with grades from sensory evaluation at various storage temperatures using DFA. Newman et al. [46] have also used DFA with electronic nose data for prediction of both sensory score and microbial counts in raw tuna. The sensory scale was condensed to four values to conform with the pass/borderline/fail system. Correct classification rate by sensory score at 1.7, 7.2 and 12.8 °C was 88.2, 82.1 and 90.0 %, respectively. This indicates that the electronic nose is able to classify correctly raw tuna samples of different quality. Microbial analysis was carried out on the same day as electronic nose analysis; replicate samples were randomly cut from the same tuna loins from which the odour samples were prepared. Microbial loads were assigned to the electronic nose values for the corresponding treatment and day. Correct classification of microbial loads by electronic nose at 1.7, 7.2 and 12.8 °C was 97.9, 91.7 and 96.7 %, respectively.

The work described shows that the electronic nose is a potentially useful tool for determination of fish quality. Development of robust measurement methods will require generation of a large database to account for product variability. A number of academic and commercial groups are involved in further development of electronic nose systems. Research is focused on development of alternative sensor formats, pre-concentration and pattern recognition algorithms. There is also a need for long term studies to investigate the effect of sensor drift on classification.

10.3.5
Advantages and Disadvantages of Electronic Nose Technology

Electronic nose technology is still in its infancy, with the technology being very application specific. However, once set up, the electronic nose offers a system which will be easy to operate, with real time analysis and the potential to be modified for at-line/on-line analysis. The main disadvantage of the electronic nose for flavour research is that it gives only an overall picture of odour and does not identify or quantify the individual components that make up the odour of the sample. Further, it is this molecular information which is required during the development of new applications for the indirect approach. Therefore the direct approach is required to support development work of the indirect approach, otherwise the system developed is prone to artefactypal information.

10.4
Direct Approach to the Analysis of Seafood Aroma

The direct approach to aroma analysis consists of three general stages:

1. Extraction and concentration of the important aroma compounds from the food matrix
2. Separation of the aroma compounds from the extract
3. Identification and quantification of key aroma compounds

10.4.1
Identification and Quantitation of Aroma Compounds

The second and third stages of this sequence are normally carried in flavour science using gas chromatography/mass spectrometry (GC/MS). However, in a few cases high performance liquid chromatography (HPLC) which is normally operated at room temperature may be a better option. In particular, certain volatiles can be heat labile which can cause peak tailing [47], or more seriously loss of signal of the true analyte and the thermal generation of heat stable artefacts. Derivatisation of the target analyte can alleviate this situation in some cases; however, this approach is unworkable for flavour systems which are being studied for the first time. A more practical alternative is to use GC systems with cryo-cooling of the column and injector ports. Alternatively, cold on-column injection may be appropriate, where the analysis of putrescine and cadaverine by GC without derivatisation has been demonstrated [48]. Cadwallader and Macleod [49] have written a comprehensive review on the techniques available for the identification and quantification of aroma compounds in muscle foods.

The sensory relevance of many volatiles separated and identified by GC-MS (and other techniques) has not been extensively evaluated. This is because the identification of key aroma compounds from the potentially large number of volatiles identified and quantified from a seafood sample is time consuming and problematic. Nevertheless, the relationship between aroma and volatile compounds can be studied using nasal appraisal of gas chromatographic effluent using a variety of techniques collectively called gas chromatography/olfactometry (GC/O). Aroma extraction dilution analysis (AEDA) where serial dilutions are performed on the extract to calculate a flavour dilution (FD) value has been used to identify the potent character-impact aroma compounds in various cooked crustacea [50, 51]. Milo and Grosch [52] using AEDA calculated odour activity values for volatiles produced from boiled cod. This technique enabled them to conclude that 3-methylbutanol was primarily responsible for the malty odour defect of boiled cod, and that (*Z*)-4-heptenal amongst other secondary products of omega unsaturated fatty acids peroxidation was (in contrast to frozen stored trout) unimportant in boiled cod. This was explained as due to the low fat content in cod.

An alternative to the GC/O dilution techniques is to measure the odour/aroma impact of a volatile by subjectively rating the intensity of the compound using an appropriate psychometric scale. Cha et al. [53] directed two trained panellists using an 8-point scale (where 0 = no odour detected, 7 = very strong) to identify aroma-active compounds in salt-fermented anchovy. Using this technique, they concluded that the most potent odourants were 1-octene-3-one (mushroom, earthy), (*Z*)-4-heptenal (rancid, boiled potato), (*E*,*Z*)-2,6-nonadienal (cucumber, melon), 3-methylbutanal (dark chocolate), 3-(methylthio) propanal (nutty, baked potato), ethyl 2-methylbutanoate (fruity, ripe apple) and ethyl 3-methylbutanoate (fruity, green apple).

10.4.2
Extraction and Concentration of Important Aroma Compounds

Although the identification and separation of volatiles is far from straightforward, the extraction stage (stage 1) may be even more problematic, and difficult choices have to made with regards to what type of extraction technique is to be used. The types of methods available are:

1. Distillation and/or solvent extraction
2. Headspace sampling of the food matrix
3. Model systems mimicking the eating process
4. Direct sampling

10.4.2.1
Traditional Extraction Techniques (Distillation and Solvent Extraction)

These techniques can in some circumstances lead to the formation of chemical artefacts. For example, the Likens and Nickerson steam distillation extraction method which is still frequently used in laboratories at normal atmospheric pressure impose the food sample to relatively high temperatures and therefore the formation of various artefacts are possible, leading to an aroma profile more relevant to the boiled sample [54]. However, vacuum distillation can minimise artefact formation, and a direct transfer system to GC/MS has been developed to analyse fish volatiles [55].

10.4.2.2
Headspace Sampling Techniques

Headspace sampling techniques are frequently divided into two categories: static headspace and dynamic headspace (or purge and trap). In each case, however, the fundamental principle is the same – volatile analytes from a solid or liquid material are sampled by investigation of the atmosphere adjacent to the sample, leaving the actual sample material behind [56].

In the static headspace analysis (SHA), the food (which is placed into an airtight vial) is allowed to reach equilibrium with the surrounding air, when a sample of the air is taken for analysis. A study of mackerel volatiles was carried out using a combination of an automated static headspace analyser connected to a Varian Ion trap GC/MS [57]. Minced mackerel (10 g) was placed into a 22 ml vial and volatiles were allowed to reach equilibrium with the headspace before automatic injection of 1 ml of headspace. Thirty two peaks were obtained. Hexanal, the most abundant type of volatile found, is known to contribute to the green plant-like and grassy aromas of most fresh fish [58]. Other volatiles identified include heptanal (fruity, sweet, spicy, wine-like), octanal (sweet, wine-like), dodecanal (floral, sweet, waxy, penetrating), 2-pentenal (pungent green, apple, orange, tomato), 2-methyl-2-pentenal (powerful, grassy, green, slightly fruity), cyclohexanone, 2-nananone, 3-methyl-1-butanol (fusel oil, whiskey), 2-penten-1-ol (butter, mild green), 1-penten-3-ol, 1-octen-3-ol (herbaceous earthy), 2-pentylfuran (green bean, vegetable). The sulphur-containing compounds such as dimethyl trisulphide increased during the storage period demonstrating its potential usefulness as an indicator of spoilage [57].

In the dynamic headspace analysis (DHA), a sample of gas (usually purified nitrogen) is passed over the food (or through the food-sometimes referred to as purge and trap) to strip off volatiles which are then concentrated on an absorbent such as charcoal or Tenax. The volatiles are desorbed prior to analysis on the gas chromatograph. Alasalvar et al. [59] used DHA/GC/MS to study the volatile aroma compounds in fresh and deteriorated mackerel. Sixty five peaks were observed. Aldehydes, ketones and alcohols were found generally in higher proportions in the fresh mackerel as compared to the stored mackerel. The sulphur-containing compounds (dimethyl sulphide, dimethyl disulphide, dimethyl trisulphide) were absent in the fresh fish samples, but were the dominant compounds in the deteriorated mackerel.

These headspace techniques generally encounter fewer artefacts as no solvents or prolonged high temperatures are employed, and generally reduce sample preparation times. However, there is a thermal desorption stage for dynamic headspace techniques, and this may be sufficient to cause artefact formation in some heat labile compounds. Commercial instrumentation may also have autosampler capability. However, unpublished work carried out by the authors has shown that the time taken to prepare a seafood sample for headspace analysis has a significant effect on results, and therefore autosampling (with some samples having larger delay times than others before analysis) needs to be carried out with caution. Carryover can be a problem with dynamic headspace. In addition, depending on the type of adsorbent used, very light volatiles and gases will not be trapped on the adsorbent resins and therefore will be missed completely from the analysis. Therefore, static headspace analysis is considered in some cases the preferred technique for very light volatiles and gases in seafoods, e.g. hydrogen sulphide, dimethyl sulphide, methyl mercaptan, the short-chain alkylamines and short-chain neutral volatiles [60]. However, the sensitivity is limited (ppm [61]), particularly with higher boiling volatiles due to their low partition into the gas headspace volume. Wampler [56] provides a more detailed discussion on the advantages and disadvantages of the types of headspace-GC used in aroma analysis.

Pawliszyn and co-workers at the University of Waterloo developed an alternative technique in the early 1990s called Solid-Phase Microextraction (SPME) [62]. Headspace-SPME is a relatively new technique for the rapid, solventless extraction or pre-concentration of volatile and semi-volatile organic compounds, using a fused-silica fibre of 1 cm in length as the adsorbant. Selectivity and sensitivity of the system can be changed by altering the phase type and thickness of the fibre coating. The overall size of the apparatus is about the same as a syringe. Further operational details of this technique can be obtained from a recent comprehensive review by Harmon [63].

Work carried out at the University of Lincoln (UK) using a 100 μm PDMS SPME fibre demonstrated no apparent advantage in sensitivity and specificity for identification of volatiles from the headspace above minced mackerel flesh (Grigor et al., unpublished work). Cadwallader and Macleod [49] reported that SPME "shows good potential for flavour analysis, its uses in the study of muscle foods is limited". This may be due to problems with quantifying compounds in complex systems, with at least experimental conditions having to be maintained precisely between samples and standards. Nevertheless, the cost of purchasing SPME is significantly less than the cost of purchasing a purge and trap concentrator; however, the flexibility of this system seems to be its real strength. From the initial studies carried out at the University of Lincoln (UK), this technique with modifications has the potential as a portable non-invasive quality indicator.

10.4.2.3
Model Systems and Direct Sampling

Other extraction techniques try to mimic the eating process by grinding the food with an analogue saliva. A good review by Taylor [64] discusses volatile flavour measurement of food during eating. Probably the most interesting approach to obtaining a representative volatile sample is by sampling the air, breath by breath, generated in the nose during the eating process. In this case identification of the odourants is carried out on an atmospheric pressure ionisation MS. The sensitivity of the system depends upon the food system, but typical detection limits have been quoted in the range of 10–100 ppb [65, 66]. To the best knowledge of the authors, this system has not been applied, as of yet, to seafood aroma analysis.

10.5
Conclusions

Seafood aroma is complex, being generated by microbial activity, endogenous enzymatic activity, thermal action, lipid autooxidation and environmental contamination, with significant variability occurring between and within different species of seafood. Flavour analysis by objective means can be carried out by direct or indirect analysis. Direct analysis requires the identification and quantification of character impact compounds, whereas indirect analysis requires the careful development and selection of sensors and the use of appropriate statistical analysis. Much effort has been directed toward developing an objective measurement for assessing the freshness of seafood; however, the seafood industry still prefers organoleptic and sensory subjective analysis. Further development is required to improve reliability in objective measurements, taking into consideration potential variability within specific species of fish or shellfish.

References

1. Sloan AE, McNutt KW, Powers M (1986) Consumers' attitudes about shelflife and technology. In: Charalambous G (ed) The shelflife of foods and beverages. Elsevier Science Publishers, Amsterdam, pp 63–72
2. Branch AC, Vail AMA (1985) Bringing fish inspection into the computer age. Food Technol Aust 37: 352–355
3. Oehlenschlager J (1992) Evaluation of some well established and some underrated indices for the determination of freshness and/or spoilage of ice stored wet fish. In: Huss HH, Jakobsonen M, Liston J (eds) Quality assurance in the fish industry. Elsevier Science Publishers, Amsterdam, pp 339–350
4. Stone H, Sidel JS, Oliver S, Woolsey A, Singleton RC (1974) Sensory evaluation by quantitative descriptive analysis. Food Technol 11: 24–34
5. British Standards Institute (1986) British standards methods for sensory analysis of foods. Part 4: flavour profile method. British standards Institution, London
6. Ryder JM (1985) Determination of ATP and its breakdown products in fish muscle by HPLC. J Agric Food Chem 33: 678–680
7. Luong JHT, Male BK, Huynh MD (1991) Applications of polarography for assessment of fish freshness. J Food Sci 56: 335–339

8. Kryzmien M, Elias L, Sim PG (1992) Development of an instrumental approach to assessing fish freshness by headspace analysis for trimethylamine. In: Bligh EG (ed) Seafood science and technology. Fishing New Books (Canadian Institute of Fisheries Technology), Halifax, pp 216–224
9. Ólafsdottir G, Martinsdottir E, Oehlenschlager J, Dalgaard P, Jensen B, Undeland I, Mackie IM, Henehan G, Nielsen J, Nilsen H (1997) Methods to evaluate fish freshness in research and industry. Trends Food Sci Technol 8: 258–265
10. Pedrosa-Menabritto A, Regenstein JM (1990) Shelf-life extension of fresh fish – a review. Part III – fish quality and methods of assessment. J Food Qual 13: 209–223
11. Rodriguez CJ, Villar-Estalote V, Besteiro I, Pascual C (1997) Biochemical indices of freshness during processing sardine for canning. In: Luten JP, Borresen T, Oehlenschlager (eds) Seafood from producer to consumer, integrated approach to quality. Elsevier Science Publishers, Oxford, pp 203–210
12. Wood R, Nilsson A, Wallin H (1998) Quality in the food analysis laboratory. Royal Society of Cambridge Publications, Cambridge, UK
13. Horwitz W (1982) Evaluation of analytical methods used for regulation of foods and drugs. Anal Chem 54: 67–76
14. Josephson DB, Lindsay RC, Stuiber DA (1984) Biogenesis of lipid-derived volatile aroma compounds in the Emerald shiner (*Notropis atherinoides*). J Agric Food Chem 32: 1347–1352
15. Josephson DB, Lindsay RC (1986) Enzymic generation of volatile aroma compounds from fresh fish. In: Parliment TH, Croteau R (eds) Biogeneration of aroma. ACS Symposium Series 317. American Chemical Society, Washington, DC, pp 201–221
16. Ashie INA, Smith JP, Simpson BK (1996) Spoilage and shelf-life extension of fresh fish and shellfish. Crit Rev Food Sci Nutr 36: 87–121
17. Ross DA, Love RM (1979) Decreased in the cold store flavour developed by frozen fillets of starved cod (*Gadus morhua*, L). J Food Technol 14: 115–122
18. Shankaranarayana ML, Raghaven B, Abraham KO, Natarajan CP (1989) Sulphur compounds in flavours. In: Morton ID, McLeod AJ (eds) Food flavours, part A. Elsevier Science Publishers, New York, pp 169–281
19. Whitfield FB, Freeman DJ, Bannister PA (1981) Dimethyl trisulphide: an important off-flavour component in the royal red prawn. Chem Ind 10: 692–693
20. Kawai T (1996) Fish flavour. Crit Rev Food Sci Nutr 36: 257–298
21. McGill AS, Hardy R, Burt RJ, Gunstone FD (1974) Hept-*cis*-4-enal and its contribution to the off-flavour in cold stored cod. J Sci Food Agric 25: 1477–1489
22. McGill AS, Hardy R, Gunstone FD (1977) Further analysis of the volatile components of frozen cold-stored cod and the influence of these on flavour. J Sci Food Agric 28: 200–203
23. Hofer T (1998) Tainting of seafood and marine pollution. Water Res 32: 3505–3512
24. Whitfield FB (1999) Biological origins of off-flavours in fish and crustaceans. Water Sci Technol 40: 265–272
25. Whitfield FB, Last JH, Shaw KJ, Tindale CR (1988) 2,6-Dibromophenol: the cause of an iodoform-like off-flavour in some Australian crustacea. J Sci Food Agric 46: 29–42
26. Persaud J, Dodd GH (1982) Analysis of discrimination mechanisms in the mammalian olfactory system using a model nose. Nature 299: 352–355
27. Gardner JW, Hines EL (1997) Pattern analysis techniques. In: Kress-Rogers E (ed) Handbook of biosensors and electronic noses: medicine, food and the environment. CRC Press, pp 633–652
28. Schaller E, Bosettand JO, Escher F (1998) Electronic noses and their application to food. Lebensm-Wiss-Technol 31: 305–316
29. Dickinson TA, White J, Kauer JS, Waltz DR (1996) A chemical-detecting system based on cross-reactive optical sensor array. Nature 382: 697–700
30. Lonergan MC, Severin EJ, Doleman EJ, Beaber SA, Grubbs RH, Lewis NS (1996) Array-based vapour sensing using chemically sensitive, carbon-black polymer resistors. Chem Mater 8: 2298–2312
31. Ali Z (1999) Acoustic wave mass sensors. J Therm Anal Calorim 55(2): 397–412

32. Sauerbrey GZ (1959) Verwendung von schwingquarzen zur wägung dünner schichten und zur mikrowagung. Z Phys 155: 206–222
33. Holmberg M, Winquist F, Lundstrom L, Gardner JW, Hines EL (1995) Identification of paper quality using a hybrid electronic nose. Sens Actuat B 246: 26–27
34. Bishop CM (1995) Neural networks for pattern recognition. OUP
35. Zadeh L (1965) Fuzzy sets. Inf Cont 8: 338–341
36. Yea B, Konishi R, Osaki T, Sugahara K (1994) The discrimination of many kinds of odour species using fuzzy reasoning and neural networks. Sens Actuat A 45: 159–165
37. Ali Z, O'Hare WT, Sarkodie-Gyan T, Theaker BJ (1999) Gas-sensing system using an array of coated quartz crystal microbalances with a fuzzy interference system. J Ther Anal Calorim 55(2): 371–381
38. Ali Z, Theaker B, O'Hare WT, Rowell FJ, Sarkodie-Gyan T, Scott S (2000) Classification of fresh edible oils with piezoelectric quartz crystal based electronic nose. Seventh International Symposium Olfaction and Electronic Nose, ISOEN 2000, 20–24th July 2000, Brighton; to be published as book by Institute of Physics
39. Shimizu Y, Takao Y, Egashira M (1988) Detection of freshness of fish by a semiconductive Ru/TiO_2 sensor. J Electrochem Soc 135: 2539–2540
40. Nanto H, Sokooshi H, Usuda T (1993) Smell sensor using aluminium-doped zinc oxide thin film prepared by sputtering technique. Sens Actuat B 10: 79–83
41. Winquist F, Sundgren H, Lundström I (1995) A practical use of electronic noses: quality estimation of cod fillet bought over the counter. Proceedings of the 8th International Conference on Solid-Sate Sensors and Actuators, and Eurosensors IX. Stockholm, Sweden: June 25–29, 1995, pp 695–698
42. Ólafsson R, Martinsdottir E, Ólafsdottir G, Sigfusson SI, Gardner JW (1992) Monitoring of fish freshness using tin oxide sensors. In: Gardner JW, Bartlett PN (eds) Sensors and sensory systems for an electronic nose. Kluwer, Dodrecht, The Netherlands, pp 257–272
43. Lindsay RC (1994) Flavour of fish. In: Shahidi F, Botta JR (eds) Seafoods: chemistry, processing technology and quality. Blackie Academic and Professional, Glasgow, UK, pp 75–84
44. Di Natale C, Brunink JAJ, Bungaro F, Davide F, D'Amico A, Paolesse R, Boschi T, Faccio M, Ferri G (1996) Recognition of fish storage time by a metalloporphyrins-coated QMB sensor array. Meas Sci Technol 7: 1103–1114
45. Luzuriaga DA, Balaban MO (1999) Electronic nose odour evaluation of salmon fillets stored at different temperatures. In: Hurst WJ (ed) Electronic noses and sensor array based systems-design and applications. Technomic Publishing Company, Lancaster, pp 162–169
46. Newman DJ, Luzuriaga DA, Balaban MO (1999) Odour and microbiological evaluation of raw tuna: correlation of sensory and electronic nose data. In: Hurst WJ (ed) Electronic noses and sensor array based systems – design and applications. Technomic Publishing Company, Lancaster, pp 170–176
47. Wilkes JG, Conte ED, Yongkyoung K, Holcomb M, Sutherland JB, Miller DW (2000) Sample preparation for the analysis of flavours and off-flavours in foods. J Chromatogr A 880: 3–33
48. Bonilla M, Enriquez G, McNair HM (1997) Use of cold on-column injection for the analysis of putrescine and cadaverine by gas chromatography. J Chromatogr Sci 35: 53–56
49. Cadwallader KR, Macleod AJ (1998) Instrumental methods for analysing the flavour of muscle foods. In: Shahidi F (ed) Flavour of meat, meat products and seafoods. Blackie Academic and Professional, London, pp 355–372
50. Cadwallader KR, Tan Q, Chen F, Meyers SP (1995) Evaluation of the aroma of cooked spiny lobster tail meat by aroma extract dilution analysis. J Agric Food Chem 43: 2432–2437
51. Chung HY, Chen F, Cadwallader KR (1995) Cooked blue crab meat aroma compared with lump meat. J Food Sci 60: 289–291, 299
52. Milo C, Grosch W (1997) Potent odourants in boiled cod as affected by the storage of raw material. In: Shahidi F, Cadwallader KR (eds) Flavour and lipid chemistry of seafoods. ACS Symposium Series 674, American Chemical Society, Washington, DC, pp 110–119

53. Cha YJ, Lee GH, Cadwallader KR (1997) Aroma-active compounds in salt-fermented anchovy. In: Shahidi F, Cadwallader KR (eds) Flavour and lipid chemistry of seafoods. ACS Symposium Series 674, American Chemical Society, Washington, DC, pp 131 – 147
54. Etievant PX (1996) Artifacts and contaminants in the analysis of food flavour. Crit Rev Food Sci Nutr 36: 733 – 745
55. Hiatt M (1997) Analysis of fish tissue by vacuum distillation GC-MS. Anal Chem 69: 1127 – 1134
56. Wampler TP (1997) Analysis of food volatiles using headspace-gas chromatographic techniques. In: Marsili R (ed) Techniques for analysing food aroma. Marcel Dekker, New York, pp 27 – 58
57. Alasalvar C, Quantick PC, Grigor JM (1997) Aroma compounds of fresh and stored mackerel (*Scomber scombrus*). In: Shahidi F, Cadwallader KR (eds) Flavour and lipid chemistry of seafoods. ACS Symposium Series 674. American Chemical Society, Washington, DC, pp 39 – 54
58. Josephson DB, Lindsay RC, Stuiber DA (1984) Variations in the occurrences of enzymically derived volatile aroma compounds in salt and freshwater fish. J Agric Food Chem 32: 1344 – 1347
59. Alasalvar C, Aishima T, Quantick PC (1995) Dynamic headspace analysis of volatile aroma compounds of fresh and deteriorated mackerel (*Scomber scombrus*). Food Sci Technol Int, Tokyo 1: 125 – 127
60. Josephson DB, Lindsay RC, Ólafsdottir G (1987) Measurement of valatile aroma constituents as a means for following sensory deterioration of fresh fish and fishery products. In: Kramer DA, Liston J (eds) Seafood quality determination. Elsevier Science Publishers, Amsterdam, pp 27 – 47
61. Alasalvar C, Grigor JM, Quantick PC (1999) Methods for the static headspace analysis of carrot volatiles. Food Chem 65: 391 – 397
62. Zhang Z, Yang M, Pawliszyn J (1994) Solid-phase microextraction. Anal Chem 66: 844 – 853
63. Harmon AD (1997) Solid-phase microextraction for the analysis of flavours. In: Marsili R (ed) Techniques for analysing food aroma. Marcel Dekker, New York, pp 81 – 112
64. Taylor AJ (1996) Volatile flavour release from foods during eating. Crit Rev Food Sci Nutr 36: 765 – 784
65. Brauss M, Linforth R, Taylor A (1998) Effect of variety, time of eating and fruit to fruit variation on volatile release during eating of tomato fruits. J Agric Food Chem 46: 2287–2292
66. Taylor A, Linforth R (1996) Flavour release in the mouth. Trends Food Sci Technol 7: 444 – 448

11 Improved Utilisation of Fish and Shellfish Waste

Tony Taylor, Cesarettin Alasalvar

Following primary processing of fish (filleting) approximately 50% of the whole fish is regarded as low value waste and mainly used for fishmeal production. This waste comprises head, viscera frame and flaps. The preparation of waste from crustaceans varies widely but in the case of scampi comprises approximately 80% of whole scampi or 30% of the tails. This chapter details three of the aspects of improved utilisation of fish and crustacean waste that have been researched at the Food Research Centre (University of Lincoln, UK).

Regarding whitening and recovered flesh, much research was carried out in the 1970s into the whitening/upgrading of fish mince without great success. However, innovative procedures and the availability of new materials have enables commercially viable procedures to be developed. Fish mince from flaps and/or frames can be whitened using titanium dioxide in a dispersion stabilised with xanthan gum. These must be reported as additives. Flaps can be successfully whitened using a hydrogen peroxide treatment prior to mincing. In the process described, this is broken down to oxygen and water and can thus be regarded as a processing aid. Both of these procedures are now in use by the industry.

There is potential for the extraction and purification of enzymes. The general procedure of partial purification of enzymes is described with the specific example of hyaluronidase from scampi waste (heads) being detailed.

An intermediate moisture pig feed, a pig feed was produced from waste skin and bones by the addition of other cheap nutrients/materials. This lowered the water activity (available water) to the level at which it is microbiologically stable and consequently resulted in a product which was stable for at least 6 months.

11.1 Introduction

In the preparation of fish for today's consumer market up to 50% of the whole fish is commonly discarded as waste [19]. Notable exceptions to this are trout and herring, which are usually sold or processed whole. The waste from most fish comprises the skeletal structure, intestinal organs and also a large amount of edible fish muscle that cannot be easily removed from the bone structure of the fish by conventional fish filleting processes. There is also additional wastage arising as a consequence of the further processing of fish fillets, for example incorrect weights and visual appearance problems such as blood spots.

The principle use for the waste has been for fish meal production, with some specific types of waste being utilised for human consumption, e.g. cod livers for cod liver oil. For the primary fish processors the result is a large difference in income between the fillets and the waste (Fig. 11.1). In the U.K. white fish (e.g. cod, *Gadus morhua*) are filleted.

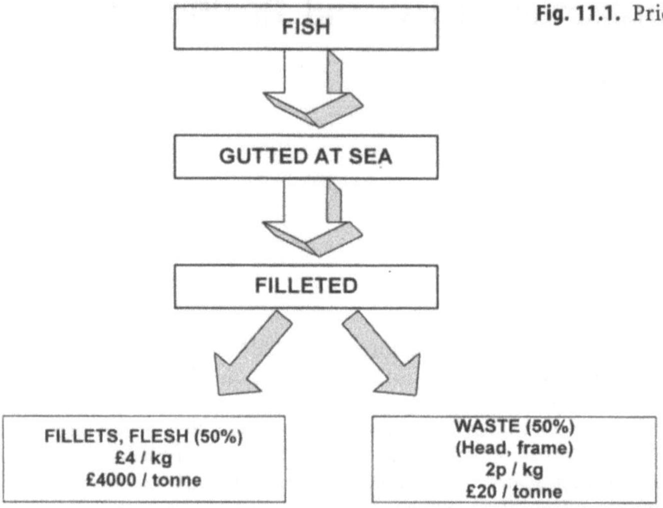

Fig. 11.1. Price of fish and fish waste

Table 11.1. Shell fish waste

	Waste (%)	Parts
Crab	75–80	Carapace, limbs and viscera
Shrimp, prawn	65–82	Head, shell and swimmarettes
Scampi	80	Head, legs, thorax and claws, and tail shell
Scampi tails	30–40	Tail shell

The world shellfish catch is estimated at 4 million tonnes. Of this, scampi catches account for 66,000 tonnes and crabs (U.K. only) 12,000 tonnes. The waste from shellfish is greater than from fish as shown in Table 11.1.

There are many ways in which the fish and shellfish waste could be better utilised, including the following:

Recovery of flesh:

Extraction of	Chitin Enzymes Oils Vitamins Pigments Flavour material
Production of	Gelatin Chitosan Fish leather

In this chapter, a few examples which have been successfully developed at the Food Research Centre are discussed.

11.2 Recovery of Fish Flesh

The mechanical recovery of the remaining flesh attached to the frame and flap, which cannot be removed by the filleting process, is a much studied field of waste utilisation and is a potential alternative to fish meal production. Most of the mechanical separation techniques are based on the physical screening of flesh from non-flesh components through a perforator filter. With the advent of drum flesh bone separators, fish mince production from the filleted fish frames and trimmings began, with up to 10% of the whole fish weight or 25% of the gutted weight of an averaged sized cod being recovered [6]. Table 11.2 shows the recovery of minced flesh from various parts of cod waste. However, the visual appearance of mince which is derived from the filleting waste (flaps and frames) of white fish such as cod or haddock is poor, principally due to the presence of pigments such as haemoglobin from blood and other haem proteins, mixed with the flesh during separation.

There are also associated quality problems, i.e. the lack of texture and the poor microbial profile that can result from the poor handling and storage of the waste and the additional processing required for the production of fish mince. Consequently, the amounts paid for the mince are generally mediocre, in the region of £800 per tonne for white fish mince. Fish mince colour partly determines retail prices and consumer acceptance, with the whiter minces attracting a higher price than those contaminated with traces of blood. For these reasons, development of a method of producing a white or whiter fish mince is commercially desirable. Washing or soaking of waste with water, prior to separation, has only a small effect in reducing the red pigmentation of the recovered mince. Direct washing, fish mince can elute part of the blood and improve the colour. Washing of mince will result in a significant loss of water soluble proteins, unless a method of recovering the proteins is applied (reverse osmosis, ultrafiltration, coagulation). Possible decolourisation of haemoglobin in fish mince via the use of high pressure has been postulated by Hoover et al. [9] but changes in texture are a possible side-effect of such a process. Consequently, three possible approaches were identified to try to overcome the problem of colour namely:

1. Remove back bone prior to flesh-bone separation
2. Whiten mince
   - Bleach
   - Titanium dioxide
3. Mask colour
   - Develop products with acceptable colour, e.g. curried, tomato flavoured

Most of the blood and discoloration is in/along the spinal cord so the effect of removal of the backbone was investigated. This provided a much better quality mince than that of the whole frames with only about 25% reduction in recovery of flesh. Whilst this works well in the laboratory it is uneconomical on a commercial scale (until an effective debackboning machine is available) due to the labour required.

Table 11.2. Recovery of minced cod fish using Baader 694 flesh bone separator

	Recovery (%)	Weight of fish (%)
Whole frame	72–82	8–10
Frame with back bone removed	55–65 (of whole frame)	6–8
Cod flaps	60–67	3–4

Masking of the colour of the mince is an acceptable method of upgrading, but suitable retail outlets have to be identified for the products such as curried cod fish burgers.

Two methods which had been unsuccessfully attempted in the 1970s were investigated and effective procedures developed.

11.2.1 Whitening of Mince Using Titanium Dioxide

The use of whitening chemicals such as titanium dioxide, vegetable fat based agents, hydrophilic colloids such as milk, gum hydrocolloids, mixtures of sugars, surfactants and fats, have been investigated. Common problems include the generation of a uniform colour (given the highly variable colour of fish mince), the possible artificial appearance of the resultant colour and the necessity to produce an emulsion or suspension which is capable of surviving the cooking/freezing process, in order to maintain the uniform colour. Consequently, Meacock et al. [12] investigated the use of titanium dioxide coupled with a variety of dispersing agents. The aim was to produce a whitener which could be added to fish mince that would produce a whiter mince, with good dispersion, and be effectively stable to freezing and frying.

To determine which suspension agents might be most suitable, a series of dispersed suspensions using titanium dioxide were prepared, using mixtures of the following, which were chosen on their existing use as suspension agents in a variety of products.

- H_2O (control)
- Vegetable oil
- Lecithin, sodium caseinate
- Carboxymethyl cellulose
- Sodium alginate
- Gelatin
- Locust bean gum
- Carrageenan
- Guar gum
- Xanthan gum
- Glycerol monostearate

Stable dispersions were achieved using locust bean gum, carrageenan, sodium alginate, but only xanthan gum gave a stable, non-odorous dispersion.

However a 'musty' taste and odour developed after a few weeks storage at room temperature of the dispersed TiO_2 suspension dispersed with xanthan gum. Thus, such dispersed suspensions should be used within 3 days of production. Fish mince produced using TiO_2 in water produces an uneven dispersion, with a toothpaste-type appearance to fish mince products after cooking.

The TiO_2/xanthan gum dispersion is easily incorporated into the mince, with excellent distribution. It gives an even increase in whiteness which is stable after frying the product or microwaving. Although at concentrations of up to 250 ppm of TiO_2 the whitening effect is negligible, the whiteness increases with further increasing concentrations of TiO_2. A level of 1 g of TiO_2/kg gives a most acceptable level of whiteness compared with the colour of cooked cod fillet. At this level no differences were detected by expert panels, triangle tests, or the texture analyser regarding the resulting texture of whitened fish mince. Figure 11.2 summarises the whitening procedure.

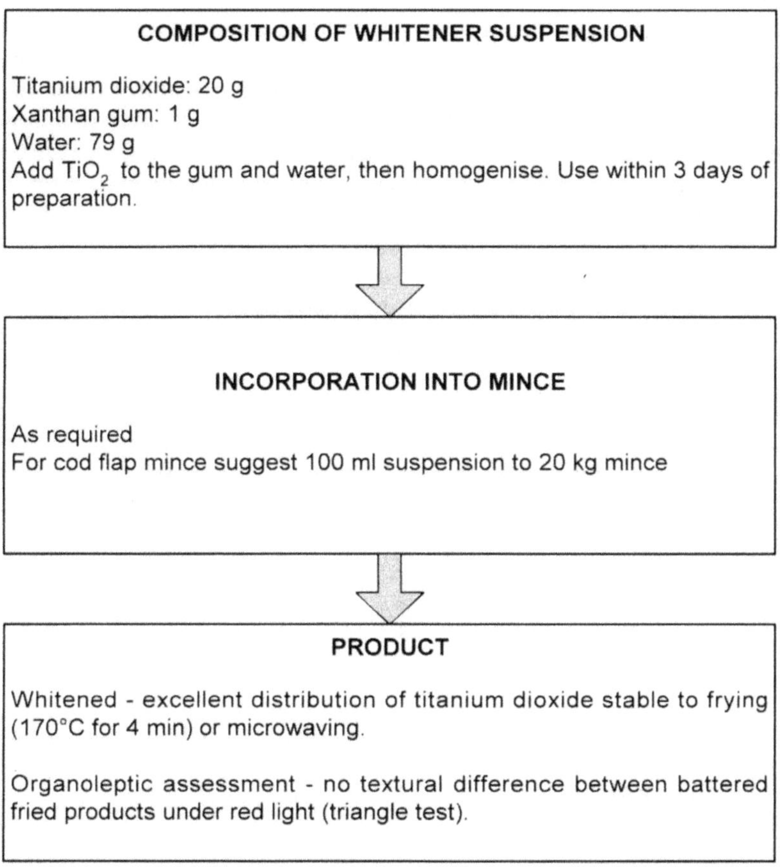

Fig. 11.2. Titanium dioxide based whitener

11.2.2 Whitening of Flaps Using Hydrogen Peroxide

Hydrogen peroxide has been used to whiten fish mince, but problems have been reported concerning textural changes and loss of proteins and amino acids through dissolution and oxidation. Also, many workers have reported the disinfecting action of H_2O_2 on various foods including fish. In spite of the reported difficulties using hydrogen peroxide, Himonides et al. [8] considered that this had a commercial and technical potential for whitening the mince.

They observed that the discoloration of flaps is mainly a superficial phenomenon and consequently treated whole flaps with H_2O_2 prior to separation for the production of fish mince. This differs from previous works in which the whitening treatment occurred after the flesh was separated and minced. The application of the bleaching agent prior to mincing should minimise protein insolubilisation and also the loss of water-soluble proteins, with minimal effect on the nutritional value or texture compared to the direct application of H_2O_2 on fish mince. The effect of concentrations of peroxide and time of soaking is shown in Table 11.3.

Samples were removed from the H_2O_2 solution after the time shown, soaked in water for 10 min and then assessed visually for colour improvement and textural damage. Immediately after treatment, flaps (particularly those of small size) may appear to have a loose flesh texture, with areas of skin that appear to be swollen due to the oxygen trapped under the surface of the skin. This textural effect, however, is minimised after soaking flaps in water, or even after leaving the flaps out of solution, for a small period of time (30 min), during which the oxygen bubbles dissipate. For industrial applications concentrations of 5–8 g H_2O_2/kg were recommended, with a soaking time of 90 min.

Visual sensory evaluation of the mince derived from standard and treated flaps (soaking for 1.5 h in 8 g/l H_2O_2) showed noticeable improvement in the

Table 11.3. Whitening effect of a range of H_2O_2 concentrations on flaps, for different time intervals

H_2O_2 (g/l)	5 min	10 min	30 min	40 min	60 min	120 min
0.5	0	0	0	0	0	0
1	0	0	0	s.i	s.i	s.i
2.5	s.i	s.i	s.i	s.i	s.i	s.i
5	n.i	n.i	n.i	3	3	3
8	n.i	n.i	n.i	3	3	3
10	3 p.t.c	3 p.t.c	3 p.t.c	3 t.c	3 t.c	3 t.c

0: no improvement.
s. i: small improvement.
n. i: noticeable improvement.
3: good whitening effect.
p. t. c: possible textural change.
t. c: textural change.

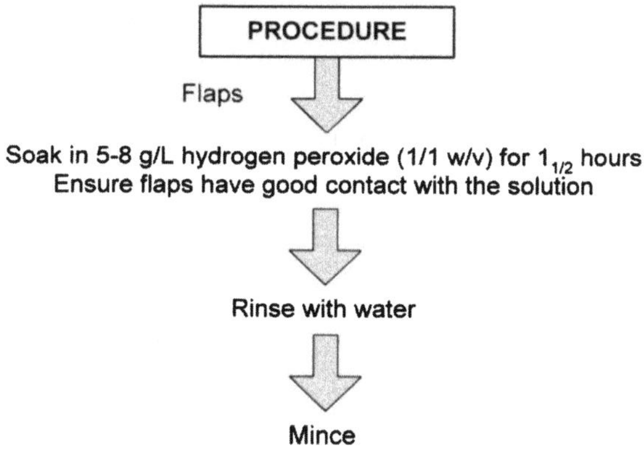

Fig. 11.3. Improved whitening of cod and haddock flaps using hydrogen peroxide

elimination of the red coloration. The degree of improvement depends on the initial condition of flaps and presumably on the depth of blood discoloration in the flesh. Colorimetric measurements confirmed a highly significant reduction of the red pigment (*a* values) and also a reduction of the yellow pigment towards the grey area (*b* values).

No significant difference ($P > 0.05$) was detected between the taste and odour of treated and standard cooked mince, by the sensory evaluation carried out before and after 8 months cold storage of the samples.

Microbiological analysis showed that treatment with hydrogen peroxide significantly reduces the total viable count of cod flaps. No residual H_2O_2 was detected in flaps immediately after treatment, using the oxygen electrode technique (the limit of detection was 3 µg/g). Immediately after treatment and washing of flaps it is possible that there may be residual H_2O_2 trapped in the flesh. It has been demonstrated, however, that hyperoxidase (catalase), which exists in the flesh cells, converts residual hydrogen peroxide into oxygen and water, particularly during mincing, due to the release of the enzyme from the cells. The existence of the enzyme was confirmed in cod and haddock mince and was found to be present in the fish mince even after the 8 months freezing stage period.

Since H_2O_2 cannot be detected after treatment and the products (water and oxygen) are non-toxic, H_2O_2 can be characterised as a processing aid rather than a food additive. As a result, and according to food legislation, the declaration of the use of H_2O_2 by the processor is not necessary. The procedure developed for and used by industry is shown in Fig. 11.3.

11.3 Extraction and Purification of Enzymes

Fish and shellfish wastes contain, as do all organisms, thousands of enzymes. Purification of any of these requires extraction and then separation from the other organic constituents extracted. This separation is usually carried out using differences in solubility, charge and size. A generalised procedure is shown in Fig. 11.4.

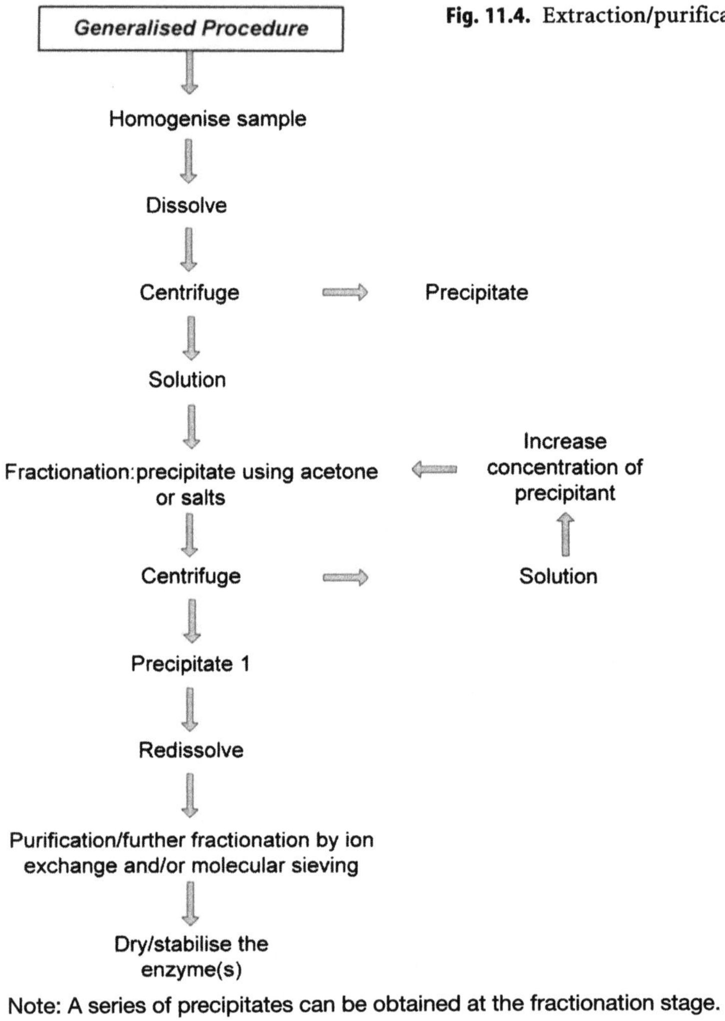

Fig. 11.4. Extraction/purification of enzyme(s)

These procedures are obviously costly with respect to time and chemicals required. Hence for this to be economically viable, the enzyme(s) extracted have to be extractable/purifiable in a combination of sufficient amount and cost per unit.

11.3.1 Extraction of Enzymes from Shellfish Waste

The total annual landing of *Nephrops norvegicus* for 1994 in the U.K. was estimated to be 30,036 tonnes [7] of which almost 75–80% was waste. Several possible ways of utilising crustacean waste have been described, with chitin being the most widely researched component. [1, 2, 13, 14]. The cephalothorax contains high levels of digestive enzymes [4, 5]. The recovery of alkaline phosphatase, β-*N*-acetylglucosaminidase, hyaluronidase and chitinase from shrimp processing waste waters of the Northern shrimp (*Pandalus borealis*) processing plants in Norway have been investigated [15].

11.3.2 Extraction and Purification of Hyalurunoglucosidase (EC 3.2.1.35)

Hyaluronidase is an endo-enzyme catalysing the depolymerisation of hyaluronic acid into short chain oligosaccharides and has been selected as an example of the potential use of recovery of enzymes from waste. This enzyme has therapeutic applications as, for example, in the cardiovascular field for salvaging ischaemic tissues following myocardial infarction [3, 16, 17]. It also has a range of other medical applications, diagnostic applications, and a minor application in the food industry as a meat tenderiser [18, 20]. It also has a high retail value when purified (up to £80/mg).

Krishnapillai et al. [11] successfully extracted and purified hyaluronidase from scampi (*Nephrops norvegicus*) waste. The solid head/waste was with all appendages, outer shell and adhering flesh removed and used as the starting material for the extraction of the enzyme. Techniques investigated included sequential centrifugal fractionation, acetone precipitation and ion exchange gel filtration. The final procedure developed is shown in Fig. 11.5, and the purification summarised in Table 11.4.

Purification of hyaluronidase (EC 3.2.1.35) from scampi hepatopancreas was achieved by acetone fractionation, ion exchange column chromatography on

Table 11.4. Summary of results of optimised purification of hyaluronidase by ion exchange chromatography on Amberlite IRA 420 followed by gel filtration on Sephacryl S-200-HR

Sample	Volume (ml)	Protein (mg/ml)	A584/ml/ 20 min	A584/mg/ 20 min	Recovery (% chromatographed)	Purif. fold	Recovery (% of original)
Crude extract	200	47.059[a] 8.053[b]	3.47	0.074 (0.43)[c]	–	1 (1)[c]	100
0.65–0.9 Acetone fraction	60	5.043[a] 2.156[b]	6.84	1.36 (3.17)[c]	–	18 (7)[c]	59
55 ml of the acetone fraction purified on Amberlite IRA420							
Ion exchange concentrate (IEC3)	34	0.472[a] 0.533[b]	8.94	18.9 (16.77)[c]	81	257 (39)[c]	48
Run 1: 12 ml of IEC purified on Sephacryl S-200-HR							
Gel filtered sample (SHR)	11.6	0.108[a] 0.075[b]	6.1	56.48 (81.3)[c]	66	766 (189)[c]	32

[a] Protein values estimated by A280/260 method.
[b] Protein values estimated by Lowry method.
[c] Results in parenthesis are based on protein values obtained by Lowry method.

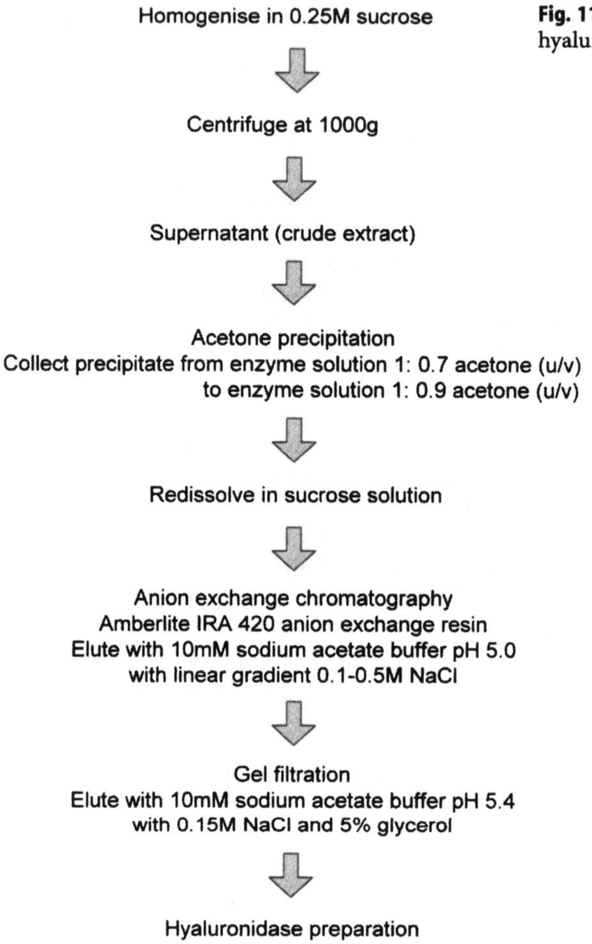

Fig. 11.5. Purification of hyaluronidase from Norway lobster

Amberlite IRA 420 and subsequently by Sephadex G-200 gel filtration. Purification of hyaluronidase from scampi hepatopancreas was optimised on an Amberlite IRA 420 anion exchange column using a gradient elution between 12.5 mmol/l to 500 mmol/l NaCl in 500 ml of 10 mmol/l sodium-acetate buffer at pH 5.4. This was followed by gel filtration on Sephacryl S-200-HR, the column being eluted with 10 mmol/l sodium-acetate buffer at pH 5.4; 763-fold purification and 32% recovery was achieved. A fraction of the highly purified extract, when subjected to native polyacrylamide gel electrophoresis (native-PAGE) with protein detected by Coomassie staining, indicated contamination by two other proteins.

Purification attempts by other methods such as DEAE cellulose, DEAE Sepharose CL-6B and DEAE Sephacel columns resulted in very low recoveries of the enzyme, possibly due to loss of enzyme by binding to the medium by the active site.

11.4 Intermediate Moisture Animal Feed (Pig Feed)

An Intermediate Moisture Pig Feed (IMPF) was developed from fish waste, which comprised mainly skin and bones (Miskin D. and Apostolidou A., unpublished report). The method used has the advantage of simplicity and low energy costs, because no heat processing (energy) is required to remove excess water. An additional benefit is that no heat damage occurs to the final product. Water absorbing materials (humectants) reduce the A_w and this, with the addition of propylene glycol, ensures the product's stability at room temperature.

11.4.1 Product Development

Fish waste (scrap) derived from white fish (cod, haddock and plaice) was used as the main ingredient in this IMPF development. The fish waste was minced, using a 4 mm mincing plate, and then it was stored at 2 ± 2 °C overnight, in order to be used the next day.

The ingredients were added progressively to the bowl chopper or blender thoroughly in the following order: fish waste, sugar, whey protein, sodium caseinate, propylene glycol and starch. They were mixed for 6–7 min. Table 11.5 shows the final recipe and cost of the IMP made of fish waste. Adequate mixing was very important for even distribution of the ingredients, especially the humectants. Storage of the resultant material at 2 ± 2 °C overnight was found to be an effective way to reduce its stickiness and make it easier to handle for the next stage, which was the forming of small pellets in the forming machine using a tablet plate of dimensions 5.0 × 2.5 × 2.0 cm. Alternatively, the Hobart mincer (3.0 mm dice) was used demonstrating that smaller pellets can be formed.

Before packing, case hardening of the pelleted pig feed was found to be necessary in order to prevent pellets sticking together. The Shrink wrapper machine was used as a tunnel drier. To give a soft but not sticky final pellet, a temperature of 45 °C proved to be appropriate for 30–40 min. During this "drying" process, the weight lost of the product found to be approximately 30%. Packaging has to be inexpensive and must protect the product from mould growth and 25 kg paper bags were successfully used. The final IMPF production line flow diagram is shown in Fig. 11.6.

Salmonella spp. analysis confirmed that the samples examined were *Salmonella* spp. free. This result was as expected, because normally fish and fish products are not natural reservoirs of *Salmonella* spp. Salmonella species are mainly isolated from the intestine of warm blooded animals and from food of animal origin [10]. Therefore, the presence of *Salmonella* spp. in the samples would be a result of poor manufacturing practices. The A_w was 0.72 (mean value, $n = 3$, SD = 0.25) as determined after the drying process of the IMPF was completed. This A_w is low enough to prevent the growth of most-organisms and gives to the produced IMPF very good microbiological stability. The final cost of the developed IMPF makes it compatible in the animal feed stuff market (Table 11.5).

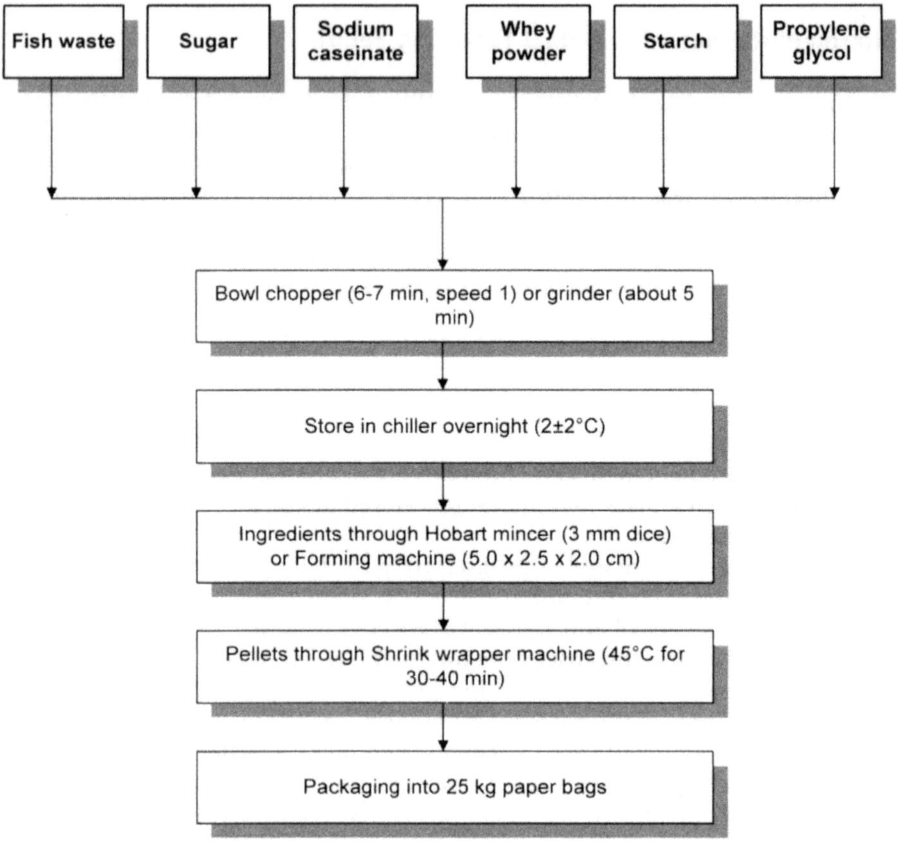

Fig. 11.6. Flow diagram of the IMPF production line

Table 11.5. Final recipe and cost of the IMPF made of fish waste

Ingredients	Weight (g)	Weight (%)	Price (£)/tonne	Price (£)/kg
Fish waste	562	56.2	0.0	0.0
Sugar	224.4	22.3	410	0.09
Whey powder	78.7	7.9	250	0.015
Sodium caseinate	56.2	5.7	4000	0.2
Propylene glycol	22.5	2.2	1000	0.021
Starch (cerestar 12012)	56.2	5.7	452	0.02

Total cost of product: £337/tonne. Prices belong to 1997.

Table 11.6. Proximate composition (%) of the produced IMPF

Water	29.7 ± 0.3
Protein	26.2 ± 0.3
Ash	7.1 ± 0.2
Lipid	trace
Carbohydrates	33.6
Calcium	1.2 ± 0.3
Sodium	0.7 ± 0.4

Data are expressed as mean±SD (n = 3).

Table 11.6 shows the results of chemical analysis of the produced IMPF after drying of the product was completed. The product has high protein and calcium values and was found to be *Salmonella* spp. free. Feeding trials with weaner piglets showed that it is very palatable and its shelf-life has been proven to be more than 6 months at ambient temperatures.

11.5 Conclusions

Waste is a widespread problem in the food industry from both economic and environmental points of view. This is particularly the case in the primary fish processing industry where about half of the expensive raw material is waste and sold mainly for fishmeal at a very low price (currently about £20/tonne). Many alternative possible uses of fish and shellfish waste have been investigated, and some are successfully being applied in various parts of the world (e.g. fish leather, chitin, recovered flesh). Nevertheless, there is much greater potential, both in terms of value and products, for use of these wastes. Further research is required to investigate and develop viable alternatives.

Acknowledgements. This work has been partly funded by EROF grants from the European Commission. This assistance is gratefully acknowledged.

References

1. Baxter DA (1990) The utilisation of scampi waste with special reference to properties chitosan. PhD thesis, University of Lincoln, UK
2. Brezeski MM (1987) Chitin and chitosan – putting waste to good use. Infofish Int 5: 31–33
3. Cairns JA, Holder DA, Tanser P, Missirilis E (1983) Intravenous hyaluronidase therapy for myocardial infarction in man: double blind trial to assess infarct size limitation. Circulation 65: 764–771
4. Cann DC (1973) Bacteriological aspects of tropical shrimps. In: FAO Technical Conference on Fishery Products. F II: FP/73/E-24, FAO, Tokyo, p 14
5. Cobb BF III (1977) Biochemistry and physiology of shrimps: effect on use as food. In: Proceedings of the Conference on the Handling, Processing and Marketing of Tropical Fish. Tropical Products Institute, London, pp 287–290
6. Connell JJ, Hardy R (1982) Trends in fish utilisation. Fishing News Books, Surrey, UK

7. FAO (1996) Year book of fishery statistics, vol. 78. Catches and landings. Food and Agricultural Organisation, Rome, Italy
8. Himonides AT, Taylor KDA, Knowles MJ (1999) The improved whitening of cod and haddock flaps using hydrogen peroxide. J Sci Food Agric 79: 845–850
9. Hoover DG, Metrick C, Papinneau AM, Farkas DF, Knorr D (1989) Biological effects of high hydrostatic pressure on food micro-organisms. Food Technol 3: 99–107
10. Kose S (1993) Investigation into toxins and pathogens implicated in fish meal production. PhD thesis, Loughborough University, UK
11. Krishnapillai AM, Taylor KDA, Morris AEJ, Quantick PC (1999) Extraction and purification of hyaluronoglucosidase (EC 3.2.1.35) from Norway lobster (*Nephrops norvegicus*). Food Chem 65: 359–365
12. Meacock G, Taylor KDA, Knowles MJ, Himonides AT (1997) The improved whitening of minced cod flesh using dispersed titanium dioxide. J Sci Food Agric 73: 221–225
13. Meyers SP (1986) Utilisation of shrimp processing waste. Infofish Market Dig 4: 18–19
14. Nair KGR, Madhavan P, Gopakumar K (1986) Novel use of chitinous waste from crustacean processing plants. Infofish Market Dig 4: 20
15. Olsen RL, Johansen A, Myrnes B (1990) Recovery of enzymes from shrimp waste. Proc Biochem 25: 67–68
16. Saltissi S, Robinson PS, Coltart DJ, Webb-Peplope MM, Croft DN (1982) Effects of early administration of a highly purified hyaluronidase preparation (GL enzyme) on myocardial infarct size. Lancet 1: 867–870
17. Sanders AB (1988) Myocardial salvage: Pharmacologic treatment. Emerg Med Clin North Am 6: 361–372
18. Stekol'Nikov LI, Shilov GG, Sevastyanov BA, Belousov AA, Mamonov ND (1980) Methods for preparing enzymatic composition for acceleration of ageing of meat products. US Pat 4,195,097
19. Windsor M, Barlow S (1981) Introduction to fishery by-products. Fishing News Books, Surrey, UK
20. Wu JJ, Dutson TR, Carpenter ZL (1981) Effect of post-mortem time and temperature on the release for lysosomal enzymes and their possible effects on bovine connective tissue components of the muscle. J Food Sci 46: 1132–1135

12 The Icelandic Way Towards Automation in Fish Processing

Kristinn Andersen, Halldor Magnusson

A review of the last 10 years in terms of automation and new technology in the Icelandic fishing industry will be presented. The main emphasis will be on the development of flow-lines and how they have been used to monitor yield, workers capacity, product-mix and quality. Flow lines have been successfully used in Iceland to improve quality, productivity and to increase both yield and production of value-added products (portion-control). The main discussion will focus on the problems the Iceland land-based factories were facing in 1996 due to competition from offshore plants and reduced quotas, and how automation was successfully deployed. The importance of pre-grading of raw material for production control will be stressed and examples taken to show how automatic portioning can be used to increase productivity.

12.1 Introduction

The rich fishing grounds around Iceland have been among the most valuable resources available to Icelanders for centuries. Despite increased diversity of the economy of the country in the twentieth century the importance of fishing and fish processing continues to be substantial as the twenty-first century begins. The export of fish products accounted for over 70% of the total exports from Iceland in 1998 [1], which illustrates vividly the present importance of the fishing and fish processing industries for the country.

While Iceland's economy has in large part been resource-based, with fishing and fish processing playing a major role, the adoption of state-of-the-art technology has been relatively rapid as it has emerged. As a result, Icelandic fish processing evolved early on as a competitive industry, seeking to streamline its operation and maximise yields in the same way other industries have done. Individual quick frozen (IQF) products were designed and manufactured early on for the relatively distant export markets on both sides of the Atlantic. The use of machine filleting started in Iceland in the 1960s and became quickly widely adopted. Flow-lines replaced pan based production systems in the 1980s and made way for more efficient processing than before.

The competitive environment of the fish processing industry and the challenges it created gave rise to new technology providers, such as Marel, which was founded in 1983. Initially the company provided hardware and software for automatic weighing and registering for the fish processing industry. Today annual sales are about 100 million ECU and well over 80% of the sales are exports to various parts of the world, to the poultry and meat industries as well as the fish industries.

Various changes emerged when the pan systems were replaced by the more streamlined conveyor systems. The overall handling and production time decreased, helping keep the product chilled and reduce drip losses. The pans were eliminated, which resulted in less space requirements, simplified work procedures and reduced need for support staff. On the other hand the initial conveyor systems allowed for only limited flexibility, and monitoring of the work of individual employees was none, or limited at best.

12.2 New Technology: Flowlines and Intelligent Portioning Machines

The introduction of Marel flow lines in 1992 opened new possibilities for monitoring, controlling and optimising fish processing. The flow line concept takes further the advantages of conveyor systems in that adverse impact on the raw material quality through transport and handling is minimised. The flow line routes raw material at automatically controlled rates to the individual workers who are the working at the line, cutting and trimming the portions. The workers return the processed portions back to the takeaway conveyors on the line and waste material is sent a separate route (Fig. 12.1).

Production data from each worker is individually monitored by a computer system, showing the capacity, yield, product mix and quality performance from that person, and collectively for the group working at the line. This gives new possibilities for paying salaries on an individual basis, according to perfor-

Fig. 12.1. Work at the Marel flow line

mance. Furthermore, the flow line design ensures minimal processing time for the material, ergonomic working conditions for the workers at the line and access for cleaning is carefully designed into the system.

Following the flow lines, the Marel Intelligent Portioning Machine (IPM) was introduced in 1994. The portioning machine uses computer vision technology to scan and evaluate the weight distribution of the raw material along the piece length. The piece is cut at appropriate positions, according to the portion weights that are requested. This machine cuts at much higher capacities than humans and at the same time the accuracy is higher. An intelligent portioning machine is shown in Fig. 12.2.

Various portioning programs are offered with the IPM, resulting in increased portioning yield. While the IPM uses high technology in computer vision and software, the principles of its basic operation are relatively simple. As a result the Marel IPM became immediately at its introduction highly competitive in comparison with other and more expensive options.

Product development of the first flow lines and the IPM was carried out by Marel in close cooperation with leading fish processing firms in Iceland. Together they were able to make systems that vastly improved the production in shore based plants which were in tough competition with fish processing at sea by the mid-1990s. Production of portions, in place of the less valuable block, became feasible because of the new technology with improved productivity, improved quality, better material handling and improved overall efficiency.

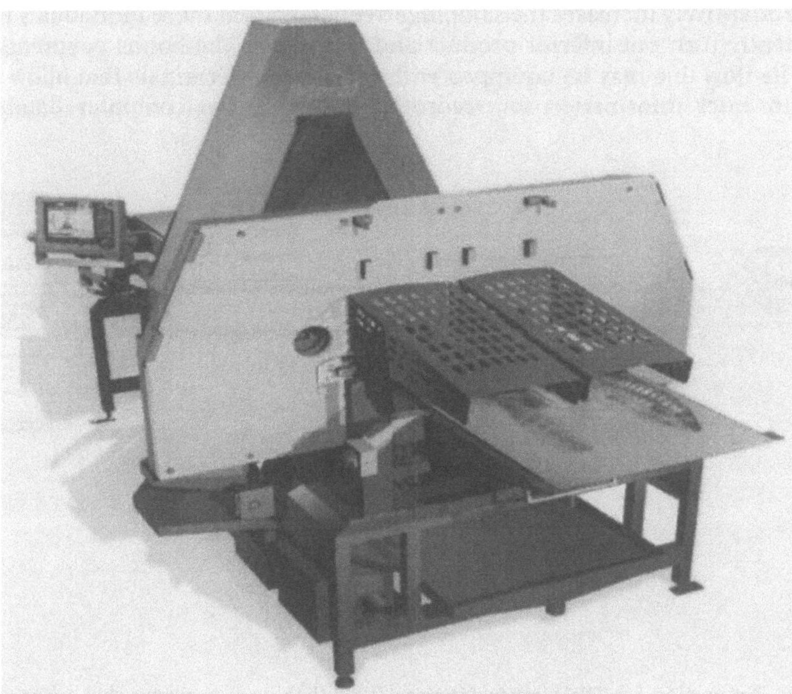

Fig. 12.2. A two lane intelligent portioning machine (IPM) by Marel

12.3 New Fish Processing Concepts

The new technology gave rise to several improvements and new concepts in fish processing. By pre-grading the raw material the following phases in the processing can be better planned and both material and equipment better utilised. All raw material entering the process is weight graded, head yield is continuously monitored, and data is recorded for real-time stock control. The raw material is stored in ice water prior to further processing.

Pre-portioning is carried out with the intelligent portioning machine, saving considerable labour at this stage. The pre-portioning ensures that less trimming is needed on the tail. Furthermore, the automation requires less handling of the material, with corresponding improvement in yield and productivity. The pre-portioning section of a production line is illustrated in Fig. 12.3.

Trimming follows the pre-portioning step. The fillet portions are automatically distributed to the trimming stations along the flow line. The amount of net product leaving each station, as well as the waste, is recorded for each worker and this information is used by the supervisor for monitoring the overall yield of the line, as well as the yield for each employee. This registration for each individual can be used in performance-based bonus payments.

Subsequent to the trimming stations is a quality control station which takes samples from the workers for statistical quality control. The quality control system tracks each sampled piece back to the appropriate trimming station. The system adaptively increases the sampling frequency from those individuals who consistently turn out inferior product and this affects the bonus payments as well. The flow line may be equipped with registration terminals that allow the users to enter information for recording into a central computer database

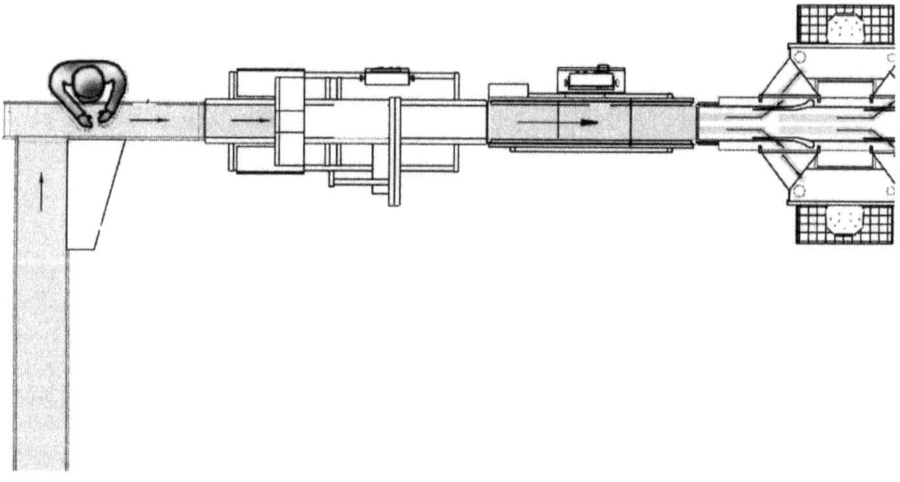

Fig. 12.3. Pre-portioning. The worker arranges fish fillets on a conveyor that takes them through the IPM where they are cut, followed by a grader for weighing the portion cuts

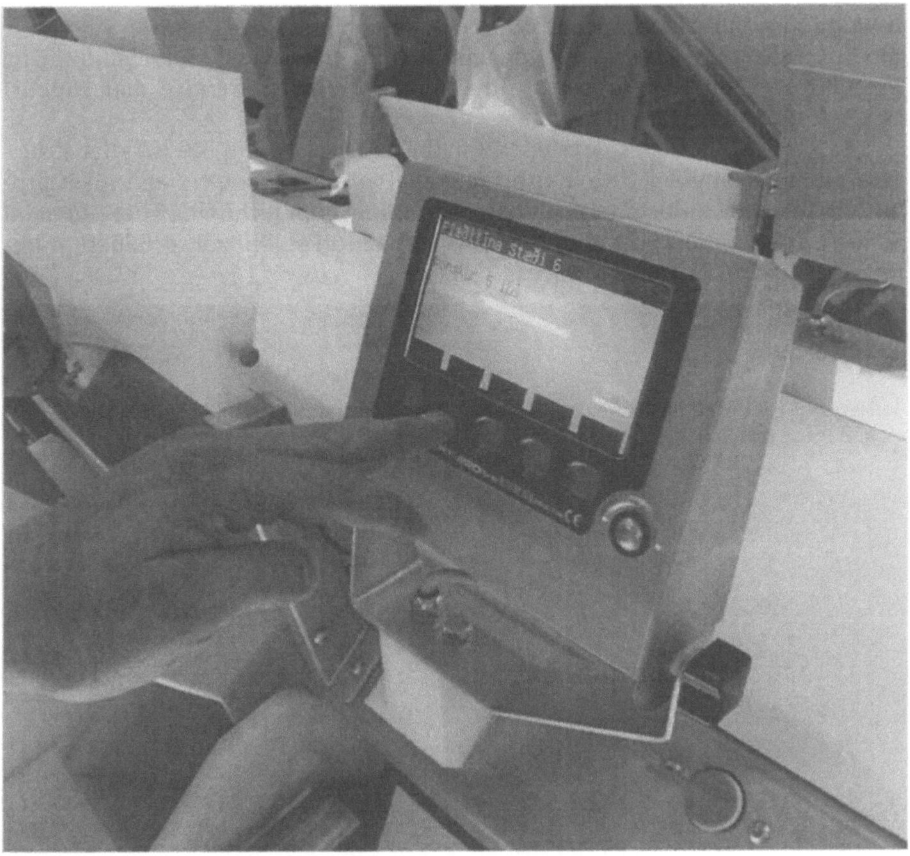

Fig. 12.4. The flow line is equipped with registration terminals, for recording data from the workers and submitting to a central database

(Fig. 12.4). The trimmed fillet pieces are routed further to a portioning machine that cuts them into the final portions.

12.4 Results and Further Development

The fish processing concept outlined above has been put to use in eight plants in four countries at the time of this writing. Generally they have increased the capacity per man hour by 50–80%. Yield of the raw material has improved by 1–3%, with less mince, less material going to inexpensive block, and more material utilised in the more valuable portions. Furthermore, improved material handling, shorter processing time and the adaptive statistical quality control have resulted in higher overall quality of the final product.

Further opportunities for development in fish processing are foreseen or already in progress at Marel. These include robots for feeding de-heading and filleting machines, equipment for bone detection and bone removal, automatic quality inspection, advanced management information system for monitoring the entire production process, and remote equipment service and support through the Internet, to name a few.

The new technologies developed for the fish processing industry have successfully been applied with appropriate adaptations to poultry and meat processing. In these industries, as in fish processing, high technology development in close cooperation with the users has resulted in significant production improvements and financial rewards.

References

1. National Economic Institute (2000) The National Economy of Iceland – Progress of 1999 and Prospects in 2000. National Economic Institute, Reykjavik: Iceland, March 2000

13 Reducing Water and Trade Effluent Costs in Fish Processing

Richard B. Watson

The Seafish Industry Authority (Seafish) is a statutory body funded by levy. Its main duty is to promote the efficiency of the UK fishing industry, whilst taking into account the needs of the consumers of fish. Coastal fish processors face a dramatic increase in trade effluent charges as a result of tightening environmental legislation. This chapter summarises the work that Seafish has carried out to reduce the costs associated with water usage and trade effluent disposal in fish processing. Detailed industry audits were carried out to identify the key problem areas in the main processing operations. The simple waste minimisation solutions identified and developed are discussed.

13.1 Introduction

In the near future, new environmental legislation will add greatly to the cost and difficulty of disposing of waste water, which will present a significant problem to the fish industry. Fish processing requires large volumes of water and similarly produces large volumes of effluent which can have a high level of organic contamination. Traditionally the effluent in UK coastal regions, where the fish processing industry largely remains, has been pumped out to sea at negligible cost but this will change as the Urban Waste Water Treatment Directive (91/271/EEC) demands that by the end of 2001 effluent must be treated before release into the sea.

In the future, coastal businesses will be charged on both the strength and volume of their effluent; the greater the quantity and the stronger the effluent, the higher the treatment costs. These new trade effluent charges will be calculated using the full Mogden formula that includes charges for the biological effluent treatment required to meet strict standards set by the Directive. This will bring coastal companies into line with charges already faced by inland businesses.

13.2 Effluent Disposal Options

In general, companies have two options: they can either discharge their effluent to the public sewer or discharge directly into the sea. Both options require a conditional consent to discharge and the payment of charges. Most businesses discharge their effluent into the sewer. The advantages of this include a low capital cost for connection; however, if the company produces a large volume of high strength effluent, the Mogden calculated trade effluent charges will be high. With direct discharge to the sea, the associated outfall and any treatment equipment required to meet the imposed consent will typically incur a very high capital cost. An expensive marine hydrographic survey of the receiving water is also required and there is a risk of prosecution should the agreed discharge consent be broken. However, once established, with the payment of relatively small annual fees this method should incur lower operating charges.

13.3 Mogden Calculated Trade Effluent Charges

The Mogden formula is the standard formula used throughout the UK to calculate trade effluent charges. This formula takes into account both the volume and the strength of the effluent produced. Typically, the water company aim to take representative effluent samples from the point at which the effluent leaves the factory. The strength of the sample is measured by two parameters: typically settled chemical oxygen demand (sCOD) which is a measure of the dissolved component, and total suspended solids (TSS) which is a measure of the amount suspended solids present (parameters may vary with different regional areas). The effluent volume is usually calculated from the water bill, minus any allowances for water which does not go down the drain, such as the water used to make ice. From industry audits carried out in 1997 it was estimated that a typical trade effluent disposal cost of about 20 p/m^3 could rise by about 500% for a typical white fish processor and by about 2500% for a typical pelagic processor if these businesses fail to implement effluent minimisation measures.

13.4 Seafish Work

To identify the scale of the problem Seafish organised brief waste surveys of 50 Humberside processors. Detailed audits were then carried out in 11 companies, representing the different sectors of industry, to identify the main problem areas and ways to minimise costs. The results of the audits showed that all processors from all sectors wasted water and produced excessively high effluent strength to greater or lesser degree. Waste minimisation at source was identified as being the most cost-effective way to reduce costs. Many opportunities to make significant reductions in both water use and effluent strength were identified, some of which have been trailed in collaboration with processors and are discussed in the following section of this chapter. Trials have also been carried out to investigate the effectiveness of the various forms of end of pipe treatment equipment, including screening and dissolved air flotation (DAF).

13.5 Waste Minimisation

13.5.1 Benefits of Waste Minimisation

Waste minimisation at source is the key to minimising both the water supply costs and trade effluent charges together, whilst generating revenue from the recovery and sale of fish waste instead of it being an effluent cost. Minimising water use not only reduces the water supply bill but also reduces the discharge costs. The discharge cost is reduced directly by reducing the volume charge and also indirectly by minimising the amount of water washing through the waste and hence the transfer of contamination to the water. Preventing waste coming into contact with the water or separating the solid waste from the effluent as close as possible to source is vital in minimising this transfer of contamination, particularly of the soluble organic materials. Once dissolved, these materials are difficult and expensive to remove from the effluent at a later stage as this requires biological secondary treatment. Minimisation at source can also reduce the cost of any further end of pipe treatment that may be required. Common and fundamental principles to prevent water wastage and high strength effluent production can be applied to most process operations in order to keep the costs to a minimum.

13.5.2 Principles of Water Use Minimisation

Water minimisation can result in dramatic savings but the necessary hygiene standards must be maintained.

Water should be turned off when it is not needed. Large quantities of water are wasted in many businesses simply through leakage and leaving hose pipes running without serving any useful purpose.

Water should be used efficiently. Most process operations consume more water than is necessary for effective operation of the process. The water flow to processes is often arbitrarily set by valves on the supply lines and is rarely controlled down to the minimum necessary. Many processes involve flooding with water or using powerful water jets, when sprays from well designed nozzles would suffice. Another example would be the fitting of trigger sprays to open ended hose pipes.

Alternative 'dry' processes should be used wherever possible. Wet processes are commonly used when there are 'dry' alternatives which consume much less water. For example, large quantities of running water are commonly used for thawing frozen material, although there are preferable air thawing techniques and purpose designed thawing equipment available. Open-ended hose pipes are still used to chase waste around the floor instead of using a squeegee, and water flumes are still used for transporting fish waste instead of using containers or conveyors.

13.5.3
Principles of Effluent Strength Minimisation

Wherever possible, working practices and equipment should stop waste coming into contact with water. Waste should be prevented from soaking in water, for example the trimmings in the bottom of the traditional filleting bench tub. This is because the soluble components of the waste such as blood and other constituents leach out and increase the strength of the effluent. Unnecessary cutting up or mashing up of the waste, such as trampling it under foot or pumping the effluent, should be avoided, as this also results in soluble material and fine pieces of fish increasing the effluent strength. Water must be prevented from washing through solid waste such as the trimmings in the basket underneath a traditional filleting bench or a skinning machine waste basket or a traditional drain catch basket. This is because the effluent picks a significant amount of dissolved and suspended material and so increases its strength.

13.6
Typical Processing Problems and Solutions

This section looks at some of the key problem areas and solutions in terms of water usage and effluent strength production which were identified during the it detailed Seafish audits.

13.6.1
Defrosting

Problems. The three common types of defrosting arrangement are shown in Fig. 13.1 A – C. Many businesses use makeshift water thawing techniques, which are largely uncontrolled and use very large quantities of water inefficiently, producing large volumes of low strength effluent. Typically fish are laid out under water sprays or are immersed in large containers of water and are left overnight with the water running. Some of the fish thaw rapidly whilst others remain partially frozen. Thawing fish in stacked containers is particularly inefficient.

Solutions. Where possible, initial thawing in ambient air can be carried out to reduce the need for subsequent use of water or heated air. Water spray defrosting systems can be improved by ensuring an even distribution of fine sprays over all the blocks. By inserting thermocouples linked to a solenoid valve in the centre of blocks which take the longest to defrost, the water can be switched off automatically when defrosting is complete. Alternatively the equipment can be linked to a timer and solenoid valve arrangement to switch the water off after the required duration. In winter the water can be heated somewhat to make the process more efficient. With container defrosting, the containers used should be purposely modified to ensure effective water circulation around the frozen blocks.

Purpose designed thawing equipment, such as that using heated moist air, uses negligible water and produces little effluent.

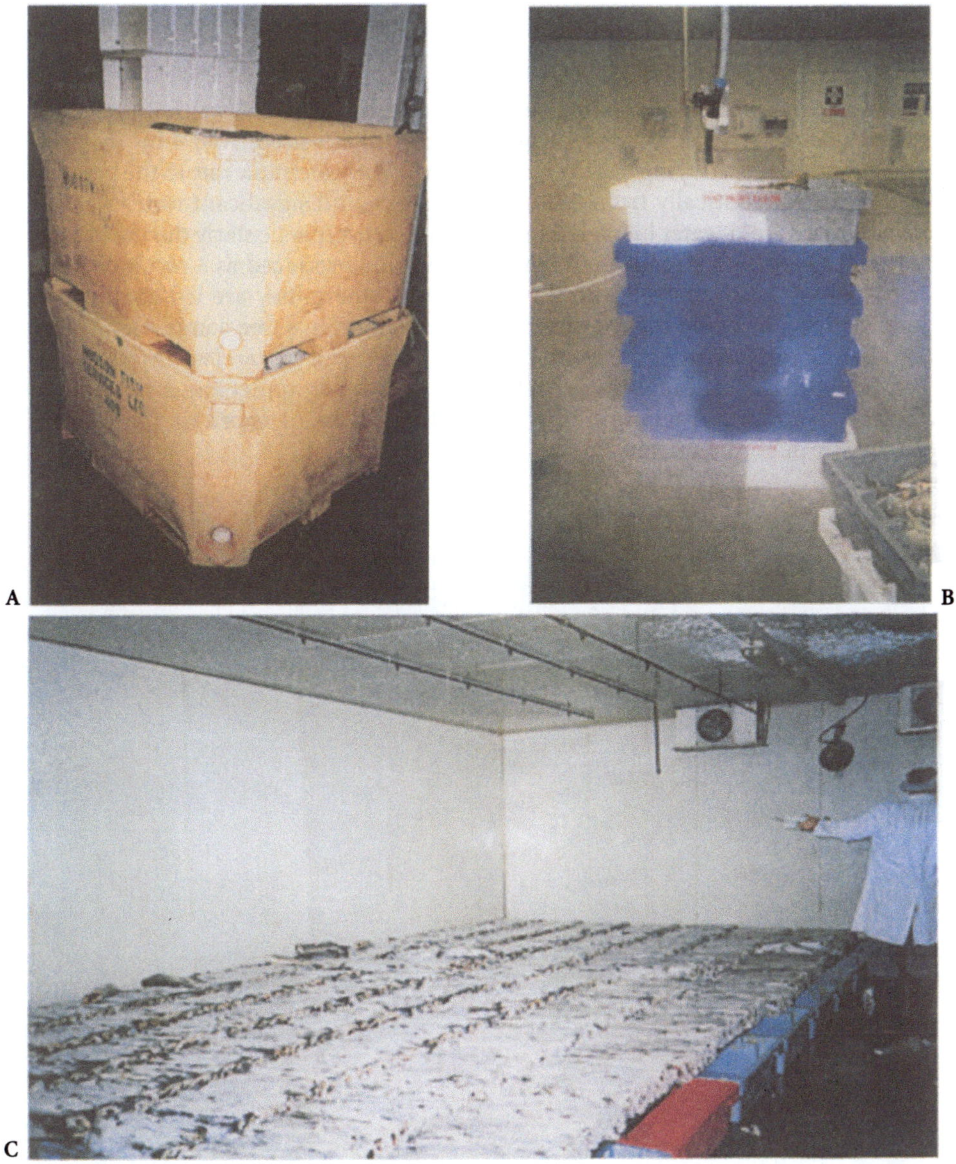

Fig. 13.1 A–C. Defrosting methods: **A** container defrosting; **B** fish box defrosting; **C** spray defrosting

13.6.2 Manual Filleting

Problems. A typical hand filleting bench is shown in Fig. 13.2. It was found that the amount of water used to produce one tonne of fillet varied from 4 m^3 to 11 m^3 whilst essentially carrying out the same process. The water flow rate to the benches also varied dramatically from 8 l/min to 70 l/min and significant water wastage also resulted from water being left on when not in use, particularly during breaks.

Excessively high strength effluent is commonly produced as a result of trimmings either being flicked into the central tub, where they are left soaking for long periods, or being flicked directly onto the floor. In some companies a large amount of waste also ends up on the floor as a result of careless throwing towards the fish meal bin. Where baskets are positioned under the drain hole in the tub to catch the trimmings, effluent strength is increased as the effluent washes through the waste.

Fig. 13.2. A traditional filleting bench

Solutions. A flow regulator (approximate cost £10 excluding fitting) set to the desired flow rate can be fitted to control excessively high water flow, whilst a solenoid valve linked to a timer can be used to prevent water being left on during breaks.

Seafish has been developing improvements to the traditional design of the filleting bench to reduce the effluent strength. Simple means of separating and collecting the trimmings have been demonstrated (Fig. 13.3 A, B). The cutting board is separated from the tub by a gap of about 50 mm and a removable catch tray

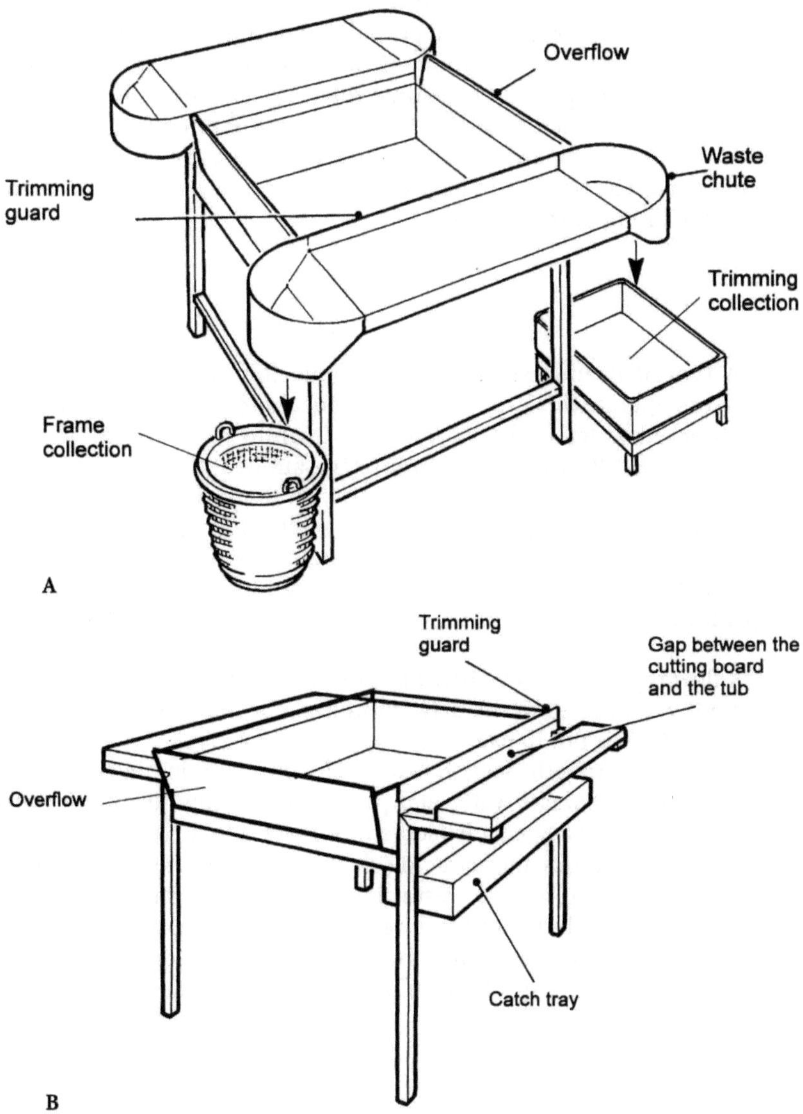

Fig. 13.3 A, B. Prototype filleting benches: A chute configuration; B catch tray configuration

(with adequate drainage) is located underneath. A trimming guard about 40 mm high is positioned on the side of the tub. The trimmings flicked towards the tub fall into the tray. An effluent overflow is incorporated into the ends of the bench. Future work will focus on the use of chutes at the ends of the cutting board to direct the waste into containers.

A few businesses use 'dry' filleting lines with an initial fish washer feeding an integrated conveyor line filleting system. The conveyors deliver the fish to a number of cutting stations and carry the product and the waste away. A flexible hose with a trigger operated spray nozzle is provided at each cutting station to keep the board clean. Potentially these lines are very efficient but in practice the fish washer design may be wasteful and poor detail design of the cutting stations may still result in a considerable amount of waste on the floor. The principles of this 'dry' filleting can be applied to separate filleting benches without conveyor systems. Seafish has modified a filleting bench to incorporate a small nozzle positioned over the cutting board. This provides the necessary knife lubrication without using a tub. The fish has to be pre-washed but the system has proven efficient and to the liking of the filleters.

13.6.3
Skinning

Problems. A typical Baader 51 type skinning machine is shown in Fig. 13.4. Many processors operate this type of skinning machine at excessively high flow rates. The observed water usage varied from 9 l/min to 70 l/min, whilst the Baader recommended flow rate is 25 l/min. One audited company used a flow rate of 10 l/min without any problems (either with the yield or the machine itself). It is also not uncommon for the water to be left running for long periods of time when the machines are not in use. Skinning machines often produce high strength effluent as the waste water washes through the basket of waste skins, picking up additional strength.

Solutions. A flow regulator can be fitted to prevent water wastage. In addition, a simple solenoid valve linked to the drive motor can be used to switch the water off when the machine is not in use.

To reduce effluent strength, Seafish has developed a simple wedge wire separator chute to divert the waste water and prevent it washing through the skins (Fig. 13.5). Wedge wire is a specialist screening material with a triangular profile, which helps resist blocking, reducing the tendency of the screen to blind. The skins slide down the modified waste chute and into the waste basket whilst the effluent passes through the wedge wire and is diverted away to drain. In trials with a Baader 51 skinning machine, the separator chute reduced the Mogden calculated trade effluent charge of the effluent produced by the machine by 50% (Fig. 13.6).

Fig. 13.4. A typical Baader 51 type skinning machine

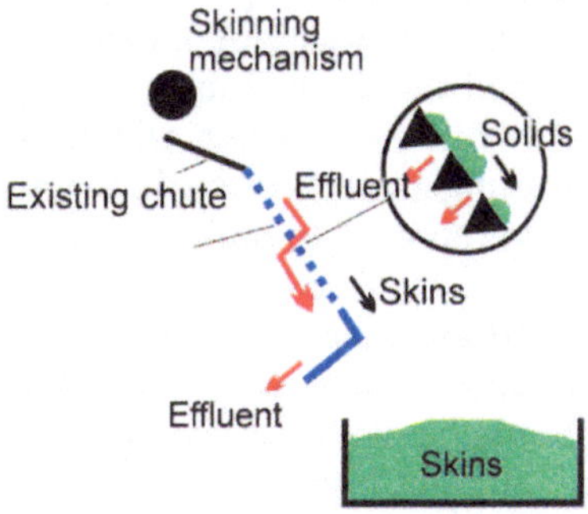

Fig. 13.5. A wedge wire separator chute schematic diagram

Fig. 13.6. A wedge wire separate chute fitted to a Baader 51

13.6.4
Secondary Processing

Problems. Some secondary processes such as enrobing can produce particularly high strength effluent. Many of the materials used such as batter mixes, cooking oil, brine and marinades have high COD values and only small amounts ending up in the drain can increase the overall effluent strength. From the audit data, the Mogden calculated trade effluent charge of discharging neat batter mix would be about £408/m^3.

Solutions. Guards and catch trays should be used to prevent high strength material ending up on the floor. Production should also be optimised to prevent the need for having to dispose of this type of waste at the end of the day.

13.6.5
Cleaning

Problems. Cleaning uses large quantities of water and it is often poorly controlled and wasteful. Open-ended hoses are commonly used to chase water around the floor. One of the most wasteful activities involves filling barrels or large bins with water, which are then tipped to swill down the floor. During cleaning, waste is often deliberately flushed down the drain. The drain covers are often removed to make disposal easier.

Solutions. Cleaning should be carried out according to a strict hygiene schedule which specifies when and how it is done and who is responsible. Squeegees should be used to gather up waste on the floor, which should then be shovelled up and put into the waste bins. Waste should not be put down the drain. Hoses should be fitted with adjustable trigger action spray nozzles to ensure water is used more effectively.

13.6.6 Drainage System

13.6.6.1 *Drain Covers*

Problems. Typical drain covers are shown in Fig. 13.7. Most drain covers have large slotted holes which are ineffective in preventing large solids from entering the drains. In addition, most drain covers can be easily lifted, this allowing large volumes of solid waste to be shovelled into the drain during cleaning.

Solutions. The design of drain covers is a compromise in order to prevent a large solids from passing through but without the holes blocking and causing flooding of the floor. Seafish has carried out trials investigating the effectiveness of both wedge wire and drilled drain covers. For white fish effluent, drilled or punch plate covers with 15 mm diameter holes taking up 11 % of the total area of the covers were found to be effective; 5 mm wedge wire covers were also ef-

Fig. 13.7. Typical drain covers

fective. Consideration should also be given to keying the covers in position so they cannot be lifted without a special tool.

13.6.6.2
Drain Catch Baskets

Problems. A typical drain catch basket is shown in Fig. 13.8. The catch baskets are often poorly designed and ineffective in preventing smaller solids from contaminating the effluent. The baskets are often poorly fitting due to either poor design or a damaged housing, allowing solids to bypass the basket. The effluent entering the basket also washes through all the solid waste, washing out small pieces of fish and picking up additional strength. The design of many baskets also results in the solid waste soaking in the effluent below the water level in the drain, resulting in the leaching out of additional soluble material. These problems are often magnified by infrequent emptying.

Fig. 13.8. A typical catch basket

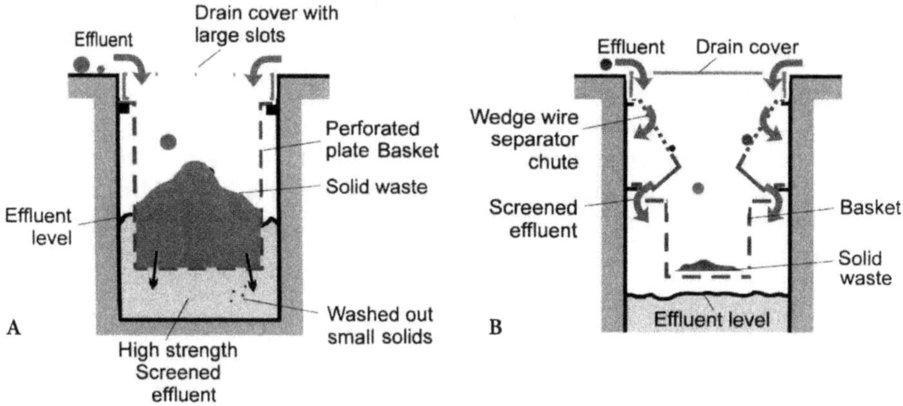

Fig. 13.9 A, B. Schematic diagrams of: **A** traditional catch basket; **B** separator catch basket

Solutions. Seafish has developed an improved design catch basket, designed specifically to prevent these problems occurring. The design incorporates a simple wedge wire screen that effectively separates the solid waste from the water (Fig. 13.9 A, B). The larger solids are prevented from entering the drain by the drain cover which is also specifically designed to direct the effluent onto the wedge wire section below. The water passes through the screen and into the drain, whilst the solids slide down the screen and are collected in a punch plate basket.

13.7 End of Pipe Treatment Equipment

End of pipe treatment equipment should only be considered after simple waste minimisation measures have been put in place, as these will greatly affect the nature as well as the quantity of the effluent to be treated. It is recommended that businesses carry out a thorough technical investigation and cost benefit analysis before investing in treatment equipment. The variations in the volume and nature of the effluent to be treated must be considered. This is particularly so for pelagic fish processing which is very seasonal. End of pipe treatment equipment which is currently in use to treat fish processing effluent includes both wedge wire screens and dissolved air flotation systems.

13.8 Conclusions

Most current processing operations waste water and produce excessively high strength effluent as a result of ineffective equipment and practices. Simple and relatively low cost waste minimisation measures have been identified and can be very effective. Once these measures have been implemented, end of pipe treatment equipment can be considered if appropriate. Processors should consider all the options carefully; a simple water and effluent audit will help to identify the key problem areas.

Seafish technology is continuing to develop effective equipment and practices to reduce water and trade effluent charges. Reports and technical data sheets will be produced to supplement the existing Seafish literature. The detailed guidance document 'Guidance for Fish Processors on Water and Effluent Minimisation' is available from Seafish or can be downloaded from the Seafish web site (www.seafish.co.uk).

14 Omega-3 Fatty Acid Concentrates: a Review of Production Technologies

Udaya N. Wanasundara, Janitha Wanasundara, Fereidoon Shahidi

Health benefits of long chain omega-3 polyunsaturated fatty acids (ω3-PUFA) have been well supported by scientific studies in recent years. In order to include ω3-PUFA in our diet, a variety of prototype foods containing ω3-PUFA and dietary supplements have been developed. To meet the demand for nutritionally and pharmaceutically valuable omega-3 fatty acids, they must be extracted, isolated or concentrated from the source materials. However, industrial-scale concentration technologies of PUFA have not yet been perfected. Production and concentration of ω3-PUFA from marine oils may be achieved using chromatography (e.g. adsorption, countercurrent, etc.), fractional or molecular distillation, enzymatic splitting, low-temperature crystallisation, supercritical fluid extraction, fatty acid solubility differences and urea complexation. The omega-3 concentrates may be in the form of free fatty acids, alkyl esters and acylglycerols. Although production of concentrates via urea complexation and molecular distillation is commonplace, products so formed are in the free acid or simple ester forms. Due to perceived advantages of concentrates in the acylglycerol form, enzymatic procedure have recently become popular and their industrial production is gaining momentum. However, the industry at this stage is using chemical procedures. This overview provides a discussion on methodologies used for producing ω3-PUFA concentrates from source materials.

14.1 Introduction

Fatty acids serve a wide variety of metabolic functions critical to all forms of life. They are rich sources of energy and carbon, and well designed as a convenient unit for energy storage. However, the importance of fatty acids in human nutrition and physiology goes well beyond their role as an energy source. Fatty acids provide the structure and hydrophobicity crucial to the maintenance of a semi-permeable membrane barrier. Fatty acids also serve as precursors to active molecules such as eicosanoids, which are capable of producing potent biological effects. Polyunsaturated fatty acids (PUFA), particularly omega-3 (ω3) and omega-6 (ω6) series, play an important role in non-energy-producing biological functions. It has been suggested that the typical "Western" diet, which is relatively high in ω6 PUFA and low in ω3, may not supply the appropriate balance of PUFA for proper biological function of the body [1, 2]. This imbalance is believed to cause a variety of diseases such as cardiovascular, hypertension, inflammatory and autoimmune disorders, depression and certain disrupted neurological functions [3–5]. In addition, ω3-PUFA, namely eicosapentaenoic acid (EPA), docosapentaenoic acid (DPA) and docosahexaenoic acid (DHA) play numerous roles within the human body. DHA and EPA have several health benefits related to cardiovascular disease, immune and renal disorders, inflammation, allergies and cancer. DHA also plays an important role in brain development and retinal function of the foetus and infants. Most of the physiological functions of DPA are still unknown. However, Tanaka et al. [6] have reported that DPA functions as a carrier of pharmaceutical compounds into the brain. Long chain PUFA are now considered "conditionally essential" for infant growth and development. In the year 2000, Food and Drugs Administration (FDA) allowed a qualified health claim about EPA and DHA in dietary supplements related to reduced risk of coronary heart disease.

The long-chain ω3-PUFA may be acquired mainly from marine mammal oils (e.g. seal and whale blubber), and fish oils (e.g. menhaden, salmon, mackerel, cod, herring, sardine, capelin and tuna), as well as marine algae or derived from α-linolenic acid by a series of chain elongation and desaturation [7]. EPA and DHA are synthesised mainly by both uni- and multicellular marine plants such as phytoplankton and algae [8]. They are eventually transferred through the food web and are incorporated into lipids of aquatic species such as fish and marine mammals living in cold waters, probably due to the ability of these fatty acids to maintain fluidity in such environments [9].

Marine oils are abundant in ω3-PUFA and have traditionally been used as the raw material for preparation of ω3-PUFA concentrates. Since marine oils are complex mixtures of fatty acids with varying chain lengths and degrees of unsaturation, separation of individual fatty acids is difficult for production of highly concentrated ω3 components. In addition, ω3-PUFA content and EPA/DHA ratios in marine oils fluctuate widely. Microalgae biomass is also suitable for extraction and purification of individual ω3-PUFA, due to its stable reliable composition. In addition, PUFA from cultured microalgae are cholesterol free, contamination-free and devoid of off-flavours. PUFA oils could be concentrated, as such, or as modified triacylglycerols (TAG) and as free fatty acids or their alkyl esters. Most of the marine oil products sold over-the-counter today have not been structurally altered and are in the natural TAG form, but products in the free fatty acids or methyl and ethyl ester concentrate forms are also being sold.

14.2 Methods of Concentration of ω3-PUFA

Numerous methods have been established to isolate (or concentrate) and recover specific fatty acids and their derivatives (i.e. esters, free fatty acids, triacylglycerols, etc.) from various naturally occurring sources, but only a few are suitable for large-scale production. The available methods include chromatography (adsorption and partitioning), fractional or molecular distillation, enzymatic splitting, low-temperature crystallisation, supercritical fluid extraction and urea complexation. Each technique has its own advantages and drawbacks. A brief background related to each of these methods is provided in this chapter. Some of the methods described in this review are currently used for industrial scale production of products with varying contents of ω3-PUFA. The challenge is now to develop cost effective procedures which produce ω3-PUFA concentrates without any isomerisation or other structural changes in the implicates involved in order to meet the growing demand of a health-conscious society.

14.2.1 Chromatographic Methods

A stationary bed chromatographic system may employ a non-polar stationary phase (i.e. reverse phase chromatographic system) or a polar stationary phase (i.e. a normal phase chromatographic system). Use of reverse phase chromatography is disclosed by Nakahara et al. [10] for production of DHA and DPA from marine microalgae (i.e. *Schizochytrium*). These authors have reported the isolation of TAG containing DHA residues by reverse-phase high performance liquid chromatography using acetone/acetonitrile mobile phase and octadecylsilane (ODS) stationary phase. This stationary phase separates the TAG based on the strength of van der Waals forces between the stationary phase and the fatty acid residues of the TAG. Teshima et al. [11] have used a silver nitrate-impregnated silica gel column to separate EPA and DHA from squid-liver oil fatty acid methyl esters. These authors were able to isolate 85–96% EPA and 95–98% DHA with a yield of 39 and 48%, respectively. Separation of fatty acids using silver nitrate-silica gel column is based on the principle that a metal ion (e.g. a silver ion) will coordinate reversibly with electrons of a π orbital of a double-bond between carbon atoms of an unsaturated fatty acid residue to form a metal complex. The strength of the complex tends to be dependent on the chain length, number of carbon-carbon double bonds, position of the double bonds and their configuration (*cis* or *trans*) in the fatty acids involved. Recently, Corley et al. [12] reported the isolation of TAG rich DHA from marine algae oil using a high performance liquid chromatographic column comprising silica gel and silver or magnesium ions. Hayashi and Kishimura [13] have isolated 63–74% pure DHA from skipjack tuna eye orbital oil by stepwise elution with *n*-hexane, diethyl ether/*n*-hexane and diethyl ether on a silicic acid column. Adlof and Emiken [14] were able to enrich the ω3 content of commercial ω3-PUFA concentrates from 76.5 to 99.8% using isocratic elution from a silver resin column. In another study the same authors fractionated 100 mg of concentrated fish oil methyl esters containing 29.1% EPA and 20.5% DHA into fractions of 87.7% EPA and 95.4% DHA with increasing amounts of acetonitrile (0–30%, v/v) in methanol. They also fractionated non-enriched menhaden oil methyl esters and fatty acids which contained approximately 12.5% EPA and 11.1% DHA. The separation was done isocratically using 40% v/v acetonitrile in acetone to yield one eluted fraction containing approximately 69% of total EPA and DHA.

Solvent choice for the separation of fatty acid esters depends on the desired purity of the eluted fractions and their end use as well as production requirements. Tokiwa et al. [15] separated 10 g of methyl esters of fish oil using tetrahydrofuran/methanol/water (25:55:20, v/v/v) to yield fractions of EPA and DHA at 91.0 and 85.5% purity, respectively. Perrut [16] used methanol/water (90:10, v/v) to separate fatty acid ethyl esters of fish oil and obtained purities of 91–96% EPA and 75–85% DHA while fatty acid methyl esters with the same solvent system yielded 86% EPA and 83% DHA [17]. Krzynowek et al. [18] obtained higher purity fractions of EPA and DHA using the tetrahydrofuran (THF) system of Tokiwa et al. [15]. However, THF oxidises readily yielding peroxides which would initiate oxidative decomposition of PUFA and is thus potentially explosive. Ethanol and water would be the solvents of choice if the end product is to be consumed by humans.

Countercurrent chromatography (CCC) or centrifugal partition chromatography (CPC) has gained much attention in recent years for isolation of polyunsaturated fatty acids [19]. CCC or CPC is a new liquid chromatographic technique that utilises liquid-liquid partition and countercurrent distribution of solute mixture between two liquid phases, in the absence of a solid support, to perform separation of complex mixture of chemical substances. Murayama et al. [20] have isolated 95.8% pure DHA from fish oil fatty acid ethyl ester. Bousquet and Goffic [21] have tested CCC separation of EPA and DHA from microalgal oil and isolated pure EPA and DHA from this oil with excellent yield. CCC is indeed a powerful method which is emerging in several areas of lipid chemistry. So far it has demonstrated its potential for the separation of lipid molecules at the level of a few grams. New instrumentation is being developed, in particular to cover the preparative area, and there is no doubt that this technique will soon allow production at kilogram levels.

14.2.2 Distillation Method

Distillation has been used for partial separation of mixtures of fatty acid esters. This method takes advantage of existing differences in the boiling point and molecular weight of fatty acids under reduced pressure [22]. This is a rather old technique and requires high temperatures of approximately 250 °C [23]. Short-path distillation or molecular distillation uses lower temperatures and short heating intervals. However, fractionation of marine oil esters is difficult since separation of these components becomes less effective with increasing molecular weight [24, 25].

The most widely used distillation procedure is fractional distillation of methyl esters under reduced pressure (0.1 – 1.0 mmHg). Even under these conditions, moderately high temperatures are required; the more highly unsaturated acids, especially ω3-PUFA, are more prone to oxidation, polymerisation and isomerisation of double bonds. Heated columns packed with glass helices or some form of metal packing are in common use despite the disadvantage of a significant hold-up and pressure drop through the column. Spinning band columns do not suffer from these disadvantages. Distillation at still lower pressures has been used in the isolation of some highly unsaturated acids, and in particularly valuable in polymerisation studies to separate monomeric, dimeric and polymeric materials and in the separation of monoacylglycerols from di- and triacylglycerol mixtures.

Stout et al. [26] have emphasised the practical difficulty of concentrating only ω3-PUFA from fish oil in the natural TAG form. The distillation of menhaden oil, as such, concentrated only EPA from an initial level of 16.0 to 19.5%. However, distillation of its ethyl esters increased the EPA content from 15.9 to 28.4%. Meanwhile, the concentration of DHA doubled from 8.4 to 17.3% in the TAG form and from 9.0 to 43.9% for the simple alkyl esters. Max [27] patented a molecular distillation method for isolation of EPA and DHA from marine oil ethyl esters and isolated DHA with a minimum purity of 90% pure or EPA and DHA together with purities ranging from 35 to 90%.

Exposure of long-chain ω3-PUFA to high temperatures during distillation may induce hydrolysis, thermal oxidation, polymerisation and isomerisation. Possible degradation products of long-chain PUFA are cyclic fatty acids and high-molecular-weight polymers [28, 29]. Privett et al. [30] and Privett and Nickell [31] found a marked decomposition of arachidonic acid (C20:4 ω6) when it was distilled slowly in a spinning band column. Even when the catalytic effects of metal parts were eliminated by using an all-glass apparatus, high temperature and exposure to oxygen caused major losses of ω3-PUFA [32]. Therefore, design of a method for preparation of ω3-PUFA concentrates involving low process temperature and time to minimise thermal damage to labile molecules is desirable.

14.2.3 Enzymatic Methods

Lipases may catalyse esterification, hydrolysis or exchange of fatty acids in esters [33]. These processes can be selected by choosing appropriate substrates and reaction conditions. Lipase-catalysed processes have attracted attention because of the mild reaction conditions under which they occur and the selectivity displayed by these catalysts. In both respects they differ from typical chemical reactions. Since enzymatic reactions occur under mild temperature and pH conditions and at ambient pressure, they generally require less energy and are conducted in equipment of lower capital cost than many other chemical processes. Another advantage of enzymatic process is related to the selectivity of many lipases which allows obtaining of products that are difficult to produce by more conventional chemical reactions.

14.2.3.1 *Lipase-Catalysed Hydrolysis*

Bottino et al. [34] have illustrated the mechanism of resistance of lipases towards long-chain ω3-PUFA in marine oils. The presence of *cis* carbon-carbon double-bonds in the fatty acids results in bending of the chains. Therefore, the terminal methyl group of the fatty acids lies close to the ester bond which may cause a steric hindrance effect on lipases. The high bending effect of EPA and DHA due to the presence of 5 and 6 double-bonds, respectively, enhances the steric hindrance effect; therefore lipases cannot reach the ester-linkage between these fatty acids and glycerol. However, saturated and monounsaturated fatty acids do not present any barriers to lipases and thus may be easily hydrolysed. Therefore, fatty acid selectivity of a lipase for EPA and DHA allows their separation and concentration from other components present in the remaining portion of marine oils. In addition, lipases have been frequently used to discriminate between EPA and DHA in concentrates containing both of these fatty acids, thus providing the possibility of producing ω3-PUFA concentrates with dominance of either EPA or DHA.

In a typical hydrolysis run, the enzyme is dissolved in a selected buffer; then oil is added to it and stirred at a predetermined temperature. Samples are withdrawn at fixed time intervals until a desired hydrolysis percentage is reached. Alcohol is added quickly to deactivate the enzyme, and the sample is titrated in order to determine its free fatty acid content. In this fashion, the percentage of enzymatic hydrolysis is determined.

Research in recent years has received much attention for using microbial lipases to produce ω3-PUFA concentrates by hydrolysis of marine oils. Tanaka et al. [35] have used six types of microbial lipases (*Aspergillus niger*; *AN*, *Candida cylindracea*; *CC*, *Pseudomonas* spp.; *PS*, *Chromobacterium viscosum*; *CV*, *Rhizopus delemar*; *RD*, and *Rhizopus javanicus*; *RJ*) to hydrolyse tuna oil and found that *CC*-lipase was most effective in increasing the DHA content in the non-hydrolysed fraction of the oil. The DHA content in the non-hydrolysed fraction was increased three times that of present in the original oil; however, other lipases did not follow suit. Hoshino et al. [36] have also used several lipases for selective hydrolysis of cod liver and sardine oils. The best hydrolysis results were obtained for the non-regiospecific *CC*- and 1,3-specific *Aspergillus niger (AN)*-lipases, but none of the lipases were able to increase the EPA content of the acylglycerols to any great extent. However, over 50% of total ω3-PUFA were produced when these two lipases were employed. Tocher et al. [37] have described the preparation of ω3-PUFA concentrates by utilising phospholipase A_2 on cod roe phospholipids. The method is based on the assumption that the majority of the EPA and DHA of fish phospholipids are located preferentially at the *sn*-2 position and the specific action of phospholipase A_2 on that position. The resulting product contained 24 and 40% of EPA and DHA, respectively, with an overall EPA and DHA recovery of approximately 60%. Shimada et al. [38] reported that hydrolysis of tuna oil by *Geotrichum candidum (GC)*-lipase increased the total content of EPA and DHA from 32.1 to 57.5%. A Japanese patent [39] describes a method based on the discrimination of lipases on EPA and DHA for preparation of ω3-PUFA concentrates. Ethyl esters from miscellaneous fish oils such as those of sardine and mackerel were hydrolysed with various lipases (*CC*, *AN* and *Mucor miehei*; *MM*). Selective hydrolysis afforded ethyl ester concentrates of up to 25% EPA and 17% DHA after separation of the hydrolysed fatty acids. Lie and Lambertsen [40] reported a similar discrimination of the *CC*-lipase among fatty acids. The C14 to C18 saturated and monounsaturated fatty acids were preferentially hydrolysed in TAG of capelin oil, whereas the long-chain monoenes of C20:1 and C22:1, and PUFA of C18:4, EPA and DHA were resistant to hydrolysis. However, lipolytic enzymes from cod guts preferentially hydrolysed PUFA over the shorter chain fatty acids which showed a completely opposite fatty acid selectivity [41]. This suggests that the fatty acid specificity of lipases is a crucial factor when considering the application of enzymes to modify marine oils.

Wanasundara [42] and Wanasundara and Shahidi [43] have carried out lipase-assisted hydrolysis of seal blubber oil (SBO) and menhaden oil (MHO) in order to enrich their content of ω3-PUFA in the acylglycerols, non-hydrolysed fraction. Table 14.1 shows the content of total ω3-PUFA, EPA and DHA in the non-hydrolysed fraction of both oils upon hydrolysis. Among lipases tested *CC*-

Table 14.1. Enrichment of total ω3, EPA and DHA of seal blubber (SBO) and menhaden (MHO) oils upon hydrolysis by different microbial lipases

Lipases	Hydrolysis time (h)	Total ω3 (%)		EPA (%)		DHA (%)	
		SBO	MHO	SBO	MHO	SBO	MHO
	0	20.2	30.1	6.41	13.2	7.58	10.1
Aspergillus niger (AN)	12	20.8	30.3	6.61	13.3	7.90	10.1
	75	23.3	35.0	7.34	13.8	9.02	10.4
Psudomonas spp. *(PS)*	12	22.4	35.0	8.58	16.5	7.73	11.8
	75	26.1	39.5	10.5	20.1	8.04	12.7
Candida cylindracea (CC)	12	40.2	40.9	9.79	17.0	19.9	15.4
	75	45.0	45.8	8.48	18.6	26.3	18.2
Rhizopus oryzae (RO)	12	24.2	39.2	5.28	14.1	13.7	17.3
	75	33.1	45.7	4.30	12.5	23.5	25.6
Geotrichum candidum	12	30.0	40.1	9.40	18.2	11.8	14.6
(GC)	75	30.0	42.2	9.30	18.4	11.8	15.5

EPA; eicosapentaenoic acid.
DHA; docosahexaenoic acid.
Source: Adapted from Wanasundara [42].

lipase significantly ($P < 0.05$) increased the total ω3-PUFA, EPA and DHA contents of SBO as the hydrolysis reaction progressed. After 75 h of hydrolysis, *CC*-lipase gave more than a two-fold increase in the total ω3-PUFA content in SBO. However, in MHO this lipase was able to increase the content of total ω3-PUFA only by 15.0% (from 30% in original oil to 45.0% after hydrolysis) over the same period of hydrolysis. In MHO, the highest contents of total ω3-PUFA and DHA were obtained upon *Rhizopus oryzae (RO)*-lipase-assisted hydrolysis. However, this lipase brought about a decrease in the EPA content of both oils during the course of reaction, perhaps due to the fact that *RO*-lipase selectively hydrolyses EPA in the oils by exhibiting acyl-chain specificity. Tanaka et al. [35] have also reported that EPA content of tuna oil was decreased upon hydrolysis by lipases from *Rhizopus* spp., *Rhizopus delemer (RD)* and *Rhizopus javanicum (RJ)*. Kotting and Eble [44] have reported that lipases from *Rhizopus* spp. are 1,3-positional specific. In SBO, the EPA content was decreased from 6.4 to 4.3% during a 75 h *RO*-lipase-assisted hydrolysis. However, upon hydrolysis of MHO by *RO*-lipase, EPA content increased with up to 12 h of hydrolysis, after which it began to decline. During 75 h of hydrolysis the content of EPA in MHO decreased from 13.2 to 12.5%. Therefore, the rate of hydrolysis of EPA from SBO was much higher than that from MHO. This may be due to cumulative effect of both 1,3-positional and acyl-chain specificity of *RO*-lipase. In SBO, EPA was located mainly in *sn*-1 and *sn*-3 positions of the TAG; however, EPA in MHO was equally distributed over the *sn*-2 and *sn*-3 positions and was present only in small amounts in the *sn*-1 position [45]. Therefore, the higher hydrolysis rate of EPA from SBO may reflect the abundance of this fatty acid in the *sn*-1 and *sn*-3 positions which is highly vulnerable to 1,3-specific *RO*-lipase hydrolysis.

In MHO, the total content of ω3-PUFA was increased from 30% in the original oil to 45.7, 45.8 and 42.2% after a 75 h hydrolysis by *RO*-, *CC*- and *GC*-lipases, respectively. Corresponding increases in the content of DHA in this oil were from 10.1% in the original oil to 25.6, 18.2 and 15.5%, respectively. In SBO maximum increase in the content of total ω3-PUFA, from 20.2 to 45.0%, was attained using *CC*-lipase under similar experimental conditions.

14.2.3.2
Lipase-Catalysed Esterification

The TAG form of PUFA is considered to be nutritionally more favourable than methyl or ethyl esters of fatty acids because experimental results have shown impaired intestinal absorption of methyl or ethyl esters of ω3-PUFA in laboratory animals [46–48]. Yang et al. [49] have shown that methyl and ethyl esters are hydrolysed slower than their corresponding TAG. From a marketing point of view, triacylglycerols of PUFA are often promoted as being more "natural" than other fatty acid derivatives.

Osada et al. [50] have employed *CV*- and *CC*-lipases for direct esterification of glycerol with individual free fatty acids, including EPA and DHA. The *CV*-lipase exhibited superiority over that of *CC*-lipase as it afforded a reaction yield of 89–95%. With the latter lipase a reaction yield of 71–75% was obtained for all fatty acids examined except for DHA which gave a 63% esterification level. Glycerolysis of ω3-PUFA, obtained from SBO, was recently studied using *CV*-lipase [51]. The degree of synthesis was up to 94% and the amounts of mono-, di- and triacylglycerols in the product were 13.8, 43.1 and 37.4%, respectively. Akoh et al. [52] were also able to incorporate up to 43% EPA into evening primrose oil (EPO) by interesterification using *Candida antarctica (CA)*-lipase. Interesterification of trilinolein with EPA and DHA esters by *CA*- and *MM*-lipases afforded 81.4 and 79.4% EPA and 79.7 and 70.5% DHA, respectively [53]. Sridhar and Lakshminarayana [54] were able to incorporate EPA (9.5%) and DHA (8.0%) into groundnut oil by *MM*-lipase-assisted esterification. All these studies point to the fact that the water content in the reaction medium is a crucial factor in determining the extent of the esterification reaction. A high water content in the reaction medium shifts the chemical equilibrium towards hydrolysis, whereas a reduced water content shifts the equilibrium towards esterification. The optimum content of water in the esterification reaction should be kept to a minimum in order to discourage occurrence of partial hydrolysis of products and formation of glycerol as well as mono- and diacylglycerols. However, the content of water in the reaction medium should be sufficiently high in order to prevent enzyme deactivation. The requirements of water for different enzymes vary considerably, typically from 1 to 4% for interesterification reactions of TAG [55]. Shimada et al. [56] have used a different approach to increase DHA level in tuna oil. They raised DHA levels of tuna ethyl esters by selective alcoholysis with lauric alcohol from 23 to 50–52% using *Rhizomucor miehei* or *Rhizopus delemar* lipase. Higher levels were obtained by starting with already enriched material (45 raised to 75% and 60 raised to 93%). EPA levels were reduced slightly during this reaction. Schmitt-Rozieres et al. [57] were able to enrich DHA content up to 80% by selective esterification of sardine oil with 1-butanol using lipozyme.

14.2.4
Low Temperature Crystallisation

Low-temperature crystallisation was originally developed to separate certain TAG, fatty acids, esters and other lipids which are highly soluble in organic solvents at temperatures above 0 °C, but become sparingly soluble at lower temperatures down to –80 °C [22]. The solubility of fats in organic solvents decreases with increasing mean molecular weight and increases with increasing unsaturation [58]. Singleton [59] and Stout et al. [26] have determined the solubility of numerous fatty acids and esters in a variety of solvents and revealed the following rules: when the acids are saturated, long-chains are less soluble than short chains; saturated acids are less soluble than monoenoic and dienoic acids of equal chain length; *trans* isomers are less soluble than *cis* isomers; and normal acids are less soluble than branched acids. The melting point of fatty acids changes considerably with the type and degree of unsaturation and thus separation of mixtures of saturated and unsaturated fatty acids may become possible [60]. At low temperatures, long chain saturated fatty acids which have higher melting points crystallise out and PUFA remain in the liquid form.

The low temperature crystallisation process may be carried out on the neat liquid in the absence of a solvent or in a selected solvent/solvent mixture. The commonly used solvents are methanol and acetone and these have been employed to separate "stearic" and "oleic" fractions. Attempts have also been made to use other solvents such as hexane and methyl formate [61]. Crystallisation in the absence of a solvent occurs by using the *Tirtiaux* process, which involves slow cooling and slow agitation, and in the hydrophilisation process. In this process, crystallisation produces a slurry of solid and liquid components, the latter being enriched with ω3-PUFA.

It has been reported that use of different organic solvents and temperatures affects the concentration of PUFA [22, 62]. Therefore, the proper choice of solvent and temperature is necessary to achieve the optimum concentration yield of the ω3-PUFA. The fungal oil extracted from *Mortierella genus* was used for concentration of γ-linolenic acid (GLA) by low temperature crystallisation [62, 63]. The concentration of GLA in different solvents was in the order of acetone (–20 °C) > *n*-hexane (–20 °C) > acetone (4 °C) > petroleum ether (–20 °C) at a solvent to oil ratio of 5:1 (v/v). Solvent crystallisation of fatty acids is an indispensable method for preparing pure fatty acids. This method requires the least number of unit operations and the simplest equipment [64, 65]. Briefly, the process consists of cooling the oil or fatty acids in a solvent, holding for a specified period of time, and removing the crystallised fraction by filtration.

Preparation of ω3-PUFA concentrates from SBO by low temperature fractional crystallisation was recently reported [42]. In these studies, SBO in the TAG or free fatty acid form was subjected to solvent crystallisation at different temperatures. Table 14.2 shows the enrichment of total ω3-PUFA following low temperature crystallisation of SBO in the TAG form using hexane and acetone as sol-

Table 14.2. Enrichment of total ω3-fatty acids (%) of seal blubber oil (SBO) upon low temperature crystallisation in different solvents

Crystallisation temperature (°C)	Triacylglycerols of SBO		Free fatty acids of SBO	
	Hexane	Acetone	Hexane	Acetone
-10	23.2	23.5	23.8	24.3
-20	23.9	26.9	24.5	25.4
-40	26.2	36.4	31.0	40.6
-60	30.5	43.8	58.3	56.8
-70	35.1	47.9	66.7	46.8

Total ω3-fatty acids content of original SBO is 20.1%.
Source: Adapted from Wanasundara [42].

vents. The content of ω3-PUFA in the non-crystalline fraction (the concentrate) was increased with lowering of the crystallisation temperature. Under all temperature conditions, acetone afforded the highest concentration of total ω3-PUFA.

Low temperature crystallisation of SBO, in the free fatty acid form, at -60°C and -70°C in hexane, resulted in total ω3-PUFA contents of up to 58.3 and 66.7% in the preparation with concentrate recoveries of 39.0 and 24.8%, respectively. However, the content of total ω3-PUFA in acetone increased up to 56.7 and 46.8%, but the recovery of the concentrates was 15.9 and 12.9%, respectively.

14.2.5 Solubility Differences of Fatty Acid Salts

Concentration of ω3 fatty acids from PUFA rich oils in the form of fatty acid salts may be achieved by using lower alcohols. The basic principle of this method of concentration is that alkali salts of saturated fatty acids crystallise more readily than those of PUFA containing four or more double bonds when the saponified solution is cooled. Thus, the total ω3 fatty acids of sardine oil was increased from 33.2 to 75.9% [66]. In order to obtain high content of total ω3 fatty acid with good recovery, the water content of the medium for this procedure should be maintained at a 3% level.

14.2.6 Supercritical Fluid Extraction

Supercritical fluid extraction (SFE) is a relatively new separation process that may circumvent some of the problems associated with the use of conventional separation techniques. A number of gases are known to possess desirable selective solvent properties when raised to pressures above that of their critical values. These pressures are very high and of the order of 1000 to 2000 psi. The region in which a substance exists as a supercritical fluid is defined by its critical pressure (P_c) and temperature (T_c). The single-component pressure-temperature phase diagram defines the critical region for the specific case of CO_2. The transport properties such as viscosity and diffusivity of supercritical fluids are generally more gas-like than those of typical liquids. Hence, because of their properties, supercritical fluids offer an attractive choice for extraction and fractionation of a variety of raw material. For food commodities, CO_2 is chosen because it has moderate critical temperature and pressure (31.1 °C, 1070 psi) and is inert, inexpensive, non-flammable, environmentally acceptable, readily available and safe [67]. The separation of PUFA by SFE is dependent on the molecular size of the components involved rather than their degree of unsaturation; therefore, a prior concentration step is needed to achieve a high concentration of PUFA in the final product [67]. Oils to be used for ω3 concentration by SFE require preparation steps of extraction, hydrolysis and esterification by conventional methods [68, 69]. The use of supercritical fluids for extraction of oil and concentration of ω3-PUFA from fish oil and seaweed has been reported [67, 70, 71]. SFE has been effectively used to refine fish oils and remove cholesterol, polychlorinated biphenyls (PCB), vitamin E and other components [72]. Several research groups have reported the fractionation of mixtures of mono-, di- and triacylglycerols using various fluids [73, 74]. Some enhancement of the content of ω3-PUFA present in fish oil TAG has been reported [75]. Stout and Spinelli [76] have demonstrated that fish oil esters could be fractionated by SFE to produce an oil with a DHA content of 60–65%. The fractionation of free fatty acids using SFE has also been reported [72]. Both of these studies have shown a low recovery of ω3-PUFA during the process, the reasons for which remain speculative. However, use of extremely high pressures and high capital costs might limit the widespread use of this method for industrial-scale concentrate production. Recently, propane has gained more interest in extraction technology especially in the nutraceutical industry [77]. However, more research and development will be required to determine the extent of its use for separation of PUFA from different oils.

14.2.7
Urea Complexation

Urea alone crystallises in a tightly packed tetragonal structure with channels of 5.67 Å diameter. However, in the presence of long straight-chain molecules it crystallises in a hexagonal structure with channels of 8–12 Å diameter within the hexagonal crystals [78]. The channels formed, in the presence of long-chain unbranched molecules, are sufficiently large to accommodate aliphatic chains. While straight-chain saturated fatty acids with six carbon atoms or more are readily adducted, the presence of double bonds in the carbon chain increases the bulk of the molecule and reduces the likelihood of its complexation with urea [79]. Monoenes are more readily complexed as compared to dienes which, in turn, are more readily complexed than trienes. Therefore, the stability of fatty acid-urea adducts parallels the geometry of the molecules involved. Any deviation from a straight chain arrangement weakens the stability of the adduct. Therefore, formation of urea inclusion compounds depends on the degree of unsaturation of the fatty acids involved. During this process, the oil (acylglycerol) is split into fatty acids using alcoholic KOH or NaOH and unsaponifiables such as sterols, vitamins A and D and xenobiotics (e.g. PCB) as well as other undesirable components which are removed from it. The free fatty acids which are mixed with an alcoholic (methanol or ethanol) solution of urea are then allowed to cool to a particular temperature depending on the degree of concentration desired. The saturated fatty acids, monoenes and, to a lesser extent, dienes are crystallised with urea, and non-crystallised fatty acids in the solution can be separated by filtration. The liquid or non-urea complexing fraction (NUCF) is enriched with ω3-PUFA. Alternatively, this procedure can be carried out using methyl or ethyl esters of fatty acids rather than free fatty acids. There are advantages and drawbacks to each of these options. For example, fatty acids are more soluble in alcohol than their corresponding esters; hence they require a much smaller volume of alcohol for processing. If the ester form of fatty acids is chosen, the re-esterification step of the concentrates is eliminated.

Han et al. [80] have tested a series of solvents (ethanol, methanol, water, formamide and acetonitrile) as wetting agents for urea. They reported that all solvents tested served as appropriate wetting agents, but water was the solvent of choice because of its low cost and lack of toxicity. Recently, urea complexation processing of seal blubber oil (SBO) was carried out in order to concentrate its ω3-PUFA [42, 81]. Among the major ω3-PUFA present, DHA was found almost exclusively in the NUCF under selected experimental conditions (Table 14.3). Although most of the EPA was recovered in the NUCF, a small proportion of it was invariably complexed with urea and ended up in the urea complexed fraction (UCF). Urea complexation of SBO, under optimum conditions, gave a total PUFA content of 92.3% in the NUCF. However, it was difficult to remove all of

Table 14.3. Contents of total ω3-fatty acids, EPA and DHA of non-urea complexed fraction (NUCF) and urea complexed fraction (UCF) of seal blubber oil

Urea-to-fatty acid ratio (w/w)	Crystallisation temperature (°C)	Total ω3 (%)		EPA (%)		DHA (%)	
		NUCF	UCF	NUCF	UCF	NUCF	UCF
2	-18	63.4	3.66	22.1	1.23	24.4	0.90
5	-18	86.7	16.2	18.1	6.03	56.8	5.00
2	0	52.3	5.59	18.3	1.86	19.9	1.97
5	0	84.6	13.7	21.6	5.59	50.7	3.54
1	-9	30.1	5.66	10.4	2.68	11.2	0.78
6	-9	85.9	14.5	20.3	5.85	54.2	3.90
3.5	-24	80.8	12.1	11.0	6.50	57.1	0.27
3.5	6	77.2	9.31	24.9	4.46	43.2	0.35
3.5	-9	86.6	16.4	8.50	6.73	65.2	4.86
Original seal blubber oil		20.1		6.41		7.58	

EPA; eicosapentaenoic acid.
DHA; docosahexaenoic acid.
Source: Adapted from Wanasundara [42].

the saturated fatty acids in order to obtain a 100% PUFA concentrate. Ratnayake et al. [82] have also reported that complete removal of saturated fatty acids by urea complexation may be impossible since some of the shorter chain saturated fatty acids do not complex with urea during the crystallisation process. Long chain monounsaturated fatty acids (MUFA), especially those of the C20 and C22, form complexes with urea more readily than those of the shorter chain saturated fatty acids (C14 and C16); thus the amount of MUFA in UCF was increased to 73% under certain experimental conditions. The enrichment of total ω3-PUFA in the concentrate, and its overall recovery, varied inversely with increasing urea-to-fatty acid ratio as well as crystallisation at lower temperatures. Therefore, these experimental variables should be carefully controlled in order to achieve a maximum content of total ω3-PUFA in the concentrate with a reasonable recovery.

The extent of crystallisation depends on the concentration of urea and the temperature of crystallisation. Wille et al. [17] reported that C18:4ω3 and DHA are concentrated more efficiently in the filtrate when crystallisation occurs at -5°C, whereas total ω3 and EPA contents were maximised at 10 and 15°C, respectively. Qualitatively, solubilities of fatty acids in the presence of urea are parallel but the values are much lower than when they are used alone. Without urea, polyenoic compounds do not normally crystallise even at the temperature of dry ice, but they will do so in high concentrations of urea above 0 °C. Successive crystallisation with increasing concentrations of fatty acids and urea at decreasing temperatures down to 13°C allows separation of DHA from other components of the oil. Interestingly, urea complexation protects these ω3-PUFA from autoxidation [83]. Complex formation is exothermic, but requires dissolution of both urea and fatty acids. Methanol and ethanol are preferred solvents for small-scale fractionation, but recently Han et al. [80] found that water may offer the best choice of solvent for large scale operations. Swern [84] reviewed urea fractionation of fatty acids of many natural oils and Patokina et al. [85] studied the thermodynamics and other aspects of urea adduct formation.

Many publications have described the application of urea complexation in both analytical and preparative applications. Iverson and Weik [86] and Strocchi and Bonaga [87] correlated fatty acid structures with their preferential order of complexation with urea. Other publications have described application of this technique for concentration of specific fatty acids such as furanoid fatty acids [88], isoprenoid acids [89], *cis-trans* isomers [90], an unusual fatty acids bearing a methyl branch and a double bond on the same carbon atom, such as 7-methyl-7-hexadecenoic acid [91], as well as preparation of ω3-PUFA concentrates from other marine oils [92–95]. It should also be noted that in urea complexation the complexed crystals are very stable and hence filtration at the very low temperatures used for solvent crystallisation of fatty acids is not required [96]. This method is also favoured by many researchers because complexation depends upon the configuration of the fatty acid moieties due to the presence of multiple double bonds rather than pure physical properties such as melting point or solubility.

14.3 Conclusions

Production of ω3-PUFA from marine oils may be achieved using a number of techniques, namely chromatography (e.g. adsorption, countercurrent), fractional or molecular distillation, enzymatic splitting, low temperature crystallisation, supercritical fluid extraction, solubility differences and urea complexation. These products may be in the form of free fatty acids, methyl and ethyl esters or acylglycerols. Although production of concentrates via urea complexation is commonplace, products so formed are in the free acid or simple ester forms. Due to potential benefits of having the concentrates in the acylglycerol form, enzymatic procedures have recently become popular and their industrial production is gaining momentum.

References

1. Simopoulos AP (1991) Omega-3 fatty acids in health and disease and growth and development. Am J Clin Nutr 54: 438–463
2. Simopoulos AP (1997) Essential fatty acids in health and chronic disease. Food Rev Int 13: 623–631
3. Dyerberg J (1986) Linolenate-derived polyunsaturated fatty acids and prevention of atherosclerosis. Nutr Rev 44: 125–134
4. Mehta J, Lopez LM, Lowton D, Wargovich T (1988) Dietary supplementation with omega-3 polyunsaturated fatty acids in patients with stable coronary disease: effects on indices of platelet and neutrophil function and exercise performance. Am J Med 84: 45–52
5. Kinsella JE (1986) Food components with potential therapeutic benefits: the n-3 polyunsaturated fatty acids of fish oils. Food Technol 40: 89–97
6. Tanaka S, Yaguchi T, Shimizu S, Sogo T, Fujikawa S (1998) Process for preparing docosahexaenoic acid and docosapentaenoic acid. Canadian Pat 2,261,231
7. Sprecher H, Luthria DL, Mohammed BS, Baykoushewa SP (1995) Reevaluation of the pathways for biosynthesis of polyunsaturated fatty acids. J Lipid Res 36: 2471–2477
8. Pigott GM, Tucker BW (1987) Science opens new horizon for marine lipids in human nutrition. Food Rev Int 3: 105–138
9. Holmer G (1989) Triglycerides. In: Ackman RG (ed) Marine biogenic lipids, fats and oils. CRC Press, Boca Raton, FL, USA, pp 140–174
10. Nakahara T, Yokochi T, Higashihara T, Tanaka S, Yaguchi T, Honda D (1996) Production of docosahexaenoic and docosapentaenoic acids by *Schizochytrium* sp. isolated from Yap Islands. J Am Oil Chem Soc 73: 1421–1426
11. Teshima S, Kanazawa A, Tokiwa S (1978) Separation of polyunsaturated fatty acids by column chromatography on silver nitrate-impregnated silica gel. Bull Japan Soc Sci Fish 44: 927
12. Corley DG, Zeller SG, James P, Duffin K (2000) Process for separating a triglyceride comprising a docosahexaenoic acid residue from a mixture of triglycerides. International Pat PCT/US00/04166
13. Hayashi K, Kishimura H (1993) Preparation of n-3 PUFA ethyl ester concentrates from fish oil by column chromatography on silicic acid. Nippon Suisan Gakkaishi 59: 1429
14. Adlof RO, Emiken EA (1985) The isolation of omega-3 polyunsaturated fatty acids and methyl esters of fish oils by silver resin chromatography. J Am Oil Chem Soc 62: 1592–1595
15. Tokiwa S, Kanazawa A, Teshima S (1981) Preparation of eicosapentaenoic and docosahexaenoic acids by reversed phase high performance liquid chromatography. Bull Japan Soc Sci Fish 47: 675

16. Perrut M (1988) Purification of polyunsaturated fatty acid (EPA and DHA) ethyl esters by preparative high performance liquid chromatography. LC-GC Mag Sep Sci 6: 914–920
17. Wille HJ, Traitler H, Kelly M (1987) Production of polyenoic fish oil fatty acids by combined urea fractionation and industrial scale preparative high performance liquid chromatography. Rev Fr Corps Gras 34: 69–74
18. Krzynowek J, D'Entremont DL, Maney RS (1988) Purification of omega-3 fatty acids from fish oils using HPLC. Proceeding of 12th Annual Conference on Tropical and Subtropical Fisheries Technology Society, pp 74–77
19. Goffic FL (1997) Countercurrent and centrifugal partition chromatography as new tools for preparative-scale lipid purification. Lipid Technol 9: 148–150
20. Murayama W, Kosuge Y, Nakaya N, Nunogaki K, Cazes J, Nunogaki H (1988) Preparative separation of unsaturated fatty acids esters by centrifugal partition chromatography. J Liq Chromatogr 11: 283–300
21. Bousquet O, Goffic FL (1995) Counter-current chromatographic separation of polyunsaturated fatty acids. J Chromatogr A 704: 211–216
22. Brown JB, Kolb DK (1955) Application of low temperature crystallization in the separation of the fatty acids and their compounds. Prog Chem Fats Other Lipids 3: 57–94
23. Berger R, McPherson W (1979) Fractional distillation. J Am Oil Chem Soc 56: 743A–746A
24. Weitkamp AW (1955) Distillation. J Am Oil Chem Soc 32: 640–646
25. Brevik H (1992) N-3 concentrates: a Scandinavian view-point. AOCS Short Courses, Modern Application of Marine Oils, Toronto, Canada, May 7–8, 1992
26. Stout VF, Nilsson WB, Krzynowek J, Schlenk H (1990) Fractionation of fish oil and their fatty acids. In: Stansby ME (ed) Fish oils in nutrition. Van Nostrand Reinhold, New York, pp 73–119
27. Max Z (1989) High-concentration mixture of polyunsaturated fatty acids and their esters from animal and/or vegetable oils and their prophylactic or therapeutic uses. UK Pat GB2,218,984
28. Ackman RG (1988) The year of fish oil. Chem Ind 3: 139–145
29. Wijesundara RC, Ratnayake WMN, Ackman RG (1989) Eicosapentaenoic acid geometrical isomer artifacts in heated fish oil esters. J Am Oil Chem Soc 66: 1822–1830
30. Privett OS, Weber RP, Nickell EC (1959) Preparation and properties of methyl arachidonate from pork liver. J Am Oil Chem Soc 36: 443–449
31. Privett OS, Nickell EC (1963) Preparation of highly purified fatty acids via liquid-liquid partition chromatography. J Am Oil Chem Soc 40: 189–193
32. Ackman RG, Ke PJ, Jangaard PM (1973) Fractional vacuum distillation of herring oil methyl esters. J Am Oil Chem Soc 50: 1–8
33. Marangoni A, Rousseau D (1995) Engineering triacylglycerol: the role of interesterification. Trends Food Sci Tech 6: 329–335
34. Bottino NR, Vandenberg GA, Reiser R (1967) Resistance of certain long-chain polyunsaturated fatty acids of marine oils to pancreatic lipase hydrolysis. Lipids 2: 489–493
35. Tanaka Y, Hirano J, Funada T (1992) Concentration of docosahexaenoic acid in glyceride by hydrolysis of fish oils with *Candida cylindracea* lipase. J Am Oil Chem Soc 69: 1210–1214
36. Hoshino T, Yamane T, Shimuzu S (1990) Selective hydrolysis of fish oil by lipase to concentrate ω3-polyunsaturated fatty acids. Agric Biol Chem 54: 1459–1467
37. Tocher DR, Webster A, Sargent JR (1986) Utilization of porcine pancreatic phospholipase A_2 for the preparation of marine fish oil enriched in ω3-polyunsaturated fatty acids. Biotechnol Appl Biochem 8: 675–679
38. Shimada Y, Murayama K, Okazaki S, Nakamura M, Sugihara A, Tominga Y (1994) Enrichment of polyunsaturated fatty acids with *Geotrichum candidum* lipase. J Am Oil Chem Soc 71: 951–954
39. Noguchi Y, Hibino H (1984) Japanese Pat 59–14,793
40. Lie O, Lambertsen G (1986) Fatty acid specificity of *Candida cylindracea* lipase. Fette Seifen Anstrichm 88: 365–368
41. Lie O, Lambertsen G (1985) Digestive lipolytic enzymes in cod (*Godus morhua*): fatty acid specificity. Comp Biochem Physiol 80: 447–450

42. Wanasundara UN (1996) Marine oils: stabilization, structural characterization and omega-3 fatty acid concentration. PhD thesis, Memorial University of Newfoundland, St John's, Canada
43. Wanasundara UN, Shahidi F (1998) Lipase assisted concentration of ω3-polyunsaturated fatty acids in acylglycerols form from marine oils. J Am Oil Chem Soc 75: 945–951
44. Kotting J, Eble H (1994) Lipase and phospholipase in organic synthesis. In: Woolley P, Petersen SB (eds) Lipases. Cambridge University Press, Cambridge, pp 289–313
45. Wanasundara UN, Shahidi F (1997) Positional distribution of fatty acids in triacylglycerols of seal blubber oil. J Food Lipids 4: 51–64
46. Hamazaki T, Hirai A, Terano T, Sajiki J, Kondo S, Fujita F, Tamura Y, Kumagi A (1982) Effect of orally administrated ethyl ester of eicosapentaenoic acid on PGI-like substance production by rat aorta. Prostaglandins 23: 557–567
47. El-Boustani S, Colette C, Monnier L, Descomps B, Paulet CA, Mendey F (1987) Eternal absorption in man of eicosapentaenoic acid in different chemical forms. Lipids 22: 711–714
48. Lawson LD, Hughes BG (1988) Human absorption of fish oil fatty acids as triacylglycerols, free fatty acids or ethyl esters. Biochem Biophys Res Commun 152: 328–335
49. Yang LY, Kuksis A, Myher JJ (1989) Lumenal hydrolysis of menhaden and rapeseed oils and their fatty acid methyl and ethyl esters in the rats. Biochem Cell Biol 67: 192–204
50. Osada K, Nakamura M, Nonaka M, Hatano M (1992) Esterification of glycerol with EPA and DHA by *Chromobacterium viscosum* and *Candida cylindracea* lipases. J Japan Oil Chem Soc 41: 39–43
51. He Y, Shahidi F (1997) Enzymatic esterification of ω3-fatty acid concentrates from seal blubber oil with glycerol. J Am Oil Chem Soc 74: 1133–1136
52. Akoh CC, Jennings BH, Lillard DA (1996) Enzymatic modification of evening primrose oil: incorporation of n-3 polyunsaturated fatty acids. J Am Oil Chem Soc 73: 1059–1062
53. Akoh CC, Jennings BH, Lillard DA (1995) Enzymatic modification of triolein: incorporation of n-3 polyunsaturated fatty acids. J Am Oil Chem Soc 72: 1317–1321
54. Sridhar R, Lakshminarayana G (1992) Incorporation of eicosapentaenoic and docosahexaenoic acids into ground nut oil by lipase-catalyzed ester exchange. J Am Oil Chem Soc 69: 1041–1042
55. Basheer S, Mogi K, Nakajuma M (1995) Interesterification kinetics of triacylglycerides and fatty acids with modified lipase in *n*-hexane. J Am Oil Chem Soc 72: 511–518
56. Shimada Y, Murayama H, Sugihara A, Baba T, Komemushi S, Moriyama S, Tominga Y (1998) Purification of ethyl docosahexanoate by selective alcoholysis of fatty acid ethyl esters with immobilized *Rhizopus miehei* lipase. J Am Oil Chem Soc 75: 1565–1571
57. Schmitt-Rozieres M, Deyris V, Comeau L (2000) Enrichment of polyunsaturated fatty acids from sardine cannery effluents by enzymatic selective esterification. J Am Oil Chem Soc 77: 329–332
58. Chawla P, deMan JM (1990) Measurement of the size distribution of fat crystals using a laser particle counter. J Am Oil Chem Soc 76: 329–332
59. Singleton WS (1960) Solution properties. In: Makley KS (ed) Fatty acids. Interscience Publishers, New York, pp 609–678
60. Haraldsson GG (1984) Separation of saturated/unsaturated fatty acids. J Am Oil Chem Soc 61: 219–222
61. Hixson AW, Bockelmann JB (1942) Liquid-liquid extraction employing solvents in the region of their critical temperatures. Trans Am Inst Chem Eng 38: 891–930
62. Yokochi T, Usita MT, Kamisaka Y, Nakahara T, Suzuki O (1990) Increase in the linolenic acid content by solvent winterization of fungal oil extracted from *Mortierella* genus. J Am Oil Chem Soc 67: 846–851
63. Kreulen HP (1976) Fractionation and winterization of edible fats and oils. J Am Oil Chem Soc 53: 393–395
64. Schlenk H (1961) Crystallization of fatty acids. J Am Oil Chem Soc 38: 728–736
65. Markley KS (1964) Techniques of separation: distillation, salt solubilities methods and low temperature crystallization. In: Markley KS (ed) Fatty acids. Interscience Publishers, New York, pp 1983–2123

66. Han DS, Ahn HB, Shin HK (1987) Separation of EPA and DHA from fish oil by solubility differences of fatty acid salts in ethanol. Korean J Food Sci Technol 19: 430–434
67. Mishra VK, Temelli F, Oraikul B (1993) Extraction and purification of ω3-fatty acids with an emphasis on supercritical fluid extraction, a review. Food Res Int 26: 217–226
68. Eisenbach W (1984) Supercritical fluid extraction; a film demonstration. Ber Bunsenges Phys Chem 88: 882–887
69. Nilsson WB, Gauglitz EJ, Hudson JK (1989) Supercritical fluid extraction of fish oil esters using incremental pressure programming and temperature programming. J Am Oil Chem Soc 66: 1596–1600
70. Yamagouchi K, Murakami M, Nakano H, Konosu S, Kokura T, Yamamoto H, Kosaka M, Hata K (1986) Supercritical carbon dioxide extraction of oils from Antarctic krill. J Agric Food Chem 34: 904–907
71. Choi KJ, Nakhost Z, Krukonis VJ, Karel M (1987) Supercritical fluid extraction and characterization of lipid from algae *Scenedesmus obliquus*. Food Biotechnol 1: 263–271
72. Rizvi SSH, Daniels JA, Bernado AL, Zollweg JA (1986) Supercritical fluid extraction: operating principles and food applications. Food Technol 40: 57–64
73. Peter S, Brunner G (1978) The separation of nonvolatile substances by means of compressed gases in countercurrent process. Angew Chem Int Ed Eng 17: 746–750
74. Brunner G, Peter S (1982) On the solubility of glycerides and fatty acids in compressed gases in the presence of an entrainer. Sep Sci Technol 17: 199–214
75. Zosel K (1978) Separation with supercritical gases: practical applications. Angew Chem Int Ed Eng 17: 702–709
76. Stout VF, Spinelli J (1987) Polyunsaturated fatty acids from fish oils. US Pat 4,675,132
77. Pinton M (1998) Propane and super critical extraction. Practical Short Course on Processing of Nutraceuticals/Functional Foods. Food Protein Research and Development Center, The Texas A & M University, Chap 16
78. Smith AE (1952) Crystal structure of the urea-hydrogen complexes. Acta Crystallogr 5: 224–235
79. Schlenk H (1954) Urea inclusion compounds of fatty acids. In: Holman RT, Lundberg WO, Malkin T (eds) Progress in the chemistry of fats and other lipids. Pergamon Press, New York, pp 243–267
80. Han D, Shin HK, Yoon SH (1997) Separation of ω3-polyunsaturated fatty acids from fish oils and stabilization of the oil against autoxidation. In: Shahidi F, Cadwallader KR (eds) Flavor and lipid chemistry of seafoods. ACS Symposium Series 674, American Chemical Society, Washington, DC, pp 255–263
81. Wanasundara UN, Shahidi F (1999) Concentration of omega-3 polyunsaturated fatty acids of seal blubber oil by urea complexation: optimisation of reaction conditions. Food Chem 65: 41–49
82. Ratnayake WMN, Olsson B, Matthews D, Ackman RG (1988) Preparation of omega-3 PUFA concentrates from fish oils via urea complexation. Fat Sci Technol 90: 381–386
83. Schlenk H, Holman RT (1950) Separation and stabilization of fatty acids by urea complexes. J Am Oil Chem Soc 27: 5001–5004
84. Swern D (1964) Technique of separation: urea complexation. In: Markley KS (ed) Fatty acids. Interscience Publishers, New York, pp 2309–2358
85. Patokina EV, Alekseev SM, Sarycheya IK, Karpova GV, Evstigneeva RP (1988) Adductive crystallization of fatty acids with urea: calculation equilibrium phase-composition in multi-component mixture of fatty acid esters. Khim Farm Zh 22: 1129–1132
86. Iverson JL, Weik RW (1967) Correlation of fatty acid structure with preferential order of urea complex formation. J Assoc Off Anal Chem 50: 1111–1118
87. Strocchi A, Bonaga G (1975) Correlation between urea inclusion compounds and conformational structure of unsaturated C-18 fatty acids methyl esters. Chem Phys Lipids 15: 87–94
88. Gunstone FD, Wijesundara RC, Schrimgeour CM (1978) The component acids of lipids from marine and freshwater species with special reference to furan-containing acids. J Sci Food Agric 29: 539–550

89. Ackman RG, Sipos JC, Hooper SN, Dube G (1977) Selection of internal standards for determining quantitative recovery of isoprenoid acids after urea complexing. J Am Oil Chem Soc 54: 199–201
90. Piconneaux A, Grandgirard A, Sebedio J (1985) Identification of an unusual polyunsaturated fatty acid in liver of rats fed with heated linseed oil. C R Acad Sci Ser 3, Sci Vie 300: 353–358
91. Ackman RG, Safe L, Hooper SN, Paradis M (1973) 7-Methyl-7-hexadecenoic acid: isolation from lipid of the ocean sunfish *Mola mola*. Lipids 8: 21–24
92. Haagsma N, Gent CM, Luten JB, Jong RW, Doorn E (1980) Preparation of ω3-fatty acid concentrate from cod liver oil. J Am Oil Chem Soc 59: 117–118
93. Grompone MA (1992) Enrichment of omega-3 PUFAs from fur seal oil. Fat Sci Technol 94: 388–394
94. Medina AR, Gimenez AG, Camacho FG, Perez JAS, Grima EM, Gomez AC (1995) Concentration and purification of stearidonic, eicosapentaenoic and docosahexaenoic acids from cod liver oil and the marine microalga *Isochrysis galbana*. J Am Oil Chem Soc 72: 575–583
95. Hayes DG, Van Alstine JM, Setterwall F (2000) Urea-based fractionation of seed oil samples containing fatty acids and acylglycerols of polyunsaturated and hydroxy fatty acids. J Am Oil Chem Soc 77: 207–213
96. Anonymous (1996) Fish oil production and potentials in Atlantic Canada' Project. Rep No 115. Fisheries Development Branch, Halifax, Canada

15 Food and Health Applications of Marine Nutraceuticals: a Review

CESARETTIN ALASALVAR, FEREIDOON SHAHIDI, PETER QUANTICK

With the growing public awareness of the nutritional, diet and health benefits of seafoods, the stage is now to set for the development of mainstream nutraceutical products. Application of marine-based nutraceuticals includes fish oil (mainly omega-3 polyunsaturated fatty acids), seal blubber oil, algal oil, shark liver oil and squalene, shark cartilage, chitin, chitosan as well as their monomers and oligomers, enzymes, peptides and related compounds, vitamins (A, particularly its precursor β-carotene, D and E), seaweed (macroalgae) and its components, protein hydrolysates and other products has become a topic of great interest for both pharmaceutical and health food industries. This review provides an account of marine nutraceuticals and their application. Where available, the health benefits of nutraceuticals of interest are also discussed.

15.1 Introduction

Nutraceuticals may be defined as health food products or extracts (part of foods) that have been clinically proven to possess health benefits including prevention and treatment of disease, and are delivered in the form of dietary supplements, functional foods or functional food ingredients. For food manufacturers, nutraceuticals are a dream come true. The global market value of nutraceutical products is speculated to be up to US$120 billion [102]. Marine nutraceuticals represent less than 3% of this market [26].

The rationale behind food fortification is a public health issue. It is to ensure that the common diet contains all essential nutrients in adequate amounts for the maintenance of good health. Diet plays an important role in disease prevention or its initiation [111] and is thought to contribute to six of the ten leading causes of death worldwide. Up to 70% of certain cancers may be attributed to diet [20]. In addition, there is evidence to suggest that high levels of saturated fatty acids, *trans* fatty acids, sodium and alcohol would increase the likelihood of cardiovascular disease (CVD), whereas a high intake of long-chain omega-3 polyunsaturated fatty acids (LC ω3-PUFA), soluble fibre and antioxidant vitamins may decrease the risk [123]. There is, therefore, an increasing interest from consumers for quality life which is fuelling the nutraceutical revolution. Consequently, the stage is now set for the development of mainstream marine nutraceutical products which have received considerable attention because of their perceived safety as well as potential nutritional and therapeutic health benefits.

Marine nutraceuticals are food or dietary supplements that contain bioactive components from marine resources. These bioactives include oils (from fish, algae, seal blubber and shark liver), some of which are rich in LC ω3-PUFA such as eicosapentaenoic acid (EPA or 20:5 ω3), docosapentaenoic acid (DPA or 22:5 ω3) and docosahexaenoic acid (DHA or 22:6 ω3), shark cartilage, chitin, chitosan and associated products, enzymes, peptides, vitamins (A, D and E), seaweeds, sea cucumbers, sea mussels, protein hydrolysates and other products [3, 19, 26, 53, 58, 68, 71, 103, 106, 107, 125, 138, 144, 156, 163, 164]. Among marine bioactives, fish oils and their LC ω3-PUFA components have received much attention in recent years.

The presence of relatively large amounts of LC ω3-PUFA (especially EPA and DHA) in seafoods and marine oils is responsible for many of their beneficial health effects [27, 93, 113, 133, 134, 171]. The LC ω3-PUFA are essential for growth and development throughout the human life cycle. High levels of DHA are found in human milk, human brain and retina [10, 182, 206]. Therefore, DHA is considered essential for normal growth and optimal brain development, particularly in premature infants [74, 152, 185]. One of the best ways to obtain these important fatty acids is to incorporate them into common foods as well as infant formulas.

This chapter summarises the use of marine nutraceuticals and their application. Nutritional aspects and health benefits of some nutraceuticals are also described.

15.2 Marine Lipids

Marine lipids originate from the liver of the lean white fish such as cod and halibut, the body of oily fish such as mackerel, menhaden and salmon, and the blubber of marine mammals such as seals and whales [165]. These oils consist of saturated, monounsaturated and polyunsaturated fatty acids, dictated by the presence and number of double bonds in the fatty acid chain. The LC PUFA are further divided into ω3 and ω6 fatty acids, which are differentiated from one another based on the location of the first double bond from the terminal methyl group of the fatty acid molecule. The LC ω3-PUFA, namely EPA, DPA and DHA, may be acquired mainly from seafoods or derived from α-linolenic acid by chain elongation and desaturation [179]. The unique feature that differentiates lipids of marine species from those of land animals is the presence of LC ω3-PUFA. DPA is present in very low levels in fish oils relative to EPA and DHA. However, it is almost as important as either EPA and DHA in seal [167]. EPA and DHA are synthesised by both uni- and multicellular marine plants such as phytoplankton and algae [148]. They are eventually transferred through the food web and are incorporated into lipids of aquatic species such as fish and marine mammals [206]. The higher content of ω3-PUFA in marine lipids is suggested to be a consequence of cold temperature adaptation in which ω3-PUFA remain liquid and oppose any tendency to crystallise [4].

15.2.1 Nutritional Aspects and Dietary Intake of ω3-PUFA

A majority of the "Western" population does not consume adequate levels of LC ω3-PUFA through natural dietary sources such as fish. More recently, the increased use of ω6-PUFA from vegetable oils (sunflower, soy and corn) and a decline in the intake of ω3-PUFA has resulted in the compromise of the balance of the ω6 : ω3 ratio to a level which is believed to be inappropriate for optimal metabolism [137]. The typical British diet has a ratio of roughly 10:1 (ω6:ω3-PUFA ratio), while recommended ratio is nearer to 6:1 [30]. Although the recommended ratio in the USA is the same as in the UK, this ratio is 20–30:1 in the diet of Americans [170]. This imbalance is believed to be unhealthy and cause of a variety of diseases [46, 92, 108, 124]. Lands [108] reported that maintaining a more even balance of ω3 and ω6-PUFA in our diet may afford many more health benefits than is generally recognised.

There is general agreement that ω3-PUFA in the diet are beneficial and necessary to keep us fit and healthy. LC ω3-PUFA cannot be easily synthesised by humans and must be ingested in the diet. The questions now are how much should we consume them and how often. Dietary intake of LC ω3-PUFA remains low in the industrialised societies; 100–200 mg/day EPA plus DHA versus some recommendations of 1.0–1.25 g/day EPA and DHA [137]. Sufficient research evidences of health benefits of EPA and DHA exist (e.g. the UK, Canada, Japan and Denmark) and has led to recommended daily allowances for these specific LC-PUFA [45, 75], typically, about 0.2% of energy from ω3-PUFA or approximately 1–2 g/day [58]. The British Nutrition Foundation Task Force [30] on unsaturated fatty acids has recommended that 5% of total daily energy supply for humans should originate from ω3-PUFA. Per capita dietary intake of ω3-PUFA in the UK averages at about 250 mg/day, which would leave a shortfall of 1 g/day. In the USA, no specific recommended dietary allowances (RDA) for either ω6- or ω3-PUFA have been established [137]. The possibility of establishing RDAs for these fatty acids should be considered in the near future [54]. Currently the dietary intake of ω3-PUFA in the USA is estimated at 150–200 mg/day, similar to other western industrialised countries [14, 150].

Consumption of ω3-PUFA-rich fish about twice a week, one of which is from oily species, has been recommended by the UK's Department of Health [44] as a means of achieving a more balanced intake. Moreover, nutritionists recommended eating between 30 and 60 g daily of the right kind of oily fish to supply our needs [137]. Table 15.1 shows the dietary sources of various ω3-PUFA.

In many countries there is a popular belief that fish oils and cod liver oil promote good health. The popularity of fish oil supplementation in many countries, particularly among the elderly, stems from its traditional use as a natural remedy and cure-all. Fish oils are so popular that they account for nearly 29% of the UK's annual vitamin, minerals and supplement category [58].

15.2.2 The Health Benefits of ω3-PUFA

The beneficial health effects of ω3-PUFA have been attributed to their ability to lower serum triacylglycerol and cholesterol [82, 93, 113, 171]. The ω3-PUFA have been found to be effective in reducing the risk of a variety of diseases including CVD, heart attacks, restenosis, diabetes, hypertension, atherosclerosis, cerebral thrombosis, multiple sclerosis, atopic dermatitis, ulcerative colitis, arthritis and

Table 15.1. Dietary sources of various $\omega 3$ fatty acids

Fatty acid	Source	Percentage of total fatty acids
α-Linolenic acid (18:3ω3)	Freshwater fish	1–6
	Marine fish	1
	Linseed/flaxseed	45–60
	Green leaves	56
	Rapeseed/canola	10–11
Eicosapentaenoic acid (20:5ω3)	Freshwater fish (tuna)	5–13
	Pacific anchovy	18
	Capelin (codfish)	9
	Mackerel	8
	Herring	3–5
	Sardine	3
	Seal blubber	7
Docosapentaenoic acid (22:5ω3)	Menhaden	1–2
	Seal blubber	4–6
Docosahexaenoic acid (22:6ω3)	Sardine	9–13
	Pacific anchovy	11
	Mackerel	8
	Capelin (codfish)	3
	Herring	2–3
	Freshwater fish (tuna)	1–5
	Seal blubber	8–9

Source: Adapted, initially, from Lee [112].

other inflammatory and autoimmune disorders [24, 31, 41, 82, 93, 113, 170, 171, 176, 202]. A growing body of data indicates that ω3-PUFA may treat and prevent depressive, suicidal and violent behaviours [77]. Hibbeln [77] also reported that women who do not eat fish may become depleted of DHA and increase their risk of suffering from postpartum depression. Furthermore, research on ω3-PUFA resulted in improved bone architecture and reduced bone loss in rats [197]. Consumption of fish oil may impart significant inhibitory effect against various cancers, including breast, colon, skin, pancreas, prostate, lung and larynx [27, 133]. Increased marine lipids consumption by the elderly decreased production of pro-inflammatory mediators PGE2, IL-1b, TNFa and IL-6 [202]. Eating fish once a week may also reduce risk of sudden death [7].

15.2.3
Essentiality of ω3-PUFA

The ω3-PUFA are now considered "conditionally essential" for infant growth as well as for vision and optimal brain development [28, 74, 87, 152, 185] and are very important in human metabolism, thus emerging as essential nutrients [165]. Nettleton [133] reported that a few of the LC ω3-PUFA are absolutely essential and without them deficiency symptoms develop, leading to growth impairment.

High levels of DHA are also found in human milk (30-fold that of cows' milk) [113, 206], human brain and retina [10, 182], testes and sperm [109]. As a structural component of brain, retina, testes and sperm, DHA appears to be linked to proper tissue function and needs to be supplied in sufficient amounts during the development and growth period [134].

Recent studies have shown that DHA supplementation during pregnancy and lactation is necessary in order to prevent deficiency of the mother's DHA status in order to meet the high foetal requirement for this fatty acid [6]. Carlson et al. [32] have shown that premature babies have lower levels of DHA in their tissues than their full-term counterparts. Thus, supplementation of infant formula with marine oil/DHA is necessary in order to provide them with as much DHA as that available to the breast-fed babies. Feeding of infants with formula devoid of ω3-PUFA results in lack of deposition of DHA in their visual and neural tissues [33]. Because of the high DHA content in the brain, DHA deficiency has also been reported to affect cognition and learning ability [205]. Therefore, maintenance and improvement of learning ability depends, in part, on adequate intake of foods containing ω3-PUFA, such as fish or fish oils, during pregnancy and early development [117, 204]. Therefore, increased consumption of marine lipids has been suggested in order to increase dietary intake of ω3-PUFA [163].

15.3 Food Application of Marine Nutraceuticals

Food application of marine-based nutraceuticals includes use of fish oil, seal blubber oil, microalgae, shark cartilage and shark liver oil, chitin, chitosan and related compounds, enzymes, peptides and related compounds, vitamins, seaweed (macroalgae), sea cucumbers and sea mussels, and protein hydrolysates in different commodities is discussed in more detail below. Figure 15.1 shows a selection of commercially available marine-based nutraceutical products.

15.3.1 Fish Oil

Fish oils, mainly their ω3-PUFA components as well as algal oils, promise to be the key to a healthy future. Much attention has been paid to the nutraceutical potential of the two ω3-PUFA, namely EPA and DHA, and more recently to DPA. Enrichment of food products with ω3-PUFA is a major opportunity for food and beverage manufacturers, provided that they can develop products that taste as good as the "real thing" and do not cost much more. There is clearly a need for responsible reporting and marketing of marine nutraceuticals. Technology has played an important role in the development of ω3-PUFA as nutraceutical ingredients, enabling scientists to extract fish lipids without any accompanying off-flavours and rancid aroma and to use them in other foods such as bread, margarine and milk drinks [123]. Today fish oils can be incorporated into foods without giving them an unpleasant taste. There is no need for people to change their eating habits or the types of fat they consume since the nutritional value of

Fig. 15.1. A selection of commercially available marine-base nutraceutical products

their food is improved [137]. The advantage of enhancement of food products with ω3-PUFA is that they are not new or totally unfamiliar ingredients and have naturally been consumed in the diet for thousand of years.

Food processing/technology has now advanced to the point where, in theory, any product with an oily or fatty component can be enriched with ω3-PUFA. The market for ω3-PUFA nutraceutical products is currently more established in Europe and Japan than in North America [58]. In the USA, most marine nutraceuticals are dietary supplements. However, in Europe and Japan, fish oils are found in a variety of foods, including baked goods, margarines, infant formulas and dietary supplements [138]. Table 15.2 displays some of ω3-PUFA enriched food products marketed worldwide. In Europe, formulated bread, margarine, pasta and infant formula enriched with fish oil have been most popular. It is now well accepted that consumption of DHA helps develop a normal visual acuity in infants fed breast milk or DHA-containing formulas [63]. Thus, formula milk products enriched with DHA by the addition of purified fish or algal oils are now commercially available in Europe, Japan and the USA. Ohshima [144] reported that the number of other fish-oil added food products in Japan now exceeds 200; these include pudding, candy, juice and others. Assorted milks, powdered milk, rice porridge, margarine, cheese, yoghurt, cocoa, soft drink, tea, confectionery and cookies have also been fortified with fish oils in Japan [144]. However, DHA and marine oils, in general, are quite susceptible to autoxidation under ambient conditions. Therefore, stabilisation of DHA and marine oils against oxidation is necessary for their commercial application in food products. Thus, stable encapsulated/microencapsulated products containing 30% or 50% DHA-rich oil have been developed [144].

Bread is considered to be an ideal medium for ω3-PUFA fortification because the carbon dioxide released in the proofing and baking process may act

Table 15.2. Some ω3-PUFA enriched food products marketed in the world

Products	Company and country	Reference
Pact spread margarine	MD Foods (UK)	[58]
Live spread margarine	Gold Vale (IRELAND)	[74]
Heart Watch bread	Functional Nutrition (UK)	[58]
Omega 3 bread	Scandinavia	[19]
Live bread	Allied Bakeries (IRELAND)	[58]
Fortified bread and juice	Bertram (GERMANY)	[135]
Fortified milk drink	Boots (UK)	[74]
Fortified milk drink	Puleva (SPAIN)	[135]
Fortified juice drink	Lactel (SPAIN)	[135]
Fortified juice drink	Parmalat (BRAZIL)	[135]
Beverages (e.g. coca-cola)	Kirin (JAPAN)	[144]
Infant formula powder	F&P-[f] (JAPAN)	[144]
Farley's infant formula	-	[58]
Karica first formula	-	[58]
Recovery nutritional bars	Power Foods (USA)	[19]
Nutritional supplement bar	BASF, (USA)	[83]
Nutritional bars	Roche Vitamins (USA)	[137]
Gold circle farms eggs	Omega Tech Inc. (USA)	[196]
Columbus healthier eggs	Deans Farm Tring (UK)[a]	-
Omega DHA eggs	The NutraSweet Kelco Co.,	[58]
Canned tuna steak	DAI-EI (JAPAN)	[144]
Tuna burgers	Aqua Cuisine Inc. (USA)	[83]
Smoked salmon burgers	Mrs. Friday's (USA)	[135]
Cakes and pasta	Functional Nutrition (UK)	[58]
Dog food	Pedigree Pet Foods (UK)	[58]

[a] Retailed by Asda food stores.

favourably to exclude oxygen and prevent oxidation while bread is at high temperatures [136]. Today, a wide range of ω3-PUFA products in oil or powder form are available for various applications. These properties together with a neutral taste and odour, make Ropufa "30" ω3-EPA oil and Ropufa "10" ω3-EPA powder, ideal for enriching foods such as margarine, reduced-fat products, milk drinks, yoghurts, salad dressing, mayonnaise, orange juice drinks and bread [137]. In Europe, consumption of breads enriched with ω3-PUFA is increasing because Europeans recognise ω3-PUFA as being healthy components of the diet, probably more than does the general population in North America [136]. For bread, the amounts recommended are 0.5–1.5% ω3 oil or 1.0–2.5% ω3 powder [136]. A typical white bread formula is given in Table 15.3. This formula yields a bread that has 0.24 g ω3-PUFA in each 125 g of finished product.

15.3.2 Seal Blubber Oil

Seal meat serves as an excellent source of nutritionally valuable proteins, lipids, minerals and vitamins [161]. Seal blubber oil, which contains small amounts of vitamin E and squalene, is rich in EPA, DPA and DHA [159, 164]. The ratio of ω3

Table 15.3. White bread formula

Ingredients	Amount (g)
Strong white flour	700
Water	450
Butter	25
Dried yeast	15
Salt	2 tea spoons
ω3-EPA powder	17.28
ω3-EPA oil	5.76

Source: Adapted from Newton and Snyder [136].

to ω6 PUFA in seal blubber oil is approximately 9.8. Therefore, most of the nutritional attributes of the seal oil lies in its high content (approximately 21 %) of ω3-PUFA, with the ability to lower low-density cholesterol and serum triacylglycerol [167].

Due to differences in the position of the LC ω3-PUFA in seal blubber oil compared to fish oil, seal blubber oil may be assimilated more effectively into the body than fish oils [161]. In addition, seal blubber oil is more stable to oxidative changes than fish oils [162]. Therefore, seal blubber oil may serve as a good source of marine nutraceutical for use in liquid, capsule or other forms.

Seal oil capsules have become popular among the consumers for their possible therapeutic benefits for blood circulation problems and arthritis pains. Besides the pharmaceutical dynamics of the seal blubber oil for disease prevention and health benefits, its direct use in foods such as salad dressings, mayonnaise, low-fat spreads, milk, juices or even as a whitener for tea and coffee is the most desirable form for general family consumption. It is hoped that these alternate seal-oil-based products will help in providing a balance of LC ω3-PUFA and LC ω6-PUFA in the diets for the discerning consumer. Recent findings have also shown that seal blubber oil is superior to fish oil in terms of its beneficial health effects [167].

15.3.3 Microalgae

Microalgae have been used as human food and as source of a wide range of chemicals for thousand of years. The use of nutraceutical products and/or ingredients from microalgae has increased dramatically over the past decade and these include lipids (mainly ω3-PUFA), carotenoids, polysaccharides, sterols, phycobilins and other bioactive compounds. The application of each nutraceutical product is provided below.

15.3.3.1 *Microalgae Oil*

Some marine microalgae are good sources of ω3-PUFA. The ω3-PUFA content of the microalgae tested are rather low compared to fish oils. However, microalgae are the primary source of DHA for fish, and some strains of microalgae produce a pure oil that contains more than 40% DHA [104, 105]. The algae used in the commercial production of DHA rich oil are of the *Crypthecodinium cohnii* strain (30% of the total fatty acid). Some microalgae belonging to the family of *Eustigmatophyceae* and *Rhodophyceae* contain EPA in excess of 44% of the total fatty acids [37].

Although fish oil is presently the main source of EPA and DHA, the supply of suitable oils is limited and their quality remains variable. Cultured microalgae could provide a more reliable source for EPA and DHA. DHA produced from cultured algae has been tested in products ranging from infant formulas to nutritional bars [19]. In a clinical trial investigating the effect of fortifying infant formulas with algal DHA oil, Hoffman et al. [81] found a significant improvement in visual acuity of infants fed on supplemented as opposed to unsupplemented formulas. A marine microalgae, *Schizochytrium* sp. ATCC20888, containing a minimum of 19% (w/w) DHA provides a useful feed ingredient for natural enrichment of animal products such as chicken, swine and cattle. Addition of *Schizochytrium* sp. to the diets of dairy cattle (150 g/day/cow) increases the DHA content of whole milk from 5 to 10 mg/l [191]. The production of ω3-DHA-containing eggs is notable in that DHA is directly incorporated into the egg by feeding the chickens microalgae rich in DHA. Such eggs are now on sale in Germany, Spain, Portugal [58] and more recently in the UK and North America (Table 15.2). In clinical trials, algal DHA oil has been shown to be safe for consumption by infants and adults [38, 86] and has acquired GRAS (generally recognised as safe) status.

The main problem with the use of unsaturated oils in food is oxidation, as noted earlier. Becker and Kyle [19] compared the various DHA-rich oils (fish, tuna head and algal) for their sensory stability in white bread (Fig. 15.2). The breads were standardised to 100 mg of DHA per slice of bread. A triangle test

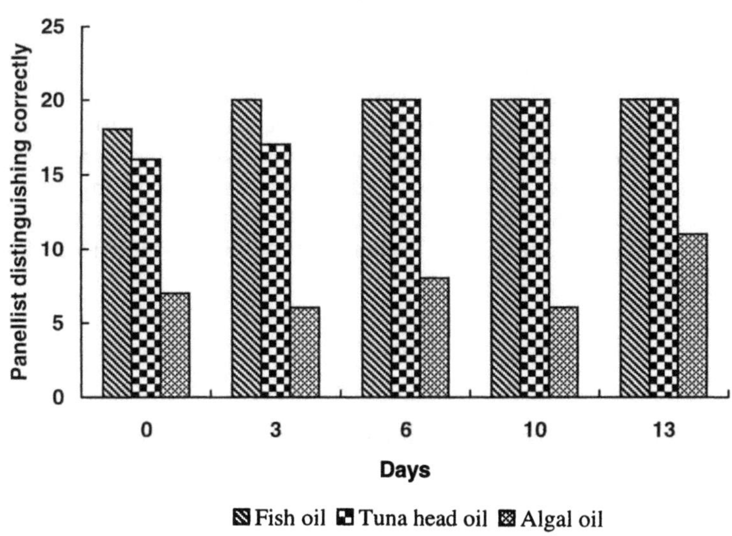

Fig. 15.2. Stability of bread. (Source: Adapted from Becker and Kyle [19])

panel data indicated that off-flavours were less likely to be detected in the DHA bread made with algal oils compared to those made with fish oils. This is probably due to a reduced accumulation of off-flavour oxidation products, perhaps due to better production standards under controlled conditions and/or possibly the presence of minor components with antioxidant potential [19].

15.3.3.2
Carotenoids

Carotenoids are a group of fat-soluble pigments and one of the main natural food colourants with widespread use [158]. The demand for β-carotene-rich foods has been on the rise due to their reported anti-cancer activity [147, 209] and health benefits [16, 21].

Cultured marine microalgae (e.g. *Spirulina*, *Dunaliella* and *Chlorella*) are known to serve as a good source of β-carotene. β-Carotene from the alga *Dunaliella salina* was the first high value algal product commercialised and there are now major producers in Australia, USA and Israel [25]. β-Carotene is sold mainly as an extract or suspension in vegetable oil, or as dried β-carotene-rich algal powder for use in the food colouring industry to prepare natural products. The health food and pharmaceutical industry also use β-carotene as a cancer preventative agent and free radical trapper. Apart from β-carotene, the ketacarotenoid astaxanthine is also one of the most important and economically valuable carotenoids due to its biological functions as a vitamin A precursor. Astaxanthine can be produced from the green algae (*Haematococcus pluvialis* and *Chlorella zofingiensis*) [18, 49, 207].

Meanwhile, carotenoids, mainly xanthophylls, zeaxanthin, peridinin and fucoxanthin, are used extensively by the aquaculture and poultry industries as a natural pigment [25, 175]. Cultured fish species require adequate pigmentation to respond to consumers' demands. Astaxanthin and canthaxanthin can be added to trout, salmon and sea bream feed for enhanced pigmentation [25, 125, 158].

Micropulverised dispersions of carotenoids are used in colouring fat-based foods such as margarine, butter, shortenings, cheese and French dressings. Water-dispersible forms of carotenoids have been developed for the colouring of water-based foods such as orange-type beverages, cake mixes, puddings, dried and canned soups. Carotenoids added to juices and carbonated beverages show adequate stability due to the antioxidant property of ascorbic acid [94, 155]. In New Zealand, milk-based formulated foods are enriched with β-carotene [141].

15.3.3.3
Phycobilins

Phycocyanin and phycoerythrin can be easily isolated from red or blue-green algae. Highly purified phycobilins are used in immunofluorescent labelling in medicine and research. Alternatively, phycobilins may be used as a natural food colouring, especially for products such as ice cream and yoghurt [25]. Phycocyanin is used for this purposes in Japan.

15.3.3.4
Polysaccharides

Microalgae produce a diverse range of polysaccharides, some of which have novel properties. Alginic acid, which exists as a cell wall component of brown algae (e.g. *Laminaria*, *Eisenia* and *Ecklonia*), is used as an effective ion exchanger in waste-water treatment [144]. Sodium alginate solutions are used as thickeners, emulsifiers and stabilisers in ice creams, jams and mayonnaise as well as in cosmetics and personal care commodities such as facial creams, toothpaste and pharmaceutical bases. Agar is composed of agarose (70%) and agaropectin (30%). It is extracted from red sea algae (e.g. *Gelidium*, *Grateloupia*, *Gracilaria*, *Hypnea* and *Gigartina*). It is mostly used as an excipient in the food industry, a microbiological culture medium and as a laxative [144]. Carrageenan is extracted from red sea algae (e.g. *Chondrus* and *Gigartina*) and its primary applications are in dairy and processed meat products.

15.3.3.5
Sterols

Microalgae produce a wide range of sterols, and many of them are unusual. However, the content of sterols in microalgae is less than 0.1% of dry weight, and to be commercially viable they would have to command a very high price [25]. Plant sterols (phytosterols) have recently been used as functional ingredients in the food industry [66, 208], and products such as benecol. Consumption of foods containing phytosterols provides health benefits. They have been known to reduce serum total and low-density lipoprotein cholesterol concentration by lowering intestinal cholesterol absorption [208]. Although the Western diet provides about 250–500 mg/day of sterols, similar to dietary cholesterol, functional foods that are fortified with sterols and consumed in the range of 1.8–3 g/day are proven to be beneficial to health [208]. Many studies showed that phytosterols are safe to be used as a functional food ingredients.

15.3.3.6
Other Bioactive Compounds

One area of interest in recent years is the production of biologically active substances by microalgae for possible application in human health products. Although screening of microalgae has been limited so far, compounds with anticancer, antibacterial, antifungal and antiviral activity have been isolated mainly from blue-green algae [25].

15.3.4
Shark Cartilage and Shark Liver Oil

The market for shark cartilage has seen dramatic increases in recent years for its perceived anti-angiogenesis properties in cancer therapy. The market for shark cartilage in the USA had an estimated retail sale of U$136 million in 1996. Although the natural/health food movement has been responsible for its initial development, sales in traditional health food outlets today only account for 18% of the total volume [125]. Chondroitin sulphate, a bioactive component of shark cartilage, is known to have several therapeutic functions, including anti-arthritis, anti-joint inflammation and anti-cancer properties [125].

Some shark species such as soupfin store enormous quantities of oil in their liver (45–70%). The soupfin shark liver is considered to the richest source of vitamin A (74,000–190,000 IU/g), while others store very little [107]. Ackman [3] pointed out that Greenland shark liver oil was found to be bioactive against cancer. Shark liver oil is also known to contain a high proportion of squalene, up to 50% [3]. There is some use in cosmetics as a skin softener and lubricant since low levels are found in our normal skin oils. It circulates in our bloodstream at low levels all the time and may also serve as a protecting agent against photo-oxidative damage [3].

15.3.5 Chitin, Chitosan and Related Products

Chitin (poly-β (1 $\Rightarrow$ 4)-*N*-acetyl-D-glucosamine), chitosan (deacetylated chitin) and their monomers and oligomers are available through further processing of by-products of the shellfish industry [97]. Shellfish processing discards (i.e. derived from shrimp, crab, lobster, prawn, squid and crawfish) contain 14–35% chitin on a dry weight basis [172]. Chitin is a by-product of the seafood processing industry with an estimated 1.2×10^5 MT (metric tonnes) annual production on a worldwide basis and total sales of chitin/chitosan were predicted to reach US$2 billion [100]. At present, most chitosan in practical and commercial use comes from deacetylation of chitin derived from crab, shrimp and krill shells [101].

The biodegradation of chitin in the crustacean shell waste is very slow. Thus, accumulation of large quantities of discards from processing of crustaceans has become a major environmental concern in the seafood-processing industry [160, 166]. Disposal of shellfish processing-discard has, thus, been a challenge for most of the shellfish-producing countries. Therefore, production of value-added products such as chitin, chitosan and their derivatives and application of products in food as nutraceutical is of great interest.

Chitin and chitosan are natural, non-toxic, high molecular weight, water-insoluble, biodegradable compounds with high water-holding capacities and ability to form films or coatings [172]. Therefore, these biopolymers offer a wide range of industrial applications, including use in food, agriculture, water treatment, pulp and paper, membranes, cosmetics, biomedical, chemical, biotechnological and pharmaceutical products and plant protection [100, 101, 114, 140, 156, 172]. Here only food application of chitin and chitosan and their use by the food industry as nutraceutical ingredients is discussed.

15.3.5.1 *Food Application of Chitinous Materials*

Conversion of processing discard into valuable and species products has been identified as a timely challenge for food research and development associated with numerous applications of chitinous polymers [153]. Chitin and chitosan are already part of our food supply as they are present in a number of food products, including mushrooms, softshell crabs, etc. [99]. Table 15.4 summarises some food applications of chitin and chitosan and their derivatives. In addition to this table, chitosan was also used to extend the preservation time of foods [40, 72, 156] and preservative coating material in fruits and vegetables [13, 62]. The US Food and Drug Administration (FDA) approved chitosan as a feed additive in 1983 [99] and its biological safety has recently been demonstrated by feeding trials using domestic animals [78]. Janak Kamil et al. [89] reported that chitosan can demonstrate an antioxidative effect in controlling lipid oxidation of seafoods. Applications of chitosan coating could be an effective method of improving the quality and shelf-life of chilled fish fillets [178].

One of the most useful properties of chitosan is related to its chelation of metal ions and thus may be used in food preparation, health care, water improvement and pharmaceutical industries [114]. Chitosan is usable not only as a biocompatible material but also as a biologically functional additive for foods [79]. Chitosan may be used in the food industry as a quality enhancer or nutraceutical in certain countries. Japan produces dietary cookies, potato chips, noodles, soybean sauce and soybean paste enriched with chitosan because of its hypocholesterolemic effect [79, 80]. Vinegar products containing chitosan are also manufactured and sold in Japan, again because of their cholesterol lowering ability [80]. Maezaki et al. [121] found that when chitosan was given (in the form of biscuits) to adult males in their diet (3–6 g/day) for 4 weeks, their serum total cholesterol level was significantly decreased. The favourable effects of a very low dose of chitosan within a short period is worthy of special attention. The chitosan intake (biscuits) by healthy volunteers brought about a significant decrease in the faecal phenols, *p*-cresol and indole, in analogy with other polysaccharides [186]. Chitosan inhibited the putrefactive activity of the intestinal microbiota, thus reducing the risk of disease states. The diet plus chitosan dietary fibre appears to be a useful treatment for excess weight gain and hyperlipidemia in obese patients and a route for weight loss [192, 193].

Use of chitin as a functional ingredient in dough fermentation for bread has been reported by Knorr and Betschart [96]. Knorr [98] reported that the loaf volume of wheat bread increased when up to 2% microcrystalline chitin was included in the formulation. Storage stability (compressibility) of bread crumbs was not decreased when up to 5% chitin was added to the bread formula [99]. Chitosan, however, resulted in a poor bread quality. This could be due to the inhibitory effect of chitosan on the fermentation of glucose by *Saccharomyces cerevisiae* as suggested by Ralston et al. [149]. Methylpyrrolidinone chitosan (MP-chitosan) was used in bread wheat and potential exists for exploitation of the selective interaction of gliadin and MP-chitosan, with a view to overcome problems of celiac disease [128]. Chitin and chitosan are also used in health foods for prevention and treatment of hyperuricemia [128]. However, chitosan-enriched food should preferably not be subjected to thermal treatment such as cooking and baking. Although biscuit cooking imparts appealing organoleptic properties, the Maillard reaction would partly destroy the primary amino group of chitosan and reduce its efficacy as dietary fibre [184].

Table 15.4. Food applications of chitin, chitosan and their derivatives in the food industry

Area of application	Examples
Antimicrobial agent	Bactericidal Fungicidal Measure of mould contamination in agriculture commodities
Edible film industry	Controlled moisture transfer between food and surrounding environment Controlled release of antimicrobial substances Controlled release of antioxidants Controlled release of nutrients, flavour and drugs Reduction of oxygen partial pressure Controlled rate of respiration Temperature control Controlled enzymatic browning in fruits Reverse osmosis membranes
Additive	Clarification and deacidification of fruits and beverages Natural flavour extender Texture controlling agent Emulsifying agent Food mimetic Thickening and stabilising agent Colour stabilisation Removal of acids from coffee Removal of lipid from cheese
Nutrition and health promotion	Dietary fibre Hypocholesterolemic effect Livestock and fish feed additive Reduction of lipid absorption Production of single cell protein Antigastritis agent Infant feed ingredient Weight loss/diet Cholesterol reduction Immuno-system stimulant
Recovery of solid materials	Affinity flocculation Fractionation of agar
Purification of water	Recovery of metal ions, pesticides, phenols and PCB's Removal of dyes
Other applications	Enzyme immobilisation Encapsulation of nutraceuticals Chromatography Analytical reagents

Source: Adapted, initially, from Shahidi et al. [156].

Research on preparation and physiological activities of chitin and chitosan oligomers has continually attracted much attention in the food and pharmaceutical field due to their versatile antitumour activity [188], immuno-enhancing effects [181], protective effects against some infectious pathogens in mice [187], antifungal and antimicrobial activities [189]. These oligomers are water-soluble and their use in different food applications is much easier. Jeon et al. [91] have recently reviewed the application of chitosan oligomers in physiological functional foods. Production of glucosamine and *N*-acetylglucosamine from chitosan and chitin, respectively, has also been achieved. These products are also used as such, and in the form of over the counter (OTC) drugs and supplements.

Thus, chitosan is no longer just a by-product from the seafood-processing industry and may be utilised by industry to solve certain quality problems and to improve existing food products, as well as to create new ones. Although chitin and chitosan and their derivatives have been considered as versatile biopolymers in food applications their potential use as nutraceutical ingredients has to be studied with broader emphasis. Chitin and chitosan oligomers may be more advantageous than chitin and chitosan as polymers in the field of food additives and nutraceuticals in human health because chitin and chitosan are not degraded in the human intestine due to the absence of enzymes such as chitinase and chitosanase [156]. Chitin and chitosan could also potentially provide other benefits of commercial importance in the food industry.

15.3.6 Enzymes

Haard and Simpson [68] have recently edited a comprehensive book on seafood enzymes. Here, only applications, uses and recovery of enzymes from seafood resources will be reviewed. Several marine enzymes are now used commercially in the food industry and some can be isolated as by-products of the seafood processing industry [71, 118]. A greater investment in research on marine enzymes and other natural products will certainly yield a plethora of products for use as nutraceutical ingredients in the food industry. Enzymes from marine resources are likely to establish a significant part of the industrial enzymes market in future as we learn more about unique properties that fulfil the needs for specific applications such as a nutraceutical ingredient [71].

Although there are many commercially available enzymes isolated from marine resources [8, 22, 43, 59, 64, 67, 76, 119, 145, 173, 174, 180], most of these are used as biochemical research reagents. The use of marine enzymes as nutraceutical ingredients in food products is a new and growing area [118].

Most of the seafood enzymes used in the food industry are either for processing or preservation. The main use is in dairy technology. The major use of enzymes is in the coagulation of milk to make cheese [118]. Bovine trypsin can prevent oxidised flavour in milk [116]. In addition, cow's milk can be "humanised" by addition of lysozyme, making it suitable as an infant milk. Lysozyme acts as a preservative by reducing bacterial counts in the milk without affecting *Lactobacillus bifius* [42]. However, other applications have been suggested such as meat tenderising for specific fish collagenases, and the enzymatic clarification of fruit juice [69].

Arctic scallop [129] contains a cold-active peptide enzyme with lysozyme-like activity that is active against both Gram positive and Gram negative bacteria. Although this enzyme has potential as a nutraceutical ingredient in food products, it will probably be necessary to produce it by rDNA technology because it is present naturally in scallops only at a very low concentration [70]. The enzyme has been recovered from scallop processing wastes and has potential for application as a preservative in refrigerated foods [71]. Psychrophilic cod trypsin efficiently strips intact carotenoproteins from shells and can then be readily heat inactivated. Squid peptidases can also be separated and used for accelerating cheese ripening. Trypsin(s) from stomachless fish may be employed for inactivation of enzymes without heat treatment [71].

15.3.7
Peptides and Related Compounds

Protamine, a basic peptide containing over 80% arginine, has been found in the testicles of more than 50 fish species [144]. It is being used as an antibacterial agent in food processing and preservation [88, 143]. The annual production of protamines, salmine and curpeine prepared from salmon and sardine, respectively, amounts to 700 MT (metric tonnes) [11].

The industrial use of collagen has been expanded and collagens are now used as materials for foods, cosmetics and biomedicine [130, 131]. The production of collagen from fish is not carried out on a large scale because of the ready availability of collagen from mammals. However, fish skin, bone and fin clearly have potential as alternative sources of collagen [130]. Fish collagen has been used in speciality applications as well as "Kosher" and "Halal" food ingredients [36, 151]. Collagen from cod swim bladders has been employed as a clarifier in the brewing of beer and wine [132].

15.3.8
Vitamins

Vitamins are essential micronutrients that were discovered in the first half of the twentieth century because their low intake led to specific deficiency diseases. Fish and fish liver oils are good sources of fat-soluble vitamins (A, D and E). Consumers have been hearing about these health benefits and have used them for decades. For example, a deficiency of vitamin A affects the function of the eye, leading to blindness; a low intake of vitamin D may lead to rickets; a deficiency of vitamin E increases the risk of atherosclerosis and coronary heart disease [199]. The amount of water-soluble vitamins (thiamine (B_1), riboflavin (B_2), niacin, pyridoxine (B_6), pantothenic acid, biotin, ascorbic acid (C) and cyanocobalamin (B_{12})) in marine foods is less dependent upon the species concerned [169].

Commercial production of cod liver oil (rich in vitamins A and D) became successful and constituted 90% of the concentrated vitamin-containing oil marketed globally [107]. Marine microalgae are also known to have nutraceutical properties for being not only a good source of LC ω3-PUFA but also of β-carotene. Among them, vitamins A (particularly provitamin A, β-carotene) and E (particularly α-tocopherol) serve as excellent antioxidants and free radical scavengers that protect cells from damage by oxidants [9]. Research has shown that vitamin E has a number of extraordinary beneficial effects as a specific antioxidant, acting together with vitamin C and β-carotene, in improving antioxidant defences in the body [60, 195]. The role of antioxidant vitamins in health and disease control has been well documented [5, 17, 47, 61, 90, 146, 190, 198, 199]. These antioxidants may also be defined as substances which interfere with normal oxidation processes in oils and fats and delay their oxidation.

Fat-soluble vitamins are present in seafoods in varying amounts, often in concentrations higher than those in the land animals. Many species of fish and shellfish store higher amounts of vitamins A, D and E in their liver than flesh with some exceptions [107]. Warm water pelagic fish species, such as tuna, have vitamin A contents as high as 10,000–250,000 IU/g in their liver oils. The flesh of fatty fish such as mackerel and herring contains higher concentrations of vitamin A (100–1500 IU/100 g flesh oil) than leaner fish such as cod (25–50 IU/100 g flesh oil). Albacore and skipjack tuna show the highest concentrations ranging from 25,000 to 250,000 IU/g of their liver oils. Fatty fish species and cod liver oil also contain significant levels of vitamin D. Cod and halibut liver oils, which were used in the early days for medical purposes, contain 100 and 3000 IU/g of vitamin D, respectively [107]. The amount of vitamin E in the edible portion of fish and marine invertebrate ranges from 0.2 to 270 mg/100 g on a wet weight basis [169]. In the flesh, dark muscle contains more vitamin E than white muscle [1].

The nutritional aspects and health effects of vitamins A, D and E are very well known. Seafoods serve as rich sources of these vitamins which are essential to life. These vitamins, although available in the form of tablets, are now in much tastier offerings in the form of food and drinks. Enrichment of common foods with vitamin-rich ingredients in production/formulation of nutraceuticals is therefore of great importance.

Vitamin A-active compounds fall into basic groups of preformed vitamin A (retinoids) and provitamin A (carotenoid). In nature, retinol forms of retinyl acetate and retinyl palmitate can be synthesised chemically and are used commercially to supplement the vitamin A content of foodstuffs [17]. Fat-based foods, particularly margarine and shortenings, are enriched by direct addition of standardised and stabilised solutions of retinyl acetate or retinyl palmitate to the oil. Nowadays, most food manufacturers use retinyl palmitate which has been shown to exhibit the greatest stability of the retinyl esters toward oxidation in fortification processes [200]. Dry preparations of synthetic retinyl esters are used in dried food products such as milk powder, infant formulas and dietetic foods [17].

Vitamin E, in the form of α-tocopherol acetate, is sometimes added to whole milk powder [85] and breakfast cereals to fortify them [200]. The vitamin E requirement increases with increased intake of PUFA; hence several types of high quality dietetic margarines are enriched with vitamin E [94].

Foodstuffs commonly enriched with vitamin D include margarine, skimmed milk powder, evaporated milk, milk-based beverages, breakfast cereals, dietetic products of all kinds, baby foods and soup powders [94].

15.3.9 Seaweeds (Macroalgae), Sea Cucumbers and Sea Mussels

Seaweeds are used in human and animal nutrition and some species are rich in their protein level, vitamins, dietary fibres and certain amino acids [53]. The annual global aquaculture production of marine algae is 6.5×10^6 tonnes (fresh products) [50]. In Asian countries, seaweeds are often consumed as marine vegetables (both fresh and dried forms). About 25% of all food consumed in Japan consists of seaweed prepared and served in many forms [142]. In Europe, algae, more particularly the brown seaweeds, are traditionally used for the production of additives or meal for animal nutrition [84].

Seaweeds show nutritional differences among species [201]. The protein content of seaweeds differs according to species and are found in low amounts in brown seaweeds (3–15% of the dry weight) compared with that of their green and red counterparts (10–47% of the dry weight) [12]. It has been reported that aspartic and glutamic acids together constitute between 22 and 44% of the total amino acids [127]. The fatty acid composition of seaweeds also differs among different groups. As far as ω3-PUFA (especially EPA and DHA) are concerned, the brown and red seaweeds are a better potential source than the green ones for these fatty acids [2, 34, 35, 142]. In addition, brown seaweeds generally contain more vitamin C than their red and green counterparts [120].

Seaweeds known under the names of "dulse", "nori", "kelp", "kombu", "wakame", "ascophyllum" and "fucus" (dry products) have been mainly used in the Asian and North American countries as nutraceutical products due to their high content of protein, amino acids, vitamins, dietary fibres, minerals and in certain cases ω3-PUFA [12, 53, 57, 126]. In Europe, the development of novel foods such as nutraceutical foods could open a new possibility for the use of seaweeds, especially from protein and ω3-PUFA-rich species, in human nutrition.

Sea cucumber and sea mussel share a very tiny portion of the marine nutraceutical market. Sea cucumber is known to be rich in mucopolysaccharides (MPS) which are the main components of amorphous substances of connective tissues surrounding collagen and elastin fibres. The MPS in the tissues are usually combined with proteins to form mucoproteins [29]. Among others, hyaluronic acid and chondroitin sulphates are the main components of the MPS fraction of connective tissues [29]. The MPS possess good physiological properties and are used as a component of cosmetics for skin care and medicine for curing of joints and eye diseases [139]. Synowiecki and Shahidi [183] stated that seal meat processing discards may also serve as a good source of MPS.

Sea mussel has a high level of chondroitin sulphate [125]. More research work is in progress in several laboratories on the nutraceutical properties of mucopolysaccharides and chondroitin sulphate.

15.3.10 Protein Hydrolysates

There are huge amounts of protein-rich discards from seafood processing plants which are discarded without any attempt of recovery. Recovery and alteration of fish muscle proteins present in the processing by-products and their use as nutraceutical ingredients in food systems is a very exciting and promising alternative. Proteins derived from fish muscle are of high quality and at a par with those of meat and poultry muscle proteins [55]. Fish muscle contains an excellent amino acid composition and a profile that is well-balanced and easily digestible proteins [194, 203].

Hydrolysates can be defined as proteins which are chemically or enzymatically broken down into peptides of varying chain length [177]. Application of enzyme technology for protein recovery in fish processing makes it possible to produce a broad spectrum of food ingredients or industrial products for a wide range of applications. These include cereals, milk replacers, protein supplements, stabilisers in beverages and flavour enhancers in a variety of products including confectionery [103, 203]. Formulas based on protein hydrolysates and amino acids have also been used in enteral diets and in formulations for the elderly as well as infant formulas [56]. Preparation of hydrolysates from fish and seal processing discards provide a means for better utilisation of resources since products so obtained may be used in a variety of applications including dietetic foods, processed meats and extruded food. Fish protein hydrolysates have also been found to possess antioxidant potential. Several studies have found powerful antioxidant activity in intact fish protein [73] and in hydrolysates [157]. These effects are probably dependent on the amino acid composition and the molecular size of the fish protein hydrolysates peptides [103]. Li et al. [115] found that a polar phenolic compound isolated from shrimp meat and waste exhibited antioxidant activity.

The functional properties of fish protein hydrolysates (solubility, water-holding capacity, emulsifying properties, foaming properties, fat absorption and sensory properties) are important, particularly if they are used as nutraceutical ingredients in food products [65, 103, 122]. Furthermore, protein hydrolysates appear useful in controlling food allergies, Crohn's disease, ulcerative colitis, short bowel syndrome, fistulas, pancreatitis and severe trauma [39, 154]. Much attention has recently been focused on natural antioxidants because of their positive health effects against cancer and heart disease [95, 168].

The use of seafood protein hydrolysates as nutraceutical food ingredients is a more recent technology and is becoming more and more popular although it has a long way to go until it becomes economically feasible and accepted by the industry and consumers. However, there is a major opportunity for this to happen, due to regulations prohibiting uncontrolled dumping of seafood processing waste. These factors should stimulate the conversion of low value fish material into more valuable and palatable products and taking advantage of nutraceutical potential of their specific preparations.

15.4 Regulatory Aspects of Marine Nutraceuticals

The regulatory aspect of marine nutraceuticals is however complicated by the fact that regulations vary from country to country. Some countries, such as Japan, have well-established regulations and guidelines for these products, whereas others, such as the USA, have no separate nutraceutical regulations and products may actually fall under several regulatory options [58].

In Europe, marine nutraceuticals fall within the Novel Food Directive approved by the European Parliament early in 1997 [48] and became binding and directly applicable in all member states. Under this definition, ω3-PUFA such as DHA produced in algae via fermentation would be viewed as a novel food and has to be approved for use as such. Those oils used in foods prior to the Novel Foods Directive, however, would not fall under these regulations. Conventional fish oils extracted and purified from fish are generally allowed for use in foods in Europe and are already being added to food products such as margarine and bread [58].

Nutraceuticals and functional foods are not defined by law or by rule in the USA and can be positioned under either the Nutrition Labelling Health and Education Act of 1990 (NLEA), the Dietary Supplement Health and Education Act of 1994 (DSHEA), or the medical foods regulations [23, 58]. ω3-PUFA were one of the original ten dietary components that were reviewed at the onset of NLEA to determine whether a health claim linking a decreased risk of heart disease was appropriate. Food and Drug Administration (FDA) recently affirmed generally recognised as safe (GRAS) status for menhaden oil as a direct human food ingredient with specific limitations [51]. The final rule allows the use of menhaden oil, provided that intakes of EPA and DHA from menhaden oil do not exceed 3 g/person/day.

Japan was the first country to develop a system for evaluating the efficacy of food ingredients in functional foods. The FOSHU (Foods for Specified Health Use) system has been in place for over 10 years and is finally gaining momentum over 10% of the functional foods in the Japanese market bearing the FOSHU logo [15, 110]. FOSHU is the opposite of DSHEA in that it focuses on foods rather than dietary supplements. In fact, one of the criteria for a FOSHU product is that it must be in common food form, not in tablet, capsule or other common supplement or drug form. The product must also be consumed on a daily basis as part of a regular diet [15]. Despite FOSHU approval for ω3-PUFA, no FOSHU food products containing these ingredients had been approved through 1997 [58]. The ω3 enriched food products on sale in Japan, such as noodles, tuna, natto (soybean paste), confectionery, beverages and infant formula are sold not as FOSHU products but rather as "health foods" [58].

In Canada, regulatory initiatives related to nutraceuticals, functional foods and natural health products are currently underway [52]. China in 1996 developed a system for regulatory control of functional foods and this one differs with the well-defined Japanese system [110].

15.5 Conclusions

Worldwide, more natural and nutraceutical products are expected in the market with the continuing discovery of novel products from marine resources. Safety, bioavailability, organoleptic quality and efficacy are main concerns when using new ingredients. Food product developers must meet these challenges and endeavour to understand and control the functionality of ingredients in a way that will allow them to manufacture products with a pleasing taste and adequate shelf-life and to provide and deliver not only essential nutrients to consumers but also health promoting ingredients.

A wide variety of food products could be enriched with LC ω3-PUFA, among others. However, each product must be considered on a case-by-case basis. In the short term, it is likely that certain food product forms may be more successful than others. More "natural" nutraceutical products, such as DHA-rich eggs and meat, may be more appealing at the beginning, as consumers become more familiar with these ingredients. From a formulation standpoint it is easier to enrich certain food product categories than others [58].

The cost of new products is one of the most important issues to be considered. The key to the success for future marine nutraceuticals lies mainly in the hands of consumers. Their reaction to these type of products is largely unknown at the moment. Therefore, industry, consumers and the public authorities need to find common ground to work together in order to boost this new and promising market. Overall, food application of marine nutraceuticals will continue to enjoy exceptional market opportunities with rising interests among consumers.

References

1. Ackman RG, Cormier MG (1967) α-Tocopherol in some Atlantic fish and shellfish with particular reference to live-holding without food. J Fish Res Board Can 24: 357–373
2. Ackman RG (1981) Algae as a source of edible oils. In: Pryde EH, Princen LH, Mukherjee KD (eds) New sources of fats and oils. American Oil Chemists' Society, Champaign, USA, pp 189–220
3. Ackman RG (2000) Shark liver oils: a review and diminishing resource. Paper presented at the International Conference on Nutraceuticals and Functional Foods, Houston, USA, September 13–17, session 15/1, book of abstracts
4. Ackman RG (1988) The year of the fish oils. Chem Ind 3: 139–145
5. Ahmad JI (1996) Free radicals and health: is vitamin E the answer? Food Sci Technol Today 10: 147–152
6. Al MDM, Hornstra G, Schouw YT, Bulstra-Remakers MEEW, Huistes G (1990) Biochemical EFA status of mothers and their neonates after normal pregnancy. Early Hum Dev 24: 239–248
7. Albert CM, Manson JE, O'Donnell CJ, Ajaani UA, Hennekens CH (1996) Fish consumption and the risk of sudden death in the Physicians' Health Study. Circulation 94, Suppl. 1: 1–578, abstract
8. An H, Vissesanguan W (2000) Recovery of enzymes from seafood-processing wastes. In: Haard NF, Simpson BK (eds) Seafood enzymes: utilization and influence on postharvest seafood quality. Marcel Dekker, New York, pp 641–664
9. Anderson R, Theron AJ (1990) Physiological potential of ascorbate, β-carotene and α-tocopherol individually and in combination in the prevention of tissue-damage, carcinogenesis and immune dysfunction mediated by phagocyte-derived reactive oxidants. World Rev Nutr Diet 62: 27–58
10. Anderson RE, Sperling L (1971) Lipids of ocular tissues. VII. Positional distribution of the fatty acids in the phospholipids of bovine retina rod outer segments. Arch Biochem Biophys 144: 673–677
11. Anonymous (1998) Marketing research on food additives. Food Chemicals Newspaper (Japan), No 1712, p 5

12. Arasaki A, Arasaki T (1983) Low calories, high nutrition: vegetables from the sea to help you look and fell better. Japan Publications, Tokyo, pp 39–42
13. Arul J, Ghaouth AE, Reddy MVB (2000) Use of chitosan for the control of postharvest diseases in fresh fruits and vegetables. In: Shahidi F (ed) Seafood in health and nutrition: transformation in fisheries and aquaculture: global perspectives. Science Tech Publishing, St. John's, Canada, pp 219–236
14. Ascherio A (1995) Dietary intake of marine n-3 fatty acids, fish intake and the risk of coronary disease among men. N Engl J Med 332: 977–982
15. Bailey R (1997) The status of foods for specified health use (FOSHU) in Japan. Paper presented at Nutracon' 97, Las Vegas, USA, July 17–18, 1997
16. Baker KR, Meydany M (1994) β-Carotene as an antioxidant in immunity and cancer. J Optim Nutr 3: 39–50
17. Ball GFM (1988) Fat-soluble vitamin assays in food analysis: a comprehensive review. Elsevier Science Publishers, London
18. Bar E, Rise M, Vishkautsan M, Arad S (1995) Pigment and structural changes in *Chlorella zofingiensis* upon light and nitrogen stress. J Plant Physiol 146: 527–534
19. Becker CC, Kyle DJ (1998) Developing functional foods containing algal docosahexaenoic acid. Food Technol 52: 68–71
20. Belem MAF (1999) Application of biotechnology in the product development of nutraceuticals in Canada, a viewpoint. Trends Food Sci Technol 10: 101–106
21. Bendich A (1993) Biological functions of dietary carotenoids. Ann NY Acad Sci 691: 61–67
22. Benjakul S, Seymour TA, Morrissey MT, An H (1996) Proteinase in Pacific whiting surimi wash water: identification and characterization. J Food Sci 61: 1165–1170
23. Betz JM (2000) US government perspective on nutraceuticals/functional foods. Paper presented at the International Conference on Nutraceuticals and Functional Foods, Houston, USA, September 13–17, session 3/1, book of abstracts
24. Bhathena SJ (1992) Fatty acids and diabetes. In: Chow CK (ed) Fatty acids in foods and their health implications. Marcel Dekker, New York, pp 823–855
25. Borowitzka MA (1993) Products from microalgae. Infofish Int 5: 21–26
26. Boudreau J (2000) Marine nutraceuticals: opportunities and challenges. In: Shahidi F (ed) Seafood in health and nutrition: transformation in fisheries and aquaculture: global perspectives. Science Tech Publishing, St. John's, Canada, pp 7–14
27. Branden LM, Carroll KK (1986) Dietary polyunsaturated fat in relation to mammary carcinogenesis in rats. Lipids 21: 285–288
28. Brenner RR (1982) Nutritional and hormonal factors influencing desaturation of essential fatty acids. Prog Lipid Res 20: 41–47
29. Brimacombe JS, Webber JM (1966) Mucopolysaccharides: chemical structure, distribution and isolation. Elsevier Publishing, Amsterdam
30. British Nutrition Foundation (1992) Unsaturated fatty acids. Report of the British Nutrition Foundation's Task Force. British Nutrition Foundation
31. Burr ML (1992) Fish food, fish oil and cardiovascular disease. Clin Exp Hypertens A14: 181–192
32. Carlson SE, Rhodes RG, Ferguson MG (1986) Docosahexaenoic acid status of preterm infants at birth and following feeding with human milk or formula. Am J Clin Nutr 44: 798–802
33. Carlson SE, Rhodes RG, Rao VS, Goldgar DE (1987) Effect of fish oil supplementation on the n-3 fatty acid content of red blood cell membranes in preterm infants. Pediatr Res 21: 507–511
34. Cheung PCK, Leung AYH, Ang PU JR (1998) Comparison of supercritical carbon dioxide and soxhlet extraction of lipids from brown seaweed, *Sargassum hemiphyllum* (Turn.) C. Ag. J Agric Food Chem 46: 4228–4232
35. Cheung PCK (1999) Temperature and pressure effects on supercritical carbon dioxide extraction of n-3 fatty acids from red seaweed. Food Chem 65: 399–403
36. Choi SS, Regenstein JM (2000) Physicochemical and sensory characteristics of fish gelatin. J Food Sci 65: 194–199

37. Cohen Z, Norman HA, Heimer YM (1995) Microalgae as a source of $\omega3$ fatty acids. World Rev Nutr Diet 77: 1–31
38. Conquer JA, Holub BJ (1996) Effect of supplementation with an algae source of docosahexaenoic acid on omega-3 status and risk factors for heart disease in vegetarian subjects. J Nutr 126: 3032–3039
39. Cordle CT (1994) Control of food allergies using protein hydrolysates. Food Technol 48: 72–76
40. Darmadji P, Izumimoto M (1994) Effect of chitosan in meat preservation. Meat Sci 38: 243–254
41. Dehmer GJ (1988) Reduction in the rate of early restenosis after coronary angioplasty by a diet supplemented with n-3 fatty acids. N Engl J Med 319: 733–740
42. Dekker RFH (1994) Enzymes in food and beverage processing. 1. Food Aust 46: 36–139
43. Delincee H, Partmann W (1979) Eel muscle carnosinase:isoelectric point and molecular weight. J Food Biochem 3: 43–51
44. Department of Health (1994) Dietary reference values for food energy and nutrients for the United Kingdom. Committee on Medical Aspects of Food Policy. Report on Health and Social Subjects. Her Majesty's Stationary Office, London
45. Department of Health (1991) Dietary reference values for food energy and nutrients for the United Kingdom. Report on Health and Social Subjects, 41, Committee on Medical Aspects of Food Policy. Her Majesty's Stationary Office, London
46. Dyerberg J (1986) Linolenate-derived polyunsaturated fatty acids and prevention of atherosclerosis. Nutr Rev 44: 125–134
47. Elliott JG (1998) Application of the antioxidant vitamins in foods and beverages. Paper presented at the Annual Meeting of the Institute of Food Technologists, Atlanta, USA, June 20–24, book of abstracts, p 18
48. European Commission (1997) Regulation (EC) No.258/97 of the European Parliament and of the Council concerning novel foods and novel food ingredients. Official Journal European Communities 1997; No L43
49. Fan L, Vonshak A, Gabbay R, Hirshberg J, Cohen Z, Boussiba S (1995) The biosynthetic pathway of astaxanthin in a green alga *Haematococcus pluvialis* as indicated by inhibition with diphenylamine. Plant Cell Physiol 36: 1519–1524
50. FAO (1994) FAO data. Food and Agricultural Organisation, Rome, Italy
51. FDA (1997) Final rule: substances affirmed as generally recognised as safe. Menhaden oil. Food Drug Admin Fed Reg 62: 30,751–30,757
52. Fitzpatrick KC (2000) Canadian perspectives on nutraceuticals and functional foods. Paper presented at the International Conference on Nutraceuticals and Functional Foods, Houston, USA, September 13–17, session 3/3, book of abstracts
53. Fleurence J (1999) Seaweed proteins: biochemical, nutritional aspects and potential uses, a review. Trends Food Sci Technol 10: 25–28
54. Food and Nutrition Board (1989) Recommended dietary allowances, 10th edn. National Research Council, National Academy of Sciences, Washington DC
55. Friedman K (1996) Nutritional value of proteins from different food sources: a review. J Agric Food Chem 44: 6–29
56. Frøkjaer S (1994) Use of hydrolysates for protein supplementation. Food Technol 48: 86–88
57. Fujiwara-Arasaki T, Mino N, Kuroda M (1984) The protein value in human nutrition of edible marine algae in Japan. Hydrobiologia 116/117: 513–516
58. Garcia DJ (1998) Omega-3 long chain PUFA nutraceuticals. Food Technol 52: 44–49
59. Garcia-Carreno FL, Raksakulthai R, Haard NF (1997) Processing wastes: exopeptidases from shellfish. In: Bremner A, Davis C, Austin B (eds) Making the most of the catch. Auseas, Brisbane, Australia, pp 37–43
60. Garewal H (1994) Chemo prevention of oral cancer: beta-carotene and vitamin E in leukoplakia. Eur J Cancer Prev 3: 101–107
61. Gerald FC Jr (1992) The vitamins: fundamental aspects in nutrition and health. Academic Press, San Diego

62. Ghaouth AE, Arul J, Ponnampalam R, Boulet M (1991) Chitosan coating effect on storability and quality of fresh strawberries. J Food Sci 56: 1618–1620, 1631
63. Gibson RA, Makrides M, Neumann MA, Simmer K, Mantzioris E, James MJ (1994) Ratios of linoleic acid to α-linolenic acid in formulas for term infants. J Pediatr 125: S48–S55
64. Gildberg A, Simpson BK, Haard NF (2000) Uses of enzymes from marine organisms. In: Haard NF, Simpson BK (eds) Seafood enzymes: utilization and influence on postharvest seafood quality. Marcel Dekker, New York, pp 619–639
65. Gildberg A (1993) Enzymic processing of marine raw materials. Process Biochem 28: 1–15
66. Gill H (1999) Functional foods-designer foods for the future. Paper presented at the 10th World Congress of Food Science and Technology, Sydney, Australia, October 3–8, book of abstracts, p 11
67. Haard NF, Dimes LE, Arndt RE, Dong FM (1996) Estimation of protein digestibility. IV. Digestive proteinases from the pyloric caeca of Coho salmon (*Oncorhynus kisuch*) fed diets containing soybean meal. Comp Biochem Physiol B 115B: 533–540
68. Haard NF, Simpson BK (2000) Seafood enzymes: utilization and influence on postharvest seafood quality. Marcel Dekker, New York
69. Haard NF (1992) A review of proteolytic enzymes from marine organisms and their application in the food industry. J Aquat Food Technol 1: 17–35
70. Haard NF (1997) Specialty enzymes from fish and other marine organisms. Paper presented at the Annual Meeting of the Institute of Food Technologists, Orlando, USA, June 14–18, book of abstracts, p 151
71. Haard NF (1998) Specialty enzymes from marine organisms. Food Technol 52: 64–67
72. Haga M, Enokida S (1988) Germicide for food and food preservative. Pat Abs Japan C (No 546) 12:30
73. Hatate H, Numata Y, Kochi M (1990) Synergistic effect of sardine myofibril protein hydrolyzates with antioxidant. Nippon Suisan Gakkaishi 56: 1011
74. Haumann BF (1997) Nutritional aspects of n-3 fatty acids. Inform 8: 428–447
75. Health and Welfare Canada (1990) The Canadian Scientific Review Committee of Nutrition Recommendations. Minister of Supply and Services, Ottawa, Canada
76. Hennessey JR, Siebenaller JF (1987) Pressure-adaptive differences in proteolytic inactivation of M4-lactate dehydrogenase homologues from marine fishes. J Exp Zool 241: 9–15
77. Hibbeln J (2000) Omega-3 fatty acids in psychiatry: the prevention and treatment of depression, suicide and violence. Paper presented at the Annual Meeting of the Institute of Food Technologists, Dallas, USA, June 10–14, book of abstracts, p 197
78. Hirano S, Itakura C, Seino H, Akiyama Y, Nonaka I, Kanbara N, Kawakami T (1990) Chitosan as an ingredient for domestic animal feeds. J Agric Food Chem 38: 1214–1217
79. Hirano S (1997) Applications of chitin and chitosan in the ecological and environmental fields. In: Goosen MFA (ed) Applications of chitin and chitosan. Technomic Publishing Company, Lancaster, USA, pp 31–54
80. Hirano S (1989) Production and application of chitin and chitosan in Japan. In: Skjak-Braek G, Anthonsen T, Sandford P (eds) Chitin and chitosan. Elsevier Applied Science, London, pp 51–69
81. Hoffman DR, Birch EE, Birch DG, Uauy R (1996) Visual function and blood lipid docosahexaenoic acid (DHA) in infants receiving ω-3 long chain PUFA. Paper presented at PUFA in Infant Nutrition Meeting, Barcelona, Spain
82. Holup B (2000) Fish and fish oils for bridging the nutrition gap towards cardiovascular health. Paper presented at the International Conference on Nutraceuticals and Functional Foods, Houston, USA, September 13–17, session 15/2, book of abstracts
83. IFT Food Expo (2000) Institute of Food Technologists Annual Meeting and Food Expo Dallas, USA, June 10–14
84. Indegaard M, Minsaas J (1991) Animal and human nutrition. In: Guiry MD, Blunden G (eds) Seaweed resources in Europe: uses and potential. Wiley, New York, pp 21–64
85. Indyk H (1983) The routine, simultaneous determination of vitamins A and E in fortified whole milk powders. N Z J Dairy Sci Technol 18: 197–208

86. Innis S, Hansen J (1996) Plasma fatty acid responses, metabolic effects, and safety of microbial and fungal oils rich in arachidonic and docosahexaenoic acids in healthy adults. Am J Clin Nutr 64: 159–167
87. Innis SM (1992) N-3 fatty acid requirements of the newborn. Lipids 27: 879–885
88. Islam N, Motohiro T, Itakura T (1986) Combined effect of heat treatment and protamine on the growth and heat resistance of *Bacillus* spores. Bull Japan Soc Sci Fish 52: 919–922
89. Janak Kamil YVA, Jeon YJ, Shahidi F (2000) Control of oxidation of cooked herring by chitosan. Paper presented at the Annual Meeting of the Institute of Food Technologists, Dallas, USA, June 10–14, book of abstracts, p 95
90. Jaques PF, Chylack LJ, McGandy RB, Hartz SC (1988) Antioxidant status in persons with and without senile cataract. Arch Ophthalmol 106: 337–340
91. Jeon YJ, Shahidi F, Kim SK (2000) Preparation of chitin and chitosan oligomers and their applications in physiological functional foods. Food Rev Int 16: 159–176
92. Kinsella JE (1987) Seafoods and fish oils in human health and diseases. Marcel Dekker, New York
93. Kinsella LE (1986) Food components with potential therapeutic benefits: the n-3 polyunsaturated fatty acids of fish oils. Food Technol 40:89–97, 146
94. Kläui HM, Hausheer W, Huschke G (1970) Technological aspects of the use of fat-soluble vitamins and carotenoids and of the development of stabilized marketable forms. In: Morton RA (ed) Fat-soluble vitamins. Pergamon Press, New York, pp 113–159
95. Knekt P, Aromaa A, Maatela J, Aaran R, Nikkari T, Hakama M, Hakulinen T, Peto R, Saxen E, Teppo L (1988) Serum vitamin E and risk of cancer among Finnish men during a 10-year follow-up. Am J Epidemiol 127: 28–41
96. Knorr D, Betschart AA (1978) The relative effect of an inert substance and protein concentrates upon loaf volume of breads. Lebensm Wiss Technol 11: 198–201
97. Knorr D (1983) Dye binding properties of chitin and chitosan. J Food Sci 48: 36–37, 41
98. Knorr D (1982) Functional properties of chitin and chitosan. J Food Sci 47: 593–595
99. Knorr D (1986) Nutritional quality, food processing and biotechnology aspects of chitin and chitosan, a review. Proc Biochem 6: 90–92
100. Knorr D (1991) Recovery and utilization of chitin and chitosan in food processing waste management. Food Technol 45: 114–122
101. Knorr D (1984) Use of chitinous polymers in food-A challenge for food research and development. Food Technol 38: 85–97
102. Koseoglu SS (1999) Processing of nutraceuticals/functional foods. Paper presented at the 10th World Congress of Food Science and Technology, Sydney, Australia, October 3–8, book of abstracts, p 7
103. Kristinsson HG, Rasco BA (2000) Fish protein hydrolysates: production, biochemical and functional properties. Crit Rev Food Sci Nutr 40: 43–81
104. Kyle D, Hoffman J (2000) DHA supplementation from an algal source significantly reduces risk factors for cardiovascular disease. Paper presented at the International Conference on Nutraceuticals and Functional Foods, Houston, USA, September 13–17, 2000, session 15/4, book of abstracts
105. Kyle DJ (1996) Production and use of single cell oil which is highly enriched in docosahexaenoic acid. Lipid Technol 8: 107–110
106. Lal M (1998) Natural seal oil emulsions. Paper presented at the 43rd Atlantic Fisheries Technology Conference: Transformation in Fisheries and Aquaculture: Global Perspectives, St. John's, Canada, July 25–29, book of abstracts, p 37
107. Lall SP, Parazo MP (1995) Vitamins in fish and shellfish. In: Ruiter A (ed) Fish and fishery products: composition, nutritive properties and stability. CAB International, Oxford, UK, pp 157–186
108. Lands W (2000) Public awareness of nutrition and disease. Paper presented at the Annual Meeting of the Institute of Food Technologists, Dallas, USA, June 10–14, book of abstracts, p 198

109. Langholz P, Andersen P, Forskov T, Schmidtsdorff W (1989) Application of a specificity of Mucor miehei lipase to concentrate docosahexaenoic acid. J Am Oil Chem Soc 66: 1120–1123
110. Lapsley K (2000) International regulations and trends for functional foods. Paper presented at the International Conference on Nutraceuticals and Functional Foods, Houston, USA, September 13–17, session 3/2, book of abstracts
111. Lee BH (1996) Fundamentals of food biotechnology. VHC Publishers, New York
112. Lee RMKW (1994) Fish oil, essential fatty acids and hypertension. Can J Physiol Pharmacol 72: 945–953
113. Lees RS, Karel M (1990) Omega-3 fatty acids in health and disease. Marcel Dekker, New York
114. Li Q, Dunn ET, Grandmaison EW, Goosen MFA (1997) Applications and properties of chitosan. In: Goosen MFA (ed) Applications of chitin and chitosan. Technomic Publishing Company, Lancaster, USA, pp 3–29
115. Li SJ, Seymour TA, Morrissey MT (1997) Isolation of a natural antioxidant from shrimp waste. In: Shahidi F (ed) natural antioxidants: chemistry, health effects and applications. AOCS Press, Champaign, USA, pp 283–295
116. Lim D, Shipe WF (1972) Proposed mechanism for the anti-oxygen action of trypsin in milk. J Dairy Sci 55: 753–758
117. Linko YY, Hayakawa K (1996) Docosahexaenoic acid: a valuable nutraceutical. Trends Food Sci Technol 7: 59–63
118. López MD, Garcia-Carrano FL (2000) Applications of fish and shellfish enzymes in food and feed products. In: Haard NF, Simpson BK (eds) Seafood enzymes: utilization and influence on postharvest seafood quality. Marcel Dekker, New York, pp 571–618
119. Luna ZG, Marzan AM, Montilla AA, Caasi PI (1968) Thiaminase in some species of fish, clams and crustaceans in the Philippines. Philipp J Sci 97: 145–151
120. Mabeau S, Fleurence J (1993) Seaweed in food products: biochemical and nutritional aspects. Trends Food Sci Technol 4: 103–107
121. Maezaki Y, Tsuji K, Nakagawa Y (1993) Hypocholesterolemic effect of chitosan in adult males. Biosci Biotechnol Biochem 579: 1439–1444
122. Mahmoud MI (1994) Physicochemical and functional properties of protein hydrolysates in nutritional products. Food Technol 48: 89–95
123. Martin C (1996) The elixir of life. Chem Br 8: 34–36
124. Mehta L, Lopez LM, Lowton D, Wargovich T (1988) Dietary supplementation with omega-3 polyunsaturated fatty acids in patients with stable coronary disease: effects on indices of platelet and neutrophil function and exercise performance. Am J Med 84: 45–52
125. Molyneaux M, Lee CM (1998) The U.S. market for marine nutraceutical products. Food Technol 52: 56–57
126. Morgan KC, Wright JLC, Simpson FJ (1980) Review of chemical constituents of the red alga *Palmaria palmata* (Dulse). Econ Bot 34: 27–50
127. Munda IM (1997) Differences in amino acid composition of estuarine and marine fucoids. Aquat Bot 3: 273–280
128. Muzzarelli RAA, De Vincenzi M (1997) Chitosans as dietary food additives. In: Goosen MFA (ed) Applications of chitin and chitosan. Technomic Publishing Company, Lancaster, USA, pp 115–127
129. Myrnes B, Johansen A (1994) Recovery of lysozyme from scallop waste. Prep Biochem 24: 69–80
130. Nagai T, Suzuki N (2000) Isolation of collagen from fish waste material-skin, bone and fins. Food Chem 68: 277–281
131. Nagai T, Suzuki N (2000) Partial characterisation of collagen from purple sea urchin (*Anthocidaris crassispina*) test. Int J Food Sci Technol 35: 497–501
132. Nagayama F (1990) Biochemical marine resources. In: Takashima F (ed) Biotechnology and high technology in fisheries. Seizando, Tokyo, pp 119–139
133. Nettleton JA (1995) Omega-3 fatty acids and health. Chapman and Hall, New York

134. Neuringer M, Anderson GJ, Conner WE (1988) The essentiality of n-3 fatty acids for the development and function of the retina and brain. Annu Rev Nutr 8: 817–821
135. New Nutrition Business (2000) The Journal for Healthy Eating, Functional Food and Nutraceuticals. Lavis Marketing, Volume 5 (10), Oxford, UK
136. Newton I, Snyder D (1997) Nutritional aspects of long-chain omega-3 fatty acids and their use in bread enrichment. Cereal Foods World 42: 126–131
137. Newton IS (2000) Long chain fatty acids in health and nutrition. In: Shahidi F (ed) Seafood in health and nutrition: transformation in fisheries and aquaculture: global perspectives. Science Tech Publishing, St. John's, Canada, pp 15–28
138. Nice DJ, Little AD (1997) Overview of marine nutraceuticals: opportunities and considerations for new food products. Paper presented at the Annual Meeting of the Institute of Food Technologists, Orlando, USA, June 14–18, book of abstracts, p 150
139. Nieduszynski IA (1985) Connective tissue polysaccharides. In: Atkins EDT (ed) Polysaccharides: topics in structure and morphology. Macmillan Press, London, pp 107–140
140. No HK, Meyers SP (1989) Crawfish chitosan as a coagulant in recovery of organic compounds from seafood processing streams. J Agric Food Chem 37: 580–583
141. Nordmark B (1999) A brief history of food fortification. Food Technol N Z 9:15–18, 20, 35
142. Norziah MH, Ching CY (2000) Nutritional composition of edible seaweed *Gracilaria changgi*. Food Chem 68: 69–76
143. Ohshima T (2000) Marine nutraceuticals and their raw materials in Japan. Paper Presented at the International Conference on Nutraceuticals and Functional Foods, Houston, USA, September 13–17, session 15/5, book of abstracts
144. Ohshima T (1998) Recovery and use of nutraceutical products from marine resources. Food Technol 52: 50–54
145. Ohshima T (1996) By-products and seafood production in Japan. J Aquat Food Prod Technol 54: 27–42
146. Padh H (1994) Vitamins for optimal health. In: Goldberg I (ed) Functional foods: designer foods, pharmafoods, nutraceuticals. Chapman and Hall, New York, pp 261–293
147. Peto R, Doll R, Buckley JD, Sporn MB (1981) Can dietary beta-carotene materially reduce human cancer rates? Nature 290: 201–208
148. Pigott GM, Tucker BW (1987) Science opens new horizon for marine lipids in human nutrition. Food Rev Int 3: 105–138
149. Ralston GB, Tracey MV, Wrench PM (1964) The inhibition of fermentation in baker's yeast by chitosan. Bioch Biophys Acta 93: 652–655
150. Raper NR, Cronin FJ, Exler J (1992) Omega-3 fatty acid content of the US food supply. J Am Coll Nutr 11: 304–308
151. Regenstein JM (2000) Fish gelation: a novel ingredient that meets religious (Kosher and Halal) dietary food requirements. In: Shahidi F (ed) Seafood in health and nutrition: transformation in fisheries and aquaculture: global perspectives. Science Tech Publishing, St. John's, Canada, pp 281–288
152. Salem N, Pawlosky RJ (1992) Docosahexaenoic acid is an essential nutrient in the nervous system. J Nutr Sci Vitaminol, special issue, pp 153–156
153. Sandford PA (2000) Food and nutraceutical applications of chitosan: functional properties of polymers, oligomers and glucosamine derived from chitin. Paper presented at the International Conference on Nutraceuticals and Functional Foods, Houston, USA, September 13–17, session 15/6, book of abstracts
154. Schmidl MK, Taylor SL, Nordlee JA (1994) Use of hydrolysate-based products in special medical diets. Food Technol 48: 77–80, 85
155. Schwieter U, Isler O (1967) Vitamins A and carotene. 2. Chemistry. In: Sebrell WH Jr, Harris RS (eds) The vitamins, 2nd edn, vol 1. Academic Press, New York, pp 5–99
156. Shahidi F, Arachchi JKV, Jeon YJ (1999) Food applications of chitin and chitosan, a review. Trends Food Sci Technol 10: 37–51
157. Shahidi F, Han X-Q, Synowiecki J (1995) Production and characteristic of protein hydrolysates from capelin (*Mallotus villosus*). Food Chem 53: 285–293

158. Shahidi F, Metusalach, Brown JA (1998) Carotenoid pigments in seafoods and aquaculture. Crit Rev Food Sci Nutr 38: 1–67
159. Shahidi F, Synowiecki J, Amarowicz R, Wanasundara U (1994) Omega-3 fatty acid composition and stability of seal lipid. In: Ho C-T, Hartman TG (eds) Lipids in food flavours. ACS Symposium Series 558, American Chemical Society, Washington, pp 233–243
160. Shahidi F, Synowiecki J (1991) Isolation and characterization of nutrients and value-added products from snow crab (*Chinocecetes opilia*), and shrimp (*Pandalus borealis*) processing discards. J Agric Food Chem 39: 1527–1532
161. Shahidi F, Synowiecki J (1996) Seal meat: a unique source of muscle food for health and nutrition. Food Rev Int 12: 283–302
162. Shahidi F, Wanasundara UN, Brunet N (1994) Oxidative stability of oil from blubber and harp seal (*Phoca groenlandica*) as assessed by NMR and standard procedures. Food Res Int 27: 555–562
163. Shahidi F, Wanasundara UN (1998) Omega-3 fatty acid concentrates: nutritional aspects and production technologies, a review. Trends Food Sci Technol 9: 230–240
164. Shahidi F, Wanasundara UN (1998) Seal oil as a novel nutraceutical. Paper presented at the 43rd Atlantic Fisheries Technology Conference: Transformation in Fisheries and Aquaculture: Global Perspectives, St. John's, Canada, July 25–29, book of abstracts, p 30
165. Shahidi F (1998) Functional seafood lipids and proteins. In: Mazza G (ed) Functional foods: biochemical and processing aspects. Technomic Publishing Company, Lancaster, USA, pp 381–401
166. Shahidi F (1997) Natural antioxidant; chemistry, health effects and applications. AOCS Press, Champaign, USA
167. Shahidi F (1998) Seal fishery product development. Science Tech Publishing, St. John's, Canada
168. Shahidi F (1997) Shellfish discard utilization. In: Shahidi F, Jones Y, Kitts DD (eds) Seafood safety, processing, and biotechnology. Technomic Publishing Company, Lancaster, USA, pp 131–138
169. Sikorski ZE, Kolakowska A, Pan BS (1990) The nutritive composition of the major groups of marine food organisms. In: Sikorski ZE (ed) Seafood: resources, nutritional composition and preservation. CRS Press, Boca Raton, FL, USA, pp 29–54
170. Simopoulos AP (1994) Fatty acids. In: Goldberg I (ed) Functional foods: designer foods, pharmafoods, nutraceuticals. Chapman and Hall, New York, pp 355–392
171. Simopoulos AP (1991) Omega-3 fatty acids in health and disease and in growth and development, a review. Am J Clin Nutr 54: 438–463
172. Simpson BK, Gagne N, Simpson MV (1994) Bioprocessing of chitin and chitosan. In: Martin AM (ed) Fisheries processings: biotechnological applications. Chapman and Hall, London, pp 155–173
173. Simpson BK, Haard NF (1985) Characterization of the trypsin fraction from cunner, *Tautogolabrus adspersus*. Comp Biochem Physiol B 80B: 475–480
174. Simpson BK, Haard NF (1984) Trypsin from Greenland cod, *Gadus ogac*: kinetic and thermodynamic characteristics. Can J Biochem Cell Biol 62: 894–900
175. Simpson KL (1982) Carotenoid pigments in seafoods. In: Martin RE, Flick GJ, Hebard CE, Ward DR (eds) Chemistry and biochemistry of marine food products. AVI Publishing, Westport, Connecticut, USA, p 115
176. Siscovick DS (1995) Dietary intake and cell membrane levels of long-chain n-3 polyunsaturated fatty acids and the risk of primary cardiac arrest. J Am Med Ass 274: 1363–1367
177. Skanderby M (1994) Protein hydrolysates: their functionality and applications. Food Technol Int Eur 10: 141–144
178. Skonberg DI (2000) Extending shelf life of fresh fish fillets with a chitosan coating. Paper presented at the Annual Meeting of the Institute of Food Technologists, Dallas, USA, June 10–14, book of abstracts, p 93
179. Sprecher H, Luthria DL, Mohammed BS, Baykoushewa SP (1995) Reevaluation of the pathways for biosynthesis of polyunsaturated fatty acids. J Lipid Res 36: 2471–2477

180. Squires EJ, Haard NF, Feltham LAW (1986) Pepsin isozymes from Greenland cod. 2. Substrate specificity and kinetic properties. Can J Biochem Cell Biol 64: 210–214
181. Suzuki S, Watanabe T, Mikami T, Matsumoto T, Suzuki M (1990) Immuno-enhancing effects on *N*-acetylchitohexaose. Proceeding from the 5th International Conference on Chitin and Chitosan, Princeton, USA, pp 96–105
182. Svennerholm L (1968) Distribution and fatty acid composition of phosphoacylglycerol in normal human brain. J Lipid Res 9: 570–579
183. Synowiecki J, Shahidi F (1994) Isolation of mucopolysaccharides from processing discards of seal and beef. Food Chem 51: 89–93
184. Tanaka M, Huang JR, Chiu WK, Ishizaki S, Taguchi T (1993) Effect of the Maillard reaction on functional properties of chitosan. Nippon Suisan Gakkaishi 59: 1915–1921
185. Tanaka Y, Funada T, Hirano J, Hashizume R (1993) Triacylglycerol specificity of *Candida cylindracea* lipase: effects of docosahexaenoic acid on resistance of triacylglycerol to lipase. J Am Oil Chem Soc 70: 1031–1034
186. Terada A, Hara H, Sato D (1995) Effect of dietary chitosan on fecal microbiota and fecal metabolites of humans. Microb Ecol Health Dis 8: 15–21
187. Tokoro A, Kobayashi M, Tatekawa N, Suzuki S, Suzuki M (1989) Protective effect of *N*-acetylchitohexaose on *Listeria monocytogenes* infection in mice. Microbiol Immunol 33: 357–367
188. Tsukada K, Matsumoto T, Aizawa K, Tokoro A, Naruse R, Suzuki S, Suzuki M (1990) Antimetastatic and growth inhibitory effects of *N*-acetylchitohexaose in mice bearing lewis lung carcinoma. Japan J Cancer Res 81: 259–265
189. Uchida Y, Izume M, Ohtakara A (1988) Preparation of chitosan oligomers with purified chitosanase and its application. Proceeding from the 4th International Conference on Chitin and Chitosan, Trondheim, Norway, pp 373–382
190. Ulbricht TLV, Southgate DAT (1991) Coronary heart disease: seven dietary factors. Lancet 338: 985–992
191. Van Elswyk ME (2000) Use of DHA from marine microalgae in the production of naturally enriched and directly fortified foods. Paper presented at the International Conference on Nutraceuticals and Functional Foods, Houston, USA, September 13–17, session 1/7, book of abstracts
192. Veneroni G, Veneroni F, Contos S, Tripodi S, De Bernardi M, Guarino C, Marletta M (1996) Effects of a new chitosan on hyperlipidemia and overweight in obese patients. In: Muzzarelli RAA (ed) Chitin enzymology, vol 2. Atec Edizioni, Ancona, Italy, pp 63–67
193. Ventura P (1996) Lipid lowering activity of chitosan, a new dietary integrator. In: Muzzarelli RAA (ed) Chitin enzymology, vol 2. Atec Edizioni, Ancona, Italy, pp 55–62
194. Venugopal V, Chawla SP, Nair PM (1996) Spray dried protein powder from threadfin beam: preparation, properties and comparison with FPC type-B. J Muscle Foods 7: 55–71
195. Verlangieri AJ, Bush MJ (1992) Effects of d-α-tocopherol supplementation on experimentally induced primate atherosclerosis. J Am Coll Nutr 2: 131–138
196. Wasik CK (2000) Turning DHA into gold. Paper presented at the Annual Meeting of the Institute of Food Technologists, Dallas, USA, June 10–14, book of abstracts, p 157
197. Watkins B (2000) Omega-3 fatty acids and skeletal health. Paper presented at the Annual Meeting of the Institute of Food Technologists, Dallas, USA, June 10–14, book of abstracts, p 197
198. Watson RR, Leonard TK (1986) Selenium and vitamins A, C and E: nutrients with cancer prevention properties. J Am Diet Ass 86: 505–510
199. Weisburger JH (1997) Vitamin antioxidants and disease prevention. In: Shahidi F (ed) Natural antioxidants: chemistry, health effects and applications. AOCS Press, Champaign, USA, pp 245–257
200. Widicus WA, Kirk JR (1979) High performance liquid chromatographic determination of vitamins A and E in cereal products. J Ass Off Anal Chem 62: 637–641
201. Wong KH, Cheung PCK (2000) Nutritional evaluation of some subtropical red and green seaweeds. Part 1 – proximate composition, amino acid profiles and some physico-chemical properties. Food Chem 71: 475–482

202. Wu D, Meydani SN (2000) Marine lipids and immune function. Paper presented at the International Conference on Nutraceuticals and Functional Foods, Houston, USA, September 13–17, session 15/7, book of abstracts
203. Yanez E, Ballester D, Monckeberg F (1976) Enzymatic fish protein hydrolyzate: chemical composition, nutritive value and use as a supplement to cereal protein. J Food Sci 41: 1289–1292
204. Yokota A (1993) Functions and clinical applications of docosahexaenoic acid. Japan J Clin Nutr 83: 619–624
205. Yonekubo A (1991) DHA in mother's milk and learning ability of a baby. Shokuryo No Kagaku (in Japanese) 161: 47–54
206. Yongmanitchai W, Ward OP (1989) Omega-3 fatty acids: alternative sources of production. Process Biochem 24: 117–125
207. Yuan JP, Chen F (2000) Purification of *trans*-astaxanthin from a high-yielding astaxanthin ester-producing strain of the microalga *Haematococcus pluvialis*. Food Chem 68: 443–448
208. Zawistowski J (2000) Phytosterols as functional food ingredients. Paper presented at the International Conference on Nutraceuticals and Functional Foods, Houston, USA, September 13–17, session 14/5, book of abstracts
209. Ziegler RG (1989) A review of epidemiological evidence that carotenoids reduce the risk of cancer. J Nutr 119: 116–122

16 Marine Nutraceuticals and Functional Foods in Japan

Toshiaki Ohshima

The utilisation of natural products from marine resources for the production of nutraceuticals and functional foods is now common. For example, formula milk products enriched in docosahexaenoic acid by adding purified fish oils are available in Japan and other countries. There are now more than 200 food products which contain added fish oil. Topics on other natural compounds from marine resources will be introduced. These include milt proteins which can be isolated from fish gonad and decrease the growth rate and heat resistance of certain spoilage bacteria and therefore used in food preservation as an antibacterial agent. Transglutaminase and ε-polylysine improve the elastic properties of heat-induced gel (*kamaboko*) produced from low grade surimi. Many advanced scientific studies on isolation and utilisation of bioactive natural products for pharmaceutical applications, including anti-microbial, anti-mould, anti-virus and anti-tumour compounds, have been carried out. Certain bioactive compounds have already been applied to pharmaceutical uses. Eicosapentaenoic acid ethyl ester encapsulated products with over 92% of purity are used for pharmaceutical for arteriosclerosis and for hyperlipidemia. Chitosan sheets are used as an artificial protector against skin damage such as cut and burns in surgical operations. This chapter summarises the use of marine nutraceuticals and functional foods in Japan.

16.1 Introduction

According to the up-to-date annual report on Japanese fisheries [34], Japanese fishery products output in 1998 amounted to 6.7 million metric tonnes (valued at 2.0 trillion yen), and has gradually decreased for the last decade. In the same year, annual imported fishery products amounted to 5.2 million metric tonnes. Japan supplied fish for 57% of its own fishery products (not including animal feed or fertiliser) in 1998, which is a 23% decrease since 1988.

Under these severe conditions surrounding the fisheries of Japan, maximum recovery from marine resources is very important because there are few under-utilised marine resources in Japanese coastal areas. In this chapter, some topics on value-added utilisation of marine resources carried out in Japan are introduced.

16.2 Fish Oils with Omega-3 Polyunsaturated Fatty Acids (ω3-PUFA)

Fish oils are produced from the whole body or guts of various fish species. Their main component is triacylglycerol which is rich in PUFA such as eicosapentaenoic acid (EPA) and docosahexaenoic acid (DHA). Epidemiological research of Dyerberg et al. [4] on comparison between the Inuit inhabitants in Greenland and the inhabitants in Denmark itself revealed that (1) in both cases 40% of the total calorie intake came from fat-based high-calorie foods and (2) death originating in coronary heart diseases (CHD) was lower among the Inuit people living in Greenland. Based on more detailed comparative studies on food consumption and the lipid compositions of the serum, they found that (1) differences in dietary PUFA were accurately reflected in the fatty acid compositions of plasma lipids and (2) the occurrence of CHD was not solely genetic but affected by EPA consumed from fish and fur seals, the diets of the Inuits. At that time, however, relationship between the frequency of CHD and EPA intake still remained unknown. After highly purified EPA became available, research has accumulated a large volume of data on physiological functions of EPA.

Much of EPA consumed from diet is β-oxidised in liver cells and synthesised *in vivo*, but some EPA is incorporated into cell membrane by the action of phospholipase A_2. Since the melting point of EPA is low at −54.4°C, the EPA incorporated in glycerophospholipids of biomembrane in this way causes physical properties of the membrane, including biomembrane fluidity. Indeed, dietary ingestion of sardine oils, which are rich in EPA [46] or DHA [30], increases the fluidity of human erythrocyte membrane. A wide range of physiological functions of eicosanoids is summarised in Table 16.1.

Dietary supplement of fish oil or EPA over a period of time has the effect of reducing blood triglycerides in healthy subjects, hyperlipidemia sufferers, labo-

Table 16.1. Physiological actions of eicosanoids

Eicosanoids	Effect
PGE_1	Inhibits platelet aggregation
PGE_2	Vasodilation, increases cAMP levels, decreases gastric acid secretion, suppresses immune response, luteotropic action
PGI_2	Relaxes smooth muscle, vasodilation, inhibits platelet aggregation, raises cAMP levels
TXA_2	Contracts smooth muscle, causes platelet aggregation, bronchoconstriction
PGD_2	Inhibits platelet aggregation, raises cAMP levels, causes peripheral vasodilation
LTB_4	Neutrophil and eosinophil chemotaxis, leakage in microcirculation, raises cAMP levels, causes neutrophil aggregation
LTC_4-LTD_4	Contracts smooth muscle, constricts peripheral airways, leakage in microcirculation, decrease camp levels
12-HETE, 12-HPETE	Neutrophil chemotaxix, stimulates glucose-induced insulin secretion
15-HETE	Inhibits 5- and 12-lioxygenase
Lipoxin A	Superoxide anion generation, chemotaxis, activates protein cell activity
Lipoxin B	Inhibits NK cell activity

Source: Adapted from Hwang [19].

ratory animals and hyperlipidemia model animals alike. The detailed mechanism of this physiological action of EPA remains obscure. When the lipoprotein composition of plasma and their constituent lipid classes were compared after dietary ingestion of fish oils to hypertriglyceridemia subjects for a few weeks, a marked reduction of very low density lipoprotein (VLDL) that bear the role of transporting triacylglycerols was noted. This was caused by a decrease in triacylglycerols level [20].

Dietary ingestion of EPA has the recognised action of inhibiting platelet aggregation. Decrease in the platelet membrane arachidonic acid (AA) with substitution by EPA leads to the decrease in production of thromboxane A_2 (TXA_2) which is effective in promoting platelet aggregation. At the same time, cycloxygenase produces TXA_3 which is not effective to antiplatelet action from EPA incorporated into membrane phospholipids. In addition to this, changes in membrane physical properties due to the incorporation of EPA causes affinity of phospholipase A_2 located in the surface of membrane and the separation of AA is suppressed [1, 54]. If the membrane supply of AA decreases with an increase in the ingestion amount of EPA, production of prostaglandin I_2 (PGI_2), which is produced from AA and has the effect of expanding arteries, also decreases [31]. In this way, EPA is important as a factor in anti-arteriosclerosis action.

Epadel (Mochida Pharmaceuticals Co., Tokyo, Japan), which contains more than 92% EPA ethyl ester, received approval for commercial production as a pharmaceutical for arteriosclerosis in 1990 and for hyperlipidemia in 1994. It is produced from sardine oils in which the original level of EPA is 15–16%. Sardine oils are generally ethyl-esterified and purified by an ultra-vacuum rectification system consisting of four fractionating towers lined in series. After this distillation process, the level of EPA ethyl ester increases to about 82%. The partially purified EPA ethyl ester is then treated by a urea-adduction process and silica gel treatment to increase the level of EPA ethyl ester to more than 92% (Fig. 16.1) [14–16]. It is then encapsulated in a gelatin capsule, and α-tocopherol is added to increase its stability against autoxidation. The final product is stable for 6 months at 50 °C or 3 years at room temperature, and its acid value remains about 0.1 mg KOH/g lipid after 3 years under nitrogen atmosphere [17].

Fig. 16.1. Refining process of EPA ethyl ester

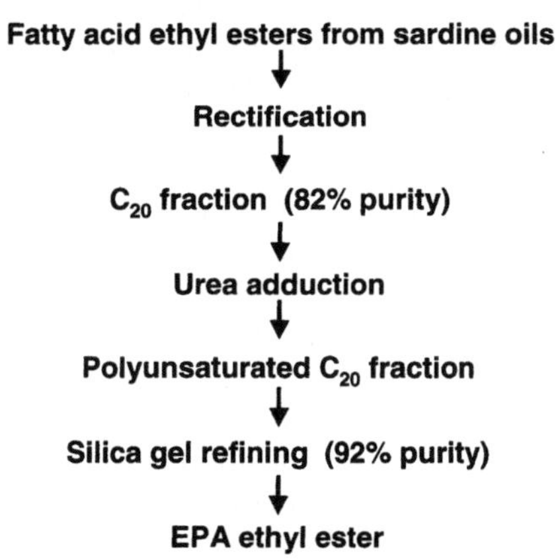

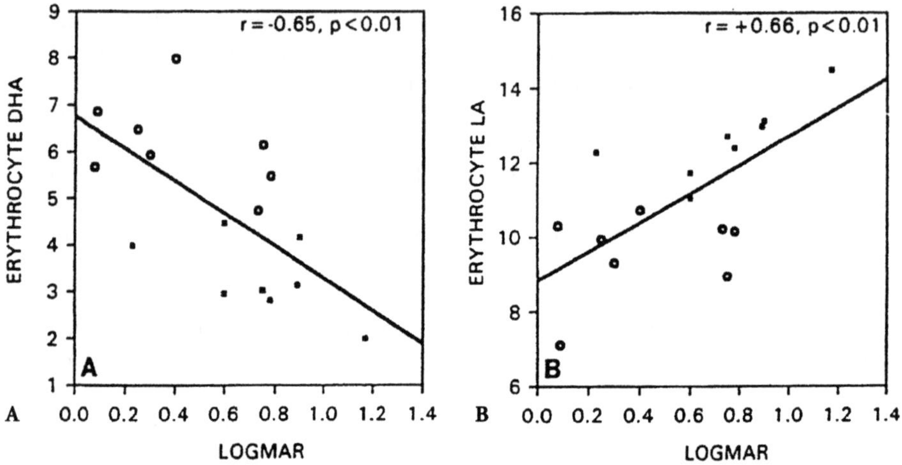

High log MAR indicates poor visual acuity and lower value implies better acuity.
A: DHA and **B**: Linoleic acid.

Fig. 16.2 A, B. Relationship between erythrocyte phospholipids DHA and visual acuity of infants: **A** DHA; **B** linoleic acid. ○: infants exclusively fed breast milk; ■: infants predominantly fed infant formula. (Source: Adapted from Makrides et al. [30])

The partially hydrogenated fish oils have a higher viscosity and are used as a raw material for the production of margarine, shortening and detergents.

Uauy et al. [57] found that the retinal functions are more or less complete in infants after 57 weeks of conception (4 months after birth) and revealed that the component ratio of PUFA with 20 and 22 carbon numbers in phosphatidylethanolamine in erythrocyte phospholipids was significantly high in the infant group fed with formula milk containing fish oil (Fig. 16.2 A, B). When the retinal potential of infants was measured in the 36th week after conception (8–13 weeks after the start of test feeding), electrical activity in the retina was found to be in proportion to the $\omega 3$ fatty acid content [57]. Thus, while the effect of DHA on retinal functions has been under some scrutiny in recent years, this shows that DHA is essential to the development of retinal functions, particularly in premature infants [10, 13]. Thus, formula milk products enriched with DHA by the addition of purified fish or algal oils are now commercially available in Japan and the USA. The number of other fish oil-added food products has now reached more than 200, including pudding, candy, juice and others. Their market value is expected to be more than 25 billion yen.

Fish oils rich in DHA (50–65%) with enzymatic modification and chemical esterification of acyl groups are commercially available. However, DHA is quite susceptible to autoxidation under ambient conditions because it has six ethylenic double bonds. Therefore, stabilisation of DHA against oxidation is necessary for commercial application in food products. Encapsulated micro-powders (20–30 μm in diameter) containing 50% or 30% DHA-rich oil were developed to prevent off-flavour development due to the oxidation of DHA during processing. They are produced as follows. Cornstarch is treated with a starch-degrading enzyme to provide elasticity [35]. A DHA-rich oil is encapsulated in the enzyme-treated starch, followed by coating with an alcohol-soluble protein obtained from corn. The oxygen permeability of the protein coat is almost 0 $ml/m^2/24\ h/atm$, so the DHA covered with the protein becomes stable against autoxidation [55].

16.3 Effects of Marine Lipids on Taste

According to Japanese traditional concepts, the best season for consuming sardine and scallop is generally between July and August, for the Pacific saury is between September and November, and for the Pacific oyster and yellowtail is between December and February. Generally, fish accumulate lipids gradually in their tissues with sexual maturation, and their lipid contents reach maximum just before the spawning season. This season is cited as "shun" in Japanese, and most consumers in this country know that fish become tasty in this particular season. In addition to this, many Japanese consumers prefer a portion of fish meat with high fat content compared to a lean portion. For example, many Japanese consumers believe that fatty tuna meat "Oh-toro" is tasty compared to a lean sample "Akami" of the same fish meat, though the pure extracted oils themselves do not have any taste. In our own sensory perception tests in humans, we obtained results showing that triacylglycerols extracted from southern bluefin tuna enhanced "Umami" taste of glutamic acid and inosinic acid in emulsion. Figure 16.3 shows the effect of DHA-rich triacylgycerols in enhancing "Umami" taste. Triacylglycerols enriches in 22:6 $\omega3$ showed a similar function to the tuna triacylglycerols [43, 59]. A similar function of marine oils in the enhancing of "Umami" taste was reported in the case of emulsions with bigeye tuna oils [27, 28]. On the other hand, emulsions consisting of soybean oils and lard and the fish extract did not reveal the "Umami" enhancing function. De-

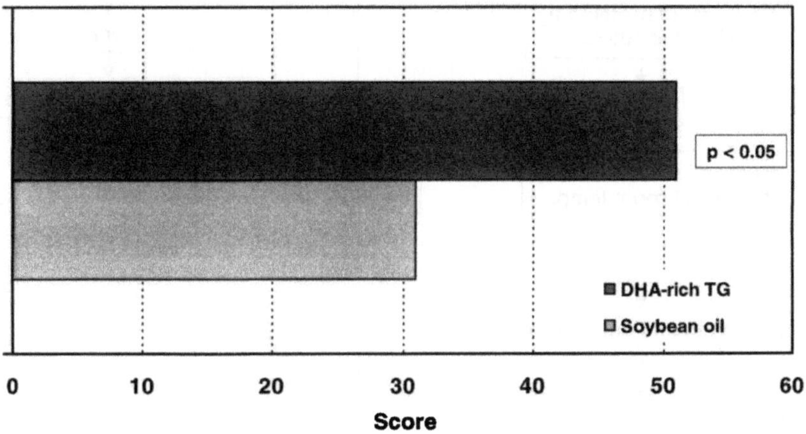

Fig. 16.3. Effect of DHA-rich triacylgycerols in enhancing 'Umami' taste

tailed mechanisms for the enhancement of "Umami" taste by marine lipids are still obscure. Gilbertson et al. [11] reported physiological evidence for the gustatory cue for fat in which the patch-clump recordings of isolated rat taste receptor cells revealed that *cis*-PUFA, including 18:3 ω3 and 20:4 ω6 inhibited delayed rectifying K^+ channels. When mouse tongue was treated by EPA or DHA, the bitter taste response of chorda timpani against quinine hydrochloride or denatonium was inhibited [39]. These results from neurophysiological studies suggest that PUFA can play a role in terms of controlling "Umami" taste of seafood.

16.4 Application of Marine Nutraceuticals and Functional Foods

16.4.1 Chitin and Chitosan

Chitin is one of the prominent components of arthropoda and mollusca tissues. The exoskeleton of crustaceans is one of the suitable raw materials for production of chitin. Demineralisation is carried out by washing the exoskeleton with dilute sulphuric acid. Proteins are removed by washing with concentrated alkaline solution, then rinsing with water. The crude chitin thus prepared is then treated with concentrated hydrochloric acid, and purified chitin is obtained as the precipitate (Fig. 16.4). Chitin is a smooth, flaky powder, and white when pure. It is insoluble in water and requires certain solvents to obtain chitin solution. Water-soluble chitosan is obtained by removing acetyl groups from chitin

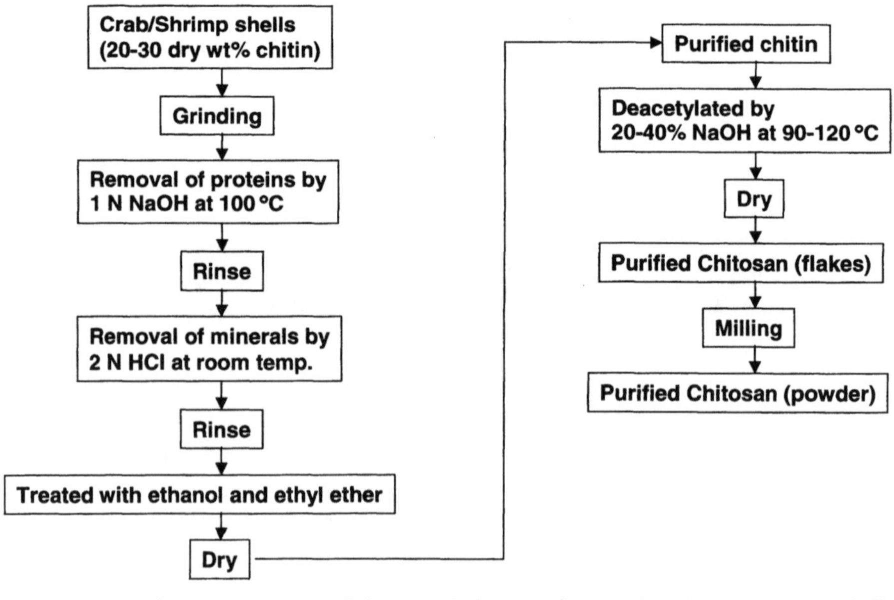

Fig. 16.4. Manufacturing process of chitin and chitosan from crab and shrimp outer shells. (Source: Adapted from Inui [21])

with an alkaline solution [21]. Annual production of chitin and chitosan is about 700 metric tonnes, and its marketability is estimated to be around 5 billion yen. About 85% of chitosan produced in Japan is used for wastewater treatment in the food industry. It removes high-BOD water-soluble proteins through flocculation.

Another notable function of chitosan is inhibition of spoilage bacterial growth in foods. Addition of 0.01% chitosan prolonged the reproductive induction period by two days compared to the control group, while the addition of 0.02% or more inhibited the growth of *E. coli* altogether (Table 16.2) [58]. Added chitosan in liquid media prevented the growth of spoilage bacteria during incubation at 30 °C for 24 h [3]. Its application for meat preservation is expected in the near future. Chitosan is macromolecular; even if it reacts with the cell wall of bacteria it would not be expected to pass through the cell membrane and react with the nucleic acid and proteins inside the cell wall. Consequently the antibacterial nature of chitosan is closely linked to the molecular weight of chitosan; the lower the molecular weight of chitosan the greater its antibacterial effect [58].

Chitin and chitosan are processed into a film for medical use as an artificial protector against skin damage such as cuts and burns [44]. Burnt skin tissues wrapped with a chitosan film regenerated faster and more favourably than those treated without the film. Artificial skin prepared from crab chitin (Beschitin-W distributed by Unichika Co. Ltd., Osaka, Japan) is commercially available. This processed film of chitin is 0.08–0.5 mm thick. However, the availability of this preparation is limited by high prices [5].

Rats fed on a diet containing 7% tallow, 1% cholesterol and 5% chitin had reduced levels of liver triacylglycerols and cholesterol and similar levels of serum and faecal cholesterol compared to rats fed on the diet without chitin, suggesting that chitin may be effective in controlling lipid absorption from intestine [60]. In hamsters the inclusion of chitin and chitosan in the diet is associated with a reduced food intake and the cholesterol-lowering effect seems mainly related to an increase in the faecal excretion of neutral sterols [56]. Ormrod et al. [45] showed a direct correlation between lowering of serum cho-

Table 16.2. Effect of chitosan derivatives on the growth of *E. coli*

Chitosan derivatives (0.004%)		Degree of decomposition (Total reducing sugar produced mg/g)	Microbial count ($\times 10^2$/ml)	
Control		–	140	++
Derivative	A	540	44	++
	B	260	29	+
	C	40	5	–
	D	8	15	–
Chitosan		4	13	–

Shaken culture at 30 °C for 24 h –: no growth, +: growth, and ++: marked growth.
Source: Adapted from Uchida [58].

lesterol with chitosan and inhibition of atherogenesis, and suggested that the chitosan could be used to inhibit the development of atherosclerosis in individuals with hypercholesterolaemia. Thus, orally administered chitosan binds fat in the intestine, blocking absorption and lowering blood cholesterol in animals and humans.

Chitosan has immunomodulatory activity. Phagocytosis of leucocyte in rainbow trout was significantly activated after injection with 100 mg/kg of chitosan in peritoneum, compared to a control injected with bovine serum albumin [49].

Other applications of chitosan include improving the physical properties of heat-induced gel of surimi, *kamaboko* [2], used as a matrix for bioreactor, strengthener for pulp sheet, and moisturiser in cosmetics (Table 16.3). More information about food application of chitinous materials can be obtained in Chap. 15.

Table 16.3. Applications of chitin, chitosan, and their oligomers

Fields	Chitin and chitosan	Oligomers
Food	Antimicrobial agent Edible film	Preservative agent
Pharmaceuticals	Protective effect on bacterial infection Antitumour agent Immuno-potentiating agent Carrier for drug derivative system	Protective effect on bacterial infection Antitumor agent Immuno-potentiating agent
Medical	Accelerator for wound healing Artificial skin Absorbable sutures	
Nutritional	Dietary fibre Hypocholesterolemic agent Antihypersensitive agent in vitro	Hypocholesterolemic agent Calcium absorption accelerator
Biotechnological	Carrier for immobilised enzyme and cell Porous beads for bioreactor Resin for chromatography Membrane material	
Agricultural	Seed coating preparation Activator of plant cell	Activator of plant cell
Others	Coagulant for water Protein recovery preparation in food processing Removal of heavy metal from wastewater Cosmetic materials	

Source: Adapted from Jeon et al. [25].

16.4.2
Chondroitin Sulphate

Chondroitin sulphate is a typical mucopolysaccharide sulphate. There are three isomers differing in the position of the sulphuric acid groups. Chondroitin polysulphate, with two sulphuric acid residues in a molecule, exists in the cartilage of sharks. It is mostly used as a base for cosmetics such as hand cream.

Chondroitin sulphate dose-dependently inhibited the pancreatic lipase activity in an assay system using triolein emulsified with phosphatidylcholine. In addition, it inhibited the palmitic acid uptake into the brush border membrane vesicles of the rat jejunum. Chondroitin sulphate caused the reduction of body weight and parametrial adipose tissue weight and prevention of fatty liver and hyperlipidemia in mice fed a high-fat diet [12].

16.4.3
Milt Proteins as Food Preservatives

Milt protein (protamine) is a basic peptide containing over 80% arginine. Protamine changes the cell morphology of certain bacteria and releases certain soluble constituents from the cells [24]. Its unique properties include thermo-stability and the ability to prevent the growth of *Bacillus* spores (Table 16.4). For this reason, protamine is being used as an antibacterial agent in food processing and preservation [23]. The preservative effects of protamine product after being added to a wide range of food, including cooked rice, omelette, cooked vegetables, salad, sweet potato, custard cream, kneaded bean jam, cooked waxy rice flower, steamed bread and white sauce were investigated [41]. Figure 16.5 shows the effect of salmin (milt protein from salmon) on the shelflife of boiled rice.

Table 16.4. Effect of milt protein from salmon (salmine) on growth of bacteria

Bacteria	Concentration (ppm)						
	0	200	300	400	500	700	1000
B. subtillis	+	+	+	–	–	–	–
E. coli	+	+	+	+	–	–	–
Sal. tphirium	+	+	+	+	+	+	–
Pichia farinosa	+	+	+	+	–	–	–
Strept. lactis	+	+	–	–	–	–	–

+: growth; –: no growth.
Source: Adapted from Nozaki [41].

16.4.4
Carbohydrates

Alginic acid is a polyuronic acid composed of D-mannuronic acid and L-gluronic acid. It exists as a cell wall component of brown algae, including *Laminaria*, *Eise-*

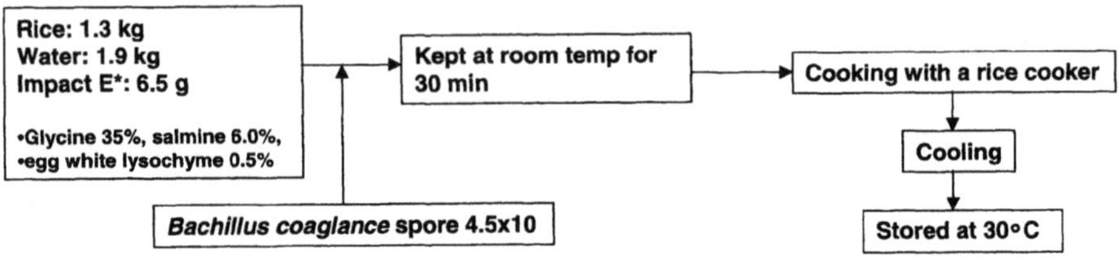

		Storage (days)			
		0	24	48	72
Control	cfu/g	10	2.2×10^4	4.0×10^7	-
	pH	6.7	6.7	6.3	-
Impact E added	cfu/g	10	5.3×10^3	2.5×10^3	4.5×10^5
	pH	6.5	6.6	6.4	6.7

Fig. 16.5. Effect of salmin (milt protein from salmon) on the shelf life of boiled rice. (Source: Adapted from Nozaki [41])

nia, and *Ecklonia*. This polysaccharide molecule contains a number of carboxyl groups and thus combines easily with cations. Therefore, it is used as an effective ion exchanger in factory wastewater treatment. More information about sodium alginate, agarose, agaropectin and carrageenan can be obtained in Chap. 15.

16.4.5 Enzymes

A commercially available transglutaminase preparation called Activa (Ajinomoto Co. Ltd., Tokyo, Japan) is added to low-grade surimi to improve the elastic properties of heat-induced "kamaboko" gel by forming ε-(γ-Glu)-Lys cross-links in the gels. The enzyme preparation is not of marine origin but is purified from the culture broth of a variant of *Streptoverticillium mobaraence* [50].

16.4.6 Others

Many compounds with both low and high molecular weight having anti-fungal, anti-virus or anti-tumour activity have been isolated from various marine organisms. Kainic acid is obtained from certain species of seaweed, *Digenia simplex* and *Centroceras clavalatum* [37] and is used in doses of 5–10 mg to exterminate an intestinal worm. Ara-A and Ara-C analogues of spongothymidine isolated from the Caribbean marine sponge, are commercially available as an anti-virus medicine.

Holotoxins A and B [53] isolated from the sea cucumber, *Stichopus japonicus*, are used as a medicine for a medical treatment of the interdigital ringworm (athletes foot). Gambieric acid is one of the polyethers isolated from the marine dinoflagellate, *Gambierdiscus toxicus*, and has anti-mould activity 2000 times higher than that of the well-known Amphotericin B, which has also been used as an anti-mould compound [38]. Its toxicity to humans is low, so medical applications are expected. Mycalamides A and B [47] from the New Zealand marine sponge *Micale* spp. and Onnamide A [51] from the Okinawa marine sponge *Theronella* spp. prevent the growth of certain viruses such as herpes simplex type 1 at low concentrations (1–2 ng/disk).

Kabiramide A~E isolated from the egg masses of *Hexabranchus* spp. [32, 33] and Mycalolide A~C from *Mycale* spp. [6] have significant anti-fungal activity against disease fungi such as *Candida*, *Trochomonus* and *Trichophyton*. However, these maclorides also have a strong cytotoxicity, and their anti-tumour activity is low. Amphidinolide B from the flagellate *Amphidinium* spp. [22] and Scytophycin B isolated from *Scytonema pseudohofmani* [36] showed a strong cytotoxicity toward leukaemia L1210 cell (IC_{50} 0.14 ng/ml) and KB cell (IC_{50} 1 ng/ml), respectively. However, these anti-tumour substances also had strong toxicity against normal cells. Halichondrin B isolated from the marine sponge, *Halochondria akadai*, has extremely strong cytotoxicity toward Melanoma B16 cell (IC_{50} 0.093 ng/ml) [18]. Its anti-tumour activity in vivo was also promising, but recovery from the marine sponge was very low (4.2 mg from 600 kg). Girodazole isolated from the New Caledonia marine sponge, *Pseudaxinyssa cantharella*, Dolastatin 10 from *Dolabella auricularia*, Bryostatin 1 from *Bugula neritina* [48] and Didemnin B from Caribbean *Trididemum solidum* [29] are promising anti-tumour compounds.

There has also been much research on anti-tumour compounds from seaweed and marine sponges to coelentrates. However, no promising compounds have been reported to date because most compounds had a significant cytotoxicity as well as toxicity toward normal cells *in vivo* [7].

Other bioactive substances found in marine organisms exhibit anti-inflammation and cardiac action. Manoalide isolated from the Palau Islands marine sponge, *Luffariella variabilis*, has anti-inflammation activity as well as inhibitory effect on Phosphalipase A_2. Its utilisation as an anti-allergy medicine is expected. Anthopleurin A from the Pacific sea anemone, *Antlopleuda xanthogrammica*, is a polypeptide with about 50 amino acid residues. Its cardiac activity is 30 times higher than that of commercially available medicines [52]. However, its utilisation in medicine has not been established because it forms an antibody *in vivo* [40].

Lectin is one of the glycoproteins with a high molecular weight. It possesses characteristics such as blood coagulation and complex carbohydrate precipitation. Lectins isolated from eels and certain seaweeds are now commercially available and used as biochemical reagents. Lectins isolated from the giant clam *Tridacna* spp. and from sea squirt have blastogenic transformation activity and antivirus activity, respectively. GL-1 lectin isolated from the alimentary tract and liver of the moray eel accelerates *in-vitro* development of a nerve growth factor [26].

Table 16.5. Bioactive substances isolated from marine organisms

Substance	Origin	Bioactivity
Antibacterial, antivirus, and antifungal activity		
Macrolactin A	Deep sea bacteria	HIV, 10 μg/ml
Gambieric acid A~D	*Gambierdiscus toxicus*	Fungus
Kabiramide A~E	*Hexabranchus* spp. egg masses	Fungus
Mycalolide A~C	*Mycale* sp.	Fungus
Mycalamide A,B	*Mycale* sp. in New Zealand	Herpes simplex type-1, 1~2 ng/disk
Onnamide A	*Theonella* sp. in Okinawa	Herpes simplex type-1, 1~2 ng/disk
Holotoxin A, B	*Stichopus japonicus*	Water insect
Eudistomin C, E	*Eudistoma olivaceum*	Antivirus activity
Squalamine	*Squalus acanthias* guts	Antivirus activity
Antitumor activity		
Amiphidinolide B	*Amphidinium* sp.	L1210 leukaemia cell, IC_{50} 0.14 ng/ml
Scytophycin B	*Scytonema pseudohofmanni*	KB cell, IC_{50} 1 ng/ml
Thyrsiferyl 23-acetate	*Laurencia obtusa*	P388 leukemia cell, IC_{50} 0.4 ng/ml
Halichondrin B	*Halichondria okadai*	B16 melanoma cell, IC_{50} 0.093 ng/ml
Okadaic acid	*Dinophysis* spp.	P388 leukemia cell, IC_{50} 1.7 ng/ml
Tedanolide	*Tedania ignis*	P388 leukemia cell, IC_{50} 0.016 ng/ml KB cell, IC_{50} 0.25 ng/ml
13-Deoxytedanolide	*Mycale adhaerens*	P388 leukemia cell, IC_{50} 0.094 ng/ml KB cell, IC_{50} 0.22 ng/ml
Bistheonellide A, B	*Theonella*	P388 leukemia cell, IC_{50} 15 ng/ml
Swinholide A	*Theonella swinhoei*	P388 leukaemia cell
Cinachyrolide A	*Cinachyra* sp.	L1210 cell growth, 0.4 ng/ml
Calyculin A	*Discodermia calyx*	L1210 leukemia cell, IC_{50} 0.74 ng/ml
Theopederin A	*T. swinhoei*	P388 leukemia cell, IC_{50} 0.05 ng/ml
Manzamine A	*Haliclona* sp.	P388 leukemia cell, IC_{50} 0.07 μg/ml
Discorhabdin A	*Latrunculia brevis*	P388 leukemia cell, IC_{50} 0.05 μg/ml
Girodazole	*Pseudaxinyssa cantharella*	P388 leukemia cell

Table 16.5 (continued)

Substance	Origin	Bioactivity
Clavulone IV	*Clavularia viridis*	L1210 leukemia cell, IC_{50} 0.3 g/ml
Punaglandin 3	*Telesto riisei*	L1210 leukemia cell, IC_{50} 0.02 µg/ml
Dolastatin 10	*Dolabella auricularia*	P388 leukemia cell, IC_{50} 0.04 ng/ml
Bryostatin 1	*Bugula neritina*	P388 leukemia cell, IC_{50} 0.89 µg/ml
Cephalostatin 1	*Cephalodiscus gilchristi*	P388 leukemia cell, IC_{50} 10^{-7}–10^{-9} µg/ml
Didemnin B	*Trididemnum solidum*	L1210 leukemia cell, IC_{50} 2 ng/ml
Patelazole B	*Lissoclinum patella*	KB cell, IC_{50} 0.3 ng/ml
Anti-inflammation activity		
Manoalide	*Luffariella variabilis*	Anti-inflammation
Pseudopterosin A	*Pseudopterogorgia elisabethae*	Anti-inflammation
Discodermin A~D	*Discodermia kiiensis*	Anti-inflammation
Cardiac activity		
Anthopleurin A	*Anthopleura xanthogrammica*	Cardiac activity
Xestospongin A	*Xestospongia exigua*	Cardiac activity

Source: Adapted from Fusetani [9].

16.5 Bioactive Reagents

There are several thousand species of marine toxic organisms. A limited number of toxic compounds have been discovered and characterised by specific conformation of the molecules and strong bioactivity against organisms. Bioactive substances and marine toxins isolated from marine organisms are listed in Table 16.5 along with their bioactivities. The mechanisms of biochemical interaction between these compounds and the live body are unique. Their have potential application as bioactive reagents in pharmacology, physiology and basic biology [8].

16.6 Conclusions

The structure of Japanese fisheries has changed over the last decade. Production from the distance water and offshore fisheries have both drastically decreased. On the other hand, the imports of fishery products in terms of quantity and value have increased. Thus, the Japanese fishing community is currently facing difficult conditions. The oceans are, however, rich in marine organisms including fish, mammals and microorganisms which all have potential as resources for value-added utilisation (not only for human consumption but also for medical applications) [42]. Cooperative research and development between industries and researchers offer an opportunity to alleviate the difficulties associated with the Japanese fisheries.

References

1. Akahane N, Ohba S, Suzuki J, Wakabayashi T, Nakahara T, Yanagi K, Ohshima N (1995) Antithrombotic activity of a symmetrical triglyceride with eicosapentaenoic acid and gamma-linolenic acid in guinea pig mesenteric microvasculature. Thromb Res 78: 441–450
2. Benjakul S, Visessanguan W, Tanaka M, Ishizaki S, Suthidham R, Sungpech O (2001) Effect of chitin and chitosan on gelling properties of surimi from barred garfish. J Sci Food Agric 81: 102–108
3. Darmadji P, Izumimoto T (1994) Effect of chitosan in meat preservation. Meat Sci 38: 243–254
4. Dyerberg J, Bang HO, Hjørne N (1975) Fatty acid composition of the plasma lipids in Greenland Eskimos. J Clin Nutr 28: 958–966
5. Feofilova EP, Tereshina VM, Memorskaya AS, Alekseev AA, Evtushenkov VP, Ivanovskii AG (1999) A new field of biotechnology: polyaminosaccharides-based wound-healing preparations. Microbiology 68: 735–738
6. Fusetani N, Yasumoto K, Matsunaga S, Hashimoto K (1989) Structures of antifungal macrolides isolated from a marine sponge of the genus *Mycale*. Tetrahedron Lett 30: 2809–2812
7. Fusetani N (1994) Marine organisms as biochemical resources for the development of unutilized resources. In: H. Reijiro (ed) Frontier researches in fisheries science. Kouseisha-Kouseikaku, Tokyo, pp 107–130
8. Fusetani N (1990) Potential drugs from marine foods. Shokuhin Kogyo 33: 22–27
9. Fusetani N (1994) Studies on exploitation of marine biochemical resources. Nippon Suisan Gakkaishi 60: 13–19
10. Gibson RA, Makrides M, Neumann MA, Simmer K, Mantzioris E, James MJ (1994) Ratios of linoleic acid to α-linolenic acid in formulas for term infants. J Pediatr 125: S48–S55
11. Gilbertson TA, Fontenot DT, Liu L, Zhang H, Monroe WT (1997) Fatty acid modulation of K^+ channels in taste receptor cells. Am J Physiol 272: C1203–C1210
12. Han LK, Sumiyoshi M, Takeda T, Chihara H, Nishikiori T, Tsujita T, Kimura Y, Okuda H (2000) Inhibitory effects of chondroitin sulfate prepared from salmon nasal cartilage on fat storage in mice fed a high-fat diet. Int J Obesity 24: 1131–1138
13. Harris MA, Reece MS, McGregor JA, Manchego JM, Allen KGD (1998) Possible roles of materanal and perintanal long-chain fatty acids in preterm birth. In: Huang YH, Sinclair AJ (eds) Lipids in infant nutrition. AOCS Press, Champaign, USA, pp 1–18
14. Hata K, Makuta M (1990) Method for continuous urea adduction and its apparatus. Japan Pat H2-180,996
15. Hata K, Noda H, Makuta M (1992) Production method of eicosapentaenoic acid or its ester with high concentration. Japan Pat H4-128,250
16. Hata K, Noda H, Makuta M (1992) Production method of eicosapentaenoic acid and its ester. Japan Pat H4-41,457
17. Hata K (1993) Application of eicosapentaenoic acid to medicine. In: Fujimoto K (ed) Properties of physiological activities of fish oils. Koseisha-Koseikaku, Tokyo, pp 101–110
18. Hirata Y, Uemura D (1986) Halichondrins-antitumor polyether macrolides from a marine sponge. Pure Appl Chem 58: 301–310

19. Hwang D (1992) Dietary fatty acids and eicosanoids. In: Chow CK (ed) Fatty acids in foods and their health implications. Marcel Dekker, New York, pp 545–557
20. Inagaki M, Harris WS (1990) Changes in lipoprotein composition in hypertriglyceridemic patients taking cholesterol-free fish oil supplements. Atherosclerosis 82: 237–246
21. Inui H (1997) Biochemical function of chitin and chitosan in mammals and higher plants, and possibilities in applications in medical and agricultural fields. Appl Biol Sci 3: 55–65
22. Ishibashi M, Ohizumi Y, Yamashita M, Nakamura H, Hirata Y, Sasaki T, Kobayashi J (1987) Amphidinolide B. A novel macrolide with potent antineoplastic activity from the marine dinoflagellate *Amphidinium* sp. J Chem Soc Chem Commu 16: 1127–1129
23. Islam NMD, Motohiro T, Itakura T (1986) Combined effect of heat treatment and protamine on the growth and heat resistance of *Bacillus* spores. Bull Japan Soc Sci Fish 52: 919–922
24. Islam NMD, Oda H, Motohiro T (1987) Changes in the cell morphology and the release of soluble constituents from the washed cells of *Bacillus subtilis* by the action of protamine. Nippon Suisan Gakkaishi 53: 297–303
25. Jeon YJ, Shahidi F, Kim SK (2000) Preparation of chitin and chitosan oligomers and their applications in physiological functional foods. Food Rev Int 16: 159–176
26. Kamiya H (1994) Utilization of high molecular-bioactive substances from marine organisms. In: Reijiro H (ed) Frontier researches in fisheries science. Kouseisha-Kouseikaku, Tokyo, pp 131–154
27. Koriyama T, Kohata T, Watanabe K, Abe H (2000) Chemical components of bigeye tuna muscle and the effects of lipid on the taste. Nippon Suisan Gakkaishi 66: 462–468
28. Koriyama T, Kohata T, Watanabe K, Abe H (2000) The effects of oils on the taste of tuna extract. Nippon Suisan Gakkaishi 66: 876–881
29. Lavelle F, Zerial A, Fizames C, Rabault B, Craudeau A (1991) Antitumor activity and mechanism of action of the marine compound girodazole. Invest New Drugs 9: 233–244
30. Makrides M, Simmer K, Goggin M, Gibson RA (1993) Erythrocyte docosahexaenoic acid correlates with the visual response of healthy, term infants. Pediatr Res 33: 425–427
31. Mann NJ, Warrick GE, O'Dea K, Knapp HR, Sinclair AJ (1994) The effect of linoleic, arachidonic and eicosapentaenoic acid supplementation on prostacyclin production in rats. Lipids 29: 157–162
32. Matsunaga S, Fusetani N, Hashimoto K, Koseki K, Noguchi H, Noma M, Sankawa U (1989) Bioactive marine metabolites, part 25. Further kabiramides and halichondramides cytotoxic peptides from *Hexabranhus* egg masses. J Org Chem 54: 1360–1362
33. Matsunaga S, Fusetani N, Hashimoto K, Koseki K, Noma M (1986) Bioactive marine metabolites, part 13. Kabiramide C, a novel antifungal macrolide from nudibranch egg masses. J Am Chem Soc 108: 847–849
34. Ministry of Agriculture, Forestry and Fisheries, Government of Japan (2000) Fisheries Statistics of Japan 1998. Association of Agriculture-Forestry Statistics, Tokyo, pp 2–14
35. Monma M, Tanamoto Y, Kainuma K (1990) Ultrastructure of corn starch-granules digested by *Chalara paradoxa* glucosamylase. Denpun Kagaku 37: 13–19
36. Moore RE, Patterson GML, Mynderse JS, Barchi J Jr, Norton T, Furusawa E, Furusawa S (1986) Toxins from cyanophytes belonging to the acytonemataceae. Pure Appl Chem 58: 263–271
37. Murakami S, Takemoto T, Zensho T, Daigo K (1955) Effective principles of *Digenea simplex*. VIII. Structure of kainic acid. J Pharm Soc Japan 75: 866–869
38. Nagai H, Murata M, Torigoe K, Satake M, Yasumoto T (1992) Gambieric acids, new potent antifungal substances with unprecedented polyether structures from a marine dinoflagellate *Gambierdiscus toxicus*. J Org Chem 57: 5448–5453
39. Nakajima S, Ninomiya U (2001) Umami of seafood and taste. In: Yamasawa M (ed) Investigation and utilization of sea food components to enhanced human health (in press)
40. Norton TR, Shibata S, Kashiwagi M, Bentley J (1976) Isolation and characterization of cardiotonic polypeptide anthopleurin-A from sea-anemone *Anthopleura xannthobrammica*. J Pharm Sci 65: 1368–1374

41. Nozaki K (1999) Preservation measures for food products. The effect of milt protein on food preservation and its application. Gekkan Fudo Kemikaru 15: 50–57
42. Ohshima T (1996) By-products and seafood production in Japan. J Aquat Food Prod Technol 54: 27–42
43. Ohshima T (2000) Preference for food lipids. Nippon Suisan Gakkaishi 66: 133–134
44. Oshima Y, Nishino K, Yonekura Y (1986) Utilization of chitin film as a covered sheet for a wound part after skin surgery. Nishinihonhifuka 48: 1119–1122
45. Ormrod DJ, Holmes CC, Miller TE (1998) Dietary chitosan inhibits hypercholesterolaemia and atherogenesis in the apolipoprotein E-deficient mouse model of atherosclerosis. Atherosclerosis 138: 329–334
46. Otsuji S, Kamada T, Yamashita T, Soejima Y, Setoyama S, Hashiguchi J, Chuman Y (1984) Effect of dietary sardine oil (eicosapentaenoic acid) on the erythrocyte membrane fluidity in diabetic patients. Rinsho Byori 32: 764–771
47. Perry NB, Blunt JW, Munro MHG, Thompson AM (1989) Antiviral and antitumor agents from a New Zealand sponge, *Mycale* sp. 2, structures and solution conformations of mycalamides A and B. J Org Chem 55: 223–227
48. Pettit GR, Herald CL, Doubek DL, Herald DL, Arnold E, Clardy J (1982) Isolation and structure of bryostatin 1. J Am Chem Soc 104: 6846–6848
49. Sakai M, Kamiya H, Ishii S, Atsuta S, Kabayashi M (1992) The immunostimulating effects of chitin in rainbow trout, *Oncorynchus mykiss*. In: Shariff M, Subasinghe RP, Arthur JR (eds) Diseases in Asian aquaculture I. Asian Fisheries Society, Manila, Philippines, p 413
50. Sakamoto H, Kumazawa Y, Toigichi S, Seguro K, Soeda T, Motoki M (1995) Gel strength enhancement by addition of microbial transglutaminase during onshore surimi manufacture. J Food Sci 60: 300–304
51. Sakemi S, Ichiba T, Kohmoto S, Saucy G, Higa T (1988) Isolation and structure elucidation of onnamide A, a new bioactive metabolite of a marine sponge, *Theonella* sp. J Am Chem Soc 110: 4851–4853
52. Shibata S, Norton TR, Izumi T, Matsuo T, Katsuki S (1976) A polypeptide (AP-A) from sea anemone (*Antlopleuda xanthogrammica*) with potent positive inotropic action. J Pharmacol Exp Ther 199: 298–309
53. Shimada S (1969) Antifungal steroid glycoside from sea cucumber. Science 163: 1462
54. Surette ME, Whelan J, Lu G, Hardard'ottir I, Kinsella JE (1995) Dietary n-3 polyunsaturated fatty acids modify Syrian hamster platelet and macrophage phospholipid fatty acyl composition and eicosanoid synthesis: a controlled study. Biochim Biophys Acta 1255: 185–191
55. Suzuki K (1995) Utilization and properties of a microcapsule DHA. Shokuhin To Kagaku 37: 1–7
56. Trautwein EA, Jürgensen U, Erbersdobler HF (1997) Cholesterol-lowering and gallstone-preventing action of chitosans with different degrees of deacetylation in hamsters fed cholesterol-rich diets. Nutr Res 17: 1053–1065
57. Uauy R, Birch E, Peirano P (1992) Visual and brain function measurements in studies of n-3 fatty acid requirements of infants. J Pediatr 120: S168–180
58. Uchida Y (1988) Antibacterial properties of chitin and chitosan. Food Chemicals 34: 22–34
59. Ushio H, Ohshima T, Koizumi C (2001) Functionality and preference of marine lipids. In: Yamasawa M (ed) Investigation and utilization of sea food components to enhanced human health (in press)
60. Zacour AC, Silva ME, Cecon PR, Bambirra EA, Vieira EC (1992) Effect of dietary chitin on cholesterol absorption and metabolism in rats. J Nutr Sci Vitaminol 38: 609–61

Subject index

A
Actin 8
Acylglycerol 170
Adenosine triphosphate (ATP) 8, 22
Adrenaline 91
Aetiological agent 98
Algae 175
Algal oil 175, 183
Allergenic 89
Allergic 90
Allergic conditions 93
Allergic reaction (s) 90
Ammonia 39
Anaphylaxis 91
Antibodies 91
Anti-fungal activity 214
Antigen (s) 90
Antihistamine (s) 95
Anti-inflammation activity 215
Anti-mould activity 215
Anti-tumour activity 214
Anti-virus activity 214
Appearance 1, 8, 37, 43
Aroma 1, 105
Aroma Extraction Dilution Analysis (AEDA) 115
ATP breakdown compounds 21, 22
ATPase activity 8, 78
Automation in fish processing 3, 137

B
Backbone 125
β-carotene 184
Binding 2, 83
Binding and texture modifying enzyme 2, 83
Bioactive components 1, 175, 185
Bioactive substances 216, 217
Bioactivity 216
Biogenic amines 22, 96
Blood discoloration 129
Bones 35
Burger's model 52

C
Cadaverine 96
Cadmium 34, 36
Calcium 84
Cardiovascular diseases (CVD) 3, 157, 177
Carotenoids 184
Catch basket 154
Causative agent 89
Chemical oxygen demand (COD) 144
Chilled storage 1, 45
Chitin 2, 3, 124, 176, 179, 186, 210
Chitin and chitosan oligomers 189
Chitosan 2, 3, 124, 176, 179, 186, 210
Chitosan derivatives 186, 211
Chondroitin sulphate 213
Chromatographic methods 159
Collagen 64
Colour 43
Compression/shearing mode 54
Computer vision technology 139
Conditionally essential 178
Connective tissue 8
Consume by 18
Cooked fish 73
Coronary heart diseases (CHD) 206
Crab stick 84
Creep and relaxation tests 49, 52, 55
Cross linking 2, 54, 84
Cross-linking of proteins 53
Crowding 10

D
Deep-water-fish 33
Defect Action Points (DAPs) 68
Deformation distances 54
Defrosting 146
Demerit points 24
Denaturation 80
Destructive 46

Diamine oxidase 96
Dietary intake 176
Dietary Supplement Health and Education Act (DSHEA) 194
Dietary supplements 3, 175, 194
Discriminant Function Analysis (DFA) 113
Dissolved air flotation (DAF) 144
Distillation procedure 160
Docosahexaenoic acid (DHA) 3, 157, 176, 205
Docosapentaenoic acid (DPA) 3, 157, 176
Drain 154
Drain cover 153
Drainage system 153
Drip loss 33
Dynamic Headspace Analysis (DHA) 116

E
Effluent 143
Eicosapentaenoic acid (EPA) 3, 157, 176, 205
Elasticity 45
Electronic nose 105
Encapsulated micro-powders 208
Enterobacteriaceae 96
Enzymatic process 161
Enzymatic splitting 170
Enzymes 1, 3, 129, 176, 179, 189
Epidemiology 98
Epinephrine 95
Esters 3, 158
European Union (EC) scheme 1, 20, 21, 28
Extended shelf life 18

F
Fatty acids 157
Fatty acids and their derivatives 158
Filleting 148
Filleting bench 146
Filleting machine 142
Fillets 35, 38
Firmness 45
Fish cakes 35, 38
Fish collagen 190
Fish content 61
Fish finger 61
Fish freshness 21
Fish mince 125
Fish nuggets 35
Fish oil 3, 175, 179, 205
Fish oil-added food products 208
Fish products 67
Fish proteins 1, 73
Fish quality 17
Flaps 128
Flavour 1, 8, 20
Flavour active compounds 106
Flavour Dilution (FD) 115
Flavour Profile Analysis (FPA) 21, 105
Flesh bone separator 125
Flow lines 2, 138
Food applications 179, 186, 188
Food Labelling Regulations 59
Forces 54
Formula milk products 180, 208
Fortified 181
FOSHU (Foods for Specified Health Use) 194
Fractional or molecular distillation 170
Frames 125
Free fatty acids 3, 158, 170
Freezing 76
Freshness 1, 13, 20
Frozen storage 73
Functional foods 3, 194, 205, 210

G
Gambieric acid 215
Gaping 8
Gas Chromatography/Mass Spectrometry (GC/MS) 114
Gas Chromatography/Olfactometry (GC/O) 115
Gelatin 74, 124
γ-linolenic acid (GLA) 165
Glutamine 2, 86
Good Manufacturing Practice (GMP) 67

H
Haemoglobin 125
Hafnia alvei 96
Hand-held pressure probes 54
Hardness 26
Hazard Analysis Critical Control Point (HACCP) 21, 22
Health applications 175
Health benefits 3, 177
Health foods 194
Heavy metals 34, 36
High Performance Liquid Chromatography (HPLC) 115
High pressure 78
Histamine 2, 89
Histamine agonist (s) 94
Histamine antagonists 94
Histamine receptors 93, 94
Histamine-N-methyl transferase 96
Histidine decarboxylase 96
Holotoxins A and B 214

Hyaluronidase 131
Hyaluronoglucosidase 131
Hydrogen peroxide 128
Hydrogenated fish oils 208
Hydrostatic pressure 79

I
Ice 27, 54, 75
Individual quick frozen (IQF) products 137
Infant formula 180
Inosine monophosphate (IMP) 107
Instrumental test 46
Intelligent Portioning Machine (IPM) 139
Intermediate moisture 133

K
K and related values 21, 22
K value 13, 24, 26
Kabiramide A~E 215
Kamaboko 205
Killing method 12
Klebsiella pneumoniae 96

L
Lactic acid 12
Leaching 154
Lead 34, 36
Lectin 215
Level (s), guidance 98
Limit (s), permissible 98
Lipase-catalysed esterification 164
Lipase-catalysed hydrolysis 161
Low-temperature crystallisation 165, 170
Lysine 2, 86

M
Marine bioactives 176
Marine nutraceuticals 3, 175, 179, 205, 210
Marine toxins 217
Menhaden oil (MHO) 162, 163
Mercury 34, 36
Microalgae 179, 182
Milt protein (protamine) 213
Mince 125
Mogden formula 144
Morganella morganii 96
Mucopolysaccharides (MPS) 192
Muscle fibre 8, 13
Muscle proteins 13
Mycalolide A~C 215
Myofibrils 73
Myofilaments 8
Myosin 8, 74
Myotomes 13

N
N-containing compounds 107
Nets 10
Nitrogen content 62
Nitrogen factors 62
Non-destructive 20, 46
Non-hydrolysed fraction 162
Non-Protein Nitrogen (NPN) 62
Non-sensory (objective) methods 1, 20, 21, 22
Non-urea complexed fraction (NUCF) 168
Nutraceutical applications 1, 179, 210
Nutraceuticals 1, 175, 194

O
Odour 20, 105
Off-flavours 107
Off-odours 107
Omega-3 fatty acid concentrates 157
Omega-3 polyunsaturated fatty acids (ω3-PUFA) 3, 157, 175, 176, 177, 205
Omega-6 polyunsaturated fatty acids (ω6-PUFA) 157, 177
Oscillatory measurements 49, 51

P
Pattern recognition 110
Peptides 3, 176, 179, 190
pH 9
Phosphate 83
Phycobilins 184
Physical instrumental methods 56
Plasticity 45
Poisson ratio 47
Polysaccharides 185
Polyunsaturated fatty acids (PUFA) 157
Practical evaluation 17
Pre-and post harvest taints 107
Predictive model 113
Pre-portioning 140
Pre-rigor 75
Pre-slaughter handling 7
Pre-slaughter stress 13
Process operations 145
Protein hydrolysates 3, 176, 179, 192
Putrescine 96

Q
Quality 1, 17, 43
Quality Index Method (QIM) 21, 43, 45
Quantitative Descriptive Analysis (QDA) 105
QUID (Quantitative Ingredient Declaration) 59

R
Rancid odour 107
Rancid/fishy 107
Recently Affirmed Generally as Safe (GRAS) 194
Red muscle 8
Regulatory aspects 193
Relaxation time 47
Respiration 9
Rheological and structural attributes 43
Rigor 12, 75
Rigor-mortis 12, 75

S
Safety 1, 99
Salt 83
Sarcoplasmic proteins 63
Scombroid 89
Scombrotoxin 2, 98
Scombrotoxin poisoning 2, 95, 98
S-containing compounds 107
Sea cucumbers 3, 176, 179, 192
Sea mussels 3, 176, 179, 192
Seafood aroma 118
Seafood enzymes 189
Seafoods 1
Seal blubber oil (SBO) 162, 163, 166, 168, 176, 179, 181
Seaweeds (macroalgae) 3, 176, 179, 192
Sell by 18
Sensory (subjective) methods 1, 20, 21
Sensory analysis 38
Sensory array technology 108
Sensory evaluation 20, 35
Sensory scoring & grading 21
Shark cartilage 3, 176, 179, 185
Shark liver oil 176, 179, 185
Shear force 46
Shore hardness 54
Skinning 150
Slaughter activity 1, 11
Slaughter procedure 1, 7, 10
Smell 43
Softness 45
Solid-Phase Microextraction (SPME) 117
Static Headspace Analysis (SHA) 116
Sterols 185
Stress 1, 9, 11
Striated muscle 8
Stroma proteins 63
Substance 216
Sulphurous aroma 107
Supercritical fluid extraction (SFE) 166, 170

T
Tasmanian Food Research Unit (TFRU) scheme 1, 20, 21, 23, 24
Taste 1, 33
Technology 1
Temperature 13
Tensile force 46
Texture 1, 8, 21, 37, 43, 45, 83
Texture analyser 54
Texture assessment 26
Texture modifying enzyme 87
Titanium dioxide 126
Torry scheme 1, 20, 21
Total suspended solids (TSS) 144
Toxicity 92
Trade effluent charges 3, 144
Trained (expert) panel 45
Transglutaminase (TG) 2, 83, 205
Triacylglycerols (TAG) 3, 158
Triangular test 45
Trimethylamine (TMA) 21, 22
Trimming 140
Tropomyosin 8

U
Umami taste 209
Untrained (consumer, hedonic) panel 45
Urea complexation 167, 170
Urea complexed fraction (UCF) 168

V
Value-added products 2, 3, 137
Vasoactive 90
Viscoelastic 47, 49
Vitamins 3, 124, 176, 179, 190
Volatile aroma compounds 105

W
ω3-PUFA enriched food products 181
Waste 2, 123
Waste minimisation 145
Waste water 143
Water-holding capacity 83
White muscle 8
Whitening 128

X
Xanthan gum126

Y
Yield 3, 141
Young's modulus 47

MIX
Papier aus verantwortungsvollen Quellen
Paper from responsible sources
FSC® C105338

If you have any concerns about our products,
you can contact us on
ProductSafety@springernature.com

In case Publisher is established outside the EU,
the EU authorized representative is:
Springer Nature Customer Service Center GmbH
Europaplatz 3, 69115 Heidelberg, Germany

Printed by Libri Plureos GmbH
in Hamburg, Germany